Library of
Davidson College

VOID

SORABJI
A Critical Celebration

SORABJI
A Critical Celebration

Edited by
PAUL RAPOPORT

with contributions by: Paul Rapoport
                         Alistair Hinton
                         Frank Holliday
                         Kenneth Derus
                         Nazlin Bhimani
                         Michael Habermann
                         Geoffrey Douglas Madge
                         Marc-André Roberge

Scolar Press

Copyright © 1992 by Paul Rapoport, except as follows:
Chapter 2 and Appendix 3 Copyright © 1992 by Alistair Hinton
Chapters 4 and 11 Copyright © 1992 by Frank Holliday
Chapter 6 and Perigraph Copyright © 1992 by Kenneth Derus
Chapter 7 Copyright © 1992 by Nazlin Bhimani
Chapter 9 Copyright © 1992 by Michael Habermann
Chapter 10 Copyright © 1992 by Geoffrey Douglas Madge and Paul Rapoport
Chapter 12 Copyright © 1992 by Marc-André Roberge

All rights reserved. No part of this publication may be reproduced, stored in a retrieval system, or transmitted in any form or by any means, electronic, mechanical, photocopying, recording, or other, without the prior express permission of the publisher and of the copyright holder.

Published by
SCOLAR PRESS
Gower House
Croft Road
Aldershot
Hampshire GU11 3HR
England

Ashgate Publishing Company
Old Post Road
Brookfield
Vermont 05036
USA

British Library and Library of Congress data are available.

ISBN 0-85967-923-3

Printed in Great Britain at the University Press, Cambridge

To Frank Holliday and Norman P. Gentieu
   sine quibus non talis liber

and

To Nicolas Slonimsky
   sine quo non tale sæculum

Kaikhosru Shapurji Sorabji in about 1945

Contents

List of Illustrations xi
Acknowledgements xiii

Part I   Discovery

1   Why Sorabji? 3
    Paul Rapoport

2   Kaikhosru Shapurji Sorabji: An Introduction 17
    Alistair Hinton

3   Sorabji: A Continuation 58
    Paul Rapoport

4   A Few Recollections and Ruminations 88
    Frank Holliday

5   "Could you just send me a list of his works?" 93
    Paul Rapoport

    A "Complete Provisional" Chronological Catalog of
    Sorabji's Compositions 105
        The Detailed Catalog 109
        The Short Catalog 175
        Sorabji's Notes 179

viii Contents

Part II   The Prose

6	Sorabji's Letters to Heseltine *Kenneth Derus*	195
	The Letters	198
	Letter Specifications	251
	Newman and Busoni	252
7	Sorabji's Music Criticism *Nazlin Bhimani*	256
	Frederick Delius	271
	Edward Elgar	273
	Arnold Bax	274
	Gustav Holst	276
	Other British Composers	278
	Conclusion	280
8	Sorabji's Other Writings *Paul Rapoport*	285
	Writings from his Two Published Books	286
	Around Music (1932)	286
	1. From "Animadversions on Singing"	286
	2. "Performance" *versus* "Celebration"	288
	Mi contra fa: The Immoralisings of a *Machiavellian Musician* (1947)	290
	1. "Il gran rifiuto"	290
	2. From "Karol Szymanowski"	295
	Unpublished Writings	297
	From Correspondence	297
	1. To Erik Chisholm	298
	2. To Norman P. Gentieu	311
	3. To Frank Holliday	317
	From the Large Notebook ("Commonplace Book")	325
	1. From the items numbered from I to CDXXXIII	325
	2. Some Sacro-Sanct Modern Superstitions (with Comments)	327

Contents ix

Part III The Music

9 Sorabji's Piano Music   333
   Michael Habermann

    Strict Contrapuntal Sections (Fugues)   346
    Sections in Variation Form   350
    Sections in the Motoric Genre   352
    Free Fantasies, Paraphrases, and Shorter Works   355
    Nocturnes   359
    Le jardin parfumé   360
        The Basic Musical Gestures in *Le jardin parfumé* 364
        Sectional Analysis of *Le jardin parfumé*   382
    Conclusion   388

10 Performing *Opus clavicembalisticum*   390
    Geoffrey Douglas Madge with *Paul Rapoport*

11 Splendour upon Splendour: On Hearing Sorabji Play   420
    Frank Holliday

12 *Un tessuto d'esecuzioni*: A Register of Performances of
    Sorabji's Works   425
    Marc-André Roberge

Perigraph To Remember Sorabji's Music:
           A Short-Form Conclusion   452
           Kenneth Derus

Appendix 1 The Texts of Sorabji's Vocal Music   460
            Paul Rapoport

Appendix 2 The Recordings of Sorabji's Music   480
            Paul Rapoport

Appendix 3 The Sorabji Music Archive   486
            Alistair Hinton

Bibliography   488
Index of Sorabji's Compositions   494
General Index   499

List of Illustrations

Sorabji in about 1945 (photo by Joan Muspratt)	Jacket
Sorabji in about 1945 (different photo by Joan Muspratt)	vi
Sorabji in 1918 (from Alvin Langdon Coburn's unpublished *Musicians of Mark*)	12
Left and right gateposts on the driveway of The Eye, Sorabji's house in Corfe Castle, Dorset (1978; photos by Paul Rapoport)	31
The approach to one doorway of Sorabji's house (1978; photo by Paul Rapoport)	35
Sorabji at his Steinway in his music room in 1966 (photo by Norman Peterkin)	35
Sorabji outside his house in 1966 (photo by Norman Peterkin)	57
Sorabji's first letter to Paul Rapoport (1974)	60
Sorabji on the slopes of Corfe Castle in about 1934 (photo by Norman Peterkin)	74
Sorabji's last letter to Paul Rapoport (1985)	85
Sorabji in 1977	92
Sorabji and Norman Peterkin at the latter's house in Surrey in the mid-1930s (photo by Marie Peterkin)	140
Sorabji's father as an engineering student in the 1880s	206
Sorabji's mother in the first decade of the 20th century	207
The planned opening of "Concerto 2", from a letter of Sorabji to Philip Heseltine (1916)	227
"Futurist Impressions of the states of mind of Colleywobbles and Great Scott after a reading of the Epistle", from a letter of Sorabji to Philip Heseltine (1916)	228
Sorabji in 1918 (photo by Alvin Langdon Coburn)	232
"Yes! I will remember to sniff in the wood", two pages from a letter of Sorabji to Philip Heseltine (1920)	237
Sorabji in 1933 (photo by "Rembrandt")	268
Erik Chisholm in 1934 (photo from a concert program)	299
Norman P. Gentieu in about 1950	315
Frank Holliday in 1942 (photo by J. Cecil Gould)	320

Michael Habermann in 1977 (photo by Alix Jeffry) 336
Gulistān, page 12 of Sorabji's manuscript (1940) 368
A letter from Sorabji to Geoffrey Douglas Madge about
　Opus clavicembalisticum (1983) 394
Opus clavicembalisticum, p. 99 of Sorabji's manuscript (1930) 408
Opus clavicembalisticum, p. 98 of the published score (1931) 409
Geoffrey Douglas Madge in 1988 (photo by
　C. Marsel Loermans) 417
Sorabji, probably in the early 1920s (photo by Hugh Cecil) 427
Sorabji and Barry Peter Ould with the *Fantasiettina,*
　newly published by Ould's Bardic Edition
　(1987; photo by Peter Dickie) 447

Acknowledgements

This book was conceived in broad outline at the first performance of one of Sorabji's works in 1980. From then until now, many people have contributed to it, both directly and indirectly.

I would like to thank first all the authors. Besides providing their chapters, they helped with many matters. In particular, many enquiries were answered by Alistair Hinton more completely than completely, and by Marc-André Roberge more thoroughly than thoroughly. Both provided many photocopies of material and many suggestions for the book; in proofreading and copy editing, the latter also proved to be the *nonpareil*.

The uniqueness of this book results chiefly from the generosity of Frank Holliday and Norman P. Gentieu. Both made available their large collection of correspondence and related material, without which only an inferior book at best could have been written. Frank Holliday in particular has been a special source of encouragement.

The composer himself, Kaikhosru Shapurji Sorabji, knowing that the book was in preparation, helped with several matters. It is regrettable that he did not live to see most of it.

I also wish to thank the following: Karen J. Mathewson (Ancaster, Ontario), Dr. Morag Chisholm and Erika Wright (Winchester, Hampshire), Donald M. Garvelmann (New York), Edward Nairn and Ian Watson (Edinburgh), Prof. Barrie Cabena (Wilfrid Laurier University, Waterloo, Ontario), Daniel G. Cooper (Toronto), Malcolm MacDonald (London), Truus Madge (The Hague), Alain Melchior (Nancy), Paul Snook (New York), Jon R. Skinner (Portland, Oregon), Alastair Chisholm (Isle of Cumbrae, Scotland), Chris Rice (Sevenoaks, Kent), Douglas Taylor (Garland, Texas), Drs. Gabriele Erasmi, Maqbool Aziz, and William Thurston (McMaster University, Hamilton, Ontario), Dr. Stephan Landis (Dundas, Ontario), Charles Maurer (Dundas), and Opus Ampersand (Ancaster).

For permission to reproduce various materials, I thank the Sorabji Music Archive, the British Library Department of Manuscripts, Charlotte Stewart-Murphy and the staff of the Archives and Research Collections of Mills Memorial Library of McMaster

University, the J. W. Jagger Library of the University of Cape Town, Dundas and Wilson (Trustees) Limited, and several photographers. Every effort has been made to contact holders of copyright material. The editor wishes to hear from any who have been missed so that proper acknowledgement may be made in future editions of this book.

For assistance in translating computer files, I thank Joanna Johnson, Coordinator of Humanities Computing Services, McMaster University. For financial assistance, I thank the McMaster University Arts Research Board.

The computer-drawn music examples were created by Ken Gee of Artset Hamilton (Hamilton, Ontario). Many photographic prints were produced by Patricia Vinton of the Audio-Visual Department of McMaster University.

Throughout the book, editorial comments usually appear enclosed in braces: { }. As these occur in footnotes, it will be apparent which footnotes are by a chapter's author and which are added by the editor. Editing of quoted texts, especially Sorabji's letters, is handled differently under different conditions. Explanations, where necessary, are given in various chapters.

The eight authors were educated in several different countries, each of which treats English usage, including spelling, a bit differently. As a compromise, most of this book adheres to Canadian usage, which itself lies somewhere between that of Britain and that of the United States. Transliterations from Greek, Russian, and Sanskrit have been prepared by the editor. Names usually retain Sorabji's spelling in his quotations (e.g. *Scriabin* or *Scriabine*) but may appear differently (e.g. *Skryabin*) in other contexts; those of Russians who lived in the West appear as they Romanized them (e.g. *Rachmaninoff* and *Stravinsky* in place of *Rakhmaninov* and *Stravinskiy*).

This book is printed mostly in 10/12 and 9/11 Utopia, a type face by Adobe Systems, Inc., with a few additional characters and modifications by the editor for the printing of some musical signs and a few words of some foreign languages.

Although the book has been carefully prepared and written, it will necessarily contain errors. I would appreciate hearing from any reader who may offer evidence for corrections to information in it or alternative perceptions of material relating to it.

Dr. Paul Rapoport
Department of Music, McMaster University
1280 Main Street West
Hamilton, Ontario, Canada

29 April 1992

And what the people but a herd confus'd,
A miscellaneous rabble, who extol
Things vulgar, & well weigh'd, scarce worth the praise.
They praise and they admire they know not what;
And know not whom, but as one leads the other;
And what delight to be by such extoll'd,
To live upon thir tongues and be thir talk,
Of whom to be disprais'd were no small praise?

       Milton: *Paradise Regained*

Why do I neither seek nor encourage public performance of my works? Because they are neither intended for nor suitable for it under present, or indeed any foreseeable conditions: no performance at all is vastly preferable to an obscene travesty.

       Kaikhosru Shapurji Sorabji:
       "A Personal Statement"

    But Beauty cannot brook
Concealment and the veil, nor patient rest
Unseen and unadmired: 'twill burst all bonds,
And from Its prison-casement to the world
Reveal Itself.
       Jāmī: *Yūsuf and Zuleykhā*

Part I
DISCOVERY

1 Why Sorabji?

Paul Rapoport

Paul Rapoport (b. 1948, Toronto) received a Bachelor's degree in linguistics and music from the University of Michigan and Master's and Doctoral degrees in musicology from the University of Illinois. He has written books on Vagn Holmboe and Havergal Brian, as well as one dealing with six composers living in Northern Europe, including Sorabji. He has also written many articles on 20th-century music, including reviews in *Fanfare* since 1977. As a composer he has a particular interest in microtonality. Currently he is on the faculty of McMaster University in Hamilton, Ontario.

He began studying Sorabji's music and prose in 1971, first corresponded with him in 1974, and visited him four times from 1976 to 1980.

In the following, *I.P.* stands for Interested Person, one experienced in listening to and reading about music. *Ed.* is the editor of this book.

I.P.: Who is Sorabji?

Ed.: There's a simple answer: a composer of the 20th century who wrote a lot of fascinating and unusual music, especially piano music, which few people are aware of.

I.P.: What nationality is he? His name sounds Indian.

Ed.: It's a Parsi name. Many Parsis settled in India after they fled from Persia over a thousand years ago. But in order to find out why Sorabji did not consider himself an Indian, indeed became enraged at being called one, I'll ask you to read Chapter 2 of this book. He was born and lived in England, by the way, but he refused equally to be labelled English.

I.P.: That sounds rather strange. But what I really want to know is whether I'd like his music. I haven't heard any of it.

Ed.: I don't know whether you'd like it, as I don't know your attitudes towards music and listening to it, or other aspects of your experiences. Even then, predicting likes and dislikes is nearly impossible. Understanding is perhaps a more worthy objective. I think that nearly anyone who has a positive curiosity about music of this century may understand Sorabji's music. But he also has his roots in many composers of earlier times, including some who were only slightly older. Do you have any interest in Skryabin, Debussy, Reger, Busoni, Liszt, Bach, early Schoenberg?

I.P.: Yes ... I like some of them. Are those Sorabji's influences? Does he sound at all like them? I can't imagine putting all those together.

Ed.: Neither can I, but Sorabji certainly was attracted to some of their music and attitudes. For example, Liszt's virtuosity, Debussy's love of sound colour, Skryabin's mystical extremism, Bach's counterpoint ...

I.P.: I get the idea, but the generalities help only a little. Supposing one were curious, what would be the best place to start? There must be several recordings, to which any newcomer would appreciate some guidance.

Ed.: There have been eight recordings, excluding reissues, plus one that was noncommercial. They're listed in Appendix 2 — and are certainly worth hearing, although some are recommendable only in part. However: a mere dozen years ago there were no recordings at all. The first was issued when Sorabji was nearly 90.

I.P.: Why so little, especially during his lifetime? How can this composer be of any significance if almost no one records his music?

Ed.: A partial answer to your first question lies in the music's extreme difficulty. More explanations are found in Chapters 2 and 3 of this book. As for the second, why are recordings, or performances for that matter, necessary for significance of a composer's music?

I.P.: Surely you're not serious. It's obviously the best music which enters the Western tradition, and it can't do that without being heard, and heard by a lot of people. If a composer's music is good, it will get around. If it isn't heard, in a sense it doesn't even exist. It certainly can't be significant. And these days any composers who don't have recordings can't be considered to be getting their music around. They won't even be known.

Ed.: You may be right if we take "significance" in a wide, public, social sense. I should have said that recordings or performances may not imply *quality*. But even if they do, more insidious is the point that lack of them does not imply *lack* of quality. In other words, splendid music doesn't always, indeed may often not get recorded or published.

What you suggest about the Western tradition is the usual view. But it's a theory only. It doesn't hold up well to examination.

To start off, you're actually putting some very simple political and economic considerations first. Which music is heard is certainly subject to them. Would you therefore really claim quality or significance on the basis of frequency of hearing? Would you say that the rarely heard piano pieces of Liszt's last years are inferior to his often played earlier ones? Mightn't some of his other symphonic poems be better too than the ubiquitous *Les préludes*, considering that conductors may be entirely unadventurous in continuing to program the same one nearly all the time?

I.P.: But conductors are not so lazy in choosing their programs. If Liszt wrote better symphonic poems, we'd hear them more.

Ed.: The sad truth is that the big-name conductors nearly always program concerts by everything else first and artistic merit second, third, or last, maybe. I don't mean they go out of their way to put on bad music. But the music that's easiest to get score and parts for, which they or their orchestra already knows (and which audiences know and will pay to hear), which is therefore the cheapest in taking less rehearsal time, which they don't have to think too hard about in the midst of dealing with too many concerts, recordings, travel plans, and who knows what else — this is the music which gets programmed; these are the overriding considerations. The problems are similar for groups smaller than orchestras and for soloists, although they should admittedly be freer of some of these pressures because their performance costs are lower.

The basic assumption that performers take every opportunity to pore over masses of unfamiliar or new scores looking for good material is false. Happily some do this from time to time, but no one can keep up with what's newly written, let alone what was written awhile ago that may have been missed. How many pianists know the music for their instrument by Ronald Stevenson? How many string quartets know the 20 quartets by Vagn Holmboe? How many conductors know the symphonies of Franz Beck, Felix Draeseke, Albéric Magnard, or Havergal Brian? The list of worthy unknowns is endless, and they're not all from this century.

I.P.: But on the whole you must agree that there's a lot of junk which happily we don't hear much, and that most of what's called the standard repertory is rather good.

Ed.: Yes, but as I said before, that's not the problem. Is everything we don't hear junk? If what we get to hear and don't get to hear is conditioned by many factors which have nothing to do with the music itself, there's bound to be fine music escaping our attention which is unlike other music which we do know.

I.P.: I suppose it's possible. I presume you'd make that claim for Sorabji's music, so let's get back to him.

Ed.: Good idea! — although we may return to these important larger issues you've raised, because he's part of them.

Sorabji wrote mostly piano music, of a sort which is unique in its scope, expression, and difficulty. I alluded to the difficulty before. It's mostly this that puts people off, presuming that they find his music in the first place. It's difficult to understand how to play it, because the music is often hard to read or to interpret, and his musical style is unusual. Once deciphered it's still fiendishly difficult to actually play, physically and mentally. And his major works last from two to eight hours, I would think. That alone puts them outside most people's experience, even outside what most would ever want to experience. Yet when played well, his works really do come across, and there's less difficulty for the listener in Sorabji than in a lot of other recent composers.

I.P.: Did you say eight hours? The man must have been crazy.

Ed.: And he virtually banned public performances of his music not for a few months or years but a few decades! From this and other "facts" ripped out of context, it's a common impression that he must have been crazy and is therefore not to be taken seriously.

The myths and rumours about Sorabji far outweigh any truth about him. Due to his mania for privacy, his reclusive nature, he's been called the Howard Hughes of music. There is, needless to say, no connection whatever beyond a superficial and entirely unimportant one. Anything for a headline! If Sorabji needed more privacy than most people do for his self-discovery and self-fulfilment, especially in an area like music, so bound up with inner worlds of imagination, who are we to say he was wrong? People automatically assume that introverts are more pathological than extraverts, but this is unreasonable.[1]

Here are some more untrue stories. Some people thought that he intended to keep the ban on performances going in perpetuity after his death — which has no foundation in what he said and no possibility under copyright law. According to some, he was wealthy and lived in a castle. Quite off the mark! And the listing of one of his works in the *Guinness Book of Records* did not exactly foster an adequate musical reputation.[2]

There's more. Many articles have misrepresented Sorabji in serious ways. A few years ago it was said that he went to hear a concert in 1976 devoted entirely to his music. Not only was there no such concert then, but Sorabji did not attend any concert at all in or around 1976. This type of mistreatment of him goes back a long way, unfortunately. In 1936 it was said that he had financed a concert of his own music, which he hadn't done either.

His self-imposed isolation helped inadvertently to spawn this sort of thing. His "legendary" qualities attract swarms of people who get a lot wrong about him and put him into ridiculously wrong frameworks. Even standard reference books aren't free of error in simple matters.

I.P.: I expect this book is better than all that.

Ed.: It certainly is! Although it can't be free from error, it tries to present Sorabji in the proper ways. There's no one right way. The book is also intended as much as a source for further thought as anything else. It presents a lot of material about Sorabji which has never appeared in print, much of it I think fascinating to read.

I.P.: Of course you would: you're the editor and one of the authors.

Ed.: That's true, but I'm involved in this book because I love the material, not the other way around. What I meant was that nearly everything Sorabji did seems fascinating. For example, many of his articles and letters are brilliantly written, often with razor-sharp wit,

---

[1] See *Solitude: A Return to the Self,* by Anthony Storr (New York: The Free Press, 1988).

[2] This is currently published in Middlesex, England by Guinness Publishing Ltd. *Opus clavicembalisticum* was listed in editions up to 1980 as "the longest continuous non-repetitive piece for piano", which it was not and in any case could never be verified as being. (Norris McWhirter, ed.: *Guinness Book of Records* (Enfield, Middlesex: Guinness Superlatives Ltd., 1979), p. 102.)

full-blown vehemence, richly elaborated exemplification, forceful opinions on anything and everything, or all four and more together. You'll find that Chapters 3, 6, 7, and 8 give a rather good representation of his writing style.

I.P.: What about his music? I hope there's a lot about that in here too.

Ed.: Almost all the chapters contain general comments on it, and Chapters 9 to 12 get specific. Chapter 9 goes into technical musical details, being the only one to focus on them. Chapter 10 is about performing one of Sorabji's biggest works; it's written by the person who has played this composition more than everyone else put together. Chapter 12 tells you who has played what by Sorabji, when and in what context.

But I must add that this isn't a "life and works" book, not even "works", because it doesn't try to give an overview of everything Sorabji wrote.

I.P.: Why not? Surely your readers deserve just such an overview.

Ed.: They do. It would be nice to have several chapters on the piano music, one on the concertos, one on the songs, one on the influence of Busoni, one on Sorabji's use of the *Dies iræ* chant, and so on. But quite honestly, there are very few people who could write such chapters yet, because the large majority of Sorabji's works is in manuscript only. A handful or two of his works have been published, and almost all of that's out of print! Don't forget that very little of his music has been performed or recorded, and even about that there's some controversy.

We could have a book about his music with many music examples from works nobody knows or is likely to see or hear in the near future, but I don't think it's time yet for that kind of onslaught. We're talking about over 100 pieces of music, *many* of them huge even beyond what that word normally means.

For this reason I've preferred to present essays which were written independently but which are frequently related just by their nature.

I.P.: What's the controversy you refer to?

Ed.: The controversy centres around the necessity of playing "exactly" what Sorabji wrote. Some of the music is extremely difficult in ways which you may discover in Chapters 9 and 10. In some places the performer must treat the overall character, mood, and sense of a passage as primary and treat more freely some details of the notation, otherwise the intent of the music — often strongly suggested by Sorabji's characterizations on his manuscripts in Italian or French — can't be conveyed. Passages with exactly notated complex polyrhythms are an example; passages written in a very large number of independent voices are another. The performer must also do a certain amount of untangling and clarifying to project the style and shape of the music. This is needed in all music, but it's crucial in Sorabji's on every page.

Then too, in much of his music, even in apparently strict procedures such as variation sets and fugues, there's an overriding feeling of improvisation in the waves of profuse decoration of the underlying themes. This must be projected, while at the same time the large-scale structure is maintained and the small details of notes, rhythms, dynamics, etc. are treated with the necessary respect.

Sorabji didn't make things any easier by the speed with which he wrote and his utter lack of concern for both performers and the reality of performances. In many of his manuscripts, especially the later ones, notes and rhythms are hard to make out: is that squiggle on the page a rest, a ledger line, or a note; and if a note, then which one, and of what duration? Dynamic and phrasing signs are as scarce as an island of rest may be in the ocean of black notes filling the page. And Sorabji often made mistakes of many kinds in his notation. So even the concept of what is a right or wrong note in Sorabji isn't simple. Similar things might be said of Ives, by the way, but for different reasons.

I.P.: These sound like sketches more than finished works.

Ed.: There's something to that. As far as I know, Sorabji never wrote sketches in the usual sense, although a few pieces were revised and a few more exist in two copies differing in little but their neatness. In a sense, then, the only copy of many of his compositions, including the biggest, is both sketch and final version. Interpretation must take that into account.

I.P.: I don't suppose that there's a solid performing tradition for Sorabji's music that would help with interpretation. Or is some of it supposed to be improvised by the performers?

Ed.: There *isn't* any obvious tradition. That's an enormous part of the problem. But improvised in performance? No. That impression must sometimes be given within adherence to what Sorabji indicated with his basically traditional notation. Deviations from the score depend on the accuracy, completeness, and appropriateness of the notation.

I'm not implying massive rewritings. We should remember, however, that Sorabji was often more interested in the large scale than in the small. Much of his music is built from the top down, so to speak, rather than from an accumulation or development of smaller gestures. You may read something about this in the chapter titled *Perigraph*, following Chapter 12.

The evidence for how he wanted his music played is scant. Some of his comments on the music of others help. These you will find in Chapters 6, 7, and 8 especially.

I.P.: Did he ever play his own music? Do any of those recordings you mentioned present him playing?

Ed.: He did play his own music, but in public only rarely, for reasons which are discussed in Chapter 3. He did make recordings, but no, they are not among the nine I mentioned. Only private tapes exist of his playing. They're listed in Appendix 2 and discussed a bit in Chapters 2, 3, and 9 as well. For various reasons, you'll see that the tapes are severely problematic if one wishes to use them to form an opinion of Sorabji's intentions for the performance of his music.

I.P.: What about students? Did he teach the piano to anyone who carried on his ideas?

Ed.: He never taught, piano or composition. He had absolutely no patience for that sort of thing. But there are people who heard him play, mostly privately, of course, as his last public appearance was in 1936. Chapters 4 and 11 are by someone who heard him play over a period of about 40 years.

I.P.: You mentioned before that Sorabji is outside the mainstream. Despite what you said about politics and economics, quality of music is important. Somehow if it's high, it will be discovered by at least a few people, and then heard by many. I don't see any period in music history where real geniuses have languished unknown for long, and masterpieces lain dormant. Their quality leads them to recognition, and composer and music enter the mainstream of music history.

Ed.: A full refutation of those points would take a long time. But let me merely state a few things. You are assuming that this mainstream of music history is somehow the unalterable truth. It isn't; it's a construct. History is not the past, but what we construe as the past. The notion of distinct periods of music (renaissance, baroque, classical, etc.), of studying them through what is magically deemed the great works of the great composers (which and who are defined by a vague and unsubstantiated concept of "immortality"), of culture developing or evolving over time in more or less a straight line, — witness the very word "mainstream" — all this is a whole lot to swallow, and actually gives more people than me indigestion. We tend to ignore the anomalous events of the past, the periphery to the enforced main line, the multiplicity of relations among many events, people, objects, and ideas. We assume certain things have a causal relationship when they do not, that the past is fixed, which in a real sense it cannot be. We simply bend or shove aside whatever does not have a neat place in what's really a frightfully simplistic, monolithic, unquestioned historical model.

To illustrate all these things is impossible in a short conversation. They demand a different book from this one for proper consideration.[3] But I draw your attention to T. S. Eliot's statement that "the past [is] altered by the present as much as the present is directed by the past".[4] To take just Beethoven as an example: Bruckner's symphonies make us rethink Beethoven's. Even more strikingly, Havergal Brian's Symphony *The Gothic* makes Beethoven's Ninth a different experience. The LaSalle Quartet played Beethoven differently because they played Webern. In other words, new discoveries constantly make us approach the past in new ways.

This means that our view of the past *must* continually change. For that, we need models of history and histories themselves which are not codified into unchallengeable law. No one point of view is sufficient, and none is infallible.

As far as masterpieces are concerned, I'm not aware of anyone having demonstrated how they are discovered, acclaimed, or

---

[3]Other books have, of course, treated these ideas already. A few which deal primarily with music history are: *Philosophies of Music History*, by Warren Dwight Allen (New York: American Book Company, 1939); *Music, the Arts, and Ideas*, by Leonard Meyer (Chicago: University of Chicago Press, 1967); *Foundations of Music History*, by Carl Dahlhaus, translated by J. B. Robinson (Cambridge, England: Cambridge University Press, 1983); *Music and the Historical Imagination*, by Leo Treitler (Cambridge, Massachusetts: Harvard University Press, 1989). Work in the last few decades in ethnomusicology, semiotics, deconstruction, and feminism also presents important challenges to traditional views of music history.

[4]T. S. Eliot: "Tradition and the Individual Talent", in his *The Sacred Wood* (London: Methuen, 1920), p. 45.

Sorabji in 1918
(from Alvin Langdon Coburn's unpublished *Musicians of Mark*)

maintained in a detailed, meaningful way that seems valid for current circumstances — let alone for all time, which is probably not possible. You can be sure, however, that a tangled complex of politics, sociology, history, philosophy, and who knows what else would enter any such discussion. There's no foundation for saying that unknown masterpieces, if you really want to use the word, cannot exist. Why may someone not write supreme music and file it away in a drawer, especially in the crazy and bizarrely heterogeneous times of the last 80 years or so, during which there have been so many irreconcilable ways of and pressures on artistic creation? Shostakovich's Fourth Symphony is a prime example; it lay unperformed for 25 years. And why may something excellent, even if it's not in a drawer, not be overshadowed or superseded by something which is simply more popular? Brian's *Gothic* Symphony, although published in 1932, was first performed only in 1961, and to date has been performed complete only four times. To many people it's superior to and more important than other music which we hear from the 1910s or 20s or which is comparable in size.

So, is a relatively unknown composition or composer necessarily inferior to others? To create a historical parallel, is the clavichord worse than the piano, an 18th-century orchestra worse than a 20th-century one? If we answered that one wrongly, we'd have the whole early-music movement pouncing on us. And deservedly too. Just because something or someone is less familiar to us doesn't make that thing or person inferior. For those who like the biological analogy so much, does the suppression or extinction of a species prove its eternal inferiority?

In the case of works of art, in the case of all these questions, who is the judge? Those who believe in the mainstream, the standard repertory, and unchangeable history ought to tell us.

I.P.: Why, the public, obviously. Despite what you've said about the past and the present, politics and all the rest, there's still an important role for the public. The culture in general is certainly shaped by it. The fact that a culture or its values may change doesn't invalidate that.

Ed.: Well, my question was rhetorical, because it has no clear answer. Yours leads to further crucial questions: what public, under what circumstances, judging in what manner; or perhaps not leading but following, and for what reasons? We should really ask these questions of someone who lived in Nazi Germany or the Soviet Union. But even totalitarian states have no monopoly on misjudgement or error. Is the public any better in this regard in the "free world" which puts more value on cars than culture?

It isn't awfully surprising that Sorabji, a highly cultured aristocrat, detested such a public. But he wasn't the only one. I think one difference between him and other composers is merely that he said publicly what many others only thought privately. Many people have called him an eccentric, but neither his attitudes nor the way he expressed himself qualifies him for that usually negative label.

But to return to the general situation, and more simply and summarily: how can one person or group anywhere be bound by the judgements of another, whether we call the latter group the public, a bunch of critics, a board of experts, or the music industry? Diversity in time and place demands continual adjustment and change of many kinds.

I.P.: If we get away for a moment from who determines what, it's impossible to say there's one judge or an identifiable group of judges, because the decision rests with a later time, a later public. In that sense we may say that the future will decide. We have to let the changes you speak of settle. We're much too close to our own time to understand everything clearly enough to make permanent judgements.

Ed.: But that leaves us in the same historicist trap as before, merely a different part of it. Why defer judgement to a time in which we may not exist? Just because we can't jump on an imaginary bandwagon? The fear of being wrong?! How can we live looking over our shoulder for a future that cannot observe the way we can?

If I may be allowed to personify time in this way, as you did, I would say that the future cannot have the access, insights, or appropriateness that we have right now. I don't mean, by the way, that the future makes worse judgements about its past than that past did when it was present, only *different* judgements, *necessarily* different, as I suggested before. For a visual analogy, to those who would say that distance produces perspective, I would also say that it produces a smaller image.

If we really don't wish to understand this or that in the arts, or if we pass off decisions to some nebulous future, we are often saying, I think, that we don't understand our relation to our own time. That may well disqualify us from making any informed judgements at all.

I.P.: I don't agree with that, but I admit that people don't like to stick their necks out.

Ed.: Well, I will. There's plenty of music of our time which is both appropriate and good enough to be heard, not just once in a while, sneaked into some program where it's hoped people won't notice it, but continually, to the point where we live and breathe it, love it and become part of it just as it becomes part of us. And at least the piano music of Sorabji deserves to benefit from such an attitude, even though it can never be mass-marketed.

I.P.: Nice of you to come back to Sorabji!

Ed.: Yes, we strayed again from our composer subject, so let's stay with him now.
   As I implied, I don't hesitate to stick my neck out for him specifically. He's one of the finest writers of piano music of the last hundred years, and unique in the whole history of the instrument. He may or may not ever be recognized as such for reasons beyond his or my control, but he has written great pieces of music, masterpieces if you like, within what I understand to be their traditions. They are not obvious traditions, by the way. They involve some ideas found more in Persian and Indian arts than Western, even though Sorabji was by no means a student of any Eastern musics.

I.P.: What exactly did he write? Somewhere in this book you must tell us how much is piano music, the title and overall plan of individual compositions, that sort of thing. One has to start somewhere, and it should be possible to learn a certain amount even from that.

Ed.: In Sorabji's case, definitely. All that's in Chapter 5. But we should be aware that there's no simple answer to the question "What music did Sorabji write?"

I.P.: Why not? Judgements of quality may be debatable, but surely he either did or did not write certain compositions, unless authorship is in doubt. *Spurious works,* I think they are called.

Ed.: There is in fact no spurious-works problem with Sorabji. You'll have to look at Chapter 5 to see what the other problems are. But you have a point; ultimately there has to be a simple list of compositions. There's one towards the end of Chapter 5, in what is called "The Short Catalog", which gives genre, title, and date of composition.
   I have a point too, though: a sizable part of Chapter 5 tells you how that list was created, the assumptions and processes behind it. The context, in other words. Don't be impatient with Sorabji or his music in trying to find out what might interest you about them. It's a long process, ultimately all the more rewarding for that. The impatient ones, I'm afraid, may miss rather a lot and come to some

erroneous conclusions like the myths surrounding Sorabji which I mentioned earlier.

I.P.: I suppose I should have asked this first, but when you get right down to it, what's significant about his music? You've begun to answer that, but there must be more to say about it.

Ed.: There is. Many answers are contained in the rest of the book. But let me add just a few more general remarks now. They start obliquely but soon come to the essence.

As I said, Sorabji has had the reputation of being a madman, especially among most people who have heard of him but have no real knowledge of him, his music, or his prose. But I've never encountered that opinion from anyone who's known him personally or who's studied what he wrote. Of the eight authors in this book, six actually met him; of those six, two knew him reasonably well. This book would not exist if we all thought he was a lunatic or a charlatan. I hasten to add that you'll not find in this book any hero worship either. The man had his problems and faults indeed. Yet a more sincere and ultimately serious individual is impossible to imagine. To those who did not know him or who offended him he could be intolerable, but to those whom he let into his world he was a wonderful, lovable human being.

All this relates to his music too. It has its flaws and limits, but it's genuine and unique. At its best it draws us in to his world in ever deeper ways, with entrancing beauty and ineluctable sensuousness, overwhelming ratiocination and alarming power.

His major compositions are mystical in profound ways. Although not especially esoteric, they become decidedly unfathomable and even unfriendly if we try to approach them armed with the munitions of history ready to battle them into submission. In such cases we will always lose.

The ideal experiencing of Sorabji's music leads to a transformation of consciousness which is pointless to try to describe. It takes an open mind and a rare ability to concentrate which is, oddly, not difficult to develop. Sorabji's music, for all its hermetic qualities, is remarkably heuristic. Like its composer, it will enrich immeasurably those who are prepared to explore but not exploit it. It can come out only to those willing to risk going into it.

Still, it is not for everybody. If you read this book and hear, study, or perform some of his music, let me know how it, you, and Sorabji all get along.

2 Kaikhosru Shapurji Sorabji: An Introduction

Alistair Hinton

Alistair Hinton (b. 1950, Dunfermline, Scotland) studied composition with Humphrey Searle and piano with Stephen Savage at the Royal College of Music, London. He has written keyboard, chamber, and orchestral music which has been played by several notable performers.

He was a major influence in Sorabji's decision in the mid-1970s to allow public performances of his music. (Sorabji dedicated to him six works, comprising everything he wrote between 1973 and 1977.) As Sorabji's literary executor and the person responsible for his estate, he established and became the curator of the Sorabji Music Archive in 1988, in order to make Sorabji's work much more accessible than it had been.

He began this article in late 1976, about four and a half years after he had met Sorabji. (At the time, there was nothing available as a general introduction to the composer which was current and correct.) Consequently, some of his statements, particularly in the early part of the article, reflect the time of their writing. They give a sense of what it was like to write about Sorabji while he was alive, and of how exasperating it was to try to find information about him when almost none was available. Explanations, where necessary, are offered in the next chapter of this book and are referenced in this chapter by footnotes, all of which have been added by the editor.

In this chapter, quotations of words by Sorabji are not direct if they are in regular type and have regular margins. Smaller type and wider margins are used for direct quotations.

Kaikhosru Shapurji Sorabji was born in Chingford in the county of Essex, England, on the 14th day of August, in the year of our Lord ... here endeth the first sentence. As all dates in this chapter are intended to be correct, it would be a pity to spoil things by committing an error merely to satisfy idle curiosity.[1] Sorabji's father

---

[1] {See pp. 58–66 for a discussion of Sorabji's birth year and his attempts to prevent its disclosure.}

was a Parsi from Bombay, a civil engineer. His mother was a gifted Spanish-Sicilian soprano. Kaikhosru was their only child.

Sorabji's earliest recollection of music was of his mother singing Marguerite in Berlioz's *Damnation of Faust* in Paris. In London, where Sorabji lived with his parents, he received his first piano lessons from his mother, probably at an early age, and began attending concerts regularly. His education was largely private; he passed through the hands of several teachers, including the music tutor Charles A. Trew, until about 1915. At that time he began to compose; from then on his development as both pianist and composer became entirely his own responsibility. His close friend of the time, the composer Philip Heseltine (Peter Warlock), was among the first to heartily encourage Sorabji to follow his own creative path.[2]

The year 1915 also marked the appearance in print of Sorabji's earliest articles and essays. Six years later came the first publication of his compositions, funded by his father, as was each publication until his death in 1932.

From 1915 to 1982, with the exception of a few years, a steady stream of works flowed from Sorabji's pen, although considering the content of many of them, it would seem (as Sorabji once put it) more like a mighty Amazon than a stream. His completed compositions include three massive symphonies for organ solo; another two for voices, organ, and orchestra; a *Symphonic High Mass* for voices and orchestra; eleven works for piano and orchestra; a number of songs; a handful of chamber works, among which is perhaps the largest and most ambitious piano quintet in existence; and a voluminous contribution to the piano literature. His piano works vary in length from some Aphoristic Fragments (only a few seconds each) to others of 20 or 30 minutes to many others intended to be the sole item in any program (if permitted to be in any program at all: see below). His largest work, the three-volume Symphonic Variations for piano solo, would actually require an entire concert for each volume, as the whole might occupy more than eight hours.

In addition to this fury of creative activity, Sorabji also wrote well over a thousand pages of reviews, essays, articles, and "letters to the editor" on a wide variety of subjects. Among these are two volumes of essays, *Around Music* and *Mi contra fa*, together with contributions to symposia on Nicolas Medtner and Ananda Coomaraswamy.[3]

---

[2]{See Chapter 6 for a discussion of Sorabji's relationship to Heseltine.}
[3]{See the bibliography for details.}

In the 1920s and 30s, in addition to being a part-time freelance writer on music and other topics, he occasionally played some of his piano music in public. An extreme dissatisfaction with the procedures of concert-giving developed to the point where he finally made up his mind (in the late 1930s or early 1940s) to withdraw from the concert platform, as had Charles Valentin Alkan before him, and possibly for similar reasons. Unlike Alkan, however, he never played in public again after that decision. He went further: he withdrew his compositions from the concert hall, in effect producing a ban which lasted nearly 40 years. I will have more to say about the ban later.

In drawing further fascinating parallels between Alkan and Sorabji in a talk he gave in 1977, Kenneth Derus once suggested that their similarity as men and musicians was such that "it is often impossible to say where one leaves off and the other begins".[4] After highlighting the further similarity between the seemingly mysterious circumstances surrounding the death of Alkan and the birth of Sorabji, he wrapped up his thoughts on the subject with "I am in fact tempted to say that at 164 Alkan is still with us ..."

* * * * *

My own association with Sorabji's music began in November 1969. As a student at the Royal College of Music, London, I made one of my regular trips to the Central Music Library (Westminster), this time to obtain for a fellow student some guitar works of Fernando Sor. While seeking the required works on the library shelf, I came across an enormous thick oblong volume bound in blue, and was puzzled to read the awe-inspiring words on the spine "*Opus clavicembalisticum* — Piano — Sorabji". Upon opening it, I was confronted with its by now well-known imperiously forbidding dedication.[5] When I began to examine the music itself, I could hardly believe what I saw: nearly 250 pages containing three huge sections comprising twelve movements written mostly on three staves presenting such staggering polyphonic and polyrhythmic complexities as to render any comparison with the most difficult pages of Busoni or Szymanowski utterly pointless. Further intense examination ensued; shortly afterwards, it seems, I was told that it was closing time for the library. The elapse of several hours had quite escaped my notice, so engrossed was I in this gargantuan

---

[4]{Kenneth Derus: "Another Alkan", a paper read to the Alkan Society of Great Britain on 21 November 1977 in London.}

[5]{See p. 135 for this.}

epic. Like many who have come across it, I was fascinated, riveted, transfixed.

A host of questions immediately arose: Who was this composer? When and where was he born? What else had he written? Was he still alive? Above all, why had I not heard of him before?

Such answers as I was able to find were more baffling than the questions. No biography of Sorabji existed; the standard reference works were full of conflicting information in the titles and dates of his compositions as well as the date of his birth. I found a few more published works in the Central Music Library, as well as one manuscript (which, it turns out, was in a copyist's hand with annotations by Sorabji). I was fortunate to find, enclosed in the pages of the published piano concerto, an article on the composer by Erik Chisholm. This boasted the authoritative ring of a scholar who had not only heard and studied the early works of which he wrote but also knew the composer as a close personal friend. Unfortunately, a quick check revealed that this unique figure in Scottish music had died in 1965.

The most unusual aspect of this perplexing case was certainly the curiously prohibitive "all rights, including that of performance, reserved by the composer" which appeared on most of the published scores. My inability to imagine what manner of superhuman executant might perform some of these works satisfactorily was reason enough why I had never seen Sorabji's name on any concert or broadcast program. For a performer of his music I could only devise a sort of Utopian recipe: "Take the polyphonic and poetic subtleties of a Godowsky, stir in the clinical accuracy of a Michelangeli, bring to boil with the staggering virtuosity and phenomenal sight-reading and memorizing of an Ogdon, simmer and cover with the seemingly unlimited resources of physical stamina and will-power of an international decathlete." Such a synthesis of intellectual and physical ability within a single human being might be even more fearsome than the music!

About Sorabji, one source stated: "has banned the public performance of all his works". I was astonished at this unprecedented step, this apparent refutation of the very purpose of music. Not even Alkan or Liszt had gone that far.

Fortunately I was able to discuss Sorabji with my professor of composition, Humphrey Searle, who recalled a great deal about him. Although he had never heard Sorabji's own piano playing, he did attend the unfortunate performance in March 1936 by John Tobin of Part I of *Opus clavicembalisticum*.[6] What should have been some 50 minutes of dynamic — and at times even dæmonic —

---

[6]{Exact dates for concerts mentioned will be found in Chapter 12.}

energy and high contrapuntal tension was apparently presented with laboured clumsiness and distended to 80 or 90 minutes. This disaster prompted a friend of Sorabji to register a written protest. Sorabji, who had allowed this performance to proceed only with grave misgivings, was reviewing another London concert on the same evening, a commitment which was probably the only beneficial circumstance of this sad affair.

In December 1936, Sorabji gave his last public recital: his *Toccata seconda* in Glasgow. Shortly afterwards came the resolve to veto further public performances of his music.[7]

Searle lent me his precious copy of *Mi contra fa*, which was out of print. Once I had picked it up I could not put it down until I had devoured its contents from cover to cover. Sorabji emerged as a writer of tremendous conviction and profound scholarship with a complete command of English. His literary manner, with its penchant for extremely long sentences of complex yet flawless construction, seemed closely related to certain of his compositional techniques. His prose suggested an utterly sincere, deeply committed, and highly opinionated musician with a fearlessly headstrong courage who refused to suffer fools at all, let alone gladly, and whose devotion to his chosen art was such that he believed it to be far above the grasp of all but a very few people blessed with an uncommonly high degree of perception, sensitivity, and intelligence — an uncompromisingly elitist view of which he was gloriously proud.

Often pungent and vitriolic, at times downright vicious, his paragraphs were wont to unleash torrents of venomous vituperation upon all and sundry, while at the same time an abrasive humour relentlessly bulldozed its way from chapter to chapter, snapping and swiping in all directions at once. On the other hand, and with no leavening of this characteristically supercharged intensity, he plainly delighted in championing the causes of various neglected composers whose music particularly appealed to him.

His unyielding contempt for the mass of people on all sides of the concert-giving business (promoters, performers, audiences, and critics alike) and his equally pessimistic views of academic musical institutions in general and the notion of "teaching" the sacred art of composition in particular combined in an effort as determined as it was comprehensive to keep himself (and his music) to himself and a few close friends. Yet despite such adamantine postulations, Sorabji was in no way a mere dogmatist. He had the courage of his many convictions to admit having made hasty false judgements, as

---

[7]{The ban is discussed further in this chapter and is treated in detail in Chapter 3.}

in the cases of some of the work of Fauré, Strauss, and Shostakovich.[8]

His essays, then, described by some as enlightening and by others as exasperatingly wrong-headed, are shot through with profound erudition and brilliant wit. They come across as highly spiced entertainment, deliciously and almost disarmingly readable by musicians and nonmusicians alike.

* * * * *

As time passed, my preoccupation with Sorabji remained. I did eventually attempt to unravel at the piano the intricate subtleties of the shorter published pieces, and even parts of *Opus clavicembalisticum*. I was amazed at the sensuous beauty of his intensely personal harmonic language, and at the early maturity of his style. Above all, I was profoundly impressed by the innate sense of pianism, in that every technical problem posed seemed to arise from the intuitive practicality of a superb executant.

My piano teacher, Stephen Savage, knew of some of the published pieces of Sorabji. As it was obvious to us both that the remotest likelihood of my ever being able to perform such work was unworthy of consideration, he suggested I might make the effort to impress upon Sorabji the impact his compositions had made on me, and perhaps even venture to persuade him to reconsider his veto in the light of the vastly changed musical climate of the 1970s.

Several days were spent carefully and nervously drafting and redrafting a lengthy letter to the composer (whose Dorset address I had obtained from Edward Johnson, a friend of the composer Oliver Knussen, whom I had met a few years earlier). I had thought of writing to him before, but how, if at all, could I hope to open a correspondence with an artist of such lofty stature who had withdrawn himself into an exclusive domain into whose privacy he plainly intended to brook no intrusion (particularly from a student at one of those "institutions for the mass production of musicians" he so despised)? What reaction might I expect from this trenchant character whose literary sentiments seemed to erupt all over the page much as did his musical ones all over the keyboard?

In my letter to Sorabji I explained as best I could that I had no ulterior aims (in regard to his work) as a pianist, journalist, lexicographer, or broadcaster, imploring that my abiding fascination for his music was entirely that of another composer. At length I took my life in my hands and mailed it to him — the letter, that is, although it seemed like both at the time.

---

[8]{See pp. 269–70 for further details concerning Shostakovich and Fauré.}

Several days later Sorabji telephoned me. While I overcame my shock after hearing him introduce himself, he thanked me for my very kind letter and issued a general invitation to visit him. His warmth and cordiality were emphasized a few days later in this letter:

Dear Mr. Hinton,

Being one of those utterly unmodish unwithit persons who set rather a lot of store by the observance of what Aldous Huxley so finely calls THE IMMEMORIAL DECENCIES I felt so strongly that your charming letter deserved a quick acknowledgement — hence my phone call to you the other morning. I take it that you are a Scot? I know another Alistair[9] a fellow like yourself of great intelligence ... NOT an "intellectual" GOD FORBID ... one of those that is educated above their intelligence and perception. [...]

You are surprised, maybe at my ban on public performance of my work? Well, allow me to quote Scripture at you ... "CAST NOT YOUR PEARLS BEFORE SWINE LEST THEY TRAMPLE THEM UNDER THEIR FEET AND TURN AGAIN AND REND YOU." AND, when I see — and hear — the sort of people who DO get performed ... AND before WHOM ... Well[,] there by the grace of God <u>GO NOT I</u>! But I have no time for more at this moment. Enclosed may tell you quite a lot that you may — or may not — want to know. It will also I hope explain why being "recognised" by the sort of crowd who think that music begins and ends at the Maltings [...] has no especial charm for me, more specially when I consider the people who HAVE [thought] and DO think well of my work ...

Kind regards, and again many thanks,

Kaikhosru Shapurji Sorabji

P.S. Where and how did you get my address? I am curious!!
K. S. S.[10]

Among Sorabji's enclosures was the card which he had printed in response to being mislabelled in several reference works. He believed passionately in racial identity and took a just pride in his possibly unique mixed heritage. Considering his loathing of lexicographers and his passion for accuracy in these matters, he

---

[9]{Alastair Chisholm, no relation to Erik Chisholm.}

[10]{Kaikhosru Sorabji: Letter to Alistair Hinton, 29 March 1972. Three dots not in brackets are Sorabji's suspension points. Punctuation has been changed from Sorabji's only where it was misleading in the original. Typing errors, of which there are many in nearly all of Sorabji's letters, have been corrected.}

24 Discovery

became incensed to the point of fury whenever he was misrepresented:

> Mr. Kaikhosru Shapurji Sorabji wishes it to be known that he emphatically contradicts and repudiates certain completely inaccurate and objectionable public references to himself as an "Indian" composer.[11]

The mere fact of his father's birth in Bombay did not make him Indian. As a Parsi, Sorabji was proudly aware that his ancestors on his father's side, driven out of their native Persia many centuries ago, remain a people held together not only by their Zoroastrian faith but also by their common racial identity. What is more, Sorabji's British nationality does not imply that he was British by race; being called British or English thoroughly annoyed him. In response to one such occasion he wrote:

> I am BY NO MANNER OF MEANS NOR IN ANY WAY ENGLISH. I have not one drop of "English" blood in my veins.
> My racial, ancestral and cultural roots are in civilisations with more millenia behind them than Anglo-Saxondom has centuries. The description "English" is thus doubly derogatory and offensive.[12]

An amusing, if not confusing addendum to this case of the blindly prejudiced leading the blindly credulous was provided some time ago by a singer who believed that only a French composer could have created Sorabji's settings of Verlaine and Baudelaire, and that *Kaikhosru Sorabji* was therefore an exotic nom-de-plume of a Frenchman. (Alkan, perhaps?!)

Another of Sorabji's enclosures related to his birthdate and names. This too was printed, intended for those who dared to suggest certain things. The composer was born Leon Dudley Sorabji; some time during the First World War he adopted officially the Parsi given names by which he is known. Behind his defensive castigation lies commonsense elucidation:

---

[11]{The most widely available reference work committing this crime is *Grove's Dictionary of Music and Musicians*, 5th edition, edited by Eric Blom (London: Macmillan, 1954): the entry on Sorabji by Terence White Gervais (vol. 7, pp. 970–71). See pp. 211 and 221 for Sorabji's earliest views on being an Indian.}

[12]{Kaikhosru Sorabji: Letter to Garrard Macleod, Manager of radio station WMUK, Kalamazoo, Michigan, n.d., sent after Sorabji saw the description of himself in the February 1975 WMUK program guide as "a Twentieth-century Englishman of Parsi, Spanish and Sicilian extract".}

TO THOSE WHOM IT MAY CONCERN, IF ANY,
AND OTHERS WHO MIND ANYBODY'S
BUSINESS BUT THEIR OWN.

Dates and places of birth relating to myself given in various works of reference are invariably false.

It is also stated that my name, my real name, that is the one I am known by, is not my real name. Now one is given one's name — one's authentic ones — at some such ceremony as baptism, Christening, or the like, on the occasion of one's formal reception into a certain religious Faith. In the ancient Zarathustrian Parsi community to which, on my father's side, I have the honour to belong, this ceremony is normally performed, as in other Faiths, in childhood, or owing to special circumstances as in my case, later in life, when I assumed my name as it now is or, in the words of the legal document in which this is mentioned "... received into the Parsi community and in accordance with the custom and tradition thereof, is now and will be henceforth known as ..." and here follows my name as now.

Certain lexicographical *canaille,* one egregious and notorious specimen particularly, enraged at my complete success in defeating and frustrating their impudent impertinent and presumptuous nosings and pryings into what doesn't concern them, and actuated, no doubt, by the mean malice of the base born for their betters, have thought, as they would say, to take it out of me by suggesting that my name *isn't* really my name.

Insects that are merely noisome like to think that they can also sting.

KAIKHOSRU SHAPURJI SORABJI.

to which the composer added (on the copy he sent me) a couplet from Pope: "But let me flap this bug with gilded wings, / This painted child of dirt that stinks and stings".[13]

Perhaps even greater misunderstanding surrounds the ban Sorabji imposed on public performances. Many have assumed that he unequivocally forbade these under any circumstances. Although his various pronouncements on this matter were never completely consistent, his basic position was that public performances be given only with his express consent. There were at least three instances in

---

[13]{Alexander Pope: *An Epistle from Mr. Pope, to Dr. Arbuthnot,* lines 309–10. Unknowingly, perhaps, just by his addendum Sorabji suggested that insects that are noisome may in fact sting. (For verification, see p. 211.) He could have added Pope's next two lines as well (Pope's capitalization): "Whose Buzz the Witty and the Fair annoys, / Yet Wit ne'er tastes, and Beauty ne'er enjoys".}

the period of the ban when the composer was prepared to sanction them.

The first was in the 1940s, when Sorabji's friends Joy McArden and her husband James Cooper urged him to allow them to broadcast the three songs he had written and dedicated to them. Sorabji was particularly impressed with the speed and facility with which Joy McArden had mastered and memorized the difficult vocal line and penetrated the fabric of the music. The broadcast might have been given but for her untimely death.[14]

The great pianist Egon Petri, a longstanding friend of Sorabji and outstanding pupil of Busoni, nurtured for many years a desire to perform *Opus clavicembalisticum* in public. Although Sorabji presented him with a copy of the score in 1932, Petri's schedule of performing and teaching never permitted him the time demanded by so monumental a task.

In 1961 Sorabji wrote a short work usually known as *Fantasiettina* (the full title is much longer) for the 70th birthday (in 1962) of the Scottish poet Hugh MacDiarmid (pseudonym for Christopher Murray Grieve). The Scottish pianist-composer Ronald Stevenson asked to play it in a concert marking the occasion and, having the manuscript on loan from Sorabji, practised it in the hope that permission might be forthcoming. Forthcoming it certainly was, but it was also slow in coming forth, for Sorabji's vital telegram of assent arrived the day after the concert. This was clearly a case where "express consent" was not express enough.

From 1936 on, a number of Sorabji devotees as determined as the composer was unconcerned that he assume his rightful position of importance in 20th-century music discussed ways of persuading him at least to record his own music — if not permit more widespread performances than he seemed willing to. Some readers wrote in to *The New English Weekly*, for which Sorabji was the music reviewer, advocating formation of a private society to arrange for him to record *Opus clavicembalisticum*. It is a pity that nothing became of this, as Sorabji was probably at the height of his powers as a player at that time.[15]

In the early 1950s, the composer's friend Frank Holliday went to an extraordinary amount of trouble to arrange for a presentation letter to be given to Sorabji urging him to make recordings. This was no ordinary letter; it took months for Holliday to circulate it literally around the world to have it signed by a distinguished group

---

[14]{She died in 1952.}

[15]{Sorabji gave several reasons for not making records, or indeed recordings of any kind: see pp. 58 and 76–83.}

of cognoscenti consisting of many friends and associates of Sorabji, and to gather their donations. The full text follows:[16]

> We the undersigned have long admired your achievements in the realms of composition and scholarship. We are familiar with your music via the printed page but we would very greatly appreciate the opportunity of hearing authentic performances of it. We hope, therefore[,] that you will accept the enclosed gift as a mark of our esteem, both to you personally, and for your contribution to the art of music, and that you may see your way to record such of your works as you may consider best suited to gramophone reproduction. You would naturally have complete control over any records so made.
> In sending you this slight expression of our warmest and most deep felt friendship and admiration, we imply no obligation whatever on you to record, but we do beg that you will see your way to accede to our request that you should do so. We have taken the greatest care to restrict the knowledge of this letter to those we know to be your personal friends and admirers[,] as we know this would be your wish. We would[,] however, add that we are convinced that there is a much larger body of people who, like us, have a genuine desire to hear your music.

Among those who signed the letter were the composers York Bowen, Erik Chisholm, John Ireland, Roger Quilter, and Bernard Stevens; the writers and editors Harold Rutland, Norman Peterkin, Clinton Gray-Fisk, Alec Rowley, Denis Saurat, and Osbert Sitwell; and the pianist Egon Petri. Enclosed with the letter was a cheque for 121 guineas.[17]

Another signatory (and the most generous contributor) was Norman P. Gentieu of Philadelphia, a science writer and editor, who had corresponded with Sorabji since 1946 and had sent him all kinds of foodstuffs, due to their scarcity for some years in post-war London.[18] In the mid-1950s Gentieu even sent Sorabji a tape

---

[16]{It was written by the critic Clinton Gray-Fisk, who was also the dedicatee of at least three of Sorabji's works. (See the bibliography for citation of his article on Sorabji from 1960.) Frank Holliday first broached the idea in writing to a few people in December 1951. Having closed the fund for donations on 3 May 1953, he sent the letter and a cheque to Sorabji on 15 May. See footnote 17.}

[17]{In British decimal currency £127.05 (equivalent to about £2000 in 1992). The two most notable absences from the list of signatories were Francis George Scott and Christopher Grieve (Hugh MacDiarmid). Holliday contacted them, but neither ended up signing.}

[18]{Gentieu continued to send things even after Sorabji had moved to Dorset and supplies were easier to obtain.}

recorder. This he managed to do after some extensive work (rivalling that of Holliday's in connection with the presentation letter) involving the use of the assets frozen in England belonging to Bernard van Dieren's son, who was in Philadelphia.[19]

Despite the presentation letter and the tape recorder, Sorabji still found himself unable to comply with the requests of his well-wishers.[20]

Fortunately for posterity, Frank Holliday was even more tenacious and patient in this affair than all the others put together. Sorabji probably enjoyed playing his music more to Holliday than to anyone else, and developed a profound respect for Holliday's judgement and understanding of his music. Holliday's unique mix of earnestness, skilful diplomacy, and sheer hard work finally paid off in the early 1960s. Having convinced Sorabji of the importance of making recordings, Holliday acquired a Ferrograph tape recorder — the best home recorder he could find — and set about learning all he could about recording procedures. Although he lived a few hours away from Sorabji by car, he made many trips to Sorabji's house to record him, after painstaking study and experimentation with tapes, microphones, microphone placement, etc. In all, six recording sessions took place, from May 1962 to April 1968. All the recordings were made in the music room of Sorabji's house, where Sorabji chose to play on his splendid Steinway, an instrument made about 1896 which he had purchased in London in 1931 for £90.

* * * * *

Without the existence of these tapes, the last item enclosed in Sorabji's first letter to me could never have come into being. This comprised a transcript, program details, and some listeners' reactions to a three-hour broadcast which Donald Garvelmann had arranged over WNCN (New York) in December 1970. This included an entire talk written by Erik Chisholm (read by Frank Holliday because the original recorded by Chisholm shortly before his death was unusable) with illustrations from Frank Holliday's recordings of Sorabji playing his own music, plus additional material supplied by Garvelmann.[21]

---

[19]{For more details, see p. 312.}

[20]{In his *Opus est: Six Composers from Northern Europe* (London: Kahn and Averill, 1978), Paul Rapoport mixed together the story of the presentation letter and the tape recorder. They involved two separate sets of events, as related here.}

[21]{See Chapter 12. The Chisholm-Holliday talk with examples of Sorabji's playing (before Garvelmann created his substantial additions) had been

[CONT'D]

Donald Garvelmann, who worked in a law office in New York, had heard a performance (unauthorized) given by John Gates of Sorabji's *Fantaisie espagnole* in 1966. Soon afterwards, in searching for material to publish in an anthology of arrangements of Chopin's *Minute Waltz*, he came across a reference to Sorabji's Pastiche on the same. After he wrote to Sorabji, his efforts received complete cooperation. Sorabji sent him the manuscript, which, after some discussions and clarifications, Garvelmann published along with twelve other *Minute Waltz* transcriptions.[22]

* * * * *

After absorbing all the material Sorabji had sent in his letter to me, I felt I was beginning to know him a bit better. Even so, I had yet to hear any of his music. Respectfully but eagerly I enquired about the possibility of hearing any of the tapes, and whether Sorabji might consider playing to me if ever I was able to visit him. His answers were contained in a second letter:

> [... Y]ou must NOT either expect or HOPE that I will inflict any of the four PIANO SYMPHONIES upon you ... They are all of them bigger than Opus Clav. and FAR worse to play ... and my fingers are not equal to them nowadays being full of rheumatism and such like. You ask about recordings[;] my very great and dear friend Frank Holliday [...] possesses all the tapes [... T]hey are Frank's own private possession, naturally as he took ASTRONOMICAL pains and trouble over them bless him!
> You ask if there has been anything since the Fourth Piano Symphony ... YES, the FOURTH TOCCATA for piano ... one of my best works I think. It is the last and shall remain my last[.] I have finished with composition for good and all, and when you see the bulk of my MSS. you will understand why I have finished with music ... it <u>bores</u> me and musicians even more ... AND remember I've been at it since I was fifteen and have been writing the blasted stuff for sixty odd years. Don't you think I deserve a rest? I want to enjoy myself now and twiddle my thumbs [...]
> I HAVE felt stirrings of fresh ideas since [1967] and have even noted them down but very quickly said to myself NO NO MORE OF

---

heard a year earlier in New York. The Garvelmann broadcast in 1970 generated an unprecedented response: more than 75 people wrote in to WNCN. (See p. 91 for some of their comments.) Garvelmann's stimulating presentation, designed to get some response, was a partial cause of this.}

[22]{See the bibliography for the full citation. Sorabji did not expect Garvelmann to publish the Pastiche; as far as he was concerned, the real one was his second version, the *Pasticcio capriccioso* of 1933.}

THIS and tore them up! WHAT a relief! To HELL with composition ... MINE at any rate!²³

When writing this letter, Sorabji seemed to have forgotten his *Concertino non grosso* of 1968, but he had certainly written no major work since the *Fourth Piano Toccata* of 1967.

After a few more exchanges of letters, I finally went (by car) to Dorset to see Sorabji — on Monday, 21 August 1972.

Once through the small Dorset country town of Wareham and into the Purbeck hills, familiar to readers of Thomas Hardy, I found the scenery changed quite suddenly. Its austere majesty provided the ideal background for the ruined castle, gaunt yet imperious, towering above the landscape on the approach to the delightful old village of Corfe, where Sorabji lived.

At the far end of the village I finally found the lane in which the composer's house was situated. Up to this point I had felt more than a little apprehensive about meeting Sorabji; by the time I had arrived at the bottom of his driveway, I was petrified. Sorabji had gone to unique lengths to discourage uninvited visitors. On the left gatepost, under the words "The Eye" (so Sorabji named his house) was the following:

> NO FLAG DAY OR
> CHARITY TOUTING
> NO
> HAWKERS, PEDLARS
> OR CANVASSERS
> POLITICAL OR OTHER.
> GENUINE CATHOLIC
> i.e. ROMAN SISTERS
> WELCOME

On the right post was an emblem, the Eye of Horus, which seemed to glower with icy truculence at the unsuspecting beholder, followed by words in French from the preface of the *Queen of Sheba* which reminded me of that sense of "Abandon hope all ye who enter here" implicit in the fearsome words of dedication in the score and the opening phrase of *Opus clavicembalisticum*:²⁴

---

²³{Kaikhosru Sorabji: Letter to Alistair Hinton, 11 April 1972.}

²⁴{For the French extract from the *Queen of Sheba* from which the editor made this translation, see pp. 31 and 191.}

Left and right gateposts on the driveway of The Eye, Sorabji's house in Corfe Castle, Dorset (1978; photos by Paul Rapoport)

> As for those impervious to
> sensitivity,
> Those insecure in
> reasoning,
> Those weak in discernment,
> Who have no right to any life,
> It is they indeed who are
> The dead among the
> living.
> On them our indifference
> More evil than a curse.
> Amen!

Added to this the fact that the house was almost concealed by more than 250 densely packed trees surrounding it on all sides (which Sorabji had planted for that very purpose), it became clear that when he said he had built himself a "tower of granite", he meant precisely that.[25] Two further admonitions were affixed to the wall on the left of his front porch: "PLEASE LEAVE PARCELS ETC. INSIDE PORCH" and "All calls and visits Strictly Barred unless previously arranged".

Correctly imagining Sorabji to be a stickler for punctuality, I waited briefly until the appointed hour of 2:30 before ringing the doorbell. The door opened to reveal an olive-skinned, energetic looking yet diminutive figure (hardly more than five feet tall) with a shock of white hair and penetrating eyes which studied me from behind a pair of very thick black spectacles. He seemed enormously pleased to see me and ushered me into his music room. Having politely enquired what sort of journey I had had, he promptly asked me my age. (As it turned out, he had expected to meet someone in his forties; I was 21.) I retained the good sense not to return the question. Having seated myself, I gazed around the room. It was a veritable antique dealer's paradise, replete with magnificent pictures, ornaments, all manner of elaborate and exotic woodcarvings, hundreds of books (some rare and beautifully bound), and two grand pianos. One of these was the Steinway mentioned earlier; the other was a splendid specimen of the American manufacturer Mason and Hamlin, dating from around 1921.

"And in there", he proudly enthused, pointing towards a large cupboard, "are scores of scores by the great masters — valuable not only because of their contents but because some of them are no longer in print, for, you see, they are not the works of your *accepted* 'great masters' but those of the really great composers — such

---

[25]{See pp. 293–95 for more on the granite tower.}

noble men as Busoni, Szymanowski, Marx,[26] Rachmaninoff — my beloved Ernest Chausson, a single phrase of whose exquisite chamber music puts practically the entire repertoire of Herr Wolfgang Amadeus' monomaniacally repetitious chamber claptrap to shame."

That is at least the gist of what he said, for he invariably spoke at a speed almost too great for intelligibility; one had to adjust one's means of aural perception to take it all in.

"You'll not find a single Schubert or Brahms symphony or Beethoven piano concerto in there. Of course I've had such things in the far distant past but rid myself of them all long ago. In another cupboard, here, I have the handful of early printed examples of the supererogatory extravagance of a certain youthful Parsi noddle, for what, if anything, they may be worth ..." Such characteristic bursts of high-velocity verbal athletics were apt to confound the unaccustomed ear, particularly when (as was often the case) they flitted without warning from one European language to another with an alarming alacrity matched only by the extraordinary lucidity of linguistic command.

In the course of our conversation, Sorabji told me a fair bit about himself — that almost all his education was private, that both his parents spoke several European languages which he eventually studied formally, that he studied the piano with his mother, that he was really helped later in his piano playing by his mother's friend, the piano teacher Emily Edroff-Smith, although he had no actual lessons from her. Very early on he made it clear that he was no infant prodigy; indeed, not even a pianist in the accepted sense of the word. For he could never go before an audience to perform Beethoven, Chopin, Schumann, etc., nor had he ever wished to. "I am able, as far as my limited keyboard facility allows, to cover the ground of my own work sufficiently well, I hope and like to think, to convey at least some idea of what I am driving at."

And so the intense verbal cut-and-thrust continued, with me firing at Sorabji a host of questions which might easily have struck him as so much busybodying impertinence concerning his studies and background, his development as a composer, public appearances as a performer, literary writings, tastes in music, his historic meeting in 1919 with Busoni,[27] and many other matters. What I received amounted to much more than mere answers. Sorabji's conversational manner shared many qualities familiar to me in his correspondence, not least the gift for keeping under

---

[26]{Joseph Marx (1882–1964), the Austrian composer.}
[27]{See pp. 253–54 for one result of this meeting.}

control long and complex sentences, the at times almost wicked sense of humour, and an innate inability to be boring.

The contemplation of this figure, walled up in his own privacy (though still keenly aware of what was happening, musically and otherwise, in the world outside), and deeply involved in the ever-increasing prolixity of his own music, prompted my curiosity as to whether his self-imposed exile had ever engendered loneliness. "No, never", came the assured reply, along with a lecture on the difference between loneliness, which Sorabji called one of the most terrible of human misfortunes, and solitude, which afforded him complete freedom to create in a permanently calm and congenial atmosphere.

A calm and congenial atmosphere had certainly struck me the moment I had entered his music room. It also found expression in his playing to me of a few fragments from three works. Although the sheer physical strength which had undoubtedly characterized the performances of his youth had clearly ebbed away somewhat, there was still a good deal of dynamism, and an astonishing dexterity and looseness of wrist in rapid pianissimo chord-playing, despite arthritic restrictions. My overwhelming impression, however, was of the sheer loveliness of the sound he made, the gorgeous sonorities, the delight of the endless riches of his pianistic invention.

Sorabji played for me on many of my subsequent visits. The impression on each of these all-too-rare occasions was as profound and indelible as was the first. He explained that he felt the piano was not just an extension of his personality, but actually part of him, so that playing it was essential as it was natural. Just as even the most eulogistic paragraphs in his most passionate essays can scarcely give an inkling of his genuine warmth and openheartedness, so the most exhaustive analysis by the eye and mind's ear cannot provide the remotest idea of the power and beauty of the actual physical sound of this music.

* * * * *

In February 1973, at Sorabji's suggestion, I went to visit Norman Peterkin, who held some phonograph records which had been made from Frank Holliday's tapes of Sorabji's playing. Peterkin (1886–1982) had first encountered Sorabji's name during the First World War, when he came across some of his articles while working in Hong Kong:

> I read his articles on music, musicians, composers, critics [...] I at once felt that here was a most powerful intellect at work writing of

Top: The approach to one doorway of Sorabji's house
(1978; photo by Paul Rapoport)
Bottom: Sorabji at his Steinway in his music room in 1966
(photo by Norman Peterkin)

36   Discovery

the contemporary musical scene in incisive and masterly fashion [...] I was so stirred and excited at his writings that I took my courage in both hands and wrote to him out of the blue to express what I felt. [...]

Soon I received a most kind and warm reply from Sorabji [...] In due course I returned to England, and then met Sorabji [...] in 1917 [...]

[My wife and I] heard him play his own works [... He was] a virtuoso pianist of international standards. If his critical writings had originally so impressed me with his intellectual powers, his actual music astounded me. I felt here was a composer (with an incredible compositional technique) whose work was as unique and individual as that of Mahler, Berg, Schoenberg, and other giants of the period — though of utterly different nature. I was certain then, and still am, that his work is a seminal force in twentieth-century music. [...]

I cannot say our life-long friendship has been a smooth one. Over various matters, musical and otherwise, mainly raised by him, we have disagreed violently and fought like cats [...] It never made the slightest difference to our affection for each other; and for me he remains a unique personality, and undoubtedly a genius of whom I am proud to be an intimate friend.[28]

Peterkin joined the Oxford University Press Music Department in 1925 and was for many years its Chief Music Editor. It was entirely due to his efforts that the 14 works by Sorabji which were published between 1921 and 1931 by three different publishers came to be available from a single publishing house: in 1938, OUP became the sole selling agent for those works (and remained such until 10 October 1988, when the last copy of any of Sorabji's works held by OUP was sold).

I had been forewarned by Peterkin that the quality of the records was inferior to that of the tapes, especially in dynamics. Nonetheless, the playing I heard on the records was in every way as masterly and exquisite as when I had heard him play the previous summer.

During my visit to Peterkin I asked if he considered that there was any likelihood that Sorabji might consider lifting the ban on public performance of his music. He was convinced that the privacy afforded by this self-imposed silence had become too firmly established in Sorabji's mind for him to give even a moment's thought to the matter. Nevertheless, I made it almost a matter of

---

[28]{Norman Peterkin: "A Note on Kaikhosru Sorabji", in program notes for the concert by Yonty Solomon on 7 December 1976 in London, pp. 8–9.}

principle to raise the subject at each of my subsequent visits to Sorabji himself.

In late February 1973 Sorabji sent me something in a large oblong envelope ... a single folio of manuscript, the *Benediction of Saint Francis of Assisi* for baritone and organ, bearing the date "xx. ii. mcmlxxiii".[29] That Sorabji had inscribed this work with a dedication to me naturally moved me deeply, but what struck me most was the fact that this marked the first time in several years he had permitted himself to compose anything at all.[30] A few weeks later he sent me some sketches for a new symphony for solo piano, his fifth, to be entitled *Symphonia brevis*. Sorabji, no longer able to stem the tidal wave of his creative imagination, was back "in gear" as a composer. Completion was announced in November, when he sent me a scrap of music paper he had "spoilt" (as he would say) with a copy of the work's poignant final cadence, adapted from the complete piano part of his incomplete Symphony No. 2 of 1930–31. I had visited him twice during the autumn, when he played me short extracts from the new symphony. His imagination showed itself to be as fecund and his expressive powers as resourceful as they had ever been.[31]

The broadcast originally given over WNCN was repeated by arrangement with its presenter, Donald Garvelmann, over KPFA in Berkeley, California in November 1973, as *Symphonia brevis* was nearing completion. A week before Christmas another letter from Sorabji informed me that the next work was under way, *Opusculum claviense* (later changed to *Opusculum clavisymphonicum*), a concerto-like composition for piano and chamber orchestra in two movements, which was eventually to take up more than 300 pages.[32]

Early in June 1974 I was able to visit Frank Holliday at his home near Eastbourne, Sussex, to hear some of the original tapes of Sorabji's playing. These certainly sounded much more like the genuine article than the records in the possession of Norman Peterkin. The whole tape collection runs over ten hours; anyone

---

[29]{Sorabji often indicated the date of completion of a work in Roman numerals. Many of his letters also carried dates in Roman numerals, and he even used them to number the pages of one work, the *First Piano Toccata*.}

[30]{Other than a few Aphoristic Fragments.}

[31]{The first three of Sorabji's major works written after his creative silence in 1969–72, including this symphony, were dedicated to Alistair Hinton. Without his interest in the composer, it is questionable whether Sorabji would have resumed composing at all, and certain he would not have done so as soon as he did.}

[32]{On the manuscript its starting date is given as 26 December 1973.}

interested in Sorabji should have intense gratitude to Holliday for creating them under very difficult conditions.[33]

February 1975 brought yet another replay of Garvelmann's Sorabji broadcast, this time arranged by Kenneth Derus over WMUK in Kalamazoo, Michigan. From April 1975 Sorabji was occupied with his Sixth Piano Symphony, another huge score. When I visited him in November 1975 he was halfway through this work. I tried resuscitating the well-worn and forbidding (if not forbidden) question about public performances by asking him if any change of heart might result from his renewed career as a composer. He was not going to fall for that, however, and dismissed any possible connection. He informed me that he had refused all requests from pianists, as well as a request to do a talk on Radio 3 of the BBC, an institution he had detested for many years.

* * * * *

In February 1976 I went to hear a performance of the Ives Second Sonata and Berg Sonata by Yonty Solomon. I had heard that he had been interested in Sorabji's music and also recalled his broadcasts of the two Ives sonatas in 1974.

After the concert, Solomon discussed his interest in playing Sorabji's music. He had first encountered it as a university student in Cape Town, where his teacher, Erik Chisholm (who was also the Dean of the music faculty), encouraged his interest in it. He had been studying *Opus clavicembalisticum* there and continued to do so from time to time since his university days. After he settled in London in 1963, he studied with some well-known pianists, travelled extensively as recitalist and soloist, amassed an extremely varied repertory, and gave premieres of many contemporary works. He had recently sought, via Oxford University Press, Sorabji's permission to play *Opus clavicembalisticum* in London's Queen Elizabeth Hall. His request was forwarded to Sorabji by Alan Frank, then head of the OUP Music Department. Permission had, of course, been denied.[34] Solomon's understandable intense

---

[33]{The original tapes are now in Mills Memorial Library, McMaster University, Hamilton, Ontario, Canada, along with virtually all of Frank Holliday's "Sorabjiana": letters, other writings, articles, etc. (mostly by Sorabji) from a period of over 40 years. Included in this material are the detailed notes Holliday made on recording Sorabji. They give an accurate idea of the extensive efforts he made.}

[34]{One reason may have been that, instead of asking Sorabji's permission, Alan Frank wrote to him (on 23 October 1974) *announcing* that Solomon was planning to play his music in London in 1975. Frank Holliday
[CONT'D]

disappointment at this outcome did not, however, dampen his enthusiasm for Sorabji's music or his desire to perform some of it in public, even though such a possibility seemed to merit no further consideration.

Nearly a month later I went to see Sorabji. I earnestly poured out to him the entire story of Solomon's long-standing boundless admiration for his music, his connection with Erik Chisholm, and the vast amounts of time Solomon devoted to preparing *Opus clavicembalisticum* for a prospective London performance he was then barred from giving. I also recounted in the warmest possible terms my recent experience of Solomon's compelling performances of Berg and Ives, and how I felt that he seemed so well equipped to tackle some of Sorabji's music.

Sorabji listened intently. After a tense, almost unbearable *lunga pausa*, he declared, "I don't recall Yonty Solomon's name. However, if he is as fine a pianist as you say ... AND if dear Erik, whose judgements and opinions I valued and respected ENORMOUSLY, and STILL DO, also thought as highly of him as he appears to have done, well ... if Mr. Solomon still feels the same way about my work and would like to write to me ... yes, I'll tell him that if he wishes to give some public performances of it, I'll certainly let him."

This long hoped-for and overdue state of affairs had come about without warning; Sorabji seemed to make this decision with surprising ease.[35]

Of course I telephoned Yonty Solomon as soon as I could, the first opportunity being around midnight that same day (23 March). At first he was none too pleased to hear from me, especially on a matter which for him had become something of a sore point. He was, however, convinced by what I told him and resolved to write to Sorabji. Sorabji telephoned him the next morning (24 March), giving him his full permission.

A few months later Sorabji heard a broadcast by Solomon of Albéniz's *Iberia*. He commented to me afterwards: "What an

---

also told Paul Rapoport that Sorabji did not like Alan Frank. If an intermediary was unacceptable to Sorabji, the intermediary's request on behalf of someone else was denied.}

[35]{According to Donald Garvelmann (in a letter to Paul Rapoport dated 27 April 1977), Sorabji had already given *tentative* approval for public performances by Michael Habermann, subject to Garvelmann's decision that Habermann was ready to play the music in public.

In any case, Alistair Hinton did not know of this tentative approval at the time, and Habermann's first "authorized" performance did not come until after Solomon's. See footnote 38.}

extraordinary MUSICIAN he is ... the tone he draws from the instrument is truly superb ... he never goes what I call 'clean through to the wood' as seems to be the done thing for so many of these blasted modern piano players ... Solomon is undoubtedly in a class far and away above any of these ... indeed I have to admit that the sound of his playing reminded me a little of that of Busoni ... and that in itself is — and most certainly ought to be — more than sufficient to make up my tiny Parsi mind about him ..."

Eventually Solomon scheduled a recital at London's Wigmore Hall for December 1976, nine days before the 40th anniversary of Sorabji's last public performance. There was plenty of advance publicity on the radio and in the press, some of it worthy, some much less so. Inevitably this included some of the "Sorabji mystique" and "legendary recluse" coverage. The recital itself was a tremendous success. After a demanding first half (of works by Busoni, Berg, John Rushby-Smith, and Wilfrid Mellers), the second half presented Sorabji's *Le jardin parfumé*, Two Piano Pieces (*In the Hothouse* and *Toccata*), and *Fantaisie espagnole*.[36] An extensive although far from error-free program booklet was produced for the occasion. The critical reviews were generally very favourable, even if scant coverage was allotted to the first half of the program.

How had it all affected Sorabji? He had already declared that he did not intend to be present on this or any similar future occasion. He flatly refused to go and "make an exhibition" of himself and certainly had no curiosity for what "johnny public" thought of him or his work. He was obviously in no way interested in collecting any public approbation for himself. He appeared to be half afraid to hear how his music had been received.[37] (His interest in the audience at this concert was limited to what it thought of Solomon.)

Among the results of Solomon's recital was a plan for a television documentary on Sorabji, to be produced for London Weekend Television by Derek Bailey, with Russell Harty as presenter. Reluctant at first, Sorabji eventually agreed, provided that any intrusion upon his privacy was restricted to the barest minimum, and that no pictures were taken. As Sorabji had never possessed a television himself, I pointed out to him that this would make for unsatisfactory viewing by the television audience. After further consideration, he agreed to the incorporation of still photographs of an interview on condition that no live filming take place. The television crew recorded the interview at Sorabji's home (The Eye)

---

[36]{All of these were published works written between 1918 and 1923.}

[37]{A telling remark; see p. 79 for more about Sorabji's fear of audiences.}

on 1 March 1977; the remainder of the program was made on 28 May at a London Weekend Television studio.

It included interviews with the writer Sir Sacheverell Sitwell, the critic Felix Aprahamian, and me, as well as Yonty Solomon playing some of Sorabji's music and illustrating its technical problems. Extracts from the interview recorded at The Eye were interspersed in the program to allow the composer to speak for himself. After a testy and prickly beginning, Sorabji gradually got into his stride and appeared eventually to enjoy the interview — so much so that he failed to notice the camera crew filming the departure from The Eye and showing quite a lively and spry Sorabji waving farewell to the television team. The broadcast was transmitted in June 1977. Sorabji never saw it.

A few weeks before the television broadcast, the young American pianist Michael Habermann (b. 1950) gave his first authorized performance of Sorabji's music, in the Carnegie Recital Hall in New York. After Donald Garvelmann had sent Sorabji a tape of Habermann playing some of the shorter pieces, Sorabji consented to public performances by Habermann, initially not to include any taking place in England. (That restriction, imposed for Yonty Solomon's benefit, was later withdrawn, although Habermann has not played in England.) Habermann's concert presented works by Haydn, Chopin, Liszt, and Godowsky, as well as Sorabji's *Fantaisie espagnole, In the Hothouse,* Pastiche on the "Habanera" from Bizet's *Carmen,* and the Fugue from his Prelude, Interlude, and Fugue.[38]

---

[38]{Habermann played published works written between 1918 and 1920, except for the *Carmen* Pastiche, written in 1922 and not published. On the program page, this piece was marked with "first authorized performance". (Habermann had in fact already played it in 1975: see p. 436.) Habermann was also noted as "the first pianist to be honored by Sorabji's granting of permission to perform his works", but, as mentioned in footnote 35, the evidence for this is indirect. Final definite consent (to play his works in the USA) came from Sorabji to Habermann in a letter from the composer to Donald Garvelmann dated 28 July 1976 (after Yonty Solomon's permission), even if discussions about the matter began or tentative approval came before that.

Nonetheless, the first pianist in this period to be given permission by Sorabji to record his music was neither Habermann nor Solomon, but Hans Kann. In response to a request from Donald Garvelmann in July 1972 that Kann be allowed to record for the Musical Heritage Society the *Minute Waltz* Pastiche along with all the other *Minute Waltz* transcriptions in Garvelmann's published collection, Sorabji consented, partly because he considered the Pastiche simply a fun piece of no importance. The recording was never made.}

This concert, his New York debut, was a great success for him and to some extent for Sorabji.

The first time any large-scale Sorabji work received a complete public performance by someone other than the composer was in June 1977, when Yonty Solomon played the Third Piano Sonata a few days after the television broadcast.[39] Solomon excelled himself on this occasion with his masterly handling of the seething tumult of this complex, convoluted, tragic, volcanic sonata, although some of its calmer moments seemed to become suffused beneath its relentless propulsion. The critics received this work with unanimous acclaim, paying tributes to Solomon's transcendent virtuosity and interpretative insight. The vexed question of duration gave rise — or fall, depending on the order of reading — to three quite different figures in as many reviews: 90, 75, and 65 minutes. The actual duration was about 73 minutes.

In September 1977 the soprano Jane Manning appeared in a concert with Solomon. She had an extensive repertoire which included much contemporary music, as well as music of composers of the English Musical Renaissance (of the early part of this century), including two whom Sorabji passionately admired: Delius and Van Dieren. After the concert she discussed Sorabji with Solomon, informing him that she had seen the June television broadcast.

Not long afterwards I visited Jane Manning at her London home, armed with Sorabji's two published sets of songs and several of his other songs in manuscript. We worked through most of these together, she sight-singing from manuscript lines of varying legibility with consummate ease, I stumbling at the keyboard through parts I had previously spent hours trying to prepare in the hope of "covering the ground" of them, as Sorabji would have put it. It is undeniable that I succeeded only in covering the ground with a Persian carpet of wrong notes and myself in embarrassment. Manning observed not only where some of my mistakes occurred but how the music should have sounded, while singing the vocal line at sight.

I recounted this episode in its entirety to Sorabji. After discussing a proposed vocal performance with Solomon and receiving a letter from Manning, he granted her permission on condition that Solomon be the pianist. The next February Manning and Solomon recorded Sorabji's two published sets of songs for a broadcast, which took place in June 1979.

---

[39]{It is of course possible that someone else played this work first, as it had been published in 1925. That is unlikely, however, given its difficulty.}

On 3 October 1977 Solomon went to visit Sorabji for the first time and played some of his music to him in his music room. Sorabji later reported, "I was staggered to hear him make my music sound just as I myself once could."

In November, the BBC broadcast Solomon playing the works he had done in December 1976, beginning with *Le jardin parfumé*, the only work that Sorabji himself had broadcast — on 22 April 1930. This marked the removal of the ban Sorabji had imposed on the BBC broadcasting his work. A few days after the broadcast, which Sorabji did hear, he sent Solomon a letter of thanks which was quoted in the program notes for his next recital, which followed in late November 1977:

My dear Yonty;

This is to repeat fortissimo what I said to you over the 'phone for your splendid playing of ME on Monday night! You have <u>everything</u> I look for in a pianist who tackles me ... unfailingly beautiful tone, complete insight and sympathy with my way of musical thinking ... and well it was perfectly satisfying in every possible way. Mille e Mille grazie ...[40]

* * * * *

In the 1950s and early 1960s, a large number of Sorabji's manuscripts were microfilmed, thanks to the initiative, persistence, and generosity of Norman Gentieu. Most of the microfilming took place in Sorabji's home, but only after a voluminous correspondence among Gentieu (in Philadelphia), Sorabji (in Corfe Castle), and Kodak (in London). Some of these microfilms are held at the University of Cape Town, South Africa; and at the International Piano Archives (College Park, Maryland), Northwestern University, Mills College, and the Philadelphia Free Library in the USA.

In 1977, Paul Rapoport asked my assistance in trying to microfilm the works which had not yet been filmed, which included a number of early works as well as everything Sorabji had written since the last filming. In the spring of 1978 Rapoport came to England to join me in completing the bulk of the filming, and bulk there was: we had to rent a sizable car in order to haul a large number of manuscripts from Corfe Castle to London, and then to the north of London for the actual microfilming. He and I sat for

---

[40]{Program notes for the concert by Yonty Solomon on 22 November 1977 in Wigmore Hall, London.}

five days opposite each other in a small room dark except for the light of a microfilming camera, engaged in the mindless and numbing act of turning thousands of pages. We began to wonder when Sorabji's Sixth Piano Symphony would ever end, something we would never have done at a performance. Some of the scores were extremely large and heavy: the full score of the *Symphonic High Mass,* for instance, would alone take up most of a first-class airline baggage allowance — high mass indeed.[41]

Since that time, more microfilms have been made in England, the USA, and Canada, as more works were completed or discovered. The microfilm collection of Sorabji's music manuscripts is now almost complete.

* * * * *

In the late 1970s and early 1980s Yonty Solomon and Michael Habermann continued to program Sorabji's music. In 1980 appeared the first commercial recording to contain Sorabji's music, with Michael Habermann playing various shorter — but by no means easy — piano works. The critics were intrigued as well as pleased with it. Since then Habermann has released two more recordings.[42]

In late 1978, Paul Rapoport mentioned the possibility of a performance in Toronto of Sorabji's *Michelangelo Sonnets* for baritone and chamber ensemble. Sorabji's permission was obtained; I sent Rapoport a photocopy of the score; he wrote out all the parts.[43] In February 1980 the performance took place, preceded (the night before) by a talk given by Rapoport on Sorabji, illustrated by Valerie Tryon performing two contrasting early works. The performance of the *Sonnets,* the first of any of Sorabji's orchestral music, puzzled the Toronto critics.[44]

---

[41]{Copies of the four reels of microfilms which were made in England at this time may be found at the British Library, Northwestern University, the New York Public Library, the University of Toronto, and the Library of Congress. Because it also has the set made in the 1950s, Northwestern University has the largest public collection of Sorabji's manuscripts on microfilm.}

[42]{See Appendix 2 for a complete list of the recordings of Sorabji's music.}

[43]{Something so problematic he swore he would never write out parts for Sorabji's music again. See the discussion about Sorabji's organ symphonies on pp. 48–49.}

[44]{Partly because of the density of the writing and certain problems in the performance. They could not understand why people came from as far away as Texas to hear the *Sonnets.*}

In 1979 and 1980 Sorabji's broadcasting "career" continued. In the second instance, this involved an interview of Sorabji, Ronald Stevenson, and me for a BBC Radio 3 broadcast commemorating the centenary in 1980 of Nicolas Medtner.

In the first instance, BBC Scotland asked for a television interview with Ronald Stevenson and Sorabji to commemorate the centenary (also in 1980) of the birth of the Scottish composer Francis George Scott. Sorabji agreed immediately.[45] The interview, filmed in June 1979, went very well, but the program as eventually shown regrettably did not include the footage with Sorabji. The occasion did, however, enable Stevenson to meet Sorabji, whose music and articles he had known for more than 20 years. Not long afterwards, Sorabji unhesitatingly gave his permission to Stevenson — for the second time — to perform the *Fantasiettina*, which Stevenson finally did in August 1981, as well as on many occasions afterwards. In the meantime, Sorabji had completed a piano work for Stevenson, *Villa Tasca*, a return to a subject he had used 50 years earlier in his Fourth Piano Sonata, which had been dedicated (appropriately enough) to Francis George Scott. I sent Stevenson a photocopy of the completed work in May 1980. He was delighted:

> Villa Tasca has been planted in Peeblesshire! She arrived this morning. The delay was caused because the Post Office found the package open and had to re-seal it. But what can you expect if you will send a whole villa through the mail?![46]

The completion of *Villa Tasca* was interrupted midway for what in some ways is the most bizarre event in this story. After nearly 65 years of composing, Sorabji received his first commission. More surprising is that the work commissioned (by Norman Gentieu on behalf of the Philadelphia branch of the Delius Society) was for flute and string quartet — not a combination Sorabji would ever freely choose.[47] Most amazing of all is that Sorabji even laid aside a piece in progress in order to get on with the commission immediately. The result, *Il tessuto d'arabeschi*, received its first performance on the occasion of the 1982 annual general meeting, dinner, and concert of the society involved, though not before some

---

[45]{Perhaps because of his love of Scott's music and his realization that this time the program would not be focusing on him.}

[46]{Ronald Stevenson: Letter to Alistair Hinton, 19 May 1980.}

[47]{As he had done previously in connection with the tape recorder sent to Sorabji and the microfilming of his works which took place in the 1950s and 60s, Gentieu financed the commission. Sorabji was paid the equivalent of US$1000 for the quintet (closer to $2000 in 1992).}

46 Discovery

sour thoughts on it had passed through the systems of both composer and performers.⁴⁸ Shortly after beginning the work Sorabji told me that

> Norman [Peterkin] giggled like anything when I told him about it over the phone. "Fancy YOU writing a string quartet." What NONSENSE[.] What I write will flout all the "CORRECT" ideas of chamber music[,] PO-MUSIC as a candidly outspoken person once called it,⁴⁹ and if I can show my dislike contempt and ridicule of the medium the better I shall like it ... and [a] few insults to the earnest highminded pompous prigs dolts and dullards who yearn and wilt over the goddam stuff ..."⁵⁰

The players all grumbled about the work's unrewarding unplayability, but the performance was a convincing one. The music, though not Sorabji at his very best, is by no means as unworthy as he suggested it might be: it has a sheer beauty in the delicate filigree of its "drawing of long lines".

* * * * *

Some chronological vacillations have been necessary in recounting the events surrounding Sorabji and his work which have come to pass since 1976, due to their overlap and number. It is necessary now to set back the clock once more, to February 1980. At that time Jane Manning gave a recital in Holland; her pianist was Geoffrey Douglas Madge.

Madge was born and had studied in Australia but left there, eventually settling in The Netherlands. Like Manning's, his repertory is unusually large and varied, embracing works by Alkan, Godowsky, Busoni, Reger, Szymanowski, Schoenberg, as well as Skalkótas, Boulez, Xenakis, Cage, and Stockhausen. Although Manning and Madge had known each other for some years, it was not until he drove her to the airport on the morning she left Holland that he mentioned his long-standing fascination for Sorabji. Manning told him of her performance of the songs and eventually put him in touch with me. On 1 April 1980 he came to visit me; we talked until the not-so-small hours of the morning about many composers and performers Sorabji had known, about pianos, and about a host of

---

⁴⁸{Norman Gentieu asked Paul Rapoport if he would copy out the performing parts for this quintet, but in view of what footnote 43 expresses, Rapoport convinced someone else (the Canadian copyist and composer Elma Miller) to do it, retaining only a supervisory role in the operation.}

⁴⁹{"Po" is a short form of *chamber pot*.}

⁵⁰{Kaikhosru Sorabji: Letter to Alistair Hinton, November 1979.}

matters concerning Sorabji, his music, and its performance. He played to me the first two movements of *Opus clavicembalisticum*, which he wanted to include in a performance.

We went to see Sorabji the following afternoon (2 April).[51] After much easily flowing conversation, Sorabji assured Madge, with no little irony, that he must not feel under any obligation to play to him after so long and tiring a journey! This became the cue for Madge to seat himself before the Mason and Hamlin to play the first two movements of *Opus clavicembalisticum*. The performance over, there followed a long and tense period of silence, after which Sorabji rose very slowly and deliberately from his seat, expressed his admiration for Madge's playing, and was immediately forthcoming not merely with permission but with encouragement to perform the whole work. Although he disagreed with a few individual matters of interpretation, he discouraged discussion of them, insisting that Madge's ideas of the passages in question were thoroughly convincing and that he had no wish for him to alter his playing of them accordingly.

Four performances of the opening two movements were then hurriedly scheduled for June 1980 in Holland. Afterwards, Madge continued his work on *Opus clavicembalisticum* in preparation for a complete performance. On Sorabji's authority he obtained a photocopy of the manuscript from the University of Cape Town. Finally the impossible was made manifest on 11 June 1982: an historic occasion more than worth the anticipation it generated. The profundity, humanity, and power of Sorabji's genius were revealed to an immeasurable degree. The entire performance was broadcast live (keeping the radio station on the air for more than an hour beyond its customary closing time) and made into a four-record set which was released in Holland in 1983.[52]

Madge's next performance of the complete work was arranged by Kenneth Derus for April 1983 in Chicago; it was followed by one in Bonn a few weeks later. The latter was a fine peformance, despite being given to an audience numbering barely 50.

Sorabji wrote his last works in the early 1980s; his very last was completed some six months before he turned 90. Even after this, although no longer able to hold a pen steadily enough or see sufficiently well to work at a score, his creative imagination remained as fiery as ever. On several occasions, and as late as his

---

[51]{Without much sleep, one surmises!}

[52]{See Chapter 10 for Madge's perspective on his initial visit to Sorabji, as well as his discussion of all of his complete performances of *Opus clavicembalisticum*.}

96th birthday,[53] he spoke of contemplating a new piano piece based on Rachmaninoff's *Vocalise* (Op. 34, No. 14).

While Sorabji himself found it impossible to continue writing, activity in the furtherance of his music increased steadily. In the 1980s Michael Habermann, Yonty Solomon, and Geoffrey Madge continued to give performances and broadcasts, Madge's taking place in several countries. Michael Habermann's two later Sorabji recordings were issued in 1982 and 1987. Other performers began to take an interest as well, with some spectacular results which will be discussed shortly.

In 1979, Sorabji's *Around Music* had been reprinted in an edition he knew nothing about and did not like. But the reprinting of *Mi contra fa*, containing a new introduction by Donald Garvelmann, was issued in 1986 with his approval. In late 1977 Sorabji had remarked on the fact that the score of *Opus clavicembalisticum* was no longer available by observing that it was "the last of my works to get into print and the first to get out of it". He was to be proved wrong in the first particular. In 1987 Barry Peter Ould, of Bardic Edition, issued a splendidly prepared "performing edition" of the *Fantasiettina*, edited by Ronald Stevenson; it is also a "teaching edition", containing Stevenson's notes and preparatory exercises. Curiously, the thread of Sorabji's music in publication was taken up in a sense in which it left off, for both *Opus clavicembalisticum* and the *Fantasiettina* are dedicated to Hugh MacDiarmid. Sorabji also described the latter work as a footnote to the former.

In 1986 Douglas Carrington, enterprising editor of the English journal *The Organ*, suggested Sorabji's First Organ Symphony for performance at the 1987 International Congress of Organists in England. Its first complete performance took place by two organists, but one, Kevin Bowyer, was so taken with it that he quickly determined to prepare the entire work for further performance. Chris Rice, of Altarus Records, who attended this remarkable occasion, decided to record the symphony with Bowyer. Bowyer performed it on his own first in Denmark in April 1988, having already made the recording which was issued later in the same year.

Bowyer considers Sorabji's three organ symphonies to be some of the most important music for the instrument since Bach. But his work in preparing all of them for performance and recording highlights one of the major problems with Sorabji's music. In the First Symphony alone, by consulting a photocopy of Sorabji's original manuscript, he unearthed well over a thousand errors in the published score: misprints, doubtful notes, and other problems,

---

[53]{After a stroke and two months before his death.}

many of which were also in the manuscript. For the other two symphonies, which were never published, he realized that his first undertaking would have to be to prepare fair copies of them longhand, making corrections as necessary. The amount of work involved in hand-copying but one of these mammoth Sorabji scores (lasting several hours in performance) is such that very few scholars or potential performers would ever consider taking it on. In the likely absence of further superhuman deciphering and copying jobs such as Bowyer's, good editions of Sorabji's larger works are very unlikely to be realized. This will obviously stand in the way of their performance.

Even issuing shorter works, some of which Yonty Solomon, Michael Habermann, and others have similarly recopied, is to most publishers a commercial impracticality. The greater part of Sorabji's œuvre will therefore probably remain entirely unknown to many listeners, unless some way is found to make it more available to the eye and accessible to the ear. Any meaningful and comprehensive assessment of Sorabji's musical output will almost certainly have to be left to the listeners and scholars of the late 21st rather than the late 20th century.

* * * * *

Sorabji received a letter from Chris Rice in May 1985 seeking permission for his company Altarus to make a commercial recording of *Opus clavicembalisticum* and informing him that Ronald Stevenson had recommended John Ogdon in the strongest possible terms. Sorabji gladly gave his consent.[54] The recording was made on a Bösendorfer Imperial Grand in 1985 and 1986, but issued only in May 1989, as the financial resources involved were considerably in excess of the norm. On some days, after playing for the microphone for 12 or 14 hours, Ogdon seemed to have more energy at the end of the session than at the beginning. This characteristic could also be observed in his first complete performance of the work in July 1988. The playing itself was utterly staggering and seemed, in defiance of all laws of nature and common sense, to increase in compelling energy in its last hour or so.[55] Stevenson declared the event a landmark in the history of

---

[54]{In 1961, he had refused Ogdon's request to perform *Opus clavicembalisticum* in a studio for broadcast. His agreeing in 1985 probably had more to do with his age and with leaving more and more of his matters to Alistair Hinton than with an active reappraisal of Ogdon's playing.}

[55]{Cf. Geoffrey Madge's comment on p. 400 about how he feels after he performs *Opus clavicembalisticum*.}

piano performance, and that he had never heard Ogdon play more wonderfully — an authoritative statement, coming from someone who had known Ogdon since 1946.

* * * * *

Sorabji's health held up well into his nineties. He managed to look after himself and his house quite successfully (with the assistance of Reginald Best, with whom he lived). During 1986, however, the onset of serious physical deterioration necessitated his giving up his home. But there was no suitable place in any private nursing homes in the area. An extended spell in a Wareham hospital followed. This experience, of having to spend several months in open wards and an overcrowded day-room, after several decades of self-imposed and self-designed calm and privacy, must have tested even his resources and resilience to the limit. As it was, I heard him only once complain bitterly of his lot — and then with the utmost brevity. Finally, in March 1987, he moved into a suitable two-room suite in a private Dorset nursing home, where, permanently chairbound, he received full-time nursing care.[56]

Early in January 1988 Kevin Bowyer arranged to visit Sorabji. He described the prospect as "like going to meet J. S. Bach".[57] After a short but fruitful and memorable meeting for both composer and organist, Bowyer remarked that he felt as though he actually *had* met J. S. Bach, reaffirming that Sorabji and his music had changed the entire course of his musical life. His subsequent visits proved to be wonderfully enriching for both these giants of the keyboard. He presented Sorabji with photocopies of his work-in-progress: copying out Organ Symphony No. 2. Sorabji kept them on a music stand where he could always see them. He once asked me "why on earth" Bowyer was going to so much trouble. I responded and added that, had the original manuscript been written as clearly as Bowyer's copy ... "Ah well, mea culpa — mea MAXIMA culpa", sighed Sorabji, making little attempt to hide an impish grin. (Actually, had Sorabji written down all his scores at Bowyer's pace, nearly three-quarters of his music would not have been written at all — in which case there might never have been any second or third organ symphonies ...)

---

[56]{Reginald Best, his junior by 17 years but also not in good health, went there as well. His death on 29 February 1988 may have precipitated Sorabji's decline.}

[57]{A reference, perhaps, to Bach going by foot in 1705 from Arnstadt to Lübeck to hear Buxtehude play. (Bowyer did not travel by foot!)}

Sorabji suffered a mild stroke in June 1988 which left him with intermittent difficulties of speech and comprehension, but other than during temporary bouts of confusion (and sometimes not even then), his mental faculties remained largely unimpaired, and his hyperactive imagination lost none of its liveliness. Six days after Geoffrey Madge's performance of *Opus clavicembalisticum* on 9 October in Paris, at a little after 7 p.m., Sorabji quietly but firmly declined his supper ... and within minutes, quietly but suddenly, his heart failed him, and his physical presence slipped away ...

Funeral services took place on 24 October: in the morning at Bournemouth Crematorium and in the afternoon at Corfe Castle Parish Church. His memorial service thus took place in the Protestant church in the village he had loved for most of his life and inhabited for more than a third of it. Sorabji was descended on his mother's side from a long line of Roman Catholics, some very high up in the Church; being the son of a Parsi, he also extolled the greatness of the teachings of Zoroaster. Furthermore, in a letter to Philip Heseltine in 1915 he proclaimed "I am very nearly a Buddhist", emphasizing the high moral standards and personal purity of both Burmese Buddhism and Zoroastrianism.[58] Having no interest in what he called the "cheapjack sentimentalitarian bunkum of the so-called 'Brotherhood-of-Man' or 'One-World Religion' variety", he described himself as "not a *humble* but a *proud* seeker-after-truth". He absorbed what he saw as the highest points of all the major world religions, their common ground.

This "monotheistic pantheism" was celebrated at the memorial, whose speakers included the church's vicar (Rev. Gerald Squarey), Ronald Stevenson, and me. The great arch-shaped musical edifice of the second movement of Sorabji's First Organ Symphony (from Kevin Bowyer's then imminent recording) formed, most appositely, the central and principal part of the service.

Obituaries appeared in at least 20 major newspapers and journals in several countries. Several artists gave their first Sorabji performances, including the young Marc-André Hamelin (b. 1961), who had already recorded Wolpe, Godowsky, and Ives, and who went on to record Sorabji's First Piano Sonata for Altarus. As mentioned earlier, John Ogdon's studio recording of *Opus clavicembalisticum* was released in May 1989 (after another live performance of the whole work by him) with an unusually large and interesting accompanying booklet which included Ronald Stevenson's deeply sensitive analysis of the work. This was written, amazingly enough, in 1961, long before all the recent performances of the work, partial or complete. Stevenson's study rested entirely on his own insight of

---

[58]{See the extensive quotation on p. 204.}

52   Discovery

mind and hand at the keyboard with the published version, together with one private hearing at his home a year and a half earlier by John Ogdon in the presence of himself and the work's dedicatee.

Curiously, decades before Ogdon's public performances and recording of *Opus clavicembalisticum*, Erik Chisholm, with what turns out to have been remarkable foresight, alluded to the performance in Stevenson's home when he wrote in the early 1960s:

> The distinguished and highly popular English pianist, John Ogdon, has indeed played the entire work privately, and by all accounts is well up to all its enormous technical and interpretive demands. If Sorabji would give permission to a pianist of Ogdon's gifts publicly to play his music, that could easily be the beginning of a public appreciation of his music.[59]

* * * * *

The only misfortune arising from increasing interest in Sorabji's work generated by public exposure was the concomitant increase in sales of these publications — misfortune because of the inevitable exhaustion of the stock of all 14 publications of Sorabji's music distributed by Oxford University Press. On 10 October 1988, the day after Geoffrey Douglas Madge's Paris performance of *Opus clavicembalisticum*, the last of Sorabji's music distributed for about 50 years by OUP went out of print. Sorabji had consistently declined reprintings, not merely by reason of the financial commitment required, but because he saw no useful purpose in reissuing error-ridden printed copies.

As a result of my discussion with Sorabji of the ironic problem of greater aural accessibility decreasing visual accessibility of his music, I founded the Sorabji Music Archive, to care for most of his manuscript scores and make copies of them and of his literature available to the public.[60] Recently, others have contributed towards renewed visibility — and legibility — of some scores by recopying them. Chris Rice is preparing *St. Bertrand de Comminges: "He was laughing in the tower"*; Marc-André Hamelin is working on *Gulistān* and the Transcendental Studies. Marc-André Roberge has finished splendid computer-produced editions of several shorter piano works, including the second and third of the 3 Pastiches of 1922. To

---

[59]{Erik Chisholm: "The Composer Sorabji" (printed privately: n.pl., [1970]), p. 3 — a talk with musical excerpts, introduced by Frank Holliday: broadcast several times, for which see Chapter 12.}

[60]{See Appendix 3 for an official statement about the Archive.}

date, the most mind-boggling feat of editing and copying has been achieved by Kevin Bowyer, who completed his edition of Sorabji's Organ Symphony No. 2 — 396 pages of A3 paper — on what would have been the composer's 99th birthday, 14 August 1991.

Hamelin is not the only one to have taken up many of the Transcendental Studies. Indeed, he began his work on them soon after hearing of the death of the only other pianist to have done so: John Ogdon, who had died on 1 August 1989, and whose involvement with Sorabji's music had just begun to achieve widespread public acclaim, through his recording and two performances of *Opus clavicembalisticum*.

Most recently, other pianists such as Jonathan Powell, Julian Saphir, and Donna Amato have performed Sorabji's music. For two months in 1990, George Ross, of Spokane, Washington, went to the Sorabji Music Archive to help prepare master copies of Sorabji literature and to begin a general index to it. Marc-André Roberge, who has also done some indexing, is planning a large biographical study of Sorabji. Plans were also in place in 1991 for further recordings to include Sorabji's music, from short piano works to the massive later organ symphonies.

* * * * *

Any serious student of Sorabji and his work must expand, even suspend received and preconceived ideas of time-scale altogether, for not only the lengths of some of the pieces themselves but the lengths of time required to present them successfully in concerts bear little relation to the accepted schedules of present-day music-making. Even such works as the 25-minute *Gulistān*, representing the essential Persian Sorabji, demand many months of detailed and painstaking study from even the most intuitive player before their complex rhythmic patterns begin to flow naturally and their subtle multilinear interweavings turn into the magical spinning of endless threads of the very finest vocal silk.

In a world of ever-decreasing circles, of cheap jargon and cliché, solution of large mathematical problems electronically in milliseconds, travelling across the Atlantic in less time than it takes to play *Opus clavicembalisticum* — an environment arguably dedicated to *reductio ad absurdum* — Sorabji's quietly dignified *Gradus ad Parnassum* cuts an odd figure indeed. His vast musical paragraphs full of beautifully constructed sentences could be seen as highly innovative, having no part of modern Western musical speech. But he pointed out more than once that the earliest expression in music was singing, and that any musician wishing to come to grips with his compositions, which are far from "primeval", must first understand their utter dependence on that earliest form of music.⁶¹

The celebrated "ban" on public performances of his music, supposedly proving his eccentricity, can also be explained. His avowal that "no performance at all is vastly preferable to an obscene travesty" is hardly an eccentric statement.⁶² Any self-respecting creative musicians would surely wish to protect their work from misrepresentation, and their listeners from the risk of misunderstanding their message. Admittedly, because Sorabji never had to earn a living as a composer, he could exercise more control over performances of his music, but to criticize the degree of his control merely because of his fortunate financial circumstances is to miss the point altogether.

Is it "normal" for a composer to expect such vast resources of patience and concentration from performers and listeners? Normal it may not be, but legitimate it has certainly proved to be. Sorabji simply found the appropriate dimensions in which to express his musical ideas. Had he merely overloaded his music unnecessarily, his longer works would amount to little more than colossal catalogs of the supererogatory and as such would be unbearably boring. No decent performance has yet, in my experience, revealed Sorabji's music to be boring.

Did Sorabji not care about his listeners? I tried attacking him over this one by reminding him that Busoni's invitation to him to play for him in 1919 declared that "music is, after all, to be heard". In the course of his answer he referred me to his two essays, "'Performance' *versus* 'Celebration'" and "'Il gran rifiuto'", in which he made it abundantly clear that public performance was by no means related to the sacred act of making or receiving music.⁶³ He also explained that just as a composer might wish to write a work — say a concerto — for a particular performer, so it should be an acceptable practice for a composer to write works for a particular listener or perhaps a few special listeners. He remained totally uninterested in writing for listeners of whom he knew nothing.

His position thus explained appears much less idiosyncratic than might at first be thought. As for the ban itself: as mentioned before, Sorabji insisted that he never imposed an outright ban in the first place, only that he demanded no public performance without his express consent.

---

⁶¹{See Geoffrey Madge's remarks about *bel canto* on pp. 392-93.}

⁶²{Hugh MacDiarmid (quoting Kaikhosru Sorabji): *The Company I've Kept* (London: Hutchinson, 1966), p. 39.}

⁶³{See pp. 288-95, where these essays are reprinted in full, and p. 244.}

He also brushed aside all suggestions that he go to a concert of his own music. He admitted to having only twice attended public concerts where others played his music — the last time being in 1928. When asked on television nearly half a century later, "Wouldn't you like tomorrow night to get into a motor car and go to London and hear that work [the *Symphonic High Mass*] done in the Royal Albert Hall?" he retorted quietly but quickly and firmly, "I wouldn't cross the road. Honestly." He did later concede that in the unlikely event of such a performance being broadcast he would at least cross the floor of his own music room to switch on the radio and listen in peaceful solitude.

He explained this determination not to attend (the concerts of his music given frequently from 1976 on) by stating that he would never make an exhibition of himself by going, that he would never give an audience the satisfaction of observing what "the other ruin of Corfe" looked like. For him the pertinent saying was "Distance lends enchantment", and the farther the distance, the greater the enchantment.

His peaceful, private, and contented lifestyle rarely changed. Nor did his spiritual or material generosity. This is from a letter to me written in late 1974:

> NOW! Will you WILL YOU TRY and understand why I am so uneasy about my friends spending money on me? ... It is a plain statement of fact that my financial position is very much better than that of those dear to me. I feel it is my bounden duty, as a gesture of thanks for my own position that I should try and help THEM insofar as I can and insofar as they will LET me and as the occasion arises ... WILL you try and get into your dear noddle that there is no "patronising" in this ... only the deep aching desire to HELP. Can you understand THAT even if you cant and/or WONT understand anything else?????????
>
> And about presents — WELL if its the RIGHT SORT of present even I won't refuse it ... I've already told you more as once that I'll take a BÖSENDORFER IMPERIAL CONCERT GRAND ... and if you'd only bought it for me when I first asked for it a year or two since you would have saved yourself two thousand quid as the price has gone up nearly two thousand since that ... NOW ISNT THAT A PITY?????[64]

* * * * *

Although I have attempted to give readers some insights into Sorabji the person — the most remarkably warm, brilliant, witty,

---

[64]{Kaikhosru Sorabji: Letter to Alistair Hinton, 11 December 1974.}

56 Discovery

and colourful personality I have known, what matters to listeners is of course the music.

I am reminded of two remarks made independently: "Mon admiration pour Sorabji est totale" (Denis Saurat)[65] and "that remarkable man, Kaikhosru Shapurji Sorabji, one of the few undoubted geniuses I have known" (Harold Rutland).[66] It is no overstated claim that this composer is the most important figure in the history of piano literature since Chopin. There is little to be gained, however, from contemplating the list of Sorabji's prodigious compositions in silent wonderment, and still less from the continual plugging of Sorabji as a reclusive eccentric and mystery-shrouded monster — music's answer to Howard Hughes. That Sorabji was larger than life and in some ways a living embodiment of the impossible is undoubtedly true. But put next to the impact made by the sound of his music, even numerous facts about him seem remarkable only for their insignificance. The sooner Sorabji is forgotten, the better. Forgotten, that is, as a controversial "mystique" figure, a legendary unusualist, an arcane improbability — and remembered as a thoroughly professional, highly gifted, extraordinary prolific composer, and an upholder and proud torch-bearer of a great creative tradition.[67]

His principal musical reputation remains based on unyielding complexity and exclusivity. There is much more to Sorabji's music than this. If the legendary intricacies of texture, polyrhythm, and many-layered polyphony come across as mere displays of mental and manual gymnastics, the work involved will have been a complete waste of time. Sorabji never wrote with any intention of focusing listeners' attention on the difficulties he sets his performers, including those of sheer physical stamina and energy required in the larger works. The musical voyeur who goes to hear Sorabji's music in hope of being entertained by a virtuoso conjuring

---

[65] {"De plus, je suis en musique d'une telle ignorance que mon admiration pour SORABJI est une foi aveugle, quoique totale." ("Moreover, I know so little about music that my admiration for Sorabji is a faith which is blind, although absolute." Denis Saurat: Letter to Frank Holliday, 12 December 1951. Saurat was telling Frank Holliday that he could not take a leading role in the matter of the presentation letter.)

[66] {*The Musical Times*, vol. 98 (January 1957), p. 22.}

[67] {Although the music certainly needs hearing, it does not have to be taken out of the context of the circumstances of its creation and divorced entirely from the personality and life of its creator, insofar as it is possible to unearth and comprehend them. Knowing (or hearing) the music without access to these things — correctly interpreted, of course — is a possibility, but even though much better than having no music at all, not the best possibility. That is one of the reasons for this book's existence.}

trickster performing preposterous feats of legerdemain upon a piano or displaying unfathomable long-distance endurance will get less than nothing out of it.

Whenever Sorabji's music is performed well and convincingly, it proves to be within the reach of a large number of listeners. Despite not wishing to understand this, he happens to have written for many more ears than ever he imagined or intended.

Sorabji outside his house in 1966 (photo by Norman Peterkin)

3 Sorabji: A Continuation

Paul Rapoport

There are three details about Sorabji which are often remembered by many people who have heard of him. Although superficial, they gain importance upon amplification:

1. Sorabji did his best to hide information about the year and location of his birth.

2. Sorabji banned public performance of his music.

3. Sorabji refused to make commercial recordings.

Why? Sorabji's essential public answers may be put quite simply:

1. These things are nobody's business. Questions about them are impertinent. I have a right to my privacy.

2. Neither performers nor audiences can treat my music properly. It is better not to have it heard at all than to subject it to mishandling or misunderstanding.

3. Once a work is recorded, I lose certain rights over it. I am also not interested in having masses of people hear my music, as I do not respect them.

Sorabji's position on these matters was wholly sincere. But all these points demand investigation, if only to answer further questions, all starting with "Why?" or "But". They come together in a completely consistent position, based on a few facts about Sorabji which are not generally known. In the following, it is not my intention to dwell on negative aspects of his character, but to try to explain what may have lain behind his behaviour.

* * * * *

Sorabji was born on 14 August 1892 in the district of Epping in the subdistrict of Chigwell in the county of Essex. His birth certificate, a copy of which is easily obtainable in London, gives precisely this information. During most of his lifetime — until he was too old for it to matter any longer — his friends, many of whom knew his age, refrained from mentioning it publicly out of respect for his wishes. He was aware that a few people knew the facts, but many more knew them than he suspected.

Spread throughout his articles and letters are remarks about events that took place when he "was a young boy" or "only a lad", etc. Some of these events took place when he was in his late twenties. Furthermore, these phrases of indirect dating often seem gratuitous, as if they are intended to serve a purpose divorced from any information required in the context. As indeed they are: to throw people off the track of his true age or birth year.

In a number of sources Sorabji's birth year is given as 1895. These may all go back to the letter he wrote to Philip Heseltine in 1922 giving that date for use in an article.[1] Before the end of that decade, Sorabji began to imply 1899 or 1900; there are a number of instances of this in his letters of the period. When I first met him in the spring of 1976, he was naturally suspicious and early in our conversation laid a trap: "I'm 76, Mr. Rapoport, but I don't think I look it, do you?"[2] This had to be false, because he would not have made a truthful revelation to a virtual stranger, even if over the decades he had not repeatedly made the point about his age being no one's business.

Nearly 40 years before, in response to Percy Scholes' using the date 1895 in his *Oxford Companion to Music*, he gently chided him, but in a rather odd way: "Your critic has a number of years erroneously clapped onto his age, but that is not the fault of Mr. Scholes[,] who is merely following a mistake that has often been repeated elsewhere."[3] Not *clapped on* at all, but *peeled from*. Perhaps Sorabji was simply trying to steer people away from the correct date to ca. 1900. Later he freely admitted having given deliberately misleading answers to questions about his age.

* * * * *

---

[1] Kaikhosru Sorabji: Letter to Philip Heseltine, 24 June 1922 (British Library ms. add. 57963).
{For the relevant parts of the letter, see p. 247.}

[2] To which I responded without hesitation: "You don't look *66!*" He didn't. (Kaikhosru Sorabji in conversation with Paul Rapoport, 14 June 1976.)

[3] *The New English Weekly*, vol. 14 (22 December 1938), p. 174.

THE EYE TOWNSEND;CORFE DASTLE;WAREHAM;DORSET Christmas Day.1974.

Dear Mr.Rapoport

First my abject apologies for being the world's WIRST typist,I have never had
th patience propecy to learn this accursed instrument, and now that thdre is
quite a lof of rheumatics in my fingers it is-if possible even WORSE....

Now to yours of December 12th for the which I thank you.

First things first,You have my full permission to send copies of the tape frcording
to FRNAK HOLLiDAY   Mf.Donald Garvelmann and Mr.Norman Gnetieu.ALSO I would like to
have one.

       Yes,I'm sure you must have foudd many major errors in O.C.and,if and
when yoh have time I'd ,uch appreciate in a list thereof.   I thikk I have
duly answered your questions,insofar as in me lies...AND my inept typist figners
to doo.For the which again renewed applogies'.

       For the rest it o lt remains for me to wish you a propitious
1975.AND if its no worse than 1974 we shall be goddam lucky shant we?

    Very kind regards;

      Yours sincerely,

      [signature: Kaikhosru Shapurji Sorabji]

Sorabji's first letter to Paul Rapoport (1974)
(see next page)

(see previous page)

THE EYE TOWNSEND: CORFE CASTLE: WAREHAM: DORSET Christmas Day. 1974.

Dear Mr. Rapoport
First my abject apologies for being the world's WORST typist, I have never had the patience properly to learn this accursed instrument, and now that there is quite a lot of rheumatics in my fingers it is — if possible even WORSE ...
 Now to yours of December 12th for the which I thank you.
 First things first[.] You have my full permission to send copies of the tape recording to FRANK HOLLIDAY[,] Mr. Donald Garvelmann and Mr. Norman Gentieu. ALSO I would like to have one.
 Yes, I'm sure you must have found <u>many</u> major errors in O.C. and, if and when you have time I'd much appreciate in a list thereof. I think I have duly answered your questions, insofar as in me lies ... AND my inept typist fingers to do. For the which again renewed apologies!
 For the rest it only remains for me to wish you a propitious 1975. AND if its no worse than 1974 we shall be goddam lucky shant we?
 Very kind regards;
Yours sincerely,

Kaikhosru Shapurji Sorabji

One reason why Sorabji steadfastly refused to reveal his age may be that he simply tired of answering questions about it. But initially, why was there not only a refusal to answer but a grand personal defense mechanism in the form of misleading answers and, even more, gratuitous misleading statements about his age? What fear was lurking; what could others do if they knew his age?

Was he just being a prima-donna in keeping the truth a secret? Many people are vain enough to state their birth year as something other than what it is, usually to appear younger in a world where youth is prized far more than age. There is certainly an element of the vain performer in Sorabji's makeup and attitude. But that is only a small part of the answer.

In his youth, but to some extent throughout his life, Sorabji was a mystic. Not in the sense of woolly-headed, or being a follower of some swami or even a philosophical movement, but in certain definable interests and pursuits which may be called mystical and in some cases occult. There is plenty of evidence for this: his articles in his book *Mi contra fa* on "Yoga and the Composer" and "Metapsychic Motivation in Music" (both of which point to connections between Tantric and Catholic ideas) and his music based on Tantric symbolism (First Piano Symphony) and the Tarot (Fifth Piano Sonata). Then there are some mysterious invocations in a few of his scores, mostly from the 1920s:

> Symphony [No. 1] (1921–22): "... and in that darkness they come."
> *Opusculum* for Orchestra (1923): "... a rite not to be spoken, a deed / of high Black Magic."
> *Le jardin parfumé* — Poem for Piano Solo (1923): "here Satan is invoked to rend asunder all such as we hate —"
> *Valse-fantaisie* (1925): "Deo gratias[,] et laudes. — / To Ganès Remover of Obstacles / Salutations and Obeisances / To Allah praise —"

For about 20 years, one of Sorabji's closest friends was Bernard Bromage, a lecturer and writer one of whose main interests was the occult. He was a member of the secret order The Fraternity of Inner Light, itself a breakaway group from the most significant British occult society, The Order of the Golden Dawn. Sorabji was aware of their work and writings, even though he was not likely a member of them and took a dim view of some of their leaders.[4]

---

[4]{See p. 245 for Sorabji's description of his anticlimactic encounter with the most notorious of these, Aleister Crowley.}

More important confirmations may be found in Sorabji's letters to Philip Heseltine and Erik Chisholm, for example:[5]

> I have a double dose of mysticism in my Spanish-Parsî origin, and what is India but the very cradle-ground and fount of all religious mysticism — "religious" in no narrow sectarian sense but in the sense in which Vedântic pantheism connotes it? "Religious" — "religion" — only the seers and mystics — the Saint Theresas, the St. Thomas Aquinases, the St. John of the Crosses, the Sri Ramakrishnas, the Meher Babas, the Abdul Bahais know what the words truly mean [...][6]

His early letters to Erik Chisholm contain many references to mental telepathy. Sorabji was sure that if Chisholm and he concentrated hard enough, they could tell what each other was feeling and thinking and even doing, although they were separated by a distance of several hundred miles. Sorabji's letters to Frank Holliday and Norman Gentieu confirm that for Sorabji religion, mysticism, and the occult were completely intertwined. He was always interested in "psychic" experiences and for a time was a member of the London Society of Psychical Research.[7]

One of the minor aspects of mysticism Sorabji was aware of was number symbolism, which forms part of every ancient set of occult beliefs. Although he wrote almost nothing about it, how else may be explained his tendency towards using certain numbers over and over for a total of variations or of pages in his major compositions? Not all such compositions exhibit such use, but the two lists below provide too much evidence for their results to be ascribed to

---

[5]{For many mentions of the occult in Sorabji's letters to Heseltine, see Chapter 6.}

[6]Kaikhosru Sorabji: Letter to Erik Chisholm, 18 April 1930.

[7]Kaikhosru Sorabji: Letter to Norman Gentieu, 5 May 1953.

Although there may be some facetiousness in the following, it is at least partly serious. Sorabji often reported "out-of-body" experiences and certainly had an interest in ghosts. On one occasion, when his companion Reggie Best was to be away, Sorabji invited Frank Holliday down to Corfe Castle:

> You shall stay IN my house and keep me from being scared stiff o'nights by the things that gang bump ... and the various sinister uncanny soft rustlings and movements of ALL THOSE who "return at evening"[.]

(Kaikhosru Sorabji: Letter to Frank Holliday, n.d. (mid-September 1956.)

chance. Both lists contain works dating from around 1920 to around 1980.[8]

Last page number

Concerto No. 3 for Piano and Orchestra: 100 (sections of 40, 20, and 40 pp.).
Concerto No. 4 for Piano and Orchestra: 100 (sections of 40, 20, and 40 pp.).
Sonata No. 2 for Piano: 49.
Symphony No. 1 for Orchestra et al.: 300.
Concerto No. 7 for Piano and Orchestra: 100 (sections of 40, 20, and 40 pp.).
Concerto No. 8 for Piano and Orchestra: 343.
Symphony No. 1 for Organ: 81.
Sonata No. 4 for Piano: 111.
Symphony No. 2 for Orchestra et al., piano part only: 333.
Toccata No. 2 for Piano: 111.
Sonata No. 5 for Piano: 343a.
Symphonic Variations for Piano: 484.
Sequentia Cyclica for Piano: 343.
Opus clavisymphonicum: 333.
Symphonic High Mass: 1001.
Symphonic Nocturne for Piano: 111.

Last variation number

Variations and Triple Fugue on "Dies iræ": 64.
Concerto No. 5 for Piano and Orchestra: 48.
Toccatinetta: 33.
Passacaglia: 100 (planned; the composition is incomplete).
Opus clavicembalisticum: 49 (one set), 81 (another set).
Symphony No. 2, piano part: 64.
Quintet No. 2 for Piano and String Quartet: 100.
Toccata No. 2 for Piano: 49.
Symphonic Variations for Piano: 81.
Transcendental Studies: 100. (There are also 100 studies in the set.)
Sequentia Cyclica: 27.
Symphony No. 3 for Organ: 49.
Un nido di scatole: 16.
Symphonic High Mass: 49. (At one time Sorabji planned 144.)
Symphony No. 4 for Piano: 49.
Toccata No. 4 for Piano: 24 (one set), 100 (another set).

---

[8]The titles here are standardized, as their exact wording is insignificant for the point being made.

Opusculum clavisymphonicum: 39 (one set), 27 (another set).
Symphony No. 6 for Piano: 64.
The Golden Cockerel Crows: Frivolous Variations [...]: 49.

In several of these instances, both pages and variations, Sorabji made errors, so that the actual total does not match his numbering. But his intentions were exactly as indicated.[9] Note especially the last page number of the Fifth Piano Sonata, 343a. Sorabji could have numbered this 344, but only 343a preserves the significance of 343.

Moreover, on several occasions he announced the number of pages or the number of variations a work would have long before the work or the variation section was completed. Many of the numbers contain replication (i.e. numeric intensity), by being squares (16, 49, 64, 81, 100, 484) or cubes (27, 343), or by containing repeated digits (111, 333).[10] Various low prime factors are found (2, 3, 7, 13), as well as non-prime factors (4, 6, 8, 10, 12). The number 1001, which is 7 x 11 x 13, also gains magic significance through the *Arabian Nights*.

Although there are too many conflicting occult numerologies to be of help in sorting all this out, one low prime is conspicuous by its absence: 5. Although 5 is a factor of 100,[11] the more obvious representations of 5, including 25, 125, 625, and 555, are rare as last page number[12] and totally absent as last variation number. This may be due to the reputation of 5 as a difficult, even dangerous number.[13]

Even if this numerology represents a tangential aspect of Sorabji's involvement with the occult, it leads us in the right direction, closer to the reason why he tried to keep his age a secret. The answer lies not in numerology *per se;* Sorabji did not run his life according to it and was not even noticeably susperstitious about numbers in his everyday life. But early on he took a considerable interest in another, related aspect of what might be called systematic occultism, viz. astrology. Writing that the deaths of major composers in 1934 indicated that the year had to be considered, in

---

[9]Some last page numbers in other works (e.g. 42, 201, 252, 432, 284, 830, 305, 149, 113, 93) do not seem to be as notable as those listed, but *every* last variation number in *all* Sorabji's works is notable for the reasons about to be given.

[10]In a letter to Erik Chisholm of 19 April 1930, Sorabji drew attention to the fact that the planned number of variations (49) in his *Opus clavicembalisticum* was a square. {See p. 303.}

[11]Which is more significantly 10 squared.

[12]Which, as mentioned, was probably unplanned in many works.

[13]See *Encyclopedia of the Occult*, by Fred Gettings (London: Rider, 1986).

astrological terms, one of "bad directions", he added: "and let no one who has had the astonishing proofs of the accuracy of this 'science' if you will, or art, in the hands of really expert practitioners that I myself have had, ridicule it".[14] In a letter to Erik Chisholm of 8 April 1930, a week or two after he first met him, he asked him for his birth date (including time) and place so that he might take the information to an astrological woman he knew.

It therefore seems that hiding his age was not the primary aim in Sorabji's ruses of chronology, except insofar as his age would obviously reveal his birth year. Astrologically, possession of the year and place of birth would give others potentially damaging knowledge about him, perhaps knowledge which he himself did not have, certainly knowledge whose use he could not control. It might therefore also lead to some kind of control over him. There are many reasons why this had to be avoided at all costs, some of which will emerge shortly. The possibility of a curse should not be ruled out: Sorabji was interested in Black Magic, even if it is not known that he practised any.

All these matters are intimately related — astrology, numerology, Tarot, Tantra, and many more. In addition, the history of mysticism, occult sciences, magic, etc. may easily be traced through the histories of religions such as Zoroastrianism and Christianity, Sorabji's ancestral religions, and Hinduism and Buddhism, in which he also took great interest.

* * * * *

In another letter to Erik Chisholm, Sorabji noted with glee his apparent victory over someone in a minor matter, and continued on a related subject:

> One must tolerate no nonsense from that type of person — it doesn't even do to treat it with contempt — one must jump on them <u>hard</u> with both feet ... <u>I do</u>! ... Nasty nature! ... Someone saw my mug in the "Radio Times" just recently and remarked to a man I know (whom they did not know knew me and who quite wisely didn't let on!) that in me was one of the cruellest most ruthless and coldly contemptuous human faces they had ever seen but didn't doubt that I could make myself perfectly charming to a very few people who took my fancy [...][15]

---

[14]*The New English Weekly*, vol. 5 (14 June 1934), p. 208.
[15]Kaikhosru Sorabji: Letter to Erik Chisholm, 5 May 1930.

Throughout his life, he gained a reputation as an eccentric, one who could be very tough and vehement, even thoroughly impossible at times. To his friends he was charming, but much more than that: kind, concerned, generous, helpful, loyal, and warmly affectionate. The verbal heaps of praise he could pour over his close friends are remarkable for their eloquence and variety. He constantly guarded against using his friends for his own purposes, with the negative example of Wagner always in mind. But he also guarded his friendships jealously, hesitating before introducing two of his friends to each other.

The above quotation shows that he cultivated extreme opposites of character, with the mean side obviously designed to keep people away, to enable him to write music and words as he wished without interference, to maintain complete control over his own life. But why did he want so often to alienate so many people? It seems hardly to have been necessary to the degree Sorabji thought it was. It was certainly part of his nature to alienate others, but that is an insufficient explanation.

The answer has many aspects, centred on the fact that Sorabji was many times an outsider in a social sense. His family environment was not conducive to stability. He was often treated as a foreigner in England due to his name, appearance, and background. He was a homosexual — at a time when memory in England of the trial of Oscar Wilde was quite fresh.[16] He was a musician in a society that did not value his abilities.

* * * * *

His mother was a fierce person.[17] Although very few independent reports of her exist, Sorabji himself told many stories of her sharp insight and prowess at cutting down opposition, admitting always that he learned much from her. Indeed, he probably had difficulty

---

[16]Havelock Ellis thought that Wilde's trial may have given some homosexuals the courage to consider themselves more positively, which was not necessarily contradicted by the harrowing precedent of the legal proceedings against Wilde. See "Sexual Inversion", by Havelock Ellis, Part 4 of his *Studies in the Psychology of Sex*, vol. 1 (New York: Random House, n.d. (ca. 1936)), pp. 63, 352–53.

[17]On the certificate of her marriage to Sorabji's father (which took place on 18 February 1892) her names are given as Madeline Matilda Wortley; on her death certificate (1959) her given names are Madeleine Marguerite Mathilde. She was probably born in 1874. Sorabji said that she was born in England but that her ancestry was Spanish-Sicilian.

living up to her standards and demands. His father[18] lived almost all of the time away from home, as far off as India, where he had much of his business dealings and, it seems, where he eventually married bigamously.[19] Despite knowing a fair amount about music, he was not in favour of his son becoming a musician. According to Sorabji, his father had prevented his mother from continuing her singing career because female singers were always associated with the image of a fallen woman.[20] At one point Sorabji's mother railed at his father: "You ruined *my* musical career; I won't have you ruining *his!!*"[21]

Anyone growing up with such interactions might well have trouble achieving a stable identity. (Sorabji was an only child.) Not helping any was the racial situation. In his letters, Sorabji referred infrequently but trenchantly to his unfortunate treatment as a youngster because of his race: he was often mocked and ridiculed by his peers and elders alike.[22] According to Frank Holliday, he kept a dossier of newspaper cuttings and correspondence marked Colour Matters.

He once sent Holliday a card on which he had taped a small newspaper photo of an Anglican cleric and then written:

> MADONNA MIA! LOOK just LOOK at this typical Anglican clerical codfish face with its putrid pomposity its "healthy openairishness" its abysmal spiritual and moral obtuseness, THEN ask yourself mon cher why the C[hurch] of E[ngland] is pour rire when it isnt pour vomir [...][23]

What has this to do with racial problems? The answer (and connection) is forthcoming. Norman Peterkin, one of Sorabji's friends of longest standing, was convinced that one incident in particular was the key to Sorabji's turbulent character:

> And the following charming incident happened to me when I was a lad in my early teens. Ma and I were in a firstclass Underground (Met) carriage. There were these, you know to well on into the

---

[18]His name was Shapurji Sorabji. He died in 1932 in Bad Nauheim, Germany; he was born in India, probably in 1863.
[19]Unknown to Sorabji until after his father's death.
[20]Kaikhosru Sorabji in conversation with Paul Rapoport, 19 May 1978.
[21]Kaikhosru Sorabji in conversation with Paul Rapoport, 14 June 1976.
[22]See also his Letter to the Editor, in *The New Age*, vol. 16 (15 April 1915), p. 653.
{This is quoted on p. 211.}
[23]Kaikhosru Sorabji: Letter to Frank Holliday, n.d. (late June or early July 1957).

twenties. Opposite us was a gaitered dignitary of the C. of E. complete with typical cod-fish-corner-of-the-mouth droop, with an elderly female with him. After staring long, rudely and offensively first at Ma then at me, he turned to the E. F. at his side and boomed ... "A BLACK BOY!" Ma is not a Sicilian for nothing and her temper erupted with Etna-like competence. Livid, she got up and went over to the old reptile (she, by the way, has even in age, a skin and complexion that is the envy and admiration of all who know her). Her reproof to this "good Christian" was shattering ... "you ODIOUS old creature," she said[,] "My son is NOT a black boy, but even if he WERE, I should thank GOD for it, if he were a gorilla or a baboon, I should thank God that he were ANYTHING rather than belong to anything or anybody that produces people like you!"[24]

Is it any wonder Sorabji execrated British society? Fortunately for him, doing so also gave him a source of strength: he could be different, and point out his superiority to those around him — resulting in an attitude which initially might have been little more than a defense against a hostile environment. Yet that is plainly what he needed.

If Sorabji was not English, what was he? He referred to himself as a Spanish-Sicilian Parsi, because he attached much more importance to heredity than to where he was born. While being called English or Indian infuriated him, Parsi he did not mind. Still, he was genealogically at best half-Parsi, in practice not even that, and in many ways closer to his Spanish-Sicilian mother. He did not embrace the Zoroastrian religion or culture of the Parsis, and even had he wanted to, he could not likely have determined what true Zoroastrianism was, as over the millenium of their stay in India the Parsis themselves mixed with the Hindus, Moslems, and Christians to the point where mid-19th-century attempts to trace genuine Zoroastrianism in India became quite difficult.[25] As Sorabji would not become enslaved to any received line of thinking, in religion or anything else, he chose from Zoroastrian culture what he wanted and no more.[26] His knowledge of it was considerable. His identification with it was limited, but more than sufficient to proclaim his difference from those around him. From mid-life he

---

[24]Kaikhosru Sorabji: Letter to Frank Holliday, 6 September 1958. "Black boy" referred to a Negroid. It was neither correct nor neutral.

[25]Dadabhai Naoroji: "The Parsi Religion", in *Religious Systems of the World*, 7th edition (London: Swan Sonnenschein, 1904), pp. 184–93.

[26]{He certainly did not like the Parsis themselves after he had gone to Bombay and observed them first-hand: see p. 222.}

was in sympathy much more with Roman Catholicism than with any other religion, but he was not a practising Catholic either.[27]

* * * * *

The fact of Sorabji's homosexuality was kept entirely private. In England during most of his life, homosexual acts between men, even in private, were illegal.[28] Sorabji may even once have been blackmailed over his orientation.[29] Nonetheless, he wrote in public occasionally about the unfair plight of the homosexual and the need for legal reform on the subject. He thought of himself as a sexual invert, not in the sense of one who adopts the reverse of a commonly expected gender role (whether in a homosexual or heterosexual relationship), but in Ellis's primary meaning, of one who has "sexual instinct turned by inborn constitutional abnormality toward persons of the same sex".[30] That he used Ellis's terminology occasionally is no accident: his mother sent him to see Ellis, probably in 1924. Ellis must have reassured him about his tendencies, as his attitude was that prosecution of homosexuals was in most cases not sensible, that

> the method of self-restraint and self-culture, without self-repression, seems to be the most rational method of dealing with sexual inversion when that condition is really organic and deeply rooted [...] The most that the physician is entitled to do, it seems to me, is to present the situation clearly, and leave to the patient a decision for which he must himself accept the responsibility.[31]

Many years later Sorabji referred to his meeting with Ellis:

> The smaller work of chamber orchestra was dedicated to the great Havelock Ellis whom I had had the honour of meeting and who was very kind and helpful to me in an intimate personal matter into which I do not propose to go.[32]

---

[27] Roman Catholicism was still an "outside" religion in England, for obvious historical reasons.

[28] Not, it seems, between women: they had been left out of the 1885 legislation.

[29] He told Frank Holliday that he had been, in a conversation in August 1955.

[30] Havelock Ellis: "Sexual Inversion", p. 1. Ellis's term is close to what today is commonly called *homosexuality*, which to Ellis had a more general meaning.

[31] Ibid., pp. 341, 344.

[32] Kaikhosru Sorabji: Letter to Paul Rapoport, 25 January 1975.

It would not be helpful here to speculate on the causes of Sorabji's condition, especially as psychology has no clear answer to the causes of homosexuality except for the probability of a decisive biological component in most cases. It is inappropriate to say that the absent father and overbearing mother promoted Sorabji's or anyone's homosexuality:

> The dominant-mother theory has come into such extraordinary prominence as to deserve a special note. For good reasons, sex researchers have never accepted the notion, but it has made quite a run in both armchair psychiatry and low-grade popular psychology [...] The dominant mother was [...] credited with causing most male homosexuality [...] implicated as well in [...] schizophrenia [...] alcoholism [...] drug addiction [...] underweight [...] overweight [...] unhappy adults [...] Certainly the mother-son closeness that sometimes occurs in homosexuality is far better interpreted as the product than as the cause of the disposition which supports it.[33]

What needs considering is how homosexuality combined with the rest of Sorabji's personality. Again, we need to guard against the simplistic notion that Sorabji assuaged his guilt by writing music, that he proved himself worthy in atonement for his sin. Dubious as such notions are in any circumstances,[34] they do not fit this case. Of guilt and sin there were none, and Sorabji appears to have decided on a music career quite some time before he became aware of his sexual orientation.

More significant is the fact that homosexuals often have trouble adapting socially. Sorabji seems to have recognized that to adapt would be impossible for him, just as he could not adapt (or repress) his hot temperament, sharp wit, love of music, or ancestry. He maintained that he was what he was, and those who could not accept him be damned. Furthermore, he had many attitudes and interests, whether deliberately chosen or not, which went against the norm; sometimes the more contrary his position seemed, the more he enjoyed having and expressing it. In this context, his homosexuality not only fitted but throve. He turned what could have been a debilitating problem into something positive, making a

---

[33]C. A. Tripp: *The Homosexual Matrix*, 2nd edition (New York: New American Library, 1987), pp. 73–74.

[34]"The artistic aptitudes of inverts may better be regarded as part of their organic tendencies than as a reaction against those tendencies." (Havelock Ellis: "Sexual Inversion", p. 295.)

virtue of a necessity while nonetheless realizing the necessity of keeping this particular virtue quiet.[35]

His anger and vituperation were thus both a genuine protest against the unfairness of society on all levels, implicitly (and sometimes explicitly) including its treatment of homosexuals, and a means of keeping away those who might weaken his fortress and seriously disrupt his life. His fierceness, as mentioned earlier, was an unavoidable characteristic developed into a good defense. Did he survive and achieve artistic success because of, or despite his homosexuality? That is the wrong question, and unanswerable. His homosexuality, just as much as other aspects of him, must have made him both regret and rejoice at various times, leading to both doubt and confidence. These reactions were more likely complementary than contradictory, relating to both his destructive tendencies and actions and his positive ones. Both kinds had to exist in this person in extremes; one of his tasks was to control the precarious balance — or more accurately, imbalance.

Was the destructive side uppermost in Sorabji? Sometimes it certainly was. He could jump to wrong, negative conclusions without looking at the facts. He could be prejudiced, unfair, stubborn, temperamental, and malicious. Neurosis based on alienation, discrimination, and insecurity does not often lead to pleasant cheerfulness or a predisposition to cool considerations. Yet destruction cannot create and maintain close friendships, nor can it produce music, let alone the music which Sorabji wrote.

* * * * *

Sorabji complained early on to Philip Heseltine that a young musician in England would have difficulty finding friends, due to the tendency of being mocked for one's musical abilities.[36] For much of his life, Sorabji the musician met with lack of understanding, cynicism, even vilification. To discuss this fully almost seems beyond possibility, not because of lack of evidence but because of its abundance. One quotation is worth special mention, as it favours everything Sorabji detested, so much so that in one of his articles Sorabji even quoted it, without comment. The author of these words was Herbert Antcliffe:

---

[35]Whenever the marriage of one of his friends broke up, Sorabji expressed complete sympathy, but often with a hint of "there but for the grace of God go I", or, as he occasionally put it, "there by the grace of God go not I!"

[36]Kaikhosru Sorabji: Letter to Philip Heseltine, 6 January 1914.
{See p. 203 for quotation of this letter.}

> [... O]ne can only wish that the young composer would give himself the very difficult task of writing a few simple melodies, a few common chords and easy resolutions of the dominant seventh, a few exercises that the ordinary player can attempt, so that we might have opportunities of knowing whether he has any creative ability and not merely an uncanny power of putting down the largest number of notes in the smallest possible space. If he can make himself do this there may be some hope for him as a composer.[37]

While there is validity to the point that Sorabji used too many notes at times, the solution to the problem is not simply to recommend the opposite. Common chords, easy resolutions, the ordinary player! Sorabji might rightly have exclaimed, "What have THEY to do with creativity?!" His way was so little the way recommended by this quotation that one may imagine him swearing at this thorough nonsense and vowing never to write any such things no matter what. He put it himself later like this:

> If the Amazon at flood sweep you away who try to breast its volume of waters, that is your misfortune, not the Amazon's fault. But you have no right to expect the Amazon to flow through a bath tap with just the force and volume you happen to be able to bear. In any case you could have kept out of the Amazon's way![38]

Although it is the easiest thing in the world to hold oneself blameless on grounds of innate something-or-other, in this instance Sorabji was right in saying that Antcliffe and his type were wrong about him. This does not justify Sorabji's music or make us like it, but it makes it more approachable, because now we know what one wrong approach is.

Sorabji wrote the Herbert Antcliffes of his world into objects of contempt. He did this in a variety of ways. One was by making a group of declarations which relates to the motto of his book *Around Music* (the quotation from Milton's *Paradise Regained*). Other members of the group are some words in a letter to Heseltine of 8 November 1921, the famous preface to *Opus clavicembalisticum*, and Sorabji's personal artistic statement from 1959.[39]

Sorabji's continual charges of inferiority against so many established musical figures from his present and past led to strong

---

[37] *The New Age*, vol. 35 (12 June 1924), p. 80.
[38] Kaikhosru Sorabji: *Around Music* (London: Unicorn Press, 1932), p. 119. The chapter containing this quotation is called "Of Simplicity".
[39] {See the first motto to the present book (p. xv) and pp. 239, 135, and 345.}

74 *Discovery*

Sorabji on the slopes of Corfe Castle in about 1934
(photo by Norman Peterkin)

criticism of his opinions.⁴⁰ But he really felt the way he wrote, partly because he was protecting his own artistic sensibilities, which ran counter to so much of what was accepted and acceptable. Whether his dislike for so much around him fuelled his music, or his music fuelled that dislike, is unknowable. What is reasonably clear is that his feelings, their intensity, and their expression derived somewhat from his environment and the particular problems of his development, both personal and musical.

* * * * *

In light of the foregoing, the famous ban on performances is more explicable. But first we must examine what it was and what it was not, beginning with the latter. Sorabji did not proclaim it to the press. He did not make an announcement to all his friends. He did not remove his published works from circulation or destroy his manuscripts. (He loved many of his works as others love their children. He was simply and completely controlling their fate; unlike children, Sorabji's music could not protect itself even a little or, more importantly, protect him.)

The only thing he did differently from the days in which he or others did or could play his music in public was to express his desire not to have public performances. However, it would be easy to misinterpret him, for he made a variety of statements on the subject of the ban over the years. Here are six of them.

> 1. I [...] have turned down quite a number of proposed performances of my own work during the past year or two [...] AND [...] have made up my mind NEVER either to perform or allow to be performed ANY of my own work in this country [...] (6 April 1944, in a letter to Cecil Gray.)
>
> 2. I have set my face against ANY PUBLIC PERFORMANCE OF MY WORK FOR GOOD AND ALL EVERYWHERE. (23 January 1948, in a letter to Egon Petri.)
>
> 3. Public performance absolutely prohibited above all in England. (1956, note in Italian on the manuscript of his *Rosario d'arabeschi*.)
>
> 4. Why do I neither seek nor encourage performance of my works? Because they are neither intended for nor suitable for it under present, or indeed any foreseeable conditions: and no performance at

---

⁴⁰{See Chapter 7.}

76 Discovery

all is vastly preferable to an obscene travesty. (14 October 1959, in "A personal Statement".⁴¹)

5. <u>I DO NOT WANT</u> PUBLIC PERFORMANCE OF MY WORK EITHER BY OGDON <u>OR ANYONE ELSE AT ALL</u>. [...] I have set out my views about this often enough AND NOTHING NOR NO ONE WILL MAKE ME CHANGE THEM. SO THAT IS THAT, ISNT IT? (ca. 7 July 1962, in a letter to Frank Holliday.)

6. [...] I remain obstinately convinced of the relative trifling importance of public performance of my works, and generally forbid it. (5 July 1971, in a letter to Michael Habermann.)

Each of these statements was made in response to a particular situation and in a particular context. The angriest, nos. 2 and 5, come from letters which are angry about other matters. No. 4 leaves room for the possibility of public performance: it is a more carefully thought out statement intended for publication, and therefore more useful as a generality. No. 6, polite and reserved, was written to someone whom Sorabji did not know at the time. None of these statements by itself may be taken to represent the ban. All of them together start to represent it. The ban varied from one of its expressions to the next just as some of the themes in Sorabji's music do.

In this case one must guard against the fallacy of *pars pro toto*. "This is what he said" is no basis for anything unless the context is respected. In the matter of the ban, Sorabji may not have intended his absolute pronouncements to apply for a long period. Children who shout in anger of the moment at their parents that they will always hate them do not usually end up doing so; their frustration subsides.

Sorabji often pointed out that he did not need to institute a formal ban. His reputation and the warnings printed in his scores were sufficient, e.g. "N.B. Public performance prohibited unless by express consent of the composer" and "All rights including that of performance reserved by the Composer" (both from the published version of *Opus clavicembalisticum*). But was he legally empowered to prevent performances (or recordings) of his work, published or

---

⁴¹{This wording differs slightly from the equivalent motto at the beginning of this book (p. xv). This one is handwritten and dated; the other is typewritten and undated.}

unpublished? Did publication give others the right to perform or record his music?[42]

As Sorabji held the copyright, he could prevent performances and recordings, regardless of publication of a score. He did refuse permission many times, but curiously he never sued for damages over unauthorized performances. He did not even seem to mind the occasional one he was informed of,[43] presumably being worried about potential gross abuses by way of bad performances of major works, rather than about performances of lesser works or about good performances. Moreover, if a friend was involved in an unauthorized performance, either as a player or as an intermediary, he did not feel threatened. Indeed, in the 1970s and 80s his permission to performers to play his music in public was provisionally granted in every case on the basis of recommendations of friends, not on the basis of first having heard someone play.[44] The personal friendship was in these cases more important than the performance.

His words were more forceful than his actions; but he liked words more anyhow. The quick and sharp retort and the extreme denunciation were more feasible, meaningful, and predictable of success than something like long drawn-out legal proceedings. Nonetheless, even throughout the period of the ban, public performances by the best performers in ideal circumstances remained at least a possibility. When he began to give permission in the 1970s, his "new" attitude amounted to less of a change than most observers thought.

Questions put to Sorabji from time to time concerning the ban's origin elicited various responses about when he decided to impose it (in whatever version). There is not yet enough evidence for any one year, although some time between 1937 and 1944 would be correct. The letter to Cecil Gray quoted as no. 1 above (in the group of six statements relating to the ban) is from the latter year. In the

---

[42]The legal answers in this section of this chapter are based on a letter of 29 June 1989 to me from Daniel G. Cooper, then of the law firm McCarthy & McCarthy, Toronto.

[43]An example: "None of the performances was authorized. However, Sorabji knew of the performances through a mutual friend and he made no objections to my playing the piece." (John Gates: Letter to Marc-André Roberge about his performances in 1966 of *Fantaisie espagnole*, 1 May 1985.)

[44]Once granted, he did not re-evaluate his permission on the basis of consequent performances. (Some of the performances given in the years 1976–85, when Sorabji could still evaluate them or understand others' evaluations, were not very good.)

earlier year Sorabji wrote to Erik Chisholm saying he would consider playing in Glasgow again. He had just been there to play his *Second Toccata*.[45]

Why did Sorabji never make commercial recordings? One reason is that he feared he would lose control over a work once he recorded it. Although this sounds fantastic, he was correct. Both the 1911 and 1956 copyright acts in Great Britain allowed anyone to record something which was already recorded, upon submission of a licence fee. This is where the matter of protection comes in. In response to requests from many readers of *The New English Weekly* to record one of his major works, Sorabji refused, citing "two bad snags". One was expense.

> The second, and from the composer's point of view, much worse snag is this. The present law of copyright in so far as it affects recorded music is a remarkable illustration of the happiness of that symbology that represents Justice as a blindfold figure, whose blows would fall with sublime impartiality upon just and unjust alike. Under this law, once a work has been recorded, the copyright-holder has no further control over future recordings, can neither stop them nor prevent some fantastic mutilation, re-arrangement or mauling of his work by anyone whomsoever and has to accept the statutorily imposed fee (which the composer has no power to alter, by the way) by way of royalty. Having had my fill of vile travesties of my work, this is not a prospect that I find alluring, as your readers can well imagine; at present I feel it is rather more to the point to safeguard myself and my work against the musical equivalent of an indecent assault![46]

It might well be argued that one's music has to stand on its own after a while, that composers may learn something when their music is performed by someone else, that they may not even be the best performers of their own music. But belief in these valid points would entail risk, for Sorabji high risk, of which he would have none if at all possible. Negative criticism stung him; no matter how

---

[45]Kaikhosru Sorabji: Letter to Erik Chisholm, 13 January 1937.

In 1960, a friend of Sorabji's claimed that the ban had lasted for just over 20 years (Clinton Gray-Fisk: "Kaikhosru Shapurji Sorabji", in *The Musical Times*, vol. 101 (April 1960), pp. 230–32). He had likely asked Sorabji about it, but Sorabji's answers about the year of birth of the ban were as variable as they were about his own year of birth — for entirely different reasons. Since no ban had ever been formally declared and the idea changed over time, there was no "birth" of it to remember. Still, 1938 or 1939 seems most probable for Sorabji's initial determination not to allow public performances at all.

[46]*The New English Weekly*, vol. 9 (10 September 1936), p. 360.

mild, it could be taken as an extreme affront. His hypersensitivity was hyperattuned to setbacks of any kind. Whether they were personal or professional (i.e. musical) made no difference.[47]

He therefore decided that there would be no recording, because high quality in one set of records could never guarantee high quality in the next by someone else playing the same music. His reputation would suffer unfairly and go out of his control. There were obviously irrationality and immaturity in this fear Sorabji had. On the other hand, he was not at all interested in the competition of the marketplace when it came to musical merit: a decidedly reasoned and mature attitude.

But what about Sorabji as a performer? He could have continued to play his music publicly while never recording it and refusing others permission to play and record it ... No, that was not possible. Even if it would have involved no legal problems, the psychological ones were just as great:

Edward Clarke Ashworth referring to Sorabji:

Unfortunately for us, as the composer says of himself, he has an almost pathological aversion from playing before an audience.[48]

Sorabji before performing his Fourth Piano Sonata in Glasgow:

What is the Hall like in which I should function — is one removed a safe and comfortable distance from the audience — on a platform for instance?[49]

Sorabji after performing his Fourth Piano Sonata in Glasgow:

I take this as an opportunity of bearing public witness to the wonderful kindness and sympathy I received on all hands. The enormously difficult and very complex work was listened to during the hour and a half of its duration with a concentrated and sympathetic attention that were an inspiration to one like myself who makes no pianistic pretensions, and who endures crucifixions of apprehension before an event of this kind.[50]

An American tour with an American booster?!!! [...] the unspeakable repugnance that the beastliness and vulgarity of that sort of thing arouses in me [...] I will not have myself rammed down the throats

---

[47]He sometimes referred to performances "of me" rather than "of my music". {See p. 43.} Bad ones could indeed constitute a personal assault.
[48]*The New English Weekly*, vol. 9 (30 April 1936), p. 55.
[49]Kaikhosru Sorabji: Letter to Erik Chisholm, 25 December 1929.
[50]Kaikhosru Sorabji: in *The New Age*, vol. 46 (17 April 1930), p. 284.

of a rabble of gaping nine-day wonderers [...] Not only do I not want mob-admiration but the thought of it sickens me with disgust and horror![51]

Under no circumstances could he be a truly public figure. Such public appearances as he was willing to make worked only if everything went the way he wanted it to, leading to a proper environment and reception for him and his music.

"No pianistic pretensions", he wrote. Others wrote that only he could play his music, or at least that hearings in private were a revelation.[52] But Sorabji always maintained that he was merely a composer who happened to play the piano. False modesty? There was almost none of that in him: "Modesty[,] that fig leaf of mediocrity", he once declared.[53]

In 1953, after he had been given by friends and admirers money towards making a recording of professional quality, he wrote to Frank Holliday that he simply could not do it, even for a private recording. He mentioned lack of time (due largely to composing), the problems his mother was causing (in what turned out to be her last years), and the fact that he had not practised regularly since 1939 and could not play his music well enough to produce a permanent preservation (i.e. recording) of it. He became appalled at the prospect of even trying, although he was practising his *Concerto da suonare da me solo* with a view to recording it first.[54]

The only direct evidence we have of Sorabji's playing is the series of private tape recordings Frank Holliday finally induced him to make in the 1960s.[55] The sound quality is remarkable, despite Sorabji's intractable music room and Holliday's inexperience in recording. The playing is something else, casual and wayward (even if often fluid and strong): runthroughs which only approximate the scores.[56] *Performances* most of them are not, although they contain enough to suggest that under the right conditions, Sorabji could have been a very fine and unusual pianist. He was 69 for the first

---

[51] Kaikhosru Sorabji: Letter to Erik Chisholm, 5 April 1930.

[52] See "The Music of Kaikhosru Sorabji", by Arthur G. Browne, in *Music and Letters*, vol. 11 (January 1930), pp. 15–16; "Music — *Opus clavicembalisticum*", by Edward Clarke Ashworth, in *The New English Weekly*, vol. 9 (30 April 1936), p. 55; and "Splendour upon Splendour", by Frank Holliday. {Holliday's article is Chapter 11 in this book.}

[53] Kaikhosru Sorabji: Letter to Erik Chisholm, 8 April 1930.

[54] Kaikhosru Sorabji: Letter to Frank Holliday, 5 October 1953.

[55] {See Appendix 2 for details of these and other recordings of Sorabji's music.}

[56] There were no retakes unless the tape recorder malfunctioned or there was some other technical difficulty.

Holliday recordings and 75 for the last, so that practising and playing then were even harder and more foreign to him. Erik Chisholm captured the situation when describing the results of his own efforts to record Sorabji early in 1962:

> About this recording you will understand — Sorabji doesn't practise the piano any more & in the 3rd Symphony makes dozens of mistakes (he himself says 100's of mistakes). Moreover, he doesn't always (actually seldom) bring out the main theme of the texture and makes rhythmical inaccuracies. Nevertheless, he gives a general impression of the sound of his music which no one else alive can do: it may sound confused, & meaningless — & does often sound this way — merely an unending stream of notes —: this impression must be corrected by referring to the score of the piece when it will at once become apparent that on the contrary no music has been better organized or thought out.[57]

Referring two and a half years later to Frank Holliday's initial recordings of Sorabji, Chisholm was even harsher:

> He is extemporising half the time and in the fugal sections he replaces the carefully worked out intellectually designed patterns with something very much freer ... [He] allows decorative or subsidiary material to completely swamp the themes: so that, judging the music on <u>sound</u> alone — most of it is unintelligible.[58]

As mentioned, in the 1950s Sorabji contemplated making a recording by himself but came to reject the idea. He protested more than once that he simply could not be expected to operate a tape recorder himself and play the piano. The former totally disrupted his relation to the latter. Equal or greater disruption would be caused by transporting his Steinway to a studio or bringing recording engineers into his home. We must wonder, therefore, whether any tape recording of Sorabji could ever have been representative or good.

When he played publicly in the 1920s and 30s, he caused a sensation as a performer, especially for his apparent power and miraculous technique, but in consideration of the preceding, one must wonder how well he played in several respects, in public at least. Some of the comments made by critics who appear to be responsible observers match those substantiated by the much later

---

[57]Erik Chisholm: Letter to Norman Gentieu, 23 February 1962. The word "inaccuracies" is the independent guess of three people, including a daughter and granddaughter of Chisholm, for an unreadable word.

[58]Erik Chisholm: Letter to Frank Holliday, 28 August 1964.

tapes: Sorabji tended to play impatiently and with little variety.[59] In his one and only performance of it, he appears to have dashed off *Opus clavicembalisticum* in close to two and a half hours. Geoffrey Madge's recording lasts nearly four hours, John Ogdon's nearly four and three-quarters.

> [It seems that] Mr. Sorabji plays his music faster than he intends to, being perhaps, as a pianist, somewhat under domination of his marvellous technic [...] Certainly the main impression created by the performance was of too little variety in the manner of utilising the keyboard for so long a work. A very large proportion of the music came to the ear as consisting of single thematic ideas lavishly decorated with whirling figures in very rapid tempo and exhibiting in themselves but little variety [... T]he restless, rushing passage work was the prevailing element in the music, and there was associated with it in performance a lack of variety in nuance.[60]

Clinton Gray-Fisk, Frank Holliday, Erik Chisholm, and others observed that Sorabji was very reluctant to record his published works.[61] Twenty years and more after they were published, Sorabji told people who wanted him to record them that they were not representative. But Chisholm and others surmised that Sorabji would not record any of his published music for fear of being checked by a score-reader.[62] Other events suggest that there may be some truth in this. The Chisholm-Holliday broadcast contains only one excerpt from a published work (the early *Le jardin parfumé*); for Donald Garvelmann's broadcast Sorabji authorized complete performances only of two unpublished compositions. In fact, on all the private tapes made by Erik Chisholm and Frank Holliday, only one published work was recorded (again *Le jardin parfumé*). Sorabji refused to record any of *Opus clavicembalisticum*. He also did not like others to stand by him at his piano when he played, even, or especially to turn pages.

For whatever reasons, Sorabji might not often have played his music *accurately* (however wonderfully he might have played in

---

[59]Particularly notable and thoughtful (although repetitious) are three anonymous reviews in *The Glasgow Herald* (2 April 1930, p. 8; 2 December 1930, p. 6; 17 December 1936, p. 13) appearing the day after each of Sorabji's three concerts in Glasgow.

[60]"Our Music Critic": "Sorabji in Glasgow / Active Society Recital / 'Opus clavicembalisticum'", in *The Glasgow Herald*, 2 December 1930, p. 6.

[61]See, for example, the letter to Frank Holliday from Clinton Gray-Fisk dated 20 October 1952.

[62]See, for example, the letter to Frank Holliday from Erik Chisholm dated 28 August 1964.

other respects), publicly *or* privately, at least from the early 1950s onwards. Although this does not mean he could *never* play it so, we must remember his disavowal of any extraordinary pianistic ability and his honest confession in 1953 (mentioned above) that he was just not up to recording the *Concerto da suonare da me solo*. He also disliked practising, especially because he could use the time to compose a new work instead. His whole approach to music, including his own, focused on deep, transcendental meaning, in which specific details often mattered much less than the whole. His impatience with those details is not surprising, but it gave us imperfect evidence of his musical intentions.

These intentions, however, seem not to have included an overly literal approach to his scores. The evidence for this is overwhelming: his own playing, his approval of others' far from literally correct performances, even the scores themselves, where making every note sound as written is often likely to give a stiff, dry, exasperating result. Regarding his orchestration, Sorabji once remarked that he often tried things just to find out what would happen.[63]

This experimental attitude also applies to his piano writing. In many places he seems to have written against the performer, but in such instances he was merely using music notation to represent his *conceptions* and not explicit *directions* to the player, who must rethink the notation, mining it for its *implicit* directions, to determine what *will* happen.

The tragedy is that he never really found out the results of most of his experiments. He merely knew that most "experimenters" were not equipped to handle them.

* * * * *

Sorabji's last public appearance as a pianist was in December 1936. His decisions to stop performing in public and not to make recordings, although involving some dissimilar issues, came partly from the same psychological base of high nervous tension and fear of being hurt. It is worth remembering too that his music is extraordinarily difficult to play well, even when his manuscripts can be read with ease (which is rarely), and that it definitely invites superficial and disastrous performances by the unwary or the

---

[63]Kaikhosru Sorabji: Conversation with Paul Rapoport, 19 May 1978.
This said, it must be admitted that some of his orchestral writing is too dense for too long stretches. Terribly difficult not to play but to project, some needs substantial editing to be performed at all.

incapable. Equally likely is incomprehension of his music by audiences.

The only known occasion on which his music was played poorly before the ban by someone else appears to have been when John Tobin played Part I of *Opus clavicembalisticum* (London, 10 March 1936). He took 80 or 90 minutes to play what should take about 50 to 55. (Sorabji thought 40!) The music was heavily criticized in the press; there were even rumours that Sorabji had financed the concert because he could not play the music himself. Even though the situation was unique, for years he had observed his playing and his music being received with everything from indifference to scorn (after his own concerts or publication of a composition).

It is possible, of course, that Sorabji fed somewhat the incomprehension of his own music. He was probably incapable of counteracting it. His reaction to others' unacceptable reactions may well have been in the other direction: with the aid of a few close friends and associates, resolving to write music even more difficult and less comprehensible.[64] Hugh MacDiarmid admitted talking to Sorabji about the suggestion from the Herbert Antcliffes of the time to write something shorter and easier:

> I strongly advised him not to do anything of the kind, if he was tempted at all. He wasn't tempted, but I strongly advised him, on the contrary, to go for bigger and bigger forms and not in any way play down to the masses [...] Why should he lower his standard to make himself popular with people of less perception, less receptivity?[65]

Who rejected whom first? Did Sorabji begin to loathe the masses because they had rejected him? As noted, his need for a feeling of superiority, given his base of what may have been severe insecurity, was a matter of psychological survival, probably developing early in his life. That he *was* superior then and later in many matters of intellect is unquestionable. Rejection by the masses was inevitable, regardless of how it came about initially.

His basic concern about performers and listeners unknown to him was therefore well founded, given his circumstances and character. The extremism of his reaction, namely near-total withdrawal, is understandable but regrettable. In addition to the

---

[64] It is a common tactic of some neurotics to increase dislike or incomprehension of themselves, thereby achieving at least some control and distinction. There was some of this in Sorabji, although it was more than compensated for by his high moral standards.

[65] Hugh MacDiarmid: *The Company I've Kept* (London: Hutchinson, 1966), pp. 42, 54.

Sorabji's last letter to Paul Rapoport (1985)
(see next page)

(see previous page)

(In this letter Sorabji answered questions concerning the dedicatee of his Symphonic Variations and the possibility of there being recent compositions of which the letter writer was unaware.)

10/1/85

Very dear Paul,
    This hasty reply not to keep you waiting! Many many thanks for yours and the extra programs!
    The dedicatee in question was
        (1) <u>Edward Ashworth</u>
    (2) No[,] fingers and eyes arent up to it! any more scrawl!!!
    Many thanks for your affectionate wish[,] most heartily reciprocated!
                                Yours Ever and Ever
                                          K.

professional issues which he could view more objectively, it involved personal issues over which he had little control. To the casual observer it may seem that he simply acted like the child who, discovering he does not like the rules of the game, picks up his ball and goes home. In Sorabji's case the games continued without him, but he was convinced that he could go on observing those he wished while being capable of playing better ones alone or with those of his friends whom he could reach.

Although his music would not have turned out the way it did had he become a calmer, more public figure, it is possible that he was not completely right. It is poignant indeed to read of his enthusiasm for several of the performers (e.g. Solomon, Habermann, Madge, Stevenson) whom he came to know in the last dozen years of his life. What might have happened if, in that period or earlier, some good friend had dragged him, literally if necessary, to a concert hall to hear his music? Or if Erik Chisholm and Frank Holliday had convinced him to allow performances by Yonty Solomon and John Ogdon years before Alistair Hinton did exactly that?

* * * * *

Sorabji's composing (as opposed to his listening) proceeded essentially in isolation, even from before the ban. It changed, but not much: his later work has a great deal in common with his earlier work. Yet his music is unique, uncompromising, and utterly amazing. Once all the difficulties are resolved in Sorabji's scores (a huge task, admittedly), there remains a body of music remarkable for its strength and beauty as much as for its extremism, infinitely resourceful in its profuse ornamentation and extraordinary textures, uncanny in its structural sense over unprecedented spans of time. It challenges us not just by its very existence but because we risk being destroyed mentally and physically in trying to grapple with it. His music is true alchemy, true magic, as dangerous as any art can be; and in a positive spiritual sense, extremely powerful and transfiguring.

He left a legacy which must not be imprisoned and yet which resists most attempts to reveal it, because it is most emphatically not for everybody. If the people for whom it exists discover it, they will know what to do with it. Recent events suggest that this may already be happening, but the task looks no easier than it ever was.

4 A Few Recollections and Ruminations

Frank Holliday

Frank Holliday (b. 1912, Belvedere, Kent) studied physics and mathematics (with a particular interest in acoustics), gaining a BSc degree. He lectured to various bodies (including the Royal Aeronautical Society, of which he was an Associate Fellow) and was in charge of training in a large engineering company. He did research into the selection of engineering personnel and had several research and other papers published. He was also consulted by Navy, Army, and Air Force authorities, and by industry. Later he taught mathematics, physics, and statistics. Now retired, he lives in East Sussex, England.

His friendship with Sorabji spanned the years 1937 to 1979.

In this chapter, Holliday refers to Sorabji as *K*, which is what all his close friends called him. He mentions the tape recordings of Sorabji playing which he made in the 1960s. Without his bid to convince the composer to make his music more widely available, even in this limited way (the tapes being intended only for restricted circulation), it is doubtful that Sorabji's music would be receiving its current attention, especially from talented performers. (A list of the tapes' contents may be found in Appendix 2.)

I first met K at Bernard Bromage's flat in London in 1937.[1] After some correspondence, he took me to his music studio in Bloomsbury Square and played to me. I was completely and utterly overwhelmed by the beauty of his music. I have been overwhelmed by the beauty of his music ever since: "Beauty that is more wisdom than the wise," as John Masefield has it;[2] "Which, without passing thro' the *Judgment*, gains / The *Heart* and all its End at once

---

[1] {Bromage was a lecturer and writer on several subjects, including music, religion, mysticism, and the occult. Sorabji's friendship with him broke off in 1942.}

[2] John Masefield: "Animula", line 21.

attains", as Alexander Pope has it.[3] Incidentally, K was greatly attracted to Pope, with whom he had a good deal in common.

I became more closely acquainted with him and met him quite often in London. We visited the Wallace Collection, etc., went to one or two shows and often had a meal together. "First table on the left; there you will find me large as life and many times more unnatural!" He was always very prompt.

He lived with his mother at 175, Clarence Gate Gardens, Regents Park, London, for many years and throughout the war. I visited him there. Later, he procured a small house for his mother at Swanage, a few miles from Corfe Castle, Dorset, a village which he had known for many years. He often took day trips from London and rented Rowbarrow, a house on the edge of Corfe Castle, with a friend, Reginald Best. I visited him there as well.

In 1956 he bought a large plot of land at Townsend, Corfe Castle, and had a house built which he named The Eye: "not a bungalow: a one-storied house!" I recall climbing the builder's ladder and walking round the boards with K when The Eye was three feet high. Later, I visited him many times there, usually once a year, sometimes twice, for two or three days at a time. (I lived at a distance, in south-west England.)[4]

On such occasions he nearly always played to me in the mornings for an hour or two. "There are only two people I like playing to: Erik (Chisholm) and yourself." Then I took him round in my car — a change for him. We made many excursions — to Swanage for shopping, to Lulworth, Kingston Lacey, Wimborne Minster, Blandford, and the villages round about. K, on seeing some wild and desolate expanse: "'Simplicity: the last refuge of the Complex', as someone once said."

We usually lunched at the Red Lion at Wareham. We shared a taste for sweet white wines, *La flora blanche* especially. We separated in the afternoon and I went round to The Eye in the early evening, when he usually played to me for an hour before we went off to Wareham for dinner. On returning, he almost invariably played to me again, often for more than an hour. I left at about 10 o'clock to sleep in digs he had arranged for me in the village, though on one occasion, Reggie being away, I slept at The Eye.

I only ever heard him play noticeably badly once. That was when we had returned from Wareham one evening and he sat down and began to play *Gulistān* on his Mason and Hamlin piano. After a short while he looked at me, I looked at him: that was enough!

---

[3]Alexander Pope: *An Essay on Criticism,* lines 156–57.
[4]{About 115 miles away. In the 1970s and 80s Holliday lived slightly further from Sorabji on the other side, i.e. to the east.}

Anyway, *Gulistān*, that exquisitely beautiful piece which he dedicated to me (as he did the Second Piano Symphony — which he declared for many years was his best work — and (retrospectively) the *Toccata* for Piano of 1928)[5] sounded better on his Steinway: he almost invariably played on the Steinway.

He rarely played other composers' work — I didn't want him to, anyway. But I recall his demonstrating Wagner's "sweep" as a response to my denigration of that composer. He also played Skryabin's *Désir:* "It's just that!"

At one time it had been arranged that we would visit his mother's grave, in Bournemouth North Cemetery, if my memory is correct. K had had some bars of Verdi's *Requiem* put on the stone above her grave because she sang in the *Requiem* so beautifully. The morning turned out wet and windy, so we didn't go. That was fortunate, for he spent the whole morning playing several of his Transcendental Studies, a number of which I later recorded.

He was never short of a more than adequate riposte: "Is it above your head, Mr. Sorabji?" asked some impertinent pianist once. "No, but it's obviously above yours" was the prompt reply.

"Passion and compassion!" he remarked as we looked at a large reproduction of the apsidal mosaic of Christ in Cefalù Cathedral: a perfect and most discriminating description. We often turned the pages of his beautiful books and handled his numerous *objets d'art*. His music room was a work of art in itself.

* * * * *

In response to a suggestion from Donald Garvelmann that he should allow a broadcast in America of some of the tapes I had made of his playing of his own compositions, I urged K that it would be better, in the first place, to broadcast a tape on him with musical excerpts. I asked him to give me permission to write to Erik Chisholm, suggesting that he write the program and I supply the excerpts — as happened. Unfortunately, the tapes of Chisholm's talk were defective through no fault of his own — he was a very sick man — and I was forced to re-record his talk myself. The talk and excerpts were broadcast in a three-hour program on Sorabji on New York radio station WNCN in December 1970.[6] They evoked what the station described as "an unparalleled response". Many of

---

[5]{Sorabji also dedicated his *Fourth Toccata* to Frank Holliday.}
[6]{See Chapter 12 for further details.}

the comments they received were printed privately in a pamphlet entitled *The Composer Sorabji (Postscript).*[7]

It has so often seemed to me that the perceptiveness of the lover of Beauty far outweighs that of the music critics. Thus (although, admittedly, it was the most stupid remark) one critic wrote of *Opus clavicembalisticum*, played in July 1988 in London by John Ogdon: "if the work has a trace of humour, it escaped me". Is there any humour in Bach's *Art of Fugue?* If so, it has escaped me, too! On the other hand, some comments from listeners to the WNCN program (referred to above):

"a long overdue tribute to this extraordinary musician".
"I enjoyed his keyboard pieces because of their timeless and peculiar tranquility."
"There also seemed to be an undercurrent of mystical sensuality throughout all his music."
"At first I thought it was so much gibberish but by the end of the program I was absolutely entranced."
"your broadcast kept me spellbound".

Many listeners asked to hear more music by Sorabji.

* * * * *

Some years ago, Mr. Garvelmann sent me a tape of Michael Habermann's playing of some Sorabji. I was greatly impressed and took it to Corfe Castle and played it to K, taking down his comments during the playing. (Later, Michael Habermann made three Sorabji discs and it is to be hoped he will make more.) Mr. Garvelmann and Mr. Habermann subsequently paid Sorabji a visit at The Eye,[8] and the latter played to K. Upon hearing Mr. Habermann's performance, he remarked: "I have just heard my music played more marvellously than I ever imagined possible." And: "Admirable, sounds like my own playing."

* * * * *

Enough!
Requiescat in pace — my wonderful and greatly loved old friend.

---

[7]Donald Garvelmann: *The Composer Sorabji (Postscript).* Printed privately: [New York, 1971].
[8]{In August 1980.}

Sorabji in 1977

5 "Could you just send me a list of his works?"

Paul Rapoport

Ever since the mid-1970s, when Donald Garvelmann compiled and circulated privately a list of Sorabji's compositions that had been microfilmed, I have been tempted to try to expand it to include a catalog of all of Sorabji's music. This temptation was wholly natural, as I had spotted a few problems in Garvelmann's list which I thought would be easy to solve. I was also interested in knowing what Sorabji wrote altogether before I tried to generalize about it.

The attempt to resolve some issues led to more problems than solutions. Through no fault of Garvelmann's, there later proved to be wrong titles, multiple versions of titles for one work, multiple versions of works with one title, works missing and probably destroyed, works supposedly destroyed but later proven not missing, early works not on his list, recent works not on his list ... And all this had to be sorted out just to identify the music.

What about the stories of an orchestral work of over a thousand pages and requiring forces larger than Mahler's? Were the page totals for the various works accurate? After all, no one could possibly have any idea of the actual duration of Sorabji's major works, as almost no one had heard any, so lengths in pages were the only possible points of comparison.

An investigation soon uncovered the fact that most of Garvelmann's data on pages were accurate and sufficient if you were interested only in the last page number of a work. But Sorabji's page numbering went astray in some cases. Although there were not enough problems to turn a large work into a small one, there was plenty to make one curious as to just what he was up to. Why did the Fifth Piano Sonata, for example, have a page 343a when 344 would do as well or better? It also turned out that there was indeed a work of over a thousand pages, precisely 1001, and another which did not have 830 pages, as many had thought by

94 Discovery

looking at the last page number, but 824, because of errors Sorabji made in numbering some pages.

Who cares, you say, about a discrepancy of six pages?

This degree of accuracy has some value in a catalog of works. Since page numbers are an important bibliographic item of reference, especially for unpublished work, presenting them correctly only makes sense. And the process of examining Sorabji's page numbering revealed some useful information about his interests and character.[1]

* * * * *

The most frustrating work over the years has been to identify (and find) Sorabji's piano concertos. The situation as far as I knew it in the mid-1970s was very simple: there was a published concerto (No. 2, written in 1920), a later manuscript in the composer's possession which had been microfilmed (No. 5, completed in 1928), and nothing further with the title *Concerto*. But no researcher could possibly be satisfied with that state of affairs. If there were a No. 2 and a No. 5, what — and where — were the others?

It looks simple: you search for Nos. 1, 3, and 4.

As expected, between Nos. 2 and 5 are two more concertos, but one is not numbered. Even worse, between Nos. 1 and 5 there is a total of not three more concertos but six, including two different works called Concerto No. 2. To confound initial impressions, there are also three concertos with identical page divisions for their three movements.

One might think that the easiest path to solutions to problems like these is via the composer. This is rarely the case. The composer created the mess in the first place: why should he want to resurrect it, let alone be able to untangle it? Most composers are far too involved with creative work to keep track of these bookkeeping-like details of their music, and it is usually asking too much of someone to know small details about and the location of things he wrote and gave away 60 years earlier.

Sorabji was of some help, however. At the time of the 1978 microfilming of many of his works, Alistair Hinton and I knew that Norman Gentieu of Philadelphia possessed an unnumbered concerto composed between the time of the published No. 2 and that of No. 5. Sorabji informed us then that he was sure he had composed *two* concertos *around the same time* for smaller orchestral forces. One was Gentieu's, the *Sīmurgh-'Anqā* concerto,

---

[1] {For both process and information, see pp. 63–66.}

written in 1924. The other, presumably also falling between the published No. 2 and No. 5, had left no trace.

Over the next decade, as the likelihood of finding more concertos by Sorabji diminished, I convinced myself that his memory about his concertos with small orchestra was inaccurate, that the missing concerto never existed. I should have known better. Hinton solved the problem in 1987. He then solved it again in 1988. Yes: in 1987 he found a concerto for small forces written in 1918, which we concluded was the "other" one Sorabji recalled in 1978. But the one he was probably thinking of then was discovered in 1988. It was written in 1922.

So Sorabji wrote not two but three concertos for small orchestra within six years (1918, 1922, 1924). On balance he was right, and I was wrong several times.[2]

* * * * *

It is often assumed that to list the works of a composer — presuming knowledge of the titles in the first place — one merely puts the titles in some kind of order. The most useful order is chronological. But already this brings difficulties, for nearly every composer has left something undated or with contradictory dates, or has revised works enough to make their placing in one position in a catalog simply and maddeningly impossible.[3]

And what happens with works which simply took many years to write? Are they listed according to the beginning or the ending date? In this catalog it is the latter, for the not very interesting reason that often the starting date cannot be determined. More sensibly, there are two other reasons for cataloguing by completion date. A composer may considerably alter a work long after it is begun (thus making its completion a more realistic chronological marker than its inception), and a completion date is obviously more

---

[2]{Rapoport made a better guess about Sorabji's unknown music in 1989, after Chris Rice had discovered the last six pages of a hitherto unknown solo piano work. Dangerously diagnosing the situation over the telephone in a conversation with Alistair Hinton, Rapoport rashly concluded that these belonged to the rarely mentioned and long disappeared (pre-First) Piano Sonata. Hinton wisely doubted this — after all, there was no title written at the *end* of the piece. Then he discovered the missing first 24 pages, a few months later in a different location. The title: Sonata, Op. 7.}

[3]{One of the most difficult cases of this in the 20th century is found in the works of the composer Rued Langgaard. See *Rued Langgaards Kompositioner*, by Bendt Viinholt Nielsen (Odense: Odense Universitetsforlag, 1991).}

useful if one wants to measure the time elapsed between composition and performance of a work. Even though most of Sorabji's works have never been performed, the principle remains valid.

An apparent exception must obviously be made for incomplete works or fragmentary manuscripts, which are listed as close to their cessation date as possible.

But the titles? It should be straightforward enough to look at Sorabji's manuscripts for those. As suggested earlier, it isn't. To begin with, there may be two or more title pages, a first page of music giving the title again, and in some cases a published version giving the title at least one more time. Among all these indications, there may be two or three different versions of the title. In this catalog, priority is given to the most prominent title page, from a manuscript if one exists.

Another colourful habit of Sorabji's is to transform a title into something else. It may, for example, run into an explanation, or a subtitle or dedication. Most people would take the instrument designation in "Sonata for Piano" to be part of the title rather than an explanation, but what about "Symphony II for Piano, Large Orchestra, Organ, Final Chorus, and Six Solo Voices"? One title in Latin even has the composer's name in it, translating literally and fully as "A Cyclic Sequence on 'Dies iræ' from the Mass for the Dead for Keyboard Use Kaikhosru Shapurji Sorabji Has Written". Despite the unassuming indication "Keyboard Use", this is far from a slight work; it is one of Sorabji's largest and finest. A much shorter, lesser work carries its title into both dedication and author identification, as well as a hint at its musical basis: "Diversified Promenade on the Name of my Dear and Kind Young Friend Clive Spencer-Bentley by his Uncle (more or less!) Kaikhosru Shapurji Sorabji".

Deciding where to cut off a title, or how to rearrange it, is nonetheless a mere diversion compared to dealing with the oddities and outright errors in Sorabji's titles, especially in some of the many Italian titles. His command of Italian, while strong in some ways, was clearly imperfect.[4] For example, he consistently spelled *capriccio* with two *p*s. As there is no point in repeating this mistake

---

[4]Although Sorabji read a great deal of foreign-language literature and his parents knew several languages, he once wrote, "I have unfortunately no ear and no special ability in mastering languages." (Kaikhosru Sorabji: *Mi contra fa: The Immoralisings of a Machiavellian Musician* (London: Porcupine Press, 1947), p. 54.) For some of his expressions, it is impossible to determine whether he was making a mistake or remembering a dialect variant. In most cases, the former is more likely.

here, the catalog corrects it. Then there is the case of the *Concerto da suonare da me solo,* whose original form is not correct Italian, having the preposition *per* in place of the first *da.*[5]

More difficult is the title of the late work of variations based on *Le coq d'or* of Rimskiy-Korsakov. On one page of his manuscript, having written "Il gallo d'oro", Sorabji then wrote "i" over his letter "o" of "gallo", followed by "n" and "o" to make "gallino", a word which does not exist in standard Italian. *Gallo* is *rooster, gallina* is *hen,* and *galletto* is *young rooster.* Sorabji did write "galletto" in a letter to Michael Habermann (10 June 1979) but wrote "gallino" to him two months later.

Here I have altered the title to *gallo* despite the fact that almost all Sorabji's indications are *gallino,* because there is no point in keeping an incorrect title unless the composer intended it to be so while remaining aware of the correct or standard version. Not surprisingly, Rimskiy-Korsakov's opera is known in Italian with *gallo.* Probably Sorabji was simply trying to remember the right Italian word. Nonetheless, the work in question contains "variazioni frivole" ("frivolous variations"), so one cannot be sure.

Obviously little but annoying questions like these could be avoided by giving only translated English titles, but then users of the catalog would lose a lot, not least the time spent looking for titles or parts of them in locations and lists which do not use translations.

Most of the errors in Sorabji's grammar and spelling on his manuscripts are probably due to his not wishing or needing to check small points with some source such as a dictionary — if indeed he kept a dictionary. The great speed with which he often wrote is part of the problem too, not only making some things very hard to read but simply reflecting his desire to get on with the task and not stop for details or matters of lesser importance. Since he composed most of these works with no intention of public performance or printing in mind, he could and did take a lot for granted in writing them down.

One slightly odd title I have left unaltered. The *Symphonic High Mass* Sorabji consistently called (in Italian) *Messa alta sinfonica,* possibly by analogy with the English (*High Mass*) or the German (*Hohe Messe*), or as distinct from the Italian *Messa bassa.* Less ambiguous Italian would use *Messa grande* or *Messa solenne.* Unfortunately, even though it may also mean *lofty, noble,* and *holy,* in this context *alta* may be taken for *tall,* and therefore *high* in that sense. Tall this work certainly is, but I doubt that this joke was

---

[5]{See the entry in the Detailed Catalog (pp. 152–53) for another anomaly in the extended title of this work.}

intended for the title of what may be Sorabji's finest choral-orchestral work.⁶

Nonetheless, there are jokes and other humorous comments, musical and other, in Sorabji's music and on his manuscripts. Although not numerous, they are often striking. One notable instruction in the work based on Rimskiy-Korsakov's opera is attached to Variation 10: "Impertinent waltz. With the elephantine grace of an English orchestra playing a Strauss waltz." Lighter but still pervasive humour runs through *Un nido di scatole* (*A Nest of Boxes*). The humour in the 3 Pastiches from 1922 is so cutting at certain points that it takes on a unique, almost frightening quality. In the same manner is the much later *Malicious and Perverse Variation on "Åse's Death" by Grieg*. Plentiful further evidence of Sorabji's humour will be found in the notes which in this chapter follow the short catalog.

One manuscript, which consists only of one undated page (and does not appear in the catalog), presents two lines of music. The first, two measures written on four staves, is marked "Full Orchestra", with the following comment below it: "Fragment for a nonexistent poem for orchestra 'Passion.' — (The bursting of the bonds.) {!!!!!!!?????} — —". If this is a joke, its object is unclear; it could even be Sorabji's own overwrought, hyperemotional writing.

The point of the second line of music is more obvious. Consisting of four measures written in a four-part chorale manner on two staves but in a tonally undefined style, it has "fin (!!!??)" at the end and this pointed remark below: "Study in 4 part writing '<u>not</u>' according to Ebenezer Prout.⁷ No prize is offered for successful solution of the tonality of this piece. Virtue must be its own reward here." The negative is underlined not once but 16 times.

* * * * *

Sorabji's songs usually have obvious titles, because they originate in others' pre-existing texts. Here, however, there are two potential additional problems: the texts themselves and the identification of their authors.

Unfortunately much of Sorabji's library was dispersed when his house was sold in 1986: valuable sources for his creative thought were lost. However, it has been possible to indicate the correct wording, spelling, punctuation, etc. of his song texts by checking

---

⁶{See p. 44 for an independent comment on this weighty matter.}

⁷{For Sorabji's blunt opinion of this pedagogue and sometime composer, see p. 208.}

many literary sources.⁸ Sorabji made errors in copying the texts into his music, just as he made errors in titles and music notation.⁹

Fortunately for the researcher, Sorabji set to music some well-known poems. Others not as famous proved a problem. Although he indicated the French translator of the stories from the *Gulistān* of Saʻdī which he set in 1926, definite errors in Sorabji's manuscript required checking against the original. A quick look at the published translation proved upsetting: for one song, he appeared to have completely rearranged some of the words.

To do that would have been so unlike him that I hypothesized he must have used another edition. Surely enough, a later edition of the same work proved that the same translator had retranslated the story in question. The later edition is the one Sorabji used.

Identification of the authors of the song texts proved no problem except in a few cases. The fragmentary song "The Wicked Gardener" contains one of the most colourful of the symbolist/decadent poems Sorabji set. He indicated its author's name unclearly: it looked like "Iwan Gwilkin". The first named looked Slavic or Welsh, but the last name was puzzling, and the poem was in French with no translator's name given.

Initial searches of literary reference books proved fruitless: there was no such person. One colleague thought that he had seen the poem somewhere and that the name must be a pseudonym, maybe for Sorabji himself. No, that did not fit. Sorabji was a magnificent writer of prose, but he was not known to be a poet, much less a published one. The name could, of course, be a pseudonym created by the real poet. A lot of help that would be!

Finally, a casual glance at one reference work uncovered the entry *Gilkin, Iwan* (far enough from the supposed "Gwilkin" to be missed). Sorabji must have misremembered the name, or perhaps his pen slipped when he was copying it. Gilkin, incidentally, was Belgian.

* * * * *

Dating is yet another major concern, especially but not exclusively for manuscripts without dates appended. It helps that Sorabji spelled his first name *Kaikhusru* until late 1919 or early 1920 — at which time he adopted *Kaikhosru*. This provides information about the period of composition of some works, even if not specific dates. It is also possible that the completion date on some manuscripts is wrong (more about an instance shortly); and there is no starting

---

⁸{Most of the texts he set to music are contained in Appendix 1 of this book.}

⁹{For comments on and examples of errors in notation, see pp. 384–85.}

date on most of them. There would not likely be any way, for example, to know how long it took Sorabji to write *Opus clavicembalisticum*, as only the date of completion appears on his manuscript. But it is clear from one of the many letters to Erik Chisholm which he wrote as he was composing *Opus clavicembalisticum* that he began it no later than mid-December 1929, and probably not much earlier.[10]

Even when the starting and completion dates are known (whether down to the day or not), it cannot be assumed that a composition took as long to write as the two dates suggest, because Sorabji interrupted some works to write others. For example, his Third Symphony, *Jāmī*, he began in 1942, while still writing the Transcendental Studies. The main score of this symphony was set aside for several others besides the Studies, some by no means small; and between the conclusion of the main large score and the conclusion of the separate small score came the entire composition of one gigantic work (*Sequentia cyclica*) and some of another (the Third Organ Symphony).

Determining just the completion date of the Symphonic Variations, piano part only, proved a perplexing matter. In the mid-1970s I noted this was August 1937 (MCMXXXVII, as Sorabji usually used Roman numerals for dates on his manuscripts), from the microfilm copy of the manuscript which was made on 12 January 1953. In 1988, however, I noticed that Sorabji's original autograph manuscript stated 1938 (MCMXXXVIII). It is possible that Sorabji altered the date when he recommenced the composition of this work for piano and orchestra in the spring of 1953, although why, no one knows. On page 361 of the score, 123 pages from the end, is the date "28 Dec. 1936". Given the circumstances, it seemed much more likely that Sorabji took another eight months to finish the work than a year and eight months. It also seemed likely that he began the orchestral version shortly after the completion of the piano part: letters he wrote in 1953 suggested so. But this still did not answer the question of when the piano part was completed.

It proved impossible to trace his movements with enough detail to know where he was in August 1937 and 1938, in view of the designation (at the end of the manuscript) of Corfe Castle as the location where he completed the work in question. But in 1989 Alistair Hinton checked a letter that Sorabji had written to Erik Chisholm in September 1937 which mentions the recent completion of the piano part. Case closed, except for the mysterious later alteration.

---

[10]{See pp. 298–311 for the letters to Erik Chisholm about *Opus clavicembalisticum*.}

Several works which have not yet been found, either in manuscript or in any other form, are noted as missing in the catalog. Still others, e.g. early songs, are completely unknown, even by title or text. No one has determined what befell the manuscript of one of Sorabji's last works, *Opus secretum*. Although several photocopies of it exist, it would be nice if the original manuscript did not live up to the work's title. Some early piano concertos are missing in a manuscript full score or first version, although apart from those, I believe now that all the concertos have been found. One substantial work is still missing altogether: the *Toccata terza*. In 1974 I asked Sorabji's friend Frank Holliday if there had been such a work, because three other large-scale toccatas (concluding with No. 4) were locatable, but in no reliable list had I seen a *Third Toccata* mentioned.

The reply came directly from Sorabji as follows (as usual, the rush of his thoughts and typing not stopping for niceties of punctuation or revision):

> Toccata three no longer exists — it was destroyed soaked and ruined owing to the criminal stupidity and neglect of people into whose [hands] his music came after his death, i.e. my dear late friend Clinton Gray-Fisk for whom it was written and [to whom] dedicated. As a specimen of crass stupidity and indifference all his music and books were left in a flimsy outhouse into which snow penetrated ruining quantities of the contents which included my Third Toccata.[11]

The date given in the catalog for this work is conjectural, based on a conversation Alistair Hinton had with Sorabji in the mid-1970s. There is no support for a date in the 1950s;[12] indeed, there is support for a date before 1946. In Eric Blom's *Everyman's Dictionary*

---

[11] Kaikhosru Sorabji: Letter to Paul Rapoport, 30 December 1974. In a Letter to Frank Holliday of 2 April 1975 Sorabji, amplifying a little, wrote that the *Third Toccata* was a work "of some size" which Clinton Gray-Fisk had had beautifully bound by Zaehnsdorf in London. Left along with "all his books and music STACKS of it" in "a flimsy garden shed" by Gray-Fisk's widow ("prize bitch and cow as ever was [...] she HATED me"), "it became a sodden <u>RUIN.</u>"

{The discovery in 1989 of some of Sorabji's music which had belonged to Clinton Gray-Fisk offers the possibility that the *Third Toccata* may yet turn up.}

[12] In some of his later lists Hinton suggests 1955, which is unlikely. See, for example, the first edition of his list in the booklet accompanying the recording of *Opus clavicembalisticum* by John Ogdon (Altarus AIR–CD–9075, issued in 1989). The dates in that list are otherwise fairly accurate.

of Music (London: J. M. Dent, 1946), three toccatas are mentioned (in addition to the early unnumbered one which forms part of the work published as Two Piano Pieces). Even though early lists of Sorabji's compositions are often full of howlers, this list is actually not bad, especially compared to the disastrous one perpetrated by the fifth edition of *Grove's Dictionary* eight years later.

Grove 5, as it is known,[13] is responsible for various serious errors, in addition to beginning the Sorabji entry with the now-famous "Indian composer" which raised Sorabji's considerable ire.[14] There are wrong titles, many obvious omissions, and works put in the wrong category. For example, the *Fantasia ispanica* and the *Tāntrik* Symphony, both for piano only, are listed as orchestral items. For many years *Grove 5* was the most widely available catalog of Sorabji's works, giving a wholly inadequate representation of them.

Even the superpersistent musical detective Nicolas Slonimsky, the most famous and justly celebrated 20th-century music lexicographer, included wrong information in his various editions of *Baker's Biographical Dictionary of Musicians*. (Not deliberately, of course; not even surprisingly, considering how difficult it must have been for him to get accurate information.) In the sixth edition is the news that Sorabji composed four symphonies for piano "with instrumental ensembles".[15] While one might think those were simply mistitled concertos, they are in fact symphonies *without* orchestra (for piano alone), given in the dictionary with one wrong date of composition, confusing the matter further. Slonimsky also misdated the last of the piano sonatas and claimed erroneously that Sorabji banned performances of his music about 1950.

He also repeated a longstanding error about *Opus clavicembalisticum*, namely that it contains a set of 44 variations. A glance at the *music* of the published score would show 49 variations. But many people do not get past its table of contents, where the erroneous indication is contained. That error came from Sorabji's manuscript, where the table of contents gives the number of variations in Roman numerals (as does the published score). The engraver of the score misread *XLIV* for *XLIX*, as Sorabji's last *X* is top-heavy, looking like a *V*.

While the seventh edition of *Baker's* corrected this and much else, it still got wrong about half the dates for the piano concertos

---

[13]Eric Blom, ed.: *Grove's Dictionary of Music and Musicians*, 5th edition (London: Macmillan, 1954). The article on Sorabji, by Terence White Gervais, is in vol. 7, pp. 970–71.

[14]{See p. 24 for one formal but abrupt result of this ire.}

[15]Nicolas Slonimsky, ed.: *Baker's Biographical Dictionary of Musicians*, 6th edition (New York: Schirmer, 1978), p. 1631.

(the real ones), gave the dates of the Third Organ Symphony to the Second Piano Quintet, misspelled some titles, omitted others, dated the missing *Third Toccata* much too late, and stated categorically that Sorabji banned all performances of his works in 1936 — still wrong, but closer to correct than 1950.[16]

We also learn from this edition that Sorabji refused to attend performances of his works, which is true, and that he "took refuge far from the madding crowd in a castle he owned in England", which is absurd. The town Sorabji lived in, Corfe Castle, had perhaps become his property! He did not own the castle for which the town is named, and could not live in it even if he did, as it is a millenium-old ruin. He lived in a beautiful one-storey house which he had built in 1956.

While slightly enlarged, the eighth edition of *Baker's* repeated all of the main errors of the seventh.[17]

Considering the availability of information at the time of publication of the various reference works, the best source before the present book may have been the article in *"Grove 6"*.[18] Aside from a too short bibliography (from which all the reference-book articles on Sorabji suffer), a few wrong dates, and a wrong title, the catalog in this article was good for its time and accompanied a better description of Sorabji's music than that in any other article of comparable intent.

Some reference books could not even get the information correct for Sorabji's published music. Following is a list of all Sorabji's compositions which were published before his father's death in 1932. The "K. S." number appears at the bottom of the pages of each score for which it is indicated. The exact place in the list of the two unnumbered works is conjectural, although their dates of publication and copyright are not.

---

[16]Nicolas Slonimsky, ed.: *Baker's Biographical Dictionary of Musicians*, 7th edition (New York: Schirmer, 1984), pp. 2167–68.
{For more on the ban, see Chapters 2 and 3.}
[17]Nicolas Slonimsky, ed.: *Baker's Biographical Dictionary of Musicians*, 8th edition (New York: Schirmer, 1992), pp. 1746–47.
[18]Stanley Sadie, ed.: *The New Grove Dictionary of Music and Musicians* (London: Macmillan, 1980). The article on Sorabji by Donald Garvelmann is in vol. 17, pp. 534–35. Coming later, the entries in *Baker's*, seventh and eighth editions, provide a more up-to-date list of works.

K. S. No.	Title	Published	Copyright
1	Trois poèmes pour chant et piano (1918, 1919)	1921	1921
none	Sonata [No. 1 for] Piano (1919)	1921	1921
none	Two Piano Pieces (1918, 1920)	1921	1921
4	Fantaisie espagnole (1919)	1922	1922
5	Quintet [No. 1] for Piano and Quartet of Stringed Instruments (1919–20)	1923	1923
6	Sonata seconda for Piano (1920)	1923	1923
7	Concerto for Piano and Orchestra (1920)	1923	1923
8	Prelude, Interlude, and Fugue for Piano (1920, 1922)	1924	1924
9	Sonata III for Piano (1922)	1925	1924
10–12	Trois fêtes galantes de Verlaine (ca. 1919)	1924	1924
13	Symphony [No. 1] for Organ (1924)	1925	1925
14	Le jardin parfumé — Poem for Piano Solo (1923)	1927	1927
15	Valse-fantaisie [for] Piano Solo (1925)	1927	1927
16	Opus clavicembalisticum (1929–30)	1931	1931

The following two works were published much later. (No others have been published.)

Title	Published	Copyright
Pastiche for Piano on Chopin: Valse Op. 64 No. 1 (1922)	1969	1969
Fantasiettina sul nome illustre dell'egregio poeta Christopher Grieve ossia Hugh M'Diarmid (1961)	1987	1987

The *Fantasiettina* appeared in a performing/teaching edition by Ronald Stevenson, with the names of the poet transposed: *Fantasiettina sul nome illustre dell'egregio poeta Hugh MacDiarmid ossia Christopher Grieve*, probably because Hugh MacDiarmid was the pseudonymous author of Grieve's poetry.

* * * * *

The aim of this chapter to this point has not been to bore readers with details with which they have no concern. It has merely been to explain that there is more than may at first be thought to the construction of a works list, especially for Sorabji. To all those who have waited for an accurate list of Sorabji's compositions: I thank them for their patience, but I also warn everyone not to believe everything they see just because it is found in print — not even the print of this book. While the catalog presented here is far more accurate and detailed than any other, it is impossible to claim that it contains no errors or omissions. Aside from those I may have caused, I expect more information about known and unknown compositions by Sorabji to appear.

A "Complete Provisional" Chronological Catalog of Sorabji's Compositions

This catalog is presented in three parts: The Detailed Catalog, The Short Catalog, and Sorabji's Notes. The Short Catalog simply lists the titles and dates by genre, and within genre chronologically; it gives a quick overview of Sorabji's works. The notes contain a variety of ancillary material, such as prefaces and performance notes, with which I chose not to clutter the Detailed Catalog, since it already contains a fair amount of information.

In the catalog is every work by Sorabji which I have examined (nearly all of them) or found mentioned in a reasonably authoritative source, such as his letters. A few works are incomplete; indeed, some titles probably represent works he never began. They are included here to give a fuller picture of his ideas and activities than their omission would allow.[19]

For the Detailed Catalog, the basic information for each work is taken from the manuscript (if more than one, the better copy). Only when none exists is it taken from the published score (if any) or a more remote source such as a letter. A raised circle (°) after a title indicates that no complete manuscript has been found, but that the complete work exists as a published score, from which the basic information is therefore taken. A raised plus sign (+) indicates that further information may be found elsewhere: in Appendix 1 if accompanied by the designation "A1"; in the "Sorabji's Notes" section at the end of this chapter if accompanied by a numeral without any letter. The number of the note in that section is given by the raised numeral after the plus sign.

Positions of compositions in the catalog have been assigned chronologically by completion date. When a date is uncertain, one is presumed on the basis of characteristics of a manuscript, a

---

[19]Not listed are two-piano arrangements of some smaller works which Erik Chisholm made. (Erik Chisholm: Letter to Frank Holliday, 28 August 1964.) None of these are known by title or have yet been traced.

comment in a letter written by Sorabji, or a guess based on other circumstantial evidence.

The titles are generally taken from full title pages; if there is none, then from the first page of the music or from the cover (if any). The punctuation shown is not always Sorabji's, as sometimes his does not translate well to the typed or typeset page. Multiple title pages complicate matters for a few works. A few titles and subtitles have been corrected; major corrections are explained in the Comments section of an entry. For the piano concertos, simple titles are suggested, assigning unique ordinal numbers to avoid confusion of identification.

Most of the translations of titles should not be taken too seriously. (The simpler titles are left untranslated.) The generic translations (with well-known terms such as *Sonata, Concerto, Fantasy*) are harmless, but the others should never be used as the real titles. They are offered only as a rough guide for those who know no French, Italian, German, or Latin at all, to indicate what Sorabji was aiming at. His titles are often unique and should be preserved, corrected if necessary but not betrayed by English translations, which are almost always inferior to his foreign-language titles.

The number of pages shown is the actual number, which may not correspond to the numeral on the last numbered page, for reasons which are explained in the Comments section of any work having this discrepancy. The method of indicating voice range for the songs presumes that Middle C is c^4, and that each octave is numbered upwards from c, with the same index for all notes in the octave comprising c and the next eleven higher pitches. Simply for convenience, it also presumes that $g^\sharp$ is higher than $a^\flat$ in the same octave (which is not always true musically).

Sometimes Sorabji wrote out the instrumentation for orchestral works on a separate page before the music begins; this has been checked, insofar as it is possible to do so, against the music itself. At certain locations in some works it is unclear exactly which instrument is playing. It may be clear, for example, that the oboe family contains regular (soprano) oboes, English horn, and bass oboe, but the music may not directly indicate which is playing or even how many, merely that a given line is an oboe part of some sort.[20] This has made it necessary, on occasion, to make inferences about the overall list of forces in an orchestral work.

---

[20] {Anyone planning to copy out parts to one of Sorabji's scores must therefore become fully conversant with his orchestral intentions from an examination of a number of his scores, and be prepared to do a lot of editing.}

Instrumentation is given in a standard format, arranged by orchestral family in score order. Any good book on orchestration or catalog of orchestral works may be consulted to decode the lists given here. One convention needs a comment: for oboes, clarinets, and bassoons, the designation "2+1" indicates 2 of the standard instrument plus 1 of the most common *larger* auxiliary instrument. For flutes, "1+2" indicates 1 of the most common *smaller* auxiliary instrument (viz. piccolo) plus 2 of the standard instrument.

The abbreviations used are the following:

alt	alto	hrp	harp
bar	baritone	obo	oboe
bls	bells	org	organ
bss	bass	pic	piccolo
cbs	contrabass	pno	piano
cel	celesta	prc	percussion
clt	clarinet	sar	sarrusophone
cor	cornet	strs	strings
flt	flute	tym	tympani
S	soprano	T	tenor
A	alto	B	bass

Dedications and inscriptions are given within quotation marks as Sorabji wrote them, with separation of lines shown by a diagonal (/). A few essential corrections are indicated on location in square brackets, in some instances set off by the word *recte*. The notation "[*sic:* ?]" signifies that a guess was made for the preceding word.

The entry for contents and pagination is the most elaborate. For every work consisting entirely of a series of variations, the individual variations are listed. Mention is also made (in all works) of any substantial fugal writing, whether or not Sorabji labelled such with a sectional heading. Many minor spelling errors of tempo and character designations, mostly in Italian, some in French, have been corrected without comment where necessary. As Sorabji's punctuation for these varies considerably, especially when he strings many together, I have standardized it to some extent. It is important to realize, in any case, that there are many more tempo and character designations in his music than those given here. For identification purposes, this catalog contains only what Sorabji gives at the *beginning* of a movement or section. An indication such as "Brioso focosamente: 1–27" (from the *Concerto da suonare da me solo*) does not imply that that marking holds for the entire 27 pages, only that it is written at the beginning (of the *movement*, in this case). If all Sorabji's markings were given here, the catalog would fill a whole book by itself, and a discussion of them most of an additional one.

The location of a manuscript is given only where it is a library or similar repository open to the public or to qualified scholars. Manuscripts in private collections do not have their location indicated, except for those many in the Sorabji Music Archive, which are listed by permission of Alistair Hinton. Recent unpublished editions by Yonty Solomon, Kevin Bowyer, Marc-André Roberge, and others are not listed, although they are also held and distributed by the Archive.

In the section for comments, a variety of additional material may be found:

1) the initial marking (tempo and character) of a work which is not divided into sections or movements. Sorabji's mistakes in these have been corrected.

2) the completion date of those works on which Sorabji indicated it — happily, nearly all. Although he never wrote dates this way, they are always given in the Detailed Catalog in the format year–month–day.

3) other information, depending on the work. For titles which exist only in secondary sources, i.e. without any extant manuscript of the music and no published edition, a source of information is mentioned.

The first public performance is listed only when it can be determined with certainty or near-certainty. In some cases a cautionary note about possible earlier performances is added.

The various kinds of information discussed above are indicated by the following abbreviations:

Auth.	Author(s)
Cont., pag.	Contents and pagination
Dedic'n	Dedication
Instr'n	Instrumentation
Med.	Medium
Med., pp.	Medium, number of pages
Ms. loc'n	Location of manuscript
Oth.	Other [title]
Perf.	Performance
Public'n	Publication
Sugg.	Suggested [title]
Transl'n	Translation

* * * * *

"Could you just send me a list of his works?" 109

I regret having to present the vast technical notes above. They are included to prevent just the kinds of misunderstanding which have surrounded Sorabji's works for many years.

The Detailed Catalog

Title, date: **[Transcription of] In a Summer Garden [by Delius] (1914)**
Med.: Piano

Ms. loc'n: Unknown.

Comments: This work may have been left incomplete. The evidence for its existence comes from Sorabji's letter to Philip Heseltine of 8 September 1914, in which he wrote: "I am attempting [...] a piano arrangement of 'In a Summer Garden'. Have got as far as ⑯ [...]"

Title, date: **The Poplars, Op. 2, No. 1 (1915)** [+A1; +1, 2]
Med., pp.: Voice and piano, 3 pp. Voice range: g^3 to b^5.

Auth., text: Jovan Dučić (1871–1943, Serbia): "The Poplars", translated by Paul Selver.

Ms. loc'n: One is in the Sorabji Music Archive, another is in a private collection. See Comments.

Comments: Initial marking: Modéré. Sombre, noir, menaçant.
Date at end [p. 3]: 1915–05–17.
Not performed.

Of the two different manuscripts, the one kept by the composer (now in the Sorabji Music Archive) has 3 unnumbered pages, the other 4 unnumbered pages. Both have the same date at the end.

Title, date: **Chrysilla, Op. 1, No. 1 (1915)** [+A1]
Med., pp.: Voice and piano, 4 pp. Voice range: $b\flat^3$ to c^6.

Auth., text: Henri de Régnier (1864–1936, France): "Chrysilla".

Ms. loc'n: Private collection.

Comments: Initial marking: Très modéré.
Date at end (p. 4): 1915–05–21.
Not performed.

At the beginning is the metronome indication of quarter-note equals approximately 40.

Title, date:	**Roses du soir, Op. 1, No. 2 (1915)** [+A1]
Transl'n:	Evening Roses
Med., pp.:	Voice and piano, 4 pp. Voice range: c^4 to $a^{\#5}$.
Auth., text:	Pierre Louÿs (1870–1925, France): "Roses dans la nuit".
Ms. loc'n:	Private collection.
Comments:	Initial marking: Lent. Date at end (p. 4): 1915-07-08. Not performed. In assigning his title, Sorabji may have misremembered Louÿs's title. On the first page is a crossed-out Roman numeral III, suggesting that this song may at one time have been Op. 1, No. 3. At the beginning of the music is the metronome indication of quarter-note equals 30.

Title, date:	**L'heure exquise, Op. 2, No. 2 (1916)** [+A1]
Transl'n:	The Exquisite Hour
Med., pp.:	Voice and piano, 2 pp. Voice range: c^4 to $g^{\#5}$.
Auth., text:	Paul Verlaine (1844–96, France): untitled poem, no. 6 in *La bonne chanson* (published in 1870).
Ms. loc'n:	Private collection.
Comments:	Initial marking: Très lent, contenu et doux. Date at end (p. 2): 1916-02-10. Not performed.

Title, date:	**Vocalise pour soprano fioriturata, Op. 2, No. 3 (1916)** [+1]
Med., pp.:	Voice (wordless) and piano, 3 pp. Voice range: c^4 to $c^{\#6}$.
Ms. loc'n:	One is in the Sorabji Music Archive, another is in a private collection. See Comments.
Comments:	Initial marking: Dans un style fantastique et quasi oriental. Date at end [p. 3]: 1916-03-23. Not performed. Of the two different manuscripts, the one kept by the composer (now in the Sorabji Music Archive) has 3

unnumbered pages; the other, which has 4 pages, has the date 1916–03 at the end (no day). The initial marking on the manuscript not kept by the composer is "Mezza di voce", which is a dialect version of the standard Italian *Messa di voce*. Sorabji may also simply have mixed the two terms *Messa di voce* and *Mezza voce*.

Title, date: **Concerto [nº 1] pour piano et grand orchestre, Op. 3 (1915–16)**
Med., pp.: Piano and orchestra, 177 pp.
Instr'n: pno / 2+3 3+1 3+1 3+1+cbs sar / 8 5 3 1 / tym prc 2hrp / 16 16 12 12 12

Dedic'n: "à Monsieur Philip Heseltine: / en témoignage d'amitié. / K. S."

Cont., pag.: I   Modéré: 1–75.
II Très lent. Toujours enveloppé d'une atmosphère de chaleur tropicale et langoureuse: 76–112.
III Impétueux et impatient: 113–177.

Ms. loc'n: The full score is in the British Library, London; a two-piano reduction is untraced. See Comments.

Comments: Date at end (p. 177): 1916–06–17.
Not performed.

An untraced two-piano reduction is mentioned in Sorabji's letter to Philip Heseltine of 6 July 1916.

Title, date: **[Vocalise No. 2] (1916)**
Med.: Probably voice (wordless) and piano.

Ms. loc'n: Unknown.

Comments: The title is editorial. The evidence for this work comes from Sorabji's letter to Philip Heseltine of 6 July 1916, in which he wrote: "I have just finished a second vocalise and have started the music-drama 'Medea'". This work is not the *Vocalise* Op. 2, No. 3, nor is it likely the *Movement* of 1927/31.

Title, date: **Medea (1916)**
Med.: Music drama

Ms. loc'n: Unknown.

Comments: This work was probably abandoned or incorporated into another. The evidence for its existence comes from Sorabji's letter to Philip Heseltine of 6 July 1916, in which he wrote: "I have just finished a second vocalise and have started the music-drama 'Medea'". The evidence for its abandonment comes from his letter to Kenneth Derus of 5 September 1983.

Title, date: **Apparition, Op. 4, No. 3 (1916)** [+A1]
Transl'n: Apparition
Med., pp.: Voice and piano, 5 pp. Voice range: $c^{\#}4$ to $g^{\#}5$.

Auth., text: Stéphane Mallarmé (1842–98, France): "Apparition".

Ms. loc'n: Private collection.

Comments: Initial marking: Modéré.
Date at end (p. 5): 1916-09-26.
Not performed.

This song was originally labelled Op. 4, No. 2.

Title, date: **Hymne à Aphrodite, Op. 4, No. 2 (1916)** [+A1; +1]
Transl'n: Hymn to Aphrodite
Med., pp.: Voice and piano, 5 pp. Voice range: $c^{\#}4$ to c^6.

Auth., text: Laurent Tailhade (1854–1919, France): "Hymne à Aphrodite".

Ms. loc'n: Two manuscripts are in the Sorabji Music Archive.

Comments: Initial marking: Modéré.
Date at end [p. 5]: 1916-10-15.
Not performed.

Instead of the standard French *Aphrodite,* Sorabji's title uses the variant *Aphrodité*. Of the two different manuscripts, one has 5 unnumbered pages; the other has no page 5 or 6, but one unnumbered page between 4 and 7; it concludes on page 8. There is no initial marking in the latter manuscript (which was probably written first); the dates at the ends of both are the same.

This song may originally have been labelled Op. 4, No. 3.

Title, date: **Chaleur — Poème, Op. 5 (ca. 1916–17)** [+3]
Transl'n: Heat — Poem
Med., pp.: Orchestra, 40 pp.

Instr'n:	2+alt flt 3 3 0 / 4 0 0 0 / 2hrp cel / strs
Ms. loc'n:	Sorabji Music Archive. Not the composer's autograph: see Comments.
Comments:	Initial marking: Très lent. Not performed. The extant manuscript of this work is not in the composer's handwriting but contains annotations in his handwriting. No manuscript in the composer's handwriting has been traced.

Title, date:	**Sonata [for Piano], Op. 7 (1917)**
Med., pp.:	Piano, 30 pp.
Sugg. title:	Sonata No. 0 for Piano
Ms. loc'n:	Private collections. See Comments.
Comments:	Initial marking: Lent. Sombre: mystérieux et sourdement menaçant. Date at end (p. 30): 1917–03–08. Not performed. This is the only manuscript which is known not to be all in one place: pp. 1–24 are in one location, and pp. 25–30 are in another.

Title, date:	**Quasi habanera, Op. 8 (1917)**
Med., pp.:	Piano, 6 pp.
Dedic'n:	"to Norman Peterkin a gifted / and sensitive musician, his friend K. S."
Ms. loc'n:	Private collection.
Comments:	Initial marking: Dans un rythme languide et indolent. Date at end (p. 6): 1917–08–10 to 14. An item on the first page which could have been a dedication is obliterated. The original title of this work was *Quasi españana,* which is incorrect Spanish and Italian.
1st perf.:	1989–02–24, NOS broadcast (Netherlands Broadcasting Corporation, Hilversum), by Geoffrey Douglas Madge.

Title, date: **L'étang, Op. 9 (1917)** [+A1; +1]
Transl'n: The Pond
Med., pp.: Voice and piano, 2 pp. Voice range: b♭3 to b5.

Auth., text: Maurice Rollinat (1846–1903, France): "L'étang".

Ms. loc'n: Sorabji Music Archive.

Comments: Initial marking: Modéré. Très sombre et toujours enveloppé d'une atmosphère d'horreur intangible. Sinistre, menaçant.
Date at end (p. 2): 1917-04-25.
Not performed.

Title, date: **Désir éperdu (Fragment) (1917)**
Transl'n: Frantic Desire (Fragment)
Med., pp.: Piano, 1 p.

Ms. loc'n: Private collection.

Comments: Initial marking: Modérément lent. Comme tourmenté d'un désir insatiable.
Date at end: 1917-09-22.

This work is complete on 1 page.

1st perf.: 1990-02-21, London, by Malcolm Rycraft.

Title, date: **Concerto II pour piano et grand orchestre, Op. 10 (1916–17)** [+4]
Med., pp.: Two pianos (reduction), 49 pp.

Cont., pag.: [I]   Modéré: 1–23.
[II]   Lent: 23–32.
[III] Galvanique mais sans trop de hâte d'abord: 32–49.

Ms. loc'n: Sorabji Music Archive. No manuscript of an orchestral version has been traced.

Comments: Date at end (p. 49): 1917-12-27.
Not performed.

Evidence for the dates of this work comes from Sorabji's letters to Philip Heseltine.

Title, date: **Concerto pour piano et orchestra da camera (1918)** [+5]
Med., pp.: Piano and orchestra, 100 pp.

Sugg. title:	Concerto No. 3 for Piano and Orchestra
Instr'n:	pno / 2 2 2 1 / 0 3 0 0 / prc hrp / 8 8 6 6 4
Dedic'n:	"To Charles A. Trew Esq.: — / his old pupil Kaikhusru Sorabji: —".
Cont., pag.:	[I] Modérément animé, avec une expression très libre et fantaisiste: 1–40. [II] Assez lent: 41–60. [III] Vif et animé: 61–100.
Ms. loc'n:	Private collection.
Comments:	Date at end (p. 100): 1918-08-25. Not performed. This work has two pages 35, and no page 34.

Title, date:	**Concerto pour piano et grand orchestre (1918)** [+6]
Med., pp.:	Piano and orchestra, 100 pp.
Sugg. title:	Concerto No. 4 for Piano and Orchestra
Instr'n:	pno / 2+3 3+1+bss obo pic clt+3+1 3+1+cbs sar / 8 5 4 1 / tym prc 2hrp / strs
Inscr'n:	[added later, probably in 1953] "This baby piece is presented (for his diversion) / to his dear friend Norman Gentieu Esq: / by his obleeged and grateful friend / Kaikhosru Shapurji Sorabji".
Cont., pag.:	I Modérément animé: 1–40 (to 101 measures). [II] Très lent: 41–60 (to 154 measures). [III] Galvanique. Animé, mais pas trop vite: 61–100 (to 263 measures).
Ms. loc'n:	George Arents Research Library, Syracuse University, Syracuse, New York.
Comments:	Date at end (p. 100): 1918-12-20. Not performed. At the end of the manuscript, the composer calls this work the second version and states that the first version (whose given dates coincide with those on the work noted as Op. 10) was destroyed. A comparison of Op. 10 with this concerto reveals only a few measures and gestures in common scattered throughout the three movements. They are different concertos.

116 Discovery

Title, date: **I Was Not Sorrowful — Poem for Voice (Dramatic Soprano or Tenor) and Piano (no date)** [+A1; +1]

Med., pp.: Voice and piano, 3 pp. Voice range: b^3 to b^5.

Auth., text: Ernest Dowson (1867–1900, England): "Spleen".

Ms. loc'n: Sorabji Music Archive.

Comments: Initial marking: With gloomy introspection, not fast. Morbid, wearily.
Not performed.

This song was probably written between 1917 and 1919.

Title, date: **Le mauvais jardinier (no date)** [+A1; +1]
Transl'n: The Wicked Gardener
Med., pp.: Voice and piano, more than 1 p. Voice range in extant part (1 p.): b^3 to $f^{\#5}$.

Auth., text: Iwan Gilkin (1858–1924, Belgium): "Le mauvais jardinier".

Ms. loc'n: An incomplete manuscript consisting of 1 page is in the Sorabji Music Archive.

Comments: Initial marking: Très lent, avec une concentration venimeuse. Dans une sonorité maladive et presque empoisonnée.
Not performed.

The extant page is p. 1. On it are two opus numbers which are obliterated; the first may be written over another number. This song was probably written in 1918 or 1919.

Title, date: **Trois fêtes galantes de Verlaine (no date)** ° [+A1]
Transl'n: Three Amorous Revels of Verlaine
Med., pp.: Voice and piano, 11 pp. Voice range: c^4 to $g^{\#5}$.

Auth., texts: Paul Verlaine (1844–96, France): "L'allée"; "À la promenade"; "Dans la grotte".

Dedic'n: "Alla mamma mia".

Cont., pag.: [I] "L'allée". Très modéré. Capricieusement avec beaucoup de rubato: 2–5. Voice range: e^4 to g^5.
[II] "À la promenade". Modérément lent: 6–9. Voice range: c^4 to $g^{\#5}$.
[III] "Dans la grotte". Modéré avec une afféterie ironique: 10–12. Voice range: eb^4 to g^5.

Public'n:	London: J. Curwen and Sons Ltd., 1924. In the bottom margin of the pages of each song respectively are the designations "K. S. 10", "K. S. 11", and "K. S. 12".
Ms. loc'n:	Unknown.
Comments:	The above information is from the published score. No manuscript of these songs has been traced. They were probably written around 1919.

Title, date:	**Fantaisie espagnole (1919)**
Med., pp.:	Piano, 23 pp.
Dedic'n:	None in primary manuscript (in the Library of Congress), but see Comments.
Public'n:	London: London and Continental Music Publishing Co. Ltd., 1922. The music is on pp. 3–32. In the bottom margin of the pages is the designation "K. S. 4".
Ms. loc'n:	One is in the Library of Congress, Washington; another is in a private collection. See Comments.
Comments:	Initial marking: Sans temps. Lent. Date at end of ms. (p. 23): 1919–03–05. Of the two different manuscripts, the earlier one, which is in a private collection and has 27 pp., has the dedication "To my very good friend Norman Peterkin, / his immeasurably K. S." The published edition has only "To Norman Peterkin". It also divides the music into three: I Prélude et introduction. II Mouvement de habanera (corresponding to the section beginning "Modéré" on p. 13 of the published score). III (Without descriptive label, corresponding to the section beginning "Modérément animé" on p. 21 of the published score.) The published edition has the title "Fantaisie espagnole for Piano" and the dedication "To Norman Peterkin".

Title, date:	**Sonata [No. 1 for] Piano (1919)**
Med., pp.:	Piano, 42 pp.
Dedic'n:	"all'Illustrissimo Maestro / Signor Cavaliere Ferruccio Busoni."

Public'n:	London: London and Continental Music Publishing Co. Ltd., 1921. The music is on pp. 2–43.
Ms. loc'n:	Library of Congress, Washington.
Comments:	Initial marking: Modéré, avec entrain. Date at end of ms. (p. 42): 1919-08-05.
	The published edition has the title "Sonata No. 1 for Piano" and no dedication.
1st perf.:	1920-11-02, London, by the composer.

Title, date:	**Trois poèmes pour chant et piano (1918, 1919)** ° +A1	
Med., pp.:	Voice and piano, 9 pp. Voice range: c^4 to a^5.	
Auth., texts:	Charles Baudelaire (1821–67, France): "Correspondances"; Paul Verlaine (1844–96, France): "Crépuscule du soir mystique"; Paul Verlaine: "Pantomime".	
Dedic'n:	"À Madame Marthe Martine."	
Cont., pag.:	[I]	"Correspondances". Lent: 3–5. Voice range: c^4 to $g\sharp^5$.
	[II]	"Crépuscule du soir mystique". Lent, avec nostalgie et langueur: 6–8. Voice range: c^4 to $f\sharp^5$.
	[III]	"Pantomime". Modéré, avec beaucoup de fantaisie: 9–11. Voice range: c^4 to a^5.
Public'n:	London: London and Continental Music Publishing Co., 1921. In the bottom margin of the pages is the designation "K. S. 1".	
Ms. loc'n:	"Pantomime" is in a private collection. No manuscript of the other two songs has been traced.	
Comments:	Dates at beginnings of songs (pp. 3, 6, and 9 respectively): 1918, 1918, 1919. There are no dates at their ends.	
	The above information is from the published score. The manuscript of the third song is 4 pp. long and at the end has the date 1919-11-02.	
1st perf.:	1921-06-02, Paris, by Marthe Martine (soprano) and the composer (pianist).	

Title, date:	**Music to "The Rider by Night" (1919)**
Med., pp.:	Voices and small orchestra, 54 pp.
Instr'n:	1 1 1 1 / 1 2cor 1 0 / prc / strs

Auth., text:	Robert Nichols: "The Rider by Night", a libretto written for Sorabji.
Ms. loc'n:	An incomplete manuscript, pp. 1–20 and 41–54, is in the British Library, London.
Comments:	Initial marking: Modéré. Date at end (p. 54): 1919-11-13. The voices are mostly speaking cues; there is some singing.

Title, date:	**Quintet [No. 1] for Piano and Quartet of Stringed Instruments (1919–20)**
Med., pp.:	Piano and string quartet, 72 pp.
Cont., pag.:	This work is in one movement, pp. 1–72.
Public'n:	London: London and Continental Music Publishing Co. Ltd., 1923 (score and string parts). The music is on pp. 3–64 of the score. The pages of each part are numbered 1–7, except for the 1st violin, where they are 1–8. In the bottom margin of the pages of the score and parts is the designation "K. S. 5".
Ms. loc'n:	Central Music Library, Westminster, London. Not the composer's autograph: see Comments.
Comments:	Initial marking: Modéré. There is no date at the end. The extant manuscript of this work, which is undated, is not in the composer's handwriting but contains annotations in his handwriting. No manuscript in the composer's handwriting has been traced. The published edition has the title "Quintet for Piano and Four Stringed Instruments" and the dedication "To my very good friend Philip Heseltine". No performances of this work have been traced.

Title, date:	**Arabesque (1920)** [+A1]
Med., pp.:	Voice and piano, 2 pp. Vocal range: c^4 to d^5.
Auth., text:	Shamsu'd-Dīn Ibrāhīm Mīrzā (dates unknown, Persia): text not located.
Dedic'n:	"À mon ami / Rex qui ne se complait [*recte* complaît] / point à [*recte* dans] ces choses[-]ci!"

120 Discovery

Ms. loc'n:	Private collection.
Comments:	Initial marking: Senza tempo: quasi improvvisato. Avec une finesse précieuse et recherchée. Très lent. Date at end: 1920-02-12. Not performed. "Rex" is Rex H. Brittain.

Title, date:	**Two Piano Pieces (1918, 1920)** °	
Med., pp.:	Piano, 20 pp.	
Dedic'n:	"To my friend Theodore Jenkins".	
Cont., pag.:	I	"In the Hothouse". Très lent: 2–9.
	II	"Toccata". D'une allure sèche: froidement animée et très précise: 10–21.
Publicat'n:	London: London and Continental Music Publishing Co. Ltd., 1921.	
Ms. loc'n:	Unknown.	
Comments:	Dates at beginnings of pieces (pp. 2 and 10 respectively): 1918, 1920. There are no dates at their ends. The above information is from the published score. No manuscript of these pieces has been traced.	

Title, date:	**Concerto for Piano and Orchestra (1920)** ° +7
Med., pp.:	Piano and orchestra, 144 pp. (published score)
Oth. title:	Concerto II (1920) pour piano et orchestre
Sugg. title:	Concerto No. 5 for Piano and Orchestra
Instr'n:	pno / 1+2+alt flt 2+1 2+1 2+1 / 4 4 3 1 / tym prc hrp / strs
Dedic'n:	(published score) "À Monsieur Alfred Cortôt [*recte* Cortot]".
Public'n:	London: F. and B. Goodwin Ltd., 1923 (score only). The music is on pp. 1–144. In the bottom margin of the pages is the designation "K. S. 7".
Ms. loc'n:	A solo piano part is in a private collection (not the composer's autograph: see Comments). No manuscript of the full score has been traced.

"Could you just send me a list of his works?" 121

Comments: Initial marking: Lent.
Date at end (p. 144): 1920–08–01.
Not performed.

The above information is from the published score. Although the full score was published, parts were not. Performances are thus unlikely to have occurred, and none have been traced.

The solo piano part is not in the composer's handwriting but contains annotations in his handwriting. It has the title "Concerto II pour piano et orchestre" and the dedication "To M. Alfred Cortôt [*recte* Cortot]: / in admiration and respect.", contains 48 pages, and is undated at the end.

Title, date: **Sonata seconda for Piano (1920)** [+8]
Med., pp.: Piano, 49 pp.

Dedic'n: "To Signor Busoni in profound veneration", to which have been added, on subsequent pages, "To Signor Busoni / in profound veneration and homage." and "al [*recte* all'] illustrissimo Maestro / Signor Ferruccio Busoni / con somma venerazione e ommaggio [*recte* omaggio] / Il Autor K. S."

Public'n: London: F. and B. Goodwin Ltd., 1923. The music is on pp. 3–65. In the bottom margin of the pages is the designation "K. S. 6".

Ms. loc'n: One is in the Library of Congress, Washington; another is in the Deutsche Staatsbibliothek, Berlin. See Comments.

Comments: Initial marking: Modéré, sans hâte.
Date at end of composer's autograph ms. (p. 49): 1920–12–24.

The published edition has the title "Sonata II for Piano" and the dedication "To Signor Busoni in profound veneration". The manuscript copy in the Deutsche Staatsbibliothek, Berlin, is not in the composer's handwriting but contains annotations in his handwriting.

1st perf.: 1922–01–13, Vienna, by the composer.

Title, date: **Sonata III for Piano (1922)** [+9]
Med., pp.: Piano, 75 pp.

Public'n: London: J. Curwen and Sons Ltd., 1925 (Curwen edition 999002). The music is on pp. 3–80. In the bottom margin of the pages is the designation "K. S. 9".

Ms. loc'n: Library of Congress, Washington.

Comments: Initial marking: Modéré.
Date at end of ms. (p. 75): 1922-05-05.

At the end of the manuscript on what would be p. 76 are two variants for the final gesture of the sonata. The published edition also has these.

The published edition has the title "Sonata III" and, like the manuscript, no dedication.

1st perf.?: 1977-06-16, London, by Yonty Solomon. The existence of the work in print could have led to an earlier performance by someone else.

Title, date: **Symphony [No. 1] for Piano, Large Orchestra, Chorus, and Organ (1921–22)** [+10]
Med., pp.: Chorus (wordless) and orchestra, 300 pp.
Instr'n: 6 5 5 5 / 8 4 1 / tym prc 2hrp pno org / SATB (choir: 50–100 ea.) / 16–24 16–24 12–16 12–16 12–16. Woodwinds include piccolo, alto flute, English horn, bass oboe, E♭ clarinet, bass clarinet, contrabassoon, and contrabass sarrusophone.

Dedic'n: "To my darling Mumsie."

Ms. loc'n: Sorabji Music Archive.

Comments: This work is written in a large score and a separate small score. The latter contains music for additional instruments which did not fit in the former. The two scores must therefore be read together.

There is no initial marking of tempo or style.
Date at end (p. 300) of large score: 1922-02-12; of small score: 1922-09-06.
Not performed.

Title, date: **Black Mass (1922)**
Med.: Chorus and large orchestra, including organ.

Ms. loc'n: Unknown.

Comments: This work was abandoned. The evidence for its existence comes from Sorabji's letter to Philip Heseltine of 24 June 1922, in which he wrote: "You can add to the list of works 'Black

Mass' for Chorus Large Orchestra and Organ — 'in preparation'[.]" The evidence for its abandonment comes from his letter to Kenneth Derus of 5 September 1983.

Title, date:	**3 Pastiches for Piano (1922)** on
	(I) Chopin: Valse, Op. 64, No. 1
	(II) Bizet: "Habanera" (Carmen)
	(III) Rimskiy-Korsakov: "Hindu Merchant's Song" (Sadko)
Med., pp.:	Piano, 17 pp.
Dedic'n:	III only: "To Christopher à Becket Williams." See Comments.
Cont., pag.:	I Valse de Chopin, Op. 64 No. 1. Avec fantaisie: 1–7.
	II Habanera [from] Carmen (Bizet). Ad libitum. Avec fantaisie et extravagance: 8–13.
	III Hindu Song [from] Sadko (Rimskiy-Korsakov). Modérément lent: 14–17.
Public'n:	I only, in *Thirteen Transcriptions for Piano Solo of Chopin's Waltz in D♭, Op. 64, No. 1 (The Minute Waltz)*, edited by Donald M. Garvelmann. Bronx, New York: Music Treasure Publications, 1969. The music is on pp. 63–78.
Ms. loc'n:	Private collection. Manuscripts of all three pastiches are in one location; another manuscript of I only is in another location. See Comments.
Comments:	Date at end (p. 17): 1922-09-29.
	The second manuscript of I is not in the composer's handwriting. Dedications have been obliterated from the title page and the first page of I (composer's autograph) and II. Placed into the manuscript (composer's autograph) is an unnumbered page containing a revision of the last 5 measures of I, derived from the *Pasticcio capriccioso* of 1933. The composer made this revision in the late 1960s for the publication of I.
	The published edition of I (in the abovementioned collection) has the title "Pastiche on Minute Waltz of Chopin" and no dedication.
1st perf.:	(?) of I: 1973-03-21, Urbana, Illinois, by Neely Bruce. The existence of I in print could have led to an earlier performance by someone else.
	of II: 1975-05-11, Oyster Bay, New York, by Michael Habermann.

of III: 1982-11, USA, phonograph record by Michael Habermann (Musical Heritage Society MHS 4811). The first concert performance of III was on 1984-11-19 in Cleveland, Ohio by Michael Habermann.

Title, date: **Prelude, Interlude, and Fugue for Piano (1920, 1922)** °
Med., pp.: Piano, 17 pp.

Dedic'n: "To R. H. Brittain".

Cont., pag.: Prelude. Dans l'allure d'un perpetuum mobile: 3–7.
Interlude. Très lent: 8–10.
Fuga [one subject]. Marqué et très décidé: 11–19.

Public'n: London: J. Curwen and Sons Ltd., 1924 (Curwen edition 909001, altered on the cover of some copies to 999003). In the bottom margin of the pages is the designation "K. S. 8".

Ms. loc'n: Unknown.

Comments: Date at end of Interlude (p. 10): 1922-10-06; of Fugue (p. 19): 1920-02-27.

The above information is from the published score. No manuscript of this work has been traced. "R. H. Brittain" is Rex H. Brittain.

1st perf.?: 1982-09-28, Baltimore, by Michael Habermann. The existence of the work in print could have led to an earlier performance by someone else.

Title, date: **Concerto for Piano and Orchestra [No.] III (1922)**
Med., pp.: Piano and orchestra, 144 pp.
Sugg. title: Concerto No. 6 for Piano and Orchestra
Instr'n: pno / 1+alt flt 1+1 1+1 1 / 1 1 1 0 / prc hrp / 8 8 6 4 4

Inscr'n: [added later] "To my own dear old / from his still Old / (not still-born!!)". See Comments.

Cont., pag.: I   Animé: 1–60.
II Lent: 61–84.
III Vif: 85–144.

Ms. loc'n: Sorabji Music Archive.

Comments: Date at end (p. 144): 1922-12-16.
Not performed.

A partly obliterated dedication reads "To Bernard", probably referring to Bernard Bromage. On pages 142a and 143a are alternative versions for the piano part on pages 142 and 143 respectively.

Title, date:	**Opusculum for Orchestra (1923)** [+11]
Transl'n:	Little Work for Orchestra
Med., pp.:	Orchestra, 36 pp.
Instr'n:	1+3 2+1 2+1 2+1 / 4 3 3 1 / tym prc hrp org / strs
Dedic'n:	"to John Ireland:".
Ms. loc'n:	Sorabji Music Archive.
Comments:	Initial marking: Modérément lent. Date at end (p. 36): 1923-05-19. Not performed.

Title, date:	**Le jardin parfumé — Poem for Piano Solo (1923)** [+12]
Transl'n:	The Perfumed Garden — Poem for Piano Solo
Med., pp.:	Piano, 16 pp.
Dedic'n:	"To my dear friend Christopher à Becket Williams."
Public'n:	London: J. Curwen and Sons Ltd., 1927 (Curwen edition 999.019). The music is on pp. 3–36. In the bottom margin of the pages is the designation "K. S. 14".
Ms. loc'n:	Library of Northwestern University, Evanston, Illinois.
Comments:	Initial marking: Libre, modéré, enveloppé d'une langueur chaude et voluptueuse. Jamais plus fort que pp du commencement jusqu'à la fin. Date at end of ms. (p. 16): 1923. The published edition has the same title and the dedication "To my friend Christopher à Becket Williams". The title comes from the 15th- or 16th-century Arabic erotic treatise (*The Perfumed Garden*) by 'Umar ibn Muḥammad, al-Nafzāwī.
1st perf.?:	1930-04-22, BBC broadcast (British Broadcasting Corporation, London), by the composer. No earlier performance by him has been traced. The existence of the work in print could have led to an earlier performance by someone else.

Title, date:	**Cinque sonetti di Michelagniolo Buonarroti (1923)** [+A1]
Transl'n:	Five Sonnets of Michelangelo Buonarroti

Med., pp.: Baritone and small orchestra, 40 pp.
Instr'n: 1 1 1 1 / – / pno bar / 2 2 2 1

Auth., texts: Michelangelo (1475–1564, Italy):
"Tu sa' ch'i' so, signor mie, che tu sai"
"Non so se s'è la desïata luce"
"A che più debb'i' omai l'intensa voglia"
"Veggio nel tuo bel viso, signor mio"
"Se nel volto per gli occhi il cor si vede"

Cont., pag.: [I] ["Tu sa'"] Lento: 1–8.
II ["Non so"]: 9–16.
III ["A che"]: 17–25.
IV ["Veggio"]: 25–33.
V ["Se nel volto"]: 33–40.

Ms. loc'n: Sorabji Music Archive.

Comments: Date at end (p. 40): 1923-12-16.

This work has two pages 11, and no page 15. "Michelagniolo" in the title is an older version of *Michelangelo*.

1st perf.: 1980-02-02, Toronto: Robert Aitken, conductor; Henry Ingram, tenor; (Toronto) New Music Concerts Ensemble.

Title, date: **Concerto per pianoforte e piccola orchestra, "Simorg-Anka" (1924)**
Med., pp.: Piano and small orchestra, 100 pp.
Sugg. title: Concerto No. 7 for Piano and Orchestra
Instr'n: Pno / 1 1 1 1 / 1 1 0 0 / prc hrp / 4 4 4 2 2

Dedic'n: "To Dr. Havelock Ellis. — / in respectful admiration, homage and gratitude."

Inscr'n: [added in 1953] "For my dear and very generous friend Norman Gentieu Esq. / January 7th MCMLIII."

Cont., pag.: I Assez animé, nerveux: 1–40.
II Lent mais pas traîné. Ordinairement très doux et "piano": 41–60.
III Très animé: 61–100.

Ms. loc'n: George Arents Research Library, Syracuse University, Syracuse, New York.

Comments: Date at end (p. 100) of piano line in score: 1924-08-10; of whole score: 1924-10-03.
Not performed.

The subtitle of the work refers to a legendary bird, gigantic and magical, who occasionally took other forms. The first half is its Persian name, the second half its Arabic name; both are French transliterations in the composer's original subtitle. (A more appropriate English transliteration would be *Sīmurgh-'Anqā.*) Since the bird figures prominently in many stories, it is impossible to determine exactly which Sorabji had in mind.

Title, date: **Symphony [No. 1] for Organ (1924)**
Med., pp.: Organ, 81 pp.

Dedic'n: "To Mrs. Emily Edroff-Smith."

Cont., pag.: I   Prelude. Modéré: 1.
Passacaglia [theme, 81 variations]. Assez modéré: 1–24.
Postlude: 24–27.
II   Introduction. Lento: 28–29.
[Quasi fugue, two subjects]. Andante: 29–43.
Coda: 43–45.
III   Moderato: 46–60.
Cadenza de' pedali. Con bravura: 60–61.
[Moderato continued]: 61–74.
Cadenza-Toccata: 74–79.
Coda-Stretto: 79–81.

Public'n: London: J. Curwen and Sons Ltd., 1925 (Curwen edition 999.009). The music is on pp. 3–107. In the bottom margin of the pages is the designation "K. S. 13".

Ms. loc'n: Library of Congress, Washington.

Comments: Date at end of ms. (p. 81): 1924-12-17.

The published edition has the title "Organ Symphony" and the dedication "To my dear friend Mrs. Emily Edroff-Smith".

1st perf.?: 2nd mvt.: 1928-05-17, London, by E. Emlyn Davies.
Entire work: 1987-07-25, London, by Kevin Bowyer (I and III) and Thomas Trotter (II). The existence of the work in print could have led to an earlier performance in whole or in part by someone else.

Title, date:	**Valse-fantaisie [for] Piano Solo (1925)** [+13]
Med., pp.:	Piano, 16 pp.
Dedic'n:	"to H. Vincent Marrot."
Public'n:	London: J. Curwen and Sons Ltd., 1927 (Curwen edition 999.018). The music is on pp. 3–35. In the bottom margin of the pages is the designation "K. S. 15".
Ms. loc'n:	Library of Congress, Washington.
Comments:	Initial marking: Modéré. Date at end of ms. (p. 16): 1925-04-17.
	This work was first titled *Wienerische Weisen*.
	The published edition has the title "Valse-fantaisie", with the additional indication on the first page of music (p. 3) "Hommage à Johann Strauss". It has the dedication "To Vincent Marrot / Salutations and Greeting".
1st perf.?:	1982-09-28, Baltimore, by Michael Habermann. The existence of the work in print could have led to an earlier performance by someone else.

Title, date:	**Variazioni e fuga triplice sopra "Dies iræ" per pianoforte (1923–26)** [+14]
Transl'n:	Variations and Triple Fugue on "Dies iræ" for Pianoforte
Med., pp.:	Piano, 201 pp.
Dedic'n:	"Alla santissima memoria / dell'ingegno trascendente e sovrumano / del divino Maestro / BUSONI — / Colla somma umiltà fede e devozione / dello scrittore."
Inscr'n:	[added in ca. 1978] "For Alistair to amuse himself with. — / from a very faithful and long burning Fire Spirit — blood relative of / 'Mongiballo.'* / ('Ignis Fatuus?' Maybe!!) / *The Sicilian dialect name / for Mount Etna."
Cont., pag.:	[PARS PRIMA]

        Thema.   Lourd, sourd: 1.
        Var. 1:   2–3.
        Var. 2:   3–4.
        Var. 3   Vivace: 4–5.
        Var. 4:   5–8.
        Var. 5   Presto: 8–9.
        Var. 6   Lento, legatissimo: 9–10.
        Var. 7   Vivo: 10–11.

Var. 8:   12–14.
Var. 9   Vivace, leggiero: 14–15.
Var. 10:   15–17.
Var. 11:   17–19.
Var. 12:   19–21.
Var. 13:   21–23.
Var. 14:   23–25.
Var. 15:   25–26.
Var. 16:   26–28.
Var. 17:   28–30.
Var. 18   Vivace assai, secco e sotto: 30–31.
Var. 19:   31–35.
Var. 20:   35–37.
Var. 21:   37–39.
Var. 22:   39–42.
Var. 23   Legatissimo: 42–44.
Var. 24   Vivace, leggiero e fantastico: 44–47.
Var. 25:   47–49.
Var. 26:   49–51.
Var. 27:   51–53.
Var. 28:   53–55.
Var. 29:   55–58.
Var. 30:   58–61.
Var. 31:   61–63.
Var. 32:   63–66.

PARS ALTERA
Var. 33   Prestissimo volante: 66–69.
Var. 34:   69–72.
Var. 35:   72–75.
Var. 36:   75–77.
Var. 37:   78–80.
Var. 38:   80–83.
Var. 39   Delicato: 83–85.
Var. 40:   85–87.
Var. 41:   87–89.
Var. 42:   89–91.
Var. 43:   92–93.
Var. 44:   93–96.
Var. 45   Laissez vibrer: 96–99.
Var. 46:   99–101.
Var. 47:   102–105.
Var. 48:   105–108.
Var. 49   Nexus: 108–110.
Var. 50:   110–112.
Var. 51:   113–115.
Var. 52:   115–118.
Var. 53   Rota: 118–120.
Var. 54:   121–123.

                    Var. 55:   123–126.
                    Var. 56   Vivace e leggiero molto: 126–128.
                    Var. 57   Le linee melodiche bene articolate con soavità e coloratura delicata: 129–131.
                    Var. 58   VII Peccata Mortalia.
                                 (i) Ira (Anger): 131–134.
                    Var. 59   (ii) Gul[a] (Gluttony): 134–137.
                    Var. 60   (iii) Avar[itia] (Avarice): 137–139.
                    Var. 61   (iv) Inertia (Sloth): 139–141.
                    Var. 62   (v) Luxuria (Lechery): 141–143.
                    Var. 63   (vi) Invidia [Envy]: 143–146.
                    Var. 64   (vii) Sup[erbia] (Pride): 146–150.

                    [PARS TERTIA]
                    Fuga [three subjects]: 150–201.

Ms. loc'n: Sorabji Music Archive.

Comments: Date at end (p. 201): 1923–01 to 1926–03.
                    Not performed.

Title, date: **Trois poèmes du "Gulistān" de Sa'dī (1926)** [+A1]
Transl'n: Three Poems from "The Rose Garden" of Sa'dī
Med., pp.:   Voice and piano, 16 pp. Voice range: a^2 to g^4.

Auth., texts: Musharrifu'd-Dīn b. Muṣliḥu'd-Dīn 'Abdu'llāh Sa'dī (ca. 1213–91, Persia): "La lampe", "La jalousie", "La fidélité"; translated by Franz Toussaint.

Dedic'n: Erik Chisholm. See Comments.

Cont., pag.:   I   "La lampe": 1–5. Voice range: $d^{\flat 3}$ to $f^{\sharp 4}$.
               II   "La jalousie": 5–9. Voice range: b^3 to g^4.
               III   "La fidélité": 9–16. Voice range: a^3 to $f^{\sharp 4}$.

Ms. loc'n: One is in the Sorabji Music Archive; another, which is fragmentary and later, is in the J. W. Jagger Library, University of Cape Town, South Africa. See Comments.

Comments: There is no initial marking of tempo or style at the beginning of any of the songs.
               Date at end of first song (p. 5 of earlier ms.): 1926–07–12.
               Date at end of third song (p. 16 of earlier ms.): 1926–09–27.
               Not performed.

               The later manuscript has the following dedication:

"Epistle dedicatory: —

Ami très cher — this dedication is not by any / manner of means an attempt to fob you off what / we have agreed to call "your" Symphony, (that is, though / still in germ, irrevocably yours) but as it may / be rather a while before you get it, this is / sent as an earnest of good faith so to speak. / Thus it goes dedicated to the dearest / best and most loyal of friends / that is / to / Erik Chisholm / from / Kaikhosru Sorabji: / cœur léal — oncques féal / April MCMXXX."

There are two dates at the end of the last page of this manuscript (p. 16): 1926-09-27 and 1930-04-13. The latter is when the composer completed the copy for Erik Chisholm. In the dedication above, the Symphony is Sorabji's Symphony No. 2, of which he completed only the piano part.

The last part of the last song has two vocal settings against the piano part in the early, complete manuscript. Although Sorabji's intentions are not clear there, the later manuscript shows only the line which is the top one (on the page) in the earlier manuscript, thus suggesting that for performance the bottom line in the earlier manuscript be disregarded.

Title, date:	**L'irrémédiable (1927)** +A1; +1
Transl'n:	The Irremediable
Med., pp.:	Voice and piano, 8 pp. Voice range: a^3 to a^5.
Auth., text:	Charles Baudelaire (1821–67, France): "L'irrémédiable".
Dedic'n:	"à l'incomparable / musicienne — / Madame Blanche Marchesi / hommage profond de l'auteur."
Ms. loc'n:	Sorabji Music Archive.
Comments:	Initial marking: Très libre et modéré. Date at end (p. 8): 1927-02-16. Not performed.

Title, date:	**Concerto V for Piano and Large Orchestra (1927–28)**
Med., pp.:	Piano and orchestra, 344 pp.
Sugg. title:	Concerto No. 8 for Piano and Orchestra
Instr'n:	pno / 6 6 6 6 / 8 6 4 4 / 4tym prc 2hrp / strs. Woodwinds include piccolo, alto flute, English horn, bass oboe, E♭ clarinet, bass clarinet, contrabassoon, and contrabass sarrusophone.

132 Discovery

Dedic'n: "Al Signor Conte Aldo Solito de Solis."

Cont., pag.:
I   Ardito — focosamente: 1–145.
II: 145–209.
III   Rude, sauvage et brutal [includes a Cadenza which comprises a fantasia, a passacaglia [theme, 48 variations], and a section marked Punta d'organo]: 209–343.

Ms. loc'n: The full score and solo piano part are in the Sorabji Music Archive.

Comments: This work is written in a large score and a separate small score. The latter contains music for additional instruments which did not fit in the former. The two scores must therefore be read together.

Date at end (p. 343) of large score: 1928–02–12; of small score: 1928–03–20.
Not performed.

This work has one page 330a.

The solo piano part has the title "Concerto for Piano and Large Orchestra No. V" and the dedication "Al Signor Conte Aldo Solito de Solis. / omaggio e amicizia / del Compositore." The page divisions given above for the full score correspond to the following in the piano part:

I   Ardito — focosamente: 1–38.
II   Lento: 39–57.
III   Rude, sauvage et brutal [includes a Cadenza which comprises a fantasia, a passacaglia [theme, 48 variations], and a section marked Punta d'organo]: 57–104.

Title, date: **Toccata [No. 1] for Piano (1928)** [+15]
Med., pp.: Piano, 66 pp.

Dedic'n: "Dedication: / To a very good, true and sincere friend: — loyal and upright — / fine of mind — sensitive and receptive of feeling: / a cultured, imaginative and keen intellect — or, in other words — / to / Bernard Bromage — / his friend. / K. S."
In 1964 the composer obliterated this and replaced it with "To my very dear friend Frank (Holliday) / with much love from his very devoted / and deeply grateful friend K. / (Kaikhosru Shapurji Sorabji)".

Cont., pag.:	[I]	Preludio-Corale. Andante: 1–11.
	II	Passacaglia [theme, 64 variations]. Solenne e pesante: 11–37.
	[III]	Cadenza: 37–41.
	[IV]	Fuga [two subjects]: 41–61.
	[V]	Coda-Stretta: 61–66.

Ms. loc'n: Mills Memorial Library, McMaster University, Hamilton, Ontario.

Comments: Date at end (p. 66): 1928-06-06.
Not performed.

On p. 66 is an alternative passage for the last measure.

Title, date: **Nocturne, "Jāmī" (1928)** [+16]
Med., pp.: Piano, 28 pp.

Dedic'n: "To my dear friend / Reginald Norman Best."

Ms. loc'n: Sorabji Music Archive.

Comments: Initial marking: Lento, languido et dolcissimo.
Date at end (p. 28): 1928-11-15.

The composer uses the French spelling *Djâmî* on his manuscript, referring to the Persian poet Nūru'd-Dīn 'Abdu'r-Raḥmān Jāmī (1414–92).

1st perf.:   1930-01-16, London, by the composer.

Title, date: **Sonata IV for Piano (1928–29)**
Med., pp.: Piano, 111 pp.

Dedic'n: "To my friend. / Francis George Scott: — / that rare being — / a musician of percipience and imagination — / his always — / Kaikhosru Sorabji: / MCMXXIX."

Cont., pag.:	[I]	Vivo — arditamente: 1–40.
	II	Lento, languido e sonnolento: 41–60.
	III	Preludio. Vivace — quasi toccata: 61–64.
		Fantasia: 64–74.
		Cadenza: 74–79.
		Fuga duplex quatuor vocibus: 80–102.
		Coda-Stretta: 102–111.

Ms. loc'n: Sorabji Music Archive.

Comments: Date at end (p. 111): 1929–03–22.

1st perf.: 1930–04–01, Glasgow, by the composer.

Title, date: **Toccatinetta sopra C. G. F. (1929)**
Med., pp.: Piano, 8 pp.

Dedic'n: "per [il] suo giovane e abbastanza piacevole amico: / Clinton Gray Fisk / musicista americano-inglese. / [Per Dio!]"

Cont., pag.: Preludietto: [1].
Piccola passacaglia maliziosa [theme, 33 variations]: [1]–6.
Fughettina. Marcato con enfasi: 6–8.

Ms. loc'n: Private collection.

Comments: Date at end (p. 8): 1929–06–24.
Not performed.

The last pair of square brackets in the dedication is the composer's.

Title, date: **Passacaglia (1929)**
Med., pp.: Piano, 41 pp. (incomplete)

Cont., pag.: Each extant section, being paginated separately, begins on its own p. 1.

I   Introduzione quasi preludio. Con impeto e focosamente: [1]–4.
II   Passacaglia. Severo, legatissimo: 1–37 [incomplete].

Ms. loc'n: Paul Sacher Foundation, Basel, Switzerland.

Comments: Not performed.

The composer ceased working on this in order to write *Opus clavicembalisticum* and probably never returned to it. It was to be in four sections: I Introduzione; II Passacaglia with 100 variations; III Cadenza fantasiata; IV Fuga. He completed the first section and went as far as the second measure of Variation 76 in the second.

The information about this work was provided by Alistair Hinton. Sorabji also mentioned the work and a similar outline in a letter to Erik Chisholm of 25 December 1929.

"Could you just send me a list of his works?" 135

This is the only extant item in this catalog which its compiler has never seen, except for a photocopy of its first page.

Title, date: **[Music for "Faust"] (ca. 1930)**
Med., pp.: Unknown (probably includes chorus).

Ms. loc'n: Unknown.

Comments: The title is editorial. The evidence for this work comes from Sorabji's letter to Erik Chisholm of 5 April 1930, in which he wrote: "It will be some time I fear before I start going in real earnest, on your Symphony. I must clear everything else off just that's on the stocks in order to devote myself entirely to it — when I say everything naturally I do not mean 'Faust'!!!" In conversation with Kenneth Derus in November 1977, Sorabji indicated that he had set the opening choruses for Faust around this time, but in a letter to him of 19 August 1978 he mentioned "the proposed FAUST CHORUSES".

Title, date: **Opus clavicembalisticum (1929–30)** [+17]
Transl'n: Work for Keyboard
Med., pp.: Piano, 253 pp.

Dedic'n: "To my two friends: — (e duobus unum) / Hugh M'Diarmid and C. M. Grieve. / likewise / To the everlasting glory of those Few / MEN — / Blessed and sanctified in the Curses and Execrations / of those MANY — / Whose Praise is Eternal Damnation. / June MCMXXX."

Inscr'n: "For my dear Erik — / with love from K. / Xmas 1931. / and now he can amuse himself noticing / the innumerable discrepancies between the / published version and the manuscript — / which ought to keep what he is pleased / to call his mind (!!?) well occupied / for a long time to come!"

Cont., pag.: [PARS PRIMA]
    [I]   Introito. Adagio. Declamato con enfasi e forza: 1–3.
    [II]   Preludio-Corale (Nexus): 4–15.
    [III] Fuga I quatuor vocibus [one subject]. Sommessamente moderato: 15–27.
    [IV] Fantasia. Scorrevole, leggiero: 27–37.
    [V]   Fuga II duplex. Animato assai, leggiero: 38–60.

[PARS ALTERA]
    VI   Interludium primum (Thema cum [49] variationibus). Legatissimo, adagissimo, grave, solenne e serioso. Sonorità piena e dolce: 60–99.

136 Discovery

	VII	Cadenza I. Allegro vivace: 100–105.
	VIII	Fuga tertia triplex. Moderato: 106–140.

[PARS TERTIA]
- [IX] Interludium B
  - [Toccata]. Rapido e uguale sempre senza ritardare né affrettare: 140–150.
  - Adagio. Grave e teneramente. Sonorità piena, dolcissima e morbidissima sempre: 150–156.
  - Passacaglia [theme, 81 variations]. Tranquillo e moderato: 156–193.
- [X] Cadenza II. Vivo: 193–197.
- [XI] Fuga IV quadruplex. Molto moderato, ma severo e austero; poi affrettare poco a poco fino alla stretta quasi impercettibilmente: 198–242.
- [XII] Coda-Stretta. Quasi organo pieno: 242–252[a].

Public'n: London: J. Curwen and Sons Ltd., 1931 (Curwen edition 999021). The music is on pp. 5–252. In the bottom margin of the pages is the designation "K. S. 16".

Ms. loc'n: J. W. Jagger Library, University of Cape Town, South Africa.

Comments: Date at end of ms. (p. 252[a]): 1930-06-25.

"Erik" is Erik Chisholm. This work was first titled *Opus sequentiale*. It has two pages 252. In both the manuscript and the published edition, the music itself does not have the indications of the three large divisions of the work, although the analytical note at the end of the manuscript does, likewise the published edition on the page labelled "Constitution of the work".

The published edition has the title "Opus clavicembalisticum MCMXXX for Piano Solo" and the same dedication as the manuscript. The listing below for the second complete performance is conjectural, as the existence of the work in print could have led to an earlier performance by someone else. Such, however, is unlikely.

1st perf.: 1930-12-01, Glasgow, by the composer.
2nd perf.: 1982-06-11, Utrecht, by Geoffrey Douglas Madge.

Title, date: **Symphony II for Piano, Large Orchestra, Organ, Final Chorus, and Six Solo Voices (1930–31)**
Med., pp.: Piano only, 333 pp.
Oth. title: Symphony for Piano and Orchestra

Inscr'n:	"For my very dear and precious Alistair / a sort of birthday present — (and how!!) / to amuse and maybe infuriate / him: / Ton tout dévoué: / K / for VI. X. MCMLXXV / All loving blessings for all time / from a Crotchetty Cross[-]Patch".
Cont., pag.:	I Prologo

                 Introito: 1–10.
                 Fantasia. Maestosamente con grandezza e importanza: 11–85.
                 Cadenza. Deciso: 86–100.
                 Coda-Stretta. Moderato: 101–110.
         II   Adagio
                 Punta d'organo. Quasi louré la mano sinistra: 111–121.
                 Notturno-Fantasia: 121–156.
                 Ritournelle–point d'orgue: 157–160.
         III Prelude. Vivace: 161–176.
                 Toccata variata [theme, 64 variations]: 176–308.
                 Cadenza-fugata [one subject]: 309–323.
                 Coda-Epilogo. Dolce, languido, mesto e nostalgico: 324–333.

Ms. loc'n:	Sorabji Music Archive.
Comments:	Date at end (p. 333): 1931-06-18. Not performed.

               "Alistair" is Alistair Hinton. The toccata has two variations 17 and no variation 41. On p. 323 is the following note: "Segue il Cantico. Durante tutto il cantico tace il pianoforte". It is possible, therefore, that the last 10 pages (324–333) were intended to follow the choral movement. The entire score as it exists, however, forms a complete piano work. At one time there may have been a dedication to Erik Chisholm, for whom it was written.

Title, date: Med., pp.:	**Movement for Voice and Piano (1927, 1931)** Voice (wordless) and piano, 9 pp. Voice range: $b\flat^3$ to $g\sharp^5$.
Dedic'n:	"To Mumsie".
Ms. loc'n:	Sorabji Music Archive.
Comments:	Initial marking: Adagissimo. Date at end (p. 9): 1931-09-28. Not performed.

               The extant copy is probably a revision.

Title, date: **Second Symphony for Organ (1929–32)**
Med., pp.: Organ, 350 pp.

Dedic'n: "To E. Emlyn Davies:".

Cont., pag.: [I] Introduction: 1–62.
 II Thema cum [50] variationibus: 62–226.
 III Finale
  Preludio: 226–241.
  Adagio: 242–251.
  Toccata: 252–265.
  Fuga triplex: 266–350.

Ms. loc'n: Sorabji Music Archive.

Comments: Date at end (p. 350): 1932-05-02.
 Not performed.
 Movement II has two variations no. 43; the last variation is numbered 49.

Title, date: **Quintet II for Piano and String Quartet (1932–33)**
Med., pp.: Piano quintet, 432 pp.

Dedic'n: "To my friend Professor Denis Saurat / in profound and respectful admiration / and homage. / MCMXXXII."

Inscr'n: [added in 1969] "For dear brother Mervyn for keeps. / K. S. S. / XXII. V. MCMLXIX".

Cont., pag.: I Introito: 1–26.
  Fantasia: 26–121.
  Coda-Finale: 121–144.
 II Preludio: 145–153.
  Passacaglia [theme, 100 variations]: 154–232.
 III Adagio: 232–300.
 IV Finale
  Introduction: 301–316.
  Allegro: 317–369.
  Intermezzo: 370–410.
  Coda-Epilogo: 411–432.

Ms. loc'n: Private collection.

Comments: Date at end (p. 432) of piano line: 1933-06-24; of string lines: 1933-07-12.
 Not performed.

"Mervyn" is Mervyn Vicars. This work has two pages 109, no page 111, two pages 364, and no page 365.

Title, date: **Fantasia ispanica (1933)**
Med., pp.: Piano, 54 pp.

Dedic'n: "To Alec Rowley."

Cont., pag.: I   Preludio-Introduzione. Con fantasia, libero e rapsodisticamente: 1–5.
II   Molto moderato: 5–16.
III: 16–29.
IV   Quasi habanera: 29–46.
V   Coda-Finale: 47–54.

Ms. loc'n: Sorabji Music Archive.

Comments: Date at end (p. 54): 1933-07-30.
Not performed.

Title, date: **Pasticcio capriccioso sopra Op. 64 No. I dello Chopin (1933)**
Transl'n: Capricious Pastiche on Op. 64, No. 1 of Chopin
Med., pp.: Piano, 8 pp.

Dedic'n: An item on the title page which could have been a dedication is obliterated. On the first page of music, the composer later added: "For Friend Donald Garvelmann".

Ms. loc'n: Sorabji Music Archive.

Comments: There is no initial marking of tempo or style.
Date at end (p. 8): 1933-08-13.
Not performed.

This is the second pastiche on Chopin's "Minute Waltz". At the end of the work is "alla carissima mamma mia per [il] suo natale."

Title, date: **Toccata seconda per pianoforte (1933–34)**
Med., pp.: Piano, 111 pp.

Dedic'n: "To my friend Norman Peterkin — / and also to take out of his mouth / the taste of the insipid baby-piece / dedicated to him years ago." In 1974 the composer added "and handed over to him with much / love Jan X. MCMLXXIV. / from his Corfe Drop".

Sorabji and Norman Peterkin at the latter's house in Surrey in the mid-1930s (photo by Marie Peterkin)

Cont., pag.:	[I]	Preludio-Toccata. Scorrevole e non troppo legato: 1–16.
	II	Preludio-Corale: 17–25.
	III	Scherzo: 26–34.
	IV	Aria: 35–39.
	V	Ostinato [theme, 49 variations]: 39–54.
	VI	Notturno. Larghetto: 55–66.
	VII	Interludio–Moto perpetuo. Riflesso del Preludio-Toccata: 66–75.
	VIII	Cadenza–Punta d'organo: 76–79.
	IX	Fuga libera a cinque voci [one subject]: 79–111.

Ms. loc'n: One is in Mills Memorial Library, McMaster University, Hamilton, Ontario; another, fragmentary manuscript is in a private collection. See Comments.

Comments: Date at end (p. 111): 1934-03-21.

The fragmentary manuscript covers p. 57 to most of p. 98 in the complete manuscript, but is numbered pp. 57 to 87, with more staff lines per page. On the first page of this the composer wrote "Take a Seidlitz / powder / the morning after: / Free Sample for / Norman / N.B. No obligation to purchase".

1st perf.: 1936-12-16, Glasgow, by the composer.

Title, date: **Sonata V (Opus archimagicum) (1934–35)**
Transl'n: Sonata V (Work of the Arch-Mage)
Med., pp.: Piano, 336 pp.

Dedic'n: "To Clinton Gray Fisk: / his affectionate friend the / author of this 'ere piece. / Epistle dedicatory: / My dear Clinton: I trust you won't take it / amiss my rededicating this work, to you, / it having borne since it was begun in / 1934 (up to now 1943) the name of one / for whom I had for 20 years regarded / as my greatest friend until he denied / all further possibility of the trust and faith that is / the very essential of friendship: but that / I place your name on it in succession / to that of one for whom for so long I had / such regard, speaks, I think you will / agree amply for the estimation in which / I hold you. Yours ever. / K. S. S. / X. III. MCMXLIII."

Cont., pag.:	PARS PRIMA: ARCANA MINORA	
	I	Fiero, ardito: 1–49.
	II	Presto, sotto voce inquieto: 50–58.
	III	Punta d'organo. Quasi adagio, oscuro, velato: 59–74.
	IV	Con fuoco, ardito e fiero: 75–123.

PARS ALTERA: ARCANA MAJORA
[V]: 124–187.
VI   Adagio. Il tutto sempre con dolcezza velenosa: 188–236.

PARS TERTIA ET ULTIMA: ARCHIMAGUS
VII   Preludio: 237–252.
[VIII]   Preludio-corale sopra "Dies iræ". Sempre oscuro, sordo e con un qualsiasi sentimento di minaccia occulta: 253–280.
[IX]   Cadenza: 280–284.
[X]   Fuga libera a cinque voci e tre soggetti: 285–343a.

Ms. loc'n: Sorabji Music Archive.

Comments: Date at end (p. 343a): 1935–05–29.
Not performed.

The subtitle of the work (*Opus archimagicum*) and the titles of the three main parts refer to the lore of Tarot. It can be determined that Sorabji originally dedicated this sonata to Bernard Bromage, as one of the prominent themes on the first page spells out an abbreviated form of his name, using the note names which may be found in it (B E r n A r D   B r o m A G E). Below this theme eight alphabetic characters are obliterated. A dedication page survives which contains massive obliterations.

This work has no page 194, two pages 196, no pages 292–299, and one page 343a.

Title, date: **Fragment Written for Harold Rutland (3 versions: 1926, 1928, 1937)**

Med., pp.: 3rd version: piano, 2 pp. See Comments.

Oth. titles: Fragment for Harold Rutland; Harold Rutland's Fragment; Fragment

Dedic'n: 3rd version: "For my friend Harold Rutland."

Ms. loc'n: Those of the first two versions are in the Library of Trinity College of Music, London; that of the third version is in the Sorabji Music Archive.

Comments: 1st version: 2 pp. Initial marking: Modéré.
    Date at end (p. 2): 1926–10–10.
2nd version: 4 pp. There is no initial marking of tempo or style.
    Dates at end (p. 4): 1926–10–10, 1928–03–26.
    Not performed.

3rd version: 2 pp. Initial marking: Moderatamente, con fantasia.
Dates at end (p. 2): 1926-10-10, 1937-06-07.

The third version is the first piece in a collection bound in one volume as "Four Short Piano Works". It is labelled the "final definitive version". The first version contains fingerings and similar markings not in the composer's handwriting, probably for the 1927 performance noted below.

1st perf.: 1st version: 1927-10-12, London, by Harold Rutland.
1st perf.: 3rd version: 1978-04-15, Greenvale, New York, by Michael Habermann.

Title, date: **Symphonic Variations for Piano and Orchestra (1935-37)**
Med., pp.: Piano only, 484 pp. in 3 volumes:
 Variations 1-27, pp. 1-144
 Variations 28-54, pp. 145-296
 Variations 55-81, pp. 297-484

Dedic'n: Although no dedication page survives, in 1985 the composer stated that the dedicatee was Edward Clarke Ashworth, thus substantiating the indirect dedication in the prominent use of the notes E, C, and A in the theme of the work.

Cont., pag.: VOLUME 1
 Tema. Quasi adagio e legatissimo sempre: 1.
 Var. 1 Vivace: 1-4.
 Var. 2: 4-6.
 Var. 3: 6-9.
 Var. 4: 9-12.
 Var. 5: 12-13.
 Var. 6: 13-17.
 Var. 7 Dolcemente mormorando: 17-20.
 Var. 8: 20-23.
 Var. 9: 23-27.
 Var. 10: 27-31.
 Var. 11: 31-35.
 Var. 12: 35-39.
 Var. 13 Sotto voce, scorrevole: 39-43.
 Var. 14 Dolcissimo mormorando: 43-48.
 Var. 15 Scorrevole sotto voce: 49-51.
 Var. 16: 52-61.
 Var. 17: 62-67.
 Var. 18: 67-70.
 Var. 19: 70-72.
 Var. 20: 73-81.
 Var. 21: 82-85.

Var. 22   Preludio-corale: 85–97.
Var. 23:   97–100.
Var. 24   Quasi Valse: 100–111.
Var. 25:   111–114.
Var. 26   Maestoso: 114–117.
Var. 27   The Garden of Irān: 117–144.

VOLUME 2
Var. 28:   145–148.
Var. 29:   149–152.
Var. 30:   153–156.
Var. 31   Sotto voce: 157–173.
Var. 32   Quasi saltando: 174–177.
Var. 33:   178–181.
Var. 34   Quasi rāg indiana. Molto libero in tempo. Nostalgico, languido e morbidissimo sempre. Lento: 182–190.
Var. 35:   191–193.
Var. 36   Molto moderato: 194–196.
Var. 37:   196–200.
Var. 38:   201–205.
Var. 39   Vivace assai: 205–208.
Var. 40:   209–216.
Var. 41:   217–221.
Var. 42:   Vivace con impeto: 221–225.
Var. 43   Legatissimo: 225–228.
Var. 44   Vivace, leggiero: 229–232.
Var. 45:   233–236.
Var. 46:   237–240.
Var. 47   Scorrevole: 241–244.
Var. 48   Libero, con fantasia e grazia tenera e dolce. Moderato in tempo: 245–249.
Var. 49:   250–251.
Var. 50:   252–260.
Var. 51:   261–263.
Var. 52:   264–267.
Var. 53:   267–269.
Var. 54   Quasi-cadenza. Passacaglia [theme, 100 variations]. Adagio: 270–296.

VOLUME 3
Var. 55   Triste e languido: 297–299.
Var. 56   Allusion to finale of B♭ minor Sonata of Chopin, a favourite work of the dedicatee's. Sotto voce, inquieto e presto sempre. Minacciosamente mormorando: 300–304.
Var. 57:   304–321.
Var. 58:   322–323.
Var. 59:   324–328.

Var. 60:	329–331.
Var. 61	Leggiero, quasi presto: 332–333.
Var. 62:	334–344.
Var. 63:	345.
Var. 64	Sotto voce: 346–347.
Var. 65	Sotto voce: 348–352.
Var. 66	Aria: 352–361.
Var. 67:	362–363.
Var. 68:	363–365.
Var. 69:	366–368.
Var. 70:	368–370.
Var. 71:	371.
Var. 72:	372–375.
Var. 73	A capriccio: 376.
Var. 74	Notturno: 377–384.
Var. 75:	384–385.
Var. 76:	386–390.
Var. 77	Leggiero e saltando: 391–395.
Var. 78	Abbastanza vivo: 396–399.
Var. 79	Cadenza: 400–408.
Var. 80	Fuga triplice a 5 voci (con licenze): 409–476.
Var. 81	Epilogue. Dolcissimo e soave: 476–484.

Ms. loc'n: Sorabji Music Archive.

Comments: Date at end (p. 484): 1937-08-30.
Not performed.

This is a work in three parts, each part coinciding with a bound volume. For an orchestral version of Vol. 1 of this work, see the identically titled one completed in 1956. The entire solo score as it exists, however, forms a complete piano work.

Title, date: **[Toccata terza] (1937?–38?)**
Med.:   Piano.

Dedic'n: Clinton Gray-Fisk.

Ms. loc'n: Unknown.

Comments: Not performed.

See the letters from Sorabji quoted in the opening discussion in this chapter. As this work disappeared or was destroyed about 1961 after the death of Clinton Gray-Fisk, who possessed the manuscript, it is unknown when it was written. The composer once suggested ca. 1937–38. The *Second Toccata* was completed in 1934. The third probably pre-dates 1946, as it is

146 Discovery

mentioned in the entry for Sorabji in Eric Blom's *Everyman's Dictionary of Music* (London: J. M. Dent, 1946).

Title, date: **Tāntrik Symphony for Piano Alone (1938–39)** [+18]
Med., pp.: Piano, 284 pp.

Dedic'n: "To dear Erik: / (Erik Chisholm) / True loyal and faithful Friend: / With Lots of Love / from / K."

Cont., pag.:
    I   Mūlādhāra): 1–64.
    II   (Svādhiṣṭhāna): 65–115.
    III (Maṇipūra): 115–151.
    IV (Anāhata Cakra). Mormorando e morbidissimo: 152–179.
    V   Viśuddha. Aria: 180–196.
    VI Ājñā: 197–206.
    VII Sahasrāra [Padma]. Fuga libera a cinque voci [five subjects]: 206–284.

Ms. loc'n: Sorabji Music Archive.

Comments: Date at end (p. 284): 1939-12-04.
Not performed.

This is Sorabji's First Piano Symphony. The movement titles refer to bodily centres and functions basic to tantric and shaktic yoga. The composer used the transliterations in *Tantra of the Great Liberation* by Arthur Avalon; above are transliterations which reflect the original Sanskrit terms more accurately.

Title, date: **Transcription in the Light of Harpsichord Technique for the Modern Piano of the Chromatic Fantasia of J. S. Bach, Followed by a Fugue (1940)** [+19]
Med., pp.: Piano, 15 pp.

Dedic'n: "To dear Aunty Edroff: / (Mrs. Emily Edroff Smith) / whose magnificent enthusiasm for the Best and lifelong devotion to the highest / in Music and whose unsparing scorn and instant detection / of pretentious incompetence and pompous humbug are / a never ending joy to those who know her and love her. / K. S. S."

Cont., pag.: Fantasia cromatica. Vivace focosamente: 1–9.
Fuga a tre voci: 9–15.

Ms. loc'n: Sorabji Music Archive.

Comments:	Date at end (p. 15): 1940-03-26.

This is the second piece in a collection bound in one volume as "Four Short Piano Works". The fugue transcription is not of the one by Bach which follows his Chromatic Fantasy (BWV 903), but of BWV 948, which may not be by Bach. |
| 1st perf.: | 1978-04-15, Greenvale, New York, by Michael Habermann. |

Title, date:	**"Quære reliqua hujus materiei inter secretiora"** (1940)
Transl'n:	"Seek the Rest of this Matter among the More Private Things"
Med., pp.:	Piano, 16 pp.
Dedic'n:	"For E. with love."
Ms. loc'n:	Sorabji Music Archive.
Comments:	There is no initial marking of tempo or style. Date at end (p. 16): 1940-05-30. Not performed.

This is the third piece in a collection bound in one volume as "Four Short Piano Works". The title and the translation given come from a line in the ghost story "Count Magnus", by M. R. James. Letters from Sorabji to Frank Holliday from around the time of writing of this work strongly suggest that "E." is Edward Clarke Ashworth. |

Title, date:	**"Gulistān"** — Nocturne for Piano (1940) [20]
Transl'n:	"The Rose Garden" — Nocturne for Piano
Med., pp.:	Piano, 28 pp.
Dedic'n:	"To Frank Holliday / greetings:". The composer later obliterated this (probably in 1979) and replaced it with "To my very dear great and / old friend Harold (Morland) / wonderful poet, translator of [*sic:* word omitted] / and a man <u>sui generis</u> if / ever there was: with much / love from Kaikhosru Shapurji Sorabji".
Ms. loc'n:	Sorabji Music Archive.
Comments:	Initial marking: Languido e dolcissimo. Il tutto in un ambiente di calore tropicale e profumato, piuttosto nostalgico. Date at end (p. 28): 1940-08-13.

This is the fourth piece in a collection bound in one volume as "Four Short Piano Works". The title refers to *The Rose* |

148 Discovery

                Garden by the Persian poet Sa'dī (ca. 1213–91). The dedication to Harold Morland in the Second Piano Symphony (1954) includes "translator of genius", which is what Sorabji may have intended here.

1st perf.:   1970-12-13, WNCN broadcast (New York), by the composer. The first concert performance was on 1977-11-22 in London by Yonty Solomon.

Title, date: **St. Bertrand de Comminges: "He was laughing in the tower" (1941)**
Med., pp.:   Piano, 16 pp.

Dedic'n: "To Ted: / (Edward Nason:)".

Ms. loc'n: Private collection.

Comments: Initial marking: Legatissimo quasi organo lontano.
                Date at end (p. 16): 1941-08-26.

                The title comes from a motif in the ghost story "Canon Alberic's Scrap-book", by M. R. James.

1st perf.:   1977-11-22, London, by Yonty Solomon.

Title, date: **[Trois poèmes] (1941)** [A1]
Med., pp.:   Voice and piano; 3 pp., 5 pp., and 5 pp. Voice range: b^3 to $b^{\flat 5}$.

Auth., texts: Paul Verlaine (1844–96, France): "Le faune"; Charles Baudelaire (1821–67, France): "Les chats"; Paul Verlaine: "La dernière fête galante".

Dedic'n: All three songs have the same words in the dedication: "à mes amis Jim Cooper / et Joy McArden Cooper."

Cont., pag.: Each song, being paginated separately, begins on its own p. 1.

                "Le faune". Temps libre modéré. Fougueux: 1–3. Voice range: $c^{\sharp 4}$ to $b^{\flat 5}$.
                "Les chats": 1–5. Voice range: c^4 to a^5.
                "La dernière fête galante". Avec afféterie. Quasi "Cooperin", léger et avec une grâce exagérée et minaudière: 1–5. Voice range: b^3 to a^5.

Ms. loc'n: Sorabji Music Archive.

Comments: Date at end of "Le faune" (p. 3): 1941-08-08/09.

"Could you just send me a list of his works?" 149

Date at end of "Les chats" (p. 5): 1941-10-06.
Date at end of "La dernière fête galante" (p. 5): 1941-10-10.
None performed.

Title, date: **Études transcendantes (1940–44)**
Transl'n: Transcendental Studies
Med., pp.: Piano, 456 pp. in 4 vols.:
    Studies 1–37, pp. 1–120
    Studies 38–63, pp. 121–240
    Studies 64–82, pp. 241–338
    Studies 83–100, pp. 339–456

Dedic'n: "To my old friend Henry Welsh: / to celebrate the renewal of a very old friendship / that lapsed through no fault of his, but of mine. / I trust he will accept this as a sort of amends; very belated I fear! / Kaikhosru Shapurji Sorabji. / XVIII. XI. MCMLXV."

Cont., pag.: VOLUME 1
    No. 1   Mouvementé: 1–3.
    No. 2   Vivace e leggiero: 4–5.
    No. 3:   6–9.
    No. 4   Scriabinesco. Soave e con tenerezza nostalgica: 10–11.
    No. 5   Staccato e leggiero: 12–13.
    No. 6:   14–16.
    No. 7   Leggiero abbastanza: 17–18.
    No. 8:   18–20.
    No. 9   Staccato e leggiero: 21–22.
    No. 10   Con brio ed impeto: 23–26.
    No. 11   Animato abbastanza: 27–28.
    No. 12   Leggiero, quasi "saltando": 29–30.
    No. 13:   31–34.
    No. 14   Tranquillamente soave: 35–37.
    No. 15:   38–39.
    No. 16:   40–42.
    No. 17   Molto accentato: 43.
    No. 18   Liscio, tranquillamente scorrevole: 44–47.
    No. 19   Saltando e leggiero: 48–50.
    No. 20   Con fantasia: 51–54.
    No. 21   Con eleganza e disinvoltura: 55–58.
    No. 22   Leggiero, volante e presto assai: 59–61.
    No. 23   Dolcemente scorrevole: 62–65.
    No. 24   Con fantasia e grazia: 66–70.
    No. 25   Vivace e secco: 71–74.
    No. 26   Dolcissimo: 75–82.
    No. 27   Staccato e leggiero a capriccio: 82–86.
    No. 28   Leggiero e volante: 86–89.

No. 29	A capriccio: 89–92.
No. 30	Con fantasia: 92–95.
No. 31	Vivace assai: 96–99.
No. 32	Legato [quanto] possibile, quasi dolce: 100–101.
No. 33	Vivace e brioso: 102–107.
No. 34	Soave e dolce, insinuante: 107–109.
No. 35:	110–112.
No. 36	Mano sinistra sempre sola: 112–116.
No. 37	Riflessioni. Moderato: 116–120.

VOLUME 2

No. 38	Con fantasia: 121–124.
No. 39:	125–129.
No. 40	Moderato: 129–132.
No. 41:	132–136.
No. 42	Impetuoso e con fuoco ed energia: 136–139.
No. 43:	140–144.
No. 44:	144–159.
No. 45:	160–161.
No. 46:	162–164.
No. 47	Leggiero e a capriccio: 165–167.
No. 48	Volante: 168–171.
No. 49	Vivace ma non troppo: 172–174.
No. 50	Per il pedale 3: 175–178.
No. 51:	179–181.
No. 52:	182–183.
No. 53	A capriccio: 184–186.
No. 54:	187–189.
No. 55:	190–192.
No. 56	Moderato: 193–195.
No. 57:	196–197.
No. 58	Leggiero: 198–201.
No. 59	Quasi fantasia: 202–210.
No. 60	Saltando, leggiero: 211–214.
No. 61:	215–217.
No. 62:	218–220.
No. 63	En forme de valse. Leggiero con disinvoltura: 221–240.

VOLUME 3

No. 64:	241–243.
No. 65:	244–246.
No. 66:	247–249.
No. 67:	250–253.
No. 68	Sotto voce: 253–255.
No. 69	La punta d'organo. Sotto voce: 256–271.
No. 70	Rythmes brisés: 271–275.
No. 71	Aria: 276–285.
No. 72	Canonica. Marcato: 286–287.

No. 73	Quasi Preludio-corale. Sonorità piena, morbida e dolcissima. Legatissimo: 288–294.	
No. 74	Ostinato. Secco: 295–299.	
No. 75	Passacaglia [theme, 100 variations]. Largo: 299–322.	
No. 76	Imitationes. Presto assai: 322–323.	
No. 77	Mouvement semblable et perpétuel. Scorrevole: 324–325.	
No. 78	Leggiero e veloce: 326–327.	
No. 79	The inlaid line. Legatissimo il tema melodico: 328–329.	
No. 80	La linea melodica. Mormorando sordamente: 330–333.	
No. 81	The suspensions. Lento quasi adagio e gravemente solenne: 334–335.	
No. 82	Sordamente e oscuramente minaccioso: 336–338.	

VOLUME 4

No. 83	Arpeggiated 4ths: 339–342.	
No. 84	Tango habanera. Leggiero, con grazia indolente: 342–350.	
No. 85:	350–353.	
No. 86	Adagietto. Legatissimo: 354.	
No. 87	Studio gammatico: 355–358.	
No. 88:	359.	
No. 89	Chopsticks. Vivace: 360–362.	
No. 90:	363–365.	
No. 91	Volante, leggiero: 366–368.	
No. 92	Legato [quanto] possibile. Velato, misterioso: 368–369.	
No. 93	Leggiero, saltando: 369–371.	
No. 94	Ornaments. Con fantasia: 372–374.	
No. 95:	375.	
No. 96:	376–378.	
No. 97:	379–382.	
No. 98	Staccato e vivace: 383–386.	
No. 99	Quasi fantasia (nello stile della Fantasia cromatica di Giovanni Sebastiano). Scorrevole: 386–406.	
No. 100	Coda-Finale. Fuga a cinque soggetti: 406–456.	

Ms. loc'n: Sorabji Music Archive.

Comments: Date at end (p. 456): 1944-02-07.

This work has two pages 349, and no page 351. There is no suggestion that it is a work in four parts; the composer merely had it bound that way.

Sorabji titled the work *Études transcendentales*. In the second word, the second *e* should be an *a*. But *transcendantales* is misleading in French; he may simply have mistranslated the English title or misremembered the last word in the title of Liszt's *Études d'exécution transcendante*.

1st perf.: Nos. 1, 10, 24: 1979-09-30, Como, Italy, by Yonty Solomon.
No. 26: 1989-02-24, NOS broadcast (Netherlands Broadcasting Corporation, Hilversum), by the composer.
The remainder have not been performed.

Title, date: **Rapsodie espagnole [de] Maurice Ravel — Transcription de concert pour piano (1945)**
Transl'n: Spanish Rhapsody of Maurice Ravel — Concert Transcription for Piano
Med., pp.: Piano, 26 pp.

Cont., pag.: I   Prélude à la nuit. Très modéré: 1–5.
II   Malagueña: 6–10.
III Habanera: 10–13.
IV   Feria: 13–26.

Ms. loc'n: Sorabji Music Archive.

Comments: Date at end (p. 26): 1945-05-30.
Not performed.

Title, date: **[Transcription of] Prelude [in E♭ by] J. S. Bach (1945)**
Med., pp. Piano, 4 pp.

Dedic'n: "per l'amico carissimo mio R. / che si dimostra sempre molto / commosso quando è suonato questo / piccolo pezzo — [il] suo tanto devotissimo / K. S. S."

Ms. loc'n: Sorabji Music Archive.

Comments: There is no initial marking of tempo or style.
Date at end (p. 4): 1945-09-20.
Not performed.

The transcription is of the Prelude (first movement) of the variant *French Suite*, BWV 815a, which may not be by Bach. "R." is Reginald Norman Best.

Title, date: **Concerto da suonare da me solo e senza orchestra, per divertirsi (1946)**
Transl'n: Concerto to be Played by Me Alone and Without Orchestra, for One's Own Diversion

"Could you just send me a list of his works?" 153

Med., pp.:	Piano, 70 pp.
Other title:	Concerto da suonare da se stesso, orchestra tacita e tacente.
Dedic'n:	"To dear Norman: (Norman Peterkin) / with love from his old / (and vastly obleeged friend) / Corfe Drop / alias Kaikhosru Shapurji Sorabji."
Cont., pag.:	[I] Incomincia l'orchestra arrogante e pomposa. Brioso focosamente: 1–27. II: 28–43. III Scherzo diabolico: 44–70.
Ms. loc'n:	Sorabji Music Archive.
Comments:	Date at end (p. 70): 1946-07-20. On what would be p. 71 is an alternative for a passage on p. 70. *Concerto per suonare*, contained in the composer's title, is not idiomatic Italian. More consistent grammar would also require its last word to be *divertirmi* (*for My Own Diversion*, literally *to Divert Myself*).
1st perf.:	1970-12-13, WNCN broadcast (New York), by the composer. The first concert performance was on 1978-06-27 in London by Yonty Solomon.

Title, date:	**Schlußszene aus Salome von Richard Strauss — Konzertmäßige Übertragung für Klavier zu zwei Händen (1947)**
Transl'n:	Closing Scene from Salome of Richard Strauss — Concert Transcription for Piano Two Hands
Med., pp.:	Piano, 25 pp.
Ms. loc'n:	Sorabji Music Archive.
Comments:	Date at end (p. 24): 1947-03-14. Not performed. This work has one page 19b, so numbered by the composer.

Title, date:	**Sequentia cyclica super "Dies iræ" ex Missa pro defunctis (1948–49)** [21]
Transl'n:	Cyclic Sequence on "Dies iræ" from the Mass for the Dead
Med., pp.:	Piano, 335 pp.

154 Discovery

Dedic'n: "To / Egon Petri: — / the greatest and most powerful intelligence / the most transcendental Master among / living Pianists. / in deepest admiration and regard. / K. S. S."

Cont., pag.: [Theme] Largo. Legatissimo sempre e nello stile medioevale detto "organum": 1–2.
No. 1 Vivace (spiccato assai): 2–11.
No. 2 Moderato: 11–15.
No. 3 Legato, soave e liscio: 15–21.
No. 4 Tranquillo e piano: 21–59.
No. 5 Ardito, focosamente: 59–65.
No. 6 Vivace e leggiero: 66–69.
No. 7: 69–71.
No. 8 Tempo di Valzer con molta fantasia, disinvoltura e eleganza: 72–93.
No. 9 Capriccioso: 93–103.
No. 10 Il tutto in una sonorità piena, dolce, morbida, calda e voluttuosa. Cantato dolcemente: 103–129.
No. 11 Vivace e secco: 130–132.
No. 12 Leggiero a capriccio: 132–137.
No. 13 Aria. Con fantasia e dolcezza: 138–150.
No. 14 Punta d'organo: 150–165.
No. 15 Ispanica. Con brio, leggiero, impertinente: 166–177.
No. 16 Marcia funebre: 178–180.
No. 17 Soave e dolce: 180–182.
No. 18 Duro, irato, energico: 182–191.
No. 19 Quasi Debussy. Dolcemente cantato: 192–195.
No. 20 Spiccato, leggiero: 196–199.
No. 21 Legatissimo, dolce e soave: 199–203.
No. 22 Passacaglia [theme, 100 variations]: 204–271.
No. 23 Con brio: 272–281.
No. 24 Oscuro, sordo: 282–286.
No. 25 Sotto voce, scorrevole, fuggitivo: 287–289.
No. 26 Largamente pomposo e maestoso: 289–299.
No. 27 Fuga quintuplice a due, tre, quattro e sei voci ed a cinque soggetti: 299–343.

Ms. loc'n: Sorabji Music Archive.

Comments: Date at end (p. 343): 1949-04-27.
Not performed.

This work has two pages 229, and no pages 231–239.

In writing *Hispanica* (without the accent) for No. 15, Sorabji probably intended the Italian word *Ispanica* rather than the Spanish word *Hispánica*.

Title, date:	**Symphony [No. 3], "Jāmī", for Large Orchestra, Wordless Chorus, and Baritone Solo (1942–51)** [+A1; +22]
Med., pp.:	Vocal soloist, chorus and orchestra, 824 pp.
Instr'n:	2+4+alt flt 4+1+bss obo 2E♭ clt+4+1+cbs clt 4+1+cbs sar / 8 6 4 2 / 4tym prc 4hrp pno org / bar SSAATTBB (choir) / 24 24 16 16 12
Auth., text:	Nūru'd-Dīn 'Abdu'r-Raḥmān Jāmī (1414–92, Persia): "In solitude, where being signless dwelt", translated by Edward Browne. See Comments.
Dedic'n:	"To my old Friend (not in age) / Mervyn Vicars. / Greetings. / K. S. S."
Cont., pag.:	[I] 1–264. II 241a–364. III 365–718. IV Cantico: 729–830.
Ms. loc'n:	Sorabji Music Archive.
Comments:	This work is written in a large score and a separate small score. The latter contains music for additional instruments which did not fit in the former. The two scores must therefore be read together.
	Date at end (p. 830) of large score: 1947-11-24; of small score: 1951-02-06.
	Not performed.
	This work has no page 136, one page 140a, pages 241a–264a between pages 264 and 265, no page 333, one page 334a, no pages 340–363, one page 601a, one page 602a, no pages 719–728, and two pages no. 780 and two no. 781 (in the order 780–781–780[a]–781[a]).
	The chorus is silent in movement II, and the baritone sings only in movement IV.

Title, date:	**Le agonie (1951)**
Transl'n:	The Agonies
Med.:	Piano.
Cont., pag.:	I Del cuore. II Della mente. III Dello spirito.
Ms. loc'n:	Unknown.

156 Discovery

Comments: This work was probably abandoned or incorporated into another. The evidence for its existence comes from Sorabji's letter to Frank Holliday of 17 March 1951, in which he wrote: "have started a short piano work called Le Agonie (Italian for the Agonies[)] ... three movements, dell'cuore [*recte* del], della mente, and dello spirito [...]".

Title, date: **Third Organ Symphony (1949–53)** [+23]
Med., pp.: Organ, 305 pp.

Dedic'n: "To my friend Norman P. Gentieu Esq.: / of Philadelphia / who combines the generosity of Haroùn er Raschid [*sic:* see Comments] / with a kindliness thoughtfulness and bonté that are / quite foreign to the Caliph, and that are as rare / in this our age as Haroùn is remote from it."

Cont., pag.: I Introito: 1–7.
     Fantasia: 8–51.
     Coda-Ripieno: 52–64.
   II Grave: 65–81.
     Corale-Fantasia: 81–109.
     Ripieno. Grave (come al principio): 109–113.
   III Toccata: 114–138.
     Passacaglia [theme, 50 variations]: 139–211.
     Cadenza fantasiata: 211–220.
     Fuga sextuplex: 221–301.

Comments: Date at end (p. 301): 1953-03-14.
Not performed.

This work has two pages 17, no page 21, two pages no. 104 and two no. 105 (in the order 104–105–104[a]–105[a]), and two pages no. 220 and two no. 221 (in the order 220–221–220[a]–221[a]). The passacaglia in movement III has two variations no. 5; the last variation is numbered 49.

The reference in the dedication is to the caliph in the Arabian Nights. The composer's spelling of his name derives from a French transliteration of the Arabic. (A more appropriate English transliteration is *Hārūn al-Rashīd*.)

Title, date: **Un nido di scatole (1954)** [+24]
Transl'n: A Nest of Boxes
Med., pp.: Piano, 26 pp.

Dedic'n: [after title] "sopra il nome del grande e buono Amico: / HAROLD RUTLAND / [...] / da Kaikhosru Shapurji Sorabji MCMLIV. A.D. / scritto e dedicato affettuosamente."

Cont., pag.: Dapprima ecco la cosa che contengono le scatole. Con impetuosità: 1.
La prima scatola. Fuggitivo: 1–2.
La seconda scatola: 2–3.
La terza scatola. Abbastanza soave: 3–4.
La quarta. [Un] pochino religioso, ma senza ipocrisia alcuna! Piccolo preludio corale tascabile: 5–7.
La quinta. La mezza via tra legato e distaccato: 8.
La sesta. Con impertinenza graziosa: 9–10.
La settima. "Omnium ecclesiarum urbis et orbis Mater et Caput": 11.
L'ottava. Arabeschi gammatici (Macché!): 12–13.
La nona. Ostinatissima come mai: 13–17.
La decima. Languido e sonnolento: 17–19.
L'undicesima. L'algolagniaco: 19–20.
La dodicesima. Con vivacissima impetuosità: 21.
La tredicesima. Con raffinamento affettato, quasi di piccola borghese che vorebbe darsi delle arie d'essere gran dama: 24.
La quattordicesima. Ein kleines Heldentenorleben. Mit Schwung, feurig: 25.
La quindicesima. Toccatissima. Si guarda un tocco sempre non legato, cioè quasi spiccato dei violinisti: 26.
La sedicesima. A rivederci! Con grande flessibilità: 27–28.

Ms. loc'n: Library of Trinity College of Music, London.

Comments: Date at end (p. 28): 1954-01-15.
Not performed.

This work has no pages 22 and 23.

Title, date: **Second Symphony for Piano (1954)**
Med., pp.: Piano, 248 pp.

Dedic'n: "With deep affection, / gratitude and heartfelt admiration for his wonderful / qualities of heart and mind: / to my very dear friend / Frank Holliday." The composer later obliterated this and replaced it with "To my very great and dear friend / Harold Morland: — / Poet of power and beauty and / translator of genius. / XI. I. MCMLXXIX."

Cont., pag.: PARTE PRIMA
I   Intrecciata politematica: 1–96.

[PARTE SECONDA]
II   Aria fiorita: piuttosto notturno: 97–132.
III Moto perpetuo: 133–149.
     Interludio: 149–158.
     Coda: 158–159.

[PARTE TERZA]
IV   Fanfare: 160.
     Introito: 161–166.
     Toccata: 166–177.
     Punta d'organo costanziata: 178–182.
     Fuga [five subjects]: 182–224.
V   Adagio-Finale: 225–248.

Ms. loc'n: Sorabji Music Archive.

Comments: Date at end (p. 248): 1954–10–25.
Not performed.

Title, date: **Passeggiata veneziana (1955–56)**
Transl'n: Venetian Promenade
Med., pp.: Piano, 24 pp.

Dedic'n: "To Mr. York Bowen / a trifling tribute of respect / and admiration."

Cont., pag.: [Barcarolla]. Dolcemente languido: 1–9.
Tarantella. Vivo: 10–15.
Notturnino. Sonnolento, languidamente voluttuoso. Sonorità sempre piena e calorosa: 16–21.
Cadenzetta. Briosissimo: 22.
[Ripresa]. Con disinvoltura graziosa ed elegante: 23–24.

Ms. loc'n: Sorabji Music Archive.

Comments: There is no date on the manuscript, but according to letters from Sorabji to Frank Holliday of 20 April and 20 May 1956, it was completed between those two dates.
Not performed.

This work is based on the *Barcarolle* from *The Tales of Hoffmann,* by Jacques Offenbach.

Title, date: **Symphonic Variations for Piano and Orchestra (1935–37, 1953–56)**
Med., pp.: Piano and orchestra, 540 pp.

Instr'n: pno / 6 6 6 6 / 8 5 4 2 / 4tym prc 2hrp / strs. Woodwinds include piccolo, alto flute, English horn, bass oboe, E♭ clarinet, bass clarinet, contrabassoon, and contrabass sarrusophone.

Cont., pag.: Introitus: 1–65.
[Theme]: 65–68.
Var. 1: 68–79.
Var. 2: 79–84.
Var. 3: 84–96.
Var. 4: 96–105.
Var. 5: 106–113.
Var. 6: 113–125.
Var. 7: 125–142.
Var. 8: 142–152.
Var. 9: 152–170.
Var. 10: 170–182.
Var. 11: 182–199.
Var. 12: 199–219.
Var. 13 Sotto voce, scorrevole: 219–231.
Var. 14 Dolcissimo, mormorando: 231–251.
Var. 15 Scorrevole e sotto voce: 251–261.
Var. 16: 261–294.
Var. 17 Tranquillo: 295–314.
Var. 18: Scorrevole: 314–327.
Var. 19: 328–339.
Var. 20: 340–367.
Var. 21: 368–377.
Var. 22: 377–402.
Var. 23: 403–414.
Var. 24 Quasi valse: 414–435a.
Var. 25 Vivacissimo: 435a–446.
Var. 26 Largamente adagio: 446–455.
Var. 27: 456–538.

Ms. loc'n: Sorabji Music Archive.

Comments: This work is written in a large score and a separate small score. The latter contains music for additional instruments which did not fit in the former. The two scores must therefore be read together.

Date at end (p. 538) of large score: 1955–06–01; of small score: 1956–09–23.
Not performed.

This work is an orchestral version of Vol. 1 of the Symphonic Variations of 1935–37. It was completed as far as the first four variations in 1937 or 1938; the remainder dates from 1953–56.

It has no pages 162, 163, 318, 319, 348, 349, and 439; and pages 431a–439a between pages 438 and 440.

Title, date: **Rosario d'arabeschi (1956)** [+25]
Transl'n: Rosary of Arabesques
Med., pp.: Piano, 45 pp.

Dedic'n: "Per [il] mio caro ed illustre amico / Sacheverell Sitwell".

Cont., pag.: I   Introito. Libero, improvvisando: 1–10.
 II Ostinato doppio: 10–27.
 III Punta d'organo. Adagissimo: 27–32.
     Cadenza. Sordo: 32–35.
 IV Tarantella. Vivo: 36–42.
 V   Coda-Ripresa: 42–45.

Ms. loc'n: Private collection.

Comments: Date at end (p. 45): 1956-11-26.

1st perf.: 1979-06-06, London, by Yonty Solomon.

Title, date: **Opus clavisymphonicum — Concerto for Piano and Large Orchestra (1957–59)** [+26]
Transl'n: Work for Keyboard and Orchestra — Concerto for Piano and Large Orchestra
Med., pp.: Piano and orchestra, 333 pp.
Oth. title: Opus claviconcertatare
Instr'n: pno / 6 6 6 6 / 8 6 4 2 / tym prc 2hrp / strs. Woodwinds include piccolo, alto flute, English horn, bass oboe, E♭ clarinet, bass clarinet, contrabassoon, and contrabass sarrusophone.

Dedic'n: "To Dr. John Ireland: / Great Musician: dear and great Friend."

Cont., pag.: I   Vivo: 1–144.
 II Toccata: 145–244.
     Cadenza fugata [one subject]: 244–273.
     Adagio-Epilogo: 273–333.

Ms. loc'n: The full score and solo piano part are in the Sorabji Music Archive.

Comments: This work is written in a large score and a separate small score. The latter contains music for additional instruments which did not fit in the former. The two scores must therefore be read together.

Date at end (p. 333) of piano line in large score: 1957-04-28; of last line in large score: 1957-11-13. The separate small score, which is undated at the end, was not completed, according to notes by Frank Holliday on his visit to Sorabji of 6 September 1959, until August 1959.
Not performed.

This work has no pages 158 and 159, and two pages no. 168 and two no. 169 (in the order 168–169[a]–168–169[a]).

The solo piano part has the title "Opus clavisymphonicum for Large Orchestra and Piano Solo" and the dedication "To my dear friend Dr. John Ireland: / in admiration respect and affection. / K. S. S. / MCMLVII." The page divisions given above for the full score correspond to the following in the piano part:

[I] Vivo: 1–46.
II   Toccata: 46–75.
     Cadenza fugata. Moderatamente vivo, deciso: 75–81.
     Adagio-Epilogo. Dolce, soave, morbido: 82–103.

The piano part has two pages 13 and no page 17.

Title, date:	**Third Symphony for Piano Solo (1959–60)**
Med., pp.:	Piano, 144 pp.

Dedic'n: "All'amico egregio: / George Richards / 'sempre con fé [*recte* fe'] sincera'".

Ms. loc'n: Sorabji Music Archive.

Comments: Initial marking: Brioso con impeto.
Date at end (p. 144): 1960-02-22.
Not performed.

This work includes a fugue [two subjects] (pp. 68–105) whose two parts are separated by an interlude (pp. 80–97), and a theme with 82 variations (pp. 106–144). There are two variations numbered 39; the last one is numbered 81. Neither the fugue nor the variations have explicit headings in the score.

Title, date:	**Suggested Bell-Chorale for St. Luke's Carillon (1961)**
Med., pp.:	Carillon, 1 p.

Dedic'n: "for my dear friend Norman Gentieu: Esq:".

Ms. loc'n:	George Arents Research Library, Syracuse University, Syracuse, New York.
Comments:	Date at end (unnumbered page): 1961-01-07. Not performed.

Title, date:	**Fantasiettina sul nome illustre dell'egregio poeta Christopher Grieve ossia Hugh M'Diarmid (1961)**
Transl'n:	Tiny Little Fantasy on the Illustrious Name of the Distinguished Poet Christopher Grieve, i.e. Hugh M'Diarmid
Med., pp.:	Piano, 10 pp., although the pages are unnumbered. See Comments.
Public'n:	Aylesbury, England: Bardic Edition, 1987.
Ms. loc'n:	Unknown.
Comments:	Initial marking: Vivo, con impeto. Date at end [p. 10]: 1961-04-10. The extant manuscript of this work is a copy made by Ronald Stevenson from 6 to 8 August 1962; the above information is from that copy. The work was written for the 70th birthday of the Scottish poet Christopher Murray Grieve (pseudonym Hugh MacDiarmid). The published performing/teaching edition has the title "Fantasiettina sul nome illustre dell'egregio poeta Hugh MacDiarmid ossia Christopher Grieve" and, like the manuscript copy by Ronald Stevenson, no dedication.
1st perf.:	1979-11-19, Roanoke, Virginia, by Michael Habermann.

Title, date:	**Messa alta sinfonica (1955–61)**
Transl'n:	Symphonic High Mass
Med., pp.:	8 vocal soloists, 2 choirs, and orchestra; 1001 pp.
Instr'n:	6 6 6 6 / 8 6 4 2 / bls 2hrp org / SATB (2 ea.) SSATB (2 choirs) / strs. Woodwinds include piccolo, alto flute, English horn, bass oboe, $E^\flat$ clarinet, bass clarinet, contrabassoon, and contrabass sarrusophone.
Texts:	Mass Ordinary with the interpolation of Pater Noster.
Dedic'n:	"Amico Optimo Carissimo et dilectissimo R. N. B."

Cont., pag.:	I	Kyrie. Allegro maestoso: 1–140.
	II	Gloria [48 variations]

                [Passacaglia: 32 of the variations]. Moderato: 141–219.

                [Interlude]. Dolce e pianissimo: 219–305.

                Di nuovo la passacaglia [the remaining 16 variations]. A tempo. Maestoso e pesante molto: 305–351.

	III	Credo. Andante, tranquillo e pianissimo sempre: 352–549.

                Offertorium. Andante, dolce e tranquillo [includes a fugue [one subject]]: 550–600.

	IV	Sanctus. Allegro grandioso: 601–720.
	V	Pater noster. Molto moderato, piano: 721–830.
	VI	Agnus dei. Molto moderato: 831–936.
	VII	Amen. Come al principio del Kyrie. Andante: 937–1001.
Ms. loc'n:		Sorabji Music Archive.
Comments:		Date at end (p. 1001): 1961-07-25. Not performed.

The Gloria has no variation no. 35; the last variation is numbered 49. The vocal soloists and choirs are silent in the Offertorium.

This work is bound in 3 volumes: pp. 1–360, 361–720, and 721–1001.

The title is presumably created on the analogy of *High Mass* or *Hohe Messe;* if so, *Messa grande* or *Messa solenne* is preferable to *Messa alta.* "R. N. B." is Reginald Norman Best.

In a letter to Frank Holliday of 25 May 1958, the composer suggested that each of the two choirs have 500 singers (100 per part), and that the orchestra consist of 180 to 200 players, with strings 32 32 24 24 24. At that time he may have been thinking of adding a separate small score to the main score, but the completed work appears not to have a separate score. He also thought of writing 144 variations in the Gloria but completed it as noted above.

Title, date:	**Fourth Symphony for Piano Alone (1962–64)**
Med., pp.:	Piano, 242 pp.
Dedic'n:	"To Harold Rutland whose independence of mind / admirable freedom from spiritual and moral besotment / by contemporary fashions of musical haberdashery / deserves all

the affection and respect of his friends among / whom I rejoice to subscribe myself. / K. S. S."

Cont., pag.:	[I]	Moderatamente allegro: 1–72.
	II	Preludio corale. Liturgicamente, molto moderato. Quasi cantico gregoriano: 73–96.
		Interludio. Perpetuum mobile: 96–105.
		Ostinato. Moderatissimo quasi lento: 106–120.
		Variazioni [theme, 49 variations, the last of which comprises Quasi cadenza–Toccata and Fuga [three subjects]]: 121–212.
	III	Finale. Abbastanza andante: 212–242.

Ms. loc'n: Sorabji Music Archive.

Comments: Date at end (p. 242): 1964-02-05.
Not performed.

Some time after the completion of the work, Sorabji replaced the dedication page with another, which reads "To my friend Harold Rutland, whose / independence of mind and freedom from monomaniacal / obsessions by current fashions of musical / haberdashery deserves all the respect and / admiration of his friends, of whom I rejoice / to be one. / K. S. S." A third dedication page is in the Library of Trinity College of Music, London, which is almost the same as the first one above: the only significant change is from "contemporary" to "'contempry'".

Title, date: **[20] Frammenti aforistici (1964)**
Transl'n: [20] Aphoristic Fragments
Med., pp.: Piano, 9 pp.

Dedic'n: "To Harold Morland: to celebrate a friendship / of more than thirty years."

Cont., pag.:
No. 69 a–c:	1.		No. 69 p–q:	6.
No. 69 d–f:	2.		No. 69 r:	7.
No. 69 g–k:	3.		No. 69 s–t:	8.
No. 69 l:	4.		No. 69 u:	9.
No. 69 m–o:	5.			

Ms. loc'n: Sorabji Music Archive.

Comments: Date at end (p. 9): 1964-02-29.
Not performed.

This series is numbered from 69a to 69u, skipping 69i. In a preface the composer says these fragments are outside the main series, which so far consists of 98 fragments. The reason for the number 69 in this group is not apparent.

Title, date:	**Toccata quarta (1964–67)**
Med., pp.:	Piano, 149 pp.
Dedic'n:	[after title] "Tema Fiorito sul nome del / carissimo amico F. H." The full name "Frank Holliday" is given on a subsequent title page and on p. 1 of the music. The composer later obliterated this and replaced it with "To Paul Rapoport: greetings and thanks. / XXVIII. IV. MCMLXIX [*recte* MCMLXXIX]."

Cont., pag.:	[I] Theme [with 24 variations]. Legatissimo, quasi adagio: 1–11.
	Nexus: 11–13.
	[II] Quasi corale. Liturgicamente, legatissimo: 14–25.
	III Intermezzo primo
	   Moto perpetuo. Vivace assai: 26–34.
	   Punta d'organo. Andante: 34–41.
	   Aria. Adagio, legatissimo: 42–50.
	IV Passacaglia [theme, 102 variations]: 50–97.
	V Intermezzo secondo. Of a neophyte and how the Black Art was revealed to him. Minaccioso: 97–103.
	VI Cadenza-Toccata. Leggiero, vivace: 103–112.
	VII Preludio adagio. Legatissimo: 112–117.
	   Fuga quintuplex: 118–149.

Ms. loc'n:	Sorabji Music Archive.
Comments:	Date at end (p. 149): 1967-05-05. Not performed. The passacaglia in movement IV has two variations no. 88 and two no. 89 (in the order 88–89–88[a]–89[a]); the last variation is numbered 100.

Title, date:	**Frammento cantato (1967)**
Transl'n:	Vocal Fragment
Med., pp.:	Voice and piano, 1 p. Voice range: b^2 to d^4.
Auth., text:	Author unknown, text not located.
Dedic'n:	"per l'Amico H. M."

Ms. loc'n: Private collection.

Comments: Initial marking: Lento. Senza misura, tempo libero.
Date at end: 1967-06-10.
Not performed.

"H. M." is Harold Morland.

Title, date: **Concertino non grosso for String Septet with Piano obbligato quasi continuo (1968)**
Med., pp.:   Piano, 4 violins, viola, and 2 cellos; 48 pp.

Dedic'n: "for Mervyn: Denise: Adrian and Kevin / with love."

Cont., pag.:   [I]   Vivace assai: 1–19.
II   Adagio: 19–24.
III   Finale. Vivace, leggiero [includes a fugue [one subject]]: 25–48.

Ms. loc'n: Private collection.

Comments: Date at end (p. 48): 1968-12-09.
Not performed.

Although Sorabji indicated two cellos in some places, there is only one line of cello music throughout. Whether he intended one or two players is unclear.

The dedicatees are the Vicars family.

Title, date: **[2] Sutra[s] sul nome dell'amico Alexis (1971, ?)**
Transl'n: 2 Sutras on the name of friend Alexis
Med., pp.:   Piano, 1 p.

Dedic'n: "Per il caro amico quasi Nipote — / Alexis."

Ms. loc'n: Sorabji Music Archive.

Comments: Date at end of first sutra: 1971-11-24.
Not performed.

The two sutras are unnumbered. The first has the title indicated, with no numeral and a singular noun. The second, which is undated, was probably written shortly after the first. The dedication appears between the two sutras; Sorabji may have intended it for the second, in place of a title. "Alexis" is Robert William Procter.

Title, date:	[104] **Frammenti aforistici (Sutras) (1962–64, 1972?)**				
Transl'n:	[104] Aphoristic Fragments (Sutras)				
Med., pp.:	Piano, 37 pp.				
Dedic'n:	"To Donald Garvelmann: bless the dear Man! / Christmas 1972."				
Cont., pag.:	Nos. 1–3:	1.		Nos. 52–54:	19.
	Nos. 4–7:	2.		Nos. 55–56:	20.
	Nos. 8–9:	3.		Nos. 57–59:	21.
	Nos. 10–12:	4.		Nos. 60–61:	22.
	Nos. 13–14:	5.		Nos. 62–65:	23.
	Nos. 15–17:	6.		Nos. 66–67:	24.
	Nos. 18–19:	7.		Nos. 68–69:	25.
	Nos. 20–23:	8.		Nos. 70–72:	26.
	Nos. 24–26:	9.		Nos. [72a]–73:	27.
	Nos. 27–30:	10.		Nos. 74–76:	28.
	Nos. 31–33:	11.		Nos. 77–79:	29.
	Nos. 34–36:	12.		Nos. 80–82:	30.
	Nos. 37–38:	13.		Nos. 83–84:	31.
	No. 39:	13–14.		Nos. 85–88:	32.
	Nos. 40–41:	14.		Nos. 89–90:	33.
	Nos. 42–44:	15.		Nos. 91–93:	34.
	Nos. 45–46:	16.		Nos. 94–97:	35.
	Nos. 47–49:	17.		Nos. 98–101:	36.
	Nos. 50–51:	18.		Nos. 102–103:	37.
Ms. loc'n:	Private collection.				
Comments:	Date at beginning: 1962. Most of the fragments were probably written by 1964. (See Comments on the Aphoristic Fragments of 1964). Not performed.				
	The fragment no. 72a is unnumbered in the score.				

Title, date:	**Benedizione di San Francesco d'Assisi (1973)** [+A1]
Transl'n:	Benediction of St. Francis of Assisi
Med., pp.:	Baritone and organ, 2 pp. Voice range: e^3 to f^4.
Auth., text:	St. Francis of Assisi (ca. 1182–1226, Italy): "Benediction".
Dedic'n:	"For my friend Alistair. / (Alistair Hinton.)"

Ms. loc'n: One is in the Sorabji Music Archive, another is in a private collection. See Comments.

Comments: Initial marking: Quasi lento, legatissimo sempre.
Date at end (p. 2): 1973-02-20.
Not performed.

Of the two different manuscripts, the one not kept by the composer (now in a private collection) is also 2 pp. and has the inscription "For Paul Rapoport Esq. / Greetings and Compliments / from Kaikhosru Shapurji Sorabji / XIX. V. MCMLXXVIII." Its initial marking is "Quasi lento".

Title, date: **Symphonia brevis for Piano (1973)**
Med., pp.: Piano, 120 pp.

Dedic'n: "for A."

Cont., pag.: [I]　Andante: 1–40.
II　Adagio: 41–48.
　Preludio quasi toccata. Vivace: 49–57.
　Aria fiorita. Dolcemente cantando. 58–66.
　Interludio. Sordamente. 67–72.
　Notturno. Lento, languido e sonnolento. Sonorità calorosa e soffocata: 73–96.
　Nexus. Abbastanza vivo: 97–99.
　Quasi fuga [two subjects]: 100–109.
　Coda-Epilogo. Punta d'organo. Dolcissimo sempre: 110–120.

Ms. loc'n: Sorabji Music Archive.

Comments: Date at end (p. 120): 1973-11-17.
Not performed.

This is the composer's fifth symphony for piano alone. "A." is Alistair Hinton. The title pages state that the first movement is marked "Movimento libero", with sections "Preludio", "Intreccio", and "Stretta", but these are not in the score.

Title, date: **Variazione maliziosa e perversa sopra "La morte d'Åse" da Grieg (1974)**
Transl'n: Malicious and Perverse Variation on "Åse's Death" by Grieg
Med., pp.: Piano, [2 pp.]

Ms. loc'n: Sorabji Music Archive.

Comments: Initial marking: Con stravaganza.
            Date at beginning: 1974.

1st perf.: 1991-07-23, London, by Donna Amato.

Title, date: **Opusculum clavisymphonicum vel claviorchestrale (1973–75)**
Transl'n: Little Work for Keyboard and Orchestra
Med., pp.:   Piano and small orchestra, 334 pp.
Other titles: Claviorchestralis; Opusculum for Piano and Small Orchestra.
Instr'n: pno / 1 1 1 1 / 0 0 0 0 / prc hrp / strs

Dedic'n: "For my very dear A. / with much love."

Cont., pag.:   I   Moderatamente animato: 1–96.
               II   Variazioni sopra il Credo in qualsiasi modo del Gretchaninoff [theme, 39 variations, of which no. 21 is an ostinato [theme, 27 variations]]. Legatissimo, adagio, liturgicamente: 97–334.

Ms. loc'n: Sorabji Music Archive.

Comments: Date at end (p. 334): 1975-09-24.
            Not performed.

            "Clavisymphonicum" and "claviorchestrale" are two Latin neologisms meaning essentially the same thing. "A." is Alistair Hinton. The ostinato has no variation no. 15, and two variations no. 22. The Credo referred to is Gretchaninoff's "Nicene Creed", from his Liturgy No. 2 of St. John Chrysostom, Op. 29.

Title, date: **Sixth Symphony for Piano (Symphonia claviensis) (1975–76)**
Med., pp.:   Piano, 270 pp.
Oth. titles: Symphonia magna; Clavisymphonica

Dedic'n: "Per L'amico caro e diletto: / A. H."

Cont., pag.:   PRIMA PARTE
               I   Introito. Adagissimo, solenne, grave e ieratico: 1–3.
                    Intrecciata. Animato assai: 4–12.
                    Interludio fugato [one subject]. Animato assai: 12–13.
                    [Intrecciata continued]: 14–90.
                    Coda-Epilogo. Sordo, oscuro: 90–96.

               SECONDA PARTE
               II   Preludio. Veloce, fuggitivo. N.B. Con pochissime "nuances": 97–99.

	Interludio placido. Legatissimo, lento, molto tranquillo. Sentimento dolce: 100–102.

        Interludio placido. Legatissimo, lento, molto tranquillo. Sentimento dolce: 100–102.
        Animato quasi scherzo. Vivace: 103–112.
        Moto perpetuo. Animato assai, uguale, senza "nuances": 113–115.
        Ostinato [theme, 64 variations]. Legatissimo: 116–166[a].
III   Quasi adagio. Dolcemente espressivo: 167[a]–187.
        Toccata–Quasi cadenza — ossia moto perpetuo. Vivace, seccamente animato: 188–192.
IV   Quasi Alkan. Moderato assai ma animato, secco: 193–208.

TERZA PARTE
V   Arabesque-Nocturne. Legatissimo e morbido sempre. Il tutto nel sentimento languoroso e tropicale: 209–227.
VI   Quasi fuga [5 fugues of one subject each, with an interlude between each pair]. Abbastanza animato, secco: 228–258.
VII   Coda-Epilogo. Quasi adagio, nostalgico: 258–270.

Ms. loc'n: Sorabji Music Archive.

Comments: Date at end (p. 270): 1976-11-11.
            Not performed.

            "Symphonia claviensis" is not a subtitle, but a Latin translation of "Symphony for Piano". "A. H." is Alistair Hinton. This work has no pages 124–133, and a second group of pages 160[a]–169[a] between the first page 169 and page 170.

Title, date: **[4] Frammenti aforistici [1977]**
Transl'n: [4] Aphoristic Fragments
Med., pp.:   Piano, 1 p.

Dedic'n: "For dear Alistair / from K. with love."

Ms. loc'n: Sorabji Music Archive.

Comments: There are no dates on this work. "Alistair" is Alistair Hinton, who supplied the date. The fragments are numbered from 1 to 4.

1st perf.:   1991-08-19, Calgary, Alberta, by Gordon Rumson.

Title, date: **Symphonic Nocturne for Piano Alone (1977–78)**
Med., pp.:   Piano, 113 pp.

Ms. loc'n:	Sorabji Music Archive.	
Comments:	Initial marking: Lento, languido, sonnolento. Date at end (p. 111): 1978-04-24. Not performed. This work has two pages no. 62 and two no. 63 (in the order 62–63–62[a]–63[a]).	

Title, date:	**"Il gallo d'oro" da Rimskij-Korsakov: Variazioni frivole con una fuga anarchica, eretica e perversa (1978–79)** [+27]	
Transl'n:	"The Golden Cockerel" by Rimskiy-Korsakov: Frivolous Variations with an Anarchic, Heretical, and Perverse Fugue	
Med., pp.:	Piano, 93 pp.	
Other title:	The Golden Cockerel Crows: Variazioni frivole sopra il grido del "Gallo d'oro" da Rimskij-Korsakov.	
Dedic'n:	"To Michael Habermann".	
Cont., pag.:	[Theme]	Acuto: 1–2.
	Var. 1	Legatissimo, abbastanza lento: 2.
	Var. 2	Animato abbastanza: 2–3.
	Var. 3	Distaccato assai: 3.
	Var. 4	Quasi lento: 4.
	Var. 5	Adagio, legatissimo. Il tutto una frase senza pausa né cesura alcuna: 5.
	Var. 6	Moderato: 5–6.
	Var. 7	Moderato, legatissimo: 7.
	Var. 7[a]	Leggiero e molto vivace: 8.
	Var. 8	Quasi notturno. Sonorità calda e morbida. Dolcemente cantando: 9–13.
	Var. 8[a]	Lugubre e sotto voce, senza crescendo alcuno: 13–14.
	Var. 9	[Un] pochino Chopinesco. Morbido e soave, languido dolcemente: 14–17.
	Var. 10	Valse impertinente. Con la grazia elefantina d'un'orchestra inglese suonante un Valzer di Strauss. Pesante parodisticamente, molto esagerato: 17–19.
	Var. 10[a]	Lento, solenne, legatissimo: 19–20.
	Var. 11:	20–21.
	Var. 11[a]	Vivo: 22.
	Var. 12	Con somma fantasia: 23.
	Var. 13	Tranquillo e legatissimo: 24.
	Var. 14	Moderatamente abbastanza. Fosco, oscuro, nebuloso. Legato [quanto] possibile: 24–25.
	Var. 15:	25–26.
	Var. 16	[Un] pochino più vivo: 26.

Var. 17	Vivace e impetuoso: 27.	
Var. 18	Passacagliettina [theme, 16 variations [a to q, skipping i]]. Legato e fosco: 28–33.	
Var. 19	Lento, legatissimo: 33–34.	
Var. 20	Vivacissimo: 34.	
Var. 21	Largamente assai: 35.	
Var. 22:	36.	
Var. 23	Abbastanza animato: 37.	
Var. 24	Adagietto. Legatissimo.: 37–38.	
Var. 25	Irato, impetuoso: 39.	
Var. 26	Volante, fuggitivo: 39–40.	
Var. 27:	40.	
Var. 28	Vivace e secco. Come una macchina da cucire: 41.	
Var. 29	Pesante e didattico: 41–42.	
Var. 30	Giocoso: 42.	
Var. 31	Quasi adagio, languido, indolente. Tranquillo: 43.	
Var. 32	Andante tranquillo: 44–46.	
Var. 33	Vivacissimo: 47.	
Var. 34	Oscuro, fosco, sordamente: 47–48.	
Var. 35	Vivace abbastanza: 49.	
Var. 36	Vivace abbastanza: 50.	
Var. 37	Meccanicamente animato: 51.	
Var. 38	Moderatamente animato: 52.	
Var. 39	Precipitato. Declamato con forza turbolenta: 53–54.	
Var. 40	Adagio e legatissimo sempre: 54–55.	
Var. 41	Leggiero: 55.	
Var. 42	Animato assai, secco: 56.	
Var. 43	Andante: 56–57.	
Var. 44	Quasi notturno: 57–64.	
Var. 45	Quasi lento: 65.	
Var. 46	Dolcemente tranquillo: 66–67.	
Var. 47	Tranquillo, meditativo: 67–70.	
Var. 48:	71.	
Var. 49	Vivace e animato: 72–80.	

Fuga eretica, perversa ed anche anarchica assai [two subjects]. Deciso, moderato: 81–93.

Ms. loc'n: Sorabji Music Archive.

Comments: Date at end (p. 93): 1979–05–20.
Not performed.

As may be seen from the above, the variations nos. 7[a], 8[a], 10[a], and 11[a] produce a total of 53 variations. *Il gallino d'oro,* contained in the composer's title, is not standard Italian. *Galletto* would be better, but the Italian title of Rimskiy-Korsakov's opera uses *Gallo.*

Title, date:	**Il tessuto d'arabeschi (1979)**
Transl'n:	The Tapestry of Arabesques
Med., pp.:	Flute and string quartet, 32 pp.
Dedic'n:	"To the Memory of Delius."
Ms. loc'n:	Private collection.
Comments:	Initial marking: Abbastanza animato. Date at end (p. 32): 1979-11-24. Commissioned by Norman P. Gentieu for the Philadelphia Branch of the Delius Society.
1st perf.:	1982-05-02, Philadelphia, by William Smith, conductor; Deborah Carter, flute; Jonathan Beiler, 1st violin; Davyd Booth, 2nd violin; Sidney Curtiss, viola; Gloria Johns, cello.

Title, date:	**Villa Tasca: Mezzogiorno siciliano — Evocazione nostalgica (1979–80)**
Transl'n:	Villa Tasca: Sicilian Noontime — Nostalgic Evocation
Med., pp.:	Piano, 47 pp.
Dedic'n:	"a Ronald Stevenson / egregio musicista e caro amico."
Ms. loc'n:	Sorabji Music Archive.
Comments:	Initial marking: Lento, morbido e sonnolento. On the previous page: Tutto questo pezzo suonato col calore languido, voluttuoso, quasi sensuale, con una sonorità ricca, dolce e piena, sempre senza durezza alcuna. Date at end (p. 47): 1980-02-04. Not performed.

Title, date:	**Opus secretum (1980–81)**
Transl'n:	Hidden Work; Occult Work
Med., pp.:	Piano, 48 pp.
Dedic'n:	"To dear Kenneth Derus: / Tante buone cose!"
Ms. loc'n:	Unknown.
Comments:	There is no initial marking of tempo or style. Date at end (p. 48): 1981-02-28. Not performed.

174 Discovery

The composer's autograph manuscript has disappeared. Only photocopies of it may be traced.

Title, date: **Passeggiata variata (1981)**
Transl'n: Varied Promenade
Med., pp.: Piano, 3 pp.

Dedic'n: [after title] "sul nome del caro e gentile giovane / Amico / Clive Spencer Bentley dallo Zio (quasi!) / Kaikhosru Shapurji Sorabji".

Ms. loc'n: Private collection.

Comments: Initial marking: Focoso, vivo.
Date at end (p. 3): 1981-04-24.
Not performed.

Title, date: **Fantasiettina atematica (1981)**
Transl'n: Tiny Little Athematic Fantasy
Med., pp.: Flute, oboe, clarinet; 2 pp.

Dedic'n: "per A. B-P. / per divertirsi! [*recte* divertirlo!]". "Per il caro e gentile amico / FRATER ANTONIUS."

Ms. loc'n: Private collection.

Comments: Initial marking: Moderato, dolce. Tempo liberamente.
There is no date on the manuscript. According to the dedicatee, the composer probably completed this piece between the end of June and the middle of August, 1981.
Not performed.

"A. B-P." is Anthony Burton-Page.

Title, date: **Passeggiata arlecchinesca sopra un frammento di Busoni ("Rondò arlecchinesco") (1981–82)**
Transl'n: Harlequinesque Promenade on a Fragment of Busoni ("Rondò arlecchinesco")
Med., pp.: Piano, 16 pp.

Dedic'n: "To Geoffrey Douglas Madge:".

Ms. loc'n: Sorabji Music Archive.

Comments: Initial marking: Vivace.

Date at end (p. 16): 1982-01-21.
Not performed.

The Short Catalog

Works not extant in a complete manuscript are marked with a black dot (•). Although so marked, the song "Le mauvais jardinier", the Music to "The Rider by Night", and *Concerto II* were probably completed. Works not extant even in part are marked with an asterisk (*). Of the seven so marked, three were probably completed: the Delius transcription for piano (1914), the *Vocalise* of 1916 (without opus number), and the *Toccata terza*. Two works are listed twice: Symphony II and Symphonic Variations, because each was to be written to include orchestra but exists as a complete work for piano solo. (See the Detailed Catalog for further information.) Other works (e.g. some of the concertos) also exist as solo works although completed in orchestral form, but they are listed only once, in the orchestral category.

For works with no date, their place is taken from that in the Detailed Catalog.

I   *PIANO SOLO*

Sonata [for Piano], Op. 7 (1917)
Quasi habanera, Op. 8 (1917)
Désir éperdu (Fragment) (1917)
Fantaisie espagnole (1919)
Sonata [No. 1 for] Piano (1919)
Two Piano Pieces (1918, 1920)
Sonata seconda for Piano (1920)
Sonata III for Piano (1922)
Prelude, Interlude, and Fugue for Piano (1920, 1922)
Le jardin parfumé — Poem for Piano Solo (1923)
Valse-fantaisie [for] Piano Solo (1925)
Variazioni e fuga triplice sopra "Dies iræ" per pianoforte (1923–26)
Toccata [No. 1] for Piano (1928)
Nocturne, "Jāmī" (1928)
Sonata IV for Piano (1928–29)
Toccatinetta sopra C. G. F. (1929)
•Passacaglia (1929)
Opus clavicembalisticum (1929–30)
Symphony II for Piano, Large Orchestra, Organ, Final Chorus, and Six Solo Voices (1930–31) [see category IVb]
Fantasia ispanica (1933)
Toccata seconda per pianoforte (1933–34)

Sonata V (Opus archimagicum) (1934–35)
Fragment Written for Harold Rutland (3 versions: 1926, 1928, 1937)
Symphonic Variations for Piano and Orchestra (1935–37) [see category III]
*[Toccata terza] (1937?–38?)
Tāntrik Symphony for Piano Alone (1938–39)
"Quære reliqua hujus materiei inter secretiora" (1940)
"Gulistān" — Nocturne for Piano (1940)
St. Bertrand de Comminges: "He was laughing in the tower" (1941)
Études transcendantes (1940–44)
Concerto da suonare da me solo e senza orchestra, per divertirsi (1946)
Sequentia cyclica super "Dies iræ" ex Missa pro defunctis (1948–49)
*Le agonie (1951)
Un nido di scatole (1954)
Second Symphony for Piano (1954)
Passeggiata veneziana (1955–56)
Rosario d'arabeschi (1956)
Third Symphony for Piano Solo (1959–60)
Fantasiettina sul nome illustre dell'egregio poeta Christopher Grieve ossia Hugh M'Diarmid (1961)
Fourth Symphony for Piano Alone (1962–64)
[20] Frammenti aforistici (1964)
Toccata quarta (1964–67)
[2] Sutra[s] sul nome dell'amico Alexis (1971, ?)
[104] Frammenti aforistici (Sutras) (1962–64, 1972?)
Symphonia brevis for Piano (1973)
Variazione maliziosa e perversa sopra "La morte d'Åse" da Grieg (1974)
Sixth Symphony for Piano (Symphonia claviensis) (1975–76)
[4] Frammenti aforistici [1977]
Symphonic Nocturne for Piano Alone (1977–78)
"Il gallo d'oro" da Rimskij-Korsakov: Variazioni frivole con una fuga anarchica, eretica e perversa (1978–79)
Villa Tasca: Mezzogiorno siciliano — Evocazione nostalgica (1979–80)
Opus secretum (1980–81)
Passeggiata variata (1981)
Passeggiata arlecchinesca sopra un frammento di Busoni ("Rondò arlecchinesco") (1981–82)

II ORGAN SOLO

Symphony [No. 1] for Organ (1924)
Second Symphony for Organ (1929–32)
Third Organ Symphony (1949–53)

III   PIANO WITH ORCHESTRA

Concerto [n° 1] pour piano et grand orchestre, Op. 3 (1915–16)
•Concerto II pour piano et grand orchestre, Op. 10 (1916–17) [orchestral score missing; two-piano score exists]
Concerto pour piano et orchestra da camera (1918) [Concerto No. 3]
Concerto pour piano et grand orchestre (1918) [Concerto No. 4]
Concerto for Piano and Orchestra (1920) [Concerto No. 5]
Concerto for Piano and Orchestra [No.] III (1922) [Concerto No. 6]
Concerto per pianoforte e piccola orchestra, "Simorg-Anka" (1924) [Concerto No. 7]
Concerto V for Piano and Large Orchestra (1927–28) [Concerto No. 8]
•Symphonic Variations for Piano and Orchestra (1935–37, 1953–56) [see category I]
Opus clavisymphonicum — Concerto for Piano and Large Orchestra (1957–59)
Opusculum clavisymphonicum vel claviorchestrale (1973–75)

IV   ORCHESTRA (excluding category III)

  IVa   Without voices

Chaleur — Poème, Op. 5 (ca. 1916–17)
Opusculum for Orchestra (1923)

  IVb   Voices and orchestra

*Medea (1916)
Symphony [No. 1] for Piano, Large Orchestra, Chorus, and Organ (1921–22)
*Black Mass (1922)
•Symphony II for Piano, Large Orchestra, Organ, Final Chorus, and Six Solo Voices (1930–31) [see category I]
Symphony [No. 3], "Jāmī", for Large Orchestra, Wordless Chorus, and Baritone Solo (1942–51)
Messa alta sinfonica (1955–61)

V   CHAMBER ENSEMBLE

  Va   Ensemble without voices

Quintet [No. 1] for Piano and Quartet of Stringed Instruments (1919–20)
Quintet II for Piano and String Quartet (1932–33)
Concertino non grosso for String Septet with Piano obbligato quasi continuo (1968)
Il tessuto d'arabeschi (1979)
Fantasiettina atematica (1981)

Vb Ensemble with voice(s)

•Music to "The Rider by Night" (1919)
Cinque sonetti di Michelagniolo Buonarroti (1923)

VI   VOICE AND KEYBOARD

VIa   Voice and piano

The Poplars, Op. 2, No. 1 (1915)
Chrysilla, Op. 1, No. 1 (1915)
Roses du soir, Op. 1, No. 2 (1915)
L'heure exquise, Op. 2, No. 2 (1916)
Vocalise pour soprano fioriturata, Op. 2, No. 3 (1916)
*[Vocalise No. 2] (1916)
Apparition, Op. 4, No. 3 (1916)
Hymne à Aphrodite, Op. 4, No. 2 (1916)
L'étang, Op. 9 (1917)
I Was Not Sorrowful — Poem for Voice (Dramatic Soprano or Tenor) and
    Piano (no date)
•Le mauvais jardinier (no date)
Trois fêtes galantes de Verlaine (no date)
Trois poèmes pour chant et piano (1918, 1919)
Arabesque (1920)
Trois poèmes du "Gulistān" de Sa'dī (1926)
L'irrémédiable (1927)
Movement for Voice and Piano (1927, 1931)
[Trois poèmes] (1941)
Frammento cantato (1967)

VIb   Voice and organ

Benedizione di San Francesco d'Assisi (1973)

VII   CARILLON

Suggested Bell-Chorale for St. Luke's Carillon (1961)

VIII   TRANSCRIPTIONS, ARRANGEMENTS, PASTICHES, ETC.

(All of these are for solo piano.)

*[Transcription of] In a Summer Garden [by Delius] (1914)
3 Pastiches for Piano (1922)
Pasticcio capriccioso sopra Op. 64 No. I dello Chopin (1933)

Transcription in the Light of Harpsichord Technique for the Modern Piano of the Chromatic Fantasia of J. S. Bach, Followed by a Fugue (1940)
Rapsodie espagnole [de] Maurice Ravel — Transcription de concert pour piano (1945)
[Transcription of] Prelude [in E♭ by] J. S. Bach (1945)
Schlußszene aus Salome von Richard Strauss — Konzertmäßige Übertragung für Klavier zu zwei Händen (1947)

IX   UNKNOWN

It is not known for what performers this work may have been intended, although it included chorus.

*[Music for "Faust"] (ca. 1930)

Sorabji's Notes

Following are various notes, quotations, warnings, etc. (other than dedications or inscriptions) which Sorabji wrote in various manuscripts. Not all this ancillary material from all his manuscripts appears here, but most of the more interesting portions do.
  All quoted material is found at or near the beginning of a work unless stated otherwise. All is from manuscripts and is printed here in a smaller typeface. All multiple underlinings have been reduced to single, but other aspects of Sorabji's spelling and punctuation are observed except where noted. Line divisions are indicated only when they are essential.
  This material is one of the sources for tracing Sorabji's attitudes towards performances of his music. As early as 1916–17 we find witty irony acting as a disclaimer for musical "meaning". This develops, through various admonitions to performers, into disillusion, even bitterness (see Note 15) and eventual sarcasm (already in Note 18) to a final defensive shot at those who would regard his music in any way other than what Sorabji would prescribe (Note 27). Most of Sorabji's works from the 1960s and 70s, it should be noted, have little ancillary material other than dedications and inscriptions.
  The line of development is not a straight or simple one. By the time of Note 27, performers and musicologists had taken some interest in Sorabji's music, with results he approved of. In a composing career which spanned nearly 70 years, we find many indications that he considered his music for some kind of performance (Notes 7, 17, 23, 26, others), as well as indications, however brief, of his interest in darker occult matters (Notes 8, 10,

11, 12) and a variety of other subjects. Note 16 contains a paean to love by one Persian poet among many to whom Sorabji often returned.

Sorabji's Latin and Italian occasionally became mixed or were erroneous for other reasons. Less often, he made up words in either language. In both cases, a comment may be made; in the former, a correction is given. The occasional words or phrases in any language needing correction (Notes 3, 9, 17, 18, 22, 24, 25, 27) are so indicated by the word *recte*, except when a mere letter is inserted, in which case a pair of square brackets is used.

1. The Poplars (1915) and other early songs

In 1978, Sorabji preferred that his early songs not be microfilmed. Alistair Hinton prevailed and they were duly microfilmed, but not before Sorabji showed his displeasure by scribbling various choice words on the title or first page as follows: "Rubbish" ("The Poplars" and "I Was Not Sorrowful"), "Muck" (*Vocalise*), "Bunk" ("Hymne à Aphrodite"), "Trash" ("L'étang"), "Tosh" ("Le mauvais jardinier"). The later Movement for Voice and Piano escaped his wrath, but "L'irrémédiable" earned "On your own head! You asked for it!! A Load of Rubbish".

Fortunately, these execrations do not obscure notes or words in the music.

2. The Poplars (1915)

The note at the bottom of the first page of "The Poplars" indicates the vocal style Sorabji was working with at the time:

> N.B. The vocal part of this Song being angular and nonmelodic in character, the executant must make no attempt at softening the outlines thereof in the interests of vocalization, such being entirely foreign to the character of the work[,] which is designed to approximate to a species of melodeclamation.

3. Chaleur (ca. 1916–17)

This is the only work for which Sorabji wrote a programmatic preface. The quotation marks may mean it was written by someone else and simply taken over by Sorabji, although in such cases he almost always acknowledged the source. For a different view on programmatic prefaces, see Note 4.

> "It is midday in a grove of Tropical India. The sun does not succeed in piercing the thick roof of leaves overhead, its rays being transformed into a green mysterious twilight. The whole life of the grove seems suspended in the tense quivering heat: not a sound to be heard but the hum of countless insects. Occasionally the subtle evil head of a krait* hovers for a moment above the dense undergrowth and vanishes with a venomous hiss. The air is heavy with the narcotic perfume of rare exotics and the languid voluptuous extasy of tropical heat pervades all things."
>
> *the deadliest serpent known. It is related to the Cobra di Capello [recte dal cappello] but is far more venomous than even the latter. It is said to be responsible for from 50 – 75,000 deaths annually in India.

Sorabji's interest in the dark side (the snake) re-emerges in some later works, even if professed images are not mentioned. (See Notes 8, 10, 11, 12.)

4. **Concerto II pour piano et grand orchestre (1916–17)**

<u>In the guise of a programme Note.</u>

> Owing to the unusually elaborate and important part played in this work by the orchestra, it has not been possible (on account of the deplorable shortsightedness of Nature in not supplying us with more fingers and hands), as a rule, to give anything more than the barest outline thereof for the second piano.
>   In playing the work through with a second pianist — should there ever be found anyone sufficiently intrepid and careless of the machinations of neighbours to do so — it would be as well to remember this fact.
>
> N.N.B.B. This concerto is based on no "programme" or "story" after the manner of the "Battle of Prague" "The Battle March of Delhi" or other masterpieces of the kind, so it would be wiser for the student of it not to rack his brains in trying to find any, but to remember the priceless maxim of the "King" in that incomparable classic "Alice in Wonderland": —
>   "'If there's no meaning in it' said the King 'that saves a world of trouble, you know, as we needn't try to find any.'"

At the end of the work:

Finis. Die XXVII. Dec. MCMXVII.

The fear of one's friends is the beginning of wisdom.

5. **Concerto pour piano et orchestra da camera (1918) [Concerto No. 3]**

At the end of the work:

FIN. Au nom d'Allah le tout puissant / le tout compatissant. 25—8—18. / À bas la bourgeoisie et la moralité de province.

6. **Concerto pour piano et grand orchestre (1918) [Concerto No. 4]**

Quoique l'orchestre ait un rôle assez important dans cet [*recte* cette] œuvre, le chef d'orchestre doit bien se garder de noyer le piano dans une trop grande amplitude de sonorité, les tutti à part. Il faut permettre au soliste une assez grande latitude de temps à cause de la très grande difficulté de la partie du piano. Éviter surtout toute hâte qui pourrait nuire à la clarté et à la précision.

At the end of the work:

Bonsoir mon très cher exécutant. Point de mauvaises [*recte* mauvais] rêves!

7. **Concerto for Piano and Orchestra (1920) [Concerto No. 5]**

Note:
For the proper interpretation of this work it is necessary to maintain a steady smooth extra-metrical prose like flow, except in such places as the contrary is clearly indicated by the character of the music: the bar lines and time signatures have no significance beyond serving as "guides âne" for purposes of study, rehearsal, and synchronization between the soloist and the orchestra. The whole must be as an elaborate fabric wherein all the threads of warp and woof are plainly perceptible although each contributing to the substance of the weft of tone.

No attempt at the memorization of the solo part is to be made by the pianist. The risks of disaster are too great and the pitfalls too many for the author to wish his executant to torture his brain with a task that the former would be the last to impose on anyone, and which he is, incidentally, quite incapable of accomplishing himself.

8. Sonata seconda for Piano (1920)

"Nec opus sit tibi null... credoni... malef..."
H. N. Sabbaticus

NOTE. This work is to be played with the strictest integrity. Rhythmic and formal pointmakings in accordance with prepossessions with which the author has no concern he severely deprecates, as also all attempts at playing the work from memory, an impossible feat. The author asks of his executant an act of interpretation and not a demonstration of a certain popular system of mental training.

Approximate time of performance 40 minutes.

In view of the extreme difficulty of this work, and the admittedly great demands on both auditor and interpreter, the former [recte latter] will do wisely to place the work — if at all — before anything else he may play.

For the timing, the number "40" is placed above the crossed-out specification "55–60".

At the end of the work:

AMÎN. FIN: — 11.25':45" P.M. 24. Dec. 1920.

9. Sonata III for Piano (1922)

At the end of the work:

P.M. 9-47. 5.5.22. il 5. [recte 5] Maggio. a Londra. tempo fino: ventoso freddo e pluvioso [recte piovoso], cioé [recte cioè] giorno da primavera inglese. FIN.

Sorabji often commented on environmental conditions at the conclusion of a work. (Cf. Note 17.)

10. Symphony [No. 1] for Piano, Large Orchestra, Chorus, and Organ (1921–22)

"... and in that darkness they come."

11. Opusculum for Orchestra (1923)

"... a rite not to be spoken, a deed / of high Black Magic."

12. Le jardin parfumé — Poem for Piano Solo (1923)

At the end of the work, under and to the left of a large ink blot:

here Satan is invoked to rend asunder all such as we hate —

13. Valse-fantaisie [for] Piano Solo (1925)

Deo gratias. et laudes. — / To Ganès [*recte* Gaṇeśa] Remover of Obstacles / Salutations and Obeisances / To Allah praise —

At the end of the work:

Finis. 17.4.25. 4.15 P.M.

14. Variazioni e fuga triplice sopra "Dies iræ" per pianoforte (1923–26)

The following were added in ca. 1978 and addressed to Alistair Hinton.

NB. NB. NB. To be kept well out of sight from all but one['s] / own sort. sc. Frank, & Norman and such ...

On the dates of composition (January 1923 to March 1926):

Can't for the life of me remember why I was so long over it!!

On the dedication to Busoni:

Exaggerated and excessive but with XVIII Century flowery Italian tradition of dedications to some great person: [...] You can lay it on yards thick in Italian!! In English it sounds just goddam silly!

On the manuscript paper:

In those days one could get very good ms. paper like this from Novello. But NOW!! Quantum mutatus ab illis!!! "Où sont les neiges (ou les papiers.) d'antan??"

On the music:

> The Seven last Variations are entitled after the Seven Deadly Sins: Don't know if at all they typify!!!
>
> You may stick to this if you like, with my love! It's not very good. much too obvious in many places.
>
> Note the paucity of "expression" (!!!) marks and dynamic ditto. The music is supposed to convey them of itself IF it does!!!

15.   Toccata [No. 1] for Piano (1928)

Motto.

"This world which is to be is none of mine:
Its Gods are not my Gods, not mine its aim.
That which it counteth honour, I hold shame;
It setteth nought by what I deem divine.
Its hopes and fears and mine are not the same;
Not mine its praises are, not mine its blame;
Its griefs are strange to me; its joys I shun,
Fear not its curse nor crave its benison.
For me, its cup is brimmed with poisoned wine,
Its light of life is as a marish flame,
That wiles through moor and fen the wandering one.
In such a world I were a soul in pine,
A disinherited, discarded son,
An unlaid ghost among an alien line.

[John Payne: "Sine Me, Liber ..."
Complete Poems:
Villon Society MCMII.]

The square brackets at the end are Sorabji's; the punctuation in the poem is from its printed edition, which differs slightly from Sorabji's.[21] Sorabji omitted the first ten lines of the poem, in which the poet suggests that happily he is too old to see the coming new era; likewise the last twelve lines, in which the poet, about to die, casts his poems "forth upon the morning air / For gift and greeting to the coming day, / Willing them fare without me where they may". (This explains the poem's title: "Without me, the book ...".)

---

[21]{For the complete citation of the item by Payne, see the bibliography to the present book.}

186 Discovery

That Sorabji omitted the first ten lines may reflect the fact that he was still young. That he omitted the closing lines is also easily explained. The action described was not for him: he would never send something out into the world without some control over its fate.

At the end of the work:

Finis: = 3.41½ P.M. 6.VI.MCMXXVIII.

16. Nocturne, "Jāmī" (1928)

"Be thou the thrall of love; make this thine object;
For this one thing seemeth to wise men worthy.
Be thou love's thrall, that thou mayst win thy freedom,
Bear on thy breast its brand, that thou mayst blithe be.
Love's wine will warm thee and will steal thy senses;
All else is soulless stupor and self-seeking."

> Jâmî
> trans. Edward G. Browne.

"Jami — at once a great poet a great scholar and a great mystic ... One of the most remarkable geniuses Persia ever produced."

> E. G. Browne.
> Lit. Hist. Pers. III.

The poetry is from *Yūsuf and Zuleykhā* by Nūru'd-Dīn 'Abdu'r-Raḥmān Jāmī. The quotation from Browne appears slightly differently in the original.²²

At the end of the work:

11.57. P.M. MCMXXVIII. Kaikhosru Sorabji Nocturnam hanc "Jami" effecit.

17. Opus clavicembalisticum (1929–30)

N.B. <u>Public performance prohibited unless by express consent of the Composer.</u>

---

²² "[... O]ne of the most remarkable geniuses whom Persia ever produced, for he was at once a great poet, a great scholar, and a great mystic." (Edward G. Browne: *A Literary History of Persia*, vol. 3 (Cambridge, England: Cambridge University Press, 1964), p. 507. This book was first published in 1902, for the first time with this title in 1928.)

At the end of the work, after a cross:

> In nomine Patris et Filii et Spiritus Sancti: — 1.50 p.m. die vicesima quinta [*recte* vicesimo quinto] mensis Junii: — A.D.N.S. MCMXXX — Kaikhosru Sorabji opus perfecit — domo suo [*recte* domi suæ *or* in domo sua]: MCLXXV [*recte* CLXXV]. Ad portum clarinensem. vicinum Hortus [*recte* Hortum] Regentis: — Londinii: apud Britannos barbarissimos et crapulosissimos.

Following this is a short formal analysis of the work, which is printed in its entirety in the notes to John Ogdon's recording of it.[23] At the end of this analysis of *Opus clavicembalisticum:*

Note: Separation and performance of any section or subsection apart from the whole work is absolutely prohibited.

> The work is only intended for pianist-musicians of the highest order — indeed its intellectual and technical difficulties place it beyond the reach of any others — it is a weighty and serious contribution to the literature of the piano, for serious musicians and serious listeners, only.

18. Tāntrik Symphony for Piano Alone (1938–39)

Envoi: or Epistle Denunciatory:

> A crore of pestilences upon all literal fools who will go rushing off to the Libraries mugging up Tantra and getting the Hell of a kick out of the dirt, the vice and all the fleshly uncleannesses that the pure ones can safely be relied on to find where and whenever they look for them, and having discovered what they will think they ought to look for (and enjoy finding above all else), will thenceforth run them to

---

[23]Altarus AIR–CD–9075. Three words were mistranscribed in the first printing of the notes, due to difficulties in Sorabji's handwriting. Under IV (*Fantasia*), for "motto" read "motive". Under IX (*Interludium alterum*), for "arises" read "arrives". Under XII (*Coda stretta*), for "web" read "weft".

The analysis is little more than a set of guidelines to the basic structure. Sorabji wrote something like this in only one other manuscript, that of his Fourth Sonata, where the actual themes are designated by letters but not given in music notation. (The notes to his *First Toccata* do the reverse: Sorabji gives the themes of the work in notation but with no further comments.) Similar analytical writing, however, may be found in the notes he wrote in the 1950s to accompany the microfilming of his music initiated and funded by Norman Gentieu. (See Sorabji's *Animadversions* in the bibliography to this book.)

earth in my Symphony. Well: "à chacun son infini;" I wish them joy and no end of outsize kicks — at least as many and big as they would get if they were to look a little nearer home, into the maggotty middens of those wholly unchemical manure-heaps their minds.

Consider well your neighbour, what an imbecile he is. Then ask yourself whether it be worth while paying any attention to what he thinks of you ... Were the day twice as long as it is, a man might find it diverting to probe down into that unsatisfactory fellow-creature and try to reach some common root of feeling other than those physiological needs which we share with every beast of earth. Diverting; hardly profitable. It would be like looking for a flea in a haystack, or a joke in the Bible. They can perhaps be found; at the expense of how much trouble!

Therefore the sage will go his way, prepared to find himself growing ever more out of sympathy with vulgar trends of opinion, for such is the inevitable development of thoughtful and self-respecting minds. He scorns to make proselytes among his fellows: they are not worth it. He has better things to do. While others nurse their griefs, he nurses his joy. He endeavours to find himself at no matter what cost, and to be true to that self when found — a worthy and ample occupation for a life-time.

Alone: (Norman Douglas)

The title "Epistle Denunciatory" balances "Epistle Dedicatory" in the Fifth Piano Sonata. (See the Detailed Catalog for the latter.)

Sorabji omitted the following where he inserted the ellipsis in the quotation from Norman Douglas's book: "Life is too short, and death the end of all things. Life must be lived, not endured." The first sentence of this did not fit his religious views; he definitely did not believe that death was the end.

Sorabji used part or all of this passage in other places. One is the preface to his book *Mi contra fa*, where the quotation is the same as that given above.

At the end of the work:

9.59. p.m. die IVa [*recte* IVo] decembris: MCMXXXIX. In the 3rd Month of the War of Financiers' Infamy.

19. Transcription in the Light of Harpsichord Technique for the Modern Piano of the Chromatic Fantasia of J. S. Bach, Followed by a Fugue (1940)

Prefatory Note:

Those half-educated neon-pedants of the Concert platform, wholesale dealers in Bach, whose principal claim to fame is that they can make more of Bach sound worse and drearier than his own worst work than had ever seemed inhumanly possible, knowing nothing of what was expected of a harpsichordist (nor of the technique of his instrument) when playing works written for that instrument — as so much of Bach's work was) — think they are preserving a punctilious puritanism of approach when playing let us say, the present work upon the piano without any substitution in pianistic terms for the many mutation and couple devices of the harpsichord, and in confining themselves to the bare written notes. As these pretentious ignoramuses have for the most part, never heard a great harpsichordist like Landowska play this piece, they can have no idea <u>how</u> it should be played upon the piano. This edition is an attempt to show them — with the more than half expressed wish that they will hear it alone. The Fugue that follows is an isolated one with a middle cadential section that relates it naturally to the Fantasia: it is an interesting and original specimen of Bach's fugal art, far superior to the dull mechanical jog-trot Fugue that usually follows the Fantasia. I acknowledge with the profoundest veneration & gratitude Busoni's great edition of the Fantasia on which in the treatment of certain sections of the Fantasia I have admittedly based my edition.

The various grammatical slips, including the extra right parenthesis, are Sorabji's. The words "hear it alone" may be "leave it alone".

20. "Gulistān" — Nocturne for Piano (1940)

Preface.

"What, sir, would you call the phenomenon of to-day? What is the outstanding feature of modern life? The bankruptcy, the proven fatuity, of everything that is bound up under the name of Western civilization. Men are perceiving, I think, the baseness of mercantile and military ideals, the loftiness of those older ones. They will band together, the elect of every nation, in god-favoured regions round the Inland Sea, there to lead serener lives. To those who have hitherto preached indecorous maxims of conduct they will say: 'What is all this ferocious nonsense about strenuousness? An unbecoming fluster. And who are you, to dictate how we shall order our day? Go! Shiver and struggle in your hyperborean dens. Trample about those misty rain-sodden fields, and hack each other's eyes out with antediluvian bayonets. Or career up and down the ocean, in your absurd ships, to pick the pockets of men better than yourselves. That is your mode of self-expression. It is not ours.'"

Count Caloveglia in "South Wind" (Norman Douglas.)

The wording and punctuation are from the printed edition of Douglas's novel, which differs slightly from Sorabji's; Sorabji introduced a few negligible errors.

Before the rededication in the score, Sorabji wrote out the text of "La fidélité" of Sa'dī, with two mistakes.[24]

21. Sequentia cyclica super "Dies iræ" ex Missa pro defunctis (1948–49)

Note. The comparative lack of what are quaintly called "expression marks" in this work is thus explained. The Composer considers that the music itself makes clear what "expression" is needed, if any in any particular passage. The "intelligence" of the player will do — or undo — the rest.

And, though usually to trust to the intelligence of performers, is to lean upon a broken reed upon which if a man — or composer lean — it will pierce his hand — and ruin his music — the enormity of <u>Sequentia Cyclica</u> is such as to place it mercifully high out of danger of the mob of gentlemen (and perfect pansies) who play with ease (as it were a nasal catarrh)[.]

At the end of the work, after a cross:

Deo gratias et laudes in excelsis: In Nomine Patris et Filii ET Spiritus Sancti AMEN. FINIS. 6.15 p.m. 27.IV.MCMXLIX. A.D. 175 Clarence Gate Gardens. London. N.W.1. Tempo freddivo [sic] brutto ventoso. di primavera inglese.

22. Symphony [No. 3], "Jāmī", for Large Orchestra, Wordless Chorus, and Baritone Solo (1942–51)

Or, gloire au seul Vivant!
Et sur le Guide des parleurs par la lettre *Dad*,
Et sur l'auteur du *Gefr* flambeau de l'intelligence,
Et sur tous les fils de la Divine Amie, nourris de pureté,
Et sur les privilégiés de l'enthousiasme et de la passion,

---

[24]{See pp. 469–70 for the text of "La fidélité".}

Et sur les amis des pensers sans fumée,
Et sur les frères sensibles de notre esprit,
La sauvegarde, les bénédictions de choix et le salam.

> Quant aux coriaces de la sensibilité, aux
> précaires de l'entendement, aux pau-
> vres de la subtilité, qui n'ont droit
> à aucune vie, ce sont ceux-là,
> en vérité, les morts parmi
> les vivants. Sur eux
> notre indifférence
> pire que la ma-
> lédiction!
>
> Amîn!

> La Reine de Saba:
> J. C. Mardrus.

The wording and punctuation are from the printed edition of Mardrus's translation. They differ slightly from Sorabji's; Sorabji introduced a few errors.[25]

At the end of the work, followed by a cross:

FINIS: PARTITIONIS MINORIS DIE VI. MENSIS FEBRUARII. A.D. MCMLI. CASTELLUM CORFIENSIS [recte CORFIENSE]: 8.30. P.M. AMÎN.

A similar note is found at the end of the *partitio major*, the large score, with the Latin for the date 24 November 1947 and for Sorabji's London address.

23. Third Organ Symphony (1949–53)

> This work is not written with that sham antique the socalled "baroque" Organ in mind: from which it is in polar antithesis in both spirit and intention. It looks towards an instrument of the tonal splendour grandeur and magnificence of the superb instruments in Liverpool Cathedral or The Royal Albert Hall, for its adequate expression.

---

[25]{For the complete citation of the Mardrus, see the bibliography to this book. For the English of "Quant aux coriaces", see p. 32.}

24. Un nido di scatole (1954)

PROIBIZIONE ASSOLUTA

<u>Non si deve fare nè vedere nè suonare nè udire da nullo altro che lui</u> [recte <u>né vedere né suonare né udire a nessun altro che a colui</u>] <u>per cui è stato scritto questo pezzino.</u>

25. Rosario d'arabeschi (1956)

NB. Esecuzione pubblica assolutamente PROIBITO sopratutto [recte PROIBITA soprattutto] in Inghilterra.

26. Opus clavisymphonicum — Concerto for Piano and Large Orchestra (1957–59)

<u>Note:</u> This work revolves around the Piano as the Solar System round the Sun. The widest latitude <u>within the framework of the sense of the music</u> is allowed to the Soloist for whose conception the Conductor is to be guided in his direction of the Orchestral part of the work. Power, massive breadth, combined with subtle variety of tone production and tone colour are called for in the performance of the Solo part.

The above is found in the separate piano part. There is no equivalent statement in the orchestral score.

The principle of the piano as centre is a basic concept in more works than this: nearly always Sorabji wrote his piano concertos (as well as his second quintet, and probably his first too) by writing the entire piano part first, and the accompanying forces later.

27. "Il gallo d'oro" da Rimskij-Korsakov: Variazioni frivole con una fuga anarchica, eretica e perversa (1978–79)

for the confoundation of e[a]rnest solemn highminded dolts and musicological pedants and bigots.

Part II

THE PROSE

6 Sorabji's Letters to Heseltine

Kenneth Derus

Kenneth Derus (b. 1948, Chicago) studied and taught philosophy at Florida State University and the University of Chicago, and from 1973 to 1978 chaired the Logic Group at the Center for Combinatorial Mathematics. Currently he is senior software consultant for U. S. Datamax Inc., in Bensenville, Illinois.

His correspondence and friendship with Sorabji began in 1975. He met him once, in 1977, when he also gave a lecture on Sorabji in London. Several years later he arranged for the North American premiere of *Opus clavicembalisticum*.

This chapter is the only one in the book besides Chapter 11 which Sorabji saw a version of, answered questions for, and commented on. He was extremely grateful to Derus for his work.

Preliminaries

And how much may we omit without not telling the truth? Depending on how slow we go. Going as fast as if everything were being omitted, nothing may be omitted without not telling the truth. Going as slow as if nothing were being omitted, everything may be omitted without not telling the truth. Gently omitting, though gently.[1]

A good place to begin is at the beginning; and nowhere are Sorabji's origins as a musician more completely revealed than in his letters to Philip Heseltine.[2]

---

[1] Laura Riding: *Though Gently* (Deyá, Majorca: The Seizin Press, 1930), p. 29.

[2] The telling of Heseltine's story is a thriving business, so there is no need to even hint at his story here. Interested readers should prefer *Peter Warlock: A Memoir of Philip Heseltine,* by Cecil Gray (London: Jonathan Cape, 1934). See footnote 86.

Thirty-eight of Sorabji's letters to Heseltine are in the British Library,[3] and 27 of these (comprising 200 manuscript pages) were written between October 1913 and August 1916. This is the period during which Sorabji composed his first musical works. Most of the remaining letters come from 1920–22. They provide a valuable picture of Sorabji approaching the height of his powers, and in particular of events surrounding his 1922 concert in Vienna.[4]

The letters should be read in bulk, but as they total nearly 36,000 words it is not practicable to present a complete edition of them here. Instead, around 20 percent of their content has been excerpted in the form of 93 annotated blocks of text. Much has had to be left out, including most references to composers and musical events, but an effort has been made to include all essential references to Sorabji's life and musical activities.

It needs to be re-emphasized that Sorabji is a composer about whom little of biographical significance is known.[5] Almost everything presented here is new. Often it is not much, but it is nearly all there is for this period of Sorabji's life.

The most exciting *facts* in the letters concern Sorabji's early piano concertos. The chronology of the early concertos has long been muddled, but the letters, together with dates on existing concerto manuscripts, clarify a great deal.

The impression of Sorabji that emerges from his letters to Heseltine will not surprise those who knew him. Most artists and writers are remarkable in spite of — or even chiefly because of — their failings as human beings. Sorabji is an exception to this rule. He was not only more intellectually gifted than most great composers: he was also more sweetly ingenuous, and his letters are refreshingly wholesome. This fact does nothing to re-introduce Sorabji to music history — but within the context of a special friendship, it bears on matters of life and death.

---

[3]Ms. add. 57963 (Heseltine Papers). Sorabji said that he destroyed the letters he received from Heseltine, at some point after the correspondence ended. (Kaikhosru Sorabji: Letter to Kenneth Derus, n.d. (mid-September 1984).)

[4]No known letters date from mid-1917 through the end of 1919. Missing, then, is everything relating to the occult doings of Heseltine's so-called Irish Period, Heseltine's controversy with Ernest Newman over Sorabji's compositions, and Sorabji's meeting with Busoni. For something about Newman and Busoni, see the end of this chapter.

[5]{This is true enough in this context, i.e. up to this point in this chapter and apart from the rest of this book.}

The smallest details of Sorabji's writing have been left untampered with in the edition that follows. Hence minor inconsistencies in punctuation and capitalization abound.

Editorial additions, deletions, and (rare) substitutions are always shown in square brackets: [ ]. Orthographically odd or incorrect characters are very uncommon; they are enclosed in angle brackets: < >. A missing diacritical mark is shown by a square bracket around a single letter having the mark; an improperly present diacritical mark is shown by an angle bracket around a single letter having the mark.

Because Sorabji's manuscripts are occasionally cacographic nightmares, a few spots in the letters may never be deciphered; but nothing in the excerpted material is unclear. Crossed out or blotted text is unusual. It is not shown, even when the underlying text is legible. The word divisions are not necessarily Sorabji's. His suspension points, having a variety of appearances (from ".." to "_ _ ..."), are always represented as "...". His underlining, occasionally double, is always represented as single.

Blocks of excerpted letter text are printed in smaller type with normal margins. They are referenced by numbers set in ordinary type. Block quotations from other sources are also in smaller type, but with increased margins.

Three other hands appear in the manuscript letters to Heseltine. One is Heseltine's, another belongs to the British Library's foliator, and the third is unidentified. (Heseltine's jottings are few and unimportant; they frequently have nothing to do with Sorabji's letters.)

Manuscript folios are referenced by numbers set in italics. A *v* suffix denotes the unnumbered verso of a folio.

Many of Sorabji's letters are partially or conjecturally dated, sometimes incorrectly, in the third hand. Dates or parts of dates deriving from other than Sorabji's own hand are identified in a table that appears towards the end of this chapter. Letters are referenced with numbers prefixed by *H*.

A block of excerpted letter text is prefixed with [+] when no material has been deleted prior to its beginning.

A paragraph sign ([¶] or [... ¶]) marks the beginning of a paragraph, in blocks of excerpted text. It identifies a *word*, virtually always indented in manuscript, not an entire paragraph.

Blocks of text are grouped under date headings which are *not* themselves text. Dates in the above-mentioned table have been similarly normalized.

A few of Sorabji's letters were written over periods of several weeks. Text prefixed by a date in brackets was written on or after the date.

Explanatory notes follow excerpted text (and sometimes date headings) in larger type. Some explanations have been shifted capriciously to the footnotes, which consist mostly of textual references. Punctuation involving quotation marks has been normalized in the explanatory notes, and paragraphs are indicated in the notes in the usual way. The inaccurate typing in Sorabji's letters to the author has been corrected without comment, and the punctuation of these letters has been systematically normalized. (Ellipses in brackets are editorial deletions; ellipses not in brackets are Sorabji's own suspension points.) People not mentioned in the letter text are rarely identified with dates.

This chapter could not have been written without the help of three old friends. Paul Rapoport, of McMaster University, invited the work, read several versions of it, and suggested many improvements. Kaikhosru Sorabji permitted excerpts from his letters to be published, lent photographs, and answered dozens of questions. Douglas Taylor, of Garland, Texas, prepared a typescript and index of all the letters, produced the manuscript illustrations, did the translations, supplied supporting documents, read the edited text more than once, and kept things moving with occasional feats of really brilliant detective work.

In addition, Patricia Brenan, of the Boston Public Library, helped date H29; Wolfgang Goldhan and Peter Thüringer, of the Deutsche Staatsbibliothek, and Hans-Günter Klein, of the Staatsbibliothek Preußischer Kulturbesitz, described Sorabji-related papers in Busoni archives; Pauline Gray and the Trustees of Cecil Gray's estate authorized the publication of part of a letter from Gray to Heseltine; Marion v. Hartlieb, of Universal Edition, and Hans Heinsheimer, of New York City, identified people involved with Sorabji's Vienna concert; François Lesure, of the Bibliothèque nationale, and Marc-André Roberge, of Université Laval, discovered valuable information, appearing elsewhere in this book, concerning Sorabji's Paris concert of 1921; Russell Thorne, of Madison, Wisconsin, located Meredith Starr materials; David Wooters, of the International Museum of Photography at George Eastman House, dated Alvin Langdon Coburn's photos of Sorabji; and the British Library microfilmed the letters. Laura Riding Jackson and Charles Musès had something to say about the ideas expressed in this work. As always, their opinions were of unusual interest.

The Letters

H1. London, 3 October 1913

Sorabji's first letter is addressed c/o *The Musical Times*, where Heseltine had recently published an article.[6]

Sorabji was 21 when he wrote it. Heseltine was a few weeks short of his 19th birthday, and about to begin his first term at Christ Church, Oxford.

1

[...] I have always freely confessed my extremely keen appreciation of, and lively sympathy with the ultra-modernist phase of contemporary music. [...] it is among the ultra-moderns that I am in my musical element, there is

---

[6]Philip Heseltine: "Some Reflections on Modern Musical Criticism", in *The Musical Times*, vol. 54 (1 October 1913), pp. 652–54.

that in their music which satisfies me completely, what it is I cannot
define, but whatever it is, this something is[,] for me at any rate, lacking in
much of the older music. [*1, 1v*]

It is interesting to have so many mostly enthusiastic references to the avant-garde (cf. 1, 5, 12, 22, 27, 32, 38), because Sorabji's later view is quite different:

> I am not a "modern" composer in the inverted commas sense. I utterly and indignantly repudiate that epithet as being in any way applicable to me.[7]

2

Skriabine is to my mind a colossal genius and there is, to me at any rate, nothing in the whole range of music quite so wonderful and strangely, w<ie>rdly <u>beautiful</u> as his marvellous music. [*2*]

Aleksandr Skryabin was the composer Sorabji admired most, at least up through 1917 or 1918. The early letters are filled with references to his music. (Twenty pages of H3 and H9 are devoted exclusively to Skryabin. By contrast, there are only five insignificant mentions of Busoni in the entire extant correspondence.)

The extent to which Sorabji later turned away from Skryabin is well illustrated by two statements. The first is from H3; the second is from something Sorabji wrote a little over twenty years later:

> I shall <u>never</u> forget the performance of Prometheus at Queen's Hall last February, under Wood. It was so sublime to <u>me</u>, as to be almost painful: the e<x>stasy and gloriousness of it! And people hissed and laughed!!!! No composer living or dead has written or could write music so transcendental as this: Scriabine stands absolutely alone, but <u>what</u> an isolation! <u>what</u> an eminence!! [*13, 13v*]

---

[7]Hugh MacDiarmid (quoting Kaikhosru Sorabji): *The Company I've Kept* (London: Hutchinson, 1966), pp. 38–39.

This statement has given composers running and barking fits. But to be modern is at most to be fashionable. *All* epigonic music is, was, or might have been modern.

> "Nothing is so dangerous as being <u>too modern</u> — one is apt to become old fashioned quite suddenly!!" said Lady Somebody in a witty Wilde play.
> (Kaikhosru Sorabji: Letter to Kenneth Derus, 26 January 1983.)

[I remember] the fury of controversy, the tremendous excitement aroused in 1913 over "Prometheus[.]" (I remember going, although then little more than a child, to a preliminary and introductory lecture by the redoubtable Mrs. Newmarch [...] on "Prometheus" and its harmonic scheme.) I remember, too, that for months I was haunted by the alleged "Mystic" chord [...] and I candidly acknowledge the stimulus to my own harmonic sense by Scriabine's researches into the higher dissonances, and remote derivatives of the dominant thirteenth, eleventh, and ninth, researches [...] that he quite failed to put to any powerfully and convincingly expressive use [...]

There is not a trace of coherent consecutive thinking in either "Le Poème de l'Extase" or "Prometheus" from first bar to last. A little idea is initiated, run for a little, or else grotesquely inflated, left, and another started after a piece of transparent and pitiful padding of the string-twiddling type [...] one never feels that the composer has made up his mind where he wants to go, or what he wants to say. [...] Of great art [Scriabine's music] has not the smallest trace, of coherent conception, of form of design, less than nothing.[8]

One of Sorabji's last public statements on Skryabin is more even-handed.[9]

3

People seem to have such a difficulty in emptying their minds of prejudices and preconceived notions. They can't let a work speak for itself. They must go and <u>compare</u> it if not actually, at any rate <u>subconsciously</u> with something they regard as a canon of excellence. [3]

---

[8]*The New Age*, vol. 55 (19 July 1934), pp. 141–42.
[9]Kaikhosru Sorabji: Letter to the Editor, in *The Musical Times*, vol. 98 (March 1957), pp. 152–53. Sorabji also made a surprisingly sympathetic reference to Skryabin's theosophy in this letter: cf. his earlier characterization of theosophy as "muddled, shoddy, illogical and confused" in *The New Age*, vol. 55 (19 July 1934), p. 142.
{And still later:

Have you perhaps heard any of the Scriabine programmes of late? I was among the very first in this country to be studying his music way back before 1914 as a lad. I SATURATED myself with it and consequently experienced a reaction which made me say some foolish and unjust things. Now coming back to it after some forty years or so I realise that he was a very great master.
And ... CHRIST ... HOW he could play the piano! ... As a boy I heard both of his London recitals in March 1914 ...
(Kaikhosru Sorabji: Letter to Frank Holliday, 15 February 1972.)}

4

[¶] My first taste of modern Music was gained some six years ago when I heard "P<é>ll[é]as et Mélisande" [...] Not so very long afterwards I had my first taste of the great Richard — "ELEKTRA"! This carried me away as it were a whirlwind. From that day to this I have devoted my attention — with the full consent of my professor, a man who fortunately for me is of the widest sympathies and most broadminded in his views — entirely to modern music. [3v]

Sorabji's music tutor was Charles A. Trew:

> Mr. Trew taught piano, harmony, et et at a small private music school in London (at which my darling Mother studied the Organ as a girl). It was called the London Organ School then.[10]
>
> I went [through] the ordinary routine, you see ... four-part, five-part harmony, counterpoint strict and free — [...] Thank God I've forgotten it *all* now — various species ...[11]

H3. London, 8 December 1913

5

[¶] I quite agree with you about Schönberg [...] It does not occur to one at all, when studying his music, as I have studied the "drei Klavierstücke" [Op. 11] with my professor, that it is humbug. That contention will not stand investigation. Let us suppose, just for a moment, that it is humbug. What is the object of it? Notoriety? But to what end? People seek notoriety for a definite purpose; raking in money as a rule; but no one can say that is Schönberg's object! No one buys his music! No one goes and hears it! He is assailed with slander calumny abuse nay even personal violence [...] No one would possibly incur all this for notoriety. It is ridiculous. [7v, 8]

Impatience with "a theory of composition ridden to death"[12] and "commonplace tortured and twisted in an endeavour to make it appear other than the commonplace it is"[13] soon brought Sorabji to a different conclusion about Schoenberg's invention, serialism:

---

[10]Kaikhosru Sorabji: Letter to Kenneth Derus, n.d. (mid-September 1984).
[11]Sorabji as interviewed on ITV's London Weekend Television (henceforth Television), 11 June 1977. Cf. the Television quotation after 49.
[12]*The New English Weekly*, vol. 5 (27 September 1934), p. 473.
[13]*The New Age*, vol. 50 (26 November 1931), p. 41.

Have you ever stopped to consider that two of the greatest hoaxes of the twentieth century, one in psychiatry and the other in music, both came from Vienna?[14]

6

We human beings are temperamentally like stretched strings. In some the material of the string is fine pure and very highly strung. In others the string is as it were coarse and heavy and slack. The former will respond to vibrating impulses so faint, so delicate as to be almost imperceptible or wholly so by others. The latter will vibrate to nothing short of an Earthquake. Now no string can vibrate, no matter how fine it be or how highly strung, to all vibrating impulses; it will only respond to a certain definite series; [...] Now because a string will not respond sympathetically to certain notes it is absurd to blame the string and unjust to call it deficient in sensitiveness or sympathetic qualities. [14]

What an odd delusion, and how prevalent, that when some composition that one dislikes has been put on the dissecting table, one will dislike it less, or, in that singularly meaningless phrase, "understand" it better. The only result of this ghoulish process, pushed to the furthest lengths of boring absurdity in the analytical programme note, is to make one dislike it even more.

It is like someone who, having introduced you to some *antipatico* person, shows you a radiograph of him, saying, "Oh you are ridiculously prejudiced against him! Just look at what a fine skeleton he has!"[15]

7

No genius has any right to lock up in one difficult and costly-accessible corner of the world, a work of supreme art [—] even his own. Great Art is universal. It should not be made the monopoly of a few. [15v]

The picture will be there for those who can bear to look upon it. [134v]

---

[14]Donald Garvelmann (quoting Kaikhosru Sorabji): "The Great Sorabji Mystique", in *The Composer Sorabji (Postscript)* (printed privately: [New York, 1971]). The reference to psychiatry is to Sigmund Freud. Serialism had of course not been invented at the time of H3.

[15]Kaikhosru Sorabji: Letter to the Editor, in *The Musical Times*, vol. 99 (September 1958), p. 490.

H4. 6 January 1914

8

You are a man after my own heart; and I am sure I have never come across anyone so completely sympathetic as yourself outside my mother, who feels and thinks as I do. (Fortunately for me I am an only child! [...] to have a brother or sister would make me expire with rage or be utterly consumed with jealousy! [...]) [19]

> My mother father and myself are all under fiery signs immediately adjacent owing to our birthdays being August 13, 14 and 15 (<u>me</u> in the middle if you please!).[16]

9

[...] where in the Devil's name do they think that a boy of 19 or 20 of musical & artistic tastes is going to find congenial companionship among his compeers of that age in <u>England</u>, where to be a musician or an artist is to be regarded as a disagreeable sort of monstrosity to be sternly reprobated and, if possible, equally sternly suppressed[?] [19v]

10

[¶] With what you say about Christianity I heartily agree. [...] I look upon it with contempt and disgust, equally now as in its past history. It is a living lie: a gigantic fraud, and an unspeakable hypocrisy. [...] Does not every one know that Christianity as embodied in the Churches has resolutely set its face against all progress in science and knowledge? Does not [...] the Roman Catholic part <u>still</u> oppose advancement as much as it did in the day of Galileo Galilei[? ...] What <u>has</u> the Church done [...] to alleviate the vast and appalling distress of the working classes in town and country? [...] Then again take that most hideous of evils[,] prostitution and immorality. What does the Church do? <u>Nothing</u>. [19v, 20, 20v]

Sorabji's later opinion of the Catholic Church was very positive (just as his opinion of the working classes was very negative).[17] He never, however, called himself a Christian.

---

[16]Kaikhosru Sorabji: Letter to Kenneth Derus, 31 July 1976.

{According to their extant passports, Sorabji's mother was born on 13 August 1874 and his father on 18 (not 15) August 1863. She died in 1959; he died in 1932.}

[17]"[...] my own reverence, admiration and respect [for the Catholic Church] is unbounded, holding as I do that most, and perhaps all, that is of any value in European civilisation is Her work [...]" (Kaikhosru Sorabji: *Mi contra fa: The Immoralisings of a Machiavellian Musician* (London:
[CONT'D]

11

I am very nearly a Buddhist. Buddhism is to me one of the most sublime of teachings. It is so pure[,] so lofty and noble, so sublime and <u>satisfying</u>, while the esoteric side is one of unimaginable grandeur and splendour. [...] The Burmese practise Buddhism in all its purity [...] Their standard of morality & personal purity, is with that of my own race — the Parsîs — whose religion [Zoroastrianism] lays very great stress on the latter — the highest in the world. Buddhism, as does our religion, practises and preaches the <u>equality of the sexes</u>; sexual subordination and slavery such as practised and declared by the Christian Churches is unknown to it. [*21, 21v*]

Something like the *practicum* of Tantric Buddhism was almost as important a factor in Sorabji's life as musical composition, with which it was closely linked. (See the notes that follow 92 and 93.)

12

[¶] On Saturday the 17th I go to see and hear Herr Schönberg! I hope to goodness the audience will behave in a proper manner and not like wild beasts like the Viennese. I am dropping a line to Mrs. Newmarch [...] asking her if she cannot make a suggestion [...] to the effect that someone be asked to come on the platform and say a few words of an introductory nature about Schönberg, and incidently asking the audience to behave themselves. [*23, 23v*]

Rosa Newmarch (1857–1940) was an authority on Russian music. Sorabji asked her to translate some Fëdor Tyutchev for him in 1912 (specifically, the verse motto for Medtner's E minor piano sonata, Op. 25, No. 2, published that year).

> The performance drew a large and appreciative audience who may or may not have been surprised by the following notice in the programme: "Herr Arnold Schoenberg has promised his cooperation at today's concert on condition that during the performance of his *[Five] Orchestral Pieces* perfect silence is maintained."[18]

Porcupine Press, 1947), p. 31.) {See pp. 327–28 and 330 for later references to the working classes.}

[18]Nicolas Slonimsky (quoting Henry J. Wood): *Music Since 1900*, 4th edition (New York: Charles Scribner's Sons, 1971), p. 233. This was Schoenberg's first appearance in London as composer-conductor, and the *press* was anything but appreciative. For Sorabji on Newmarch and Medtner, see *34v* and *Around Music*, by Kaikhosru Sorabji (London: Unicorn Press, 1932), p. 60.

H5. London, 3 February 1914

13

Yes! I and my mother (we are always together, quite inseparable in fact) were at the Philharmonic and I heartily agree about the Delius. They were exquisite dreams of beauty. What more can be said? One can hardly utter what one feels in words; one must "<u>sense</u>" another's feelings in the occult meaning. [26v]

14

I have [...] got the 4 hand arrangement of the Opus 16. (Schönberg) [*Five Orchestral Pieces*] but they sound <u>frightful</u> on the piano. [...] I hope you have got [Schönberg's] Opus 19 just published? Six little piano pieces. [...] VI is really quite beautiful. [26v, 27]

15

[...] I find that English people — whom with all due respect to your honoured self and my own dear mother, herself English, I detest, "en masse" — do not respond to music of a deep profound nature. [27]

16

Your accounts of Public School and University Life are truly ghastly. Fortunately for me I have escaped both. I could not possibly remain away from my mother for long periods of time [...] Besides a Public School would have about killed me but not before I should have contrived to knife somebody like poor Shelley. [...] I am so pleased to hear that you are coming to London, and am dying to meet you and hope you will often come and see me. I am very lonely; I have no friends at all, except my mother's, and <I>t will be indeed a joy to find such a keenly sympathetic soul. [27v, 28, 28v]

17

[...] I have this year given up my other scholastic studies to devote myself entirely to musical study with a view of becoming a "<u>critic!</u>" I passed the London Matric. some years ago, and intend now to work for Inter. Mus. with an eye to Mus. Bach. An academic qualification is an enormous help over here, where people are so impressed by <u>tangible</u> results. Moreover the Standard at London Univ. is very very high as I know to my cost and pain when working for the Matric, which is equal to a Cambridge B.A. in difficulty: so there is some credit in getting a London degree. [28v]

Sorabji's father as an engineering student in the 1880s

Sorabji's mother in the first decade of the 20th century

Sorabji changed his mind about pursuing the degrees, and in later years he strongly deprecated mass education.[19] Heseltine began studies at London University in October 1914 but abandoned them about three months later.

18

No! I do not compose! I have not yet reached that stage. I am plowing through "Ebenezer"! [29]

> Ebenezer Prout ... Great Gods, what a name! As well expect one with a name like that to be a musician as expect another with the name of Martin Tupper to be a poet, as the great Lord Chesterfield so well understood.[20]

19

[...] My name is a curious one. It is either Sorabji-Shapurji or Shapurji-Sorabji but as people make such a ghastly hash of it we generally call ourselves Sorabji 'tout court'. We have been called among other things Swabby; Soggy; Soralli, Swabby [sic], Sorbi, Soppy[,] Serabby; Sorabeeji, etc: etc: etc: etc. to 40 places of decimals!! [29v]

In the letters, Sorabji's name is signed these ways: Dudley Sorabjî Shapurjî (H1); Dudley Sorabji-Shapurji (H2); Dudley Sorabjî-Shapurjî (H3, H4); D. Sorabji Shapurji (H5); D. S. (H6, H10); Dudley Sorabjî (H7); C. L D S Sorabjî (H8); Dudley S. (H9); Dudley Sorabji (H11); C. D. S. S. (H12); C L. D S. Sorabji (H13); D. K. Sorabji (H14, H17); K. L. D. S. S. (*C* over-written with *K*; H15); K. L. D. S. S. (H16); D K S. (H19, H22); D. K. S. (H20, H21, H23); K. S. (H29; cf. 71). H26 is signed with a symbol formed by superimposing the diagonals of *K* on *S*. For a note on how the other letters are signed, see the comments after 72.

---

[19] {He agreed with Norman Douglas, who, in his book *How about Europe?*, described compulsory mass education as "a State-controlled manufactory of echoes". (Kaikhosru Sorabji: *Mi contra fa*, p. 128.)}

[20] Kaikhosru Sorabji: *Mi contra fa*, p. 47. Ebenezer Prout (1835–1909) was a well-known teacher and author of books on music theory. Sorabji went on to deride his compositions for "*naïveté*, ineptitude and sheer incompetence".

H6. London, [possibly February] 1914

20

[¶] I hope I am not such a fool as to allow myself to be deceived into misestimating a work merely because it is badly rendered!! All the mutilations in the world cannot hide the genius of a great work from a seeing eye. [62]

21

Tell me what you look like so that I may be able to recognize you. For myself I am very "sombre": les "cheveux noirs foncés": of which there is a mop: and gold specs. You cannot mistake me. [62]

H7. London, late February 1914

22

[¶] I am rather surprised at your apparent attitude towards the ultra-modern movement in painting. Surely you cannot expect this art to escape the general upheaval! Surely it is most undesirable that it should! Moreover what do you suppose that all the modern painters are aiming at? All of them: Expressionists: Fauvistes: Orféistes: Post-Impressionists; Cubists; Futurists? Why just what Sch[ö]nberg and all the others are fighting for in music, greater freedom and power of expression. Perhaps you have not paid over a dozen consecutive visits to one ultra-modern exhibition as I have, otherwise I do not think you would be so adverse. [...] One thing that impressed me very much about these Exhibitions was the marvellous atmosphere or I ought more properly — I suppose — to say "aura" — (for it is an occult thing that atmosphere) of intense life, vitality, or "aliveness" about the work of these men as contrasted with the dead effete flabby nerveless flaccid stuff paraded annually on the walls of the R[oyal] A[cademy ...] [30v, 31, 31v]

H8. London, early March 1914

23

How many times have I subsequently been compelled to change my opinion about a singer or instrumentalist whom on a first hearing I have thought to be indifferent or bad, when it has only in reality been one of their bad days. Why even in my own small way, there are days when I cannot touch the piano and my fingers will simply not go. [37v]

24

[14 March] I also went to Benno Moiseiwitsch's recital to hear the first performance of John Powell's remarkably fine "Sonata Teutonica". It is a monumental work taking up over an hour in performance, but such is the high quality of the music that one was [not] — i.e. I was not, conscious of any abnormal length, and it did not seem any too long. Indeed I have heard many a Beethoven Sonata one tenth its length which seemed a hundred times as long as this Sonata. [38]

The *Sonata teutonica* (1906–13) by the American John Powell (1882–1963) was published several years ago in an edition that eliminates one-third of its playing time, on the grounds that its original length makes intolerable demands on most listeners.[21] Particularly to be regretted is the loss of the work's eight-minute fugue.

> The man who has scarcely the energy and guts for a thumbnail sketch naturally sneers at him who can fill a decent-sized canvas. Talk about "bulk," with a sneering implication, tells me much more about the sneerer than about the sneered-at, other things being equal, for I think it is sufficiently obvious that it takes more creative power to produce a lot of good stuff than a little good stuff.[22]

25

It is very disgusting to see how Europeans pilfer bits from Oriental and particularly Hindû philosophy, trick it out in their own words which no one can understand — which is perhaps as well — and palm it off as the results of their own philosophic speculations and researches. [38v]

26

[¶] The Cyril Scott was there looking round for recognition and admiration. He looks one of the people who ought to have a herald in front of them crying out "Room! Room for the one and only the almighty Cyril Scott". [...] But do you not always find the third rate ones so? The really great ones are modest and reticent about their work and in their demeanour ... conceit, arrogance, affectation, insincerity, and swelled-head: all these I have found invariably go together. They excite in me nothing but loathing and disgust. [...] But oh! dear, how fearfully prevalent they are over here!

---

[21] John Powell: *Sonata teutonica*, edited by Roy Hamlin Johnson (New York and London: Oxford University Press, 1983).
Benno Moiseiwitsch (1890–1963) performed Powell's sonata on 7 March 1914 in Bechstein Hall.
[22] *The New English Weekly*, vol. 10 (8 April 1937), p. 514.

[...] One day I will tell you some tales of what Indians have to endure at the hands of British arrogance; but not now. [*39v, 40*]

Cyril Scott (1879–1970): the composer.

> As a Parsi, may I be allowed to express my hearty endorsement of the following [...], "The English nation to a man, and, certainly, to a woman, is persistently nasty to all foreigners"? I will go further and assert that they are so for certain of their own fellow-subjects, pre-eminently to Indians. Their attitude towards us is one of carefully-studied and calculated hatefulness, here as well as in India.
>
> If we go in the train, the 'bus, the street, we are greeted with rude, insolent stares. Insulting and offensive remarks are passed about us in loud tones, we are ridiculed and laughed at to our very faces. They make no attempt of concealing their behaviour. Oh, dear, no, that would never do, for it would fail in its design of wounding, offending and hurting us if they did so.[23]

27

The extreme bigotry of ultra-modernism, i.e. Futurism is surely just as bad as the bigoted academicism of the Corders and Bridges n'est-ce pas? [*40*]

Frederick Corder (1852–1932) and Frank Bridge (1879–1941). Corder was a pedagogue. Both men were composers.

28

[20 March] When a man thinks it necessary to wrap up his thoughts in complicated verbose phraseology one is bound to become suspicious. If he has really something of value to say he will not swaddle it up in a mass of verbiage. We can now-a-days very quickly detect the composer who having nothing to say takes 1½ hours to say it like the late Gustav Mahler! [*41*]

Mahler (not Powell!) might seem a likely early inspiration for Sorabji's own big works, but Sorabji did not become a great champion of Mahler until after the correspondence with Heseltine ended. (See 85.)

---

[23]Kaikhosru Sorabji: Letter to the Editor, in *The New Age*, vol. 16 (15 April 1915), p. 653. See the note that follows 50, including footnote 38, for Sorabji's later realization that Parsis were not Indians.
{See also pp. 68–69 for a more personal expression of racial condescension.}

29

[¶] March 28th[.] I was so delighted to meet you that Friday. I will be honest with you. I was a little bit afraid [...] lest you were a rather formidable person! [43v]

H9. London, 14 April 1914

Heseltine was staying with Delius at this time.

> I vividly recall my dear friend Heseltine writing to me when we were both boys, he then in a very ecstasy of Delius enthusiasm, staying at Grez-sur-Loing helping with the making of parts [...][24]

30

[...] I wish I had your charming style. Unfortunately I have only the power to write down my ideas as they come, and cannot fashion them into a presentable literary shape. [46]

31

We must not allow our likes and dislikes to run away with our fairness and justice. After all it is quite conceivable that a work may be a good one in the opinion of someone quite as competent to form a valid opinion as ourselves[.] [46v]

Sorabji, needless to say, went on to run wild with his own likes and dislikes. But he was not always condemned for doing so:

> [...] being himself a man of great intelligence, sensitive over a wide field, remarkably true in his intuitions, [Sorabji] naturally suspects omniscience. And this causes him to be disinclined to accept anybody's word but his own, and the music critic's least of all. It is a perfectly understandable position [...][25]

The notion that good criticism has to be fair is parochial at best. Boulez is not fair. Arthur Cravan, on the Paris scene in 1914, was out to *insult* talent, not identify it:

---

[24]*The New English Weekly*, vol. 19 (29 May 1941), p. 63.
[25]Scott Goddard: Review of *Around Music*, by Kaikhosru Sorabji, in *Music and Letters*, vol. 14, no. 3 (July 1933), p. 288.

If I write it is to infuriate my colleagues, to get myself talked about, and to make a name for myself. A name helps you succeed with women and in business. [...] Treat me with respect or I'll twist your private parts.[26]

(Cravan, of course, is a great deal more charming than Boulez, but both are writers of substantial historical importance.)

Readers with no conception of how critics have written in other times and places should nevertheless be willing to say of Sorabji what Sorabji once said of Ernest Newman:

> I submit that these observations [...] made by any Tom, Dick or Harry [...] would not be worth the paper they are written on, but being made by Mr. Newman they are of great interest *and value* [...][27]

32

[15 April] [The Futurists] apparently combine the daring colour harmonies of the Post-Impressionists with the extreme abstraction of form of such Cubists as Picasso and Braque. I find it amazingly interesting. And whether one understands it or not, it is most fascinating and it is <u>alive</u>! [...] It is their colour grouping that I find especially fascinating and stimulating [...] Picture a room with a black ceiling — why should a ceiling for ever be white?? — vivid orange carpet — gleaming yellow walls [—] purple painted wood work and a few touches here and there of scarlet — cushions or upholstery. Who could feel miserable in such a room? You see[,] being an Oriental I have all the Orientals' colour-sense, in which Englishmen are lacking, and I feel quite at ease and at home in juxtapositions [...] at which the ordinary person pretends to be horrified. And after all what is the accepted scheme of colour grouping but another convention such as that of consonance and dissonance which the ultra-modern artists and musicians are seeking to upset. [*49, 49v*]

---

[26]Mina Loy: *The Last Lunar Baedeker*, edited by Roger L. Conover (Highlands, North Carolina: The Jargon Society, 1982), pp. li, 331. The editor is quoting Arthur Cravan.

Cravan invented Dada several years before Tristan Tzara. He was a forger, a professional boxer, and a master of disguise, as well as an art critic and a nephew of Oscar Wilde. Like Ambrose Bierce, he disappeared in Mexico.

[27]*The New Age*, vol. 45 (10 October 1929), p. 286. Something of Newman's reputation can be gathered from the section on Newman and Busoni at the end of this chapter.

33

[¶] May 22nd. [...] I have been fearfully busy, among other things helping my mother <u>flat</u>-<u>hunt</u>! Then my father has just returned after an absence of <u>six years</u>!![28] [*51*]

H11. London, 8 September 1914

34

One great thing will come out of [the War] together with the "Summum Bonum" of the crushing of Germany and that will be the explosion of the ridiculous myth of German "culture". [...] Real culture is a nation's progress towards higher morality and humanity and it gives one great satisfaction to see the English — whom they have always ridiculed and insulted as they do everybody a bit better than themselves — as far above them in these respects as the sun above a farthing rushlight. [*63, 63v*]

35

[¶] I am attempting — how you will jeer!! — a piano arrangement of "In a Summer Garden". Have got as far as ⑯ where it gets so big that one pair of hands cannot cope satisfactorily with it, though I am trying to manoeuvre it so that they can. It is an exquisite work. I know a lovely garden on a hillside at Robin Hood's Bay in Yorkshire where it might have been written and every time I see that lovely garden I think, Oh! to hear "In a Summer Garden" in such surroundings! All the languourous heat and quivering intensity of such a spot on a sultry summer's afternoon are conveyed with marvellous fidelity and power in this most perfect work. It is always a matter of great regret to me that Mr. Delius should have wasted such glorious music on the preposterous drivel and senseless stuff of Nietzsche's Zarathustra. A truly great and glorious work could he write around say, some of the Vedic Hymns [or] the Zarathustrian Gathâs (the real thing & not N's piffle.) The beauty of the language and richness of imagery of these last are inconceivable and must surely prove an inexhaustible fount of inspiration to such an one as Mr. Delius. [*64v, 65*]

The Delius transcription might be Sorabji's first musical work. (It is the first for which there is any evidence.) Heseltine transcribed *In a Summer Garden* for two pianos in 1912.

---

[28]See 36 and the comments following it.

36

[My father] had gone just recently (3 weeks before the War, to be precise) to Bad Nauheim for treatment for heart trouble but had to return after having completed but two weeks' of his 6 weeks' cure [...] the little benefit that had accrued from the two weeks' cure was entirely annulled by the turmoil and worry of his perfectly appalling return journey [...] [65, 65v]

Sorabji once referred to his father, with evident pride, as "the worst human man in Bombay";[29] but he denied that his father left him a rich man when he died in 1932:

> He did nothing of the sort. His Indian whore and a set of rascally Indian lawyers rooked me and my beloved mother of what should have been ours [...][30]

37

[15 September] [¶] I will now draw to a close with a quotation from Sabanéiev. [...] There are many instances such as this of notes outside the keyboard compass and often as much as a 6th outside. [67v, 68]

Sorabji's quoted piano music of Leonid Sabaneev (1881–1968) includes two Gs immediately below the normal low A. It is natural to suppose that Sabaneev was writing for the eight-octave Bösendorfer Imperial Grand, the lowest note of which is C below the usual A. Sorabji eventually wrote for the Imperial Grand, possibly influenced by Sabaneev's example.

---

[29]Television, 11 June 1977.
{Sorabji appeared to be saying "the worst man" and "the worst human being" at the same time.}

> I'm a half-Sicilian you know ... and much more than that temperamentally and psychologically. Much more my beloved mother's son than my father's though <u>he</u> was very like a Sicilian in temperament <u>and</u> temper ... and even looked like one ...
> (Kaikhosru Sorabji: Letter to Kenneth Derus, 21 August 1977.)

[30]Kaikhosru Sorabji: Letter to Kenneth Derus, 4 June 1983.
{His father appears to have married bigamously; after his death Sorabji had to travel to India to try to straighten things out. What money Sorabji and his mother received from his father after his death came not from any inheritance but from a trust fund established in 1914. According to Sorabji, the inheritance went to the bastard son of his father's "Indian whore"'s sister. After his father's death Sorabji referred to him more than once as "late and wholly unlamented".}

H12. London, 27 December 1914

38

[¶] With infinite difficulty and after promenading Maida Vale from end to end, asking 4 policemen and 6 postmen I discovered Southwold Mansions, which — wretch! — you carefully omitted to tell me were half a mile from Maida Vale and left with the Porter at 32. a parcel for you containing "Blast." [69]

Blast I — Wyndham Lewis's "puce monster" — was published near the end of June 1914. Nestled among Lewis's vorticist manifestos and art are contributions by Ford Madox Ford, Rebecca West, Ezra Pound, Henri Gaudier-Brzeska, and Jacob Epstein.

H13. London, 11 January 1915

39

I should be only too pleased to write articles about Louis Aubert, Charles Koechlin and Albert Roussel [...] If you would care to entertain the idea, I might try my hand at a short article on Sabaneiev [...] I have only written an article once or twice before and am rather afraid it would not meet with your approval! [71, 71v]

Aubert (1877–1968), Koechlin (1867–1950), and Roussel (1869–1937) were French composers.

40

I am quite convinced that before long we shall witness the introduction of instruments with a smaller division of the octave than the semitone[,] say 22 notes to the octave as the Hindûs have. Everything points to it. [...] The stupendous revolution that will then take place will only be comparable to the <E>ffect of the revolution caused by the establishment of your present Occidental equal temperament. It will of course postulate a finer aural sense. More than the cycle of 53 to the octave however <it> is impossible and is likely to be for thousands of years impossible for the human ear to distinguish. Helmholtz maintains that with a little practise it is perfectly easy to distinguish the various degrees of the 53 note octave. Unfortunately it is not practicable as yet owing to the impossibility of maintaining such small intervals accurately tuned. However I don't see why we shouldn't at once have the 31 or 22 note octave. String players would not be very much bothered by it while the wind instruments could give their natural series without any appreciable difference between them and the strings being observable.³¹ [74, 74v]

41

[+¶] I wonder if a piano on the principle of the resonophon[e] bell is a practical possibility? You know this do you not? A long plate of Bronze is fixed above a resonating chamber of bronze, a <u>circular tube</u>. The tone is of the utmost depth[,] richness, beauty and power. The modern pianoforte, splendid instrument that it is, is not quite all that is wanted especially against a great orchestra. [74v, 75]

The resonophone was a bass glockenspiel. Hawkes and Son built it for Percy Grainger, who used it for the first time in Bournemouth in February 1914, in his orchestral arrangement of *Molly on the Shore*.

H14. London, 24 January 1915

42

[¶] Herewith enclosed is an attempt — to be greeted by you & your fellow conspirators with howls of derision — at a bit of scribble about Louis Aubert. I told you what to expect so you will only have yourself to thank. [76]

H15. London, 2 March 1915

43

[¶] The <u>possibilities</u> of the pianola are tremendous. They are as yet, however[,] possibilities only; and anyone who tries to conceal that is only committing a piece of self-deception. [¶] Now the <u>Welte-Mignon</u> is really a marvel. When the ordinary foot controlled or driven pianola attains <u>that</u> stage then it will really be something great. [80]

> One had thought and hoped at one time that the pianola had ended the age of the Horowitz type ... and I once heard [...] Reginald Reynolds [...] produce <u>marvellous performances</u> from a pianola [...]

---

³¹{Sorabji had been reading Hermann Helmholtz's *On the Sensations of Tone*, as indicated in H8. He nonetheless underestimated the problems of these alternate tunings for musical instruments. His interest in these matters led to no theoretical or compositional results.}

As that ghastly female Dietrich might have said but didn't ... "Where have all the pianolas gone?"[32]

44

[¶] I have no intention of endorsing your statement that there are no female English singers whatever. This is merely a silly exaggeration and quite unworthy of you as a profound and discerning critic. [... ¶] My mother who is anything but a lover of English singing or singers and herself a competent authority having for long been the pupil of delle Sedie — one of the very greatest of singing masters — has heard the "Ring" about a dozen times in London[,] 11 times with all the famous Continental exponents of that work participating and once with English singers, and assures me that never was it so finely or so beautifully done. The music was really sung, not barked, spluttered and coughed à la Bayreuth. [*81, 82, 83, 84*]

Enrico delle Sedie (1822–1907): the Italian baritone and singing teacher.

H16. London, March 1915

45

The remarkable feature of Delius' music is that it sounds glorious even on the monochrome piano — and let me tell you that in my opinion, that is the supreme test of orchestral music — its sounding well in a piano arrangement. By skilful orchestration an empty commonplace can be made to sound quite interesting. [*91, 91v*]

46

[¶] I hope some day to give you in my poor way a feeble presentation of the new works of Scriabin. Opp. 71. 72. 73. 74. [*91v*]

H17. London, 12 May 1915

47

[¶] You will doubtless in your own forceful and vigorous parlance think me a "bloody fool," but do you remember what you said to me the other day

---

[32]Kaikhosru Sorabji: Letter to Kenneth Derus, 16 October 1978. Reynolds was a pianola operator for the Aeolian Hall. By March 1916, Heseltine was planning a Pianola Society.

about chucking the "Daily Mail" at some future time? You asked me if I would care to take it on. I refused at the time, but have pondered since that at any rate it would be something as a start. [... ¶] But seriously, if I were you, I don't think I should "chuck it." At any rate it is safe and secure. It enables you to go to a quantity of concerts and hear heaps of music gratis, and you need have no feelings of shame or pricks of conscience in writing your notices for it [...] in order to make money out of the most thoroughly sordid mercenary rag that ever issued from a printing press. [94, 95v]

Heseltine wrote approximately 30 articles for the *Daily Mail*, from February to June 1915.

H18. London, 24 August 1915

48

I have also been reading some extremely absorbing pamphlets published by the I[ndependent] L[abour] P[arty]. I have got all the most interesting concerning the manufacture of the war by the various groups of blackguards who "govern" the wretched peoples of Europe. The sight of thousands of young men going off to sacrifice their lives, and inflict on others (when not receiving themselves) hideous suffering and mutilation fills me with horror: and to think that it is all for the sake of the skins and pockets of the bloody swines who "run" countries and peoples for their own profit! Oh! it is hideous! Horrible. [...] M. Suhrawardy would do well to pour the vials of his scorn on the "Allies" side of the case: their fight for the "sanctity of treaties" remembering <u>Oudh</u>, <u>Persia</u>, <u>Korea</u>, <u>Morocco</u> and <u>Turkey</u>; and their mission of bringing freedom help and all and every blessings to oppressed nations remembering <u>Ireland, India, Persia, Poland, Finland</u>, the <u>Ukraine, South Africa, Egypt</u> etc. etc. (oh and the <u>Congo</u>, the happy hunting ground of those dear and noble Belgians. I suppose you never read the Casement report? If you want your blood frozen with horror and to have sleepness nights for weeks <u>read</u>!) [98]

> Lawrence and Frieda have been here again, and they brought with them [...] an Indian, called Sarawadi [*sic*], who is at Oxford, and who is a friend of Heseltine. [...] He is extremely anti-English, but like all Indians quite foreign and remote, though he seems more substantial and self-confident than most of his race.[33]

---

[33] Ottoline Morrell: *Ottoline at Garsington: Memoirs of Lady Ottoline Morrell, 1915–1918* (New York: Knopf, 1975), p. 77.

Lawrence called the Pakistani politician Hasan Suhrawardy (1893–1963) his "pair of Indo-Persian eyes", and invited him to Florida.[34] It has been suggested that Suhrawardy had a role in the notorious "Café Royal incident" fictionalized to Heseltine's disadvantage in *Women in Love*.

49

[¶] The Concerto progresses with measured tread and slow [—] the first section is nearly complete!! [99]

> When I was 15, my old Master said to me, "Look," he said, "you ought to start composing." "Oh," but I said, "I never had a thought of doing any such sort of thing." Well he said, "Look here, forget all the things I've taught [you]." [...] So I thought, "All right," and I started writing sort of short cadences — you know, very much *à la* Ravel — and he said, "Oh, yes, yes, yes, you must go on," so the next thing was a concerto! I never had a lesson in orchestration in my life — and yet people say that I've got a marvellous command of orchestration [...][35]

The following scheme is used to refer to Sorabji's first five piano concertos:[36]

C1   Concerto, Op. 3 (April 1915 – June 1916).[37] Cf. 49, 50, 52, 56, 57, 70.

C2   A concerto begun by 6 July 1916 and finished by June 1917. Cf. 60, 65, 70. Dating this concerto has partly depended upon dating H28 and H29; for how this was done, see the notes that precede 64 and 66. A two-piano reduction exists (labelled "Concerto II", Op. 10, June–December 1917), but the original orchestral version is lost.

C3   Concerto for piano and chamber orchestra (June – August 1918), not mentioned in this collection of letters.

C4   "Concerto I" (September–December 1918), second version. The first version is lost or destroyed. Cf. 76, 84.

---

[34]D. H. Lawrence: Letter to Lady Cynthia Asquith, 3 December 1915, in *The Letters of D. H. Lawrence*, edited by Aldous Huxley (London: Heinemann, 1932), p. 284.

[35]Television, 11 June 1977.

[36]{For fuller information about them, see Chapter 5.}

[37]{Over many decades Sorabji often implied he was born around 1900. (See p. 59.) Given this subterfuge about his age, the above quotation suggests that his first concerto was indeed C1.}

C5   "Concerto II" (completed 1 August 1920). The *published* concerto. Cf. 84.

(The titles given here are simplifications.) It can be seen from this list that Sorabji was continually employed writing piano concertos between April 1915 and December 1917, as well as from June to December 1918. There is *no* evidence in the letters that he composed a piano concerto in 1913 or 1914, as has sometimes been claimed.

H19. London, 11 February 1916

50

[¶] It is exceedingly good and generous of you to suggest sending the Concerto [C1] to M. Delius and I feel I ought to accept. [...] I shall <u>dread</u> the verdict!!! And I <u>command</u> you that you on <u>no</u> account send it to M. Delius unless you can in all truth, honesty and sincerity, say it is worthy of such a man's attention. If you deceive me I will <u>never</u> forgive you!!! <u>La vérité! La Vérité</u>!! And remember whatever may hap — I <u>will</u> <u>not</u> be called a "<u>British</u>" composer. Heart mind body and soul I am Indian and would wish to be nothing else, though duly grateful for the soupçon of Spanish — "avec un peu d'Espagne autour"! Dear me what a very egotistic rigmarole nicht wahr? [*100v*]

Delius may never have seen the concerto. Sorabji later changed his mind about being Indian:

> Who was it who said the English were the silliest race in Europe after the Swedes? How long is it going to be before they get it into their goddam silly heads that a Parsi is not never was and never could be Indian. That those who were born within the confines of India are citizens of that beastly place is their misfortune and not their fault [...][38]

---

[38]Kaikhosru Sorabji: Letter to Kenneth Derus, 27 November 1980.
Sorabji had nothing good to say about Indian music, regardless of the level of his understanding:

> [...] the Indian musician has no power of getting any organic growth out of his material. He goes on with a maddening Stravinsky-like repetition of a small melodic fragment with the slightest variations at each repetition, which add rather than divert attention from his complete sterility of resource and lack of inventive faculty. The same vice of the mechanical repetition of one device is to be seen in Indian carving, the carver smothering the entire surface of whatever

[CONT'D]

Despite his high regard for Parsi culture, Sorabji had a low opinion of the Parsi community in Bombay:

> Our own people, the Parsis[,] who thank God are not "Indians" also appear to have gone pretty rotten ... and as far as I can discover no one ever reads an intelligent book [...], nor talks about anything but the doings of other members of the community, whom they have married[,] who not, what they are doing — it should be who — who has been born and who is dead — unhappily not the whole crew — ...[39]

51

[¶] I picked up recently a beautiful edition of Flaubert's "Tentation de Saint Antoine" <recently> containing all 3 versions. It is one of 100 copies of the "Édition definitive" exquisitely printed on "papier de Chine[.]" What a work! I mean to try and set it "un bel d[ì]." [101]

Heseltine's friend Cecil Gray (1895–1951) got the same idea at the same time. Unlike Sorabji, Gray did complete a massive setting of *The Temptation of Saint Anthony*, but only after several decades of thought and work.

Sorabji's seventh piano concerto ("Simorg-Anka", 1924) might be a setting of a single episode from Flaubert's work, rather than a generalized celebration of a mythological creature.

---

has to be covered with an infuriating pointless and formless repetition of the hackneyed lotus-motive [...]
(*The New Age*, vol. 52 (9 March 1933), p. 224.)

This lack of form-sense is the prevailing weakness of Indian art and culture in general. [...] No other great Eastern people suffers from it, neither Persia — whence came all the best in India's civilisation probably — nor Arabia, at any rate, the Arabia of the great days — nor China nor Japan.
(Ibid., pp. 223–24.)

{His opinion of the Hindu Indians eventually went lower: "That pestilent foul crew the Hindus (scum of the earth if ever there were!) [...] We Parsis have always loathed and detested them." (Kaikhosru Sorabji: Letter to Norman Gentieu, 7 September 1954.)}

[39]Kaikhosru Sorabji: Letter to Bernard van Dieren, n.d. (summer 1932 or 1933), written in Bombay.

H20. London, 23 February 1916

52

[¶] Now what about Bechstein's one morning for the Concerto [C1]? or rather I should say one afternoon? [...] You will be doubtless vexed with me to learn that under no circumstance will I allow it to be published in England. [...] any sort of English reputation has no attractions whatever for me except with such select souls as your own dear self, and such as you are in a proportion of perhaps 1/100,000. As I have already told you, we intend at some future date to take up our abode either in France or Italy. We suffocate, we choke here, especially my poor mother who loathes England with intense loathing and has for years desired nothing better than to escape. [*102, 103*]

Escape they did, but not for nearly 35 years, and then only to Dorset, where Sorabji had made many visits and lived for the last 38 years of his life.

Many years after writing H20, Sorabji offered Cecil Gray an explanation of why he stayed in England:

It is often said to me "well, since you detest us so much (sc. the English) why on earth do you live here?" ... To which I reply "detest? But who said so? Does it occur to you that in order to live among you, endure the worst climate, foulest cooking and worst manners in Europe (à peu près) I am robbed of half my income NOT ONE PENNY OF WHICH IS [...] DERIVED FROM THIS COUNTRY? Does it not occur to you that I must be very very fond of this country to sacrifice so much in order to live here? AND as I do the paying-through-the-nose for that dubious privilege does it also not occur to you that I am entitled to speak my mind occasionally as to the quality of my purchase???"[40]

53

[¶] "The Rainbow" is a <u>wonderful</u> work. It has one supreme fault. That style, that mode of expression cries out for the French language. The author himself seems to have felt that unconsciously. The book is full of idioms with a decidedly Gallic flavour and the turns of many phrases are thoroughly Gallic [... ¶] The suppression of this work is a monstrous absurdity. [...] All, and the worst that can be said of such an action is <u>how English</u>! [*103, 102v*]

Heseltine was staying with D. H. Lawrence at the time.

---

[40]Kaikhosru Sorabji: Letter to Cecil Gray, 15 April 1944, British Library ms. add. 57786 [75].

224 The Prose

H23. London, 21 April 1916

54

[¶] Yes I was at the Goossens concert. Who the Devil told you I was upstairs and what did they mean by doing so? Is one never to slip in anywhere unnoticed??? I know you will think me a perfect pig for not waiting but I loathe the crowd who come surging out so much that I go to any lengths to avoid them. I am a silly fool no doubt — but I am what I am voilà tout. [*106*]

H24. London, 3 May 1916

55

[¶] You did not say who disclosed my presence at the Aeolian Hall the other night????? Who was it???? Mr. Blom swears it was not he. [*112v*]

Eric Blom (1888–1959): the writer on music, editor of the fifth edition of *Grove's Dictionary of Music and Musicians*. (Cf. 54. Works by "that amazing genius" [*106v*] Eugène Goossens (1893–1962) had been performed.)

H25. London, 31 May 1916

56

Will you let me dedicate the Concerto [C1] to you instead of the group of French songs? [...] Please <u>do</u> let me do this there's a good soul. I shall be very upset and hurt if you refuse!!! Madre mia agrees that I am quite right in asking this. I await your reply with violent impatience. [*113, 113v*]

C1 *is* dedicated to Heseltine. What the group of songs might be is unknown. H22 [*105*] contains the final chord from Op. 2, No. 3: Sorabji's first vocalise, completed on 23 March 1916. (The date written on H22 (23 March 1917) in an unknown hand is incorrect.)

H26. London, 6 July 1916

57

[¶] I am going to pay Mr. Scherek a visit shortly to talk about the Concerto [C1]. [¶] Of course if I cannot secure the Copyright for all countries I shall not risk having it done [...] I suppose I had better make a fresh 2 piano 4 hand version, as the one you have does not correspond with the full score as I have told you. [... ¶] It would be very nice, if — later on — the Orchestrelle Co. thought it worth their while — they would take the rights of reproduction for Mechanical instruments! But no such luck. If such a thing did happen, <I>t would I suppose have no effect on the subsequent disposal of Copyright to a publisher? All these things have to be made sure of, and as I am quite a novice it behooveth me to go warily. [114]

No two-piano or other reduction, fresh or not, has been found. Sorabji eventually had a number of works published in which he retained the copyright (but not this concerto).

58

[+¶] Yes, I think I castigated Hugh Arthur [Scott] quite nicely: you remarked his frenzied wrigglings????[41] [114, 114v]

[...] Mr. Scott is evidently one of those people to whom a melody is — well — *not* a melody if it is other than strictly diatonic. He speaks a great deal about melodies, tunes, and themes without clearly defining what he means by any of them. The term *melody* he apparently restricts in a manner not in the least warranted. How, one would like to know, would Mr. Scott classify the following Indian fragment [...] This typical specimen of our vocal melody certainly does not fit in with Mr. Scott's "tunes which everybody can get hold of," nor has it the smallest feature in common with anything to be found in Bach, Mozart, Beethoven, Schumann, Schubert, Chopin, &c. It is therefore not a melody according to Mr. Scott!

What you and your readers will observe in the quotation above is its very striking affinity with many a theme from ultra-modern Occidental music — a fact of the very highest significance.[42]

59

[+] I have just finished a second vocalise and have started the music-drama "Medea". [114v]

Sorabji abandoned *Medea* fairly quickly.[43] There is no trace of a manuscript of either it or the second vocalise.

---

[41] Hugh Arthur Scott: "The Melodic Poverty of Modern Music", in *The Musical Times*, vol. 57 (1 June 1916), pp. 276–79.
[42] Kaikhosru Sorabji: Letter to the Editor, in *The Musical Times*, vol. 57 (1 July 1916), p. 332. Cf. 62.
[43] Kaikhosru Sorabji: Letter to Kenneth Derus, 5 September 1983.

60

[+¶] In the meanwhile, there seetheth at the bottom of the cauldron of my mind the plan of Concerto 2 [C2]!!!!! But this is as yet quite nebulous and vague: — [See p. 227.] [¶] This is how it will commence I think. It is in my usual mood of ungovernable violence as you will remark from the above fragment! [*114v*]

The music in this letter resembles closely the opening of the solo piano in the only extant version of C2, a two-piano reduction.

H27. London, 27 August 1916

61

[¶] I think it would be best to keep the affair private or semiprivate, that is, not announce it widely but canvas as it were for subscriptions among a chosen circle and people whom the scheme is likely to appeal to [...] a little introductory lecture [...] helps break down the absurd barrier between the audience and the artists, which however justifiable it may be in the case of such a rabble as form the average Queen's Hall Audience — and the farther apart the artists keep from that sort of "canaille" the better — is quite out of place in the case of an intimate affair such as that which you are proposing. [*115, 116*]

Heseltine was in Gloucestershire in August, engaged in affairs of an altogether different sort:

> [...] if one wishes to avoid arousing "rustic curiosity" so very much, a good plan is to refrain from riding a motor-bicycle through the village streets at midnight at a speed of about sixty miles an hour, stark naked, and from having in the house attractive young persons of the opposite sex who could not, even on the most charitable assumption, be considered to be the lawful and wedded wives of any of the inmates — inmates, I think, is the right word [...][44]

It is probable that the concert being planned was Bernard van Dieren's historic one. That concert took place six months after Sorabji wrote H27. (See 66 and the note that follows 67.)

---

[44]Cecil Gray: *Peter Warlock*, p. 103.

The planned opening of "Concerto 2", from H26 [114v]
(see previous page)

62

[¶] I forgot to tell you this morning that I had heard from the Mc<n>aught creature who now wants to publish my letter versus Colleywobbles and Great Scott in an abbreviated expurgated form.[45] I have consented solely on <u>2</u> conditions, that a footnote be appended indicating that the letter as published is greatly abbreviated <u>and</u> that the unexpurgated original <u>be either sent or shewn</u> to Colleywobbles and Great Scott, who, he informs me are "valued contributors", precisely for what reasons is not forthcoming [... ¶]

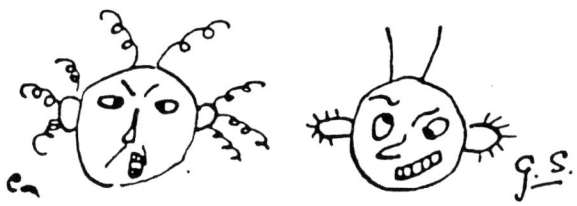

Futurist Impressions of the states of mind of Colleywobbles and Great Scott after a reading of the Epistle. [*116, 117v*]

Henry Cope Colles (1879–1943) wrote books about music. William Gray McNaught (1849–1918) was editor of *The Musical Times*.

> That a melody is not a melody because any Tom, Dick, or Harry cannot grasp it as such, I repudiate. The right of the melodies of practically all your great European masters to be considered as such was denied by some of their contemporaries. [...] Mr. Colles considers my Indian fragment somewhat irrelevant. I wonder why. Mr. Scott appears to postulate a melody among other things as "a tune which everybody can get hold of," and, so far as I can see, would deny that title to one which does not conform to his condition. My quotation is typical of Indian vocal melody of a simple form, but does not conform to this condition. Where is the irrelevancy! If a melody is a melody in one place, it can scarcely cease to be so somewhere else![46]

---

[45]H. C. Colles: "Melody and Modern Music", in *The Musical Times*, vol. 57 (1 August 1916), pp. 360–62 (a reply to Sorabji's July attack on Hugh Arthur Scott).
Hugh Arthur Scott: "The Melodic Poverty of Modern Music".
[46]Kaikhosru Sorabji: Letter to the Editor, in *The Musical Times*, vol. 57 (1 September 1916), p. 410. "Lack of space compels us to abbreviate the much longer letter sent by Mr. Sorabji. — ED., *M.T.*"

63

[¶] Do you think my interpretations of Scriabine are good? It is so difficult to tell oneself, when one is playing. For although as far as I am concerned I put my <u>whole heart and soul</u> into them and I feel every note as few people can, yet I am by no means certain that I convey those feelings to my "auditoire". Of course I know that I could do them <u>ever</u> so much better were I not so hampered technically and physically, and I feel pretty certain that if I had the requisite technique I could interpret them probably as finely as any one living. It is cruel and diabolically tantalizing to find one's powers of expression gagged and throttled by defective media and sometimes a great disgust seizes me, and I feel I will never play another note!! [*117*]

> I have never made any pretension about being a pianist. I get over the ground in my own work. All I do or can is to give a general <u>coup d'oeil</u> of it [...][47]

H28. [London, June or earlier 1917]

The first three pages of this letter are missing, but the references to Skryabin, Ravel, and Cyril Scott place it immediately prior to H29, which has related references.

64

[¶] It is the greatness of Scriabine and Ravel that they have such, so to say, super human emotions and can express them, Scriabine especially — with such amazing force and power. Only those with a considerable degree of inner vision and marked supernormal receptiveness can hope to grasp and sense such music, which is the reason that both these composers appeal so powerfully to Indians, in whom by right of birth these qualities are inherent to a degree far beyond that of humanity in the rest of the world [... ¶] It is odd that Cyril Scott, profound and sincere occultist as he truly is has no power of musical utterance in that respect. [*140, 140v*]

65

[¶] Will you come one day to Bechstein's and hear the Sonata and parts of the new Concerto? I should love to hear what you think of them. You may damn them utterly but I shall not mind. I have said what I wanted and what I felt in my own way and am satisfied — as for the others, if they

---

[47] Kaikhosru Sorabji: Letter to Kenneth Derus, 26 January 1983. Cf. 87. {Also pp. 33 and 79–83.}

don't like what I say or my way of saying it be damned to them, it is no business of theirs!! [*140v, 141*]

The concerto is C2.

This is the only reference in the letters to the piano sonata predating the published Sonata I (itself completed on 5 August 1919). The "pre-first" sonata has been mentioned elsewhere at least once:

> [Sorabji] only started composing in 1915, and all works prior to 1918 he has suppressed. These compositions included a piano concerto, a sonata, several piano pieces, an orchestral work, and a couple of dozen songs. They were interesting, but not significant, those that I have seen being strongly reminiscent of the contemporary French school and more particularly Debussy.[48]

H29. [London, June 1917]

This letter has an incorrect date "March 1915" not in Sorabji's hand (reflecting the letter's position in the collection immediately after one of March 1915 which *is* dated in Sorabji's hand). H29 can be conclusively dated by virtue of the magazine references in 67 and 68. (Sorabji wrote five letters which mention Delius to the *Musical Standard* in 1917, but only one contains a reproof of the kind described in 68.)

66

Many thanks for music and "Review." Although as you know I violently disagree with you on many points it is such a relief to read something by one who does know what he is talking about. [...] It was an absolutely false step on your part to issue tickets to the critics. The very conditions make what they say worthless. You should never have deigned to notice their existence. Having done so you might have explained your attitude in the N[ew] A[ge]. [*92*]

Bernard van Dieren (1887–1936) conducted his Overture and *Diaphony* on 20 February 1917 in Wigmore Hall. The event was aggressively promoted by Heseltine and Cecil Gray — and notices were largely negative, at least partly as a consequence of the promotion itself. Heseltine's reply to the concert's critics appeared in *The Palatine Review*'s March issue:

---

[48]Christopher à Becket Williams: "The Music of Kaikhosru Sorabji", in *The Sackbut,* vol. 4 (June 1924), p. 315.

The illustrious composer of "I know of two bright eyes" (not to mention "Ma curley headed babbie") expressed, in "The Observer," great indignation that the authors of the programme, after several months' study of the difficult music to be performed, should so far impugn the infallibility of first impressions as to say a few words about [V]an Dieren and his relation to his contemporaries. The "Musikalisher Kritik" [sic] of the "Daily News" looked to the programme for guidance but was only thereby the more perplexed: while his "colleague" of "The Star" acknowledged his indebtedness to the programme for what little he did manage to write of the bewildering music.[49]

67

[+] I have sent a letter partly supporting you against the cretinous F[rederick H.] E[vans] mentioning a few facts about you which should have an "effet écrasant" on the microbe. [92]

Heseltine had published an article in *The New Age*, and Frederick H. Evans (1853–1943) had written a letter to the editor to complain.

(Between 8 March and 28 June 1917, 14 letters and four articles by or about Sorabji, Heseltine, Gray, Van Dieren, and the sculptor Jacob Epstein appeared in twelve issues of *The New Age*. Only Sorabji's contributions are too inoffensive to be of much interest.)[50]

68

[+] You might also keep your eyes on the M[usical] Standard for next week. I am administering reproof to an individual who has the effrontery to claim Delius as a British composer. [92]

> Delius, as everyone knows, is not of British *race* [...] and it is [...] absurd to claim him as such [...] Almost as absurd as the remark people have made to me — a remark meant, let us hope, to be amiable and flattering! — "Oh! yes, Mr. Sorabji, Coleridge-Taylor was

---

[49]Fred Tomlinson (quoting Philip Heseltine): *Warlock and Van Dieren* (London: Thames Publishing, 1978), p. 13.

[50]Alfred Stieglitz called Evans the best architectural photographer in the world. Evans was also an inventor of pianola mechanisms; Sorabji praised one of his instruments in 1926. Alvin Langdon Coburn and Evans were old friends — and equally enthusiastic about pianolas — but Evans nevertheless ridiculed Coburn's Lewis-inspired vortographs (the first totally abstract photographs ever created) at around the same time he was attacking Heseltine.

Sorabji in 1918 (photo by Alvin Langdon Coburn)

one of your people too, wasn't he?" I am too polite to record my muttered remarks.⁵¹

69

No. I did not mean [Cyril Scott] was an occultist of the calibre of our very good friend Meredith Starr and I ought not to have made use of words giving that impression. That he is a deeply sincere one and that it means much to him I believe, from what he said to me. [*92v*]

At the time Sorabji knew him, Starr (1890–?) was preoccupied with occult and religious matters:

> There are some herb-eating occultists, a Meredith Starr and a Lady Mary ditto: she is a half-caste, daughter of the Earl of Stamford. They fast, or eat nettles: they descend naked into old mine-shafts, and there meditate for hours and hours, upon their own transcendent infinitude: they descend on us like a swarm of locusts, and devour all the food on the shelf or board: they even gave a concert, and made the most dreadful fools of themselves in St Ives[.]⁵²

He was a sort of theosophist: a bit of a humbug I think!⁵³

70

Yes the Personal Equation is <u>Everything</u>. <t>he rest is nothing. For myself, my own work means to me just this, <u>the expression of my own emotions and individuality as I will, with all the force sincerity and conviction at my command</u>. I don't know if it is what is called "swelled head" but I find my own work satisfies me more completely than anyone elses. Should this be so I wonder? Yes I think it should. It is a sort of guarantee as it were! [¶] I don't know what you will think of Concerto II. I am bursting to play it to you. I think it is <u>miles</u> beyond I. The orchestra is as "megalomaniac" as

---

⁵¹Kaikhosru Sorabji: Letter to the Editor, in *The Musical Standard*, 30 June 1917, p. 439. Coleridge-Taylor's father was African. Sorabji's target, Christopher à Becket Williams, later became a good friend and the dedicatee of *Le jardin parfumé*. Cf. footnote 48.

⁵²D. H. Lawrence: Letter to Lady Cynthia Asquith, 3 September 1917, in *The Collected Letters of D. H. Lawrence*, edited by Harry T. Moore (New York: Viking, 1962), p. 523. Lawrence was writing from Tregerthen, about two months before he was expelled from Cornwall.

⁵³Kaikhosru Sorabji: Letter to Kenneth Derus, n.d. (mid-September 1984).

Starr was also, unfortunately, a poet: "O oft-kissed lips and soul-remembered eyes, / O stricken heart — the old love never dies!" (Meredith Starr: in *Equinox*, March 1912, p. 291. *Equinox* was Aleister Crowley's publication; cf. 88.)

Later in life, Starr became a psychotherapist.

234 The Prose

before with the addition of <u>Organ</u> a <u>4th Trombone</u> a <u>picc. Clarinet</u> a <u>Bass Oboe</u> (!!) and <u>Caisse Claire</u>[,] but it is used very sparingly. [*93, 93v*]

See the list after 49. Sorabji is describing C2 (for which only a two-piano reduction exists) and comparing it to C1.

71

[¶] Thanks for the "Kaikhusru". No more D. K. please[.] K only please. I abandon D to the <u>outer</u> darkness.⁵⁴ [*93v*]

H30. London, 26 January 1920

72

[¶] You poor soul! Ten thousand sympathies is all I can offer you, but take them with all my heart! [... ¶] Shiva open his eye of wrath on them who mar your peace, the Rakshasas rend their astral bodies and burn them with monstrous unquenchable desires in Kama-loca: is the prayer of the ever faithful and affectionate [¶] Hircus Olens. [*118, 118v*]

I <u>can</u> and <u>do</u> feel very very deeply for my friends ... sentimental? I don't care a bloody damn if it is ...⁵⁵

You see, I'm <u>not</u> like Wagner, who thought his friends existed only or chiefly for his personal benefit ...⁵⁶

"Hircus Olens" (Redolent Goat)⁵⁷ is an allusion to an adopted name of Sorabji's, used by him over a period of seven years in the letters: ""<u>Gote</u><.> a friend has nicknamed me" [*89*]. *Gote* appears in H15, H16, H18, H24, H25, H27, H28, H31, H32, and H34 to H38. H33 closes with "Hircus hoc tuus S[ü]ffelein" (This your goat, the tipsy one).⁵⁸

---

⁵⁴{See p. 25 for Sorabji's later elucidation of his names.}
⁵⁵Kaikhosru Sorabji: Letter to Kenneth Derus, 30 December 1977.
⁵⁶Kaikhosru Sorabji: Letter to Kenneth Derus, 23 October 1980.
⁵⁷*Smelly* is probably not meant! *Olens* is also *fragrant*. "[...] the Parsî is the purest and cleanest living individual on the face of the earth [...]" [*33v*].
⁵⁸{Sorabji has piled his grammatical genders together: the first and third words are masculine, the second and fourth neuter.}

73

[...] now that you, my sole intermediary in the affair of the "Nightmare" of our friend Robert the Devil or Nikola, are gone, how shall I hear what happens in that quarter: & what about the "<u>music</u>" thereof? Have you it safely? [*118v*]

> [...] Rider by Night was a play by — if I recall — Robert Nichols and I wrote some so-called incidental (<u>accidental</u>) music for it [...] It was of no importance at all.[59]

> [Heseltine] urged on me that I should write librettos for Sorabji and for Bernard van Dieren, each of whom happened to need a libretto in a hurry [...] My librettos for *The Rider by Night* and *The Tailor* were (in Hollywood studio slang) "so gosh-awful they was jus' t'rrible." There was, I hold, a genuine idea in each, but Philip, in tyrannic mood, only allowed me about a week (if that) for the first and something less than a fortnight for the second.[60]

74

[+] And dare I hope for the long promised article on my own unworthy self in the not too distant future? [*118v*]

Two and a half years later Sorabji provided information for Heseltine's article. (See 93.) This is part of what Heseltine published:

> It is of interest to note that [Sorabji's compositions] are written straight down in fair copy — in the case of the orch[estral] works, in full score. No sketches are made, nor is even the figuration of the piano music determined at the keyboard. One is reminded of Blake's methods in composing the *Prophetic Books;* but these, we are told, were dictated by angels. If we are to say the same of S[orabji]'s music we must use the word in its literal sense of "messenger" without its usual connotation of celestial origin and moral intent.[61]

(See the note that follows 92.)

---

[59]Kaikhosru Sorabji: Letter to Kenneth Derus, 19 August 1978.

[60]Robert Nichols (1893–1944), the English writer: in *Peter Warlock*, by Cecil Gray, p. 77.

[61]Philip Heseltine: "Sorabji, Kaikhosru", in *A Dictionary of Modern Music and Musicians*, edited by A. Eaglefield-Hull (London: J. M. Dent, 1924), p. 469. Heseltine also wrote an article about Sorabji for the *Weekly Westminster Gazette* (18 August 1923).

H31. Bournemouth, 21 August 1920

75

We must talk about the "Sackbut" concert on which I have set my heart. [119]

The second Sackbut concert, 2 November 1920, at which Sorabji premiered Sonata I in his first public performance.[62] No reviews of the concert have been discovered.

76

Have made up my mind to get the Concerto cut and am going to see the Aeolian Co. as soon as I get back about it[.] [120]

Presumably C4. Late in his life Sorabji did not remember this plan to make a piano roll of a concerto.

77

[+¶] Sonata II. grows steadily[:] 7 pages of the 49 completed!! Ein staunendes [W]erk Schätzlein![63] [120]

The first indication that Sorabji often decided on the length of his works before completing them. Sonata II was finished on 24 December 1920. The manuscript *is* 49 pages long.[64]

H32. London, 8 November 1921

78

[¶] Poor [V]an Dieren is very very bad again ... I went up and saw him on Saturday and it is really heartbreaking: in a week or two he has lost all that he had gained and looks almost as bad as ever ... but still I hope, although one hardly dares to think it, I may have been the instrument of procuring him, indirectly[,] alleviation from his sufferings. [121]

> A martyr in the latter years of his prematurely shortened life [...] to renal calculi and to agonising physical suffering — his case was

---

[62]Cf. *The Sackbut*, vol. 1 (September 1920), p. 231.

[63]Sorabji's German is not right: *erstaunendes*, not *staunendes*. He means "An astonishing work, darling!"

[64]{Cf. 84. The number of pages itself is also significant: see pp. 63–65.}

"Yes! I will remember to sniff in the wood",
from H31 [*119v, 120*] (see previous page)

almost a clinical *locus classicus,* and he must have endured a sum total of pain that appals the mind — [Van Dieren's] astounding fortitude was on a par with the greatness of his personality as a whole. [...] There were [...] vile rumours sedulously propagated by certain English "musicians" (!) [...] because, to give him a short respite from pain such as not one in a million could endure and remain sane, his doctor was compelled to give him an occasional morphia injection, the commonplace of every hospital and infirmary ward anywhere in the world.[65]

79

It's just like the Debussy "period" some 1½ decades ago: when anyone who used a couple of consecutive triads, fifths or sevenths was sure to have "Debussy" shrieked at him. They are doing it to me over <u>Sonata I.</u> Everything now — except the Concertos [—] is in the Press or going to be very soon. I'm going to Vienna in a few weeks. Whom shall I descend on there? One wants a few hints of that kind. The Symphony goes on well — p. <u>164</u>. now: but there still remain the Chorus and Organ parts to do which will occupy a small subsidiary score apart from the main one. [*121v*]

Symphony (No. 1) for Piano, Large Orchestra, Chorus, and Organ, completed in 1922. (See 84.)

Vienna-related hints were also solicited from Cecil Gray, who wrote to Heseltine a few weeks later:

Ah, yes. I am giving Sorabji an introduction to Her[t]zka — how does one address the old bird [...] Let me know <u>by return</u> as The Gote leaves very shortly. I always feel that if I address people wrongly or use the wrong formula, nothing happens, as in magic [...]

    Kaik[h]osru played to me his 2nd sonata last Sunday & occasioned me acute distress. Being one of them stoics I showed no sign of what I was undergoing.[66]

Emil Hertzka (1869–1932) was the director of Universal Edition.

80

[+] I had Willie Walton and Sachie Sitwell here the other afternoon and dosed them with Sonata II. which they <u>said</u> impressed them enormously. I think it is a good work — much better than no. I. [¶] Did I tell you that the first 3 month's sales of the Sonata [Sonata I] produced £14.10? Rather astonishing. <u>44</u> copies! [*121v*]

---

[65] Kaikhosru Sorabji: *Mi contra fa*, pp. 149, 153.
[66] Cecil Gray: Letter to Philip Heseltine, dated "Dec. 1921" but not in Gray's hand, British Library ms. add. 57962 [*23*].

The English writer Sacheverell Sitwell (1897–1988) remembered meeting Sorabji in 1918:

> I formed an instant liking for him, and I think we really became great friends. I used to often go and see him, have tea with him — and his mother I remember well too. They lived in Clarence Gate Gardens, in Marylebone [London], in the same block of flats as T. S. Eliot, who was also a friend of mine, and I think that I combined visits to both on the same day sometimes. [...] [Sorabji and his mother] seemed very comfortably well off, [...] and they lived in this very nice comfortable flat. [...] I must say this with reverence because I'm sure it had a history attached, but I do seem to remember there was a stuffed pug dog under the piano [...][67]

> It was in the days of Busoni's wonderful and inspiring piano recitals in London [...] at this time I had many talks with Kaikhosru[,] who greatly revered Busoni [...] Kaikhosru will then have been in his late twenties, and a most vital, amusing and energizing influence in all he said or wrote [...] On those far off days I had the experience on three or four occasions of hearing Kaikhosru play [...] I have another memory of meeting him and his mother on the long staircase up to the Aracoeli church in Rome. I go there now on occasion and never pass below the church without thinking of that.[68]

81

Willie Walton who told me he was at the rehearsal this morning said that the <u>whole</u> time over 4 hours was taken up with the macro-cosmohydrocep[h]alic Universe of Holst. Willie and S[acheverell Sitwell] promenaded the Corridor doubled up with laughter [...] Surely a feebler production never diarrh<a>e<o>aed from the pen of [a] British composer??? I had also at that concert an interesting lesson in bacteriology[. T]wo creations of God — I suppose — came and buttonholed Willie under my nose in a manner that made one think of a very ill-trained bad mannered charwoman laying dishes in front of one — he afterwards told me that they were Herbert Howells whose music gives me pains in my Bowells and Armstrong Gibbs. [¶] Howells, I hear in concert with a few other lewd fellows of the baser sort have conspired together to do me the honour of publicly expressing their execration of me. This is quite the most encouraging thing I have heard for a long time and still further convinces me — if that were necessary — of my own value. [*122, 122v*]

---

[67]Television, 11 June 1977.
[68]Sacheverell Sitwell: "Kaikhosru Sorabji", in program notes for the concert by Yonty Solomon on 7 December 1976 in Wigmore Hall, p. 7.
    See *Musical Chairs: or, Between Two Stools*, by Cecil Gray (London: Home and Van Thal, 1948), p. 285 for an appropriate, Heseltine-related memoir of William Walton (1902–83) in 1918.

Gustav Holst (1874–1934), Herbert Howells (1892–1983), and Cecil Armstrong Gibbs (1889–1960).

H33. Vienna, 2 January 1922

82

[¶] I'm here as you see. I've met and played to Dr Wellecz who <u>appeared</u> greatly impressed and have also seen old Hertzka and his Kalmuck nephew alias Herr Doctor Kalmus<s> — who is seeing to all the arrangements of my little 5 oclock concert in the small hall of the Musik Vereins Gebäude on January 13th. I shall play the 2 sonatas ... it will last about an hour and a half in all and is by invitation only: I thus hope to rope in some of the most interesting people. Dr Wellecz has promised to act as turner over of pages. [*123*]

"Wellecz" was Egon Welle*s*z (1885–1974), the composer and musicologist. He did not turn pages and by 1983 Sorabji could not remember who did. Alfred Kalmus (1889–1972) was Hertzka's eventual successor at Universal Edition, and went on to champion Berio, Boulez, and Stockhausen.

83

[+] Schönberg has not answered nor acknowledged the copy of the Sonata I sent him. Alban Berg I have not got at yet but hope to do so through Dr. Wellecz. [*123, 123v*]

Sorabji did not meet Berg in Vienna, or at any later time.

> [Berg] told Erik [Chisholm] how much he was interested in my work — that was how Erik put it.[69]

84

[¶] Everything is now arranged[,] for all the big works are in the press: the Second Sonata is going and the 2nd Concerto [C5] ... There remains now only Concerto I [C4]. and the as yet incompleted Symphony the flames of

---

[69]Letter to Kenneth Derus, n.d. (late September 1983). Erik Chisholm (1904–65) was a Scottish composer and one of Sorabji's dearest friends. He arranged most of Sorabji's few public concerts, before leaving Glasgow for Cape Town.

{See pp. 298–311 for letters of Sorabji to Chisholm from 1929–30 about *Opus clavicembalisticum*.}

which have however risen as far as page 230 of the 300 allotted span. [*124v*]

The manuscript score of the Symphony (No. 1) *is* 300 pages long.

85

[+] I don't like Vienna: it is depressing drab and a ridiculously pretentious gimcrack city — the only tolerable part of it is of course the Innere Stadt where the shops are quite amusing. [...] worst of all is this bloody Mahler orgy. [...] Even the art shops have abominable etchings [...] based on the "Lied von der Erde"! [¶] Still Mahler is better than Arthur Piss and I suppose one ought not to be astonished that the Viennese musicians have a Mahler to play with when ours have a pen__[70] (I mean a Piss! pardon! ...) But still no one has yet thought of renaming Lyons Corner House Piss House — they <u>might</u> of course very appropriately and proceed to enthrone 22 effigies of Arthur and Leigh clasped in a loving embrace. "Righteousness and Piss have kissed each other" ... [*124v, 125, 125v*]

> [My dear mother] used to say, never forget people who are nice and kind to us, and with lightning glances we never forget those who are *not*.[71]

"Arthur Piss" is Arthur Bliss (1891–1975). "Leigh" is Leigh Henry (1889–1958), the conductor and author.

Writers tend to approach Sorabji as timidly as E. W. Lane approached the *Arabian Nights*. But bowdlerization obscures a glorious Sicilian heritage. Sorabji's outbursts are spontaneous and graceful. They contain no hint of the clumsy spitefulness that makes some of Schoenberg's letters so depressing. Then too, Sorabji's robust intolerance is explained and justified by physically alarming circumstances — in which bad or inadequate art can be deadly as well as distressing. (See the notes that follow 92 and 93, and especially footnotes 93 and 94.)

86

There is a flamboyant green whore in the hotel. The waiter on being questioned by my mother as to the status & identity of this baggage informed us with gusto that she was "une dame terrible": [...] that in a month she had brought nine different messieurs in with her. Business must <u>indeed</u> be bad if a French strumpet in Vienna can't catch more than 9 men in a <u>month</u>! [*126*]

---

[70]I.e. "penis".
[71]Television, 11 June 1977.

H34. London, 12 April 1922

87

[¶] I played the <u>2 Sonatas</u> only at 5 oclock on Friday Jan. 13 in the Kammersaal of the Musikvereinsgebäude. The audience was small — all by invitation <u>only</u> not a hundred people or any where near it but they were <u>such</u> an audience ... pupils of Schönberg and Dr. Wellecz ... old Hertzka and Co. including the Kalmuck Litmus his nephew ... this creature's mouth makes me think of a baby's bottom or a pan of chicken and ham sausages superimposed lengthwise — and everybody came swarming round me after expressing the utmost amazement and ébahissement first at the music then of my playing of it ... Dr Wellecz said ... "it is so difficult to us so new and strange, that you must give us time ... such things in music we have never before heard: it is an order of mind and feeling we have never realized to exist" ... through his bad English this is what he said. Another man Bechert said he had never heard or dreamt of either such music or such playing — Becker of W[aldheim-] E[berle] said I was a virtuoso of an order they had never heard ... that the things that happened were astounding ... breathtaking & so on ... and I find that echoes have reached London about it. [...] It appears my dear ... that <u>Holbrooke</u> yes <u>Joe</u>, holy Joe, has an enormous admiration for me [...] — this strains my credence as much as <u>can</u> be! [*127, 127v, 128*]

Joseph Holbrooke (1878–1958) was a flamboyant English composer and writer. Paul Bechert wrote the concert's only review:

PERSIAN COMPOSER-PIANIST BAFFLES.

It is with some reluctance that I refer to a recital given by a young Persian composer, Kaikhosru Sorabji, before a small circle of musical professionals. Mr. Sorabji, who lives in London, played his two piano sonatas, and frankness compels the statement that, at least on first hearing, they are absolutely beyond the grasp of ever so modern a hearer, who still expects from a composition such ancient things as form, rhythm and thematic or harmonic treatment of any kind. There seem to be some interesting oriental colorings in these sonatas, and a few of their passages "sound" beautifully, but the feeling one derives from them is, in short, that compared to Mr. Sorabji, Arnold Schönberg must be a tame reactionary. Withal, the impression Mr. Sorabji creates is that of a fully sincere personality, in whose madness there must be some sort of method. Just what that method implies, future generations may perhaps be able to discover.[72]

---

[72] Paul Bechert: "Persian Composer-Pianist Baffles", in *Musical Courier*, 2 March 1922, p. 7. Sorabji's scores were printed by the firm of Waldheim-Eberle.

88

[+¶] Crowley I missed in Cefal[ù] and in Paris but one of the priestesses said he was coming to London so I have written to him expressing my desire and yours to meet him when he <u>does</u> come. [128]

> I visited the creature at Heseltine's insistence in Cefalù (Sicily) and found there only two females ... who I was afterwards told were his trollops [...] Largely a figure of fun, largely a humbug and charlatan I felt then as a very young man and later on when I attained (if I ever <u>did</u>) more years of shall we say <u>more</u> discretion.[73]

Aleister Crowley (1875–1947), the occultist, wrote many books and professed magical powers. Today he is remembered with great enthusiasm by specialists in drug addiction and sexual perversion. His poetry is worse than Meredith Starr's.[74]

89

[+¶] The Symphony — the main score, is finished. There remain the <u>Chorus and Organ</u> parts to do, and Sonata 3. is more than half done and, I hope will overtop no[.] 2 as much as 2 does 1. I have planned out my work for the next few years and shall be kept pretty busy. [128]

90

[¶] <u>What</u> a climate after Palermo! Clumps of Maidenhair fern growing lustily and bigger than ever seen in hothouse here in <u>open air</u> there in <u>February</u>! And what crystalline clear and pure air: <u>and</u> those ineffable mosaics the Cap[p]ella Palatina I saw on a blazing sunny morning: it glowed like a gorgeous jewel. [¶] This is my 3rd visit to Italy and never have I marvelled at and admired that incomparable country more. [128v]

> [...] my four-times great grand uncle [was] Cardinal archbishop of Palermo about the first two decades of the last century ...[75]

---

[73]Kaikhosru Sorabji: Letter to Kenneth Derus, 23 January 1982.
[74]{See "The Beast Himself", by Colin Wilson, in his *The Occult* (St. Albans: Granada, 1979), pp. 457–91.}
[75]Kaikhosru Sorabji: Letter to Kenneth Derus, 11 March 1975.

H36. London, 19 June 1922

91

[¶] Robert Lorenz who is a dear creature and one that I like persuaded me to go to Allinson's studio and there play the 1st and 2nd Sonata in his Allinson's [...] Harvey Grace's and another man's hearing. [¶] Allinson says I do not sufficiently consider the "limitations of the human ear" — my leng<ht>, complexity and "lack of contrast" seem to upset him. Harvey Grace sighs for "diatonic discords" — like expecting a cat to have the penis of a paradoscure — otherwise quite sympathetic and reasonably intelligent. "The limitations of the human ear!" Why the bloody hell should I consider them when conscious of no such limitations in my own ear? Because one of the principles of <u>a certain form</u> of musical design is a continual alternation of contrasting sections why should I, who<,> exist in a realm entirely outside those principles[,] be controlled by them? Judge me if you like but I claim, and demand to be judged by the relation of my own work to its implied standards whatever they may be. That they are <u>not</u> those of 99 out of 100 composers ought to protect me from such singularly and irritatingly inept criticism. Again: "if you make your work of such monstrous difficulty no one can play it but the finest pianists." What if it is only for the "very finest pianists"? What if it is for no one at all but its creator? In the last resort there is the pianola. Says A. "you don't paint a picture to lock up in a cellar". Where is the analogy?? All the Sonatas are in process of publication or <u>will</u> be. The picture will be there for those who can bear to look upon it. "You are limiting your appeal so much it seems to me" — Is it not conceivable that in its very nature and essence this music <u>can</u>, and <u>must</u> only appeal to an extremely restricted audience? Supposing it is not good or meet that the mass should be able to hear it. Oh! the idleness of all this chatter as to what the artist should or should not do, resolving itself in the end into what others not fit mentally & spiritually to lick his arse would <u>like</u> him to do. [¶] I shall go on as I have begun; regarding no ones taste & prejudices or wishes on earth but my own. I should scarcely consult the Art critics on the question of what sort of a ... wife I should take unto myself were I of the breed that takes wives unto themselves the which praise be to God that I am not — still less shall I allow them to influence me in the infinitely more important matter of creating my monsters! [*133, 133v, 134, 134v, 135*]

Robert Lorenz (1891–1945) was a businessman who wrote intelligent articles about music. Sorabji dedicated *Around Music* to him in 1932. (The dedication — "you with your vehement and stentorian public protests" — is calmly factual. Lorenz liked to raise his voice at Queen's Hall concerts.) Adrian Allinson (1890–1964) was a painter, and a friend of Heseltine's. Harvey Grace (1874–1944) was by then editor of *The Musical Times*. He had already reviewed Sonata I, and would review Sonata II after its publication. Calling the former "probably the most difficult pianoforte work in existence", he suggested that "music of this type should be written for an automatic instrument" such as a player-piano.[76] He repeated this suggestion for Sonata II after despairing of getting anything out of its printed pages.[77]

The essence of Sorabji's powerful artistic credo may be found in something he published five years earlier:

> The artist, by the very fact that he is an artist, is on a higher evolutionary level than his fellow men. He sees things and feels that which is outside the spiritual or emotional purview of ordinary mankind. Small wonder that when he gives artistic expression to his experiences, people are puzzled and fail to understand him. It is as absurd and unjust to quarrel with him on that account as it would be to quarrel with a great mathematician because he could not make the theory of geometric progression intelligible to a person ignorant of the elementary principles of algebra.[78]

92

[+¶] The 3rd Sonata is finished — a gehenna like work of some hour and a quarter's duration [—] a piano symphony which I hope to have the joy of playing to my Phee at a not too distant date. [¶] The Beast Salvarsan [Crowley] is the dullest of dull dogs.[79] He talked like Ralph Waldo Trine & the Theosophical Society. It was most depressing. He wants however to hear me play and when I[']m finished with my Solstitial Fast which started last night Sunday at 6 and ends <u>next</u> Sunday at 6 P.M. he is coming to hear some of my demons. [¶] He had on a red poplin silk waistcoat with gold buttons and his face is sunburnt up to the hat-line, above it's lighter, making him look like a mask in a Chinese play. His face is that of a prosperous overfed fox-hunting tory squire — the unteachable in full pursuit of the unwearable. [*135, 135v, 136*]

---

[76]Harvey Grace, in *The Musical Times*, vol. 62 (1 November 1921), p. 781.

[77]Harvey Grace, in *The Musical Times*, vol. 65 (1 June 1924), p. 520.

[78]Kaikhosru Sorabji: Letter to the Editor, in *The Musical Standard*, 30 June 1917, p. 439.

[79]Crowley liked to call himself The Great Beast 666. Paul Ehrlich's antisyphilitic compound 606, discovered in 1909, was also known as Salvarsan.

> [...] in view of his sexual shall we call them "activities" I nicknamed him The Beast Salvarsan [...]
> (Kaikhosru Sorabji: Letter to Kenneth Derus, 23 January 1982.)

See also 93.
Ralph Waldo Trine (1866–1952) was an American writer on religion.

246 The Prose

> [...] they say I practise black magic [...][80]

Religion, morality, and the occult enter the personal equation of Sorabji's art in ways that are apt to be thoroughly confusing. For one thing, Sorabji was a man of profound religious knowledge but no identifiable set of religious beliefs; and his impatience with the vulgar trappings of esoteric doctrine was extreme. A composer less like Olivier Messiaen or Dane Rudhyar would be impossible to imagine:

> [...] those musical maunderings we are occasionally asked to accept as conscious and deliberate transcripts of a transcendental fourth dimensional music, turn out, as often as not, to be the feeblest and dreariest of commonplace gone a little queer in the head, along with a shoddy and incompetent technique. Certain egregious theosophisticated examples will occur to the minds of most musicians, and although in all fairness, the reproach of technical incompetence and jejune platitude does not attach to it, to such a degree, the heaving rainbow-tinted protoplasmic jelly that is so much of the later orchestral work of Scriabine is a case in point. The stuff barely and precariously exists, in two, let alone four dimensions![81]

For another thing, Sorabji's notions about the business of composing were not at all romantic:

> I absolutely refuse to regard the very deliberate, very intellectual, and, as the sentimental amateur who imagines the artist paddling and plopping about in inspiration like a duck in warm cow-dung would say, very cold-blooded processes of music-making, as a sort of substitutional self-abuse, a mystical masturbation, a psycho-sexual whoremongering.[82]

What Sorabji was up to can be explained without recourse to the supernatural. When he composed, he pushed himself — physiologically — significantly beyond what even the most hyper-productive writer would call "white heat", and he did so for reasons which have nothing to do with the creation of art. The techniques Sorabji employed were largely mechanical and have been well understood, in the East and the West, for thousands of years. They are best called Tantric; but here again, thinking in terms of

---

[80]Television, 11 June 1977.
[81]Kaikhosru Sorabji: *Mi contra fa*, p. 75.
[82]Kaikhosru Sorabji: *Around Music*, p. 227.

stereotypes would be a mistake.[83] The techniques themselves did not correspond in any macroscopic way to known Tantric ritual; but what resulted, in any case, was a condition of mind and body very much the opposite of that popularly called hypnotic. While in these yogic states, Sorabji wrote down his music at unbelievable speed: almost always without sketches, without planning, without looking ahead or back, and without blotting a note. The music literally flew to the page, for all its great contrapuntal and organizational complexity.[84]

H37. London, [24 June 1922]

This is the penultimate letter in the collection.

93

[¶] Yes. Salvarsan is a good name for him: for he's as much a fraud as that much boomed "remedy". [... ¶] Tomorrow — Sunday evening at the Canonical Hour of Vespers I break my 7 day fast. It's been an ordeal but I've done it — which is more than old Syph-Salv could ever do. [¶] Now about the biographical snips. Born 1895 — Mother Spanish[,] Father Parsî — in Essex. Educated privately with tutors. Commenced composing in 1915: but has discarded all works prior to 1918 including a large number of songs and 2 piano Concertos etc. [... ¶] You can add to the list of works "Black Mass" for Chorus Large Orchestra and Organ — "in preparation[.]" [*138v, 139*]

---

[83]See the preface to his *Tāntrik* Symphony for Sorabji's comments on the general misconception of Tantric matters {pp. 187–88}.

[...] the substance of [Tantrism] is far removed from what in the West we know as idealism, spiritualism, mysticism. It resembles most, in the words of Sir Charles Eliot, in *Hinduism and Buddhism*, the deserted mansions of Herbert Spencer.
(Kenneth Rexroth: *With Eye and Ear* (New York: Herder and Herder, 1970), p. 58.)

[84]Cf. footnote 93.
By itself, this is nothing more than sleeping on a bed of nails — for tourists. Yoga, assiduously practised, does not facilitate art. Sorabji's music might have ended up sounding exactly the same if it had been written down in a more normal way.

So, essentially, ends the correspondence.[85] But Sorabji would remember it, years later, when it was time to remember Heseltine:

> A song writer of exquisite delicacy, jewel-like craftsmanship, and flawless rightness of instinct, he has been equalled by few and surpassed by far fewer, and those happy recipients of quaint postcards inscribed in a freakish manner so typical of him in a microscopic, dainty, and delicate handwriting, typical of the perfect orderliness and complete lack of loose ends about any part of his personality, have poignant reason for cherishing these memorials of him now.[86]

As Cecil Gray points out, there was good reason for the correspondence to end when it did:

> Each man kills the thing he loves, wrote Wilde in one of his rare moments of insight, and no one ever did so more thoroughly than Peter Warlock. Everything Philip had cared for most intensely became in the end the target of his sharpest and most envenomed darts. It was about 1921, then, that the secondary personality, hitherto in abeyance, begins to gain the mastery, both in the man and in the musician. He gradually dropped his old friends, and their place was taken by a vast horde of superficial acquaintances and boon companions.[87]

At present, Gray's ideas about Heseltine and Warlock are not very popular:

> Supposing Heseltine and Warlock to be, as it were, separate individuals, Gray's differences are mainly superficial; i.e. H. a vegetarian — W.'s favourite dish "Steak Tartare"; H. drank sweet and sticky liqueurs — W. only drank beer; H. was an internationally-minded pacifist — W. was a bellicose and insular Englishman; H. was fond of children — W. affected to loathe them; H. was credulous and

---

[85] {With Sorabji giving out a false birth date and implying he might destroy or have destroyed works which are extant today.}
The *Black Mass* never materialized: "Abandoned this silly idea!!" (Kaikhosru Sorabji: Letter to Kenneth Derus, 5 September 1983.)

[86] *The New Age*, vol. 48 (15 January 1931), p. 128. Recall footnote 3.
{Heseltine committed suicide on 17 December 1930 at the age of 36. In this obituary notice Sorabji implicitly rejected the idea of suicide, claiming Heseltine's death occurred "through a wretched accident". Sorabji's view was not accepted then, nor is it now. See footnote 94.}

[87] Cecil Gray: *Peter Warlock*, pp. 236–37.

superstitious — W. a cynical blasphemer; H. a romantic idealist not particularly successful with women — W. a hedonistic "Don Juan."[88]

[...] these differences between Heseltine and Warlock were little more than the differences between Philip sober and Philip drunk.[89]

This is not the whole truth either, but it may be the part of it that was most important to Sorabji:

In his latter years I saw little of Philip Heseltine. I found myself growing more and more out of sympathy with the Peter Warlock side of him with all that beer and boozing [...] I can't stand the smell of a public bar and beer — it is [an] aesthetic not a moral objection!! I always say that British Public House pallyness and Beery Bonhomie are violently antipathetic to me! Mass Merry Making sends my spirits into deepest depression!!! High spirits give me low spirits!!![90]

Heseltine never prospered after he drifted away from Sorabji, and in this case Gray's explanation has not been quarrelled with:

[...] there is no doubt whatever that at this time [ca. 1918], and for some time after, perhaps always, Philip was an ardent believer in the objective reality of the phenomena of the magical arts, and that he practised them [...][91]

From these activities Philip undoubtedly suffered certain psychological injuries from which, in my opinion, he never entirely recovered, and in saying this it is not necessary to subscribe to any definite belief in the objective reality of the phenomena with which the occult sciences profess to concern themselves.[92]

Heseltine's fate can be known with great exactness, if it is imagined in terms that apply to Sorabji:

In Tantric Buddhism, yogic manipulations have clearly defined alchemical concomitants. Like Thomas and Rebecca Vaughan — locked in a Tantric embrace in the Pinner of Wakefield three centuries before — Sorabji is performing a chemical experiment, as he composes, in a way less metaphorical than commonly thought.

---

[88]I. A. Copley: *The Music of Peter Warlock: A Critical Survey* (London: Dennis Dobson, 1979), p. 32.
[89]Ibid., p. 25.
[90]Kaikhosru Sorabji: Letter to Kenneth Derus, 5 September 1983.
[91]Cecil Gray: *Peter Warlock*, p. 164.
[92]Ibid., p. 163.

His partner — his *soror mystica* — is his art. They balance each other perfectly.[93]

People who do this sort of thing usually come to bad ends, for reasons which can be understood in straightforward medical terms. The Vaughans were careful, intelligent, and devout — but disciplined and dangerous gymnastics of the spirit ultimately killed them.

That Sorabji has survived into his tenth decade is less a tribute to his skill than a tribute to his moral integrity. The yogic texts of several cultures are all very clear about this. Overriding unselfishness is an essential pre-condition for avoiding catastrophe. That a man so outwardly ferocious could be inwardly gentle, generous, and filled with kindly good humor is hardly surprising. Had he been otherwise, he would have perished a long time ago — in some equivalent of a laboratory accident.[94]

---

[93]Anyone who jogs down a roadway is doing brain chemistry, of a rudimentary kind, by means of simple physical exercise. The most characteristic exercises of Tantric yoga are elaborately choreographed varieties of sexual intercourse; and to these exercises there corresponds an elaborate brain chemistry — the reaction products of which are pharmacologically compelling indeed. (Alchemical talk — of an interior ballet of flasks and retorts, corresponding to an exterior ballet of sex — is ultimately no more metaphorical than anything in contemporary biochemical physics, where, for example, one gets "vessels" from reacting and diffusing matter much the way one gets numbers from classes in logic.)

Sorabji's yogic exercises were calligraphic: they involved a hand moving very rapidly across music paper. This is why his *scores* have a magical look. (Sorabji's *music* is not magical. If anything, it has an almost Diderotian appeal.)

A less ample art, less rich in calligraphic opportunity, might have *failed* Sorabji ... chemically.

[94]Kenneth Derus: Program notes for the performance of *Opus clavicembalisticum* by Geoffrey Madge on 24 April 1983 in Chicago, pp. 7–8 (in slightly different form).

Lovers can be calisthenically mismatched, for Tantric purposes, and in a similar way artists can fail to balance their art. Peter Warlock was an outsized Tantric work of art. He exercised Heseltine with routinized but awkward physical and moral vigour. The chemical consequences were lethal and in one sense murderous.

States of mind mediate brain chemistry, and conversely. But the states of mind and body that result from mismanaged yogic activity leave diminished scope for volition. At best, they can be entreated, not willed. This explains the Tantric tradition of personifying material and mental capacities. Genuine entreaties engage genuine persons. Stereotyped yogic manœuvres ensure that the same consequent persons keep coming back, throughout history, frequently with the worst of intentions.

[CONT'D]

Letter Specifications

The table below enumerates all the letters in a more correct chronological order than the order in which they have been foliated. Following it are exact points of origin for the letters when these are known.

Dates in italics are not in Sorabji's hand. Dates in bold italics are newly assigned. (The dates they replace appear under *Comments*.) H6 may follow H7; otherwise the chronological order is certain. *Ms. pp.* excludes postcard versos and manuscript pages with nothing in Sorabji's hand. One manuscript page counts as two folios when text crosses the midline of a leaflet.

No.	Date	Ms. pp.	Folios	Comments
H1	3 Oct. 1913	7	*1–4*	
H2	30 Oct. *1913*	3	*5–6v*	
H3	8 Dec. 1913	22	*7–18*	
H4	6 Jan. 1914	14	*19–25v*	
H5	3 Feb. *1914*	8	*26–29v*	
H6	***possibly Feb.*** *1914*	1	*62–62v*	*Feb.–June* [postcard]
H7	*late Feb. 1914*	8	*30–33v*	
H8	*early Mar. 1914*	24	*34–45v*	
H9	14 Apr. *1914*	28	*46–59v*	4 pp. missing from ms.
H10	28 June 1914	4	*60–61v*	
H11	8 Sep. *1914*	11	*63–68v*	unknown no. of pp. missing
H12	27 Dec. *1914*	3	*69–69v*	
H13	11 Jan. 1915	9	*71–75*	
H14	24 Jan. 1915	4	*76–77v*	
H15	2 Mar. 1915	12	*78–89v*	
H16	Mar. 1915	4	*90–91v*	
H17	12 May *1915*	6	*94–97v*	
H18	24 Aug. 1915	2	*98–99*	
H19	11 Feb. 1916	4	*100–101v*	
H20	23 Feb. 1916	4	*102–103v*	
H21	*17 Mar. 1916*	1	*104–104v*	in French [postcard]
H22	*23 Mar.* ***1916***	1	*105–105v*	in French [postcard]; *1917* [postmarked 1916]

It is therefore neither superstitious nor childish to suggest that Heseltine was "visited" in his Chelsea flat, some time before seven on the morning of 17 December 1930. One could even look to an Indian or Tibetan *grimoire* and give the visitor a name.

H23	21 Apr. 1916	10	*106–111*		
H24	3 May 1916	2	*112–112v*		
H25	31 May 1916	2	*113–113v*		
H26	6 July 1916	2	*114–114v*		
H27	27 Aug. 1916	4	*115–117v*		
H28	**June or earlier 1917**	3	*140–141*	n.d.; first 3 pp. missing	
H29	**June 1917**	4	*92–93v*	*March 1915*	
H30	26 Jan. 1920	2	*118–118v*		
H31	21 Aug. 1920	4	*119–120v*		
H32	8 Nov. 1921	4	*121–122v*		
H33	2 Jan. 1922	8	*123–126v*		
H34	12 Apr. 1922	5	*127–129*		
H35	28 Apr. 1922	3	*130–131*		
H36	19 June 1922	9	*132–136*		
H37	**24 June** *1922*	4	*138–139v*	Saturday	
H38	28 July *1922*	2	*137–137v*		

Points of Origin

25A, High Street, St. John's Wood, London N.W.	H1–H5, H7–H9
29, Clarence Gate Gardens, London N.W.	H10, H11
10, Gt. Russell Mansions, London W.C.	H12–H15
177, Clarence Gate Gardens, London N.W.	H17, H18, H20, H23
175, Clarence Gate Gardens, London N.W.	H24–H27, H30, H32, H36, H37
Boscombe Pier Hotel, Bournemouth	H31, H38
Hotel Krantz, Vienna	H33
n.pl. [London]	H6, H16, H19, H21, H22, H28, H29, H34, H35

Newman and Busoni

Sorabji's most dramatic public association with Heseltine occurred within the context of a rancorous and largely private debate with Ernest Newman. In the latter part of 1919 Heseltine sent Newman some Sorabji and Van Dieren scores in manuscript and became angry when Newman failed to take much interest in them. (Newman's letters are in the British Library. Heseltine's letters have not been preserved.)

The *Observer* declined to publish a letter from Heseltine attacking Newman, so Heseltine created an opportunity to rehash the matter almost as soon as he became editor of *The Sackbut*. Sorabji sent a letter to the *Sunday Times* which was not printed; Heseltine printed it in *The Sackbut* in June 1920 (pp. 55–56):

> Sir, — [...] I can give from personal experience some highly interesting and instructive information regarding the way in which Mr. Newman pursues his search after the potential masterpieces of British or any other music.
>
> Having taken to show Mr. Newman some work of my own which had previously been strongly commended to him from an outside and independent quarter, I was informed that Mr. Newman did not look at [...] manuscript scores.
>
> There was a time when one thought Mr. Newman the most alert and enterprising of the critics, but this one staggering revelation of his methods shows that the others are not more like themselves than he is like to them.
>
> Not a week after this incident, Signor Busoni — to whom my work went entirely without introduction or recommendation of any kind — asks me to play certain of my compositions to him, and, as a result, is kind enough to give me a letter of high commendation wherein he expresses himself as greatly interested in what I had played him, describing at length the qualities in my work that had seized his attention.

Heseltine went on to quote the letter of Busoni (which Sorabji cherished for the rest of his life) and to compare Busoni favourably to Newman in the matter of seeking out "potential genius".

> Mr. Kaikhusru Sorabji eut la bonté de me jouer au Piano une <u>Sonate</u> de sa composition. À juger d'après une première impression — assez surprenante, d'ailleurs — le talent de Mr. K. S. se comptait dans la complexité harmonique et profusement<->ornamentale, qui semble lui être naturelle et facile. — La liberté qu<'>y règne, apparaît encore d[é]sordonnée et exub[é]rante; sa Musique — consciencieusement écrite — est inconsciente de ses qualités irr[é]gulières — surtout dans les proportions —: en se d[é]barrassant des "traditions" elle franchit un seuil qui n'est plus purement européen, capable de produir[e] une végétation d'un aspect presque<->exotique. (Pas dans le sens de nos "charmantes" Danses orientales, par exemple!)
>
> Somme toute: un talent naissant d'une espèce encore nouvelle, qui donne à penser et à espérer ...
>
> <u>Ferruccio Busoni</u>
> Londres, Novembre, 1919.[95]

---

[95]This text is based on the facsimile of Busoni's letter included in the notes for Marc-André Hamelin's recording of Sonata I (on Altarus [CONT'D]

(Mr. Kaikhusru Sorabji was kind enough to play for me at the piano a Sonata [Sonata I] of his own composition. To judge from a first impression — quite amazing, moreover — Mr. K. S.'s talent was felt in the harmonic and profusely ornamental complexity which seems to be natural and easy for him. The freedom which prevails in it seems as yet disorderly and exuberant; his music — conscientiously written — is oblivious of its irregular features — especially in its proportions — in freeing itself from "traditions" it crosses a threshold which is no longer purely European, capable of producing vegetation of an almost exotic nature. (Not in the sense of our "charming" Oriental Dances, however!)

In all, a rising talent, of a still new kind, which makes one think and hope ...
Ferruccio Busoni
London, November, 1919.)

Busoni wrote to his wife about Sorabji on 25 November 1919, confirming his tentatively favourable impression despite some implied reservations:

Kaikhusru Sorabji hat sich als ein ganz junger *Indier* entpuppt: — dem gab ich, auf seinen Wunsch, einen Empfehlungsbrief. Ein feiner, nicht gewöhnlicher Kopf, trotz seiner häßlichen Musik: einem Urwald mit vielem Unkraut und Dornengestrauch, aber fremdartig und üppig — ...[96]

(Kaikhusru Sorabji turns out to be an Indian, quite young. I gave him a letter of introduction for which he asked me. A fine, unusual person, in spite of his ugly music. A primeval forest with many weeds and briars, but strange and voluptuous ...)[97]

Writing to Emil Hertzka on 5 January 1920, Busoni emphasized his positive impressions:

At the same time I became the dedicatee of a piano sonata (from the pen of a 20-year-old [!] Indian, Kahushru Sorobdji [*sic*]) with tropical ornamentation, luxuriant foliage, absorbing.[98]

AIR–CD–9050). {The letter as printed in *The Sackbut* differs slightly from the original.}

[96] Ferruccio Busoni: *Briefe an seine Frau*, edited by Friedrich Schnapp (Erlenbach-Zürich and Leipzig: Rotapfel, 1935), p. 367.

[97] Ferruccio Busoni: *Letters to his Wife*, translated by Rosamond Ley (London: Edward Arnold, 1938), p. 289.

[98] Ferruccio Busoni: *Selected Letters*, translated and edited by Anthony Beaumont (New York: Columbia University Press, 1987), p. 303. The brackets are Beaumont's. Elsewhere (ibid., p. 300) Beaumont misidentifies the sonata that Sorabji played for Busoni.

Sorabji recalled much later that after he played Sonata I, Busoni said he could not have played it better.[99] A copyist's score of Sonata II, dedicated to Busoni, is in the Busoni Collection of the Deutsche Staatsbibliothek.

---

[99] Kaikhosru Sorabji: Letter to Kenneth Derus, n.d. (late January 1985). Sorabji wrote an important memoir of his meeting with Busoni for his friend Alistair Hinton. It is also included in the notes for the recording of Sonata I mentioned in footnote 95.

7 Sorabji's Music Criticism
Nazlin Bhimani

Nazlin Bhimani (b. 1959, Kampala, Uganda) is Head of Music Acquisitions and Services at the BBC Library in London. Previously she was a librarian at the Royal Academy of Music (London) and the Universities of Western Ontario and of British Columbia. She holds BMus and MA degrees from the University of British Columbia, as well as a Master's degree in library science from the University of Western Ontario. She has published articles on music manuscripts and librarianship.

This chapter derives from and adds to her master's thesis *Kaikhosru Sorabji's Writings on British Music in "The New Age" (1924–34)* (MA, University of British Columbia, 1985).

Although many people have mentioned the published writings of Sorabji, few have examined many of them in detail, perhaps because they are scattered in several different serial publications and books, many of which are out of print or otherwise not easily found. As a result, the literature dealing with Sorabji's journalism is minuscule, principally comprising a two-page article by Arnold Whittall,[1] a paragraph by Paul Rapoport,[2] an article on Sorabji's criticism of English opera in *The New Age* by John Steane,[3] and a few sentences in music reference books.

This chapter focuses on Sorabji's articles on contemporary composers published in the newspapers *The New Age* and *The New English Weekly*, which contain much more of his music criticism than any other serial. *The New Age* contains some of his earliest critical writings, produced when England had rediscovered its musical personality by breaking away from the continental

---

[1]Arnold Whittall: "Sorabjiana", in *The Musical Times*, vol. 107 (March 1966), pp. 216–17.

[2]Paul Rapoport: *Opus est: Six Composers from Northern Europe* (London: Kahn and Averill, 1978), pp. 162–63.

[3]John Steane: "English Opera Criticism in the Interwar Years: Sorabji of *The New Age*", in *Opera*, vol. 36 (June 1985), pp. 623–31.

influences which had bound it since the death of Henry Purcell. By the first decade of the century, the results of this English Musical Renaissance, a particular English style encompassing romantic and impressionist idioms as well as some native influences, could be heard in the music of such composers as Delius, Elgar, Bax, and Ireland. Their distinct styles were much appreciated by Sorabji; having been born and educated in England, he witnessed all the changes in music there.[4] This is why his writings provide a valuable perspective on British music criticism and musical life from the 1920s to the early 1940s. These writings also help us understand the music Sorabji wrote, as there is an intimate relationship between his critical aesthetics and his compositions.

* * * * *

At various times Sorabji was a frequent contributor to leading papers and music journals in England, including *The Sackbut* (1920–21), *The New Age* (1924–34), *The New English Weekly* (1932–45), *The Musical Times, The Chesterian, Music Review,* and *Musical Opinion.* He revised and reprinted some of these writings in his two books, *Around Music* and *Mi contra fa: The Immoralisings of a Machiavellian Musician.*[5]

In addition to over 650 contributions to music journals (and his two books), Sorabji also wrote letters to some well-known musical and literary people, including Philip Heseltine, Hugh MacDiarmid (pseudonym for Christopher Murray Grieve), Bernard van Dieren, Ferruccio Busoni, Erik Chisholm, John Ireland, Joseph Holbrooke, and Alan Bush.

Those who knew Sorabji's critical judgement had immense respect for it. As early as 1932, A. R. Orage, the influential editor of the two weekly newspapers for which Sorabji wrote the most, recommended him highly as a first-rate critic who could communicate his enthusiasm with vivid descriptions of music:[6]

> As I continued to read Mr. Sorabji's articles [...] I became gradually aware of an increasing authority in his opinions, of an increasing

---

[4]{In spite of this, he refused to be called British or English: see p. 24.}

[5]London: Unicorn Press, 1932; and London: Porcupine Press, 1947 respectively.

[6]{Orage left the editorship of *The New Age* in 1922 and moved to the USA in 1923. He started *The New English Weekly* as editor in 1932 upon his return to England but died two and a half years later. In its last years, *The New Age* was devoted almost entirely to social-credit economics and politics.}

respect for and submission to his judgments [...] and I do not remember that he has ever failed me.[7]

Shortly afterwards, Clinton Gray-Fisk, later the chief critic of *Musical Opinion,* acclaimed Sorabji as one of the leading music critics in England, surpassing both George Bernard Shaw and Ernest Newman.[8] The composer Bernard van Dieren wrote a letter to Sorabji expressing admiration for his writings:

> I am very flattered indeed to read your high opinion of my work in general and your very penetrating and clear observations regarding the performance of the pieces on this occasion. Wit, brevity, understanding and forceful prose are such rare things every one of them that it is a memorable experience to find them contained in one single criticism [...] I am more than ever anxious to tell you how very greatly I value your criticism and what a very high opinion I have of your literary powers not to mention your musicianship and erudition.[9]

Some 30 years later, in his autobiography Hugh MacDiarmid referred to Sorabji's two books:

> Where else in any book published in Britain, or in any British periodical, in the last half-century will you find musical criticism of this quality? It has an unmatched authority, derived from the fact that the writer understands the creative process from inside, and has himself made great contributions to the art or arts he writes about and is on a level with the greatest of those he criticises.[10]

Sorabji was a "modernist" who promoted not only certain contemporary British composers but Alkan, Mahler, Medtner, Busoni, and Szymanowski, all of whom were heard infrequently in England at the time Sorabji was writing. His advocates described him as being the most direct, just, honest, and reliable of music critics, one who would not put up with nonsense or with what the "trend of the times" seemed to be, one who could and did cut the pretentious down to size. He was thus an important and influential

---

[7]A. R. Orage: Foreword to *Around Music,* by Kaikhosru Sorabji, pp. x–xi. It is unlikely that Sorabji's career as a music critic would have been as successful if such an imposing figure as Orage had not supported him.

[8]*The New Age,* vol. 52 (16 February 1933), p. 189.

[9]Kaikhosru Sorabji: *Mi contra fa,* pp. 154–55.

[10]Hugh MacDiarmid: *The Company I've Kept* (London: Hutchinson, 1966), pp. 66–67.

critic among his colleagues and close acquaintances, even if their number was not large.

However, not all of his readers praised his criticism:

> Sir, — The language of fish-porters applied to musical criticism would be more tolerable if Mr. Sorabji's distribution of ecstatics and abuse were discriminate [...] I suggest that Mr. Sorabji's personal idiosyncrasies, masquerading as criticism, are not sufficiently interesting to carry the weight of the riot of words in which they are set down.[11]

> I have never been so disgusted as I am now at the venomous and ignorant articles by that foreigner Sorabji.[12]

> I rather think that the circulation might increase among people who matter if, for instance, the violent opinions of Sorabji were omitted [...][13]

In spite of comments like these, Sorabji's critical writings appeared for another nine years in *The New Age*.

* * * * *

The New Age, a "weekly review of politics, literature and art", had a long and complicated history.[14] It began in London in 1894 but due to severe financial difficulties (which were prevalent over its lifespan) ceased publication in 1938. It had the reputation of a brilliant and provocative, radical weekly. Orage established this reputation by publishing some of the most unorthodox and opinionated writings, sometimes shockingly straightforward and crude. The journal was often informative in regard to the progressive ideas of the time, entertaining to read, and a sheer delight for the uninhibited manner of much of its prose.

Its contributors were often highly accomplished figures in arts and letters, e.g. Oscar Levy and Anthony Ludovici, George Bernard Shaw, G. K. Chesterton, H. G. Wells, Hilaire Belloc, Havelock Ellis, Arnold Bennett, and John Galsworthy; in music Ezra Pound, Herbert Hughes (critic for *The Daily Telegraph*), and Cecil Gray. The

---

[11] *The New Age*, vol. 36 (30 October 1924), p. 10.
[12] *The New Age*, vol. 36 (4 December 1924), p. 71.
[13] *The New Age*, vol. 38 (19 November 1925), p. 35.
[14] See *Orage and The New Age Circle: Reminiscences and Reflections*, by Paul Selver (London: George Allen and Unwin, 1959), and *A. R. Orage: A Memoir*, by Philip Mairet (New Hyde Park, New York: University Books, 1966).

contributors worked for the most part without pay. Sorabji, having been supported by his father during his father's lifetime and by a trust fund after his death (and therefore not forced to earn a living by regular employment), could afford the luxury of saying anything he wanted without fear of loss of income.

The New Age emphasized current much more than historical activities. In addition to musical events in London, Sorabji wrote about the state of music education, music criticism, and copyright. (He also wrote occasional letters about hotly debated nonmusical topics such as social-credit economics, racism, birth control, abortion, unemployment, and British rule in India.[15]) His critiques, whether positive or negative, could rouse the feelings of even the most passive readers. What performer, for example, would not dream of receiving praise, enthusiasm, and encouragement in a review that starts like this?

> On Sunday evening, 8th, for a short half-hour, some millions of people were admitted into the inner shrine of music — one says admitted, rather should one say, the doors thereof were opened to them through the transcendent power and greatness of Egon Petri's Bach playing. Imagine the superb precision, the gigantic controlled power of movement of some great engine, the fineness of line, the matchless balance of mass against mass, the incomparable draughtsmanship, the sense of design of a Dürer engraving in terms of sound, and perhaps this will convey some idea of Petri's Bach playing.[16]

But Sorabji could also write in the most satirical, denigrating manner, proving himself a "Master of Insult" with his scathing salvos:

> [...] the Bach sung and played by Misses X. and Y. [...] I do not propose to give them the honour even of disparaging mention by name in a periodical of such distinction as ours, hence the X. and Y. Sufficient be it that the one is a popularish soprano of the ballad type, the latter a still more popular chorybantic pianist of the writhing, intense type, the kind that plays with every part of her body, naturally except the part most concerned, her fingers. Her success, I am convinced, is chiefly due to her sinuosities, our

---

[15]{He was an enthusiastic supporter of birth control, legalized abortion, and social-credit economics. He deplored unemployment and racism. His opinion of British rule in India is more complicated: he did not like what the British had done to India, but he liked what the Indians were doing to it even less.}

[16]*The New Age*, vol. 45 (26 September 1929), p. 261.

audiences being far too much concerned with the sinful lusts of the eye to enable properly to attend with their ears [...]

Neither possesses the glimmerings of a perception of the need of the most absolute technical precision, that drawing of fine, steady, firm, clean lines without which Bach interpretation does not begin. Neither can hold a phrase without letting it sag in the middle like a clothes-line, and each has recourse to injecting into the music that extraneous and hideously inappropriate "feeling" that is the hallmark of a bad performer and a proof that the root of the matter is not in him or her.[17]

Sorabji's career as music critic for *The New Age* began in March 1924. By this time he had established himself as knowledgeable through his letters to the editor, had performed his first two sonatas in public, and had several works published. When asked many years later why he had written music criticism, he answered, "For the fun of it."[18] A letter to Philip Heseltine shows that he had contemplated becoming a critic as early as 1914.[19]

But by 1930 he had already begun to withdraw by attending fewer concerts. He was disillusioned by low standards of concert performance and by dull, uninteresting programs.[20] As a substitute, he turned gradually to gramophone recordings, which he believed would eliminate the need for him to hear second- and third-rate performances. He wrote several articles discussing various radios and record players and was one of the first music critics in England to encourage technical advances in recording. From the middle of

---

[17] *The New Age*, vol. 43 (30 August 1928), p. 215.

[18] Paul Rapoport (quoting Kaikhosru Sorabji): Letter to Nazlin Bhimani, 2 March 1983.

{Sorabji once put it this way, although it was certainly not the whole story:

You wonder [...] why I bothered to go to concerts and write about the unspeakable? Well ... it gave me quite a lot of malicious fun believe it or not. AND as I did it all for NIX ... I was able to go to such things as I wanted to ... get a good laugh ... for its always MUCH greater fun to laugh when you're not really MEANT to ...
(Kaikhosru Sorabji: Letter to Paul Rapoport, 23 January 1976.)}

[19] {For the relevant excerpt, see p. 205.}

[20] Many historians would agree that the standard of performances in England at this time was low, partly because mass music education programs had thrust many unqualified amateur performers onto the London stages. See, for example, *A Social History of English Music*, by E. D. Mackerness (London: Routledge and Kegan Paul, 1964), and *The English Musical Renaissance*, by Frank Howes (London: Secker and Warburg, 1966).

1931 the majority of his reviews in *The New Age* were of recorded performances or radio broadcasts. (By far most of his reviews for *The New English Weekly* were also of these.) By 1932 he was established as a well-known record reviewer whose judgement was relied upon by some of the leading record manufacturers. After the middle of 1934 he tended to write reviews of public concerts only when they included a musician or composition of some stature.

Years of critical writing, however, gradually left him feeling weary and depleted. He eventually gave up writing reviews when doing so was more of a chore than an enjoyable and stimulating activity. In 1945 he ceased regular reviewing, occasionally submitting his views to various journals in correspondence columns.

Sorabji did not write for *The New Age* or *The New English Weekly* every week, but only when he considered a particular concert or musical event or topic deserving of his attention. Often he would combine reviews of several concerts, broadcasts, or recordings in one long article. Other activities also affected the frequency of his contributions: when he spent some months away from England, his journal writing understandably lessened. His most productive reviewing years for *The New Age* were 1928 to 1930, for *The New English Weekly* 1936 to 1938.

* * * * *

During the 19th century, English music criticism stagnated because of the conservative tastes of critics such as H. F. Chorley and James William Davison, who dominated critical opinion in London for nearly half a century (1830–79).[21] To them Germany was the foremost musical nation, with Beethoven and Mendelssohn its leaders. These and similar ideas buried even the most heroic attempts of English composers of that time. But at the end of the century Shaw and Newman aroused the English musical establishment: Shaw with his imaginative literary style and Newman with his wide-ranging musical knowledge and championing of many contemporaries. Thus the serious, inquiring, and literary manner of music criticism on the continent, which had reached an apex in the writings of François Joseph Fétis, Hector Berlioz, Richard Wagner, Eduard Hanslick, and Hugo Wolf, finally had an influence in England. Apart from Shaw and Newman, important music critics in England in the early 20th century included Ezra Pound, Cecil Gray, Philip Heseltine, Bernard van Dieren, and Neville Cardus.

---

[21]Winton Dean: "Criticism", in *The New Grove Dictionary of Music and Musicians,* edited by Stanley Sadie (London: Macmillan, 1980), vol. 5, p. 40.

The name of Sorabji must be added to this company of writers who contributed to the development of English music criticism, not only for his style, but also for his continued promotion of neglected composers (as mentioned: Alkan, Mahler, Medtner, etc.) who eventually became much more widely performed and understood. Moreover, the scope of Sorabji's reviews was often wide, encompassing many aspects of performance and composition. For example, in his review of the Covent Garden *Ring* cycle in 1927, he wrote about the orchestral playing, the singing and acting of the main performers, the stage design and sets, the lighting, and of course the music, all in great detail.[22] Newman's review of the same productions focused exclusively on the music.[23]

Sorabji's perceptions also provide valuable commentary on performance techniques, tastes, and standards. His record reviews, some of the first published in England, are a notable contribution to the history of recorded music.

* * * * *

What were Sorabji's general musical affinities? Without an understanding of these and his attitudes towards criticism, his judgements may initially seem inconsistent, even irrational. An examination of his work for *The New Age* gives an accurate picture of his concerns, approaches, and opinions.

In a letter to Philip Heseltine from 1913, he confessed his sympathy with contemporary music, the ultra-modern (as he called it) satisfying him more than much of the older music.[24] The validity of this admission remained, *for the music it referred to:* Sorabji always promoted the works of many composers active during the period of that letter: the impressionists and post-impressionists (Debussy, Ravel, Delius, Szymanowski), the post-romantics (Mahler, early Strauss, early Schoenberg). For Sorabji these were the ultra-moderns. Later ultra-modern or avant-garde composers he disliked immensely: he condemned Stravinsky, the later Schoenberg, Hindemith, and Bartók. He detested particularly the powerful, pounding rhythms of Stravinsky, his loud orchestral effects, unusual chordal combinations, and lack of a sustained musical line. The following is typical in its side-swipe at Stravinsky:

> The great operatic event has been the return of "Elektra" [...] One realises again still more acutely that "Le Sacre du Printemps" is after

---

[22]*The New Age*, vol. 41 (26 May 1927), p. 45.
[23]Ernest Newman: *Testament of Music* (London: Putnam, 1962), p. 286.
[24]{For the relevant letter, see pp. 198–99.}

this the mere stammering fumbling of an intellectual baby. There is more brain power in the first five pages of "Elektra" than in all Stravinsky's work put together [...][25]

Sorabji also condemned any music influenced by Stravinsky, for example Honegger's *Le roi David*:

A very typical specimen of the work turned out by the epigoni of Stravinsky — as textureless and incoherent as the worst works of their master with a crudity and clumsiness of workmanship that goes beyond even his. There is the same "stunning monotony of rhythm" (to quote a devout disciple) which in this case has not even the passing pathological interest it has in his, since with them it is a sort of malingering.[26]

Although Sorabji greatly admired the early works of Schoenberg (*Verklärte Nacht, Gurrelieder,* Second String Quartet), he did not like his later harmonic and vocal experiments. A review of his *Das Buch der hängenden Gärten* (1909) shows his parochial dislike and basic lack of understanding of Schoenberg's new style:

[... T]he "songs" as a whole are all but a denial, a negation of the human voice, springing from that perverse anti-vocal obsession of the latter-day Schönberg, although the strangely impressive power of many of them is not to be denied. On the whole, the frigid intellectual contortions of the music seem a curious æsthetic reaction to these warmly, richly coloured poems.[27]

Subsequent reviews of Schoenberg's music also reflected Sorabji's inability to accept serialism. Much later he offered this opinion:

As for serialism ... well! This is nothing but a jigsaw in terms of notes instead of words. They are always prattling of the intense logic of it all ... Ebbene ... it is possible to construct an argument that is syllogistically flawless from premises that are inherently nonsensical, reaching a logically sound conclusion but one that is factually nonsensical. So it is with the tone-rowers, serialists, and all the rest of them.[28]

He was also shocked at the "barbarism" of Bartók's music. Despite professing "respect and admiration" for Bartók's ideals, in his music

---

[25]*The New Age*, vol. 37 (11 June 1925), p. 68.
[26]*The New Age*, vol. 40 (7 April 1927), p. 273.
[27]*The New Age*, vol. 46 (21 November 1929), p. 32.
[28]Hugh MacDiarmid (quoting Kaikhosru Sorabji): *The Company I've Kept*, pp. 61–62.

he wondered whether "such a bluntness tending often to an uncouthness, is really compatible with musical expression at its highest."[29]

Among the better-known composers of the 19th century, Sorabji's heroes were Berlioz, Liszt, and Wagner. He adored warm, dense, rich orchestral colours, a vigorous, passionate, intense style, and strong chromatic harmony that abounded with daring dissonances and modulations within the established harmonic language of the late common-practice period. He was impressed with the huge formal structures of Wagner's *Der Ring des Nibelungen*. He was astounded by Berlioz's *Requiem Mass:*

> This mighty and overwhelming work, a granite rock-hewn temple, is one of the most amazingly powerful and original conceptions in all of music. One does not know what to admire and marvel at most, the triumphantly successful use of the four brass orchestras added to the main one, the astonishing daring of the treatment as a whole, the volcanic power and burning intensity of the inspiration, or the originality of every note of it. I would give the whole of the Symphonies of Beethoven for one page of the Requiem.[30]

Sorabji also favoured Mahler and the Strauss of *Salome* and *Elektra*. He wrote often of his longing to hear the Mahler symphonies, complaining bitterly about the overall neglect of Mahler by the English. He lauded the symphonies' gigantic structures, richness of detail, extraordinary orchestral colours, long lyrical melodies, and intense and sincere expression. The first English performance of Mahler's Eighth Symphony, which he found uninspired, he nonetheless called "one of the greatest experiences of a lifetime".[31] Of other post-romantics, he retained an affinity for Sibelius, whose Seventh Symphony he admired for "its stark laconic qualities, its freedom from frills, and its aloofness from all the fashionable jargon of the day".[32]

Of newer trends, Sorabji was in sympathy with the impressionist music of Debussy and Ravel. He praised the subtle, delicate, and evocative imagery of such works as Debussy's Nocturnes, *Pelléas et Mélisande*, *La mer*, and *Ibéria*, and Ravel's *Daphnis et Chloë*. He was not favourably impressed by either composer's more abstract neo-classical style, as exemplified by most of their work after about 1913, including Debussy's last sonatas and Ravel's *Le tombeau de*

---

[29] *The New Age*, vol. 46 (23 January 1930), p. 137.
[30] *The New Age*, vol. 40 (10 February 1927), p. 177.
[31] *The New Age*, vol. 47 (1 May 1930), p. 7.
[32] *The New Age*, vol. 42 (5 January 1928), p. 117.

Couperin. As for the well-known earlier classical composers such as Mozart and Haydn, or Brahms and most of Beethoven, Sorabji's later characterization (writing of himself in the third person) presents his position fairly starkly:

> [...] the bulk of German Lieder infuriate him [...] the click-clack symmetries of Haydn and Mozart turn him into a homicidal maniac in any but the most homœopathic of doses [...] the square-toed flat-footed pompostities of Brahms impress him about as much as the stately and completely inane [...] verbiage of a more than usually portentous *Times* leading article [...] Beethovenian drubbings, growlings, gruntings do NOT as far as he is concerned suggest, or evoke the ultimate sublimities, the bottomless profundities or whatever it is they ARE supposed to do [...][33]

He was, however, duly impressed with Bach's B minor Mass and Beethoven's *Missa solemnis* and late piano sonatas.

Considering the rapid changes taking place in music during the 1920s and 30s, Sorabji's tastes turn out to be rather conservative. But he was not alone in his views, for in some ways it was not until after the Second World War that England took in developments from the rest of Europe. Many of Sorabji's reviews of music by contemporary British composers reveal the same principles behind his reviews of the composers already discussed. As suggested earlier, those who wrote in an original manner using a post-romantic or impressionst language he generally treated favourably; the radical new styles he condemned.

* * * * *

Sorabji's writings in *The New English Weekly*, "a review of public affairs, literature and the arts", were generally longer and more detailed than his writings in *The New Age*. For whatever reason, he found it necessary to justify his opinions more, to describe vividly, to illustrate through comparison, rather than merely begin and end with unsupported judgements. Also noticeable in the later reviews is a feeling almost of acceptance within the profession, for he often referred to other critics, especially Newman, as being within the same class and sharing similar sentiments. His reputation was as secure as it ever would be. When his critical output tapered off in the mid-1940s, readers complained.

In *The New English Weekly*, on the whole, he showed a more mature and accepting attitude, especially with respect to the music

---

[33]Kaikhosru Sorabji: *Mi contra fa*, p. 115.

of some younger composers. Certainly his writing style was mellower. Vengeful caustic outpourings, although not totally forsaken, were few and far between.

These changes may have been occasioned by his reviewing many more recordings and broadcasts than live performances, the standard of performance in the former two being much higher generally than in the last. He could certainly praise a performance of music he did not like:

> More Mozart, the A minor piano sonata, by that most interesting and simpatico figure among the younger English pianists, Denis Matthews, who has a mind of his own and a point of view about what he plays, and has made one listener at any rate listen with patience and even interest to a work that, in other and less admirably competent hands, would have made him scream with boredom at its tick-tack, click-clack — its deadening and deadly "correct" symmetrical antitheses.[34]

Clearly this suggests a fairer and more tolerant critic willing to let the music speak for itself, given sympathetic performances of it. However, this is not to say that Sorabji had softened completely. His views on most of the composers previously discussed remained consistent. Brahms' G minor Rhapsody, for example, he found timid, conventional, and lacking in inner necessity.[35] Gustav Mahler remained a great composer; in fact, Sorabji continued to defend him from other English critics such as Eric Blom:

> Mr. Blom is "not convinced," let us say, that Mahler is as great a Master as his admirers think. He calmly ignores the fact that a large number of the greatest critics and musicians of Central Europe regard Mahler as one of the outstanding figures in music, and that, as Mr. Newman has well pointed out, the Mahler chorus may be small, but it is remarkably select, including, as it does, musicians and critics of the highest rank.[36]

Sorabji's reviews of Busoni's music continued to illustrate his ideals in a musical composition. One such review, of Busoni's Indian Fantasy, is a good example of his later critical style. In one particular paragraph it moves from praise of Busoni's orchestration and harmony to deprecation of Schoenberg and back again to Busoni, concluding with this specific point:

---

[34]*The New English Weekly*, vol. 23 (15 July 1943), p. 115.
[35]*The New English Weekly*, vol. 26 (26 October 1944), p. 15.
[36]*The New English Weekly*, vol. 2 (23 February 1933), p. 446.

Sorabji in 1933 (photo by "Rembrandt")

> Observe, in this connection, the gradual spicing of the harmony, the gradual introduction of foreign and remote elements, after the *Andante quasi Lento* section of the Fantasy. We start quietly off in a demure G major, gradually passing right out of the diatonic system altogether, without having noticed it, almost.[37]

Sorabji's strictures on later Schoenberg remained, even in his non-serial music, e.g. in this review of Schoenberg's adaptation of music by Georg Monn in a Concerto for Cello and Orchestra:

> [... I]t is a monstrosity, and is the musical equivalent of an indecent assault. All Schönberg's now effete and antiquated tricks of instrumentation, constant and pointless cuivré brass, constant tinkling celesta, and melodic leaps an octave and [a] ninth apart instead of a second abound in the work, which sounds like nothing so much as a dance-band director's nightmare of a piece of classical music [...] It was a grotesque and humourless exhibition such as only a monomaniac like Schönberg could inflict upon us.[38]

Sorabji was not, of course, the only one who found it difficult to appreciate Schoenberg's music. Rollo Myers and Constant Lambert encountered the same problems, as did the general public.

Stravinsky's changes of style and borrowings from music of the past signified for Sorabji a lack of originality and continued to grate on his critical fabric. Several reviews denounce Stravinsky in a comparison of his techniques to others' which Sorabji found more valid. The following comments are found in a review of an all-Sibelius concert:

> How different this from the unedifying picture of Monsieur Igor (one had almost said Igrigious) Stravinsky sitting at the piano fuddling to find "funny" chords and hooting with delight when, in the course of his messing-about, he strikes upon something that sounds wild and woolly enough to find a place in the latest mistress-piece of "absolute" music! It is like the Paris *couturier* who, stumped for ideas idiotic and eccentric enough to titillate even the average woman of "fashion," revives a style of a century ago, and palms it off upon their boob-*clientèle* as the smartest, the ultraest ever![39]

Sorabji also wrongly condemned Shostakovich for a similar reason (lack of originality) stemming from a different situation: the composer in a totalitarian state. Unable to fathom how a composer

---

[37] *The New English Weekly*, vol. 6 (25 October 1934), p. 42.
[38] *The New English Weekly*, vol. 8 (28 November 1935), p. 135.
[39] *The New English Weekly*, vol. 9 (24 September 1936), pp. 393–94.

could let the political situation govern his artistic output, he castigated Shostakovich for giving in.

Of French composers, Sorabji continued to write favourably about Debussy and Ravel, but his rediscovery of the music of Fauré is more significant. In a review of Fauré's A major Violin Sonata he enthused:

> This work with its enchanting beauty of melodic line, the masterly draftsmanship of its structure represents French musical art at its most seductive best, and, by the way makes me ashamed and anxious to make amends for certain ill-considered and unjust remarks of my own made — I must plead — many years ago — about this fine Master who is Gabriel Fauré.[40]

His sincere and humble apology certainly points to a mature mind. He admired the performance of the sonata (by Jascha Heifetz): it is therefore once again understandable to find him appreciating the music. One wonders how much of his critical judgement of a new or unfamiliar composition relied too much on the performance of it.[41]

*****

Sorabji wrote a great deal on contemporary British music in both of Orage's weeklies. In his articles for *The New Age* he discussed about 24 British composers, most frequently mentioning Delius, Elgar, Bax, and Holst. His treatment of these composers' music will now be examined, with reference to both *The New Age* and *The New English Weekly*.

---

[40]*The New English Weekly*, vol. 18 (26 December 1940), p. 114.

{Sorabji felt sufficiently uncomfortable about this to apologize again in *Mi contra fa* (p. 162) for what he had written about Fauré in *Around Music* (p. 144). In *Around Music* (p. 73) he had also apologized for an erroneous earlier impression of the Hans Pfitzner Piano Concerto, modified by "a remarkably fine performance". Late in his life he even reconsidered Shostakovich ("this pretentious dunderhead, this ideology-besotted prig": *Mi contra fa*, p. 88), admiring things in his Fourth Symphony, First Violin Concerto, and Tenth Symphony, according to Alistair Hinton.}

[41]{It is very unlikely in most cases that he examined the scores of such works in advance or followed the scores at a concert, as he almost never wrote as if he had done either.}

Frederick Delius

Sorabji dealt with many compositions of Delius (1862–1934), the majority of which he praised lavishly. In his opinion Delius was the creator of "radiant masterpieces",[42] "the greatest and purest Nature-poet that music has ever known";[43] he was a master who could "express musically the mood of ecstatic and transcendent contemplation which in India they call *Samādhi*".[44]

It is understandable that he would like Delius's music, as it combined the romantic, post-romantic, and impressionist traits for which Sorabji felt a strong affinity: especially rich orchestral colours and chromatic harmony; exoticism, evocative imagery, and subtle formal structures. Early in his reviewing career Sorabji said this about Delius's *Paris:*

> a glorious and glowing mood poem; it is one of the orchestral masterpieces of our time, at once vivid and subtle, highly-coloured and yet sensitive, [...] alight and burning with a white hot imagination, exultant, and is shot through with that nostalgia, that "tristezza," which is such a characteristic of Delius [...][45]

Much later he added a more specific observation:

> The superb orchestral poem "Paris" written in 1899 stands [...] outside the currents of music of that time [...] I discount heavily the Wagnerian influence in the earlier Delius [...] As in the case of Mahler, if Wagnerian processes are used (and much more so in the earlier Mahler) they are applied to wholly unWagnerian ends, saying wholly unWagnerian things.[46]

Many works by Delius from the first decade of the century also received high praise from Sorabji: he described "A Walk to the Paradise Garden" from *A Village Romeo and Juliet* as having "piercing and heart-stabbing beauty";[47] *Sea Drift* was "one of Delius's most moving and poignant nature poems".[48] His praise for *A Mass of Life* was absolute:

---

[42] *The New Age*, vol. 36 (2 April 1925), p. 273.
[43] *The New Age*, vol. 38 (25 March 1926), p. 250.
[44] *The New Age*, vol. 46 (14 November 1929), p. 20.
[45] *The New Age*, vol. 36 (19 March 1925), p. 246.
[46] *The New English Weekly*, vol. 19 (29 May 1941), p. 63.
[47] *The New Age*, vol. 41 (9 June 1927), p. 70.
[48] *The New Age*, vol. 40 (28 April 1927), p. 310.

> Than Delius' "Mass of Life" I feel convinced there has been no greater nor more truly lofty and sublime work since the B minor Mass. Although as Pagan as the B minor Mass is Catholic [...], yet a deep religious emotion quite indefinable and inexplicable of analysis breaks through every note, and the work is as much a great celebration as a High Mass. The power and sweep of the genius manifested in it, the sustained level of ecstasy, the "elevating excitement of the soul," the radiant and glowing quality of the work [...][49]

However, not all of his reviews of the music of Delius contain such positive reports. The later Cello Concerto and Second Violin Sonata, which employ classical formal structures, lost some of the wonderful, magical qualities which had earlier led Sorabji to be so enthusiastic. Despite having some good things to say about the concerto, Sorabji spotted a weakness:

> The trouble comes when Delius remembers he is writing a concerto and that a concerto ought to have a quick section. Then he falls into one of those jog-trot crotchet-quaver movements that are rather a cliché with him, manifestly ill at ease [...] and only watching an opportunity to return to the prevalent mood and style that he should never have left.[50]

He preferred the earlier Violin Concerto and Double Concerto. His last review of Delius's music (in 1944) praised its inner inevitability, beauty, warmth, and aloofness.[51]

Sorabji often challenged the attacks of others upon Delius's formlessness, amateurishness, and lack of technical competence. He lashed out at someone who misunderstood *A Song of the High Hills*:

> [... A]n otherwise intelligent amateur [said] the work was formless because quite probably it does not lend itself to the sort of "formal analysis" beloved of the programme-note gentry and the Musical Appreciation Supply Stores. The ineffable loveliness of the work, its supreme spiritual beauty, its utter "rightness" within its own sphere and according to the standards of its own universe were lost on him [...][52]

He also attempted to put Delius in a wider context by comparing him on one occasion to Sibelius, in a frank appraisal of the

---

[49] *The New Age*, vol. 36 (23 April 1925), p. 308.
[50] *The New Age*, vol. 45 (12 September 1929), p. 239.
[51] *The New English Weekly*, vol. 26 (7 December 1944), p. 71.
[52] *The New Age*, vol. 50 (24 December 1931), p. 92.

Edward Elgar

The common view of Elgar (1857–1934) in England is that he succeeded in creating a personal style that combined the techniques of romantics such as Wagner, Brahms, Schumann, Berlioz, and Franck: less adventurous than Richard Strauss could be, but still typically romantic in his luxurious, powerful, and grand manner. Elgar's success stemmed partly from his use of musical materials which appealed to the general public: strong march rhythms, traditional harmonic language, some ideas in a popular style.

Sorabji's evaluation of Elgar's music was generally positive, for he believed that Elgar possessed a "very great musical mind, broad, deep and powerful".[54] But the popular characteristics in it did not appeal to him in the least. In fact, their inclusion in his music Sorabji regarded as a serious weakness because they were so prominent. *The Kingdom* contained some of Elgar's best and worst qualities:

> Occasionally the music rises to heights of etherealised, rarefied purity and beauty, to descend promptly into the worst Elgarian maudlin of the amorous sections of the "Cockaigne" overture or the detestable bombast of his jingoisms, such as "Land of Hope and Glory."[55]

Later, Sorabji went further in generalizing that all music containing nationalistic elements created a serious conflict between the purely musical considerations of a work and the nationalistic propaganda it promoted. Sorabji and others of his circle (e.g. MacDiarmid and Van Dieren) also believed that having music succumb to the inferior tastes of the general public belittled the creative, spiritual qualities granted to music: music was intended for the appreciation of an elite class, a higher group of individuals who were spiritually aware of its importance.[56]

Sorabji's preferred compositions of Elgar were his Violin Concerto, Second Symphony, and *Falstaff*. He liked the concerto partly because it did not contain mundane popular characteristics

---

[53] *The New English Weekly*, vol. 12 (16 December 1937), p. 194.
[54] *The New Age*, vol. 46 (3 April 1930), p. 261.
[55] *The New Age*, vol. 37 (14 May 1925), p. 18.
[56] {See "'Performance' *versus* 'Celebration'", from *Around Music*, pp. 288–90 of the present book.}

geared to appeal to the general public. He was infatuated by its ardent sweetness, luscious melodic content, and mystical sensuousness, as well as its virtuoso elements.

Although, like others, he found Straussian ideas behind *Falstaff*, Sorabji preferred it to much of Strauss because it was a less literal translation of something external. He claimed that "the Strauss works are much more pictorial in an external way — so much so that enjoyment of them is much enhanced by a knowledge of the programme", whereas the Elgar was "an end in itself [... telling] its own tale without needing nor wishing to translate that tale into verbal concepts".[57] He found *Falstaff* contained

> a richness and suppleness of ideas and treatment not reached by the composer before nor since [...] a great and powerful piece of music, full of dark, sombre, and often sinister emotions [...] No Falstaff ever did or could go through the immense spiritual experiences of which it seems to me "Falstaff" is the expression, and superb expression.[58]

Arnold Bax

In spite of the inherent romantic and impressionist tendencies in the early works of Bax (1883–1953), many of Sorabji's *New Age* reviews of them are negative. He felt Bax to be overrated, a composer lacking in imagination, sincerity, and structural strength. The Second Piano Sonata, which Sergei Rachmaninoff and Artur Schnabel may have thought highly of,[59] Sorabji found "thick and gruff" and too influenced by Edward MacDowell.[60] Despite others' admiration for Bax's Piano Quintet, and its obvious romantic gestures and textures, Sorabji wrote severely of this and the Oboe Quintet:

> The two principal works played on this occasion [...] are calculated to give the worst possible opinion of this composer. They are compact of a tepid viscous glucosity, completely lacking in firmness of outline and line drawing, and over all broods that marsh miasma of foggy-headedness that used, I believe, to be called the Celtic

---

[57] *The New Age*, vol. 46 (3 April 1930), p. 261.

[58] *The New Age*, vol. 44 (15 November 1928), p. 30.

[59] Lewis Foreman: *Bax: A Composer and his Times* (London: Scolar Press, 1983), p. 363.

{The high opinion of the sonata was attributed to the two pianist-composers by Harriet Cohen in a program note for a concert of hers in 1956.}

[60] *The New Age*, vol. 35 (12 June 1924), p. 79.

twilight, producing a singularly repellent result. The composer fails completely to gain that essential and inner coherence which alone constitutes "form," and lack of which no ingenious and specious jerry-building with "thirds," "first and second subjects" and all the rest of the programme analyst's claptrap will conceal or substitute for — indeed, in default of it these devices are a very minor and palpable piece of artistic dishonesty, so transparent that one is astonished at anyone imagining us simple-minded enough to be impressed, let alone taken in by them.[61]

It is certainly possible that the performance influenced his judgement considerably. Others have pointed out the difficulty of interpreting Bax and the jumble resulting from inadequate sympathy for it.[62]

In the 1920s Sorabji admired most Bax's Symphonic Variations for Piano and Orchestra. In June 1924 he called it "the best large work for piano and orchestra of any contemporary composer roped in by that accommodatingly elastic adjective "British".[63] But in October 1924 an inferior piano performance brought mutterings about its Wagnerian influence and "perilous approach to banality of theme" in the midst of general praise for the work as a whole;[64] a review a few years later made Sorabji question the orchestral playing, with no direct mention this time of the work's imposing stature.[65]

But in the 1930s the work that captured his attention was Bax's Sixth Symphony:

It is, in my opinion, in all respects the most mature and powerful work of Bax that I have ever heard [...] It is at once eloquent, reserved, rich, and sumptuous, yet austere and has a finer sense of form than I ever remember to have encountered anywhere else in Bax's work, with the exception of the first version of the Symphonic Variations for Piano and Orchestra. I know of no other contemporary composer who has a richer, more diversified nor more subtle harmonic sense than Bax. That tendency to a kind of slack diffuseness [...] that at one time was apt to mar Bax's work is certainly not here. The whole work marches irresistibly and irrevocably from point to point with the inevitability of complete mastery.[66]

---

[61] *The New Age*, vol. 42 (10 November, 1927), p. 22.
[62] Lewis Foreman: *Bax*, p. 119, and Norman Demuth: *Musical Trends in the 20th Century* (London: Rockliff, 1952), p. 157.
[63] *The New Age*, vol. 35 (12 June 1924), p. 80.
[64] *The New Age*, vol. 35 (23 October 1924), p. 308.
[65] *The New Age*, vol. 41 (15 September 1927), p. 238.
[66] *The New English Weekly*, vol. 8 (12 December 1935), p. 174.

[CONT'D]

Alluding to the performance problems mentioned above, Sorabji went on to claim that most critics, who could not "apportion blame between composers and performers", wrongly accused Bax of "turgidity" which was due "not to Bax but to his often detestable performers and execrable performances".

Sorabji's reviews of Bax in *The New English Weekly* are markedly more favourable than those in *The New Age*. He even relaxed his prejudices against string quartets to call Bax's First "a pleasant work";[67] his Third Symphony he described as "an attractively sombre-toned work, very original in design and cast".[68] His change of attitude may be explained by the fact that the majority of his reviews in *The New English Weekly* were of records, and of reasonably good performances. It is also possible that he simply preferred some of the works of Bax that he reviewed later: his mention of the earlier "slack diffuseness" in his review of the Sixth Symphony suggests so.

Gustav Holst

Of all the British composers about whom Sorabji wrote, Holst (1874–1934) received the most negative reviews. Sorabji detested his music, considering him to be "a manipulator of arrant clichés loosely tacked together with no organic essential or inherent cohesion, a set of ideas devoid of intrinsic distinction or individuality in expression".[69] Consequently, Sorabji reserved some of his most colourful criticisms for Holst's music, written in prose which may at times even have embarrassed some readers. He classified *At the Boar's Head* as

> perhaps the feeblest work ever written for the operatic stage [...] a crazy, clumsy, jejune patchwork of meaningless fragments, utterly devoid of coherence or sustained sense of continuity, an incompetence of handling almost [...] unbelievable; vocal writing so atrocious, so bad that it was impossible to hear more than an isolated word or two here and there, and this with false stresses, misplaced accents; no trace of style is to be found in the work from the first bar to the last, and the amateurish *gaucherie* of the whole would disgrace a student.[70]

{See p. 341 for Sorabji's opinion of the differences between the two versions of the Symphonic Variations.}

[67] *The New English Weekly*, vol. 20 (15 January 1942), p. 114.
[68] *The New English Weekly*, vol. 25 (8 June 1944), p. 71.
[69] *The New Age*, vol. 38 (19 November 1925), p. 32.
[70] *The New Age*, vol. 37 (14 May 1925), p. 18.

In addition to the obvious reasons for Sorabji's displeasure, he would not have appreciated Holst's adoption of folk tunes for the melodic content of the work.

Holst's Choral Symphony fared no better: Sorabji even used some of the same words to criticize it.[71] He complained further that critics admired in Holst what they did not like in others. In this case, the more obvious Stravinsky influence may have annoyed Sorabji. He also stated that

> his harmonic and melodic ideas waver between diatonic commonplace on the one hand, and polytonal commonplace on the other. His potterings about and fiddlings with chords in fourth structures have no more merit or interest than Rebikov's affairs of ten or twelve years ago [...][72]

In *The Hymn of Jesus*, Sorabji felt the problem was also philosophical:

> Nothing short of the highest possible sources of inspiration do for Mr. Holst — an entire Cosmos in the Planets' Vedāntic thought in the Ṛig-Veda Hymns and the Apocryphal New Testament in the Hymn of Jesus, and indeed they do "do for" him in quite another sense by showing his lamentable inability to deal with them or catch even a fleeting glimpse of the shadow of a reflection of their greatness.[73]

This work, austere even for Holst, has little of the richness, warmth, or ardent emotionalism that Sorabji identified with.

In his writing for *The New Age* and *The New English Weekly*, almost the only positive comments on Holst are applied to his *Ode to Death*, a more romantic and traditional work which "showed indications of an imaginative sensitiveness and subtlety" that Sorabji had not found in his other music.[74] Even Holst's death brought almost no charitable remarks, only that he "had at least a largeness and width of aim that was in complete and startling contrast to that fashionable at the time". Not surprisingly, Sorabji again found him inadequate for his aim. He summed up his work this way:

> Over all his work [...] was a general nondescriptness, a lack of well-marked physiognomical characteristics, that made it, at least, for one

---

[71] *The New Age*, vol. 38 (19 November 1925), pp. 31–32.
[72] *The New Age*, vol. 38 (19 November 1925), p. 32.
[73] *The New Age*, vol. 45 (27 June 1929), p. 104.
[74] *The New Age*, vol. 50 (10 December 1931), p. 66.

among his audience, impossible to be able to say of any page or bar, that it was signed, definitely and unmistakeably, as any page of Elgar, Delius, or any other of the really outstanding figures of music.[75]

In the same article, he stated that he could see little value in the "legendary [...] amazing orchestral technique" of *The Planets:* the orchestral treatment he found "as wholly and essentially unoriginal and tame as the matter of the music" and far inferior to the orchestration of Sibelius's Fifth Symphony.

The following year Sorabji brought out another charge (which he laid against more composers than Holst):

> As for the Holst "Oriental" (!!!!!) Suite ("Beni Mora") it is the sort of thing one would expect from the musical Cook's tourist. Here we have the usual European's disordered aural impression of that which he mistakes for the "gorgeous East" [...] It is really time that a league was started for the artistic protection of the East against this kind of indecent assault by half-baked European dilettantes.[76]

Even in his last review of Holst, Sorabji found that even a fine recorded performance of *The Hymn of Jesus* could not save it from its "scrappy, disjected, episodic form" and its too obvious borrowings from other composers.[77]

Other British Composers

Sorabji discussed many other British composers. Of the better-known ones, he generally had good things to say about Vaughan Williams, Walton, Lambert, Heseltine, Ireland, and Bush, although he did not like the work of Walton and Lambert which seemed influenced by Stravinsky, Schoenberg, or Bartók; and certain works by Vaughan Williams and Ireland he found inferior to others by them.[78]

---

[75] *The New English Weekly*, vol. 5 (14 June 1934), p. 208.
[76] *The New English Weekly*, vol. 6 (11 April 1935), p. 538.
[77] *The New English Weekly*, vol. 25 (28 September 1944), p. 191.
[78] {Much later he admitted an inability to like Vaughan Williams' music:

"a temperamental disharmony, I suppose ... Its all too English by half for my taste! I have spasms from time to time when Anglo-Saxonishness acts on me like a dog on a cat and my fur all bristles ... silly and irrational ... but there ... what would you from such an utter oddity as a Spanish-Sicilian Parsi?
(Kaikhosru Sorabji: Letter to Norman Gentieu, 16 May 1955.)}

But much of Sorabji's admiration went to some composers who were relatively unknown then and remained so, e.g. York Bowen and Bernard van Dieren. His response to the latter's Chinese Symphony is worth quoting extensively for its contrast to his opinion of other "Eastern" music as noted above in connection with Holst, and its mixture of praise for Van Dieren with dismissal of many others in a colourful and overwrought style:

> I have no hesitation at all [...] in calling this work a very great masterpiece. It is a most lovely thing, of a texture of the rarest, finest, and subtlest; glowingly interwoven like a priceless piece of Chinese embroidery or painting upon silk. Van Dieren here has not, in the idiotic cant "captured the spirit" of China; artists of that dimension need to "capture" no spirit but their own, and do not deal in local colour as an oil-and-colour shop deals in blue-bag, Dolly-dyes and washing-soda. Such artists as Van Dieren, to use the preposterous and egregious Whitman's for once apt and happy phrase "absorbing, translating," take into themselves the matter of their "inspiration" (another damnable cant-catch-phrase) or rather their point of artistic departure, they psychically and spiritually digest it, and turn it into bone of their own bone, flesh of their own flesh, and blood of their own blood. But it is only the greatest artists who can do it, not your Rimsky-Korsakovs, or de Fallas or those your "nationalist" anthologists miscalled composers, who go trotting off to the nearest musical-theatrical costumiers buying their local colour by the yard, feet or even inch. Van Dieren by virtue of an intensity of emotional and spiritual insight, and a technique and a mode of expression, that in its matchless fineness of craftsmanship, its firmness of line-work, its delicacy of tint, its perfect form and balance recall the triumphs of Chinese craftsmanship (in fact, such craftsmanship as belongs naturally to the *Extrême Orient*). The subdued nature of the orchestral colouring, with, at the same time as complete a lack of any vague "impressionism" as there is in any Chinese art itself (such nonsense does not flourish among a people as utterly realistic, and rational as the Chinese, but belongs to the Maeterlinckian morasses of mid or Northern Europe where the ground is never properly dry, nor the air free from misty and mistifying exhalations) is something completely unique in contemporary or nearly contemporary orchestral music, or music of any sort at all for that matter.[79]

A variety of other well-known and less-known composers Sorabji almost always treated negatively, e.g. Arthur Bliss, Benjamin Britten, Cyril Scott, Herbert Howells, and Rutland Boughton. Of the last-

---

[79] *The New English Weekly*, vol. 11 (22 April 1937), p. 35. {The ragged punctuation and sentence structure of the original are not repaired here.}

named's opera *The Immortal Hour,* which received 216 consecutive performances in the early 1920s, Sorabji had this to say (after some comments on Schubert's Fourth Symphony):

> [... O]ne had but to listen (if one could bring oneself to it) to two excerpts from Mr. Rutland Boughton's "Immortal Hour," written when he was already old enough to be the father of the Schubert of the Fourth Symphony. The one is the rather raw youth of genius, the other a manifestation of the so prevalent and admired infantilism which trades under the name of simplicity.[80]

Conclusion

This study of Sorabji's music criticism has revealed a critic who, mindless of the consequences of his writings or his acceptance within the musical establishment, wrote what he believed in the clearest language possible. He left no doubt about his opinions. Seen in historical perspective, Sorabji also supported the music of many less-known British composers at a time when much of the musical establishment was ignoring them. He certainly gained their respect: Ireland, Bowen, Bush, and others sent him scores to review, presumably knowing that he was not afraid of telling the truth, good or bad.

Several of the composers he favoured, some very well known, also knew and admired his music. When Delius heard Sorabji's 1930 broadcast of *Le jardin parfumé,* he wrote to him at once: "I listened to your 'Jardin parfumé' on the Wireless last night and wish to tell you that it interested me very much. There is real sensuous beauty in it."[81] Walton was impressed with the First Organ Symphony:

> I enjoyed so much hearing the movement from the Organ Symphony, and only wish that I could have heard it all. I was much struck to find it so clear, logical, and easy to follow (a fact, which you may admit, does not seem obvious when it is seen on paper), — and it makes the most beautiful patterns of sound, especially towards the end — and the climaxes are very exciting [...][82]

It should not be surprising that the composers whom Sorabji admired admired him, not for political but for musical reasons. There was an intimate relationship between his critical aesthetics and his music: his compositions contain many of the characteristics

---

[80] *The New Age,* vol. 43 (27 September 1928), p. 261.
[81] Frederick Delius: Letter to Kaikhosru Sorabji, 23 April 1930.
[82] William Walton: Letter to Kaikhosru Sorabji, n.d. (ca. May 1928).

he championed in the music of other composers, e.g. baroque structural principles, romantic and post-romantic harmony and grandeur, impressionistic colour, subtly flexible rhythms without regular barlines, virtuosity and ornamentation which are integral to the musical conception, seamless musical forms, music which is deeply serious or even religious in its effect, and so on. Of the influences of serialism and neoclassicism or of Stravinsky's rhythmic and structural innovations there is no trace in Sorabji's music or in most of the music he reviewed positively.

Looked upon as a foreigner in England, Sorabji did not have to defend that which was British for reasons of national pride. He did not care to belong to any established group and owed allegiance to none. But even though he often denigrated British music and musical life in a manner as independent as it was forceful, he was by no means always alone in his views. They overlap to some extent with those of critics who became his friends (e.g. Heseltine, Van Dieren, Gray, Gray-Fisk), as well as of others. He was far from the only critic to devalue some of Delius's concerto writing, or, on the positive side, to uphold Delius's more successful works against charges of formlessness. Nor was he the only one to find some of Bax's music excessive, Holst's Choral Symphony structurally problematic, Vaughan Williams' Fourth and Fifth Symphonies richly rewarding, or Schoenberg's serialism anti-musical. His generally conservative tastes were in fact widespread among British critics who did not welcome atonality, serialism, the extremes of German expressionism, or neoclassicism.

In part, Sorabji's music criticism was influenced by his highly emotional outlook and subjective sense of what constituted true and sincere music. He was quite aware that he was alone in his approach, whatever the results:

> It is my office, as I see it, to set down without any *arrière-pensée* of, I hope, idiot or ideological prejudice, of classical or modern prepossessions [...] certain observations, and to set them down as completely and uncompromisingly as possible, so far as my own faculties of expression and observation will enable me to do. In the course of doing all this, I shall be — I do not doubt — on occasion, coarse, vulgar, crude, venomous, spiteful and a number of other things that no one who tries to get round a critics' circle ought to be. Perhaps I'm trying to do something worse, ... square ... or even by-pass it![83]

---

[83]Kaikhosru Sorabji: *Mi contra fa*, pp. 15–16.

He also knew he could never be polite in order to avoid telling musicians the truth, for that was a lie which only helped breed the incompetence he frequently observed. To some extent, Shaw and Newman would have agreed, but they were less often as direct as Sorabji. Sorabji's "black and white" beliefs and methods often led him to relentless extremes of either negative or positive criticism, as many of the excerpts in this chapter show. He did not waffle, he did not shy away from controversy.

It is this emotional severity and contrast that are both fascinating and disturbing in his music criticism. Possibly they may be explained simply by his general situation as an outsider in England and English musical life. But he also found the English racist in their attitudes towards foreigners like himself who could tell them things about themselves and their institutions which they did not wish to hear. It was one thing to be a foreign musician, quite another a "foreign", dark-skinned critic, especially one as vigorous and unfettered as Sorabji. On more than one occasion he was either not invited or refused admission to a concert. This could be for personal or other reasons, but Sorabji always harboured suspicions of racism and was in fact more than once the subject of racist criticism.[84]

Despite or because of his opinions and style, Sorabji was at least partially successful as a critic. One example of a reader's devotion to him came in a letter of thanks to *The New English Weekly:*

> Sir,— Mr. Sorabji fears that he has "bored and wearied long-suffering readers." May I be allowed to tell him through your columns that I, for one, have read his articles for a number of years with never failing pleasure and admiration? He possesses what is, to my mind, the greatest quality open to a popular musical critic, in that he can persuade a layman like myself that I understand the technical problems which he discusses and the praise and dis-praise which he distributes. I have hoped for a very long time for an opportunity to thank him for the pleasure he has given me; and here it is.[85]

---

[84]See, for example, his Letter to the Editor, in *The New Age*, vol. 16 (15 April 1915), p. 653; and the quotation referenced by footnote 12.

{For the letter, see p. 211 of this book. There are also items in Frank Holliday's collection of "Sorabjiana", now at McMaster University, which show that Sorabji was the subject of decidedly racist verbal attacks as a response to his music criticism.}

[85]*The New English Weekly*, vol. 20 (25 December 1941), p. 88.

{Sorabji wrote a letter to the editor (which appeared the next week) thanking this writer, C. E. Bechhofer Roberts, for his letter.}

His success may be attributed to several things, in addition to those already mentioned about his vigorous and colourful style. His writing was largely informal. MacDiarmid noted that he could imagine Sorabji actually saying in conversation anything in his published criticism.[86] He rarely used technical language, decrying its prevalence in certain places:

> All that infantilistic babble about "form," "subjects," "development" and all the rest of the classroom claptrap, tells us less than nothing about the music [...] It is high time to declare roundly that all that pseudo-anatomical nonsense of the text-books and the analytical programme is so much pernicious and noxious rubbish, confusing the issues and darkening counsel. It distracts attention from what matters — the music — to subordinate and subsidiary matters that, in the totality of the music, are as germane thereto as a man's skeleton to the whole of him.[87]

His writing was basically descriptive, vividly and memorably recounting what he considered the essential details of the music, based on important (if difficult) considerations such as these: "how is the work made? — is it a well-planned, masterful structure? — has it absolute mastery of all its means? — does it move inevitably and with conviction and power? — has it the authentic glow of great music?"[88]

The essential details, of course, did not interest him if the music did not strike him as "authentic" in the first place. In such instances he was able to include more of his powerful negative adjectives in a single sentence than most critics dared to use in an entire review: "The Toch concerto I did not hear. I know the work, however, to be beneath contempt. It is a fair specimen of the infantile ineptitudes of the young hopeless of modern Germany — sterile, vapid, vacuous and null."[89]

* * * * *

Sorabji has not received the attention accorded many of the English music critics, partly because most of his reviews are tucked away in the radical Orage weeklies, which never had a large circulation. Certainly his writing itself precluded formation of a large number of

---

[86] Hugh MacDiarmid: *The Company I've Kept*, p. 67.
[87] Kaikhosru Sorabji: *Mi contra fa*, p. 15.
[88] *The New Age*, vol. 42 (9 February 1928), p. 175.
[89] *The New Age*, vol. 46 (6 March 1930), p. 209.
{Sorabji does not otherwise identify the work by Ernst Toch, although it is his First Piano Concerto.}

supportive relationships. But there are other reasons for the neglect of his criticism, related to his isolation as a composer. His huge, complex, difficult compositions gained him the reputation of being unrealistic, and his ban on performances of them that of a crackpot. These characterizations led to his lack of recognition by others (whether he would have wanted recognition or not), without which no serious consideration would likely be given to other sides of his work such as his music criticism.[90]

In spite of this, his highly witty, racy, cutting, and amusing writings are both entertaining and informative. In Sorabji we see a critic who is more than just a brilliant polemicist, for he knew the art of music at its deepest level. Unlike George Bernard Shaw, Ernest Newman, Neville Cardus, and Samuel Langford, Sorabji was a practitioner of the art. A study of his music criticism is therefore of fundamental importance for what it reveals both about musical activities in England between the wars and about Sorabji the composer.

In John Steane's words:

> [... S]omewhere between the extremes of the passionately beating pendulum of his judgments, there existed a man of good sense and remarkable integrity. His critical skirmishes with the "execrable taste" of the "crapulous age" had nothing in them of that superior boredom which is the real deadliness of criticism, and his hatred of mediocrity was the necessary obverse of his love of excellence. He was an extraordinary man.[91]

---

[90]{Equally likely is the converse. Many who read Sorabji's reviews may also have rejected him as a composer.}

[91]John Steane: "English Opera Criticism", p. 631.

8 Sorabji's Other Writings

Paul Rapoport

This chapter provides a taste of Sorabji's writing from a variety of sources. He was as prolific a writer of prose as of music: in addition to his music criticism he contributed many articles and letters (usually on the arts, politics, or religion) to a wide variety of journals and papers, e.g. *The European, The Catholic Herald,* and local newspapers; and his private correspondence was immense. Anything he came across that caught his fancy, or more likely that caused his displeasure, seemed sufficient to set his pen to paper or send his typewriter into action.

The excerpts below are not intended to be representative, much less comprehensive, but merely to present some of the many concerns he had and the ways in which he treated them. Often the good is mixed with the bad in his opinions: rarely did he write a stream of praise without comparing his praised item to something worse. The variant repetitions, tangential remarks, and almost throwaway jibes and similar expressions which populate his writing are entirely characteristic of it; Sorabji's more tightly organized writing tends to be less lively, personal, and interesting.

The second and third excerpts presented below (No. 2 from *Around Music* and No. 1 from *Mi contra fa*[1]) together form a kind of statement of artistic belief. Less obviously revealing are his comments on his music: he was no analyst and had no desire to be one. (Most composers are often the least capable of discussing their own music in any depth, even those who are expert analysts.) More colourful, certainly, are Sorabji's comments on a variety of nonmusical matters, including the notions of democracy, Black Magic in the Church, and an oversized cabbage. Anyone who wishes to understand this complex, crafty, ebullient, and abundant

---

[1]*Around Music* was published in London by Unicorn Press in 1932, *Mi contra fa* in London by Porcupine Press in 1947. Both have been reprinted. {See the bibliography for further information.}

person or his music will find much that is revealing in his writings, however unrelated they may seem to be to the music itself.²

Writings from his Two Published Books

Around Music (1932)

1. From "Animadversions on Singing"

Because his vocal music is a minor and virtually unknown part of his output, writers on Sorabji often ignore the considerable (if biased) knowledge he had about singing and singers of his time, much of it originally gained from his mother. The following is offered as a brief indication of his passion for good singing, which was the equal of his passion for good piano playing.³

To begin with, what *is* singing? It is astonishing that it should be necessary to say it, but it is a stream of vocal tone, even, pure, homogeneous, free, bright, clear and steady — and that it is necessary to define it, Sir Henry Wood's admirable "Gentle Art of Singing" amply demonstrates. But to such a pass have things arrived that one asks oneself how often does one actually hear this stream of pure, steady, bright, clear tone? Or if the singer does succeed in emitting it for a few notes, how long can he or she keep it up without letting it dro[o]p and sag in the middle after about a couple of bars? The still more monstrous consequence of this inability to stay the course is the wobble. This is *not*, as it is so often miscalled, *vibrato* or *tremolo* — two totally different things, legitimate and established musical devices, but an affirmation of incompetence pushed to the lengths of a dogma, as Gounod said in another connection. It is the

---

²One of the better summaries of Sorabji's character, amply illustrated by the material in this chapter, is by Hugh MacDiarmid:

keenly sensitive [...], rebellious, irreverent, humble and acutely civilised. There is about him a perpetual tension, a trigger-ready quality that may explode at any moment. He is imbued with a reckless courage and a furious lust for life [...] He says what he thinks and lives the way he wants to live. There's nothing false about him. His honesty is almost shocking.
(Hugh MacDiarmid: *The Company I've Kept* (London: Hutchinson, 1966), p. 64.)

³The full title of the chapter from which it comes is "Animadversions on Singing in General, with Remarks on the Misuse of the Term 'Coloratura'". This excerpt is found on pp. 40–43 of *Around Music*.

result of the inability to exercise the uniform regular and steady muscular pressure required to produce a good firm solid tone. This often is the result of physical defects, but of that more later. But to such an extent have ears been corrupted by this universal and ubiquitous vice that its *absence* — the most elementary requirement of good singing — is actually regarded as a fault, and voices which are very properly without it will be called unsympathetic or some such nonsense. [...]

Coming now to physical defects: the present mania among women for the figure of a half-starved and consumptive hobbledehoy may or may not be æsthetically defensible, but it is an utterly impossible physical equipment for a singer. The poor, thin, cottony little thread of sound that will issue from such might get across a drawing-room sixteen feet square, but as a vehicle for the interpretation and execution of great music it is impossible. Generations of bad feeding coupled with the present Bedlamite notions of symmetry have further frequently so crippled the physical apparatus that no improvement is possible, a permanent dwarfing and stunting having taken place, but to go fully into this would need at least a chapter to itself. Sufficient for the moment is to say that it is in England where these preposterous notions have obtained the firmest hold and have wrought the worst damage — as every medical man knows.

The astounding myth especially prevalent among musicians who know nothing about singing (and they scarcely ever do), that it is easy to learn how to sing, easier than to learn to play some instrument, is so extraordinary that one wonders where and how it ever arose. That it is possible for persons to make vocal exhibitions of themselves upon a concert platform after perhaps shorter periods of study than would enable an instrumentalist to do so is undoubtedly true, but no one in his senses calls them singers.

It is not too much to say that of all branches of executive musicianship, the path to becoming an accomplished singer is more difficult, more thorny, more beset with fatal traps and deadly pitfalls than any other. In the singer's case it is the very instrument itself that is at stake if a false step is made. A pianist, for instance, may bring on an attack of neuritis through wrong or excessive methods, but he can conceivably recover; the singer risks his very voice as well. And anyone who has the most elementary physiological and psychological knowledge will know how very excusable and comprehensible are the whimsies, real or reported, of various great singing artists, when the slightest physical derangement — in complete dejection, oppressive atmospheric conditions, emotional disturbance, or irritation — exercises an instantaneous and harmful effect upon the vocal apparatus. I invite anyone to imagine the state of mind of a highly-strung artist — and no artist worthy [of] the name is not — who perhaps has passed a sleepless or restless night, rising limp and weary with nerves on edge, with all the consciousness of what that will probably mean to her vocal form, and knowing she has a rôle like Lucia, Gilda, Norma, Isolde, or the Second or Third Brünnhilde's before her the following night! Our critics, unhappily, have scarcely ever either the insight or competence to tell whether a defect of performance be due merely to indisposition or vocal incompetence.

To return, however, to the question of the singer's period of study as compared with that of the instrumentalist. Genuine singing study means the sort of thing Farinelli went through with the great Porpora, seven years on one page of exercises, and that great artist Dinh Gilly's three years to sing the vowel *ah*. Observe in this last connection that Monsieur Gilly does not say that it took him three years to make a more or less ah-like noise on a more or less definite pitch, but to sing it. Caruso never ceased working at and studying certain technical points all his life. So much for the ease of learning to sing.

2. "Performance" *versus* "Celebration"

Sorabji's point in the following article becomes clear, even if it takes him a while to make it. There has been no attempt to remove the contradictions in his view of sport, nor to alter the considerable length and wandering of some of his sentences. Mingled among them is a strong statement of his artistic credo.[4]

More and more with the progress of time one feels that the hope for music in this country is for a radical and most improbable change of attitude to it on the part of the listeners — that is, that it shall be raised to the dignity of a sport, since that is the only thing English people can be induced to take, think or talk about seriously — for sport to them is as much as religion is to other peoples. Anyone watching the myriads who crowd to great football or cricket matches cannot fail to be struck with the intense and portentous seriousness of their expressions, impressing one with a full sense of the high gravity of the proceedings — the solemn nature of the ritual at which they are about to assist. How different from the audience going to a concert — the careless chattering, the grins, the laughter, the general air of being *en fête*. Each attitude is equally grotesque and inappropriate to its own circumstances — that is why I say that the only hope for music in England is that it become a sport so that the attitudes be reversed or interchanged. In certain parts of Northern England, Lancashire and Yorkshire especially, music is already a sport — witness the competition festivals, the festival choirs, and so on, the struggle to outdo the choir of the neighbouring town — the fact that no pains are spared, no fatigue or effort, to attain this end, all demonstrate the truth of the description. But these people are purely and simply interested in what may be called the athletics of music. For music as an art there is ample evidence to show that they have little or no feeling at all. Their interest in it is purely physical — it is a manifestation of mass psychology, the herd instinct, the fondness for doing things in crowds; as they go to football and cricket matches, on their holidays, in crowds, so they practise choral singing. One would imagine that this at least would cause them to take an

---

[4]The entire chapter is reprinted here (pp. 198–200 of *Around Music*).

interest in other music than that which they make themselves; but this is not the case, for a rare visit to their districts of such a superb musician and artist as Sir Thomas Beecham has taken place to half-empty houses. There is no reason, of course, on reflection, why they should be interested seeing that music — or, rather, what they know of it, choral singing — is merely a means of scoring off rival choirs. From regarding music as a sport, however, to regarding it as a religion, would be in this country but a very small step, if any step at all, since sport is here taken with a quasi-religiousness which brings me to the kernel of my topic, which is whether music is to be regarded as merely a very high-class and superior form of entertainment, different only in degree and not in kind from any other entertainment, or whether it is to be looked upon as a holy and sacred thing to be approached with devoutness, seriousness of mind, and intent — but not, of course, the hypocrite mock-solemnity of our provincial festivals with performances in cathedrals stolen from their rightful owners and perverted to uses for which they were neither built nor meant, throwing a spurious sanctimoniousness over the proceedings (a barbarous and stupid attempt to blend the rites of two faiths, that of the Church and that of Music), and that, in fact, great works be no longer *performed*, but *celebrated* like a religious ritual, that attendance at their celebration be looked upon as participation in the rites of the Church. Music and its public execution should, as Busoni wished, be surrounded with an atmosphere of peculiar sanctity and reverence — opportunities for hearing it decreased, not increased, and the approach to the art should be surrounded with every difficulty and obstacle, so that only the most worthy could ever reach to the level of priest — that is, as we now call it, public performer. For it is thus that a performer, to my mind, functions. He is the medium, the consecrated medium, of intercourse between the Faith and the believers. Through his unworthiness the Faith and its Teaching suffer as through lying priests. They are the false prophets who disguise, conceal, and distort the truth to which they have not the spiritual greatness to give expression. By their sacrilegious and blasphemous vanity they exalt and puff themselves up above the Faith which is alone the beginning and end of their justification, their reason for existence; thus it is that in our time the true priests can scarcely reach the altar to fulfil their function, the way thereto being choked up by the false prophets — they who are not worthy to sweep and clean the temple floor and who, usurping the place of the rightful priests, fight and squabble among themselves as to which of them shall get to the altar to go through a blasphemous and impious parody of the sacred rites — unanimous in this alone[,] that they as one man bar the way to the true priests — for once let the rightfully consecrated ones celebrate, and the blasphemous pretence of all the others becomes manifest, for they, the consecrated ones, alone can bring about that *verbum caro factum est* — the others scarcely can utter the word but it choke them.

For this is what music, perhaps above all other arts, most really and truly is — a religion, a way to enlightenment to the spirit, like devout meditation and contemplation — Samadhi [*recte* Samādhi], as it were. Only thus regarded, thus approached, can all its grandeur and beauty enter into the soul, giving thereunto glimpses of Nirvana [*recte* Nirvāṇa], the state wherein all opposites, all contraries, are reconciled, all discords resolved, where the veils of illusion are torn asunder and the inner eyes opened to the peace which passeth all understanding.

Mi contra fa: The Immoralisings of a Machiavellian Musician (1947)

1. "Il gran rifiuto"

Regardless of whether one agrees with Sorabji's assumptions or his logic, one has to admire the consistency of his position not to allow performances of his music in circumstances he deemed unfit for them. The previous excerpt and this one explain well his general attitude on the matter. Whether this attitude resulted from disinterested purity of spirit or dispirited insecurity of mind is discussable: probably both.[5] Nonetheless, there is much truth in what Sorabji says about music, its environment, and its importance.[6]

i)	*Reasons for not going to Concerts*
ii)	*Reasons for having nothing to do with Musicians*
iii)	*Reasons for living in a Granite Tower*

i) Reasons for not going to Concerts

After quite a long slice of pre-adolescent, adolescent, and post-adolescent life spent in frequenting concert halls, to have arrived at a stage when the inside of a concert hall scarcely knows one's presence once in a year is a state of affairs one's friends find puzzling, disconcerting, or downright annoying, according to their temperaments. Holding that by far the most important reasons for doing or not doing a thing is that one wishes or does not wish to do it, or that having once wished to do it one finds one has now ceased any longer to wish, that seems to me in and of itself an all-sufficient answer. When all is said and done, going to concerts, provided one is a free agent, and not under the unholy necessity of writing about the wretched things, can hardly be said to come under the category of a duty, though it is, more often than not, even more unpleasant, which is the reason why perhaps one's friends so disapprove of one's absenting oneself therefrom. Irremovably rooted in the English mind particularly, is the conviction that what is unpleasant is in some strange way "good" for you, like the cold bath first thing in the morning. Demonstrate that the

---

[5]{See Chapter 3 for fuller discussion of these points.}
[6]The entire chapter is reprinted here (pp. 141–48 of *Mi contra fa*).

cold bath first thing in the morning is a thoroughly nasty, unhygienic habit (and it is quite easy to do so) and you will be henceforth as a monster of moral perversity.

Now I think that I have heard as much — possibly more — public music-making in my several decades of concert and opera going than most people of my age, and it must be remembered that I was quite monstrously precocious in the matter, starting quite a time before the age of two;[7] enough may or may not be as good as a feast, but it is often more than bad enough for indigestion. However, as "rationalising," that is to say the finding or forging of reasons and excuses for what one does or does not do, is a favourite contemporary pastime, like crosswords (which it not a little resembles in its tortuous attempts to establish connections where none exist), let us see what sort of a showing this produces in my case.

To begin with, as I grow older, I find my dislike of my fellow-creatures increases by leaps and bounds: I find my own failings and foibles as much as I can bear with a becoming equanimity; those of others added I find an intolerable burden. The sight of them in their various degrees and kinds of physical and mental ugliness is a distasteful and humiliating reminder that I am one of them; that displeases me. I know it, I don't want it underlined. I find also that the vocal and phonetic noises with which they think it necessary to announce to the world that their brains are working — quite irrespective, of course, as to whether (a) their brains ARE working, and (b) whether there are any brains there to work — do not, so far as I am concerned[,] make a suitable, pleasing nor helpful background against which to listen to music.

Again, in that mælstrom of concerts that occurs in an average London season, it is safe to say that, under the conditions that prevail nowadays, not one in several hundred will be of a first-class order. I find it impossible, and indeed wholly unnecessary, to try and work up interest in a musical event which repeats, for the thousand and first time, with all the average and mediocre indifference of performance of all the other thousand, what one may hear once or twice in years, superlatively well done at the hands of the Masters of the Art. As for those concerts at which the very latest and newest of second-hand music is done, those aquaria of goggle-eyed goldfish so very much in the swim, as one knows quite well beforehand how second-hand it all is, why submit to the boredom, irritation and waste of time betaking oneself to an event at which one stands the slenderest chance of being agreeably disappointed?

Aldous Huxley has put the matter quite inimitably as he always does:—

"I simply don't want to be up-to-date. I have lost all desire to see and do the things the seeing and doing of which entitle a man to regard himself as superiorly knowing, sophisticated and unprovincial; I have lost all desire to frequent the places a man simply *must* frequent, if he is not to be regarded as a poor creature hopelessly out of the swim. Why should I have my feelings outraged? Why should I submit to being bored and

---

[7]{Whether this means ca. 1894, ca. 1897, or ca. 1901 is anyone's guess: see p. 59.}

disgusted for the sake of somebody else's categorical imperative? Why? There is no reason. So I simply avoid most of the manifestations of that so-called 'life' which my contemporaries seem to be so unaccountably anxious to 'see.' I keep out of the range of the ART they think it so vitally necessary to 'keep up with.' ..."

Lastly, as a final incentive to my avoidance of concerts: to the concerts to which I do not wish to go, go all the people whom I do not wish to see, and to whom I do not wish to talk. I think all that makes a very good show as a "rationalisation."

(ii) Reasons for having nothing to do with Musicians

In addition to the reasons and/or excuses already set out above, and which are *a fortiori* reasons for avoiding musicians also, there are in addition, these.

It is extremely rare, even rarer among musicians than among other folk, I think, that a musician is a man of all-round high intelligence. As often as not, owing chiefly to physiological abnormalities not far removed — if at all — from the pathological, he is a dexterous manipulator of some instrument, the psychological abnormality being apparently linked with some hypertrophy of the particular area or lobe of the brain controlling the abnormal organs, so that he performs technical executive feats with as little working of a real intelligence, as unconsciously, as involuntarily almost as those fantastic mathematical monsters who will give you instantaneously the product of a couple of factors involving a dozen digits, or the cube root of a nine-figure number on the spot, while being in all other ways nit-wits. Intellectual or spiritual contacts in such cases are neither interesting, profitable nor pleasing.

Bernard van Dieren used to say that music was the last refuge of the feeble-minded, and with no little reason, as is brought home to one when one sees the children who, indicating the presence of little or no normal intelligence in any other direction, are turned over to some unhappy music teacher; the idea being, apparently that, having shown almost total incapacity to learn anything else they might at least learn music. Astonishing to relate, some of them sometimes do, if they have the good fortune to get into the hands of an inspired teacher like a very dear old friend of mine, Mrs. E. Edroff Smith, whose manner with the children's parents is as inimitable as it is with the children themselves. The devastating felicity and perfect appositeness wherewith she could — and I hope still does — put the semi-imbecile parents of almost totally cretinous children in their place, had to be seen — and heard — in action, for its full savour to be relished. Having one of these incarnated suet-puddings dumped on her for "music" lessons, and divining, by a rare clairvoyance, some small shreds of brain, she would set herself to bring these to light and such small fruition as they were capable of. The parents, in the fatuous pride of seeing their brats miraculously raised to the level of the normally silly — prodigious progress — have disordered visions of their becoming Carreños, Menters, Rosenthals, and Heaven knows what all. To them my old friend says that she is not teaching their children MUSIC, that God

Almighty could not do that. ... She is teaching it, or them, to use its brains. She, I think, would feelingly endorse Van Dieren's *mot*.

If one listens — or rather accidentally overhears — I cannot imagine anyone with anything better to do deliberately *listening*, except from an interest purely pathological and possibly psychiatric — to the conversation of average musicians gathered together in the name of Barclay and Perkins or Worthington,[8] Bernard van Dieren's remark seems not in the least exaggerated: if they are executants (and most musicians are), the principal topic of conversation is engagements and press notices (the store so many of them set by these is an extraordinary comment on their intelligence), that is to say "shop" of the dullest and most uninteresting kind, far less interesting and instructive than the "shop" of local farmers over their pints in a Dorset village. Efforts to divert the conversation into channels of a more general significance and interest end invariably in failure, the conversation petering out miserably in monosyllabic interjections. Again, the conventionality and timidity of the ordinary musician's outlook in matters of general import is deeply depressing. One is so often misled into thinking that because a man or a woman has embarked on a career like music, that is sufficiently far removed from the avocations of the multitude, he will for that reason be a person of rather more than ordinary interest, of rather more than ordinary force of character, individuality of outlook and independence of judgment. Vain delusion! In most cases, except for the fact that he is a musician he might be anybody, with anybody's ideas about anything, as avid and as uncritical a mopper-up of press dope as the generality; and to sum up, with no qualities of mind or personality that make any time passed in his neighbourhood, let alone in his company, anything other than spiritually and morally profitless, a waste, null and void.

(iii) Reasons for living in a Granite Tower

One hears a lot about the *tour d'ivoire* as the spiritual home of those creative artists who say with Horace "Odi profanum vulgus, et arceo" — the implication being that their seclusion, while it may be very decorative and graceful, is fragile and brittle like ivory. It is an unfortunate simile, having I think very little relation to the truth of the matter: speaking purely for myself, I want no "ivory tower," but a Tower of Granite with plentiful supplies of boiling oil and molten lead handy to tip over the battlements on to the heads of unwanted and uninvited intruders on my privacy and seclusion. Not nearly enough has been said — if anything at all — in favour of the creative artist, provided he be so minded, deliberately withdrawing from contacts with his fellows, eschewing the society alike of his colleagues the other composers, who make music (sometimes), and of those who still more often mar it, the performers.

The East, which sees (or did) further and deeper in these matters than the present-day West, sees in artistic creation a form of religious activity, or

---

[8]{Sorabji's footnote} They don't often soar as high as Bass or Guinness.

as it is said in India, Yoga — Karma Yoga. Some of the greatest and profoundest treatises upon Yoga give preliminary directions as to circumstances and environment that would fill many Westerners with deep astonishment, prone as they are to associate any form of religious activity with a masochistic asceticism.[9] One of the most authoritative and important of the great Yoga treatises enjoins upon the chela [*recte* celā] the primary necessity of avoiding uncongenial unsympathetic contacts of a personal nature, and disharmonious surroundings of an impersonal nature. The artist, the Karma-Yogin, is far more like to find — more especially if he is a man and personality of conspicuous force and power — those uncongenial unsympathetic and disharmonious personal contacts among other musicians and musical practitioners, especially among those whose inferiority to himself in artistic stature gives them the best, which are also the worst, of reasons for ill-will towards him.

The lot of the creative musician has always seemed to me the least enviable of any, unless he have either the will, courage, and ability, or all three, to make as regards that exceedingly small, exceedingly mean, exceedingly petty "great world of music," *il gran rifiuto*, by declining to have anything to do with it, in so far as his own creative work is concerned. Consider for a moment the cycle of events in the course of the ordinary composer's life. He completes a work after many months, possibly years, of labour. This he proceeds to hawk around like a bagman, to this conductor and that, pestering this performer and that, getting the while the most shocking and humiliating of rebuffs — and what some of our leading composers endure, are even willing to endure, the abject importunities they have recourse to in seeking public performances of their works, would arouse astonished unbelief were I at liberty to recount the instances known to me. Next come the rehearsals (assuming the composer and his work to have got that far, after a plentiful plying of the conductor with his pet booze). He has frequently to put up with agonies of misreading and misinterpretation of his musical intentions, scarcely daring to hazard a suggestion to some stick-swishing swashbuckler, for fear of upsetting that personage, and either having his work deliberately and utterly ruined at the performance (this has happened more than once of recent years if the composer has dared to differ from the conductor at the rehearsals), or having it struck off the programme.

But what a feeling of release, of liberation, to any composer who has the stamina to turn his back on all that, and henceforth, as they say in India, determines to devote himself wholly to his Dharma — that subtle untranslatable word meaning at once inborn ability and the obligation, the moral duty to develop it and practise it to the fullest of one's power. Behold him henceforth for ever emancipated from the unpleasant necessity of waiting hat in hand upon conductors, performers and such cattle, or from having to listen with a pose of respectful attention to the learnedly idiotic gibberings of critics. What a relief no more to have to dine and wine

---

[9]{Sorabji's footnote} Particularly if they have the misfortune to be infected with the Protestant-Puritanic heresy.

star conductors of the tenth magnitude, or listen with an air of simulated interest to the outpourings of egotistical and vanitous trash from performers obsessed with themselves!

I make bold to say that our composers would be the better for devoting themselves to composition alone — and not trying to combine that with the various forms of sycophancy, toadyism and lickspittling that are the prerequisites to securing performances at the hands of those by whom, in many cases, it were far better never to be performed at all.

Moreover, it has to be remembered that the public concert, the public performance of music — apart from the Church, which is another matter altogether — is a very recent development in the millenial history of music. There seems no reason to consider it as either an inevitable development or a lasting and permanent one; indeed a considerable case might be made out for regarding it as little more than a morbid and unhealthy excrescence on the body of music. Even during the period of the development of the public concert, there have been at all times a certain number of works that were neither written nor intended for public performance, but which were addressed to musician-scholars in the quiet, privacy and *recueillement* of the study; there seems no valid reason why those composers who to-day think seeking an audience and performers not only not worth the time and energy which they feel could be put to far better uses, but degrading and humiliating to their self-respect as artists, should not renounce the public performance and the audience deliberately, and devote themselves to the writing of music, first, last, and all the time. This would also tend to introduce a more wholesome and *convenable* atmosphere into the composer-performer relationship, a relationship that tends at present to be extravagantly and disproportionately weighted on the performer's side. There can very well be composers without performers, but no performers without composers. It is neither becoming nor fitting that this primordial primacy should be forgotten, least of all by the composers. What the performers think is seldom of much importance — to music — however much it may be to that feather-headed tribe themselves.

2. From "Karol Szymanowski"

Sorabji rarely praises as highly as he does here. In this excerpt his urge to make comparisons with baser music is held almost entirely in check. Those who find distressing his frequent vituperative criticism and suspect he likes little or nothing ought to read what he says in various places about Rachmaninoff, Medtner, Mahler, Godowsky, Francis George Scott, Van Dieren, Busoni and his pupil Egon Petri, the singers Dinh Gilly and Blanche Marchesi, or the entire article from which the present excerpt comes. Even though they do not explain or justify by appeals to logic, history, or analysis, it is not hard to agree with A. R. Orage's statement (in his introduction to *Around Music*) that Sorabji's "articles for a sensitive reader were almost as vivid as the music they described".[10]

Karol Szymanowski is by general consent of his cultured and art-loving fellow-countrymen reckoned to be their greatest composer since Chopin. It is an estimate that is very much an understatement. Szymanowski's range and scope was immensely greater than that of Chopin, for it embraced every form of musical composition, symphony, opera, ballet, chamber and piano music and songs, and in all these branches his achievement is of the very first order. [...]

The *Third Symphony*, subtitled *Le chant de la nuit*, is a great choral-orchestral work with an elaborate choral part and an extended tenor solo. The poem is from the Dīwān of Jalāl al-Dīn Rūmī, one of the greatest of Irān's mystical poets.[11] That supreme Persian scholar, Edward G. Browne (whose death was mourned in Persia as a national calamity, so greatly was he esteemed and loved there, so great the store set by his services to Iranian literature) says of him: "The greatest of all the Persian Ṣūfī poets. His Mathnawī and Dīwān are among the great poems of all time." Szymanowski has taken a poem from the Dīwān, a poem celebrating the beauty, the enigmatic and transcendental beauty of an Eastern night, the like of which is to be found perhaps nowhere in Europe except in Sicily, which belongs as much to the East as it does to the West. Around this poem, Szymanowski has written music of a radiant purity of spirit, of an elevated ecstasy of expression, music so permeated with the very essence of the choicest and rarest specimens of Irānian art — the whole score glows with gorgeous colour, rich, yet never garish nor crude, like a Persian painting or silk rug — that such a feat is unparalleled in Western music. Here is no European in Eastern fancy-dress, but one who, by a penetrating clairvoyant insight and sympathy, an astonishing kinship of spirit, succeeds in giving us in musical terms what we instinctively know and recognise as the essence of Persian art. And that wonderful blend of ecstasy and languor of which only the great Irānian poets have the secret, to find it expressed with this degree of intensity, this authentic accent, by a Western musician is something the like of which we are not likely soon to see again. The score of the *Third Symphony* is a marvel — firm in structure and essential cohesion, yet disembodied and transparent as gossamer; glowing with the utmost of scintillant luminosity, yet rich in deep dark velvety shadows, elevated and lofty in expression, yet without a hint of magniloquence, pomposity, or the striking of attitudes, rising to a climax of enormous power by the most sovereign mastery of musical means and the ineluctable inner urge, the irresistible interior logic of the very stuff of music, yet with no superfluity, overstress or point-labouring. *The Song of the Night* combines in perfect accord the most discrepant, disparate, and antithetical of qualities. In a word, it remains, as it begins — from its deep murmured unforgettable opening through its sublime heart-stirring climax to its

---

[10]The following excerpt comes from pp. 178 and 183–84 of *Mi contra fa.*
[11]He lived from 1207 to 1273.

unforgettable close, fading out in the deep blue luminousness of the Eastern night, in passages for whose beauty one scarcely dares to breathe — a perfect and incomparable masterpiece.

Unpublished Writings

From Correspondence

If Sorabji wrote one letter every three days from 1915 to 1985, he would have written more than 8,500 altogether. In reality he probably wrote tens of thousands.

The speed with which he must often have produced his letters could give his handwritten efforts the appearance of an indecipherable scrawl. As for his manipulations of a typewriter, Sorabji complained that he could never "learn this accursed instrument"; the results were what his friend Norman Peterkin called not typed but "tryped".

In the letters presented here, the punctuation, spelling, and underlining remain as faithful as possible to the source, in order to give the best representation (short of facsimile reproduction) of Sorabji's writing style. The only significant typographical change is the reduction of Sorabji's rare double underlining to single. The occasional odd punctuation, awkward repetition, grammatical lapse, etc. in the English are not corrected when they do not obscure meaning. They are an essential component of the *ex tempore* nature of Sorabji's prose.

The few editorial additions are enclosed in square brackets. Three dots in brackets, i.e. [...], attached to a sentence or paragraph indicate that part of it is omitted; the same bracketed dots on a line by themselves indicate that a paragraph or more has been skipped over. Three dots without brackets represent Sorabji's own points of suspension, which range in appearance from ".." to "_ _ ..." and other varieties. The dates, which are given at the beginning of each excerpt, have a standardized format which does not necessarily reflect Sorabji's practice.

The letters are printed in small type, comments in large type. The comments are kept to a minimum. (Simple spelling errors or anomalies go unnoted, such as *its* for *it's* and *dont* for *don't*.) The letters almost speak for themselves, whether they are friendly or not, reflective or vehement, formal or intimate. Sorabji read widely and wrote richly: creativity jumps out off every page of these letters. Of the hundreds I have examined, very few are uninteresting.

Although the addressees of these letters all maintained a correspondence with Sorabji for about 40 years, it came to a close in each case for different reasons. The correspondence with Erik Chisholm ended with his death in 1965, that with Norman Gentieu because of the infirmities leading to Sorabji's death in 1988, and that with Frank Holliday because of a quarrel in the late 1970s (although there are a few letters to him from the 1980s).

The selection of letters offered here by no means gives an adequate representation of Sorabji's relationship to the addressees, nor of the very high regard in which he held each of them.

1. To Erik Chisholm

Erik Chisholm (1904–65) was an energetic teacher, author, composer, and administrator, principally in Scotland and South Africa. Much of his correspondence with Sorabji comes from 1929–31, when Chisholm lived in Glasgow and Sorabji in London. Sorabji met him for the first time when he travelled to Glasgow to perform his Fourth Piano Sonata (on 1 April 1930) for Chisholm's Active Society for the Propagation of Contemporary Music. After that meeting, his letters to Chisholm became longer and more intimate. It is clear that the intensity in some had as much to do with his esteem for Erik Chisholm, whom he referred to once as his "other soul", as for the music he was writing or hearing. Chisholm and Sorabji remained life-long friends, although their correspondence diminished after Chisholm married and eventually settled in South Africa.

Chisholm preserved what appears to be most of the Sorabji side of the correspondence. These letters from Sorabji discuss anything and everything, giving a vivid representation of his personality, beliefs, problems, and activities, as well as those of a number of his contemporaries as he saw them.

Rarely do we find a composer writing about his own composition almost as each section of it is written. In the case of *Opus clavicembalisticum*, we have Sorabji's comments both during the writing of the work and after, the latter in the form of a short analysis of it appended to its manuscript.[12] More valuable by far are the former, in a series of letters to Chisholm written over a period of exactly six months, from shortly after the work was begun until the day it was completed. These are the excerpts printed here. Although they provide no analytical insights, no solutions to manuscript difficulties, and no direct clues for performance of the work, they

---

[12]Published in the insert notes to John Ogdon's recording of *Opus clavicembalisticum* (Altarus AIR–CD–9075), pp. 21–27.

Erik Chisholm in 1934 (photo from a concert program)

reveal the environment of *O.C.*'s creation — often its composer's ways of thinking about matters both musical and other which were wrapped up with the composition he was writing. Although there is a lack of superficial "information", there is a wealth of psychological inference to be gained from these letters. One conclusion emerges readily: were it not for Erik Chisholm, *O.C.* might have been a quite different work, at least in its Parts II and III, comprising the seven movements which were all written after Sorabji had met him.

During the composition of *O.C.*, Sorabji was in the habit of writing to Chisholm frequently. Sometimes he started a letter, wrote for several pages, returned to it after a few hours or a day or two, and eventually mailed it. The pauses between parts of a letter were sometimes filled by composition of pages of *O.C.*, or to put it the other way around, sometimes Sorabji filled the time required to let the ink on a page of *O.C.* dry by writing a few more lines or pages of a letter. Sometimes the result was a concatenated letter of 20, 30, or more pages.

Not all of these letters are extant in Sorabji's handwriting, but fortunately, when Chisholm was Director of the South African College of Music in Cape Town, he had a secretary transcribe many on a typewriter — an arduous task, considering Sorabji's difficult script. In the presentation below, heading dates with an asterisk indicate a letter which could be examined only in typescript. The others are transcribed from Sorabji's originals. It is likely that all were written in London, although only a few of those quoted actually indicate so.

25 December 1929

Actually I am very much involved and wrapped up in a very large and complex new piano work <u>Opus Sequentiale</u> inspired admittedly by the Fantasia Contrappuntistica of Busoni with which I presume to flatter myself it has a mood feeling not at all un-akin. Here is the scheme of this portentous work

    I.   Introito
              – Nexus – leading to
    II.   Preludio Corale –
    III.   Fugue I (2 c[ounter] subjects developed independently)
                   completed as far as this fugue.
    IV.   Toccata-Fantasia
    V.   Fuga II. (duplex)
    VI.   Interludium I
    VII.   Cadenza I
    VIII. Fuga III. (Triplex)

IX.   Interludium II
X.   Cadenza II.
XI.   Fuga IV. (quadruplex)
XII. Coda. Stretta.

                                          ?!!!!!!!?!?

It is significant that at most a few weeks before he would have begun *O.C.*, Sorabji had heard and reviewed Egon Petri's performance of Busoni's *Fantasia contrappuntistica*.[13]

Even though by 25 December Sorabji had already laid out the plan of the work, he had completed only about eleven percent of it. Many other works were also completely planned in overall form before much, if any, of the music was written — with very little or no alteration later to the plan.

There are only minor differences between the plan above (as far as it goes) and the finished work. Sorabji deleted *Toccata* from the *Fantasia* of section 4 (IV). *Nexus* became attached to section 2 rather than section 1. Only later did he determine the shape of the two interludes, which became gigantic.

At this time, Sorabji was also writing a *Passacaglia* for piano and his Second Organ Symphony, and was considering a Second Piano Quintet. The latter two were eventually finished; he put all three aside until *O.C.* was completed. The *Passacaglia* apparently remained incomplete; an unfinished manuscript of it came to light early in 1989.

---

[13]Sorabji wrote as follows:

The rather terrifying quality of the work, its monumental grandeur, its severe and ascetic splendour, its eerie magnificence, its utter uniqueness were realised in a performance of such insight, such mastery, such vast power that it seems a human being cannot accomplish more [...] It is useless to talk of the prodigious variety of style yet unified with such utterly satisfying completeness, of the brain staggering complexity of its unprecedented structure — a choral prelude, a sequence of three fugues, single, double, and triple, in succession, an Intermezzo with three variations, a Cadenza, a fourth and quadruple Fugue, a repetition on an astonishing pedal figure of the Chorale from the choral prelude, and finally a cataclysmic Stretta — of the almost unendurable "excitement of the soul," a performance such as this never-to-be-forgotten one of Petri's gave one.
(*The New Age*, vol. 46 (21 November 1929), p. 32.)

2 February 1930

I have finished the 4th movement or section of the <u>Opus Sequentiale</u> and have begun the second (and double) fugue. It is already 44 pages long and there are 8 more sections to come!!

14 March 1930

The second fugue of the Opus Sequentiale completed yesterday after a perfect Hell of a stretto — 4 forms each of 2 themes c. subject: c. subject from 1st fugue and other such delights — it's already 60 pp. long and I'm not half way through it yet!! There follows an Interludium (theme and variations) on a sombre grave para-diatonic theme ... all of which is more or less what!

The second fugue reintroduces the subject and first countersubject from the first fugue, while itself offering two new subjects and one new countersubject.

5 April 1930

It gives me great joy to think I have spurred you on to work. I am a little slow to get back to mine — have only done two variations on the 1st Interlude of the Opus Sequentiale — which by the way is to be renamed <u>Opus Clavicembalisticum.</u> I had meant to play you the first 60 pp. and indeed carted it up to Glasgow with that end in view — but there was so much other to do and talk about that it was pushed into the background. It will be longer than the 4th Sonata. I'm not yet ½ way through it and it already totals 62 pages!.

Sorabji had just returned to London from Glasgow, where he had played his Fourth Piano Sonata (on 1 April). The first 60 pages of *O.C.* contain all of Part I, up to the end of Fugue 2. Sorabji appears not to have written any of *O.C.* between 14 March and the time of the results reported in this letter, which must have come from between 2 and 5 April. This is not surprising, given his preparation and travel for the Glasgow performance.

11 April 1930

Yes. I will come to Glasgow next Season for another recital if you really want me to, but I think the Opus Clavicembalisticum would be better. It ought to be done in 2 or 3 months now, although the biggest and most intricate parts are yet to come. i.e. the 3rd and 4th Fugues with the

Passacaglia and Stretta. It is the sternest most uncompromising work I have ever done, austere, ascetic — it ought to be liked in Glasgow I think, dark and menacing in feeling. I like it very well myself — [...]

In the margin, in reference to the possible recital of *O.C.* in Glasgow, Sorabji wrote "<u>but don't say anything to a soul yet</u> <u>about it!! On your life, silence!!</u>"

Chisholm had suggested a performance of Sorabji's Variations and Fugue on *Dies iræ*, which Sorabji objected to because it was too long: "I should be a <u>corpse</u> if I played that work! it is half as long again nay nearly double the length of the 4th Sonata!" Clearly he had not yet realized the ultimate dimensions of *O.C.*: see the letter from 20 April.

18 April 1930
[Sorabji noted it only as Good Friday]

[...] how mortally weary I am after some very high pressure work — 20 pages of most intricate and closely wrought stuff in little over 9 days out of which take 2 for copying your <u>Trois Poèmes</u> and another day or two when I did not write anything at all — [...]

Sorabji sent Chisholm a copy of his (Sorabji's) *Trois poèmes du Gulistān de Saʻdī* as a show of good faith, as he put it, before writing a symphony for him. The symphony he never completed, but the complete piano part, from 1930–31 and forming a work in itself, is extant.

19 April 1930
[Sorabji noted it only as Holy Saturday]

I have turned the 32nd variation of the 1st interlude of the "Clavicembalisticum" today — there are to be 49 of them (49 = 7 x 7 i.e. a perfect square) — the most nerve-wracking portion of the work (in the triple and quadruple fugues) is still before me. Still if I can keep up my present furious pace I shall have the 2nd interlude i.e. following the 3rd Fugue well under way by the time I come to Glasgow. Do you want me to bring it with me so you can have a smell at it? I am very well content with it — it is I think thoroughly mature and "established" so to speak, in musical physiognomy.

Sorabji went to Glasgow on 23 May; see the letter of 12 May.

20 April 1930
[Sorabji noted it only as Easter Day]

I am now on Variation 35 — and so it goes Heigh oh dear Erik, the other page is dry so I leave you for a space.
[...]
Later: (after Variation 36) Loud and enthusiastic applause! 4 variations today ... at this rate anything may happen. Eblis himself is to be invoked in 49. The second Interlude is to be a Toccata Adagio and Passacaglia — form finally cast ... the work I estimate at about 200 pages of MS. as near as possible, or nearly twice as long as the 4th Sonata ...

The Islamic Eblis (Iblīs) is equivalent to Satan. Once a rebellious angel, he became the demon ruler of the devils. As completed, O.C.'s Variation 48 seems a more likely home for him than Variation 49.

21 April 1930

Another day of it — (up to Variation 42 now!) all very good I feel sure, but My God I'm getting tired! Tomorrow evening is that blasted B.B.C. affair about which I told you. I shall rejoice when it is over and done with.

On the next day Sorabji performed *Le jardin parfumé* in what turned out to be his only performance over the BBC.

23 April 1930

I have just for the first time discovered that admirable Scotch liqueur (albeit of originally French origin) "Drambuie" — I don't know when I have tasted anything I like so much. "Drambuie" is surely indicated between the "Fyltes" of the Opus Clavicembalisticum — i.e. Opus = a work: Clavicembalum = a cymbalon with keys: plus termination = isticum = adjectival indicating belonging to or pertaining to. See what a classical education does for (or to) you!!! Fortunately I escaped Greek and consequently any risk of Græcomania or græcophobia.

24 April 1930

Started Variation 45 today: hope to have the whole set finished by Sunday — then for the 3ple Fugue!! ... Once again I take leave of you — [...]

On 23 April, Sorabji had become distraught because he could only find paper that was five-eighths of an inch wider and half an inch narrower than the Italian manuscript paper he had been using for *O.C.* Having run out of this, he did not want to continue the work on the new paper and be forced to have the two sizes bound together when it was completed. As a fastidious bibliophile, he could not contemplate such a "constant eyesore shame and irritation". He was even prepared to recopy the already written 90 pages of *O.C.* onto the new paper in order to avoid "a bookbinding atrocity that no selfrespecting bibliophile can contemplate without horror". Fortunately, the following day he went to Zaehnsdorf bookbinders (in London), who explained how it was possible to bind the two sizes without anyone noticing the difference. He was immensely relieved.

Anyone who has seen the extraordinary bindings of many of Sorabji's manuscripts or knows of his care over and understanding of the art of binding will readily appreciate this story. This was a serious crisis. Had it not been as short-lived as it was, it might have altered *O.C.* in some ways — even if it seems from these letters that nothing could stop its course.

3 May 1930

[...] I've been unwell — tormented with an inflamed throat (septic) ... a visit to my old leech today revealed violent inflammation, he also found me feverish — hence stern orders to take things quietly (as if I could, of all people!!) and menaces against overwork. ... [...] Well — I've done it i.e. the 49 variations of the 1st Interlude and the 1st Cadenza: today drew the subject (1st) of the Third (and triple) fugue (p. 106 of MS.) The work is amazingly good: much better than Dies Irae as I'm sure you'll agree when you see what's done of it.

5 May 1930

Now dearest Boy I must return to the Triple Fugue for a space ... it is dry and calls in reproachful contrapuntally plaintive tones! ... so I go where it calls me damn it and blast it I am going to hate it before its done!! Three intricately wrought Fugue pages today: I feel so nervy and restless tonight [...]

Needless to add, perhaps: when Sorabji wrote "it is dry", he meant the ink and not the music itself.

9 May 1930

The Opus Clavicembalisticum progresses — 1st section of the 3rd and triple Fugue finished: I'm immensely pleased with it all as will you be my Angel! (Perhaps! "Angel" I mean for Perhaps!)

10 May 1930

Op. Clavicem. is tiring me out badly ... I feel very jaded these days, must, I quite see, go slow — I never do, of course[.] I only talk a great deal about doing so. It generally means that I'm going to slog away at higher pressure than ever. [...] I break off to drink tea.
Later: I've drunk my tea and now come trotting back to my Werk Tisch to chatter to you again before getting on with the 3rd Fugue.

12 May 1930

The second part of the triple Fugue is completed. I shall have quite a good deal to show you on Friday week ... how blessedly near it is! I think I shall have a three-cornered fit when the Day arrives!

*28 May 1930

Now I leave you for a space to get on with the Second Interlude — last left in room 41!!
[...]
Two more pages to dry:
[...]
The Toccata just finished
[...]
The toccata is now five pages longer than it was when you saw it on Monday — very well proportioned I think — now comes the Adagio grave and tenderly serious as it will be I hope ...

*29 May 1930

Now to the Adagio though how I am going to write this afternoon God knows — my mood of exaltation has all gone and left me right down in the "Well of Loneliness" (apologies to that clever authoress Radclyffe Hall!)[.] Still — here goes — at it!
[...]
Schéhérazade-Kaikhosru resumes his (her) tale — she sees the dawn is breaking — that is to say a page more has to dry and she interrupts the story of her Adagio to continue her more or less artless prattle about other

things. But the page has dried quicker than she expected so the <u>Adagio</u> — a very beautiful and interesting story about the Shark and his friend the handsome young prince Nureddior* — continues [...]

Footnote *Mirza el. Akbari and Fakreddin ul. Mulk following the Baghdad commentators say that this name should be spelt "E"—"R"—"K" an "I" being suggested for the elided letter.

Radclyffe Hall's *The Well of Loneliness* (London: Jonathan Cape, 1928), a novel of lesbian love, was banned in England as obscene shortly after its publication.

Although the source typescript almost certainly misspells the names in Sorabji's own mock-footnote,[14] his spoof of the *Arabian Nights* is clear enough.

1 June 1930

The Adagio of the Interlude II finished yesterday night in a stately procession of 37 chords in ever changing harmony right down from the top of the keyboard on a held C♯ major chord — very impressive I think. I've just done the 8th variation of the Passacaglia which is going to go very well a nice cranky theme with <u>one</u> even bar in three.

3 June 1930

Twenty variations of the Passacaglia since I started this. My head is burning inside and I'm trembling ... [...]

*5 June 1930

"Clavicembalisticum" grows apace 39 of the 81 passacaglia variations are now done. It will be about as long as <u>Dies Irae</u> if not, only a very little less, but <u>miles</u> and <u>miles</u> beyond it in every way. I shall probably indeed I am seriously thinking of destroying <u>Dies Irae</u> — I have been looking on it with a sour cold eye and I don't think <u>really</u>, it pleases me any more ... and write an entirely new work thereon later. How's that for an idea? Digest it and tell me what you think of it.

Sorabji eventually did write a new work on the same theme, the *Sequentia cyclica* of 1948–49. Fortunately he did not destroy the *Dies*

---

[14]"Nureddior", for example, should probably be *Nureddin*.

iræ Variations mentioned here. Throughout his life he was attracted to the *Dies iræ* chant; it is found in several of his major works.

*9 June 1930
[Sorabji noted it only as Whit Monday]

A few words to you before I go to bed ... I've just come in ... and a little concentration you-ward ... I'm getting more weary every day 56 variations now done ... I feel sometime I can hardly hold out to the end the spread is so great and yet it goes [...]
   [...]
64 Variations completed up to date ... 17 more only — then Cadenza II. THEN Fugue IV!

*10 June 1930

I'm going to be a thorough wet-blanket today ... I'm full of weary bitterness, most intense morbid despondency ... I don't know what's happening to me ... my rest grows steadily worse ... ½ past three this morning before I got to sleep and wide awake again for good at ½ past six ... Clavicembalisticum at the 181st page! But oh! God how can I finish it in time? ... I'm a miserable creature! ... a wretched worm for all my proud spirit.
   [...]
I'm one mass of jangling nerves all over — touch me anywhere and it sets my teeth on edge ... my head aches — my eyes ache my back legs and arms ache ... I'm an incarnate perambulating ache ... What a lot! Nevertheless I've completed 76 variations today ... and so it goes — [...]

The first performance had by now been scheduled for December 1930. Sorabji's high-strung nervousness was doing him in. The distresses, or at least his relating them in such colourful terms, may well have helped him in some way to get on with *O.C.*, at least at the speed he deemed necessary.

*11/12 June 1930

Kyrie Eleison! the 81st variation — a tremendous thing in broken alternating chords in "♩'s" up and down the keyboard finished this pomeriggio verso le 2.!!! now the second cadenza and Fugue IV only.
   Later. Young Gray Fisk to tea with me — overwhelmed at the spectacle of Clavicembalisticum. Have just added an epilogue to the passacaglia a quiet repetition of the theme over slow moving darkly coloured harmony — most effective! Very pleased with the whole work. The thing I feel has an

imperious majesty of movement and breadth of style that I don't think I have yet reached in any of my other works — don't you think so too? the second Interlude <u>has</u> worked out longer than the first — but the necessity of the form demanded it[. I]t means I suppose an extra ¼ hour or twenty minutes on the performance — it can't be helped. The musical necessities and not the convenience or comfort of the audience are what matters in these high regions of Brahman manifesting as Art.

The Italian means *afternoon about 2*. Obviously the typist did not know much Italian, for in the extant typescript this phrase reads "porneiggio versole 2". Also, *Brahman* is spelled *Brahmah*. Other mistakes in the typed copies, especially in foreign phrases, are likely, although in many places they seem carefully transcribed.

The American-born Clinton Gray-Fisk (1904–61) later became an important music critic in England and remained a friend of Sorabji's the rest of his life. Sorabji dedicated several works to him.

15 June 1930

I started the last fugue today and finished Cadenza II (it's now 200 pp. long!!!) but it <u>is</u> a marvellous work although I say it as shouldn't! And it is getting on my nerves and it <u>is</u> wearing me down!

16 June 1930

I hope you can read this — I took a double dose of my sleeping medicine last night and feel in consequence rather drugged and stupid this morning — and the bloody pen must need go and run dry into the bargain. <u>Damn</u> and <u>Blast</u> everything!

19 June 1930

I have a headache that has lasted 6 days up to date — something of a record meseems: Clavicembalisticum now at 223rd page third section of 4uple Fugue well underway.

21 June 1930

This letter does not progress with great fluency <u>does</u> it? Am today started on the 4th part of the quadruple fugue <u>a quattro soggetti</u>. It's now in 5 voices continuously — the first time I have done a 5 voice fugue in a piano work.

310 *The Prose*

23 June 1930

Last section of 4ple fugue well under way. Shall have reached the Coda Stretta tomorrow.

25 June 1930

With a racking head and literally my whole body shaking as with ague I write this and tell you I have just this afternoon early <u>finished</u> Clavicembalisticum (252 pages — <u>longer</u> than Dies IRAE and immeasurably better ... the final Coda Stretta <u>is</u> an achievement with the 4 forms of each subject running through the fabric linked with quotations of earlier fugue subjects declaimed with massive vehemence. The closing 4 pages are as cataclysmic and catastrophic as anything I've ever done — the harmony bites like nitric acid the counterpoint grinds like the mills of God to close finally on this implacable monosyllable:—

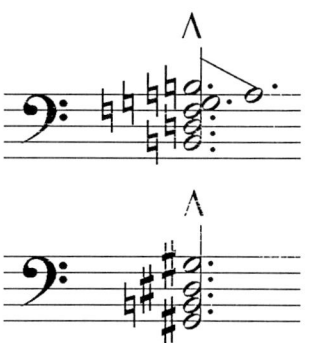

"I am the Spirit that denies!"
But <u>how</u> it's drained me ... I feel like Christ when he said Virtue has gone out of me! And I too: all my courage all my strength!! God! I am a half dead thing!

"Ich bin der Geist der stets verneint!", from Goethe's *Faust*, Part I, line 1338. This quotation and the one from the Bible Sorabji had already linked in his letter of 18 April, where he associated the Biblical idea with "utterly forespent weariness and bitter despondency [...] in some great effort of activity of [the] higher faculties". His meaning on 25 June is clear enough, even though he misused the line in a way that is predictable from the line itself. This King James version of Luke 8:46 is misleading (as the King James often is, despite its poetry); "virtue" is an obsolete translation of a word which suggests the power of faith, and "gone out of" suggests loss or draining, which has nothing to do with the Biblical situation.

One would think that Sorabji took a long rest after this ordeal. Indeed, he went on to write, in the letter of 25 June:

> And now a rest I <u>must</u> have for a space before I set about the E. C. Symphony ... and the rest of the 2nd Organ Symphony ... I shall I think do no more composition this side of September ...

But his very next words were

> unless ... unless ... I take some to Corfe Castle with me [...]

He began the "E. C." symphony on 1 July, but, as mentioned earlier, never completed more than its piano part. It is gigantic (333 pages).

2. To Norman P. Gentieu

Having read *Around Music* just after the Second World War, Norman P. Gentieu (b. 1914), at that time of Lansdowne, Pennsylvania, wrote to express his admiration for it to its author, offering to send him some goods to help alleviate the shortages which persisted in England after the war's end. Sorabji replied immediately; in a letter of 10 March 1946 he thanked Gentieu for his sentiments: "I am deeply touched by the impulse so kind, considerate[,] thoughtful and generous that prompts your charming offer." Over the next four decades, Gentieu continued to send Sorabji a great deal of food and other things, even after the shortages ceased, as gestures of heartfelt friendship.

In the early 1950s Gentieu offered to pay for the microfilming of Sorabji's complete works and to place a few copies of the films in selected libraries, thereby ensuring a virtually permanent existence of Sorabji's scores. Because he suspected that Sorabji would refuse his offer on grounds that it was too generous a gift from one person, he formed a Society of Connoisseurs to be the financiers. He was virtually the sole member (a fact that he kept from Sorabji but which Sorabji eventually figured out). He even wrote Society letters on a striking red and black letterhead, created by the former master counterfeiter Baldwin S. Bredell, showing figures of Thoth and Isis.

As for the offer to microfilm his music, Sorabji could scarcely believe it:

"Macch[é] ... macch[é] ...What AM I to say of the microfilm project. OF COURSE ITS ADMIRABLE ... BUT the COST ... MY DEAR DEAR MAN!!!! the works you mention are 300 and 400 odd pages long <u>EACH</u> ... Its utterly beyond MY remotest capacity ... financially I mean. But I CANNOT believe that the Society of Connoisseurs are willing to finance such a project ... without, that is, fully real[is]ing what the poor dears are letting themselves in for. Anyway, if I have misunderstood, misinterpreted or otherwise mentally garbled their intentions, please disabuse me[.][15]

The plan apparently started as one to microfilm Sorabji's major piano works, soon became one to microfilm all of his unpublished piano music, and eventually expanded to include all his unpublished manuscripts.[16]

A few years later Gentieu formed a second plan: to send Sorabji a tape recorder. (By this time the Society of Connoisseurs had become The Criterion Club, but the subterfuge was the same.) He paid the required funds to Bernard van Dieren Jr., who was living in Philadelphia. Van Dieren then had the equivalent taken out of his English account to have the machine bought there — necessary because at the time there were strict limits on how much sterling one could take out of the country, and Van Dieren needed the money. There remained the problem of getting the recorder to Sorabji in Dorset, and the bigger problem of inducing him to record something on it. The former was solved, the latter not.

Frequently in his letters Gentieu asked Sorabji if he could visit him in Dorset. Sorabji was eager for this to happen, but one thing and another always prevented Gentieu from going. He finally went to see Sorabji in 1985.

Although he lived far from Sorabji and saw him only once, his insight and generosity did Sorabji a world of good. Sorabji responded warmly to anyone who appreciated him in what he felt was the right way for the right reasons. Norman Gentieu was certainly such a person.

---

[15]Kaikhosru Sorabji: Letter to Norman Gentieu, 1 October 1952.

[16]{Some pieces were not filmed, either because Sorabji did not have them, did not uncover them, or thought little of them. Gentieu continued to have microfilms made of Sorabji's works up to and including the *Fourth Toccata*, completed in 1967. Many unfilmed works were microfilmed by Paul Rapoport and Alistair Hinton in 1978.}

London, 27 November 1947

Your remarks anent the "spiritual energy" emanating from a great interpreter and his audience chime with a pet theory of my own. I have long held that not only the written notes, as Busoni said, are merely a clumsy shorthand for the musical substance they are intended to communicate, but that even performance itself also is a <u>hint</u> of what IS there, a hint limited by instruments ears and all such things. It is the psychic impact of the performers' mind upon those of the sensitively attuned that really communicates the musical meanings through the obstructing media of ears, instruments and all. Does this sound VERY transcendental and far-fetched?

You know, I DONT believe music is promoted by having it laid on like water, gas, electricity and plumbing! ... When a thing is vulgarised, even in the original derivatively classical sense of the word, by being spread among the "vulgar" ... "vulgus ..." the crowd, there happens to it what happens to pound-notes, dollar-notes and such, in ceaseless circulation ... they get grubby, crumbled greasy and thoroughly nasty in the end ...!... No ... if people WANT music, they should go AFTER it ... as well bring a baseball field to everyone's apartment, a fishing stream to everybody's kitchen garden and so on ... as well ... AND AS ILL! [...]

Now, as always you overwhelm me with kindnesses already in transit or proffered! Such utterly disinterested generosity and kindness one does not often encounter in one lifetime. Its the essence of real Fransiscan [*recte* Franciscan] Christianity and charity and I am deeply touched and appreciative of it. No thank you very many times, I do not smoke so your generosity will not be trenched upon for any thing of THAT kind. But, since you are kind enough to ask me I'd deeply appreciate a spare head for my <u>SCHICK SUPER</u> and a spare head for my latest model <u>LARGE HEADED SHAVEMASTER. (MODEL "S".</u>) My Roto I've disposed of to a friend, as these two latter (the Schick and the new Shavemaster are QUITE THE most wonderful shaving instruments I've ever come across).

[...]

Your story of John Barrymore amused me vastly. There is one analogous to it told of Sir Herbert Beerbohm Tree. When playing Wolsey in Henry VIII he spotted a man in the stalls ostentatiously reading the sporting edition of some evening paper. Advancing with a stately Cardinalian swish to the footlights, he hissed at the man "WHO WON THE TWO THIRTY?" ... After a moments petrified silence he declaimed magnificently, to the audience ... "HE DOESNT KNOW!" ... Imagine how the house roared, and the discomfiture of the illmannered one!

[...]

I see no reason at all why one should refrain from sharpening one's wits and amusing oneself and one's friends by acid comments upon the multifarious manifestations of human, especially musically human imbecillity!!! I'M always doing it ... but what can you expect from me ... a Latin twice over from my Iranian ancestry on my father's side ... "where the cats and carpets come from["] ... and therefore catty, like the former ... and Latin from my mother's Sicilian family origins ... And whatever Latin

mirth may be its always well barbed ... and hardly "innocent fun"!!!!! My Cardinal-Archbishop four-times-great-Grand-uncle who was Cardinal-Archbishop of Palermo in Nelson's time and was a gorgeous old blackguard who lived to the ripely sinful old age of ninety-eight and a half was wont to say that the reason why he wasnt kicked neck and crop out of the Church ... for Black-Magical dabblings ... I possess his ring, by the way[17] ... was that the Holy Father couldnt make up his mind which was worse, the scandal of a top-notcher Cardinal being hoofed out of the Church or quietly allowing him to pursue his nefarious course technically INSIDE it, to the great undoing of souls ... The perfect balance of the Holy Father's uncertainty kept dear Cardinal four times great grand uncle safely in his Cardinal's stall! ... At this very moment, I am the proud possessor of a sweet old great-Aunt who is the Abbess of a convent in Sicily, an enclosed order; I cant go inside to see her, but that doesnt prevent her blowing kisses to me from windows in the walls when my Mother goes inside to see her[.] A thoroughly realistic and Latin combination of the exigencies of religious obligations and family affectional ones! This sort of thing is apt to shock Northe[r]ners who lack Latin "souplesse" in these matters!
[...]
But I think I've inflicted more than enough upon you for one sitting; I'll take my leave and say again how delighted I always am to hear from you and to express for the forty-eleventh time my sensibility to your unfailing kindness and generosity to

                    Yours very sincerely;

                    Kaikhosru Shapurji Sorabji.

The first paragraph of the letter above relates closely to what Sorabji wrote in "'Performance' *versus* 'Celebration'" in *Around Music*,[18] and to what he often wrote about Busoni.

Sorabji attached much importance to his ancestry. There is more than a little of his Cardinal Archbishop in him. Whenever he described himself as a transplanted tropical plant or a Persian cat, Sorabji usually added in some colourful way that his emotions did not recognize moderation.

Corfe Castle, 31 July 1959

For me, I work now continually (more or less!) on the great symphonic HIGH MASS, am now in the midst of the SANCTUS getting on towards the 700th page of full score. I am also feeling full of spiritual pride and

---

[17]According to Sorabji, there was a curse on the ring if any female member of the family wore it.

[18]{See pp. 288–90 of the present book for the entire article.}

Norman P. Gentieu in about 1950

arrogance having lately completed a six day fast ... I used to do this sort of thing every year before the War, but dropped it during that world-lunacy. Then, in 1957 I decided I was getting or had got, slack and determined to take them up again. I always used to do them at the solstice i.e. in mid June so started with four days, then last year five, now this, six[.] Next year it will be seven. Holding as I do that the only discipline worth undergoing, if you have the pride of Satan (as I have!) is a self-imposed one, I do this sort of thing, or used to do for that reason alone, not health or dietetic; although important results of that kind often follow, but they are not my primary nor even secondary concern. So there you are! I recall, many years ago, before the World Lunacy, when I was about to start a long one (nine days) I mentioned this to a fanatically vegetarian female I used to know ... She killed her own very gifted and clever husband with this mania of hers ... and she remarked "Oh how wonderful Mr. S!" and knowing that I was NOT a vegetarian said "Of course you lose all your perverted desire for meat you know doing these long fasts!" Now as at that time I had already been at this game for YEARS and knowing it to be a COMPLETE MYTH, I could not resist replying "Dear lady, that be damned for a tale, I dont lose my taste for flesh food AT ALL[.]" "Oh?" she said terribly shocked ... "But dont you look forward eagerly to the beautiful fruit with which you will break your fast?" (You of course know that a long fast must be broken so and not with anything that imposes any more strain upon a digestion that has been dormant for so long a time[)]: "Yes," I said ... I regard the fruit with mild interest ... but what sets me a-dribble is the smell and thought of my first bit of flesh food and the smell of it tastily cooking!" Poor dear ... she was most TERRIBLY shocked! AND when I told her that as a babby the thing that was given to me AS A LAST RESORT WHEN THEY THOUGHT I WAS GOING TO CONK OUT BEING UNABLE EITHER TO RETAIN OR DIGEST MILK OF ANY KIND IN ANY SHAPE OR FORM, WAS THE BLOOD OF RAW MEAT, on which I throve and which I showed every sign of immensely enjoying as other babbers enjoy milk ... she was frankly APPALLED!!!! ... Poor souls! The one-idea'd ... WHAT harm they do to themselves and everybody else!

There may well have been some malice in the fun of the conversation Sorabji reports. He was quite capable of enjoying having others squirm at his conversational repartees.

Corfe Castle, 21 August 1972

The most idiotic question that I get asked by friends who still live (God help them) in what I call the INTERNATIONAL HUMAN RUBBISH DUMP sc. London is "what do you find to DO in the country?" ... When I tell them that I have a very big correspondence, do all my own housework[,] my godbrother ... I call him that because he's my late beloved Mother's godson ... so he MUST be my godbrother mustnt he? ... does the cooking and very well indeed he does it. That and shopping which has to be done in the small country market town of Wareham some miles away and the time is pretty fully occupied[.] THEN in good summer weather yes, it DOES OCCASIONALLY OCCUR EVEN HERE! ... a little excursion to some village or vicarage garden party or fête or a visit to some lovely house or garden that's open to the public during the summer months at intervals, and the time is VERY fully occupied. Then of course there is listening to the radio ... AND by the way WHAT my dear friend CAN be said for Master John Cage??????? I listened to a bit of an alleged composition the other evening for forty-eleven harpsichords ... Now in SOME cases of the "contempry" practitioners one can get a laugh out of them for the first few minutes ... but Johnny Cage wasnt funny for any time at all, only UNUTTERABLY DULL TIRESOME AND DREARY. One is told of his enormous influence on contemporary American music ... in THAT case, all one can say is GOD HELP CONTEMPORARY AMERICAN MUSIC! But it seems we live in a time when the most demented twaddle is accepted and seriously discussed. Did you hear of an occasion at a Donau[es]chingen "Festival" of, of course CONTEMPRY stuff about a certain work done there? A group of players come on to the platform playing any old thing in any old way joining in at any old time while the "composer" shies EGGS at a blackboard. At the "rehearsal" of this piece the composer expressed himself as highly satisfied with the result ... BUT ... at the performance some joker good luck to him GOT HOLD OF THE EGGS TO BE USED IN THE PERFORMANCE AND HARD BOILED THEM!!!!!!!

3. To Frank Holliday

Frank Holliday (b. 1912) met Sorabji in London in 1937 through the writer and lecturer Bernard Bromage. They soon became good friends. Over the years Sorabji often said that he depended on Holliday's understanding, advice, and company more than on those of anyone except Reginald Best.[19] The only four people for whom Sorabji liked to play the piano included Holliday,[20] who probably heard him play over a longer period than anyone else except Best.

The correspondence from Sorabji to Holliday is extraordinarily rich, containing discussions of every conceivable subject. Among other things, it reveals how much Holliday did for Sorabji's music. He was the dedicatee of three works written between 1940 and 1967 and became the "retrospective" dedicatee of another.[21] Over the course of 17 months, from late 1951 to the spring of 1953, he organized and circulated to Sorabji's distinguished friends and

---

[19]With whom he lived for the last 38 years of his life.

[20]The others being Erik Chisholm, Reginald Best, and later Alistair Hinton.

[21]Which had been written long before they met. Sorabji obliterated the dedication to Bernard Bromage and rededicated the work to Holliday.

associates all over the world a presentation letter to be signed by these people urging him to make a recording, and gathered funds to help Sorabji do so. But Sorabji did not record at that time.[22]

Finally, after trying for about two decades (his efforts went back at least to the early 1940s), he convinced Sorabji to record his own music on tape, going to more trouble to make those recordings himself than it is possible to describe here. He helped create the broadcast program on Sorabji which brought Sorabji and his music to the attention of many American listeners. He took care of various administrative matters for him. Although he wisely did not try to promote a Sorabji "cause", he was always available to discuss his music privately and to assist those interested in it, tasks which took up much of his time and which he performed with no other aim than to further the cause of his friend's creations.

In the mid-1970s, however, their friendship became strained, after arguments over the appropriateness of some of Sorabji's intents and actions, and finally broke in 1979. In 1988, not long after the death of Holliday's wife, Brenda, Sorabji, infirm in a nursing home, expressed a desire to write to Holliday, but apparently he did not do so. He died shortly afterwards.[23]

[London], 8 November 1942

My very dear friend Frank;

It was a VERY GREAT PLEASURE to see once again your very individual and personal "fist" upon an envelope, and I rejoice that you will accompany me in partaking of a soupçon of smut, to wit, FINE & DANDY. I dont suppose I'll be able to secure decent seats before Nov. 21st, at the earliest, I'll apprise you of developments as soon as I've been to the box office.

By the way, why the whiff of chilliness in your letter and the retrogression to a formal & bleakly courteous "kindest regards"?????? Alas, alas am I no longer so charming as I <u>once</u> was ... (and how bloody much was THAT?)

The symphony about which you ask is a tremendous affair involving work upon paper of forty staves for the <u>main score</u> and later a subsidiary score of about twenty more. It is for an enormous orchestra, eight part chorus, barytone solo, organ and piano. The chorus are <u>wordless</u>

---

[22]{See pp. 78–83 for the reasons; for more about the letter and funds eventually presented to Sorabji, see pp. 26–28.}

[23]{See Chapter 4 for Frank Holliday's memories of Sorabji, and Chapter 11 for his impressions of his playing. Despite the hurt of the broken friendship, they contain no rancour.}

throughout, only the barytone soloist has any words to sing the "In solitude where Being signless dwelt" of Jàmi, towards the close of the work. The genre is your "Gulistan" raised to the nth. power and translated into orchestral-choral terms with orchestration of extreme elaborateness and intricacy, with subdivided strings and every subtelty that a perverse and subtle Oriental like myself can imagine. It contains, though I sez it some GORGEOUS music, and I feel it ought MUCH more be dedicated to YOU than the man to whom it IS dedicated, a very good creature, fine musician and all that but far too indoctrinated with the gospel of Communist Naziism for it to be good for him!! [S]ixty pages of it so far exist, pages two feet high by sixteen inches wide, so you can form some idea of the sheer labour involved, also when I tell you that I am nowhere NEAR half-way through it yet! Our dear E. came over to see me yesterday afternoon; I see him more or less regularly about once a week; he picked your letter up from the letter-box [—] this sounds nonsense, — what it DOES mean is from off the floor on to which the letter-slit debouches! WHY do you suggest that you are a boring anything? I can assure you that I do not nor ever should find you so, and E. is wholly of my opinion. You have far too much of the essential human qualities i.e. REAL civilisation as opposed to a factitious veneer over a fundamental barbarism which usually passes for that.

My respectful salutations and greeting to Madame.
Ever yours affectionately

Kay.

Sorabji's concern and assumptions over a more formal manner show his acute sensitivity to relationships and hint at his insecurity over them. He expected loyalty and intensity in his close friendships; his doubts may also have led to a desire for greater control at times than most other people would accept. He routinely refused to "mix friends"; he hesitated before introducing one of his friends to another.

What Sorabji wrote about his *Jāmī* Symphony he carried out over the next nine years. It developed into the biggest orchestral work he had yet written, which he obviously suspected it would be. "E." is Edward Clarke Ashworth. The Symphony is dedicated to Mervyn Vicars, who remained, along with his wife Denise, a friend of Sorabji's for the rest of his life.

Corfe Castle, 25 October 1952

It took well over a year to fulfill the plan to give Sorabji the presentation letter and funds mentioned above. Given the literally widespread adventures of the letter, it was nearly impossible to keep the plan a secret from the recipient.

Frank Holliday in 1942 (photo by J. Cecil Gould)

At the time of this letter, which is friendly despite the obvious annoyance, Norman Gentieu had asked Sorabji to find out the cost of microfilming his works, so that this could be carried out in England with financing arranged by Gentieu. Frank Holliday lived in North Devon.

> I have got particulars of microfilming, so dont bother. You put yourself to MUCH too much trouble on my behalf ... and it makes me feel <u>acutely</u> uncomfortable ... <u>And what is going on behind my back</u>??? ... During my recent visit to London I was asked not once nor twice ... "I hear you are going to record" ... and by dint of angry persistence plus threats to the parties concerned ... I extorted an admission about NORTH DEVON! ... You DEVIL! ... It MUST be you! What do you MEAN by it????????!!!!!!!!!!! ... I promised you I would MAKE ENQUIRIES about the possible cost of recording ... and ... to absolve myself of the charge of a broken promise I've done so to THREE QUARTERS ... one of which, THANK GOD ... has said they do not do it ... I have similar hopes of the other two ... BUT ... <u>I PROMISED NOTHING MORE</u> ... You are a very bad ... but all the same a very DEAR fellow ... DAMN you! ...

Holliday wrote back on the 27th with a friendly but firm refusal to divulge details, deploring others' breaking of confidence. One of the people who had mentioned recording to Sorabji, probably inadvertently, was Erik Chisholm.

[Corfe Castle, a few days after 19 January 1956]

> ... in the throes of a foul headache ... AND in the midst of an enormous complicated choral fugue which forms the last part of the KYRIE. This part alone is bound to be over 100 pages long ... the whole running into six or seven hundred at least, excluding the elaborate AMEN that is planned to which at the supreme climax I think of adding a thunderous brass chorus of about 16 trumpets twelve trombones twelve horns and the entire family of Tubas or between forty and fifty in all over and above and outside the main orchestral allowance[.] Of course EVERYBODY will be busting themselves the Organ ALL OUT ... And if the roof falls in on top of the whole bloody lot ... well all the better ...

The orchestra is, by implication, both acceptable and foul at the same time. Such an imagining was likely necessary, for how else could a composer write music for performers, whom he often said he detested? (Cf. Frank Holliday being both "very bad" and "very dear" in the previous letter.)

The elaborate *Amen* to the Symphonic High Mass was written in 1961, but without the added brass.

[Corfe Castle, 10 or 11 May 1957]

This letter was prompted by its accompanying advertisement for plant growth tablets called *Plantoids*, in a newspaper showing the results: a cabbage of over 16 pounds and nearly 3 feet in diameter.

Frank dear! MY CHRIST LOOK AT THIS ... Why why WHY????? This inane worship of SIZE disregardless of everything else[.] In France for instance the VERY BEST petit[s] pois really ARE petit[s] pois the choicest being "petit[s] pois extra fins" ... Here au contraire the demand is for a bloody great thing as big AND as succulent as a golf-ball and as often as not even harder ... AND those fruit and vegetable shows ... FIRST PRIZE for a vegetable marrow (unfit for human food any how) that dwarfs any self respecting hippopotamus ... first prize for bright yellow butter because its colour looks "rich" ... the only goddam thing about it that IS ... WHAT sodding business HAS butter to look like egg yolk any old way? And so on and so on [...] O TEMPORA O IMMORALES MORES ...

One might well ask: what is a composer who writes gigantic compositions doing complaining about a gigantic cabbage? Well, Sorabji never asked anyone to eat his music ... despite the fact that it shows much more taste than this cabbage probably had.

His general attitude towards food and health was remarkably — and for its time unusually — sane.

[Corfe Castle,] 14 May 1962

AND, now I solemnly authorise you to use the recordings AS AND WHERE YOU SEE FIT. EXCEPT to keep them well out of reach of hearing of any B.B.C. scum ... miserable venial scribblers called "critics", and such untouchables ...

I ENJOYED doing this for YOU ... you and Erik are the ONLY TWO people for whom I would EVER do it ... For the rest ... FUCK them ... But I dont want to ... much too good for 'em ... I LOVED seeing you and entertaining you to the best of my ability ... such as it was and be ... Madonna mia ... HOW lucky I am in my friends ... YOU above all who are next in my affection and treasuring to my dearly beloved Godbrother, as I call him ... Reggie. Your miraculous insight and understanding SIMPATIA are, as I have often told you immeasurably precious to one of MY temperament with that smouldering Mount Etna in my heart ... as dear Ma always said of us ... Being as and what I am, if my friends like and understand my work THAT IS ALL I WANT AND SEEK ... For the rest ... I dont care a piss shit and fart for them ... their opinion good bad or indifferent I regard as a piece of presumptuous impertinence, of such utterly insignificant NOTHINGNESS do I regard them. And thats all for this nonce ...

Blessings gratitude and ever so much love to you;

K.

What Sorabji says he enjoyed is making a few tape recordings for Frank Holliday.[24]

Sorabji was rarely as vulgar as in this letter; his extremes of language are an extreme defense. The trouble was that his strongly expressed views often gave extreme offense to those who did not know him. His close friends, however, enjoyed his complete loyalty and often spoke of his warmth and generosity, of which there is plentiful evidence in these letters.

[Corfe Castle, 21 October 1968]

Monday

My dearest Frank;

Yours just received this morning. Orders have AT ONCE been sent to the BIOSTRATH people for the IMMEDIATE DESPATCH to you of FOUR BOTTLES OF THE BIOSTRATH DROPS.

Since my return I have been nursing a quite severe wasp sting on my ankle which has made it wellnigh impossible to put on outdoor shoes on account of the swelling ... but have now got it down to vanishing point by MY OWN METHODS without any goddam bluddy DOCTOR (!!!!) messing me about!

God bless you both; your devoted

C Drop

Over the decades Sorabji found a number of aids and procedures to prevent and defeat illness which were not well known or much accepted in England. His own constant advice was to "avoid orthodox doctoring as much as you can".[25]

This letter also reveals a very practical side of Sorabji. Far from being an eccentric to those who knew him, he was straightforward and resourceful as well as clever and persistent. This combination often led to his discovery of various things, from razors to

---

[24]{For the complete list of recording sessions, of which Sorabji refers here to the first, see Appendix 2.}

[25]"Alternative medicine" and even preventative medicine on a large scale did not become important concepts in the Western world until much later.

medicinal drops to investment plans to magnificent artifacts, the last often acquired at quite low prices.

One of his private names for himself was The Corfe Drop; others included Diabolus Ipsissimus, Catamountain (or Catamontanus Corfiensis), Kak Corf (or Kakodaemon Corfiensis), The Corfe Castle Crack-Pot, The Demoniac Devotee of Dorset, The Korfe Karsell Katastrophy, The Purbeck Panda, The Purbeck Pisspot, The Warlock of Wareham, and Il gatto persiano del Castello di Corfe.[26]

[Corfe Castle,] 2 [October] 1971

Sorabji wrote this letter after his first visit to the Hollidays in Hardham Cottage, the house which they had bought in December 1970.

Frank dear, and if it comes to that dear BOTH of you!

I DID enjoy my visit to HARDHAM COTTAGE which I think delightful, to say nothing of your and Brenda's kindness to me. Rather ashamed of myself for being taken with one of my PIDDLY attacks, which Dr. Gilbert says are simply nerves and elimination, but it CAN be berluddy embarrassing occurring at importune times. It went off completely and have had no further botheration since.

The eye treatment MOST successful. The troublesome cloud has virtually disappeared. Got back in quite good order last Tuesday and found Mizzy in quite good shape bless him. Also some snaps from Norman ... I've THREATENED him if he sends that goddamorful one of me at the piano showing my scraggy neck I'll THROTTLE HIM WITH HIS OWN GUTS! ...

I have tried three times to ring you, twice today and once yesterday. Perhaps you have gone off to Brenda's aunt at Hove isnt it? I wanted to thank you viva voce for all your loving-kindness and the beautiful food you fed me on. Down THIS way we NEVER get lamb tasting like yours, AND its ALWAYS as tough as HELL! ...

Was too really QUITE impressed with my own playing on your admirable tapes though I sez is! Pity though I didnt take you to the Greek place in Bolton Road and give YOU a better lunch[.] Never mind, we'll do that, ALL THREE OF US on my next check up visit to Brooks Simpkins MAYISH or JUNEISH.

---

[26]Some of his names (also private) for places, concepts, items, institutions, and people he did not like were Uncle Sham; Demuckracy; The Times Nitwittery Supplement; the Bum Boys' Club; the Archfish of Cant, Sir Midnight Divorce, John Dustbin, Rancid Fricassee, Blue Serge Prokofiev, Dimitri Sonnovabitsch, and Aram Katchaskatchcanrian.

{Arthur Piss is mentioned on p. 241.}

And by the way, my 9% Treasury Loan was bought in June for 96 and a bit! So quite a tidy rise! And thats all for this nonce.
God bless you both, and VAST affections;

K

"Mizzy" is Reginald Norman Best, with whom Sorabji lived in Corfe Castle. "Norman" is Norman Peterkin, Sorabji's friend of more than 50 years, whom he would not harm, but with whom he could certainly have sharp disagreements.[27] Brooks Simpkins was Sorabji's "eye man" in Eastbourne.

Sorabji and Holliday often traded financial recommendations.

From the Large Notebook ("Commonplace Book")

with the following motto, dedication, and subtitle/identification:

> To the Pure all things may or may not be pure: / To the Puritan — Nothing.

> Given to my very dear Frank Holliday as a sort of sour / Christmas Gift. / MCMLXV.

> The Fruits of Misanthropy: / being: the Animadversions of a / Machiavellian — / by / Kaikhosru Sorabji: / MCXXV–MCXXX et sequitur:

This handsomely bound notebook contains handwritten items numbered in Roman numerals from 1 to 433, which range in length from one sentence to several pages. The numbering is problematic, however; there are around 300 items altogether. Some of them were published in Sorabji's books or elsewhere. Part of the subtitle is found in the subtitle of his second book. The motto is Sorabji's adaptation of an Arabic proverb at the front of Richard Burton's translation of the *Arabian Nights*, which he much admired.

1. From the items numbered from I to CDXXXIII

I. When Englishmen exhort one "to play the game" it is quite unnecessary to ask what game and whose — for no Englishman can conceive any other game than the one he plays and for himself.

---

[27]{The photograph on page 35 is not the one which Sorabji was complaining about.}

XIV. No artist worthy of the name accepts advice. If he is an artist it is superfluous and if he is not it is useless — it cannot make him one.

XLV. It is said that only a definitely abnormal man can fully appreciate the astonishing and poignant beauty of young naked manhood: but whether this is always true or not, and it is of course readily understandable that the homosexual man with his special emotional-erotic bias will be of necessity curiously and intensely conscious of it[.] There is no doubt but that masculine beauty has been most perfectly expressed by artists whom we know were homosexual — da Vinci and Michelagniolo. Greek statuary too emanated from a civilization with an emphatically homosexual cast[,] a fact often bunked or ignored, but without a frank recognition of which many phases of Greek art and thought are meaningless or incomprehensible.

LXXVII. To Hell with all "Purity" mongers "Cleanlifers" and such tedious tiresome killjoys! The cartoonist and scribe of the public lavatory contributes powerfully to the gaiety of life and any attempt to suppress him must be stoutly resisted. What if he does use "rude" words draw "rude" pictures — his repertoire is[,] it must be confessed[,] not usually especially wide or exciting, still he does often depict for us that most heartening and delicious spectacle in a dull and naughty world a fine large penis in erection — and one suspects that in this lies the reason of the rabid ferocity of the Purity mongers ... who it is impossible to conceive possessing fine large penes ... and who lacking that delightful possession are unpleasantly envious of its possession or graphic depiction by other people. And when the possessor of the fine large penis commits the still further outrage of being young and attractive virtuous indignation naturally knows no bounds. One always feels that Societies for the Suppression of Vice are really Societies for the Suppression of Penes.

CXXIV. Relations were given us in order that we might value our friends the more.

CCLXXVIII. Was there ever a stupid old tag so misused as that about half the loaf? When the half loaf is as it usually is mouldy and worm eaten it is much worse than no bread at all.

CCCXXVIII. The monstrous lopsidedness cruelty and injustice to the female of Nature's arrangements for the propagation of the species — arrangements of fantastic wastefulness barbarous stupidity incredible clumsiness and danger by the way, evidently struck the early mythologues and mythopœists, hence the legend of the "fall" with the prominent part therein alleged to have been played by woman, though why the whole of female creation should have become involved in the supposed sin of Eve is not explained, either by way of appeal to justice or reason. But one hardly looks to professional theologians any more than to any other sort of specialist for appeals to justice and reason.

CCCLXXIX. "Beauty is Truth[,] Truth Beauty" — sheer nonsense — both are raw material for Art — if you like, but that is absolutely another thing beyond Beauty and Ugliness — beyond Truth or Falsehood — in fact the realm of Art is akin to the release of the Vedântic and Brahmin philosopher [—] it is "freed from the pairs of opposites" of worldly illusion.

CDIX. Do you not think it is wiser to form attachments with places and things than persons? Places and things do at least keep quiet. The great danger of attachment to persons is that it gives them some power over oneself — and that is intolerable to anyone with any proper pride or self-respect. The same holds good of course of places and things, but to a far lesser degree. Places and things do at least stay where they are put, when they are no longer wanted.

2. Some Sacro-Sanct Modern Superstitions (with Comments)

These follow the entry in the notebook carrying the Roman numeral CDXXXIII. They are numbered simply from one to ten (in lower-case Roman numerals), under the heading "Some Sacro-Sanct Modern Superstitions". Frank Holliday noted on Sorabji's typed copy that it came from late 1950 or early 1951; that is the copy which is used for reprinting here (but with Arabic numerals, for convenience). The handwritten version in the notebook was written in about 1964 and is essentially the same as the typed, with the principal exception noted after No. 4.

1. That a devout and practising Catholic is a sort of intellectually benighted bushman compared with the "enlightened" "modern-viewed" readers of LEFTISH LEANINGS, MEANDERINGS AFTER MARX, THE FIFTH COLUMN RED WAGGER and so on.

Is it really more difficult to believe in what St. Thomas Aquinas, Maritain, Father d'Arcy, Cardinal Mindeszenty [recte Mindszenty], the reigning Holy Father and the sixteen thousand martyred priests and nuns of "free" Republican Spain stand and stood for than what the "liberators" of Poland, Esthonia, Latvia, Lithuania, Czechoslovakia, Hungary stand for, or that belief in the Immaculate Conception and Transsubstantiation is any more difficult than believing in "democracy" either of fore or aft-Iron Curtain varieties? Speaking personally, I find it child's play.

2. That only what is called "Labour" does what it calls REAL WORK.

I have not found any member of what are called "the working classes" who has the faintest notion of the toil, mental and, yes, physical of writing down a few pages of a complex modern orchestral score, let alone hundreds of them; the preliminary years of drudgery on the top of innate ability, plus unlimited and unpaid overtime at <u>all</u> times. One of them once said to me, "But naturally you cant understand our point of view, you're not a member of the working classes!" "No, indeed!" I spat at him, "I am NOT! I WORK!" ... I went on ... "When your hours, but not your work, are finished, off you go gleefully boozing or whoring or both. When MY work is finished, I am so drained and exhausted that I cant sleep for nights on end. YOU cant understand THAT either CAN you, <u>honest toiler</u>?"

3. That the conception of Original Sin is a libel on mankind.

All recorded history apart from the lives of that ultra-microscopical minority the Saints proves to admiration that it is a detached, objective, fearless and realistic recognition of the unpleasant facts about humans in the mass.

4. Equality.

"A society in which all shall be equal" ... thus the <u>beau</u> [*recte* <u>bel</u>] <u>idéal</u>. And equal to what, to whom, if you please? One cannot be "equal" in the air <u>et in vacuo</u> just like that; we are then told that we shall all be "equal" to one another ... But WHAT, WHICH others? St. John of the Cross, Jami, da Vinci, Dante, Byng [*recte* Bing] Crosby, Miss Gracie Fields, Mr. Solomon Wulkan-Stanley? "I'm as good as <u>you</u>" — the typical yelp of miscegenate mongrelism, whose perceptions, blunted, besotted and rudimentary <u>comme tout</u>, never fail to reveal to him the presence of his betters. And for them he has no forgiveness, no mercy just because they ARE so plainly, so undeniably so irrevocably his betters. "As good as" what? What for? As a sponge for soaking up brewers' swill or Fleet Ditch bilge? Leave him gladly, wallowing in his pre-eminence.

In the ca. 1964 version, Sorabji omitted the last three names in his list and inserted in their place "the Beatles" and "Strumpet Keeler".

5. Education; the advantages of it.

For whom, the educatees, the educators, the promoters of the whole business? Now the geneticists have told us that only a one figure percentage of humans are mentally capable of mastering more than the elements, reading, writing and simple arithmetical processes. According to the investigations of the American War Department, the vast majority of that country, with the highest known standard of living — go through life with the mental development they reached at the age of ten; all that education then and all that more of it constantly being administered cannot be for the sake of the educatees. For the educators? Ah, much warmer this time. The ever growing number of jobs for educators must obviously be useful to them assuming that they like educating better than breaking stones on the road or picking cakum. For whom, then, is it sovereignly advantageous to have a mass of reflex conditioned human automata, a crowd that will instantly and unthinkingly react to a stimulus in a desired way as to a pin stuck in their bottoms? Now we are hot on the scent ... THEY, as Mr. Douglas Reed calls them, "the Internationalists" as Mr. Pasco Langmaid and the distinguished Catholic priest, and authority on money, Father Dennis Fahey call them — men who belong to every country and none, and who have every country rather more than less, in their pockets.

6. "Popularising the Arts" ... "Bringing Art to the People" ... "Spreading Culture" as it were muck or weed-killer.

"GIVE NOT THAT WHICH IS HOLY UNTO THE DOGS NEITHER CAST YOUR PEARLS BEFORE SWINE LEST THEY TRAMPLE THEM UNDER THEIR FEET AND TURN AGAIN AND REND YOU."

7. The "immorality" of artists.

When people in England talk about "immorality" they never mean the Major Sins, Lying, Treachery, Cruelty, Envy, Malice, Avarice ... it is always and only sex. A classic example of this occurred in the courts some years ago. Prosecuting counsel said of some scoundrel of a woman charged with forgery, perjury, swindling and robbing her benefactors that there was no suggestion against her moral character.
 Now artists we all know are "hot stuff", "dirty dogs", live in unmarriage, seduce other men's wives, and far more thrilling than all, even sometimes get involved in "nameless" scandals, "unspeakable" vices and so on, with relish and unction.
 The fact that in any village you could, if your noseyness were supported by a sufficiently pornographic and virginal persistence, find all those going on all round you, among people with the remotest connection with art or artists doesnt in the least lessen the kick you get from occasionally finding your own swinishness in circles far above the shadow of your normal night: it is the rarity of an occurrence that makes it noticeable, particularly to the eyes of malice; for as has been said, it makes Caliban furious to see his own face in the mirror.

8. "Such a cultured person".

I have an uneasy feeling that a "cultured" person and a "cultured" pearl bear much the same relation to the real thing in each case.

9. "Think themselves so much better than anyone else!"

Thus the voice of malignant envy, of the base and mean of spirit about their betters. We indignantly repudiate the suggestion! We THINK nothing of the sort. We KNOW it.

10. The "proletariat".

It produces offspring, that is to say, by implication little else; as it were the spawning of herring, mackerel or cod whom one were tempted to say it so much resembles in appearance and intelligence, were this not being unjust and unkind ... to the herring, the mackerel and the cod.[28]

---

[28]In April or May 1972 Sorabji wrote a further ten points under the title "The Disbelief of an Anti-Democrat". Although they do not appear in his large notebook (this having been giving to Frank Holliday in 1965), they relate clearly to ideas in "Some Sacro-Sanct Modern Superstitions", e.g.:

> 3. I disbelieve that counting heads, regardless of what is — or is not — inside them — achieves any result other than ... counting the heads. The mathematicians tell us that nothing multiplied by infinity still remains for ever nothing. Similarly one empty head remains empty multiplied by no matter how many millions.

> 10. I believe in the rightness of caste, not class divisions. AND Caste does NOT mean banking account ... it means birth, breeding tradition. No great culture has ever been without them. And the old Brahmins were never more right than when they laid it down that the shadow, the mere shadow of a low-caste man was defilement and pollution to the High Caste man.

Part III

THE MUSIC

9 Sorabji's Piano Music

Michael Habermann

Michael Habermann (b. 1950, Paris) has lived in Mexico, Canada, and the United States. Currently he resides in Baltimore, where he teaches piano. He holds an Associate Arts and Sciences degree from Nassau Community College, a Bachelor of Music degree from C. W. Post College of Long Island University, a Master's degree in composition from the same institution, and a Doctorate in piano performance from the Peabody Institute.

In July 1976, after some years of correspondence involving him, his friend Donald Garvelmann, and Sorabji, the composer gave Habermann permission to play his music in public. Since that time Habermann has given a great many recitals which have included Sorabji's music and has made three recordings devoted entirely to it.

This chapter derives from his doctoral dissertation *A Style Analysis of the Nocturnes for Solo Piano by Kaikhosru Shapurji Sorabji with Special Emphasis on "Le jardin parfumé"* (DMA, Peabody Institute of the Johns Hopkins University, 1985).

Not often is one so baffled by the printed page. Mr. Sorabji would have done better to publish it straight away as a player-piano roll.[1]

The extreme difficulties of sight-reading and deciphering Sorabji's intricate music provoked most critics in the early part of this century to dismiss it immediately as being the work of a musical madman. First impressions revealed little but "a chaos of incoherence and over-elaboration", and subsequent examination of "two handsful of notes, each handful satisfactory in itself, but bearing little or no relation to the other" led reviewers to further negative conclusions.[2] Many critics found nearly everything at fault. They claimed that the music was self-defeating not only in its technical difficulty but in its unprecedented length, as well as lack

---

[1] Harvey Grace: Review of Sorabji's Sonata No. 1 for Piano, in *The Musical Times*, vol. 62 (1 November 1921), p. 781.

[2] Harvey Grace: Review of Sorabji's Organ Symphony No. 1, in *The Musical Times*, vol. 67 (1 July 1926), p. 616.

of contrast, simplicity, clear-cut structure, thematic design, rhythmic definition, and personal style. Even those sympathetic to Sorabji's efforts found flaws:

> One page will look like an effort of the medieval "organum" experimentalists; then another [...] will express a voluptuousness that seems foreign to the classical conception of the bulk of the work.[3]

Fortunately, there has been a noticeable discrepancy in response between those who judged the music exclusively through study of the printed score and those who had the opportunity to hear the music played by the composer or others.

> [... W]ithout hearing this music we can neither praise nor blame it legitimately [...] Mr. Sorabji can play his own music, and those parts of the Piano Concerto I have heard in this way seemed to justify Sorabji's complicated method of expression [...] Hearing part of the Concerto showed how useless it is to judge Sorabji's music only on paper.[4]

Sorabji's musical style reflects the influence of many of the composers whom he admired and emulated. Since little of his music has ever been heard on a regular basis, critics, in an attempt to describe what Sorabji's music sounds like, mention composers from Bach to Messiaen:

> What I hear [...] is by turns absorbing and vastly entertaining. A flippant way to convey an impression of it might be: take some Liszt, Busoni, Scriabin, Satie and Ives: shake well before using.[5]

To others, the music sounds like (a) "an exotic cross-breeding between Bach and Ravel", (b) "Debussy played with Schoenbergian dissonances", (c) "Lisztian improvisations on Ravel", and (d) "a collaboration between piano virtuoso Busoni and exotic harmonist Messiaen".[6] But his music is more than an amalgam of styles.

---

[3] Edmund Duncan-Rubbra: "Sorabji's Enigma" (review of Sorabji's *Opus Clavicembalisticum*), in *The Monthly Musical Record*, vol. 62 (September 1932), p. 148.

[4] Arthur G. Browne: "The Music of Kaikhosru Sorabji", in *Music and Letters*, vol. 11 (January 1930), pp. 15–16.

[5] David Hall: Review of *Piano Music by Kaikhosru Shapurji Sorabji* (Musical Heritage Society MHS 4271), in *Stereo Review*, December 1981, p. 128.

[6] (a) Robert Jones: "The Crusaders", in *New York Daily News*, 26 June 1977, Leisure Section, p. 17, col. 1; (b) Jim Aikin: "Of Special Interest:
[CONT'D]

Rather, it synthesizes in a unique way the tendencies of all these styles combined, and forges ahead into hitherto unexplored territories. There is something undeniably original in his style:

> His music is essentially the language of late 19th-century Romanticism colored by Impressionist timbres and braided with a relentless striving for the unique in complex harmonic situations. The music is sometimes reminiscent of Ravel, or at times contains a quality similar to that found in the works of Charles Ives. For the most part, however, Sorabji's compositions lie between the poles of easy categorization, [being] saliently individual.[7]

Despite the generous number of articles written by now about Sorabji and his music, few writers have dared to analyze his music. Fifty years ago, a statement like the following was not unusual: "any attempt at thematic or formal analysis is not only superfluous but impossible".[8] And even today his music may appear equally enigmatic:

> [... R]epeated excursions through the virtually unchartable waters of this analysis-defying piece obstinately refuse to yield any definable reasons for its undeniable inner cohesion ...[9]

The key to appreciating Sorabji's art lies in understanding the musical objectives for which he was striving and how he achieved these through his original fusion of various musical styles and techniques. With this in mind, the present chapter will give an overview of his piano music and will explain how inner logic and unity are achieved in it by way of the example of his composition titled *Le jardin parfumé*.

Kaikhosru Shapurji Sorabji" (review of *Piano Music by Kaikhosru Shapurji Sorabji*), in *Contemporary Keyboard*, May 1981, p. 62; (c) Irving Lowens: "The American Liszt Society", in *High Fidelity / Musical America*, March 1979, p. MA 34; (d) Robert Finn: "Pianist Rises to Composer's Challenge" (review of the piano recital by Michael Habermann on 6 October 1978 at Center for the Arts, Midland, Michigan), in *The [Cleveland] Plain Dealer*, 20 October 1978, p. 29.

[7]"Sorabji by Habermann" (review of the piano recital by Michael Habermann on 19 September 1978 at Long Island University, Greenvale, New York), in *Cakes and Ale*, vol. 11, no. 3 (1978), p. 2.

[8]Cecil Gray: "Sorabji, Kaikhosru", in *Cobbett's Cyclopedic Survey of Chamber Music*, edited by Walter Cobbett (London: Oxford University Press, 1930), vol. 2, p. 437.

[9]Alistair Hinton, in program notes for the piano recital by Yonty Solomon on 16 June 1977 in Wigmore Hall, London.

Michael Habermann in 1977 (photo by Alix Jeffry)

A brief examination of his critical writings reveals his musical orientation. As a music critic for over 40 years, his knowledge of music, its composers, and performers was impressive. He was aware of every latest trend and new development in Europe. His avowed purpose as a writer on music was "to exhort musicians and music-lovers to think, and think hard about their art".[10]

His essays, like his music, are generally stimulating, entertaining, witty, as well as informative. His writing style is elaborate. It employs a large vocabulary and a complex sentence structure, characteristics which are reflected in his music. His unique critical and musical styles were, to some extent, the result of his completely inflexible elitist stance. He ignored "all fashionable conventions and standards" so that he could pursue his own ideals.[11] Through his stubbornness, perseverance, and the barriers which he erected between himself and the world, he was able to withdraw into a solitude which allowed him to devote himself completely to his musical projects.

His curious likes and dislikes are in some respects difficult to explain. He sometimes contradicted himself, sometimes completely changed his opinions. He was, however, a champion of neglected works and of neglected composers. He consistently waved the banner for Busoni, Alkan, Liszt, Medtner, Reger, Delius, Mahler, Rachmaninoff, Szymanowski, and other composers who at that time were not popular in England.

As Sorabji was not given to "obsessional grovelling before the 'best' Teutonic models",[12] occasionally one senses his impatience with the music of some of the established "masters". He thought that the classical and some of the romantic composers relied too much upon formal compositional techniques at the expense of free invention.[13] Such composers as Haydn, Mozart, Schubert, Mendelssohn, Brahms, Saint-Saëns, Chaykovskiy, and Beethoven (in his early years) were not among his favourites. That he could fail to respond to the melodic beauties of the work of the classical composers is difficult to understand, but he stated his lack of affiliation with this style very clearly:

[... F]or me the click-clack symmetry, the rhythmic and melodic poverty (yes, even that!) of much of Schubert, Brahms or Schumann

---

[10]Kaikhosru Sorabji: *Mi contra fa: The Immoralisings of a Machiavellian Musician* (London: Porcupine Press, 1947), p. 71.

[11]As he wrote of the composer Nicolas Medtner in his *Around Music* (London: Unicorn Press, 1932), p. 71.

[12]Kaikhosru Sorabji: *Mi contra fa*, p. 122.

[13]Ibid., p. 159.

is unendurable except in the smallest doses [...] The symmetry and formal perfection which others find so exquisite, incomparable or marvellous, I find infuriating.[14]

Much of Sorabji's music employs tonal elements and is at least tonally oriented, yet he organizes his music in unusual ways, seldom resorting to the traditional system of key relationships, which he thoroughly disliked. He owes a great deal to Debussy's "emancipation" of music from the tonal system.

Most 20th-century developments, such as jazz, nationalism, neoclassicism, and serialism, Sorabji disdained. He rejected the twelve-tone approach and its ramifications on the basis that it was constructed upon artificial precepts. He could not identify with composers such as Bartók, because their procedures consisted partly of the incorporation of folk materials into their works. His approach to music was essentially conservative. His image of himself was of a composer pitted against society, working in isolation, not in an ivory tower, but in a "Tower of Granite with plentiful supplies of boiling oil and molten lead handy to tip over the battlements on to the heads of unwanted and uninvited intruders on my privacy and seclusion".[15] This dramatizes his position as an arch-romantic at heart.

But he was also influenced by the impressionist composers, especially in their concern for fluid, sensuous textures. He admired the music of Ravel, Debussy, and Delius. The imaginative, improvisatory, deceptive casualness or effortlessness, understatement, and non-dramatic qualities of their music are also present in Sorabji's work. He much preferred the French "mélodie" to the German "Lied"; his favourite song composers were Berlioz, Chausson, Duparc, and others of the French tradition. The vocal works of the baroque were also very dear to him. He advised composers to study this repertory in order to get a working knowledge of the potentialities of decorative melodic writing (*fioritura*) in free rhythms. He favoured supple melodies of uneven lengths and of an ornamental character. (See example 1, p. 339, the beginning of one of Sorabji's melodies.)

Regarding his early works, he freely acknowledged that Skryabin had introduced him to "the higher dissonances".[16] The early works also contain many written instructions such as "déchirant",

---

[14]Ibid., p. 159; *The New English Weekly*, vol. 6 (13 Dec. 1934), p. 200.
[15]Kaikhosru Sorabji: *Mi contra fa*, p. 145.
{For the entire chapter in Sorabji's book from which this comes, see pp. 290–95 of the present book.}
[16]*The New Age*, vol. 55 (19 July 1934), p. 141.

Ex. 1. *Gulistān:* p. 1, sys. 1.[17]

"désordonné", "sobre", etc., which Skryabin frequently employed, and many Skryabinesque harmonies which betray the young composer's admiration for the Russian's music.[18]

Many people, including the publisher Norman Peterkin and critic Cecil Gray, have pointed out that Sorabji's art is equally influenced by Eastern and Western concepts, the former reflecting his heritage, the latter his domicile. But Sorabji's "exoticism" has nothing to do with the showy and superficial orientalism in works of composers of the 19th century. Eastern elements are an integral part of his music. His Parsi and Spanish-Sicilian background accounts for his love of

---

[17]Examples of published works come from published scores, with one exception; all others come from manuscripts. The exception is example 2, from the manuscript of Sorabji's *Fantasiettina.* {The published version is a performing/teaching edition by Ronald Stevenson which differs considerably from the manuscript copy he wrote out in 1962. Sorabji's original manuscript has been missing for many years.

A list of the published works may be found on p. 104. Those which were for a long time available through Oxford University Press have all been out of print since late 1988. Almost all the unpublished works have been microfilmed. For details of the locations of partial sets of microfilms, see p. 44.

The location of most of the manuscripts themselves may be found in the Detailed Catalog of Sorabji's music in Chapter 5 of this book; further information is available from Alistair Hinton of The Sorabji Music Archive, where most of Sorabji's manuscripts reside. The Archive's address is given in Appendix 3.}

In all the examples of his music, Sorabji intends an accidental to be valid only for the note immediately following, except for repeated and tied notes. {What he actually does with accidentals may be a different matter!}

[18]{See Chapter 6 for a more extended consideration of Sorabji's opinion of Skryabin.}

Eastern aesthetics and philosophies and his identification with the Latin outlook on life. His music mirrors this in its spacious proportions and luxuriousness of texture. Despite the frequent atonality and searing dissonance of some of his early works, the overall impression received is one of serenity. His music contains none of the tension and anxiety that were a driving force in the music of many post-Wagnerian composers, and which are usually associated with highly dissonant music.

The influence of the East also manifests itself in: (1) unusually supple and irregular rhythmic patterns, the basis for (2) asymmetrical and prose-like phrase structure; (3) abundant ornamentation; (4) a sense of the improvisatory (despite Sorabji's dislike of the act of improvisation) and of timelessness; as well as (5) the unusual length of many of his compositions. Eastern practices utilizing melodic arabesque also had a decisive impact upon Sorabji's work. The filigree and embellishment which crowd almost every page are inseparable from the framework and nature of the composition. Such is the abundance of decorative material in his works that ornamentation itself assumes a very important role in shaping the texture and content of his music. Harmonic progression, which in pre-20th century music was usually one of the most important elements in defining the shape of a passage or piece, is relegated to a secondary position.

Another important influence upon his work is the musical outlook of Liszt. The dazzling virtuosity of composer-pianists in the Lisztian tradition, such as Ferruccio Busoni and Leopold Godowsky, further inspired Sorabji to write music that would make the utmost technical and musical demands upon the interpreter.

Above all, he was in awe of the largest, most majestic, and most complex works of Bach, Berlioz, Wagner, and Mahler. What he appropriated from the music of the post-romantics, such as Mahler and Reger, was the complexity, inventiveness, grandiosity, and sense of freedom displayed in their works. Sorabji himself rivalled them by composing works of equally imposing proportions. Extensive use of counterpoint coupled with decorative figurations, fluctuations between free atonality and tonality, extreme textural density, technical difficulty, complex formal layout, and complicated rhythmic structures are all present in his compositions: a bewildering mixture at times. Nevertheless, the primary effect produced by Sorabji in such music is one of unique and satisfying beauty.

Sorabji's textures are incredibly varied. In this respect, they ought to be compared with those of Gustav Mahler. Generally Sorabji equated variety and abundance with creativity and quality. His goal appears to have been to pack into each work more detail than seems humanly possible to absorb. To him, the "endless fascination of the masterpieces" lay in their "infinite richness", in which another aspect and some detail which had previously been unnoticed were always being discovered anew.[19] This being the basic premise, he set out to dazzle by inventing as many patterns as possible, combining notes in endless permutations, and avoiding almost any semblance of exact repetition. To achieve this goal, he felt free to employ as many notes as he pleased: "Sorabji never uses one note where a dozen or two will serve just as well."[20] Basically a developer rather than an innovator, he intended to surpass (rather than overthrow) every composer he knew, in every way. He deliberately made many of his pieces more elaborate than any that he knew of.

Sorabji therefore placed great emphasis on the importance of complexity in music. Simplicity was, to him, synonymous with ingenuousness. He never strove for it: "[... T]hat the supreme things in art are ever the simplest [...] can be demonstrated by references to the great masterpieces of all art to be entirely false."[21] Sparseness of texture, economy of means, and brief statement in music he viewed as the manifestation of a dry, academic approach to composition. Size, technical difficulty, and textures thick with overloaded detail he seemed to equate with greatness, importance, richness, and intellectual activity. Just as in the case of his prose, Sorabji seldom edited or kept short his musical compositions, nor did he want to. His music was notated directly onto the manuscript without recourse to preliminary rough drafts or to trial "testing out" at the piano.[22] Of composers who revised their works by cutting, Sorabji wrote:

> It is a great pity that the composer [Arnold Bax] has allowed himself to be persuaded into shortening the work [Symphonic Variations for Piano and Orchestra] by cutting out certain very beautiful and interesting variations. Unlike literature, music always seems to suffer by this kind of editing, for I cannot think of a single example in which the gain by the excisions has not been, as far as I am concerned, of the most questionable and dubious.[23]

---

[19]Kaikhosru Sorabji: *Around Music*, p. 118.
[20]Stephen Kennamer: "Music" (review of the lecture-recital by Michael Habermann on 29 March 1980 at the University of Richmond, Virginia), in the *Richmond Times-Dispatch*, 31 March 1980, section B, p. 1.
[21]Kaikhosru Sorabji: *Around Music*, p. 115.
[22]S. Grew: "Kaikhosru Sorabji — *Le jardin parfumé:* Poem for Piano", in *The British Musician*, vol. 4 (1928), pp. 85–86.
[23]Kaikhosru Sorabji: *Around Music*, p. 70.

Clinton Gray-Fisk was not exaggerating when he wrote of Sorabji:

> All the piano works, indeed, plumb the instrument to its depths and display a command of infinitely varied sonorities, inventive figuration and imaginative decoration as yet unequalled by anyone of any period.[24]

One result of all this elaboration is piano music which is seemingly impossible to learn. It is not unreasonable or exaggerated to state that Sorabji's music is terrifying in its demands, both technical and interpretive. Although Liszt, Busoni, Godowsky, Rachmaninoff, and the French impressionists are the chief influences on Sorabji's piano writing, his use of the instrument is even more elaborate and daring. As the years progressed, his work became even more complicated. Of *Opus clavicembalisticum* one writer has understandably remarked: "The work is almost a challenge to the audience and to the performer — perhaps even an affront [...] It is safe to say that Sorabji writes with no regard whatsoever for the performer."[25]

Sorabji purposefully made his work especially difficult in order to make it inaccessible to all but those who would (by necessity) be totally devoted to learning it. Example 2 (p. 343) is typical of many pages of Sorabji's music. At first it looks unmanageable, but careful study reveals that the passage actually "fits" two normal hands quite comfortably.[26]

Regarding form, Sorabji believed that content should create its own: form and substance must be intertwined. Standard ideas of form were no substitute for organic structure. He hoped to create "a music that shall stand by its own interior logic and coherence, and not by any reliance on controversial or more or less free developments of academic conceptions of musical form."[27] He frequently stated that the material cannot successfully be poured into the mould of "form", often attacking academicians and their espousal of classical forms, for example:

---

[24] Clinton Gray-Fisk: "Kaikhosru Shapurji Sorabji", in *The Musical Times*, vol. 101 (April 1960), p. 232.

[25] Robert J. Gula: "Kaikhosru Shapurji Sorabji (1892–   ): The Published Piano Works", in *Journal of the American Liszt Society*, vol. 12 (December 1982), pp. 48–49.

[26] In all examples, ↑ signifies music to be played an octave higher than written, ↓ an octave lower.

[27] Christopher à Becket Williams: "The Music of Kaikhosru Sorabji", in *The Sackbut*, vol. 4 (1924), p. 317.

Ex. 2. *Fantasiettina sul nome illustre dell'egregio poeta Christopher Grieve ossia Hugh M'Diarmid* (from the ms. copy; see footnote 17): p. 8, sys. 2.

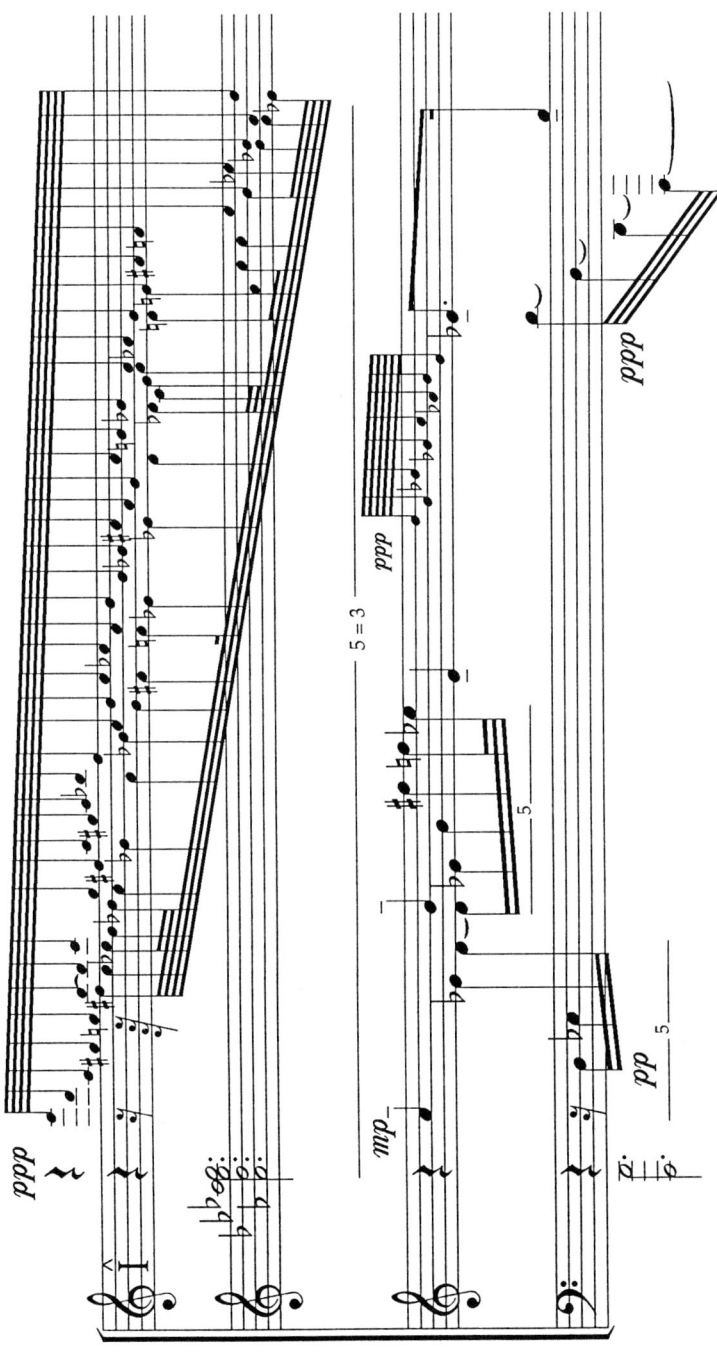

> [... T]he rigidly classical rondo is one of the most lamentable aberrations of musical design, without either technical [or] architectonic [...] interest [...] but rather [...] unspeakable boredom and tedium.[28]

Yet he was always very concerned with attaining discernible form in his works. Generally, he followed the frequently employed romantic procedure of creating form through a progression of successively greater peaks, culminating in climactic statements in the concluding part of the work. Many of his pieces begin at low dynamic levels and gradually build momentum and energy towards the end.

His large works are subdivided into sections with titles borrowed from the baroque: *Toccata, Preludio, Interludio, Cadenza,* etc. One of the active influences here was likely that of the neo-baroque spirit of the many Bach transcriptions and of original works such as the *Fantasia contrappuntistica* and *Toccata* by Ferruccio Busoni, a composer and pianist whom Sorabji revered.

Sorabji attempted to achieve inner cohesion in his works without recourse to traditional motivic or formal procedures of development. He often compared composing with weaving a rug; of his late work *Il tessuto d'arabeschi* (*The Tapestry of Arabesques*) he wrote:

> It is designed [...] as a SEAMLESS COAT ... what I call a TESSUTO IN SOUND, from which the threads cannot be disassociated or, if you like, disentangled without destroying the Tessuto ... same as what happens if you pulled out strand by strand of a Persian rug until the rug qua rug no longer remained.[29]

Closely linked with his conception of organic structural unity was his demand of himself and of other composers for logical, consecutive thinking:

> The great masters of organic technique, Berlioz, Delius, Sibelius, Van Dieren, pursuing intensely orderly cohesive trains of musical thinking [and] instinct with vital and living ideas, mould and shape their forms in accordance with the growth, development, and proliferation of these ideas.[30]

---

[28]Kaikhosru Sorabji: "The Greatness of Medtner", in *Nicolas Medtner*, edited by Richard Holt (London: Dennis Dobson, 1954), p. 130.

[29]Kaikhosru Sorabji: Letter to Norman P. Gentieu, quoted in the program notes to the concert sponsored by the Delius Society, Philadelphia branch, on 2 May 1982 in Philadelphia.

[30]Kaikhosru Sorabji: *Mi contra fa*, p. 52.

One of his main criticisms of many modern composers was that they were unable "to maintain one logical and coherent train of thought much longer than a few seconds".[31] He found this particularly so in Skryabin's work.[32]

How did Sorabji consider himself?

> I am not a "modern" composer in the inverted commas sense. I utterly and indignantly repudiate that epithet as being in any way applicable to me. I write very long, very elaborate works that are entirely alien and antipathetic to the fashionable tendencies prompted, publicised and plugged by the various "establishments" revolving around this or that modish composer. [...]
>
> Why do I write as I do? Why did (and do) the artists-craftsmen of Iran, India, China, Byzantine-Arabic Sicily (in the first and last of which are my own ancestral roots) produce the sort of elaborate highly wrought work they did? That was their way. It is also mine. If you don't like it, because it isn't the present-day done thing, that is just too bad, but not for me, who couldn't care less. In fact, to me your disapproval is an indirect compliment and much less of an insult than your applause, when I consider some of your idols.[33]

To Sorabji the act of composition was a "holy and sacred thing to be approached with devoutness [and] seriousness of mind".[34] He condemned all forms of music that deviated from this ideal, such as popular and commercial music. He wanted to create "pure music, music which does not pretend to say this or that — a musical transcript of verbal or ideological concepts [...]".[35]

*****

The works of many composers have frequently been divided into stylistic periods, often early, middle, and late. Although in principle this categorization may be applicable to Sorabji's music, it is far more helpful to organize his piano works in a different way: strict contrapuntal sections (fugues); sections in variation form; sections

---

[31] Kaikhosru Sorabji: *Around Music*, p. 96.

[32] {See pp. 199–200.}

[33] Hugh MacDiarmid: *The Company I've Kept* (London: Hutchinson, 1966), pp. 38–39. {The word *modish* at the end of the first paragraph has been changed from *modern* in MacDiarmid's book, as the former is what Sorabji wrote in both surviving drafts of this statement. See also p. xv of the present book for part of the statement omitted here.}

[34] Kaikhosru Sorabji: *Around Music*, p. 199.
{For the entire chapter in Sorabji's book from which this comes, see pp. 288–90 of the present book.}

[35] Ibid., p. 25.

in the motoric genre; free fantasies, paraphrases, and shorter works; and nocturnes. Each of these will now be discussed briefly in turn.

Strict Contrapuntal Sections (Fugues)

The fugues are the most cerebral of his conceptions. Consistency of texture, rhythmic drive, counterpoint, and the building of climaxes seem to be uppermost in importance. Variety in patterns, clarity of phrase structure, and harmonic definition are not priorities. Erik Chisholm writes: "Sorabji's fugues are enormous architectural structures — 'living embodiments of elaborate intellectual processes' — to quote a remark of his own in another connection."[36]

Sorabji's counterpoint stems from that of Max Reger and Ferruccio Busoni. These composers attempted a synthesis of Bach's polyphony and Wagner's harmony in their own compositions. Sorabji carried the process one step further. His contrapuntal writing is even thicker and more unwieldy, though perhaps not as turgid as that of Reger can be. His conception of ideal counterpoint seems best expressed in the following passage about Busoni's music:

> The possibilities of the counterpoint are here surely pushed to their extreme: every imaginable scholastic device is turned to use, but with such logic, such conviction, such inevitability, that in the majestic and stately onward flow of this superb work one is no more immediately conscious of the minor [sic] architectonic skill and ingenuity that has gone to its making than one is of how many millions of gallons of water flow by every hour when watching the flow of a great river.[37]

There is little in Sorabji's thematic counterpoint that is compositionally unexplainable. His contrapuntal treatment is basically conservative. He begins all his fugues with the subject in its original form and develops his material in a traditional way. In some works, every alteration and transformation of a subject is labelled or bracketed (by the composer) in the score, whether it be an inversion, retrograde, retrograde inversion, stretto, or other variant. Occasionally Sorabji employs numbers to identify the various thematic elements throughout a movement, as in the first movement of his *Tāntrik* Symphony.

---

[36]Erik Chisholm: "Kaikhosru Shapurji Sorabji" (London: Oxford University Press, ca. 1938). Reprinted privately: n.pl., [ca. 1964], n.p.

[37]Kaikhosru Sorabji: *Around Music*, pp. 26–27.

Sorabji's fugues have as many as five different subjects, which are combined in the final stretto section. Generally, the fugues begin with slow-moving subjects in long note values irregularly grouped. There are few areas in the fugues in which the entire subject is not present. Usually building to four or five voices, the texture gradually thickens as the composer adds doublings at various intervals. Having reached a climax, the second subject, in faster-moving note values, is introduced. It is manipulated in a similar way: the texture becomes increasingly complex, and the music again builds to a dynamic peak. The procedure applied to the first two subjects is repeated with any remaining subjects, each often being in successively smaller note values. In the final, massive section of his fugues Sorabji combines all the subjects in a section often labelled *Coda-Stretta*. Occasionally, the concluding section is preceded by a *punta d'organo*, in which a pedal point (often several pages in duration) may declaim a tonal centre. Markings such as *Quasi mixtures* show that Sorabji might be thinking in terms of the grandiose sound of the organ (an instrument which he also dearly loved). One wonders whether such grandiosity is possible on the piano, and whether the polyphony can be heard at all when six or seven staves, one above the other, are overloaded with notes, all intended to be played with only two hands and two or three pedals — as in the following example.

Ex. 3. *Sequentia cyclica:* p. 334, sys. 1.

348 *The Music*

The fugues are the most atonal sections of his compositions, as Sorabji's intention in them is to create music which is exclusively the consequence of the interaction of melodic lines, without serial techniques to organize the music. Since he does not avoid intervallic parallelisms, the resultant harmonies may range from extreme harshness to those suggesting a modal influence. The overall musical result is, however, harmonically consistent and satisfying.

Sorabji's fugue subjects are among the most unusual, if not perverse, of his melodic constructions. Some subjects consist solely of a gradual ascent or descent, without the overall change of direction which usually occurs in melodic writing. Other fugue subjects are surely the longest ever penned, and upon first hearing strike one as being an emotionless succession of notes. Yet they make an impression, not only because of their unusual and uncompromising nature, but because of the eventual comforting familiarity they provide in the otherwise forbidding labyrinth of polyphony they generate. Even if some of the thinner textures in the fugues sound tentative, the fugues' formal interest is regenerated by effective forward motion provided by some textural variety and rhythmic impetus.

Ex. 4. Five fugue subjects from *Sequentia cyclica.*

a) p. 299, sys. 3.

Sorabji's Piano Music 349

b) p. 304, sys. 1–2.

c) p. 309, sys. 1–2.

d) p. 314, sys. 1.

e) p. 320, sys. 1.

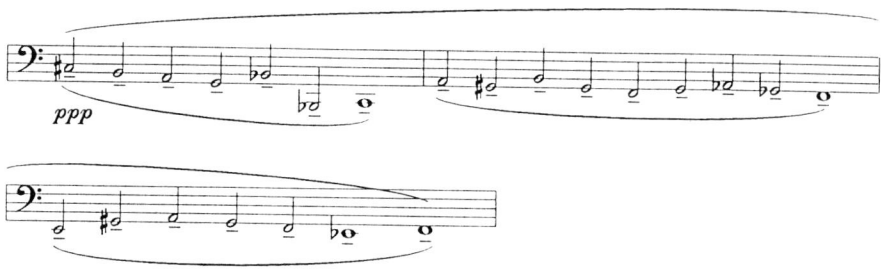

Sorabji often uses the fugue as a climactic texture at or near the end of a major section of a work, from the early Prelude, Interlude, and Fugue (1920, 1922) to the late *The Golden Cockerel Crows* (1978–79).[38]

Sections in Variation Form

The sets of variations are unique in their wide diversity of patterns, rhythms, textures, and harmonies. Sections from the large-scale works entitled *Variazioni, Passacaglia, Basso ostinato,* or *Preludio corale* feature constant variety in melody, rhythm, and texture in conjunction with each repetition of an unchanging *cantus firmus.* The procedure is akin to the baroque rather than to the classical concept of variation.

The melodic ideas upon which these works are based generally move by step instead of by leap. They are concise, occasionally consisting of two complementary phrases, as in example 5 (p. 351).

The variation sets often contain 49, 81, or 100 individual variations. Long as they are, the sets are effective. The enormous range of expression is presented in a structured manner; each musical idea is clearly separated from the next. Each variation is built upon a specific rhythmic, textural, or technical pattern which persists from the beginning to the end; occasionally two or three successive variations explore one basic style or technique. Tonal elements are much more prevalent in these sections, since Sorabji does not restrict himself to polyphony as the sole constructive element.

---

[38]{*The Golden Cockerel Crows* is the title of the work found on the first page of music, better than the one on the title page: see p. 171.}

Ex. 5. Theme of the Variations from *Opus clavicembalisticum:* p. 59, sys. 1.

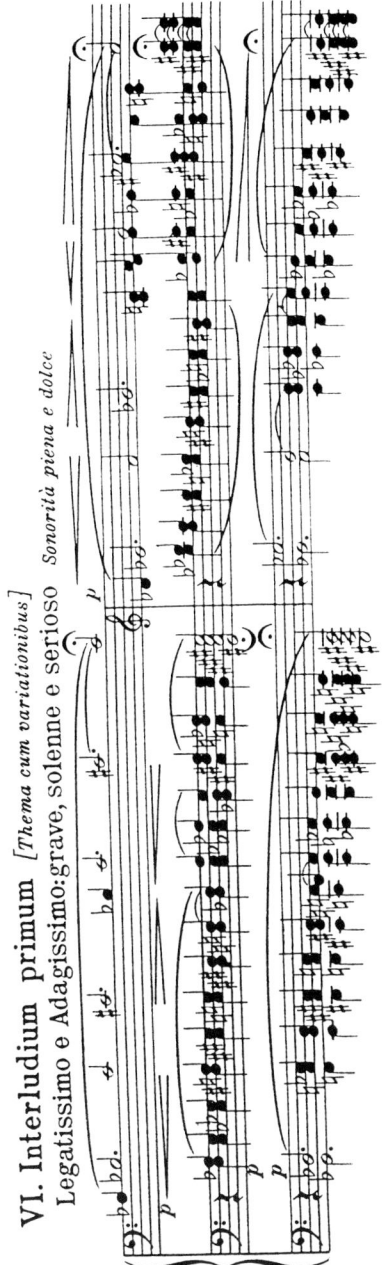

Almost identical to the sets of variations are those sections entitled *Passacaglia* and *Ostinato*. The main difference between these and the variations lies in the basic thematic line stated at the onset being adhered to more closely in the passacaglias and ostinatos and thus more clearly audible in these. *Preludio corale* denotes a freer set of variations, written in the style of a piano transcription of an organ work. Sorabji's chorale preludes are considerably shorter than his other types of variations. Thematic material in these sections is usually stated in broad note values and is often restated in resonant diatonic chordal settings. Decorative figurations doubled at various intervals suggest the off-unison or mixture stops of an organ, as seen in example 6 (p. 353).

There are several complete works in variation form, from the early *Dies iræ* Variations (1923–26) to the *Golden Cockerel* Variations (1978–79). Variation sections, as well as passacaglias, ostinatos, and chorale preludes, are similarly found throughout Sorabji's piano music.

Sections in the Motoric Genre

The sections in the motoric genre, such as the toccatas, preludes, perpetual motions, fantasias, and cadenzas, being relatively short in their rapid tempos, generate excitement in their relentlessness and impulsiveness. They consist primarily of an enormous number of brilliant running 16th-note figures. (See example 7, p. 354.)

As in the fugues, the predominant dynamic scheme is *crescendo* towards the end, although there are exceptions, e.g. the Prelude from Prelude, Interlude, and Fugue; and the second movement of Sonata No. 5, marked *Presto: sotto voce inquieto*. Both are meant to be played quietly throughout. Possible prototypes for these scurrying movements are the "perpetual motion" from Carl Maria von Weber's Sonata No. 1, Op. 24, the last movement of Chopin's Sonata No. 2, Op. 35, Alkan's *Le chemin de fer*, Op. 27, and Busoni's *Perpetuum mobile*, the solo piano version of the second movement of his Concertino for Piano and Orchestra.[39]

Toccatas differ from preludes and perpetual motions in that they display freer rhythmic treatment, as well as declamatory phrases in accented, longer note values set above or below the quick figurations. Cadenzas are freer yet, at times combining the swift motion of passage work with long pedal points. Cadenza II from

---

[39] {The *Perpetuum mobile*, BV 293 is derived from the *Scherzoso* of the *Romanza e scherzoso*, BV 290, which forms the Concertino, BV 292 when it is added to the *Konzertstück* for Piano and Orchestra, BV 236.}

Ex. 6. *Preludio corale* from *Opus clavicembalisticum*: p. 14, sys. 2–3.

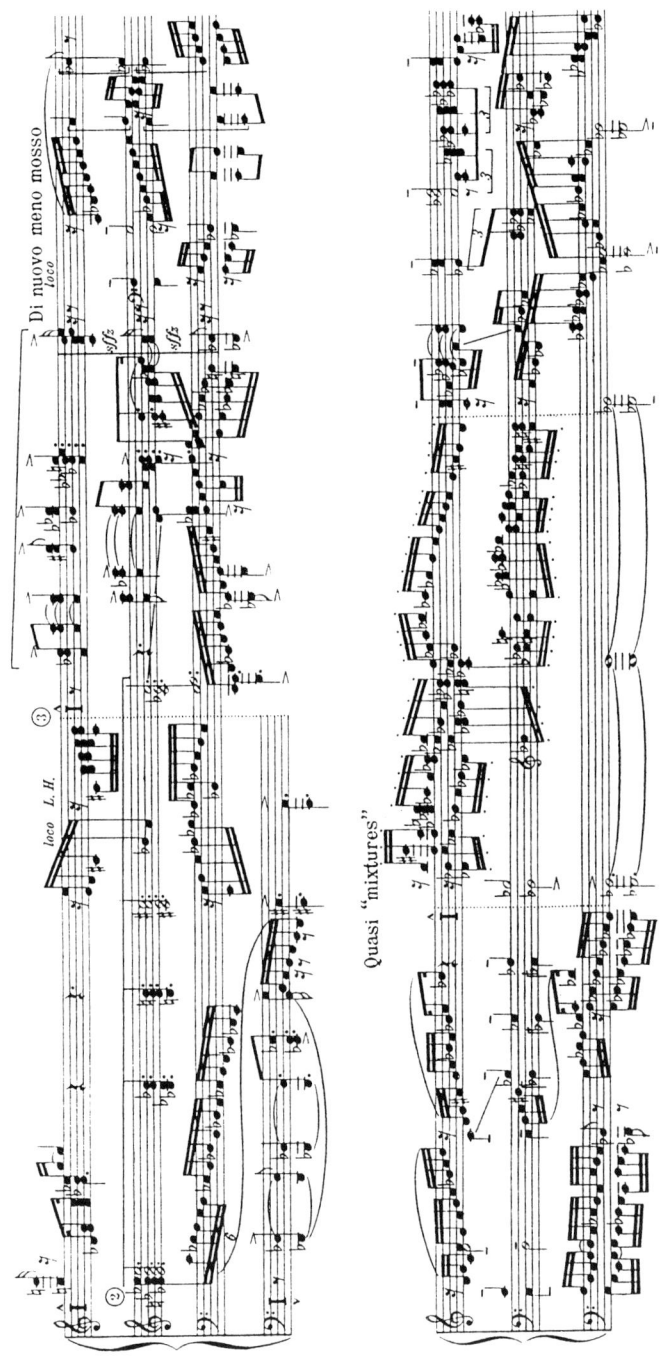

354 *The Music*

Ex. 7. Prelude from Prelude, Interlude, and Fugue: p. 3, sys. 1.

Opus clavicembalisticum, for instance, combines rapidly moving chords in various groupings of eighth-notes with a repeated pedal point, both of which help build a powerful climax.

The most daring type of motoric work is found in the fantasias. Relentless determination and obsessive perseverance are aspects of Sorabji's character which are revealed in these sections. The penultimate Transcendental Study is a wild fantasy closely modelled upon the *Chromatic Fantasia* by Bach.

Free Fantasies, Paraphrases, and Shorter Works

The three early sonatas are free inventions in which unbridled creative delirium in all musical dimensions nearly threatens unity and coherence. Lengthy, almost formless written-out improvisations, they are sonatas only in name. Sorabji himself declared that "strictly speaking, the sonata is merely a generic label for any extended or large-scale work for one or more than one solo instrument".[40] These sonatas are anomalies in his output because of their near lack of structural and thematic clarity. They seem to belong to an experimental phase in his composing career.

The First Sonata might tax the listener's patience, as it is the least interesting, being stylistically and harmonically uneven and inconsistent. The multiple peaks and expressive frenzy are not the result of musical logic. The Second Sonata, a more inventive work, especially at the intervallic level, shows that Sorabji had begun to think more in an expressive musical sense. The phrase structure is somewhat clearer.

Far more successful still is the Third Sonata. In contrast to the paucity of musical thoughts in the first, this sonata teems with ideas. Every page looks interesting, but one wonders whether any relationship among the numerous thematic ideas exists. What Robert J. Gula wrote about the early works is especially applicable to these three sonatas: "almost everything about these early works bespeaks excessiveness — excessiveness coupled perhaps with exuberance and extravagance".[41]

Two programmatic works of interest, both based on ghost stories by M. R. James, are *St. Bertrand de Comminges: "He was laughing in the tower",* based on "Canon Alberic's Scrap-book", and *Quære reliqua hujus materiei inter secretiora,* based on "Count Magnus". These are attractive, in part because they are not excessively long (16 pages each), also because the musical ideas upon which they

---
[40] Kaikhosru Sorabji: *Around Music,* p. 54.
[41] Robert J. Gula: "Kaikhosru Shapurji Sorabji", p. 49.

are built recur frequently and can easily be identified by an attentive listener. Although Sorabji mocked those who saw programmatic content in his *Le jardin parfumé*,[42] he nevertheless took the time to compose these two illustrative pieces. He may have been influenced by the example of Ravel's *Gaspard de la nuit*, also of a sinister nature, based on three poems by Aloysius Bertrand. In one other early work, Variations and Fugue on *Dies iræ*, Sorabji again uses music to attempt a description of a non-musical topic: Variations nos. 58 to 64 each allude to one of the seven deadly sins.

With a few exceptions, the individual pieces from the Transcendental Studies are relatively short. Roughly equivalent in length to most of the individual variations in the longer sets such as *Sequentia cyclica super "Dies iræ"*, they are constructed in a similar way. The basic pattern which the composer reiterates throughout a study, however, is more of a technical and pianistic nature than of a strictly musical one. Prototypes for this collection of studies are perhaps Busoni's *Klavierübung* and Godowsky's 53 Studies on Chopin's Etudes.

Each of the 104 *Frammenti aforistici* from the collection begun in 1962 are the shortest of Sorabji's compositions.[43] In fact, they are so minute (as brief as the tiniest piece by Webern) that calling each a separate piece is an overstatement. (Perhaps they are only incipits.) This compilation of phrases and short periods is an ideal starting point for the analyst who wishes to understand the mature Sorabji style: it is almost a dictionary of the composer's musical vocabulary. (See example 8, p. 357.)

The Fragment for Harold Rutland, "a sort of musical sample", is one of the few of his pieces that Sorabji heard performed by someone else. Perhaps this was the main reason why he revised it twice. (One can only speculate what direction Sorabji's composing might have taken had he been able to listen to his other compositions in good concert performances.) In its final version, it is based upon two contrasting motives which are stated simultaneously at the beginning. The opening section is fiery and dramatic, the second quiet and contemplative. Although it is only two pages long, it is very satisfying both structurally and musically.

A much later composition, *Fantasiettina sul nome illustre dell'egregio poeta Christopher Grieve ossia Hugh M'Diarmid* (1961), resembles the Fragment for Harold Rutland in both scope and bipartite structure.[44]

---

[42]Kaikhosru Sorabji: *Mi contra fa*, p. 24.

[43]{Along with the other fragments, in sets of 4 and of 20 items.}

[44]It is regrettable that Sorabji's output does not contain many other works of reasonable length.

Ex. 8. No. 4 from *[104] Frammenti aforistici:* p. 2, sys. 1.

Surely the most accessible of Sorabji's works are the parodies, transcriptions, and paraphrases upon well-known themes by other composers. Several other composer-pianists, such as Liszt, Alkan, Reger, Busoni, and Godowsky, delighted in commenting on and transforming popular melodies into brilliant and entertaining keyboard pieces. Sorabji emulated them by writing several virtuoso arrangements of works by Bach (*Chromatic Fantasia and Fugue*), Ravel (*Rapsodie espagnole*), and Strauss (closing scene from *Salome*). These works are, without a doubt, extremely effective in live performance, although Sorabji modestly stated that he wrote the latter two for his own amusement, with no thought of public performance.[45]

Sorabji viewed transcription as an opportunity to transform the familiar into the unusual. He was impressed by Busoni's "uncanny

---

[45]Kaikhosru Sorabji: Letter to Michael Habermann, 1 August 1979.

power of seizing upon material of a quite ordinary character, and so taking possession of it [...] that it loses all its own identity and becomes merely a medium for him".[46] In Sorabji's paraphrases too, worn-out melodies receive a new life and character.

Busoni's work was occasionally a specific influence on Sorabji's choice of material for reworking. For instance, Busoni's Sonatina No. 6, based on themes from Bizet's opera *Carmen,* and his edition of Bach's *Chromatic Fantasia and Fugue* were respective sources of Sorabji's Pastiche on the "Habanera" from *Carmen* and his own transcription of the same Bach work. (Sorabji, however, appended to it and transcribed a different fugue.)

There are several compositions, such as *Variazione maliziosa e perversa sopra "La morte d'Åse" da Grieg,* which are parodies of famous tunes. These are primarily tonal pieces overlaid with chromatic decorative material. The set of three pastiches includes a version of Chopin's *Minute Waltz,* the Bizet "Habanera", and "The Hindu Merchant's Song" from *Sadko* by Rimskiy-Korsakov. Not only did Sorabji write two arrangements of Chopin's *Minute Waltz* (the other being *Pasticcio capriccioso sopra Op. 64 No. 1 dello Chopin*), but he also quoted portions of it in other works of his, for example, *Passeggiata veneziana.* This piece, in the manner of a 19th-century opera fantasy, is a free paraphrase in several sections on the *Barcarolle* from Offenbach's *Tales of Hoffmann.* In the middle movement, the languid theme is transformed into a brilliant tarantella. (A second tarantella appears in *Rosario d'arabeschi.*)

Sorabji used another dance model, the Viennese waltz, as a springboard for his wild improvisations in such works as *Valse-fantaisie,*[47] Transcendental Study No. 63 ("en forme de valse"), and others.

His love of Spain is manifested in several compositions which employ Iberian dance rhythms. Aside from the very early and less interesting *Quasi habanera,* the *Fantaisie espagnole* is the simplest and most melodic of these. Undoubtedly influenced by the Spanish works of Liszt, Albéniz, Granados, and Debussy, it is, nevertheless, a worthwhile composition. It is tonally oriented despite the abundance of added-note harmonies and fierce dissonances. Its three large sections are introduced and separated by improvisatory-sounding cadenza bridges. Above the rhythms of the *habanera* and *tango* in the left hand, melodic phrases alternate with brilliant "filler" figurations. The ending of the last section, a *jota,* is a good example of how brilliantly Sorabji outdid even Liszt in providing dazzling endings to his pieces.

---

[46]Kaikhosru Sorabji: *Around Music,* p. 28.
[47]Possibly inspired by Ravel's *La valse.*

Music in a Spanish style also appears in parts of later works, e.g. some of the Transcendental Studies and the *Sequentia cyclica super "Dies iræ"*.

Nocturnes

The kinder side of Sorabji's character comes through in his articles of praise and admiration for his favourite works and composers. Musically, this outpouring of approval is given shape in his nocturnes. They seem to have been written to please, with their enticing melodies and luxurious harmonies, rather than to demonstrate a particular compositional technique pushed to its extremes. They are extended, meditative, sensuous, impressionistic pieces. The harmonies are luscious, the textures varied, and the phrases asymmetrical. But above all, the melodic content is truly inspired. Surrounding these sinuous chant-like melodies are imaginative decorative figurations, pedal points, and haunting repetitive patterns that create hypnotic moods.

Undoubtedly, the nocturnes are the most successful and beautiful of Sorabji's compositions. All of the musical components effectively interact to produce music that has both unity and variety. Coherence is the result of the intuitive stream of musical, as opposed to "intellectual" thought. Rhythms, melodies, and textures are always in a state of flux, each in its turn providing interest. Only the dynamic level is fixed; the nocturnes — dreamy, flowing pieces — are meant never to be played louder than mezzo-forte. The neutral dynamic level does not interfere with harmonic and rhythmic progressions; it does not superimpose upon the music a false sense of direction. The nocturnes are not lengthy, and the main melodic line guides the listener through the sonorous maze.

Their general atmosphere is best expressed in Sorabji's description of a work by Delius, which reveals Sorabji's love of rich, lavish, and mysterious music:

> [... T]he "Arabesk" is not only unique among Delius' work. It is surely one of the most astonishing evocations in sound of poisonous, perverse, tuberose-like beauty that exists. It is indescribably insinuating and haunting, and the mood of the subtly beautiful poem, with its deadly perfume, "the poisonous lily's blinding chalice," is expressed with miraculous insight and power.[48]

---

[48] *The New Age*, vol. 46 (7 November 1929), pp. 8–9.

In Sorabji's larger works, the section in nocturne style may take the place of the traditional slow movement, as it does for the first time in his Sonata No. 4. This style is found in a very wide variety of his works: as an entire composition (e.g. *Jāmī, Gulistān*, and the Symphonic Nocturne), as a movement (e.g. *In the Hothouse*, the second movement from the *Concerto da suonare da me solo*, and the *Notturno* movement from the *Symphonia brevis*), as a section (e.g. several variations in the Variations and *Passacaglia* parts of *Opus clavicembalisticum*, and several of the Transcendental Studies).

Closely related to the nocturnes are the sections labelled *Punta d'organo*, in which nocturne-type music is heard against an extended pedal point. "Le gibet" from Ravel's *Gaspard de la nuit* is such a piece; it may have been the initial model which Sorabji took and occasionally expanded into mammoth proportions.

These pedal-point sections are also found throughout Sorabji's piano works.

Le jardin parfumé

Le jardin parfumé was composed in 1923 and published by Curwen in 1927. It was dedicated to another composer, Christopher à Becket Williams, who wrote an article on Sorabji's music in 1924 for *The Sackbut*.[49] The work's title alludes to the Arabian love-manual written by Sheik al-Nafzāwī in the 15th or 16th century. The book was translated into English by Sir Richard Burton, famous for his translation of the *Arabian Nights*. Several other nocturnes by Sorabji were also inspired by poets and poetry of the Middle East. The Nocturne *Jāmī* is named after the Persian scholar, poet, and mystic Jāmī (1414–92). *Gulistān (The Rose Garden)*, written in 1258 by the Persian poet Sa'dī (ca. 1213–91), gives its title to one of Sorabji's most beautiful nocturnes.

In 1930, Frederick Delius wrote Sorabji a letter, admiring the "real sensuous beauty" of *Le jardin parfumé*, which he had just heard in Sorabji's performance on the BBC.[50] Clinton Gray-Fisk was referring to Sorabji's nocturne style when he wrote: "He can, when he wishes, make sheer sensuous beauty of sound his primary consideration and surpass Debussy and Ravel in exotic harmonies, colouration and evocative power [...]."[51] Erik Chisholm described *Le jardin parfumé* as having "strange and indefinable beauty", being (in the words of critic Hugh Reid) "the expression of a rare and

---

[49]Christopher à Becket Williams: "The Music of Kaikhosru Sorabji".
[50]{See p. 280 for Delius's complete comment.}
[51]Clinton Gray-Fisk: "Kaikhosru Shapurji Sorabji", p. 232.

significant poetic mirage".⁵² Soon after the work was published, another critic praised it highly, although he was frustrated by its technical difficulties:

> I cannot review this piece [...] I cannot play the music, nor yet read it. It eludes my translating eye as it completely eludes my fingers. Only this is clear, that given a piano of celestial tone, a pianist whose technique is transparently delicate, sure and strong, and whose mind is that of a poet-musician, the piece must prove fascinating.⁵³

There are a number of notational ambiguities and apparent misprints in the published score which need clarification and correction. Yet a comparison between the printed edition and the manuscript, which is now located in the music library of Northwestern University in Evanston, Illinois, does not help solve many problems: the two are almost identical. Correction of these errors is found in the appendix to the dissertation from which this chapter comes.

Many of Sorabji's compositions from the period 1920–30 are experimental, unsettling, and violent works. *Le jardin parfumé*, however, is a very soothing piece. The marking at its beginning reads: "Jamais plus fort que *pp* du commencement jusqu'à la fin", although a mezzo-forte is seen on page 17. Concerning the relative paucity of dynamic and expression markings in his scores, Sorabji wrote elsewhere:

> The comparative lack of what are quaintly called "expression marks" in this work is thus explained. The Composer considers that the music itself makes clear what "expression" is needed, if any in any particular passage. The "intelligence" of the player will do — or undo — the rest.⁵⁴

But dynamic fluctuations within this restrained range are needed to give coherence and shape to phrases and to relieve possible monotony. Also, changes in volume are implied by both rhythmic activity and variety in texture, which ranges from solitary monodic lines to pages of great density. Thickness of texture also has a structural function: high points in textural density and the following easing of tension are the primary delineators of the shape of phrases, sections, and of the whole work.

---

⁵²Erik Chisholm: "Kaikhosru Shapurji Sorabji".
⁵³S. Grew: "Kaikhosru Sorabji", pp. 85–86.
⁵⁴Prefatory note to *Sequentia cyclica super "Dies iræ"*.
{For the rest of this note, see p. 190.}

Sorabji's own performance of *Le jardin parfumé*, privately recorded by his friend Frank Holliday in the 1960s, is inadequate. There is often little resemblance between what is notated and what is played. When I wrote to Sorabji about his performance, he replied:

> You say in your kind letter of 22nd. that you perceived marked liberties and deviations in performance (by self) of my JARDIN PARFUMÉ. I dont doubt it for ONE MOMENT! I am not ... repeat N O T a pianist and make no pretensions to being one. I get over the ground in my own music, and within my limitations EMPHATIC AND DECIDED as they are claim to do no more than give a birds eye view of the music. Such liberties as I take — <u>and who has better right to do so than myself in my own music?</u> — are dictated by the condition of my fingers at any particular time when I was recording; then I modify and alter AS SUITS ME. That's all there is to it. The music as printed embodies my INTENTIONS.[55]

Sorabji's conception of the use of the piano as a singing instrument was in agreement with that of the romantics and impressionists. Like them, he treated the piano non-percussively. To him, such composers as Bartók and Stravinsky had a "percussion obsession" with regard to the instrument, an approach he did not like.

Sorabji seldom expressed his views on how his music was to be interpreted. The preface to the piano part of his published piano concerto, a work written a few years before *Le jardin parfumé*, prescribes mostly a "steady, smooth extra-metrical prose-like flow", using the barlines solely for counting, and recommends against memorizing the solo part.[56]

In spite of this recommendation, it has been this writer's experience that only when Sorabji's compositions have been completely memorized can they be given an adequate performance. This has always been an arduous task, but amply rewarding: the pianistic difficulties and technical aspects of his music are always subservient to the musical idea. Although it seems that the difficulties in Sorabji's music might be mitigated in two-piano settings, his writing for solo keyboard is very idiomatic and does not lend itself easily to transcription. Perhaps the only medium

---

[55] Kaikhosru Sorabji: Letter to Michael Habermann, 28 February 1972. The suspension points are Sorabji's.

[56] Kaikhosru Sorabji: Prefatory note to the solo part of the Concerto for Piano and Orchestra (1920).
{Published as No. 2, this is actually Sorabji's Fifth Piano Concerto. For the entire preface, see pp. 182–83.}

besides solo piano for which the music might be suitable is that of computer-assisted synthesized sound. Several segments from *Opus clavicembalisticum* were executed by Paul Rapoport on a computer in 1974. This experiment showed that Sorabji's complex music lends itself to musically effective realizations in the electronic studio.[57]

Meter signatures are not used in *Le jardin parfumé*, nor are they necessary. Sorabji generally notated with great exactitude the speed at which the notes are to be played. The constant variety in rhythmic values and the frequent shifts in the content of the beat embody his ideal of a music with a "prose-like flow". To avoid unmusical rhythmic angularity in performance, the shifts in note values should not be taken too literally but be understood as written approximations of a flowing "rubato" style of performance. However, carefully planned shaping of phrases and sections is absolutely necessary in order to counteract the lurking aimlessness of this work.

A principal melodic line is usually present throughout each of Sorabji's works. If in performance this line stands out clearly while the surrounding decorative material is subdued, then the interpreter will have avoided one of the errors that Sorabji loathed to hear in pianists:

> [...] Lisztian *fioriture* delivered with the inanely grinning impudence and slapstick slickness of the clown-juggler drawing yards of multicoloured paper ribbons from his mouth, with no realisation at all that the *fioritura* decoration is not something stuck on to make a nitwit virtuoso's numskull audience stare and gape, but belongs as integrally to the work as the fretted marble lacework of Santa Maria in Valverde, of the Casa Professa in Palermo to Sicilian baroque architecture.[58]

Despite its length (34 pages in the published score) and seemingly discursive and improvisatory nature, *Le jardin parfumé* is actually carefully shaped. Of its musical structure Sorabji wrote that

---

[57]See "Sorabji and the Computer", by Paul Rapoport, in *Tempo*, no. 117 (June 1976), pp. 23–26.

{Created because of the unlikelihood at the time of there ever being a performance of *Opus clavicembalisticum*, much less a recording, this computer realization, despite containing some effective parts, is deficient in many ways, and certainly inferior to a good recording by a "human pianist". A better computer realization is also possible now, as the author of this chapter suggests.}

[58]Kaikhosru Sorabji: *Mi contra fa*, p. 113.

"the entire work is woven [from] a theme worked in one form or another into the fabric of almost every page".[59]

His solution to the problem of achieving both variety and unity in this work was to base it upon a *number* of musical gestures which permeate the whole composition. These musical-pianistic ideas, presented in the opening pages of the work, are defined chiefly by their general outline. Matching pitch sequences or characteristic rhythmic patterns are of less consequence than the overall contours of the ideas. Constantly varied, developed, combined, and juxtaposed, the gestures resemble leitmotifs. But these musical gestures are different: their presentation and subsequent development permeate and define the whole texture, whereas leitmotifs function rather as landmarks within a texture. The form of the piece is a direct outgrowth of the organic development of the basic shapes with which the composer has chosen to work. As a result, an intuitive sense of continuity pervades the music.

The Basic Musical Gestures in *Le jardin parfumé*

The number of *idées fixes* in each of Sorabji's compositions varies. In *Le jardin parfumé*, for example, there are 15 basic gestures. (See table 1, p. 365.) The most important is the melodic idea to which Sorabji accords a traditional role of primacy. Other gestures include pianistic-musical ideas which function alternately as background, decorative, transitional, and episodic material. The work is the result of free association and meditation upon these recurrent basic ideas. The treatment and function of every gesture vary with and depend upon the particular musical context. Although the gestures are clearly defined, they are all interrelated in several ways.

---

[59]Kaikhosru Sorabji: Letter to the Editor, in *The Musical Times*, vol. 69 (1 December 1928), p. 1120.

Table 1. Musical gestures in *Le jardin parfumé*.

1. Main melodic material.
2. Accompaniment figure.
3. Ostinato figures (slow tremolos).
4. Chains of tremolos and trills.
5. Arpeggios.
6. Ascending passages followed by trills or tremolos.
7. Short motives: i) grace notes.
      ii) ascending and descending figures.
      iii) repeated notes and chords.
8. Single-note passages, ascending and descending.
9. Passages for one hand in which single notes alternate with chords.
10. Passages divided between the hands.
11. Passages which are repeated identically in different registers.
12. Rapid scales and glissandi.
13. Double notes.
14. Retrograde patterns.
15. Chords with added notes.

Each of the 15 basic gestures will now be discussed.

1. The melody, appearing in many different guises, retains its identity chiefly due to its rhythmic and melodic shape, and partly because of its pitch content.

Ex. 9. Main melodic material, *Le jardin parfumé*: p. 4, sys. 1–3. (Cf. p. 372.)

The melodic phrase features alternations between long, held notes and sections of florid notes of shorter value. At times the rhythmic progression moves gradually from long to shorter note values, but it generally adheres to no specific pattern. The rhythmic treatment is suggestive of the *cante hondo* of Spanish music and also recalls the improvisatory concept of Indian melodic inspiration. The *legato* articulation and the long notes of the main melodic material counteract the jagged rhythmic spurts to produce a wonderfully freely moving melodic line which aurally is easily recognizable. An abundance of tied values distracts the listener's attention from the basic beat. Added flexibility is provided by the frequent division of the beat or the half beat into five or seven parts. Changes in the unit of the beat itself, from the prevailing quarter-note unit to a dotted quarter-note or a dotted eighth, also contribute a great deal to the sense of freedom. But such rhythmic acrobatics do not merely indicate a "rubato" style of performance: see example 10 (p. 367).

The main melodic material in this excerpt must be played in "strict" time for it to be synchronized with the steady ostinato figure in the same hand. Meanwhile, the right-hand figurations must be played with clarity and evenness.

The shift in the content of the beat creates the illusion of a change in the tempo, which in turn contributes many additional rhythmic possibilities, within a unified framework. Coupled with other sub-groupings (such as five 16th-notes against four) and combinations thereof divided between the hands, the variety is staggering. Perhaps this, and not the formal structure of the composition, is what accounts for the seemingly improvisatory, beatless character of *Le jardin parfumé* and Sorabji's other nocturnes. The rhythmic structures within brackets predate the complicated rhythms of Messiaen and Stockhausen.

In Sorabji's later works the rhythmic complexity is even more staggering. The writing is far more contrapuntal, and many keyboard registers sound simultaneously. A fine example may be seen in *Gulistān*. (See page 12, system 2 in the reproduction of Sorabji's manuscript on p. 368.)

The other delimiting factor in the melodic writing is the treatment of pitch. The overall melodic direction is one that descends or revolves around a main pitch — or, rarely, ascends. Unlike the shape of many of Sorabji's fugue subjects, the descending melody of *Le jardin parfumé* twists and circles, constantly changing direction, taking its time to unravel. Descending chromatic lines may be traced by deleting intervening ornamental pitches.

The composer explores the sundry paths which avoid the obvious in melodic delineation. When pitches are repeated, they invariably appear in a different rhythm or in a different part of the beat. Intervallically, the motion is predominantly conjunct, although the

Ex. 10. Rhythmic complexity, *Le jardin parfumé*: p. 25, sys. 3.

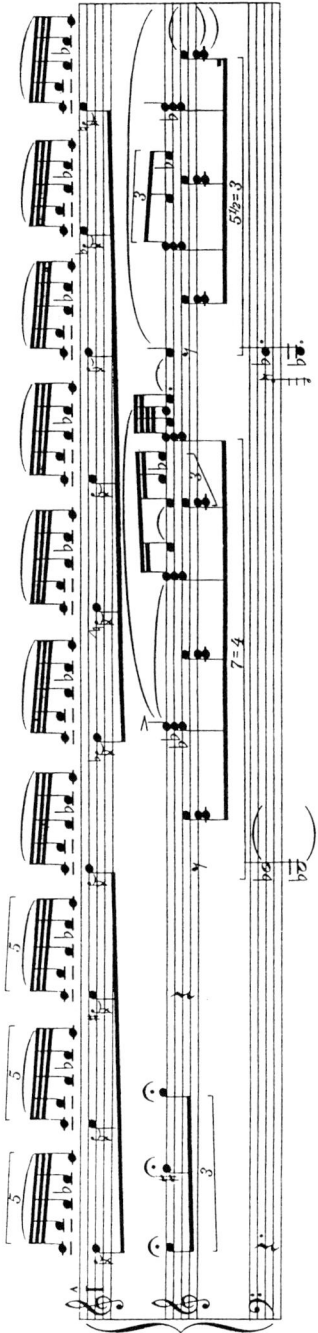

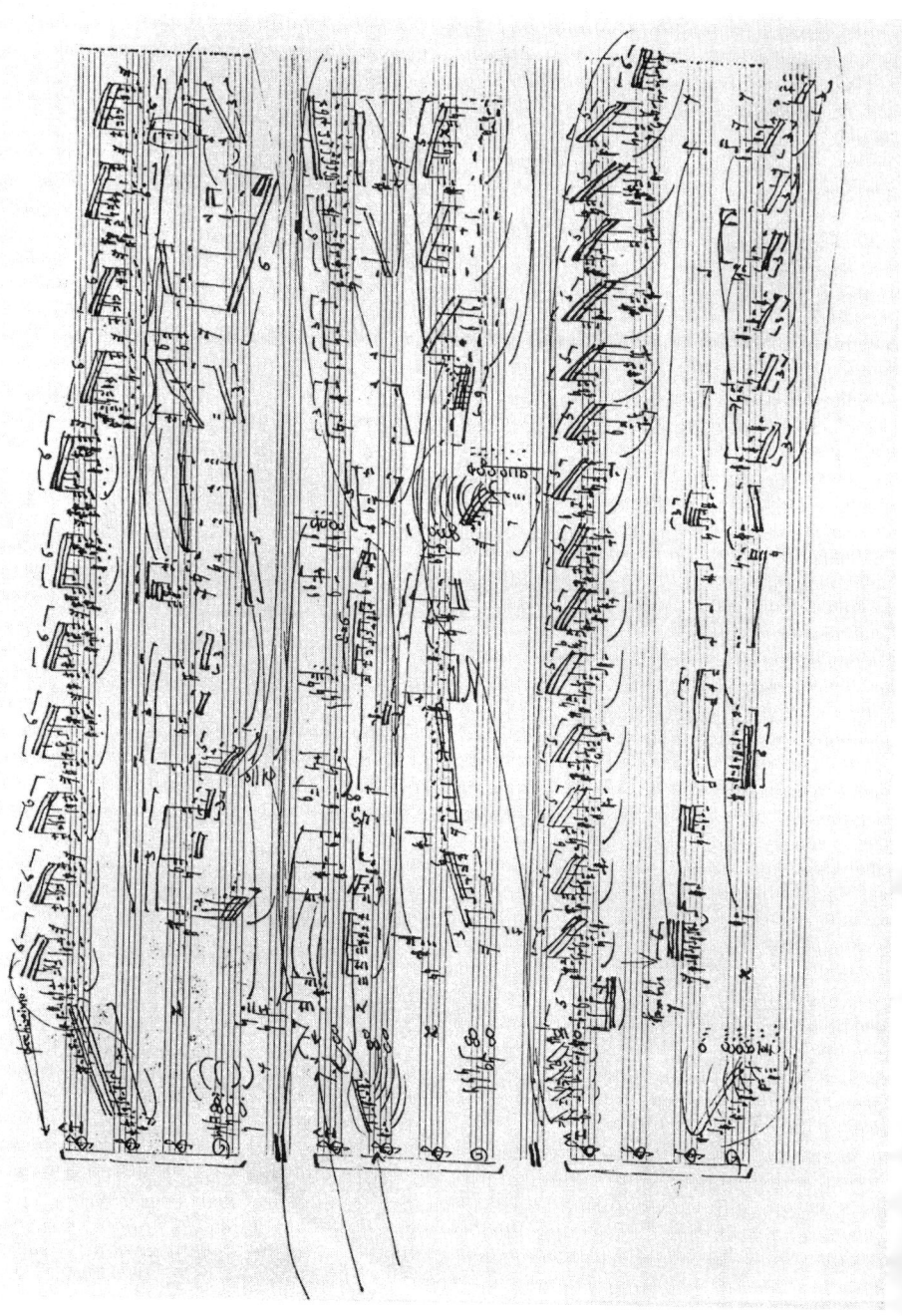

Gulistān, page 12 of Sorabji's manuscript (1940)

cell of a minor third and modifications thereof are present in many of the melodic variants.

Initially the melody is three phrases long, or 21 quarter-notes. But other statements may be only three quarter-notes in length. Similarly, its range varies from a span of three octaves to a mere major third. In those instances in which the melody revolves around a main pitch, this pitch is usually the longest note in the phrase, giving a sense of tonal orientation.

Most frequently the melodies are stated in the middle register, but the final appearance of the main chant-like melody is in the bass. Its elongated note values give it the additional function of a supporting harmonic root for arpeggios which appear above. The melody resonates with such solemnity, profundity, and gravity, that further appearances of it in any guise would be ineffective.

2. The accompaniment figure provides contrast to the highly ornate rhythms of the main melodic material. It seems to owe much to those arpeggio accompaniment figurations in the nocturne-like passages of Chopin and Liszt, as may be seen on examination of the two parts of example 11 (p. 370).[60]

Rhythmically the two-part writing on page 26, systems 2 and 3 is related to the accompaniment figure. The single occurrence of this sparse counterpoint provides striking textural relief. Effective use of such two-part writing is also found before the final climax in *Jāmī*.

3. The ostinato consisting of an alternation of two chords or pitch sets is an element which contributes much to the eerie mood of this work. (An ostinato appears at the beginning of Sorabji's earliest published composition, *In the Hothouse*, and is used throughout *Jāmī* and *Gulistān*.) The oscillation of two chords is employed as an event in its own right as well as a backdrop for sinuous melodies. Although the chords may be very dissonant, their reiteration establishes familiarity and harmonic stasis, and the usually consonant supporting bass and subdued dynamic level ensure lack of harshness. This gesture serves the structural purpose of providing areas of repose and stability. (The initial accidentals of example 12, measure 2 (p. 371) apply throughout the passage, even if not notated. Note Sorabji's unusual spelling of major and minor triads.)

4. The ostinato alternation of chords resembles a tremolo played very slowly. Closely linked is the next gesture, illustrated by example

---

[60]Example 11a is from Liszt's First Concerto for Piano and Orchestra, second movement, in *Franz Liszts musikalische Werke*, pt. 1, div. 4, vol. 13 (Leipzig: Breitkopf und Härtel, [ca. 1914]), p. 16.

370 The Music

Ex. 11. Accompaniment figure.

a) (left) Franz Liszt: Piano Concerto No. 1, second movement (*Quasi adagio*), measures 9–13.
b) (right) *Le jardin parfumé:* p. 3, sys. 1.

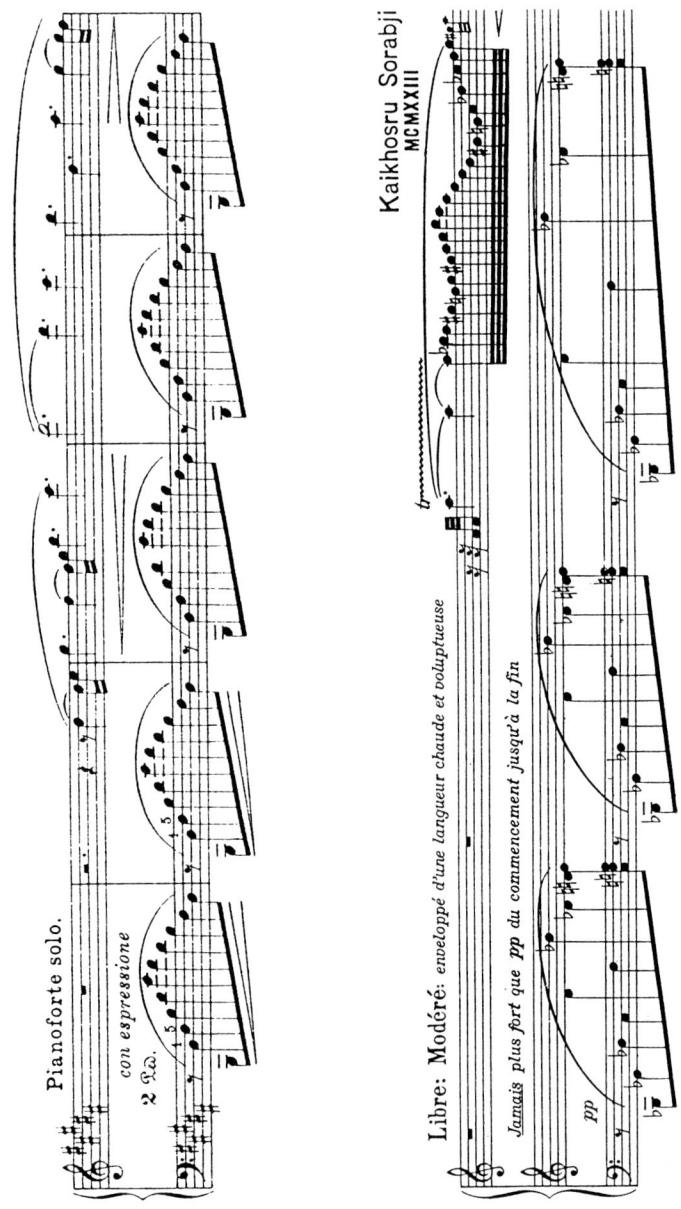

Ex. 12. Ostinato figure, *Le jardin parfumé:* p. 11, sys. 1–2.

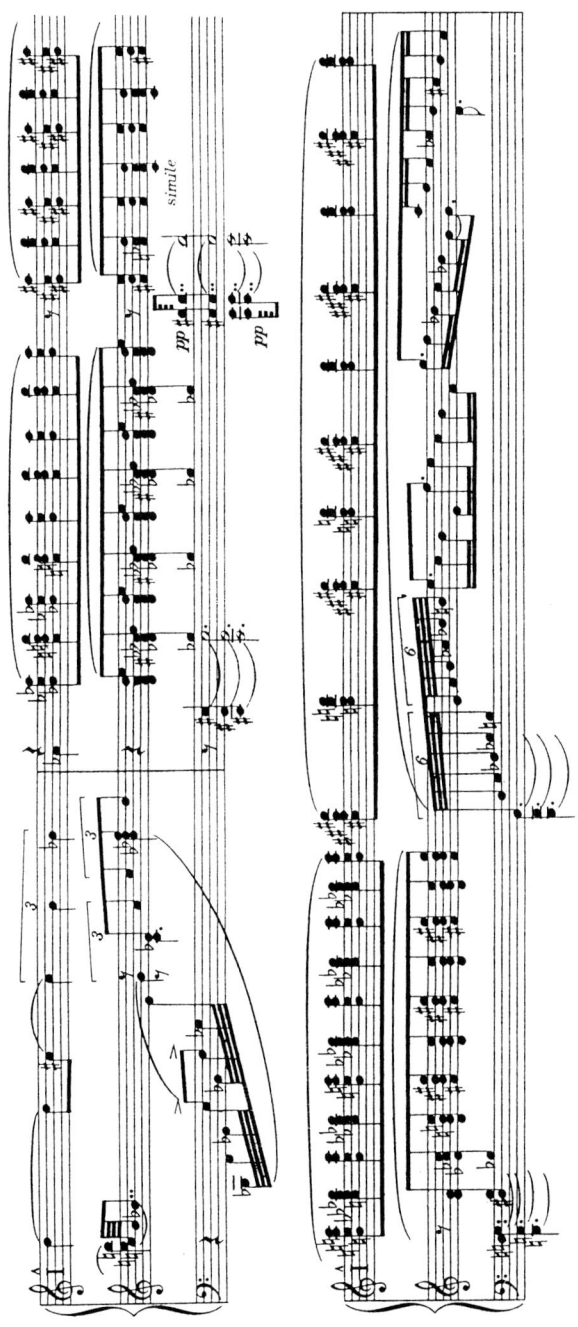

372 *The Music*

Ex. 13. Chains of tremolos and trills, *Le jardin parfumé:* p. 4, sys. 3 to p. 5, sys. 1. (This example is continued on the next page.)

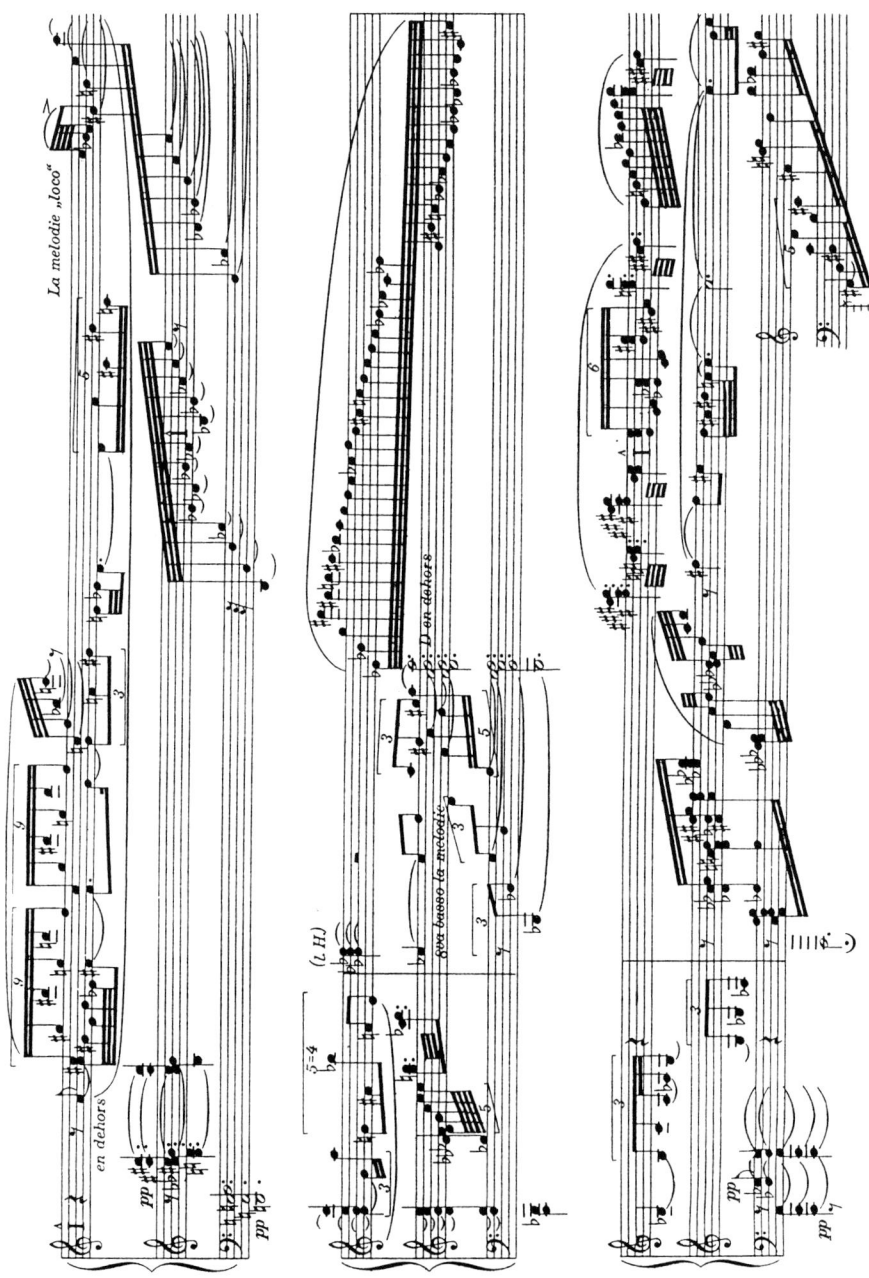

374 *The Music*

13 (pp. 372–73): unbroken chains of rapid tremolos and trills, which are used throughout the work and provide another level of unity. They serve as either foreground or a continuous background against which the melody stands out.

5. Arpeggios, almost always ascending, also pervade this composition. They sound like a refracted overtone series; the upper harmonics are chromatically altered. The arpeggios are constructed from the superposition of major, minor, augmented, and diminished triads, and ascend most frequently by thirds (possibly influenced by Busoni's explorations in such works as *Fantasia contrappuntistica* and *Prélude et étude en arpèges*), as in example 14. They serve both to accompany the main melodic material and to provide harmonic material for non-thematic but structurally essential passages. In contrast to the accompaniment figure, the arpeggio figure appears in free rhythms and is never repeated twice in succession.

Ex. 14. Arpeggio figure, *Le jardin parfumé:* p. 22, sys. 1.

6. An ascending upbeat figure followed by a downbeat trill or tremolo is another motive that is often found in Sorabji's nocturnes. Whereas the arpeggio figure is rhythmically free, the ascending figure followed by a trill generates a strong upbeat-downbeat response in the listener. (See example 15, p. 375.)

Ex. 15. Ascending figure leading to a trill, *Le jardin parfumé:* p. 23, sys. 2.

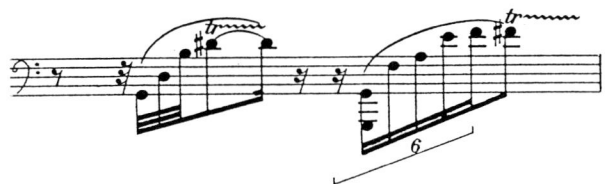

7. Highly contrasted to the six elements of the work so far described are a number of short motives which embellish and add complexity to the score, both texturally and rhythmically. These individual interjections, found everywhere, punctuate textures and supply inner unity. These motives may be divided into three categories, differentiated primarily by their rhythmic or melodic shape.

i) Grace notes (melodic ornaments preparing the arrival of downbeats) add rhythmic subtlety and roundness.

Ex. 16. Short motives: grace notes, *Le jardin parfumé:*

a) p. 12, sys. 2.

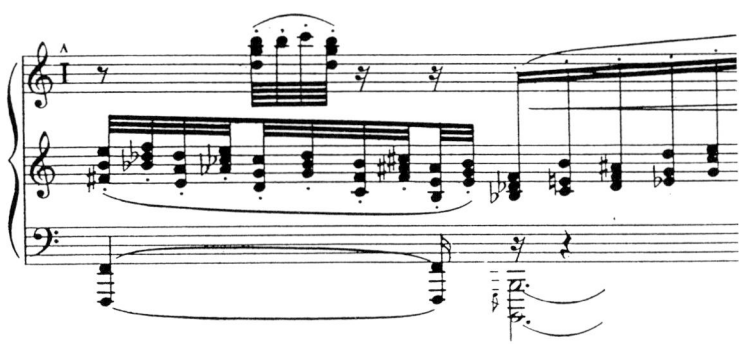

b) p. 26, sys. 1.

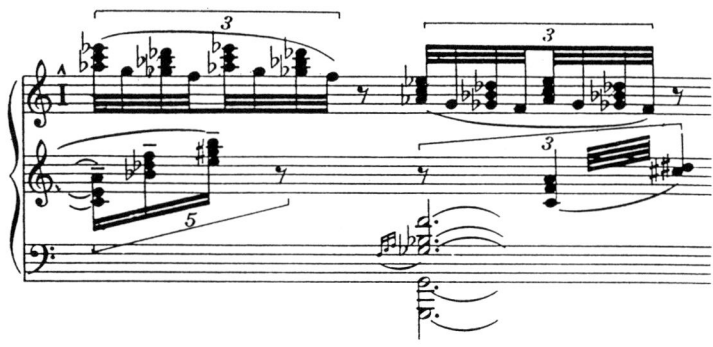

ii) Brief ascending and descending figures in 32nd-notes, generally outlining an arpeggio, frequently surround melodic statements.

Ex. 17. Short motives: ascending and descending figures, *Le jardin parfumé*:

a) p. 12, sys. 1.

b) p. 15, sys. 1.

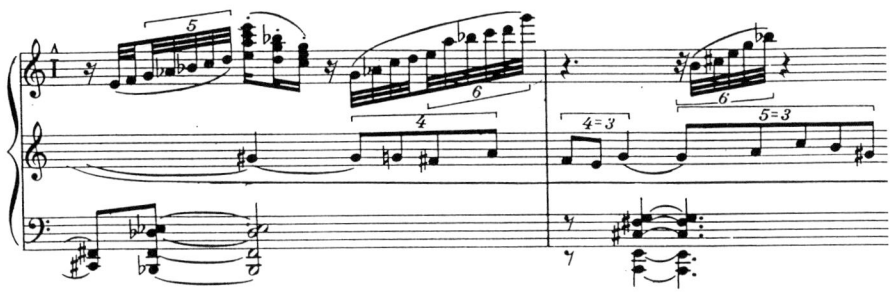

iii) Repeated notes are found in places where the attention is focused on other musical events (examples 12, measure 2 (p. 371) and 18).

Ex. 18. Short motives: repeated notes, *Le jardin parfumé:* p. 18, sys. 1.

The opening flourish of the piece begins with a repeated note. The combination of note repetition with the alternation of two pitches produces a figure similar to that at the opening of "Ondine" from Ravel's *Gaspard de la nuit*, yet it seems to be a natural and logical outgrowth, intrinsic to *Le jardin parfumé* (example 19, p. 378).

8. The fascinating variety in the ordering of the pitches in every scale may be the direct result of Sorabji's response to Busoni's proposal in his book *Sketch of a New Esthetic of Music,* for the

Ex. 19. Combination of note repetition with the alternation of two pitches, *Le jardin parfumé:* p. 29, sys. 1.

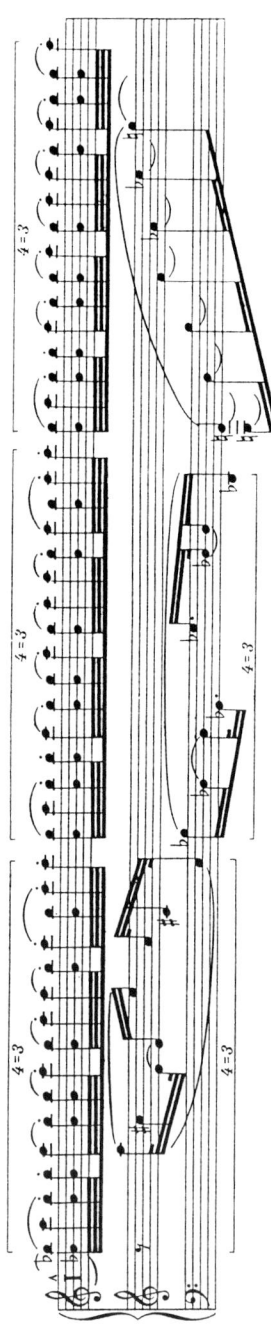

creation and exploration of new scales.[61] The opening flourish (a trill followed by a sweeping ornamental figuration) seems to have an inherently wild, improvisational quality which provides an effective foil to the reiterated and controlled accompaniment figure which appears below it. The combination of these two opposing elements is pursued further on in the work. An eerie descending passage on page 4 not only fills the space between one long melody note and the next, but adds ghostly glitter to a texture consisting of the descending chant-like melody supported by slow-moving harmonies. (See p. 372.)

As Sorabji's style matured, the inner structure of the music became more organized. He was generally able to avoid the imbalance produced from the excessive production of new material, by defining his material more clearly through immediate repetition: identically in successive registers, transposed up or down the steps of the whole-tone or chromatic scale, or transposed using the circle of fourths or fifths.

Ex. 20. Passage work generated by transposition.

a) Using the circle of fifths, *Jāmī*: p. 12, sys. 2.

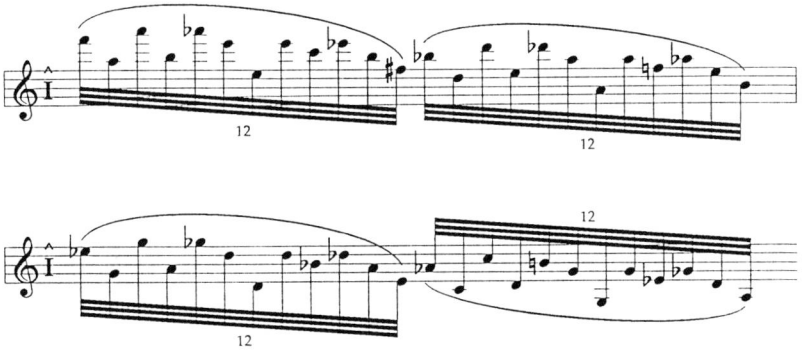

---

[61] Ferruccio Busoni: "Sketch of a New Esthetic of Music", translated by Theodore Baker, in *Three Classics in the Aesthetic of Music* (New York: Dover Publications, 1962), pp. 75–102.

b) Using the whole-tone scale, *Gulistān:* p. 1, sys. 2.

c) Using chromatic patterns, *Gulistān:* p. 4, sys. 1.

9. Similar to the single-note passages are those in the midst of which the pianist is required to play chords, perforce with the same hand.

Ex. 21. Passage work for one hand, consisting of single notes alternating with chords, *Le jardin parfumé:* p. 8, sys. 2.

Such a detail may seem more pianistic than musical, yet the added chords have more than technical or coloristic use. These passages reflect Sorabji's interest in the post-romantic aesthetic of voluptuous sound. But the rapid succession of unrelated consonant triads against a more static bass harmony also creates polytonal combinations. The concluding two pages of *Le jardin parfumé*

illustrate how Sorabji employs this simple musical-pianistic figure to build a coherent musical passage.

10. Passages are frequently divided between the hands. The dissolution of boundaries between the technical and the musical is admirable. The flickering, haunting, and delicate effect produced may be observed on page 5, systems 2 and 3 (the continuation of example 13, p. 373).

11. Exact duplication of passages in various registers is derived from the repetition established at the beginning of the piece. Sorabji allows his material to expand in many different directions, being oblivious to conventional time frames. Any pattern may be subject to immediate repetition.

Such a procedure seems rather self-indulgent, but fortunately his power of concentration upon the basic musical gestures and his sense of overall form make these seemingly random compositional decisions even more alluring and effective. No matter what the musical complexities are, the logic of the compositional operations is present in the sound of the music, and perceivable to the listener. As opposed to the work of many avant-garde composers, in which logic resides exclusively in the written score (even hidden in it, not perceivable by the ear) and has to be "explained" in prefatory program notes, Sorabji's musical ideas are clearly stated. One does not have to analyze the score or read about the piece in order to understand what is happening in the music.

12. Glissandi, both diatonic and chromatic, are often used in this quiet work. Even some of the fingered scales sound almost like glissandi and should be considered exclusively decorative. However, in the later nocturne *Jāmī*, glissandi are more of an integral element.

13. Similarly, passages in mixed double notes for one or two hands, although sparingly used in *Le jardin parfumé*, are the norm in many later works.

14. The retrogression of a short series of chords or single notes will be discussed in the next section of this chapter. This technique, which generates a variant of the accompaniment figure, tends to retard musical motion.

15. Tenths, solid or broken, are used throughout the work. More often than not, the thumb of either hand is required to play simultaneously the ninth as well. At times, even three adjacent keys (white, black, or mixed) are to be played with a single finger. Added notes to chords in open position are used so often throughout Sorabji's piano music that these alone mark the music as his.

Ex. 22. Chords for the left hand, *Le jardin parfumé*:

Although Sorabji's piano music is completely idiomatic, there are some chords, in the chains of tremolos, which perhaps only pianists with the longest fingers (a stretch of a twelfth) could truly negotiate.

Ex. 23. Difficult stretches for the right hand, *Le jardin parfumé*: p. 18, sys. 2.

Sectional Analysis of *Le jardin parfumé*

The recurrence of the accompaniment figure clearly signals the beginning of each section. There are only 87 barlines in this work, placed at irregular intervals, but these generally indicate the beginning and ending of phrases and subsections. Table 2 (p. 383) provides an overview of the structure of the work.

Table 2. *Le jardin parfumé* partitioned.

PART ONE: p. 3 to p. 17, sys. 2.
    Subsection 1: p. 3 to p. 9, sys. 3.
    Subsection 2: p. 10, sys. 1 to p. 15, sys. 3.
    Subsection 3: p. 15, sys. 3 to p. 17, sys. 2.

PART TWO: p. 17, sys. 3 to p. 28, sys. 3.
  First Half
    Subsection 4: p. 17, sys. 3 to p. 20, sys. 2.
    Subsection 5: p. 20, sys. 2 to p. 24, sys. 3.
  Second Half
    Subsection 6: p. 24, sys. 3 to p. 26, sys. 2.
    Subsection 7: p. 26, sys. 2 to p. 28, sys. 3.

PART THREE: p. 28, sys. 3 to p. 36.
    Subsection 8: p. 28, sys. 3 to p. 32.
    Subsection 9: p. 33 to p. 36.

The first subsection, consisting of seven phrases of varying length and musical content (pp. 3–9), comprises several settings of the main melodic idea. Each setting is separated by an episode whose dual function is to provide relief from and elaboration upon the material just played. Each new phrase explores patterns, rhythms, pitches, registers, and textures that were neglected in the previous phrase. The order of these ideas and their development are governed by the composer's structural instinct and his ideal of constant variation. Adjacent phrases balance each other through contrast in all regards, yet are not unrelated. Tendencies inherent in one phrase are explored in the next. The varying levels of textural, rhythmic, and harmonic activity in each phrase create a feeling of tension and release which give the music organic shape. Unity is assured by confinement to the basic musical gestures established at the onset. The interaction among the different musical gestures further intensifies the cohesiveness of the work. A comparison of the first two phrases can clarify this point.

Whereby the bass register of the first phrase (p. 3) is occupied by the repeated accompaniment figure in eighth-notes and by a six-note chord on a relatively weak beat at the end of the phrase (p. 3, sys. 2), the bass register of the second phrase is rhythmically contrasting. A four-note chord placed on the downbeat begins the second phrase (p. 4, sys. 1–3) and is followed by three upward-sweeping pedalled arpeggios in varying smaller note values. The left hand of the second phrase has greater rhythmic variety and lacks the stability of the first phrase provided by repetition and rhythmic continuity. The material in the right hand is equally contrasting. The opening figuration — two trills separated and followed by passage work — prepares the entrance of the main melodic material in the second phrase. The only element incorporated from the first phrase is a rapid descending scale, which fills the space between one long melodic note and the next. In the first phrase speed is relegated primarily to the right hand. In the second, spurts of fast notes are given to both hands. The phrases complement each other in a very satisfying way.

The second subsection of the piece, almost five pages long (p. 10 to p. 15, sys. 3), begins with a passage for left hand alone, somewhat similar to the beginning of Skryabin's Nocturne, Op. 9, No. 2 (for left hand alone). A three-note cell, spanning a major third and consisting of a minor second and a minor third, spelled in various ways, is present not only throughout this passage (p. 9, sys. 3) but on almost every page of *Le jardin parfumé*.

The second phrase of the third subsection (p. 16, sys. 3) is poorly notated. The rhythmic notation is so ambiguous and arithmetically inaccurate that only the vertical lineup of notes on the three staves can give the performer an approximate idea of how fast they should be played. The addition of brackets indicating the duration of a group of notes relative to the beats (e.g. a triplet sign) does not solve the problem. Consultation with the composer only raised further unanswered questions. Example 24 (p. 385) illustrates the problems, the first of which is this: the first seven pitches on the top (from C to F), comprising six 16ths, seem equal to five 16ths (top staff, 32nd-rest to tied note E) as well as eleven 16ths (bottom, 16th-rest plus first five eighth-notes in the left hand).[62]

Some figures which play a minor role in *Le jardin parfumé* are used in other works to great effect. For instance, the descending triplet figure of notes repeated in several octaves which is heard only once in this work (example 25a, p. 386) becomes one of the main unifying gestures of *Jāmī* (example 25b, p. 386).

Part two of *Le jardin parfumé* (p. 17, sys. 3 to p. 28, sys. 3) resembles a development section and functions as an interlude which prepares the entrance of the final, climactic part of the work. It may be divided in two halves, each consisting of two subsections. The basic gestures are developed, combined, and juxtaposed in seemingly haphazard ways, but only for the purpose of providing contrast to the more clearly organized opening and closing of the work. The overall effect created by the wide range of fluctuation in

---

[62] {In many other complex passages in Sorabji's music one must constantly examine the number of notes in a beat (or larger span) and the vertical alignment of notes, because the two are often contradictory. Furthermore, in Sorabji's manuscripts, some notes could be any one of several possible pitches.}

Ex. 24. Poorly notated passage, *Le jardin parfumé*: p. 16, sys. 3.

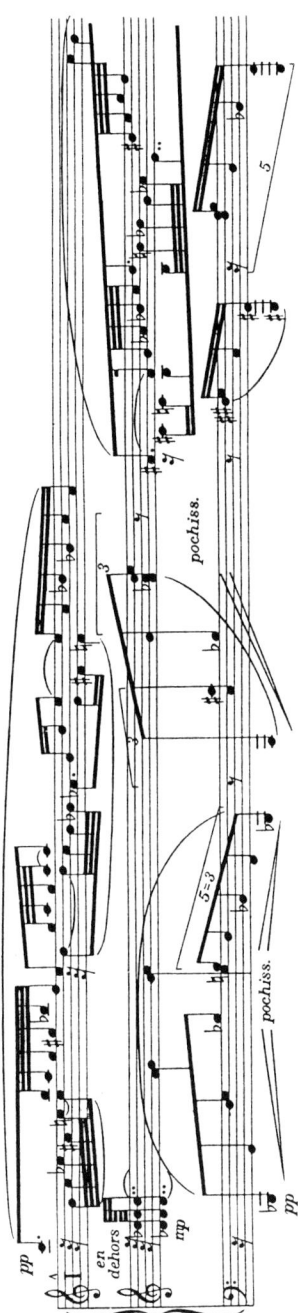

Ex. 25. The same motive in two different pieces.

a) *Le jardin parfumé:* p. 26, sys. 3. (The missing clef for the top staff is treble.)

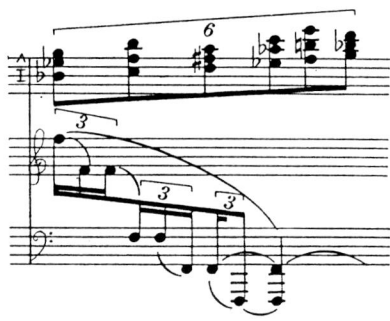

b) *Jāmī:* p. 1, sys. 1.

harmonic rhythm and between thematic and non-thematic material is a pulsation between areas of motion and stillness, atonal instability and tonal security. A sense of upbeat and downbeat pervades the unfolding of the music. The interplay of opposites gives this music its essential vitality.

The fourth subsection is similar to the fourth phrase of subsection 1 in that it is practically devoid of any melodic content. Three basic gestures are developed: the chain of tremolos, the ostinato alternation of two chords, and the short rhythmic motives.

The fifth subsection contains two passages employing techniques usually found in Sorabji's fugal writing. One is illustrated in example 26, top system (p. 387): the retrogression of a short series of chords, which produces harmonic stasis. Several variants of the accompaniment figure are also obtained with this procedure (p. 16, sys. 2 and p. 25, sys. 1).

Ex. 26. Retrogression of a series of chords and canon by inversion, *Le jardin parfumé:* p. 21, sys. 2–3.

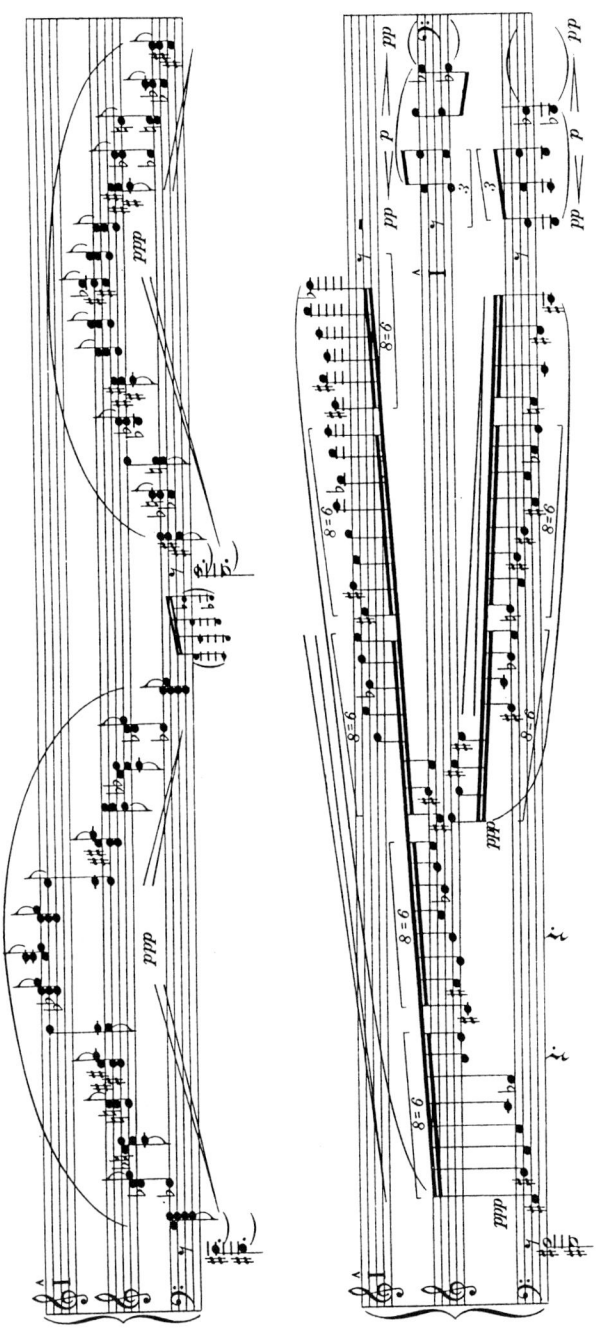

The next phrase resembles a short canon by inversion: the right hand figuration is given to the left hand, inverted and transposed down a major third (example 26, bottom system (p. 387)).[63]

The disparate collection of phrases in this fifth subsection seems to bring the music to a complete halt, but the fragmentary nature of the opening half of this section is complemented by a flowing second half, beginning with yet another variant of the opening two gestures (p. 24, sys. 3).

The rhythmically varied repetition of six chords in the upper register of the second phrase in the seventh subsection provides tonal stability and direct contrast to the atonal opening phrase in two voices (p. 26, sys. 3).

The high point of the piece occurs in part three. The climax is achieved through increased rhythmic activity (pp. 29–30), increased textural density (pp. 31–32), and extension of the length of each phrase.

The final section of *Le jardin parfumé*, a dénouement — melancholy and reflective — begins with the last recurrence of the accompaniment figure (with the same pitches as those of the first time) and another variant of the decorative passage-work above it (p. 33).

Conclusion

One of the most perplexing problems facing the analyst of Sorabji's music is the unusual coexistence of both atonal and tonal elements on any one page, with no domination by either. The fusion of tonality and atonality into a third and workable "concept" is one of Sorabji's main contributions. His music seems to be what the conductor Dimitri Mitropoulos hoped for, "a kind of twelve-tone music filled with Ravel-like flavour and appeal".[64] In Sorabji's music, triadic sonorities function only in the vertical sense; half- and whole-step progressions in the voice leading control chordal succession. Varying rates of harmonic activity create tension-release patterns that propel or retard the musical action and give it additional definition. Slonimsky's term *pantonal*[65] and Sorabji's own

---

[63]{Given this observation, it is likely that in the bottom system the G♮ immediately above the *ppp* should be an A.}

[64]Rudolf Réti: *Tonality — Atonality — Pantonality* (London: Barrie and Rockliff, 1958), p. 119.

[65]"The term 'pantonality' denotes the use of all major and minor keys with complete freedom and without preference for any particular tonality."
[CONT'D]

term *metadiatonic* are the most accurate for describing the harmonic procedures in Sorabji's nocturnes. Erik Chisholm noted that "metadiatonic" meant that "the chords can all be explained within the diatonic system, but [...] the *relation* of the chords to one another is in the plane of no particular 'key'".[66]

Free use is made of all triads, but in the absence of functionality, "a multitude of tonical relationships intensify, counteract, and annul each other, so that finally their spirit rather than their mechanism is a compositional directive".[67] It is because of the liberal use and frequent intermingling of triadic, diatonic, and atonal elements that intervallic pattern matching is not a pressing condition which must be met in order to create a coherent musical statement. Basic shapes and their manipulation assume this role of primary importance in the structuring of Sorabji's nocturnes.

* * * * *

By imposing a ban upon the public performance of his own music, Sorabji denied himself the opportunity of receiving response from others, which ultimately is a very vital and nourishing experience for a composer. Furthermore, his own renditions of his works, being probably highly unsatisfactory, served to alienate critics. Not until performers bring Sorabji's music to the public's attention will a balanced appraisal of his contribution be possible. Fortunately, awareness and interest in this composer's music in professional circles seem to be growing. His music is of unusually high quality in both craftsmanship and musical inspiration and is worthy of the high praise lavished upon it by such musicians as Delius, Heseltine, Stevenson, and Ogdon.

(Nicolas Slonimsky: *Music since 1900,* 4th edition (New York: Charles Scribner's Sons, 1971), p. 1475.)

[66]Erik Chisholm: "Kaikhosru Shapurji Sorabji".

[67]Rudolf Réti: *Tonality — Atonality — Pantonality,* p. 118.

10 Performing *Opus clavicembalisticum*

Geoffrey Douglas Madge with Paul Rapoport

Geoffrey Douglas Madge (b. 1941, Adelaide, Australia) studied piano with Clemens Leski at the University of Adelaide. After winning first prize in an Australian Broadcasting Corporation piano competition, he moved to Europe, settling in the Netherlands in 1970. Currently he is Senior Lecturer in Piano at the Royal Conservatory of Music in The Hague.

He has gained a reputation as an extraordinary pianist, especially for his performances of works which are extremely demanding in technique and expression and venture into new aesthetic territory. He has championed the piano music of neglected composers such as the Russian futurists, Sorabji, Stefan Wolpe, Nîkos Skalkótas, Giacinto Scelsi, and Iannis Xenakis. He has won awards for his recordings, e.g. of music by Xenakis, Busoni, and Sorabji. He has played innumerable concerts for audiences in many countries as well as for radio and television.

This interview between Geoffrey Madge and Paul Rapoport took place by telephone, in person, and by letter in phases over several years, beginning in 1984 and ending in 1989. *Opus clavicembalisticum* is referred to throughout as *O.C.*

P.R.: When did you first come across the score of *O.C.?* When did you first try to play it?

G.D.M.: The answer to both questions is 1960, when I was studying at the Conservatory in Adelaide, Australia. I remember the great excitement with which I opened the package from London containing the printed score. After looking through the music, I put it on the piano stand and left it there, as if it would play itself ... at the same time imagining how it would sound. I was immediately determined to be able to play it, but I also wondered whether it really was playable. A friendly colleague at the Conservatory confused and irritated me by pronouncing it unplayable. Naturally, that only increased my stubborn determination to play it.

My first move was to go through it mentally, imagining someone actually performing it. (Through this, I discovered that musicality and technique exist in the mind; in a sense they are not physical.) For weeks I proceeded like this, not playing a note of *O.C.*, just reading it — partly because I was busy preparing a performance of the Brahms Second Concerto. Eventually I tried the easier passages from Part I of *O.C.*

P.R.: How did that go? What did you learn from it?

G.D.M.: The temperature was extremely hot, I remember. Windows wide open. (Wonderful for the neighbours.) For sure it must have been an incredible din.

Several major problems impressed me. Obviously the sheer stamina needed to retain control had to be developed, possibly a new way of playing that would give a tremendous range of dynamics without tiring the pianist. Although I was then studying many of the works of Busoni and Alkan, *O.C.* needed something new, more like a yoga technique than anything else. I remember that while trying to play the most difficult parts, I just let my breath go and my muscles relax — with the result that there was no separation between my body and the keys. They became one. This later proved to be a good approach. Gradually I became more familiar with the themes and the main idea of the total form. One thing that impressed me very much was the almost spidery figuration of the *Fantasia*. I still think of it like that.

P.R.: Did you play through the whole work at that time?

G.D.M.: At the end of the year I did, for a small group of "initiated people". I had the feeling that I might be able to play it if I should ever receive permission from Sorabji himself. But that was in the period of the ban. In any case, I saw no reason to impose upon him the burden of listening to me, and there was a good chance he would not like my playing anyway. Strangely, as the years drew on I became more obsessed by the idea of performing it.

P.R.: Nearly everyone, I think, who tries to get to know this work suffers from an obsession of sorts about it. What led to your first public performance of it?

G.D.M.: Nearly 20 years after the events I've described, I was invited to give the world première of the complete 32 Piano Pieces of Nîkos Skalkótas in Athens — a nonstop performance of about one hour 40 minutes and of great complexity. This was my first experience of giving a marathon recital of this difficulty. Following this there was a long concert at the Holland Festival in 1979. I had a still more strenuous program in the 1980 Festival, in which I wanted to include the first two sections of *O.C.* The problem was how to get in contact with Sorabji. As chance would have it, I was working with the wonderful singer Jane Manning, who knew Alistair Hinton, a personal friend of Sorabji. Contact was made, and within a few weeks I was playing for him at his residence in Corfe Castle.

P.R.: What did you do with *O.C.* after you played the first two sections at the 1980 Festival?

G.D.M.: I made plans to play the entire work. My first complete performance was in the 1982 Holland Festival, in Utrecht. Subsequently I've given complete performances in Bonn, Chicago, Montréal, and Paris, and performances of various parts in several other cities.[1]

P.R.: Let's return to the subject of your visits to Sorabji. What did you gain besides the necessary permission to play *O.C.?*

G.D.M.: Sorabji was always very helpful, both on my visits to him and in our telephone conversations. When I first saw him, I played a fair amount of *O.C.* for him, first on his Mason and Hamlin, then on his Steinway. At the end he just said, "My dear boy, it's absolutely fantastic", and gave me permission to play all of *O.C.*, not just the first two sections. He also said that he found the composition had more in it and was better than he had realized. Later we discussed many other subjects, including details of how certain parts of *O.C.* should be performed.

Playing on his Steinway was a delight in itself. I still associate it very strongly with my idea of the Sorabji sound.

P.R.: Can you explain what that is?

G.D.M.: It's very hard to describe, but it has a great deal in common with *bel canto* singing, a subject Sorabji had an immense knowledge of and which we discussed frequently. Once he went over to his Steinway and started playing for me — small excerpts from *O.C.* Of course he was at an advanced age; nonetheless, his playing had a certain style. The way he played chords and the way he pedalled were notable. His sound was not harsh but warm, much more related to *bel canto* technique than to virtuoso piano

---

[1]{For details see Chapter 12.}

technique, which may be surprising, considering the extraordinary technical difficulty of *O.C.*

To study *O.C.*, I think it is very important to listen to recordings of singers of the early part of the century, to appreciate their skill in the art of phrasing and tone production. *O.C.* is unfortunately more famous for its technical difficulty than for its singing qualities, but it is in fact just what Sorabji said, a colossal song. Just listen, for example, to the theme of the Variations or the *Adagio*, or any of the fugue subjects, to see how they sing. I think that these are the climactic moments of the composition as a whole, not the huge technical dramas!

P.R.: Did you try to model your own playing of *O.C.* after how you heard Sorabji play, either live or on tape?

G.D.M.: Only in regard to the *bel canto* ideal, aiming for a form of speech in tones. In this connection, it is important to have the fingers act on the keys the way the tongue articulates speech. This is one aspect of *bel canto* which is often neglected in instrumental performance: the notes from the piano should sound like a form of sung speech.

But Sorabji himself preferred me to follow my own inclinations and certainly not to imitate his playing: he wanted to hear what I would make of *O.C.* Indeed, I doubt that anyone *could* imitate him, so why try? Anyhow, he would have been appalled if I had tried to imitate him, and his private recordings were made when he was advanced in age, when he was less technically accomplished. I did, however, take his advice to absorb his influences.

P.R.: For the complete performances of *O.C.* in Utrecht and Chicago, you had a prototype of a new Yamaha concert grand brought in, in the first instance driven in from Hamburg and in the second flown in from Tokyo. What attracted you to this piano for *O.C.?*

G.D.M.: To answer that, I must go back to Sorabji's Steinway. It sounds different from any instrument I've heard by a modern maker. Its sound is like the sound of many old instruments, very warm. It's very transparent; chords never sound thick. Some of the new Yamahas have a similar transparent sound. They also have an extremely strong frame, and a different kind of pin which enables the instrument to stay in tune for a long time and through very difficult conditions, such as a performance of *O.C.* The instruments I played it on needed tuning afterwards, but the situation was not disastrous by any means.

2 March 1983

My dear Geoffrey

I was appalled to hear that you had not received my telegram giving you full permission to do all you asked in respect of O.C. However I now confirm my complete consent to your requests in that matter. So go ahead straightaway!

Much love and all blessings.
Yours Ever.

Kaikhosru
(Sorabji)

A letter from Sorabji to Geoffrey Douglas Madge about *Opus clavicembalisticum* (1983) (see next page)

(see previous page)

28 March. 1983

My dear Geoffrey

I was <u>appalled</u> to hear that you had never received my telegram giving you full permission to do all you asked in respect of O.C. However[,] I now confirm my complete <u>consent</u> to your requests in that matter. So go ahead straightaway!

Much love and all [*sic:* ?] blessing!
Yours Ever.

Kaikhosru
(Sorabji)

For the first performance I also needed a technician (not just a tuner) with the instrument: this too was a significant factor.

P.R.: What was this Yamaha action like?

G.D.M.: Almost as good as a well-regulated Steinway. I've now played *O.C.* on both makes; my preference is still the Steinway, for its neutrality and power. By the way, this composition is the best test of a concert grand that I know. Any imperfection in the action becomes clear within the first hour, annoying in the second, and unbearable in the third, tiring the performer and making it impossible to go on. Certainly the quality of the regulation of the action influences greatly the accuracy of the performance.

One important thing is the relationship of the speed of the key descending to the mechanics within the instrument: there's a certain speed, a certain momentum ... This is crucial, because I make use of the rebound of the key for the energy needed to play. The action must be tight to get this rebound in the fingertip.

P.R.: Did Sorabji take any interest in the instruments you used for *O.C.?*

G.D.M.: He always asked full details — how were the bass, the treble, the overall tone, how did it orchestrate ... His own Steinway is what I call a neutral instrument. No register stands out; it does not sound like several instruments joined together under one keyboard. Because of that, you can get any sound you want from it: horns, violins, oboes, etc. in any range.

I think that it would be really amazing to hear *O.C.* played on a good Steinway from around 1900 to 1930. My experience with these instruments makes me believe that the whole composition would then really sound as it should. But to find such an instrument is another matter, let alone one in good condition.

P.R.: Did the two of you ever talk about improvements that you would like made in piano construction in view of the nature and demands of his music?

G.D.M.: Yes we did. In fact there are about half a dozen such improvements I could list. First, pins which retain the tension of the strings so that the instrument does not lose its tuning — better than the Yamahas, even. The fall board of the piano could also be farther back, so as to create more key surface. The top registers of the instrument need to be equal in power to the bass without giving a sound which is too metallic.

P.R.: What about the pedals? I know you're always interested in the finest details of their action.

G.D.M.: It should be possible to have separate sustaining pedals for bass and treble, and it would be marvellous to be able to enhance the effect of the third pedal by use of magnets above the dampers. As specified by some preprogrammed arrangement, they would automatically trigger the dampers and hold them up as long as necessary. Just imagine, a new keyboard polyphony!

P.R.: Is there any other change in construction which you see as desirable for performances of *O.C.?*

G.D.M.: There is one more thing: we need a simple but effective device for page-turning, or page-sliding in the case of loose sheets.

P.R.: Somehow I don't think that page-turners of scores the size of *O.C.* would mind being put out of a job. Speaking of the score, in preparing for the first complete performance of *O.C.*, did you find there were erroneous notes and other markings in the printed score? You got a copy of Sorabji's original manuscript, didn't you?

G.D.M.: Yes, with his help I got a copy of it from the University of Cape Town. I spent quite a lot of time with it and discovered that there were dubious notes and so on in both manuscript and printed score. I spoke to Sorabji about the first page, for instance — the chords which have an octave and a third in the printed score, but only octaves in the manuscript. He said to play it as it was in the printed edition, although I think the reading in the manuscript would have more power. I must say that in general I like the printed version more. Sorabji probably revised and improved his manuscript for publication.

P.R.: That does seem to be true, and the corrected proofs of *O.C.* substantiate it. In any case, the manuscript is far from being the ultimate authority on every page.

G.D.M.: That's exactly my point.

P.R.: What sort of practising did you do before the first performance in Utrecht? Are there some general principles involved here which you believe are especially important for *O.C.?*

G.D.M.: Precise planning is very important. All physical movements at the keyboard must be coordinated so that playing proceeds naturally, with simple economy, without any unnecessary tension. How the music sounds as a whole and the whole spirit of the performance depend very much on the ease with which we coordinate these movements. Being preoccupied with the subjective mechanics of playing certain notes or passages will eventually create ruinous physical tensions. I remember too that Sorabji was very concerned that I not injure myself!

One of the first things which influences the sound, as well as the way we hear while playing, is the way we sit at the instrument. I prefer to start working in a chair with an almost vertical back and no cushioning — just a hard wooden surface — the body perfectly balanced, the shoulders almost against the back of the chair.

P.R.: What does all that enable you to do?

G.D.M.: It helps direct the energy from the shoulders and the back of the chair, bringing the power and sonority through the stomach and buttocks; and it enables you to play outwards and upwards, not inwards and downwards. In this way I begin practising with lower dynamic levels (maximum *mf*), producing only the slightest possible attack in the notes. The feeling is that the arm is a light bridge between the fingers and the stable body.

This lets me direct the energy to groups of notes more than to individual ones, and it helps develop awareness of physical relaxation, even when playing the most strenuous passages. After beginning like this, it is no longer necessary to sit against the back of the chair — I can lean slightly forwards, but with the neck still relaxed. At this point, I introduce greater dynamic differences, but without being able to perceive physical differences in the arms or body between *ff* and *pp*, i.e. with hardly any difference in energy. The playing must remain as economical as possible, and must be able to create all dynamics without going beyond the escapement level of the keys.

In time, the sound produced appears to open up, projecting a great distance. This is the beginning of what I call "objective listening". Not only is the body freer, but the ears become less foggy!

This is still an early stage. But it's different from a self-conscious, critical listening, which tends to make us tense rather than loose, contracting rather than expanding. Eventually we are able to just look on in a relaxed manner, as if someone else is playing for us. The critical faculty too should operate spontaneously, without our being conscious of it: the body must find intuitively its own wisdoms that parallel the musical ideas of the composition.

P.R.: As you said awhile ago, it seems as if a lot of this is more mental than physical.

G.D.M.: Absolutely. It is possible to develop a way of concentrating and working so that the performance is just there. The spirit takes over all functions. As a result of this, in playing *O.C.* I can be totally unaware of doing anything technically. I don't mean to be immodest, but really, I'm not aware of the difficulties any more when I play it. In performance it now seems very short to me, about an hour and a half, not the actual four hours. Audience members everywhere have told me they have exactly the same experience in listening: it sounds much shorter than it is.

P.R.: Having heard three of your five complete performances, I couldn't agree with you more. Going back to the time before the first performance, were there specific technical things you worked on? I know these are of lesser importance to you than the larger concerns you've just talked about, but I am curious: were there identifiable problems which you had to solve?

G.D.M.: Yes, there were, the main one being that a technical problem taken out of its context is difficult to reinsert into its surroundings. Well before the Utrecht performance I tried to work in long sections, because after all this was the first major problem — the total line. My aim was to keep the flow with as much clarity and simplicity as possible. Sound qualities must develop from this.

As I went on I uncovered more specific difficulties: long running passages, extended *ff* chordal passages, polyphonic voice leading, how difficult it is to let some passages flow through all the notes.

When necessary, I worked at a slow tempo, slow enough not to feel the difficulty, even simplifying the text if needed. Each time through I increased the speed, gradually introducing more notes of any simplified passages. This practising manœuvre is of course well known to every performer.

But I discovered that the quickest way to solve most situations was to clarify the character and message of each passage, so that the body seemed to find its own solution without interference. (As a test, I would pick any point in the score of any technical difficulty, throw my hands on the keyboard, and play with the required expression, just letting my hands and arms work everything out for themselves.) The clearer I was about what Sorabji wanted, the easier this became. It sounds simple, but I'm sure it's right, and not only in Sorabji's music — what about the fugue in Beethoven's *Hammerklavier* Sonata? As soon as the musical meaning is understood, the music becomes playable. For a pianist, of course.

Quick changes of hand positions and other playing manœuvres may have helped, but mainly I tried to understand what Sorabji meant in the music and made my own "choreography" correspondingly. Discovering the relationship of each phrase to its surrounding phrases was particularly important for discovering the line of the total work. It's an obvious method, perhaps. But it makes each phrase doubly important within its context, increasing its potential for characterization far beyond what the text of the moment states, and transcending the limitations of its notation. This implies that Sorabji is an extraordinary architectonic composer — which he is.

P.R.: I find this revealing, because even at the first performance you made most of *O.C.* look normal as far as difficulty is concerned. That's quite something, considering the stupendous challenges on nearly every page, not to mention the stamina required to get through all 248 of them.

G.D.M.: There were things about the Utrecht performance, however, which were quite difficult. There was so much publicity in all the media, and the concert was broadcast live and taped for records. It was enough to put the most hardened performer completely off the idea. Playing *O.C.* through for a group of friends and playing it under these conditions are two totally different experiences which draw on different mental powers entirely.

The hour before the performance was a nerve-wracking one. There was no way for me to know what it would be like to perform *O.C.* in a huge hall under the tremendously stressful conditions I've mentioned. What would happen if a string broke? Repeating a whole section would ruin the whole flow, so despite the reserve concert grand standing at the ready, this was a further thought for anxiety. And of course I didn't know what the public's reaction would be to this music as they heard it for the first time.

It was necessary to have planned a way to keep my energy going, to create a concentrated energy that was self-producing; but still, I might have been unable to go further after one and a half hours.

These things changed in the later performances. I don't concern myself with them any more. Indeed, I always *gain* energy from a performance of *O.C.*, so that immediately afterwards I feel that I could easily repeat it. But there were these necessarily unknown factors which made the conditions immensely difficult before the start of the first performance.

P.R.: What else is different about the performances which came after the first one?

G.D.M.: I now feel more at ease and do a lot more. The first performance was a "total-line" performance more than a detailed one. I wanted to bring out the line of the whole composition, to show what the architecture was, rather than be distracted too much by the "scenery". I think too that Sorabji just wanted the scenery to take care of itself.

Now, however, some tempos are different, dramatic timings are slightly different, the sound is in certain ways deeper and more resonant. I play with more "orchestration" now and bring out the contrapuntal side of the work much more clearly.

P.R.: Can you give any examples of these differences?

G.D.M.: The *Fantasia* goes faster now, played in the way a spider moves. The fugues are generally faster, but their climactic passages are a little broader; and the middle voices get more of my attention. In the first performance I was concerned about what the physical feeling and pacing would be in performing *O.C.*, especially after a few hours of it. Now I can look a little more to the scenery.

There's another significant difference. It is possible to sound a line so that it is not quite together with the other voices, and yet keep that effect from the audience, which hears the music as if everything were being played together. In other words, a melodic line can be played a fraction earlier or later than the surrounding accompaniment without the difference being noticed, even in the first row of seats in the hall. With this, the possibility is increased of playing all the notes with more attention to contrapuntal clarity, as are the possiblities for greater tonal expression in general.

P.R.: That technique must be a problem when a work is recorded.

G.D.M.: It can be. If microphones are put too close to the piano, these things may be heard, which would be disturbing. They're not heard in the hall. In any case, a good performance has a certain projection in it, which is heard best about 15 meters or more away from the piano. Microphoning too close would give the wrong impression. This is one reason why I "kept a low profile" in the differentiation of lines in the first performance, which I knew was to be issued on records.

P.R.: I'd like now to go over the individual sections of *O.C.*, asking some general questions about your approach to them, as well as specific questions about certain passages or certain musical elements or performing techniques.

Let's begin with the *Introito*. What can you say about the very beginning? Obviously it is a very important moment in *O.C.*

G.D.M.: The *adagio* at the very beginning should be slow: very slow, with several fingers playing each note. They should produce a psychological intensity which is much more important than the actual *ff* that's written. This should create an idea of the power that you will later be experiencing in the composition. It's difficult to get this intensity, but it can be done.

The rest of the *Introito* should not be too loud. In fact the dynamics are often marked *mf*.

P.R.: What do you do with the *non troppo f* lines on page 6 of the printed score? It strikes me that the upper-register chords will always have to struggle to be heard over the noise going on in the bass.

G.D.M.: Oddly enough, it's because of that that you hear them! Of course you can reduce the sound a little in the left hand and use a careful vibrato pedalling to control the low C#s. But the upper line may also be meant more as a colour or a reflection than as a theme. There are many places in this work where notes must be played without drawing too much attention to them.

P.R.: I presume your overall approach to the *Introito* is different if you play only the first two sections, as you did at the 1980 Holland Festival.

G.D.M.: That's quite true. You should begin a complete performance by making the introduction seem like the beginning of an epic. But that would be making too much of it in a partial performance. In that case, the very beginning could be faster.

P.R.: What about the tempo of the *Preludio corale* in a complete performance?

G.D.M.: That shouldn't be too slow. In the chorale at the bottom of page 8 you must sing without delaying. The *pp* chords on the second line of page 10 should all be held in the third pedal while the triplets are pedalled almost note-to-note with the sustaining pedal. This is very difficult because they move very quickly. The same pedalling is used in similar situations, such as the next two lines on page 10. In fact, this Busonian type of pedalling is necessary on practically every page of *O.C.*

P.R.: How can you maintain intensity right to the end of this section and the thinner textures at the top of page 19?

G.D.M.: The organ point there should be kept in tempo until the *rallentare*. Sorabji himself advised that. He also told me that the bass line at the bottom of page 18 should be very clear.

P.R.: That line, of course, has been heard in the *Introito*, and is closely related to the theme of the 49 Variations.

G.D.M.: It is also heard more exposed earlier in the *Preludio corale*, on page 16, for instance.

P.R.: How would you characterize the First Fugue?

G.D.M.: This is a dark fugue, to be kept dark as long as possible. Only on page 24 with the *tranquillato* part does that begin to change. The beginning of the fugue must sound very deep. The notes are very low, but you can play them so that they will not sound deep, which would be missing the point of the sonority.

P.R.: The First Fugue has three themes: the subject itself and two countersubjects. Should it be played so that all three have equal importance, or so that one or another of them assumes greater importance as the fugue progresses?

G.D.M.: There are places in the fugue where a different form of the subject (such as an inversion) or one of the two countersubjects assumes greater importance. You can't continue to emphasize the initial form of the subject. There is something of an epic quality, an organic development, which keeps the momentum going. The changing roles of the three themes are part of this.

P.R.: You've often said that despite the length of the fugues in *O.C.*, Sorabji shows a very alert sense of timing in them. Can you illustrate this with the First Fugue?

G.D.M.: Consider the dramatic pause right after the unresolved chord on G under the fermata on page 29. Or the way he prepares the fast descending bass octaves just after that by the accentuated descending octaves at the bottom of the previous page. The different marking on page 28 is very important; the speeding up of those lines on page 29 then becomes very vital and exciting. And then there's the juxtaposition of A and D♯ near the end of the fugue, on page 30. The repeated A recalls the close of the *Preludio corale*, and the D♯ the goal of the opening theme of the work on page 5.

P.R.: The *Fantasia* seems like a complete contrast.

G.D.M.: That's just it; it should sound unexpected. I would hold the initial chord longer now, so as to further that effect. It's a Hoffmannesque type of fantasy; it makes my hair stand on end. If it doesn't do that, the playing may be right but probably sounds wrong. The quality of being almost unbelievable is important too on page 35, which should sound somewhat out of place.

The whole thing should be very fast, perhaps even gain in tempo, until page 38. The F♯s on the second line there should start a slightly slower tempo so as to bring out more clearly the reiterated bass notes, especially the As, and to clarify the denser texture towards the end. The ending must have an elemental power, implying more than we have heard during the composition up to this moment, like a volcanic outburst.

P.R.: You play the Second Fugue rather quickly. Can you explain why?

G.D.M.: The markings *animato assai* and *leggiero* suggest a fast tempo. But more than that, the music itself suggests a rushing onwards, a leap forwards after the climax of the *Fantasia*. Sorabji also puts in quite a few *rallentando* markings subsequently, so he must want a very fast tempo at the start. I think it might even move at the cost of some clarity.

P.R.: You once said that there was a problem in the middle of this fugue. Where exactly did you mean, and what is the problem?

G.D.M.: One of the difficult things in this fugue is beginning the second part, on page 49, where the new subject is marked *diminuendo subito*.

P.R.: Is this not an issue with every new subject after the first one in all the multi-subject fugues?

G.D.M.: Not really. On page 49, after the long and tremendous climax in the first part of the fugue, one has somehow got to go back to nothing, also playing more slowly and clearly. And if you listen to the new subject without the score, it's very difficult to understand those rhythms. It also doesn't seem to do very much, even in some of its later elaborations.

P.R.: This, then, may be a weaker place in the composition.

G.D.M.: It's very difficult to make it sound right in performance.

P.R.: The Second Fugue brings us to the end of Part I, and presumably an interval of rest and recovery for you and the listeners. At the performances I heard, however, you kept both intervals fairly short.

G.D.M.: Yes, just long enough for the piano technician to do his work. *O.C.* must not be halted too long; it is an entity. It may even be possible to play it without any breaks if the instrument is exactly right.

P.R.: You have said that the Variations from Part II and the *Adagio* from Part III form the twin hearts of *O.C.* What does this mean as far as the Variations are concerned?

G.D.M.: After the short pause which follows Part I of *O.C.*, it is an amazing feeling to walk out on the stage and start again with the theme of the Variations. It has such great solemnity and nobility. I understand it as a profoundly dedicatory passage; it stands out as the spiritual centrepiece of the work.

P.R.: So the theme itself is the main reason for your feeling about the whole section.

G.D.M.: Yes. It also has to do with its position in the work. Up until this time we have not had such an extended chordal passage as this, descending so slowly and so deeply. The next time we get this is in the *Adagio* (from section 9), whose ending is an extension of this descending idea in the theme of the Variations. In fact, both this theme and the *Adagio* end on the same chord, that very deep C♯ major. And the rising alto line of the theme here reaches way back, of course, to one of the themes of the *Introito*, as we mentioned earlier.

    I should add that I play the low chords of the theme differently now, more like the way Busoni might have done them. I catch them in the third pedal, releasing the fingers after the chords have been sounded, and use both the *una corda* pedal and the sustaining pedal for the less important notes, so that it all sounds like some mysterious orchestration.

P.R.: Does this prove useful anywhere else in the Variations?

G.D.M.: The chords in Variations 24 and 38 might receive a similar treatment. It's important to their sound. They should seem more like a reflection, quite weird in a way. In the first performance I was too careful with them.

P.R.: What further importance do the Variations have as a whole?

G.D.M.: This is the first section of the piece where you can make quite clear what kinds of music there are in *O.C.* The Variations have an extremely wide range. One sees many sides of Sorabji in them — his mysterious side and his Godowsky side, for example. The end, by the way, in Variation 49, should not be too strong. Otherwise you destroy the flow of the whole work.

P.R.: The first *Cadenza* looks a bit like the *Fantasia*, but you don't play it the same way. Do you find less of the fantastic or the grotesque in the *Cadenza*?

G.D.M.: Yes I do. The *Cadenza* develops much more grandly and should be played very smoothly. There should be almost no accents in it; it must just build up in a great surge.

P.R.: Except, I suppose, in the brief bit marked *con sentenziosità didattica, pesante e pomposo*. What is that doing in this otherwise relatively untroubled *Cadenza I*?

G.D.M.: Occasionally Sorabji moves from one extreme to another. We see this certainly in the Variations and the *Passacaglia*. It's part of his style, his way of thinking. He can write something terrifying one minute and something quite lyrical the next.

P.R.: No contrasts of this sort occur in the *Fantasia*, so perhaps this aspect of the *Cadenza* is affected by the preceding Variations. At any rate, the *Cadenza* is followed by another sharp contrast, the Third Fugue. How do you view it as a whole? It's longer, of course, than the first two fugues, but is there something else that makes it different?

G.D.M.: I think this is a softer fugue. It should be kept fairly quiet and unobtrusive, even in the entries of the subjects. Most of the time one needn't even be aware that this is a fugue, except for places like the top of page 111, where things become a bit stronger. There are certain places too, like the cadence on A at the top of page 113 and the arrival on G at the top of page 117, which recall similar events in the First Fugue. Somehow you must make these relationships clear in performance. In the long scheme of things, these are rather dramatic moments.

Another remarkable spot is at the top of page 121, where all the lines descend, as though everything is collapsing. This change of direction should be marked very clearly, especially as it foreshadows the descent at the beginning of the third subject and another passage later on in the third part of this fugue ...

P.R.: You must mean those 16 four-voice canons near the end of the fugue which begin at the top of page 130.

G.D.M.: Yes, that's it precisely.

P.R.: It seems as if the fugue stops here to make some gargantuan point about *stretto*.

G.D.M.: The individual canons too always go and then stop. One must vary the tempos some; then the canons have tremendous urgency.

P.R.: On the whole you play them quite fast.

G.D.M.: If you go too slow, you lose the line of the whole thing. Even now, though, I feel that building the tension here is very difficult. The notes themselves are not difficult; the problem is how to avoid holding everything up here. This whole passage must really move on.

P.R.: Since the Third Fugue ends Part II, you get another well-deserved rest after it, assuming you want it. The beginning of Part III is quite unlike the beginning of Parts I and II, isn't it?

G.D.M.: Definitely. It's an amazing feeling here too, coming out onstage and playing that low D♯ minor chord. It's incredibly dramatic, and incidentally recalls the first low chord of the *Introito*. The whole *Toccata* should "burst the seams" and be almost out of control: very fast, very frenzied. The runs over held chords, for example on pages 146–47, should just roar up and down the keyboard.

408 The Music

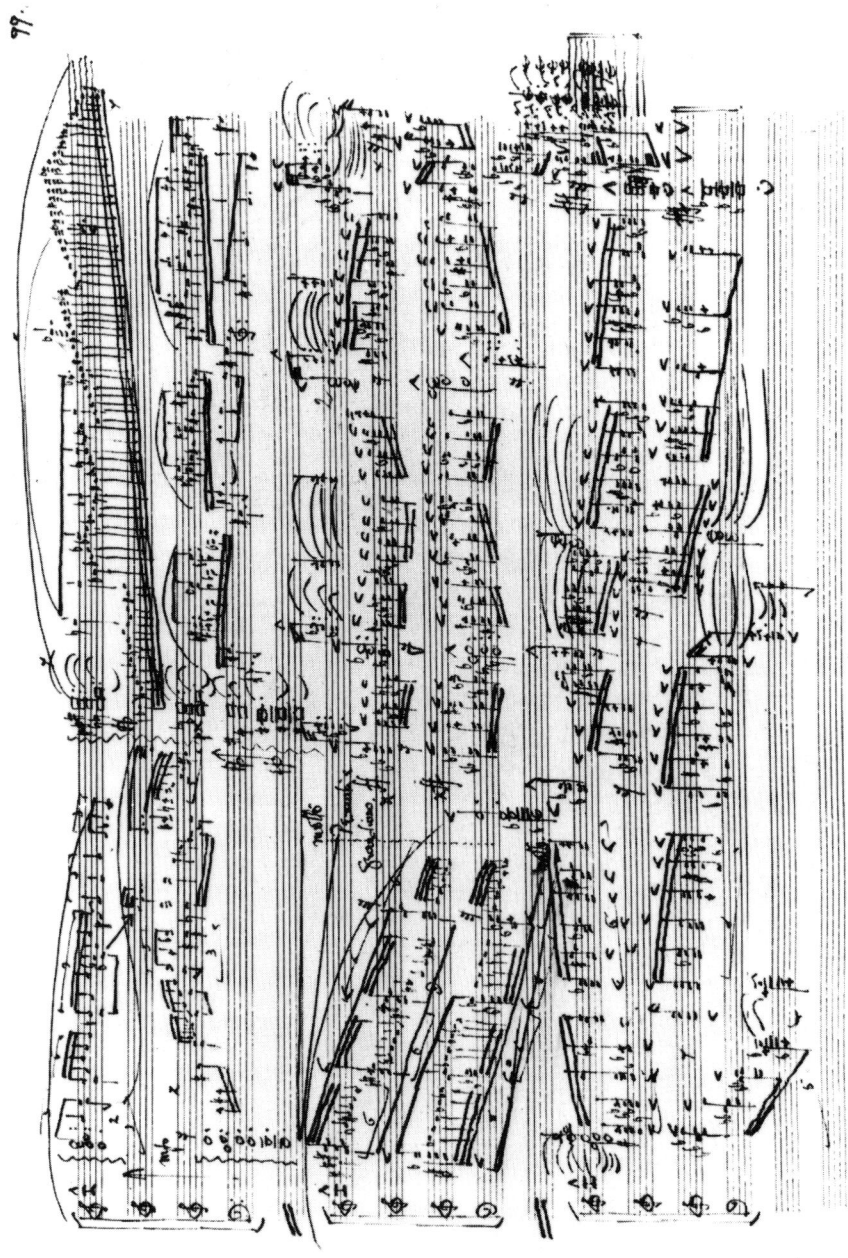

Opus clavicembalisticum, p. 99 of Sorabji's manuscript (1930), corresponding to p. 98 of the published score (see next page)

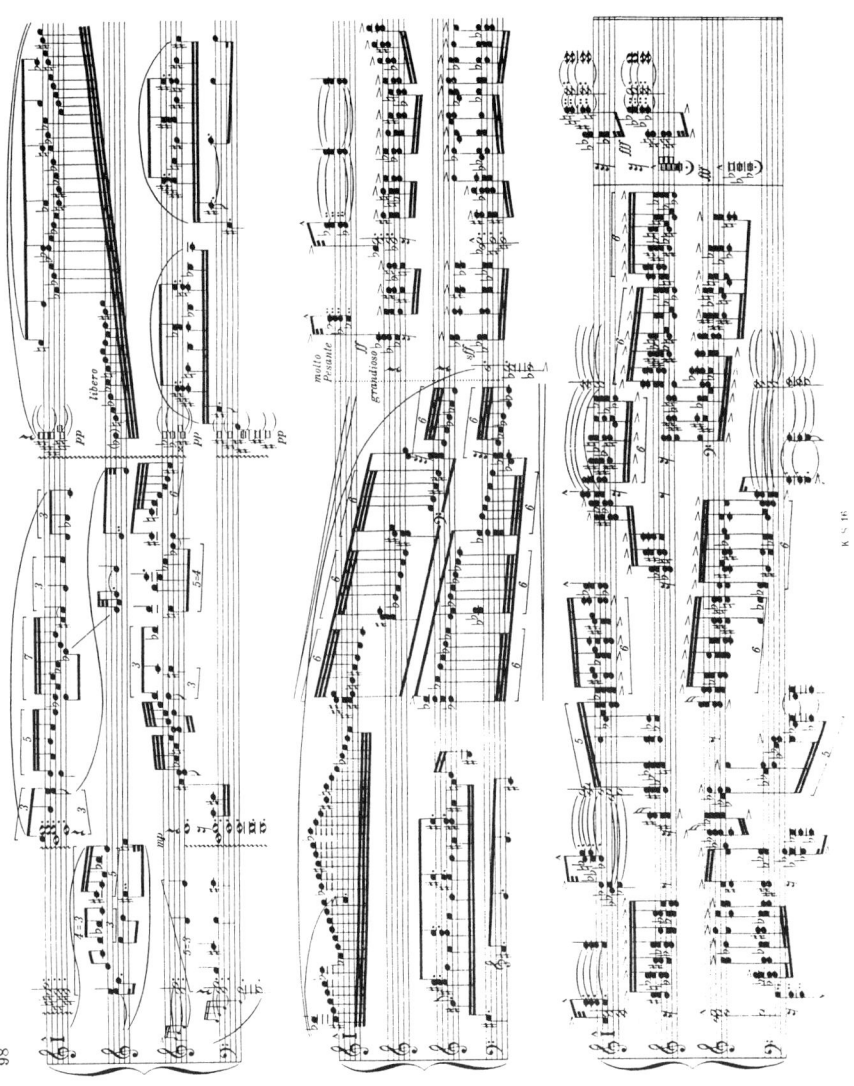

Opus clavicembalisticum, p. 98 of the published score (1931), corresponding to p. 99 of Sorabji's manuscript (see previous page)

Incidentally, Sorabji rather liked the idea of doing the *Toccata*, *Adagio*, and *Passacaglia* as an entity, as an excerpt from the whole work.[2] After the racing *Toccata*, the *Adagio* should sound as if it is on another planet, as if it is about 50 times slower. One should not go too deep in the keys. There should be no mechanical noise whatever in the *Adagio*, until the last few chords of the descending passage of 36 chords at the very end of it, where some percussive noise of the key against the key bed may be reintroduced. Those final 36 chords with their *crescendo* remind me of the beginning of *O.C.*: they bring things back to reality. They must make the walls of the hall move.

P.R.: In the *Adagio* we find the most differentiated simultaneous rhythmic patterns, such as 11 notes in the time of 9 in one hand, simultaneous with a succession of 8 in the time of 3, 10 in 3, and 7 in 3 in the other hand. I conclude that the numbers are guides to flexibly articulated note groupings rather than a direction to subdivide the beats precisely. The numbers tell you how many notes there are over a given span — if he's counted properly! — but not exactly where to place each note.

G.D.M.: I think that's absolutely right. Sorabji seems to indicate a new sort of rhythmic freedom here. The individual notes should not be too pedantically placed; the groupings are more important. Actually, these rhythms are not so difficult to play. If you keep track of the main pulse, everything seems to fall into place. A greater difficulty is achieving transparency with all the interweaving lines, deciding which lines are more important in any given passage. Above all, it must have a feeling of improvisation about it.

P.R.: The *Passacaglia*, like the Variations, has an enormous number of elaborations over one theme. In your view, how is it different?

G.D.M.: In several ways. The *Passacaglia* is more contrapuntal. The theme itself is almost frivolous in comparison with the theme of the Variations. This is the first time in *O.C.* that we hear a theme that is so clearly triadic. Since there are so many thematic statements in the *Passacaglia*, it becomes very important to group them, and especially to make it clear when the placement of the theme moves. It starts in the bass but moves up through the middle and eventually to the top.

---

[2]{When he wrote the work, Sorabji proscribed partial performances: see p. 187.}

P.R.: Are there any parts of the *Passacaglia* which particularly stand out as you recall it?

G.D.M.: There are so many, really. The whole *Passacaglia* is always thrilling to play. But variation 50 is certainly unique. The theme should be caught in the third pedal; the *quasi pizzicato* notes around it should try to disturb it. Variation 52 is absolutely scintillating, and is followed by the marvellous *quasi tambura* no. 53, very Eastern, very mystical. Variation 70 should sound like Glenn Gould; I can imagine him playing that one. There are some very exciting variations towards the end, but Sorabji closes the *Passacaglia* with a short, quiet epilogue. It's a remarkable thing to do after the fireworks of variations 79 to 81.

P.R.: You play *Cadenza II* in a special way, sitting almost still and letting your arms dash about doing all the work. Why?

G.D.M.: Just as the *Cadenza* itself has a fixed harmonic anchor on the note A, I anchor myself and just play it, without moving at all. By doing that, there is a point of non-movement which you can use as a resistance to go against. You hold your back still; it should be strong but not tense. The dynamics are then brought out against your back and buttocks! You shouldn't feel it; the whole thing should come out as if you're playing a Czerny study. I mean visually — not, of course, in sound. (God forbid!)

P.R.: How do you determine tempo in the Fourth Fugue?

G.D.M.: I choose a basic tempo for each of the four parts. The choice depends on several things, such as harmonic language. More rapidly changing harmony sometimes requires a slower tempo. Higher dynamics sometimes need a steadier tempo.

P.R.: The second subject looks like it could go quite fast, but you don't race through it.

G.D.M.: One reason is the harmonic one I just mentioned. Another is the syncopations. If they're rushed, you can't hear them.

P.R.: As the fugue goes on and more and more thematic material is brought back, do you try to make the listener aware of these new soundings of subjects from earlier parts of the fugue?

G.D.M.: Yes, absolutely; for example, at the top of page 233. But in another way, the more the fugue develops, the more the total effect is important: the harmonic ideas rather than the individual lines. On page 228, for example, the longer notes must be very clear. The 16th-notes are subsidiary, whether they are part of a theme or not. They are fast enough to be heard anyway.

P.R.: The fourth subject, like the second, suggests a rapid tempo, especially with its marking *irato, impaziente.*

G.D.M.: This one, in fact the whole fourth part of this fugue, I do try to take quite fast. If it's not fast, somehow it sounds very slow and clotted.

P.R.: The beginning of the *Coda stretta* looks unplayable as written, not because of impossible hand stretches but because there is so much going on. There seem to be many problems here of tempo, polyphonic clarity, overall expression, and so on, with conflicting solutions to those problems. The records are not entirely satisfactory here. Do you play this differently now?

G.D.M.: Yes, I do what I mentioned earlier. I keep three different pulses going. Certain themes might be played a fraction before or after certain other lines, depending on length of notes, among other things. As I said, these differences in moment of attack must remain inaudible to the audience. But it means that a lot more is playable in this *Coda* — almost all of it, actually. Nonetheless, it is absolutely vital to get the expression right in the *Coda*. It's more than a lot of notes and lines. There is a case for omitting things that are not playable or not audible; I would prefer, though, to try to do what may be very difficult or even impossible and actually play them. The attempt at playing them gives a certain expressive tension in itself, as it must have done in the first performances of the *Große Fuge,* or as it still does in Xenakis.[3]

The beginning of the *Coda stretta* must really move. Otherwise the long bass notes will get lost, and certain metrical contrasts with them will not be possible. It is obviously the physical climax of the piece (the spiritual climax belongs to the Variations and the *Adagio*), but it is important not to sound pompous, not to make a great deal of noise without any content. Rather, I try to create higher tension in the listener with less sound in the instrument.

---

[3]{On the subject of playability, and of the physical choreography at the keyboard which Madge mentions several times in this interview, see "L'éloge de la difficulté", by Cyril Huvé and Geoffrey Madge, in *Le monde de la musique*, no. 119 (February 1989), pp. 116–18.}

The pedalling is important in this and can be quite daring — sometimes pedalling over totally different fundamental chords.

P.R.: At the very end of *O.C.*, in the last three pages, I've always felt that the increasingly important triads held in the outer parts should resound spectacularly, like aural fireworks. What is your impression? Are those triads in 32nd-notes on page 251 a little too slow on the records? You certainly played these pages differently in Montréal.

G.D.M.: Yes; they should be faster. That brings up the whole matter of the records, which I would like to say a few things about.

P.R.: You mean apart from the performance itself.

G.D.M.: Yes. For example, I was informed that some recording problems developed in the live performance of the Fourth Fugue, so on the records they substituted my reading of a few days earlier, from the entry of the second subject to the end of the work. Although this substitution had been recorded without any retakes, I think that artistically it was a pity that it was used, because the electricity at the live event was, as I remember, very much stronger.

P.R.: Your earlier reading was done, however, in the same hall (of the Vredenburg Muziekcentrum) and on the same piano.

G.D.M.: Yes, but that was *before* the first performance, and therefore different. As I said, I wish now that the records did not contain that substitution; it doesn't sound right to me in the context of the rest of the first performance. But I am glad that all of the rest of that performance is on records, without any editing, because, despite some technical deficiencies, its spirituality was right. People say it sounds electrifying!

P.R.: Nonetheless, mightn't a recording done entirely in a studio be better?

G.D.M.: I doubt it. Perhaps one could use a studio performance as the basis for a recording but combine it with parts of a live performance (if it is acoustically possible to do so). The studio setting would certainly provide better recording quality, less noise, and probably fewer extremes and exaggerations.

But in a work of this immensity, the tensions in a live performance are very high; they could not be expressed in a studio performance. The electricity generated by the live performance brings out the architectonic qualities of the music.

P.R.: I find it curious that you haven't said that the main advantage of the studio is the opportunity to correct errors.

G.D.M.: Obviously that is an advantage, but on the other hand it is vital in a performance to take risks. Studio performances encourage sterile accuracy, which bores me completely. Errors which occur in a live performance may in fact reflect the great emotional intensity and therefore be quite acceptable, even necessary. Let's get away from the sterile methods of "corset" recording.

O.C. also needs excellent microphoning, better than we had for the records, and it would benefit greatly from digital technology. Did you know that as an experiment, Part I of the Utrecht performance was also recorded digitally? It was one of the first digital recordings in Holland.

P.R.: No I didn't. You mean, then, that they recorded digital and analog versions simultaneously, but only for Part I?

G.D.M.: Yes. I believe the digital recording has been broadcast in Holland, although I haven't heard it. Undoubtedly the digital process would improve the dynamic range greatly. I'm sure you noticed that the range on the records is rather limited; yet listeners to the live broadcast informed me that they had never heard such wide dynamics, not even in the hall!

P.R.: The power of the performance in the hall as I remember it does not come over so well on the records. I'm afraid, therefore, that anyone listening to the records who has never heard you play O.C. live is bound to be misled in this regard.

G.D.M.: The original tapes sounded very good, with a wide dynamic range. But the producer wanted over 30 minutes on some sides to get the whole work onto four records. Consequently the sound quality suffered a good deal.

P.R.: What about the other complete performances?

G.D.M.: They have all been different. You see, this piece always takes on the characteristics of its environment: it is affected not only by the attitude of the audience, but by the hall, the lighting, the chair I sit on, the weather, of course the piano ... Everything counts in O.C. — everything.

P.R.: Just about all the things you mentioned were a problem in Montréal, unfortunately. I thought the lights were too hot, there was too much light altogether in the hall, the audience was too close to you, the audience chairs were too noisy, the piano bench was much softer than your usual, and the Yamaha piano was inferior to the ones in Utrecht and Chicago.

G.D.M.: There was a problem in finding a concert grand in the first place. The Bechstein that was available was totally inadequate technically, so at the last moment other arrangements had to be made. And due to scheduling problems, the only instrument I could use couldn't be placed in the hall until the day of the concert, and I couldn't play it there until that afternoon. That is simply not enough time, for either me or the piano.

Also, I think that the Montréal audience was not prepared like some of the others for what they were about to hear. The papers did not give nearly the same information before the event as they did in the other cities. This is no reflection on the organization in Montréal. There was just a conservative publicity machine. Still, the electricity came about after Part I.

P.R.: What difference does pre-concert publicity make?

G.D.M.: If the audience doesn't know what to expect, it is very difficult or even impossible to recreate the proper architectural line of emotional development in *O.C.* I have to convince people and bring them from the outside into the experience. That's the wrong approach for this work.

P.R.: I felt that Utrecht was quite different in that respect.

G.D.M.: In Utrecht there was an awe-inspiring silence before the first notes. The electricity was right — just taken right out of the air. This electricity isn't a matter of nervousness, by the way. If the proper spiritual intensity is in the air, then my muscles need not be felt to participate; I just draw on that intensity. But if I must create it, then I must work hard on fixing the "atmosphere", and there's much less left to play the music in a way that allows it to be itself in its proper environment.

The sound in performance should echo back to the performer with an energy that comes from the audience. Especially in the slower, more sustained passages, I feel the most response and energy from the audience.

I should add that the size of the audience has nothing to do with it. One of the best performances was in Bonn, where all the arrangements for the concert went perfectly, but where the audience was the smallest by far. Chicago went well also, but the audience there was smaller too than the one in Montréal.

P.R.: From what you said before, *O.C.* becomes easier as you play it more. Is there any way in which it becomes harder?

G.D.M.: As I mentioned earlier, the technical problems seem to disappear. But it becomes harder to bring out more and more of the depth that is there in the composition. Playing *O.C.* should produce more than a performance, more than a presentation of a long composition written for or against the performer or the public. It must be a communion.

P.R.: What about Paris? How was that performance different?

G.D.M.: It had a very strong architectural line. The preparations of climaxes in the fugues were carefully graded in dynamics and tempo, each above the previous one, so that the last fugue was really stupendous in effect. The softer, more lyrical sections had their highlight in the *Adagio* of Part III.

I believe this was the best of the five complete performances I have given.

P.R.: What was the piano sound like?

G.D.M.: According to members of the audience, the sound was excellent, made even more exciting by the wonderful acoustics and intimacy of the Opéra comique. I heard people talking of a Lipatti-like sound. The instrument was a Steinway grand, the best in Paris, I was told. It had superb qualities and was better than the other instruments on which I had played *O.C.* previously.

P.R.: Did the pre-concert publicity meet your requirements this time?

G.D.M.: The organization was perfect and the audience was large. *Le monde* printed a big interview a week before. The program notes were a little short on information, but otherwise good.

P.R.: What about your own pre-concert preparations? Did you have to do more work, not having played the whole composition for four years?

G.D.M.: I did have to do more work, but there were also advantages to not having played it for so long. I could see the work as a whole

Geoffrey Douglas Madge in 1988 (photo by C. Marsel Loermans)

better. I also worked out all my choreography beforehand: the method of moving was consistent and connected to the sound needed for each passage, simplified to the most economical way of playing. The music sounded closer to the way I wanted it, yet I think the larger form was grander too. All this was helped, as I mentioned, by the good acoustics and the incredible piano.

P.R.: You've said that this might be your last complete performance. Five of these represent a stupendous amount of work yet hardly seem enough. And I'm sure many people want you to play it again.

G.D.M.: One of the main difficulties has been the long periods between performances. As I just mentioned, new technical work and new concentration are needed each time. The ideal is to have two or three performances within a fairly short period; except for the Chicago-Bonn pairing, this has never happened. Another difficulty is that my other concert work comes to a near standstill for at least a month prior to a performance of *O.C.* In any case, far too few concert organizations and pianists have realized the importance of *O.C.* on a technical basis, let alone otherwise.

Furthermore, I don't want a reputation based solely or even mostly on *O.C.* When you play this music you are very quickly put into a category of musical heavyweight, which is meaningless and quite contrary to my ideas. People begin to forget that you do other things equally well.

Finally, the extreme length of the whole work requires the speed of some parts in actual performance to be too fast. I think Sorabji was concerned about this too. The *Passacaglia* and most of the fugues are, I think, the main difficulty in this respect. The *Toccata* also, but at least it is called *Toccata!* For these reasons I could well imagine a studio performance of the whole work lasting about a half hour longer.

In any case, especially with the faster speeds it is too easy for a naive listener to hear only the cascades of notes and miss the important inner musical logic or the piano playing as a total art.

I will continue giving performances of some sections, which may even give a better idea of what Sorabji intended. He agreed on my selection of parts and even suggested that playing them may be better than playing the whole thing.

P.R.: What parts may you play separately?

G.D.M.: The *Introito, Preludio corale, Fuga I, Fantasia, Interludium primum,* and *Interludium alterum,* perhaps including the *Passacaglia,* perhaps not.

P.R.: What about a studio-based recording from you of the entire work?

G.D.M.: No, I don't think so, really. I was offered one, but I turned it down.[4]

---

[4]{Since his 1988 Paris performance of the entire *O.C.*, Madge has not played Sorabji's music in public. In February 1989, however, a tape of him playing two short works was broadcast in the Netherlands. See Chapter 12 for details.}

11 Splendour upon Splendour: On Hearing Sorabji Play

Frank Holliday

This article was originally printed privately in 1960 with an essay on Sorabji by Clinton Gray-Fisk which had appeared in *The Musical Times* in April 1960.

Frank Holliday knew Sorabji for a very long time, during which Sorabji played to him on many occasions.

When one looks at the masterpieces of interior decoration, like the Gothic Rathaus chambers in Lüneburg, the Saracen Cappella Palatina in Palermo, the Renaissance dining-room of the Gonzaga Palace or the Rococo drawing-rooms of Sans Souci in Potsdam, one finds that every inch of wall and ceiling has been covered with ornament, every door, every architrave, every door knob and key plate, every latch, every sconce.

The Platonic saying that only the like can understand the like also holds true in interior decoration. Only riches can enhance riches. Only sumptuousness can be coupled with sumptuousness. Only splendour can underline splendour.[1]

The twin questions of elaboration of detail and the conception of the whole have often been discussed in the arts (for example, by Matthew Arnold in the 1853 preface to his *Poems*, in connection with poetry and drama), but almost invariably as if they were antitheses, alternatives. Yet in the great traditions, or at least some of the great traditions of Western culture and art, *were* they antitheses, *were* they mutually exclusive? I think not.

The great mosaics may have been inlaid small piece by small piece so that they have a beauty of detail that delights the eye, but

---

[1] Edith Templeton: *The Surprise of Cremona* (London: Eyre and Spottiswoode, 1954), p. 162.

in addition, *in toto,* they create an awe-inspiring spectacle in the design of cathedral or church as a whole. To take an example near home: walk round Westminster Cathedral. Study the detailed loveliness of the Lady Chapel and then ask yourself whether that detracts from the impressiveness of the cathedral as a whole. There can be only one answer: it certainly does not. The detail is not extraneous, it is an integral part of the architectural conception of this great cathedral, essential to it and enhancing the outlines of the interior.

One could go further and argue that it is only when a culture becomes decadent — tired and introspective — that the fragmentation occurs which sees beauty of craftsmanship and detail as antithetic to boldness and grandeur of overall design.

The wellsprings of Sorabji's music lie in those traditions that knew not this fragmentation, this antithesis: the cultures of his Parsi father and his Spanish-Sicilian mother. With the great works of the illuminators such as the Bedford Book of Hours, *Les belles heures du duc de Berry;* with the works of craftsmanship and beauty of the finest gold and silversmiths, such as Fabergé, of the damasceners and the technically consummate carvers in ivory; with the marble and mosaic-embellished interiors of the *Duomo* of Monreale, of the *Cappella palatina* at Palermo, of Westminster Cathedral — with all these, Sorabji's work is one. It could be said to be their expression in music. They stand together: riches piled on riches, splendour upon splendour.

As for that music that reaches its peak with our modish composers; that painting that reaches its apex in Picasso (and, of course, began in 19th-century France); that Freudianism that is the last word on the human mind; that logic that can no higher go than in the negative illogicalities of Logical Positivism; that "functionalism" of contemporary packing-box architecture — as for all these: what have they to do with a Sorabji? What has he to do with them? What indeed? Just as much, in fact, and that is precisely nothing at all, as they have to do with such things as the B minor Mass of Bach, the work of Giovanni Bellini, of Aquinas, the apsidal mosaic at Cefalù ...

Power — creative plenitude — does not *seek* to impress: it *does* impress. There is nothing outré, nothing gauche, nothing seeking to impress about the Taj Mahal. Neither is there about Sorabji's music. It has the sanity, the wholeness,[2] the creative plenitude and finality

---

[2]Sorabji quoted to me on more than one occasion the words of the 15th-century Persian poet Jāmī: "... One Being was / Exempt from "I-" or "Thou-"ness, and apart / From all duality; Beauty Supreme, / ...".

[CONT'D]

of all great art. When you have heard it, you endorse the saying of the prophet Isaiah: "and thy heart shall wonder and be enlarged"; than which, ultimately, there can be no higher praise.

Sorabji's music is different in kind from the "playing with sounds" of so many modish composers.³ The impression made by this sort of noise is that its compounders, sitting statically on bare floorboards, are experimenting fortuitously with various sounds — their compositions going round and round, as time goes on, in ever decreasing circles until they end ... Well, the reader may be left to conjecture just where they end. So much cacophony, so much sound and fury, so much froth and pother, so much signifying so little, as "... their lean and flashy songs / Grate on their scrannel Pipes of wretched straw".⁴

How one is reminded of the old tag: "Il dit tout ce qu'il veut, mais malheureusement il n'a rien à dire." Hence, presumably, the novelty masquerading as originality, the desolating spiritual vacuum: poverty piled on poverty, emptiness upon emptiness to its logical conclusion: *omnia vanitas*.

Just as in one of the cathedrals mentioned we may at one moment be overwhelmed by the beauty of the detail — the friezes, the figures and faces of the saints, the geometrical mosaics, where no two faces, no two figures, no two patterns are exactly alike, but there is endless invention, endless variation — to not the slightest detraction from the magnificence of the whole; so too, despite the often elaborate complexity of the scene at any one moment, we never cease to be aware that Sorabji's music moves purposefully forward, the detail being an integral part of the overall design. At no time are we in the presence of the work of a static ear-tickler, a static experimenter with sounds who will shortly, we feel sure, be left regarding his own navel. Direction, movement towards its appointed end, is felt from the beginning no less (and it couldn't be more) than in a Palestrina Mass. Detail that may be said to be the expression in music of daedal beauty in marble, mosaic, and precious metals goes hand in hand, in many of this incomparable composer's works, with sweep and grandeur, as in a great cathedral.

I hope that nothing I have written has given the impression that Sorabji's music is "foreign" or, worse, "oriental", or even "strange". Well do I remember the first occasion the composer played to me

---

{For the rest of this section of the poem *Yūsuf and Zuleykhā*, see pp. 477–79.}

³Admirably summed up in one of Sorabji's own *mots* in a different though similar context: "That sort of thing gets you nowhere — and proceeds out of nowhere!"

⁴John Milton: *Lycidas,* lines 123–24.

in about 1937. At that time I was profoundly attracted to the music of the Roman Rite: the rendering of the Psalms as at Westminster Cathedral (under Sir Richard Terry), and as at Solesmes (on the gramophone records I had bought); and to the polyphonic music of Palestrina and others.⁵ As a youth of little cultural background and no musical knowledge whatever, but as one loving music as almost a necessity, this was a revelation to me. When Sorabji played to me — his *Jardin parfumé*⁶ — I was staggered, absolutely staggered by the beauty of what I heard; but it did not strike me as "strange" by comparison with the polyphonic music by which I was so moved. Something in it, in fact, struck me as being so profoundly natural that, after hearing it, so much other music — with the exception of that mentioned above — sounded not only "wrong" but, all too often crudely, coarsely, and monotonously "wrong". This impression has been strongly underlined in hearing Sorabji play his own compositions for many hours since.

One is always aware, in hearing his work, of what for want of a better word one may call its great "immemoriality" — and this despite the extent to which he is a developer. This is no mushroom growth, no bastard growth one feels; it has its roots deep. It may be partly this that accounts for what I imagine might be considered by those who have the misfortune to know his work only through his published scores (i.e. his earlier work; his later work is unpublished⁷) a rather surprising and curious fact: the sense of peace with which one is often left after having listened to his work (except when the composer intends otherwise) — the scintillating fireworks notwithstanding. It is music that can live with silence. True, a contributory factor may be the refreshing absence of the interminable monotony of the *beat*; but I was interested to be told, on entering his music room for the first time one year and remarking on its very marked peacefulness, that that identical comment had been made a short time before by a musician visitor and his wife.

The prime and overriding impression made by Sorabji's music is of its great beauty, range, and variety; the second, of its essential dynamicism. It is always moving, always evolving, and that is why any comparison with the static arts is so hopelessly inadequate. If, at any one moment of time, a cross-section of a particular

---

⁵{Indeed, Frank Holliday became a Roman Catholic in 1956.}

⁶The work that drew high praise from Delius when broadcast by the composer (in April 1930).

⁷{This was completely true when Holliday wrote this article; it is still largely so, as only one short work written after 1930 (the *Fantasiettina*) is published.}

composition of his may be compared with a mosaic, the composition as a whole may be said to resemble a series of seamlessly joined moving mosaics passing across one's aural "field". Kaleidoscopic patterns of great beauty are held and turned for a while in the hand, like a many-faceted jewel, only to dissolve and give way to further and yet further patterns — the whole exhibiting an apparently illimitable inventiveness.

For example, in parts of his *Passeggiata veneziana* (*Venetian Promenade*), a wholly charming and delightful piece growing from the germ of the *Barcarolle* from the *Tales of Hoffmann,* in which his evocation of "atmosphere" is unerring, the images are fresh and diaphonous, light as butterfly wings. (The nocturne, in its different way, is of superlative beauty.) In *Gulistān* (*The Rose Garden*), on the other hand, played softly by the composer, it is as if in a flowing panorama of dreamlike beauty, we behold and are thoroughly immersed in all the exotic magic of Iran: the Shah Mosque of Iṣfahān, the poetry, the incredibly lovely works in porcelain, silver, and gold, its exquisitely carved works of ivory and wood, and, of course, the scented loveliness of the roses of Shīrāz. This work evokes in a masterly fashion delicious and at times almost overpowering whiffs of Iran's "sweet rose-haunted walks", to use a phrase of Ḥāfiẓ.

Listening to Sorabji's work one never tires. Boredom, irksomeness, monotony are unknown. Whether this is because of the *movement* of his work (as contrasted with the staticism of so much other music), the endless variety of his invention, its polyrhythmic nature, or all three, I leave to musicians, merely recording my experience that this is so.

The *last* impression made by such of Sorabji's music as I have had the privilege of hearing is that of dissonance. Not that there are not parts, such as the glittering scherzo of the *Opus clavisymphonicum,*[8] that are astringent and tart — there are — but by and large the impression is one of concord, not discord: great and often moving beauty, utter "rightness".

That discerning scholar and author, the late Denis Saurat, wrote to me of the composer: "Mon admiration pour Sorabji est totale."[9] With that affirmation, I have the honour to associate myself most whole-heartedly.

---

[8]{Presumably the *Toccata* of the second movement: see pp. 160–61.}
[9]{For the fuller statement by Saurat, see p. 56.}

12 *Un tessuto d'esecuzioni:* A Register of Performances of Sorabji's Works

Marc-André Roberge

Marc-André Roberge (b. 1955, Montréal) received his BA in music history and literature from Laval University (Québec City) in 1979, his MA in musicology from McGill University (Montréal) in 1981, and his PhD in musicology from the University of Toronto in 1988. Currently he is Assistant Professor of Musicology at Laval University.

Among his interests are large-scale works for the piano written since 1850 and late romantic German music. His MA thesis was on Busoni's Piano Concerto; his PhD dissertation was on the periodical *Die Musik.* From 1984 to 1990 he was on the editorial board of *Sonances,* a Québec music journal, in which he published articles about Alkan, Busoni, Godowsky, Sorabji, and Stevenson, as well as Korngold, Schreker, and Zemlinsky. In 1991 Greenwood Press published his bio-bibliography of Busoni.

He is studying Busoni's activities in his American years and his relationships with French-speaking countries. He is also writing a critical biography of Sorabji and preparing critical editions of some of his works.

In most cases, a list of performances of works by significant 20th-century composers would be almost impossible to compile because of the magnitude of the task involved. It might also be rather uninteresting. In the case of Kaikhosru Shapurji Sorabji, however, performances until recently have been so infrequent since his Glasgow recital of 16 December 1936, that such a list can be prepared without an inordinate amount of research, though not without difficulties. In addition to documenting the increasingly positive reception of this prodigious composer, a list of performances enables us to see that, in the 40 years or so before Yonty Solomon's landmark Wigmore Hall recital of 7 December 1976, there had been a few unofficial performances which, to this day, have remained mostly undocumented.

426   *The Music*

The following list, which draws its title from Sorabji's chamber work *Il tessuto d'arabeschi*, was prepared using data provided in the Sorabji chapter in Paul Rapoport's book *Opus est*, but was vastly augmented by reference to articles published in various (mostly British) music journals and newspapers and by data kindly provided by the performers themselves, to whom I would like to extend my warmest thanks. I am also very much indebted to Alistair Hinton and Barry Peter Ould for bringing to my attention many items which distance prevented me from becoming aware of as rapidly as I would have hoped, as well as to Paul Rapoport.

In creating this list, I had to omit some performances that are reported to have taken place but could not be documented by articles, concert notices, letters, programs, reviews, etc.[1] It seemed preferable to reduce the list by a few items in order not to add to the numerous apocryphal stories already circulating around the composer.[2]

Performances which were not given in a concert hall but were broadcast from a recording studio are included, as are repeat broadcasts thereof. Broadcasts of concert performances (including repeat broadcasts), whether live or delayed, are noted. However, broadcasts of commercially available records, cassettes, and compact discs are not.

Lecture-recitals or conferences which were illustrated by live, privately recorded, or commercially as yet unreleased excerpts are included. In events containing one or more of these kinds of commercially unavailable recording, the parenthetical notation "also included:" gives information about commercially released recordings which were also heard.

The history of Sorabji's music in performance may be conveniently divided into six periods. The first covers November 1920 to December 1936 and, with three exceptions, consists of performances given by the composer himself, mostly in London and Glasgow, but also in Paris, Vienna, and Bombay. The first exception is a performance of the Fragment by its dedicatee, Harold Rutland,

---

[1] In this category are performances at the University of Cape Town South African College of Music when Sorabji's friend Erik Chisholm was Dean of Music there.

[2] {It would nonetheless be lunacy to assume that the register of performances is complete or completely accurate; and its compiler is no lunatic. The editor will be grateful for additions and corrections, substantiated by photocopies of programs, announcements, reviews, etc. as applicable, to pass on to Dr. Roberge. In the past five years, during which the number of performances has increased steeply, it has become difficult for one person to document every one of them.}

Sorabji, probably in the early 1920s (photo by Hugh Cecil)

at an Aeolian Hall recital on 12 October 1927. The second is E. Emlyn Davies' rendering of the second movement of Organ Symphony No. 1. The third exception is the frequently mentioned "reading" by John Tobin of *Pars prima* of *Opus clavicembalisticum* at Cowdray Hall on 10 March 1936, a performance with which the composer and others expressed dissatisfaction.

The second period covers May 1946 to March 1973. During these years, a few scattered performances, mostly of short works, took place, such as John Gates' performance of the *Fantaisie espagnole* at Carnegie Hall on 20 October 1966, which was the only well-documented event during this period at which Sorabji's music was played to a substantial number of people. (A notable, yet hardly noticeable event, due to its very nature, was a private reading of *Opus clavicembalisticum* by John Ogdon at Ronald Stevenson's home on 1 December 1959.) But it was a radio program consisting of remarks by Donald Garvelmann, a talk by Erik Chisholm (read by Frank Holliday), and piano music performed by Sorabji himself that really contributed to creating interest in the composer. (This program, prepared by Donald Garvelmann and broadcast on 13 December 1970, was repeated a few times afterwards.)

The third period covers July 1973 to June 1976, during which Michael Habermann gave numerous "unofficial" performances of various short works, including the *Fantaisie espagnole* and the first two sections of *Opus clavicembalisticum*. This series of preparatory performances eventually culminated in the first official (authorized) American recital to include Sorabji's music, given at Carnegie Recital Hall on 22 May 1977.

The fourth period covers December 1976 to April 1980. Its beginning corresponds to Yonty Solomon's first Sorabji recital at Wigmore Hall. It was the first performance of music by Sorabji authorized by the composer in several decades, and the first in London since John Tobin's 1936 performance. During this period, Solomon and Habermann, each in his respective country, gave first hearings of several short and medium-size works. On 2 February 1980, in Toronto, the probable first performance ever of a chamber work by Sorabji, the *Cinque sonetti di Michelagniolo Buonarroti*, was given by New Music Concerts at the University of Toronto.[3]

---

[3]Sorabji's First Piano Quintet was scheduled to be performed by the University of Toronto's Hart House String Quartet and pianist Norah Drewett at Aeolian Hall in New York on 29 November 1925 as part of a concert organized by Edgard Varèse's International Composers' Guild. The performance was cancelled for reasons which have not yet been fully ascertained but which may have much to do with the difficulty of the work.
[CONT'D]

The fifth period, covering June 1980 to April 1984, contains as its high point the first complete modern performance of *Opus clavicembalisticum*, given in Amsterdam by the Australian-born pianist Geoffrey Douglas Madge on 11 June 1982. This memorable performance, later released on records, had been preceded by six performances by Madge of the first two sections. On 9 October 1988 in Paris, Madge gave his fifth and, by his own decision, last complete performance of the work; this was also probably the first time any music by Sorabji was heard in a concert in France since the composer, together with the French soprano Marthe Martine, gave the premiere of his *Trois poèmes* on 2 June 1921. Two other interesting events of this period are: (1) a performance of the *Fantasiettina sul nome illustre dell'egregio poeta Christopher Grieve ossia Hugh M'Diarmid* given in Glasgow on 23 August 1981 by Sorabji's friend Ronald Stevenson, who, in 1987, published a performing/teaching edition of the work; and (2) the premiere, on 2 May 1982 in Philadelphia, of another chamber work, *Il tessuto d'arabeschi*, Sorabji's only commissioned composition.

The sixth period, from June 1984 to the present, confirms the increasing interest in Sorabji's music. Pianists such as Raymond Clarke, Victor Sangiorgio, and Marc-André Hamelin have begun playing Sorabji in public. A few other pianists, such as Julian Saphir, Jonathan Powell, and Donna Amato, added their names to the list in 1990 and 1991, partly as a consequence of the availability of copies of manuscripts through the Sorabji Music Archive. An important event in this period was the first complete performance of Organ Symphony No. 1 by Kevin Bowyer and Thomas Trotter on 25 July 1987. The most memorable achievement, however, remains Ogdon's performance of *Opus clavicembalisticum* on 14 July 1988, which constituted the first complete hearing of the work in England.

Both the recent performances and the recordings of Sorabji's music have helped to dispel the numerous legends that have surrounded his music for years. It had long been thought by many that Sorabji's music was largely unplayable. This rumour could be plausible at a time when aural images of the scores were accessible only to a minority. The artists, mainly pianists, whose names are mentioned above, have proved that it is not only playable, but also overwhelmingly beautiful and viable — *Gulistān* immediately comes to mind. It is worth noting that many pianists who have played Sorabji (such as Stevenson, Ogdon, Solomon, Madge, Habermann, and Hamelin) have also been, to varying degrees, exponents of the

---

{It is still possible that this quintet has been performed, as it was published in score and parts in 1923.}

music of some composers greatly admired by Sorabji, such as Alkan, Busoni, and Godowsky, and that they are also known for their interest in large-scale works for piano, such as those by Liszt, Skryabin, Reger, Ives, Medtner, Wolpe, Messiaen, Xenakis, Boulez, and Stevenson.[4]

It is true that many works by Sorabji will remain inaccessible to musicians except those gifted with the prerequisites to play the kind of music written by composers such as those just mentioned. Obviously, this is likely to reduce considerably the number of opportunities to hear the music. On the other hand, it gives us some assurance that Sorabji's works will not become commonplace and will still be listened to in a special atmosphere that is conducive to better understanding. In this respect, one might compare a performance of a work by Sorabji, especially a major work, to one of those infrequent productions of the opera *Doktor Faust* by Busoni, a composer for whom Sorabji's admiration was boundless.

The following outlines the format of the entries in the register of performances.

Part 1: *Date* (year–month–day), *city* (followed by state or country, if necessary), *hall, occasion* (special concert, festival, concert series, sponsoring body, etc.). Performances are listed up to the end of 1991.

The * denotes a live studio broadcast; if in parentheses, a simultaneous broadcast of a live performance in a concert hall. The • denotes a broadcast of a prerecorded tape. (Broadcasts of commercially available records, cassettes, and compact discs are not noted.) Unless stated otherwise, broadcasts are radio, not television. The ° denotes a private reading.

Part 2: *Performer(s), works* played (listed in chronological order of composition, where possible). The letter *x* in parentheses denotes an excerpt.

In the register the performers are listed without indication of their instrument or vocal range. The following is a list of all performers in the register, grouped by instrument or voice, along with the date of their first known performance of a work (or excerpt) by Sorabji.

---

[4]In this respect, see my article "The Busoni Network and the Art of Creative Transcription", in *Canadian University Music Review*, vol. 11, no. 1 (1991), pp. 68–88.

Pianists

Donna Amato (1991-07-01)
David Branson (1961)
Neely Bruce (1973-03-21)
Raymond Clarke (1984-11-23)
Cecil Ewing (1946-05-17)
Douglas Finch (1991-12-01)
Elvira Froese (1991-03-30)
John Gates (1966-09-28)
John Gibbons (1988-10-06)
Michael Habermann (1973-07-12)
Marc-André Hamelin (1989-03-19)
Alistair Hinton (1979-11-19)
Maurice Katz (between 1934 and 1938)
Robert Keeley (1984-07-17)
Geoffrey Douglas Madge (1960)
Jean-Bernard Marie (1989-02-25)

Robert Nasveld (1991-03-01)
Martin Offord (1984-06-30)
John Ogdon (1959-12-01)
Jonathan Powell (1990-05-24)
Gordon Rumson (1991-08-19)
Harold Rutland (1927-10-12)
Malcolm Rycraft (1990-02-21)
Victor Sangiorgio (1986-01-10)
Julian Saphir (1990-03-01)
Christopher Seed (1990-02-20)
Yonty Solomon (1976-12-07)
Kaikhosru Sorabji (1919-11)
Ronald Stevenson (1981-08-23)
John Tobin (1936-03-10)
Valerie Tryon (1979-11-06)

Organists

Kevin Bowyer (1987-07-25)
E. Emlyn Davies (1928-05-17)

Thomas Trotter (1987-07-25)

Sopranos

Christine Cairns (1986-12-15)
Janice Lewis (1991-03-30)
Jane Manning (1979-06-03)

Marthe Martine (1921-06-02)
Hieke Meppelink (1991-03-01)
Jo Ann Pickens (1989-02-25)

Tenor

Henry Ingram (1980-02-02)

Conductors

Robert Aitken (1980-02-02)

William Smith (1982-05-02)

Chamber ensembles (for the names of the specific performers in these groups, see below)

MPO   Members of the Philadelphia Orchestra (1982-05-02)
NMC   New Music Concerts (1980-02-02)

432 The Music

For the *Cinque sonetti di Michelagniolo Buonarroti*, the New Music Concerts ensemble of Toronto consisted of Fiona Wilkinson, flute; Alexandra Pohran, oboe; James Campbell, clarinet; David Carroll, bassoon; Henry Ingram, tenor; Victor Martin, Fujiko Imajishi, Joseph Pepper, David Zafer, violins; Rivka Golani Erdész, Douglas Perry, violas; Peter Schenkman, Coenraad Bloemendal, cellos; John Taylor, string bass; Marc Widner, piano; and Robert Aitken, conductor.

For *Il tessuto d'arabeschi*, the Philadelphia Orchestra members were Deborah Carter, flute; Jonathan Beiler, violin; Davyd Booth, violin; Sidney Curtiss, viola; Gloria Johns, cello; and William Smith, conductor.

Abbreviations of works performed

CDS	*Concerto da suonare da me solo e senza orchestra, per divertirsi*
CF	Transcription in the Light of Harpsichord Technique for the Modern Piano of the *Chromatic Fantasia* of J. S. Bach, Followed by a Fugue
CSM	*Cinque sonetti di Michelagniolo Buonarroti*
DÉ	*Désir éperdu*
FE	*Fantaisie espagnole*
FHR	Fragment Written for Harold Rutland (followed by the appropriate numeral, 1 to 3, referring to versions)
FSN	*Fantasiettina sul nome illustre dell'egregio poeta Christopher Grieve ossia Hugh M'Diarmid*
G	*Gulistān*
J	Nocturne, *Jāmī*
LJP	*Le jardin parfumé*
OC	*Opus clavicembalisticum* (Roman numerals refer to parts, Arabic numerals to sections)
OS	Organ Symphony (followed by the appropriate numeral, 1 to 3)
P	Pastiches 1 = on Chopin: *Valse*, Op. 64, No. 1 (the *Minute Waltz*) 2 = on Bizet: "Habanera" (from *Carmen*) 3 = on Rimskiy-Korsakov: "Hindu Merchant's Song" (from *Sadko*)
PIF	Prelude, Interlude, and Fugue (numbered 1, 2, and 3 respectively)
PV	*Passeggiata veneziana*
QFA	*[4] Frammenti aforistici*
QH	*Quasi habanera*
Rd'A	*Rosario d'arabeschi*
S	Sonata (for piano, followed by the appropriate numeral, 0 to 5)
StB	*St. Bertrand de Comminges: "He was laughing in the tower"*
Sy	Symphony (for piano solo, followed by the appropriate numeral, 1 to 6)
T	Toccata (followed by the appropriate numeral, 1 to 4)
Td'A	*Il tessuto d'arabeschi*
TFG	*Trois fêtes galantes de Verlaine* (numbered 1, 2, and 3 respectively)

TP	*Trois poèmes pour chant et piano* (numbered 1, 2, and 3 respectively)
TPP	Two Piano Pieces
	1 = *In the Hothouse*
	2 = *Toccata* (precedes the numbered toccatas)
TS	Transcendental Studies
VF	*Valse-fantaisie*
VMP	*Variazione maliziosa e perversa sopra "La morte d'Åse" da Grieg*

For P, PIF, TP, and TPP, the absence of a numeral indicates a performance of the complete work. So far, it appears that P has not been performed in its entirety on one program.

1919–11–??°	London; home of Maud Allan, in the presence of Ferruccio Busoni.	
	Kaikhosru Sorabji	S1
1920–11–02	London; Mortimer Hall. Second Sackbut concert.	
	Kaikhosru Sorabji	S1
1921–06–02	Paris; Société des agriculteurs de France, Société musicale indépendante.	
	Marthe Martine, Kaikhosru Sorabji	TP
1922–01–13	Vienna; Musikverein, Kammersaal.	
	Kaikhosru Sorabji	S1, S2
1924–05–13	London; Contemporary Music Centre. British Music Society.	
	Kaikhosru Sorabji	S2
1927–10–12	London; Aeolian Hall.	
	Harold Rutland	FHR1
1928–05–17	London; Westminster Congregational Church.	
	E. Emlyn Davies	OS1: II
1930–01–16	London; Westminster Congregational Church.	
	Kaikhosru Sorabji	J
1930–04–01	Glasgow; Stevenson Hall. Active Society for the Propagation of Contemporary Music.	
	Kaikhosru Sorabji	S4
1930–04–22*	London; British Broadcasting Corporation. London Regional broadcast.	
	Kaikhosru Sorabji	LJP

434 *The Music*

1930–12–01	Glasgow; Stevenson Hall. Active Society for the Propagation of Contemporary Music.	
	Kaikhosru Sorabji	OC
1931–04–29	Glasgow; Stevenson Hall. Active Society for the Propagation of Contemporary Music.	
	Kaikhosru Sorabji	J
1932–10–19*	Bombay.	
	Kaikhosru Sorabji	An improvisation
1932–12–07*	Bombay.	
	Kaikhosru Sorabji	An improvisation
1933*	Bombay.	
	Kaikhosru Sorabji	An improvisation
	Note: Doubtful event.	
1936–03–10	London; Contemporary Music Centre, Cowdray Hall.	
	John Tobin	OC: I
1936–12–16	Glasgow; Stevenson Hall. Active Society for the Propagation of Contemporary Music.	
	Kaikhosru Sorabji	T2
between 1934 and 1938?°	Philadelphia; Studio of Maurice Katz.	
	Maurice Katz	OC
1946–05–17	Bristol; University of Bristol, Reception Room. Annual Concert.	
	Cecil Ewing	TPP1
1959–12–01°	West Linton, Scotland; home of Ronald Stevenson.	
	John Ogdon	OC
1960 late°	Adelaide, Australia; home of Geoffrey Douglas Madge.	
	Geoffrey Douglas Madge	OC
1961	Rye, Sussex. Lecture-recital.	
	David Branson	LJP (x), Unidentified sonata(s) (x)
1962 or 1963	Location unknown. Lecture-recital.	
	David Branson	LJP (x), Unidentified sonata(s) (x)

1966–09–28	Greenfield, Indiana; Le Blazer Studio Club.	
	John Gates	FE
1966–10–09	Indianapolis; Indianapolis Museum of Art.	
	John Gates	FE
1966–10–20	New York; Carnegie Hall.	
	John Gates	FE
1969–12–08•	New York; WBAI broadcast of Erik Chisholm's "The Composer Sorabji" read by Frank Holliday, with recordings of Sorabji playing his own music. (Duration about 55 minutes.)	
	Kaikhosru Sorabji	LJP (x: pp. 3–9); J (x: beginning, end); Sy2 (opening of 1st movement); PV: Barcarolla (x), Notturnino; Sy4 (x: end of Chorale Prelude)
1969–12–13•	New York; WBAI broadcast of "The Composer Sorabji".	
	Kaikhosru Sorabji	(see 1969–12–08)
1970–12–13•	New York; WNCN broadcast of Donald Garvelmann's radio program, which comprised 1969–12–08 plus material supplied by Garvelmann. (Duration about 3 hours.)	
	Kaikhosru Sorabji	LJP (x: pp. 3–9); J (x: beginning, end); G; CDS; Sy2 (opening of 1st movement); PV: Barcarolla (x), Notturnino; Sy4 (x: end of Chorale Prelude)
	Note: This program was broadcast subsequently on several other American radio stations, as noted below.	
1971–12–12•	New York; WNCN broadcast of Donald Garvelmann's radio program.	
	Kaikhosru Sorabji	(see 1970–12–13)
1972–12–10•	New York; WNCN broadcast of Donald Garvelmann's radio program.	
	Kaikhosru Sorabji	(see 1970–12–13)

1973-03-21	Urbana, Illinois; University of Illinois, Smith Music Hall. Phoenix 73: New Music for Keyboard. Neely Bruce　　　　　　　　　　　P1
1973-07-12	Glen Cove, New York; Glen Cove Hospital, School of Nursing Auditorium. Michael Habermann　　　　　　　　FE
1973-11-08•	Berkeley, California; KPFA broadcast of Donald Garvelmann's radio program. Kaikhosru Sorabji　　　　　　(see 1970-12-13)
1974-11-26	Roslyn, New York; Bryant Library. Michael Habermann　　　　　　　　FE
1975-02-19•	Kalamazoo, Michigan; WMUK broadcast of Donald Garvelmann's radio program. Kaikhosru Sorabji　　　　　　(see 1970-12-13)
1975 (Spring)	Urbana, Illinois; University of Illinois, School of Music Building. Illustrated lecture by Paul Rapoport. Taped computer realization by Paul Rapoport　　　　　　　　　OC (x)
1975-05-11	Oyster Bay, New York; Christ Church Parish Hall. Michael Habermann　　　　　　TPP1, P2
1975-06-18	Rockville Center, New York; Nassau Conservatory of Music. Student recital. Michael Habermann　　　　　　　　FE
1975-06-20	Rockville Center, New York; Nassau Conservatory of Music. Student recital. Michael Habermann　　　　　　TPP1, P2
1975-07-01	Westbury, New York; Westbury Library. Die Kammermusik-Gesellschaft. Michael Habermann　　　　　　　　P2
1975-10-20	Edmonton, Alberta; University of Alberta, Fine Arts Building. Illustrated lecture by Paul Rapoport. Taped computer realization by Paul Rapoport　　　　　　　　　OC (x)
1976-03-12	Rockville Center, New York; Molloy College, Quealy Hall. Michael Habermann　　　　　　TPP1, P2
1976-03-21	Roslyn, New York; Bryant Library. Michael Habermann　　　　　　TPP1, P2

1976–04–27	Westbury, New York; Westbury Library. Honours student recital.	
	Michael Habermann	P2
1976–05–03	Garden City, New York; Nassau Community College, Music Building. Lecture-recital.	
	Michael Habermann	TPP1, FE, P2
1976–05–08	Rockville Center, New York; Molloy College, Quealy Hall. New York State Music Teachers' Association annual recital.	
	Michael Habermann	FE
1976–05–10	Garden City, New York; Nassau Community College, Music Building. Lecture-recital.	
	Michael Habermann	TPP1, FE, P2
1976–06–18	Rockville Center, New York; Nassau Conservatory of Music. Student recital.	
	Michael Habermann	FE
1976–06–19•	Collegeville, Minnesota; Minnesota Public Radio broadcast of Donald Garvelmann's radio program (over KSJR, Collegeville; KSJN, St. Paul / Minneapolis; KCCM, Moorhead, Minnesota / Fargo, North Dakota; WSCD, Duluth, Minnesota; KRSW, Worthington, Minnesota; KLSE, Rochester, Minnesota / Decorah, Iowa).	
	Kaikhosru Sorabji	(see 1970–12–13)
1976–08–23•	New York; WFUV broadcast.	
	Michael Habermann	Various pieces, titles unknown
1976–12–07•	London; British Broadcasting Corporation. Radio 4 "PM" news program broadcast.	
	Yonty Solomon	LJP (x)
1976–12–07	London; Wigmore Hall.	
	Yonty Solomon	FE, TPP, LJP
1977–02–08	Greenvale, New York; Post College, Great Hall. Student recital.	
	Michael Habermann	P2
1977–04–03	Great Neck, New York; Great Neck House.	
	Michael Habermann	TPP1, FE, PIF3, P2
1977–04–17	Rockville Center, New York; Molloy College, Quealy Hall.	
	Michael Habermann	TPP1, FE, PIF3, P2

1977–04–24	Farmingdale, New York; South Branch Public Library.	
	Michael Habermann	TPP1, FE, PIF3, P2
1977–05–18•	New York; WNYC broadcast.	
	Michael Habermann	TPP1, P2
1977–05–20*•	New York; WQXR. "The Listening Room" broadcast.	
	Michael Habermann	TPP1, FE (x), P2
	Note: TPP1 and FE (x) were broadcast live, P2 on tape.	
1977–05–22	New York; Carnegie Recital Hall.	
	Michael Habermann	TPP1, FE, PIF3, P2
1977–06–11•	London; London Weekend Television. "Aquarius" program broadcast.	
	Yonty Solomon	TPP1, FE (x), S3 (x, incl. opening page), LJP (x), OC: 1 (x: opening)
1977–06–16	London; Wigmore Hall.	
	Yonty Solomon	S3
1977–10–11	Belfast; University of Ulster, Assembly Hall.	
	Yonty Solomon	FE
1977–10–17	Nottingham; University of Nottingham, Cripps Hall.	
	Yonty Solomon	FE, S3
1977–11–07•	London; British Broadcasting Corporation. Radio 3 broadcast (studio recording).	
	Yonty Solomon	FE, TPP, LJP
1977–11–13	Merrick, New York; Merrick Library.	
	Michael Habermann	P2
1977–11–18	Brentwood, New York; St. Joseph's College. Classroom presentation.	
	Michael Habermann	P2
1977–11–22	London; Wigmore Hall.	
	Yonty Solomon	FE, G, StB
1977–11–22	Greenvale, New York; Post College, Great Hall. Student recital.	
	Michael Habermann	P2

1978–01–07	Cape Town; Baxter Hall. Yonty Solomon	FE
1978–04–15	Greenvale, New York; Post College, Great Hall. Michael Habermann	TPP2, OC: 1–2, FHR3, CF
1978–05–08*•	New York; WQXR. "The Listening Room" broadcast. Michael Habermann Note: FHR3 was broadcast live, the others on tape.	PIF1, OC: 1–2, FHR3
1978–05–08•	New York; WFUV broadcast. Michael Habermann	TPP1, P2
1978–05–11•	New York; WNYC broadcast. Michael Habermann	PIF3, FHR3
1978–05–13	New York; Carnegie Recital Hall. Michael Habermann	TPP2, OC: 1–2, FHR3, CF
1978–06–27	London; Wigmore Hall. Yonty Solomon	CDS
1978–07–25	Cambridge, England; University of Cambridge, Music School. Yonty Solomon	CDS
1978–09–19	Greenvale, New York; Post College, Great Hall. Michael Habermann	FE, TPP, P2, OC: 1–2, FHR3
1978–09–27	Garden City, New York; Nassau Community College, Music Building. Michael Habermann	FE, TPP, P2, OC: 1–2, FHR3
1978–10–06	Midland, Michigan; Midland Center for the Arts. American Liszt Society Festival. Michael Habermann	FE, TPP, P2, OC: 1–2, FHR3
1978–10–30	Newport, Wales; Dolman Theatre. Newport Music Club. Yonty Solomon	P1
1978–11–15	Glasgow; University of Glasgow, Concert Hall. Yonty Solomon	TPP1, FE

1979-05-19	Greenvale, New York; Post College, Great Hall.	
	Michael Habermann	FE, P2
1979-05-20	South Huntington, New York; South Huntington Library.	
	Michael Habermann	FE, P2
1979-06-03•	London; British Broadcasting Corporation. Radio 3 broadcast.	
	Jane Manning, Yonty Solomon	TFG, TP, G
1979-06-06	London; Wigmore Hall.	
	Yonty Solomon	Rd'A
1979-08-09	College Park, Maryland; University of Maryland. International Piano Festival. Lecture by Cecil Ewing, recital by Michael Habermann.	
	Michael Habermann	FE, TPP, P2, OC: 1–2, FHR3
1979-09-30	Como, Italy; Salone Villa Olmo. 13° Autunno musicale.	
	Yonty Solomon	FE; LJP; TS: 1, 10, 24; CDS
1979-11-06	Hamilton, Ontario; McMaster University, Convocation Hall. Lunchtime Concert.	
	Valerie Tryon	TPP1
1979-11-19	Leicester; Leicester Polytechnic. Illustrated lecture by Alistair Hinton.	
	Alistair Hinton	LJP (x), OC: 1 (x)
1979-11-19	Roanoke, Virginia; Hollins College, Talmadge Hall.	
	Michael Habermann	TPP1, FE, P2, FSN
1979-12-16	Bloomfield, New Jersey; Bloomfield Public Library, Vogt Theater.	
	Michael Habermann	TPP1, FE, P2, FSN
1979-12-19	Greenvale, New York; Post College, Great Hall.	
	Michael Habermann	P2, LJP, FSN
1980-02-01	Toronto; University of Toronto, Walter Hall. New Music Concerts. Illustrated lecture by Paul Rapoport.	
	Valerie Tryon	TPP1, P1
	Taped computer realization by Paul Rapoport	OC (x)

1980-02-02	Toronto; University of Toronto, Walter Hall. New Music Concerts. NMC — CSM
1980-02-11	Baltimore; Peabody Institute. Doctoral degree recital. Michael Habermann — LJP
1980-03-28	Richmond, Virginia; Women's Club Auditorium. Michael Habermann — P2, LJP
1980-03-29	Richmond, Virginia; University of Richmond, Modlin Fine Arts Building. Illustrated lecture by Michael Habermann. Michael Habermann — PV: Notturnino, Unidentified pieces (x) Note: The unidentified pieces represent tape recordings.
1980-04-30	London; Wigmore Hall. Yonty Solomon — TS: 1, 10, 24
1980-06-01	Utrecht; Muziekcentrum Vredenburg. Holland Festival. Geoffrey Douglas Madge — OC: 1-2
1980-06-05	Amsterdam; Centrum Bellevue. Holland Festival. Geoffrey Douglas Madge — OC: 1-2
1980-06-09	Almelo, The Netherlands; Cultureel Centrum de Hagen. Holland Festival. Geoffrey Douglas Madge — OC: 1-2
1980-06-11(*)	The Hague; Koninklijk Conservatorium, Schönbergzaal. Holland Festival. Geoffrey Douglas Madge — OC: 1-2 Note: Simultaneous broadcast on NOS.
1980-07-24•	Sydney; Australian Broadcasting Corporation. Television broadcast. Geoffrey Douglas Madge — OC: 1-2
1980-08-10•	Toronto; Canadian Broadcasting Corporation. Broadcast of 1980-02-02 and part of 1980-02-01. Valerie Tryon — TPP1 NMC — CSM

1980-10-12	Newtown, Pennsylvania; home of William Marsh. Meeting of the Delius Society (Philadelphia branch). Illustrated lecture by Paul Rapoport.

Valerie Tryon   TPP1, P1
Taped computer realization by
  Paul Rapoport   OC (x)
Note: All the above items represent tape recordings.

1980-11-20	Baltimore; Peabody Institute. Doctoral degree recital. Michael Habermann J
1981-03 and later•	US National Public Radio. "Grand Piano" broadcast on many stations of 1979-08-09. Michael Habermann FE, TPP, P2, OC: 1-2, FHR3
1981-03-09•	Baltimore; WBJC. "Focus on the Arts" broadcast. Michael Habermann Various excerpts, titles unknown
1981-04-22	Baltimore; Peabody Institute. Doctoral degree recital. Michael Habermann FE
1981-07-05	Middelburg, The Netherlands; De Vleeshal. Festival Nieuwe Muziek. Geoffrey Douglas Madge TPP, PIF1, PIF3, OC: 1-2
1981-07-10	Baltimore; Back Door II. Michael Habermann TPP1, FE, P2
1981-08-23	Edinburgh; Saltire House. Edinburgh International Festival (Fringe). Ronald Stevenson FSN
1982-05-02	Philadelphia; Old Pine Street Church. Delius Society (Philadelphia branch). MPO Td'A
1982-06-11(*)	Utrecht; Muziekcentrum Vredenburg. Holland Festival. Geoffrey Douglas Madge OC Note: Simultaneous broadcast on NOS.
1982-06-28	London; Priory Church of St. Bartholomew-the-Great. St. Bartholomew's Festival. Geoffrey Douglas Madge OC: III

1982-08-25	Philadelphia; WUHY broadcast of 1982-05-02 and other items: NMC CSM Kaikhosru Sorabji G MPO Td'A (also included: OC: 1–2 from Michael Habermann's record)
1982-09-09	Perth, Australia; University of Western Australia, Octagon Theatre. Lunchtime Concert. Ronald Stevenson FSN
1982-09-28	Baltimore; Peabody Institute, Leakin Hall. Michael Habermann PIF, VF, J
1982-10-07	Cambridge, Massachusetts; Harvard University, Paine Hall. American Liszt Society Festival. Michael Habermann PIF, VF, J
1982-10-20	Shippensburg, Pennsylvania; Shippensburg State College, Memorial Auditorium. Noon Music. Michael Habermann PIF, VF, J
1983-02-06	Hamilton, Ontario; McMaster University, Convocation Hall. Explorations Concert. Michael Habermann PIF, VF, J
1983-04-24	Chicago; University of Chicago, Mandel Hall. Contemporary Concerts. Geoffrey Douglas Madge OC
1983-05-10	Bonn; Beethovenhalle. XXXI. Internationales Beethovenfest. Geoffrey Douglas Madge OC
1983-07-14•	Washington; US National Public Radio. "All Things Considered" broadcast. Michael Habermann PIF1 (x) (also included: LJP (x) from Habermann's record)
1983-08-08•	New York; WFUV broadcast. Michael Habermann PIF (also included: J from Habermann's record)
1983-08-22•	New York; WFUV broadcast of part of 1983-04-24. Geoffrey Douglas Madge OC: IXc (Passacaglia)
1983-08-29•	New York; WFUV broadcast of part of 1983-04-24. Geoffrey Douglas Madge OC: 11–12

1983–11–02   Århus, Denmark; Chamber Hall. International Society for Contemporary Music, World Music Days.
Geoffrey Douglas Madge   OC: III

1983–11–24   Nottingham; University of Nottingham, Great Hall.
Yonty Solomon   TPP

1984–04–07•   Chicago; WFMT broadcast of 1983–04–24.
Geoffrey Douglas Madge   OC

1984–04–30•   Edinburgh; British Broadcasting Corporation. Radio Scotland broadcast.
Ronald Stevenson   FSN

1984–06–30   London; Purcell Room.
Martin Offord   TPP1, PIF, LJP

1984–07–17   London; British Music Information Centre.
Robert Keeley   TPP1

1984–07–20   Old Field, New York; State University of New York, Sunwood Estate. Sunwood Summer Series concert.
Michael Habermann   J

1984–08–14•   London; British Broadcasting Corporation. Radio 3 broadcast.
Yonty Solomon   S1

1984–11–09   Montréal; McGill University, Redpath Hall. Les événements du neuf.
Geoffrey Douglas Madge   OC

1984–11–14   Toronto; York University, Department of Music, McLaughlin Hall.
Geoffrey Douglas Madge   OC: 1–2

1984–11–14   Toronto; Music Gallery.
Geoffrey Douglas Madge   OC: 1–2

1984–11–19   Cleveland, Ohio; West Shore Unitarian Church. Rocky River Chamber Music Society.
Michael Habermann   P1, P3, PIF, VF, J, StB

1984–11–23   Cambridge, England; University of Cambridge, Trinity College Hall.
Raymond Clarke   FE

1985-01-06•	Montréal; Radio-Canada. "Musique de notre siècle" broadcast of 1984-11-09. Geoffrey Douglas Madge OC
1985-01-23•	Baltimore; WBJC. "Music in Maryland" broadcast of 1982-09-28. Michael Habermann PIF, VF, J
1985-01-30	Oxford; University of Oxford, Holywell Music Room. Raymond Clarke FE
1985-03-05	Hamilton, Ontario; McMaster University, Convocation Hall. Lunchtime Concert. Ronald Stevenson FSN
1985-03-13	Fredonia, New York; State University of New York College at Fredonia. Ronald Stevenson FSN
1985-04-11•	London; British Broadcasting Corporation. Radio 3 broadcast (repeated from 1984-08-14). Yonty Solomon S1
1985-05-18	Nottingham; University of Nottingham, Music Studio. Raymond Clarke FE
1985-07-02	London; British Music Information Centre. Raymond Clarke FE
1986-01-10	London; Purcell Room. Young Artists and Twentieth-Century Music. Victor Sangiorgio FE
1986-08-02(*)	Viitasaari, Finland; Youth Hall. Fourth International Summer Academy and Festival: Time of Music. Geoffrey Douglas Madge OC: 1-2, 4 Note: Simultaneous broadcast on Finnish television.
1986-12-15•	Edinburgh; British Broadcasting Corporation. Radio Scotland broadcast. Christine Cairns, Ronald Stevenson TFG3
1987-04-05	Baltimore; Maryland State Music Teachers' Association, Towson Chapter. Michael Habermann LJP (x) (also included: LJP from Habermann's record)

1987-06-10•	London; British Broadcasting Corporation. Radio 3 broadcast. Yonty Solomon StB
1987-07-25	London; Holy Trinity Chuch. International Congress of Organists. Kevin Bowyer, Thomas Trotter OS1 Note: The 1st and 3rd movements were played by Bowyer, the 2nd movement by Trotter.
1987-08-14•	London; British Broadcasting Corporation. Radio 3 broadcast. Yonty Solomon S3
1987-09-01	Edinburgh; Edinburgh Society of Musicians. Ronald Stevenson FSN (twice)
1987-10-23	London; British Music Information Centre. Ronald Stevenson FSN (twice)
1987-11-18	York, England; University of York, Sir Jack Lyons Concert Hall. Ronald Stevenson FSN
1987-12-26	Middelburg, The Netherlands; Kloveniersdoelen, Centrum Nieuwe Muziek. Geoffrey Douglas Madge FSN
1988-01-15	Kelso, Scotland; Kelso Music Club. Ronald Stevenson FSN
1988-01-22	Amsterdam; De IJsbreker. Geoffrey Douglas Madge FSN
1988-02-10	Leicester; Leicester Polytechnic. Yonty Solomon S1, LJP
1988-02-12	Oslo; Universitets Aula. Norsk tangentfestival. Geoffrey Douglas Madge OC: 1–2
1988-04-28	Århus, Denmark; Århus Cathedral. Kevin Bowyer OS1
1988-07-14	London; Queen Elizabeth Hall. John Ogdon OC
1988-07-15•	London; British Broadcasting Corporation World Service "Outlook" program broadcast. John Ogdon OC: 1 (x)

Sorabji and Barry Peter Ould with the *Fantasiettina*, newly published by Ould's Bardic Edition (1987; photo by Peter Dickie)

1988–07–16• London; British Broadcasting Corporation World Service "Outlook" program broadcast.
John Ogdon OC: 1 (x)

1988–07–24• Århus, Denmark; Danish Radio broadcast of 1988–04–28.
Kevin Bowyer OS1

1988–07–26 Dorking, England; Cleveland Lodge. Organists' Summer School. Illustrated lecture by Alistair Hinton.
Raymond Clarke FE (x)
Yonty Solomon FE (x), S1 (x), G (x)
Jane Manning, Yonty Solomon TP1, TP3
NMC CSM (x)
Kevin Bowyer OS1: II (live performance), I (x), III (x)
John Ogdon OC: I (x), II (x)
Kaikhosru Sorabji G (x)
Ronald Stevenson FSN
MPO Td'A (x)
(also included: P2 from Michael Habermann's record)
Note: All the above items represent tape recordings except for the two noted otherwise (Bowyer and Habermann).

1988–08–22 Edinburgh; Richard Demarco Gallery.
Ronald Stevenson FSN

1988–09–04 Largs, Scotland; Barrfields Pavilion. Largs Viking Festival.
Ronald Stevenson FSN

1988–10–06 London; Royal Academy of Music, Duke's Hall.
John Gibbons TPP1

1988–10–09 Paris; Opéra comique. Festival d'automne à Paris 1988.
Geoffrey Douglas Madge OC

1988–10–24 Corfe Castle, Dorset; Parish Church. Memorial service for Sorabji.
Kevin Bowyer OS1: II (x) from the CD about to be issued
(also included: other recordings)

1988–11–02 London; Skinners' Hall; Cornhill Festival of British Music.
John Ogdon OC

1989-01-18•	London; British Broadcasting Corporation. Radio 4 "Kaleidoscope" broadcast.	
	Kevin Bowyer	OS1: I (x)
	John Ogdon	OC: 11 (x)
1989-02-24•	Hilversum; NOS broadcast.	
	Geoffrey Douglas Madge	QH, FSN
	Jane Manning, Yonty Solomon	TFG
	Yonty Solomon	LJP (x)
	Kevin Bowyer	OS1: I (x), II (x)
	Kaikhosru Sorabji	TS: 26
	MPO	Td'A
	(also included: OC: IXb (Adagio) from Madge's records)	
1989-02-25	London; Serpentine Gallery.	
	Jo Ann Pickens, Jean-Bernard Marie	TP
1989-03-19•	London; London Weekend Television broadcast.	
	John Ogdon	OC: 6 (x), 12 (x)
1989-03-19	Hamilton, Ontario; McMaster University, Convocation Hall. Celebrity Concert.	
	Marc-André Hamelin	S1
1989-05-31	Québec City; Université Laval, École de musique, Salle Henri-Gagnon. Annual conference of the Canadian University Music Society.	
	Marc-André Hamelin	S1
1989-10-31	New York; Weill Recital Hall. League of Composers / International Society for Contemporary Music, US section.	
	Marc-André Hamelin	S1
1990-02-05	Ottawa, Ontario; National Arts Centre, Opera. Celebrity Recital.	
	Marc-André Hamelin	S1
1990-02-20	London; Royal College of Music, Concert Hall.	
	Malcolm Rycraft	DÉ, TPP1, FHR1
1990-02-20	London; St. John's, Smith Square.	
	Christopher Seed	TPP1
1990-03-01	London; Royal College of Music, Lecture Room. Lecture-recital.	
	Julian Saphir	OC: 1

(also included: excerpts from recordings by Michael Habermann, Kevin Bowyer, and John Ogdon)

1990-04-11	Adelaide, Australia; University of Adelaide, Elder Conservatorium of Music. Lecture-recital.	
	Martin Offord	PIF
1990-04-21	London; Trinity Church, Golders Green. Hendon Music Society.	
	Yonty Solomon	LJP
1990-05-21	London; Royal College of Music, Recital Hall.	
	Julian Saphir	OC: 1-2
1990-05-24	London; British Music Information Centre.	
	Jonathan Powell	S1
1990-08-02	Saint-Irénée, Québec; Domaine Forget. Festival international du Domaine Forget.	
	Marc-André Hamelin	S1
1990-08-23	Husum, West Germany; Rittersaal/Konzertsaal im Schloß vor Husum. Raritäten der Klaviermusik im Schloß vor Husum.	
	Marc-André Hamelin	S1
1990-10-20	St. John's, Newfoundland; Memorial University, M. O. Morgan Music Building.	
	Marc-André Hamelin	S1
1990-11-14	Lancaster, Pennsylvania; Franklin and Marshall College, Hensel Hall.	
	Marc-André Hamelin	S1
1990-12-05	London; Steinway Hall. Invitation Recital Series.	
	Julian Saphir	TPP
1991-02-27	Oxford; Oxford University, Lecture Room A. Oxford University Contemporary Music Group. Illustrated lecture by Alistair Hinton.	
	Yonty Solomon	FE (x), S1 (x)
	Jane Manning, Yonty Solomon	TP1
	NMC	CSM (x)
	MPO	Td'A (x)
	(also included: OS1: I (x) from Kevin Bowyer's discs)	
	Note: All the above items represent tape recordings except for the one noted otherwise (Bowyer).	

1991–03–01	Amsterdam; De IJsbreker. Hieke Meppelink, Robert Nasveld	TP
1991–03–30	Waterloo, Ontario; Wilfrid Laurier University, John Aird Recital Hall. Student recital. Janice Lewis, Elvira Froese	TP
1991–06–18	Cambridge, England; Gonville and Caius College. Jonathan Powell	S1
1991–07–01	London; Church of St. Martin-in-the-Fields. Donna Amato	FE
1991–07–09	London; British Music Information Centre. Donna Amato	FE
1991–07–23	London; Purcell Room. Donna Amato	FE, VMP
1991–08–19	Calgary, Alberta; Pleasant Heights United Church. "Largely Liszt" recital, Program I. Gordon Rumson	QFA
1991–09–11•	Hannover; North German Radio broadcast of 1990–08–23. Marc-André Hamelin	S1
1991–09–20	London; Church of St. Martin-in-the-Fields. Donna Amato	VMP
1991–09–25	London; British Music Information Centre. Donna Amato	VMP
1991–09–27	Bath; The Pump Room. Donna Amato	VMP
1991–10–30	Off the coast of Spain; Pacific and Orient ship Canberra. Donna Amato	FE (in two concerts)
1991–12–01	Winnipeg, Manitoba; University of Manitoba, Eva Clare Recital Hall. Douglas Finch	FSN

Perigraph

To Remember Sorabji's Music: A Short-Form Conclusion

Kenneth Derus

This article, which could equally be called Chapter 13 or Appendix 1, is presented as poetic philosophy, although its aim is not necessarily poetic or philosophical. It is partly a response to Sorabji and his accomplishments, given to provoke, thoughtfully, with new ideas leading to and from new ideas, related to the ineffability of the experience of the imminence and immanence of Sorabji's music.

George Flynn encouraged this work and composed *Glimpses of Our Inner Selves* in response to it. Some of the material was presented in the form of a lecture called "Remembering Music", given by Kenneth Derus at a DePaul Composers' Forum, 13 February 1990 in Chicago.

Perigraph is used here not in the obsolete sense of *inscription* but in a combination of senses derived from a Greek noun having several meanings, including *outline*, *limit*, and *termination*.

Kaikhosru Sorabji is about as misunderstood as he ever was. It used to be fashionable to compare him to a host of lesser composers, based on a facile appreciation of the most superficial aspects of his least characteristic music. Now it is routinely suggested that the works of his maturity are utterly unique by virtue of their duration — when this, too, is precisely not the case.

A performance of Sorabji's largest piano piece could easily take eight hours, and a dozen other of his compositions are at least half this size. But Sorabji's intent was not to create wholly new kinds of musical experiences, in which the element of time on a vast scale is somehow important. It was, in fact, to create just those sorts of experiences which cannot result from merely listening to music of exceptional duration.[1]

* * * * *

Each of Sorabji's characteristic works has a symmetric design compounded of melodies, not notes. The designs are evident as patterns on paper. Pictures created from Sorabji's scores look like tilings. Melody shapes cover paper with very few gaps or overlaps. Adjacent picture segments of appropriate width appear to rotate, reflect, or translate the same shape material.[2]

A design-related picture segment consists of a combination of interlocking melody shapes, together with the heads and tails of additional shapes. Not every patch of interlocking melody shapes is a shape combination. Small sets of melody shapes never generate symmetric patterns on paper.

Melody shape combinations can always be identified in different ways. The different ways involve relaxed isometries on different sets of melody shapes.[3]

---

[1]Sorabji never said much about how his music is supposed to work, but he did say this:

> I deny [...] the right to talk romantically and windily about Music, to indulge in fantasy-sodden theorisings that can by no conceivable means be tested for their validity by reference to any body of ascertained or ascertainable fact [...] The place for the imagination, brothers, is *in* the music, not all round outside it.

(Kaikhosru Sorabji: *Mi contra fa: The Immoralisings of a Machiavellian Musician* (London: Porcupine Press, 1947), p. 14.)

[2]Specific notes are rarely essential to specific melodies, in much of Sorabji's music. Hence patterns of Sorabji's note shapes can be almost random even when patterns of his melody shapes are symmetric.

Sorabji's designs suggest Morton Feldman, a composer fascinated by rug patterns and memory. (See his *Essays,* edited by Walter Zimmermann (Kerpen, Germany: Beginner Press, 1985), pp. 124–27.) Some of Feldman's later works have durations of many hours.

[3]Isometries are distance-preserving spatial transformations. Relaxed isometries are approximate isometries. See *Tilings and Patterns,* by Branko Grünbaum and G. C. Shephard (New York: W. H. Freeman, 1987).

Symmetric patterns need not be predictable. Sorabji's melody shapes often rotate about a centre in adjacent shape combinations. This makes rotations easy to anticipate; but it is generally impossible to anticipate *specific* rotations.

Relaxed isometries can be present if pairs of melody shape combinations are viewed from a reasonable distance.⁴

Melody shape combinations represent melody combinations. Melody combinations often consist of hundreds of notes. Only a small number of notes can be present parts of hearing experiences.⁵ Hence melody combinations can never be present. Hence pairs of melody combinations can never be present. Hence musical changes associated with relaxed isometries of melody shape combinations

---

⁴Something is present in an experience if it is recognized without inspection. Every part of a present experience is present. Sights and sounds are present experiences. Something can be recognized without being named. (No one needs to name notes to recognize notes.)

Looking at Sorabji's *scores* from a distance has been done before:

At first sight his works appear to be a sort of chaos of incoherence and over-elaboration, but this is not so. It must always be remembered that he is an Oriental, and his music must be looked at from a distance as it were. It is like an intricate piece of Benares work or Chinese ornamentation. The arabesques, which are a feature of such work, when examined closely are exquisitely conceived, but appear meaningless; yet from some way off they sink into their place and the whole design becomes apparent. So it is with these works [...]

(Christopher à Becket Williams: "The Music of Kaikhosru Sorabji", in *The Sackbut*, vol. 4 (June 1924), pp. 315–16.)

⁵Cf. the Leipzig experiments of Wundt and Dietze (in *The Principles of Psychology*, vol. 1, by William James (New York: Dover, 1950), pp. 612–13). Sounds can be parts of very long notes, but usually notes are sounds or parts of sounds. Short melodies can be parts of sounds, but sounds are more commonly parts of melodies. Very short works can be parts of sounds, but sounds are almost always parts of works. None of this means that hearing experiences are always fusions of nothing but sounds. Most works have rests and pauses as present parts.

(Notes, melodies, and works overlap sounds. So do hearing experiences. Notes, melodies, and works are fusions of their parts. So are hearing experiences. For more about mereology, see *Parts of Classes*, by David Lewis (Oxford: Basil Blackwell, 1991) and *Parts: A Study in Ontology*, by Peter Simons (Oxford: Oxford University Press, 1987).)

can never be present.⁶ Hence Sorabji's symmetric designs can never implicitly uncoil.⁷

But memories of melody combinations can exist, and so can memories of pairs of melody combinations.⁸

Memories are present experiences — like sights and sounds. Hence remembered melody combinations can be present, even though melody combinations can never be present.⁹

Memories usually have parts. The parts are always present. No parts of memories are ever parts of sights or sounds. (Remembered notes are never notes. Remembered cats are never cats.

---

⁶Change can be present. (Nonsimultaneity can be recognized without inspection.)

Any change associated with Sorabji's isometries is at least a change from one melody combination to another. No such change can be present unless at least pairs of melody combinations can be nonsimultaneous parts of a present part of a hearing experience.

Melody combinations need never seem served up in pairs, because fusions of present experiences need never be present.

⁷All music uncoils in terms of individual notes. A design implicit in the uncoiling of something is a local design. For Babbitt and Beethoven, musical designs are local designs.

Sorabji's symmetric designs are necessarily nonlocal. Nonlocal musical designs never accumulate. (The ear, in calculus class, always fails to find an integral.)

One kind of design need not exclude another. Most of Sorabji's music has some sort of compelling nonsymmetric local design. (More counterpoint can be clearly distinguished, by ear, in Sorabji's keyboard music than in Conlon Nancarrow's music for player pianos.)

⁸This means that melody combinations can be subjects of memory, and so can pairs of melody combinations. And this means that implicitly remembered durations can radically exceed memory durations. Cf. footnote 20.

⁹Remembering involves more than present experience. Not all remembered melody combinations are present, because not all remembered melody combinations are memories of melody combinations. Some remembered melody combinations are fusions of memories of parts of melody combinations. Fusions of memories need not be memories.

In what follows, a remembered melody combination is always a memory of a melody combination — and a remembered pair of melody combinations is always a memory of a pair of melody combinations. But remembered works are *not*, in general, memories of works. (This means that remembered melody combinations and remembered pairs of melody combinations are always present; but remembered works are rarely present.)

Memories can be more than experiences. Memories can be judgements involving the past. This fact is irrelevant: what matters is that almost all present experience is memory experience.

Remembered melodies never have notes as parts. A coloured afterimage is not a memory.)

Some parts of memories are counterparts of sights and sounds. A remembered F♯ is a counterpart F♯.

A counterpart F♯ is (in many ways) more like a counterpart C♯ than an F♯. But a counterpart F♯ is more like an F♯ than anything else that is sometimes part of a memory.[10]

Notions of memory that trade on counterparts are thoroughly bankrupt.[11] Few memories consist of counterparts, or even have counterparts as parts. Few memories consist of things like things that are seen or heard.[12]

Only a small number of remembered notes can be present parts of memories. Hence remembered notes are never parts of remembered melody combinations.[13]

The number of melodies in a pair of melody combinations always approximates the number of remembered notes that can be present in memories. Hence remembered melodies can be parts of remembered pairs of melody combinations when remembered melodies are simples.[14] Hence counterparts of changes associated with Sorabji's isometries can be present in memories.[15]

---

[10] The debt to David Lewis is staggering, but no one should suppose that what counts as a counterpart here would count as a counterpart for Lewis. (Cf. his "Counterpart Theory and Quantified Modal Logic", in *Journal of Philosophy*, vol. 65 (1968), pp. 113–26.)

[11] See *Memory and Mind,* by Norman Malcolm (Ithaca: Cornell University Press, 1977) and *Consciousness Explained,* by Daniel Dennett (Boston: Little, Brown, 1991).

[12] See footnote 13. But some qualities of parts of memories are also qualities of parts of sounds. The counterpart gunfire in a memory of loud, rapid gunfire is rapid, even though no part of the counterpart gunfire is loud.

(Qualities are not parts. The qualities of notes include pitch, duration, timbre, and intensity. These qualities are not *parts* of notes.)

[13] No parts of remembered melody combinations are counterparts of things that are heard. This means that Sorabji's "harmonic" vocabulary consists of varieties of many simultaneous and nonsimultaneous note combinations remembered together — not well-known chords individually heard and appreciated. It also means that Sorabji's melodies are in some respects notated more exactly than they need to be.

[14] Structures have parts; simples do not. (Notes are simples, except insofar as they change. Notes with temporary parts can change. Notes without temporary parts never change.)

If remembered melodies had to have parts, then remembered pairs of melody combinations would have too many parts to ever be present.

[15] This presumes that remembered melodies are as easy to recognize as remembered notes. (Cf. footnote 4. Recognition involves sensing, not

[CONT'D]

If pairs of melody combinations consisted of fewer notes, then remembered pairs of melody combinations would have parts irrelevant to Sorabji's symmetric designs.[16] If pairs of melody combinations consisted of more notes, then remembered pairs of melody combinations would lack parts relevant to Sorabji's symmetric designs.[17]

Counterpart "counterpoint" — involving remembered melodies — exists in fusions of remembered pairs of melody combinations. Fusions of memories can be parts of remembering experiences. Hence counterparts of Sorabji's symmetric designs can implicitly uncoil in remembering experiences the same way counterpoint implicitly uncoils in hearing experiences.[18]

---

saying.) It also presumes that melodies are experienced when Sorabji's music is heard. (Cf. footnote 4. Not all hearing experiences are present experiences.)

Any counterpart of a change associated with Sorabji's isometries is at least a change from one remembered melody combination to another. No such change can be present unless at least pairs of remembered melody combinations can be nonsimultaneous parts of a present part of a remembering experience. Cf. footnote 6.

[16]Remembered melodies would have parts; hence not every present change would be a counterpart of a change associated with Sorabji's isometries.

[17]The smallest parts of remembered pairs of melody combinations would have more than just single melodies as subjects; hence counterparts of changes associated with Sorabji's isometries would not be present. Cf. footnote 14.

For works like Feldman's *Triadic Memories* the question is obvious: Does what has to be remembered correspond to what can be remembered?

Giacinto Scelsi had little genuine control over the *structure* of notes, in works like *Quattro pezzi per orchestra (ciascuno su una nota sola)*. Sorabji had complete control over the structure (if any) of remembered melodies.

[18]Cf. footnote 9. Counterpart "melodies" — of remembered melodies — exist in fusions of memories. (The memories are present; the fusions are not.)

Only *relations* are counterparts in counterpart "melodies" and counterpart "counterpoint". (Cf. footnote 13. Remembered melodies are never counterparts of melodies, insofar as they exist as parts of remembered melody combinations.) Hence counterpart symmetric designs are compelling only because the qualities of remembered melodies are compelling. (See *The Qualities of Melodic Simples*, by Kenneth Derus: a work in progress.)

Counterpart symmetric designs are local designs, in fusions of remembered pairs of melody combinations. Cf. footnote 7.

The duration of a melody combination is measured from the first note of the melody that begins first through the last note of the melody that ends last. Pairs of melody combinations sometimes have durations of more than sixty seconds. (*Gulistān* and *Le jardin parfumé* consist of almost nothing but such lengthy melody combinations.)

The duration of a remembered pair of melody combinations is measured from the remembered melody that begins first through the remembered melody that ends last.[19] Remembered pairs of melody combinations typically have durations of at most three seconds.

Opus clavicembalisticum consists of roughly five hundred pairs of melody combinations, involving subsets of several dozen types of melody. (The duration of a pair of combinations averages thirty seconds.) The work is a fusion of sounds, with a duration of roughly four hours.

An appropriate fusion of remembered pairs of *Opus clavicembalisticum*'s melody combinations constitutes a remembered work, with a duration of at most 25 minutes. Symmetric local design is evident in present parts of this remembered work.[20]

Indirectly, this was never less than Sorabji's intention. He always wanted to give his music the special virtues of modestly proportioned work he admired, and he modelled *Opus clavicemba-*

---

[19] Remembered melodies do not consist of remembered notes, at any rate in remembered pairs of melody combinations.

[20] Cf. "The Intentionality of Sensation", by G. E. M. Anscombe, in *Metaphysics and the Philosophy of Mind* (Minneapolis: University of Minnesota Press, 1981), p. 3. Anscombe's example of *no longer current* English usage can be paraphrased: the fusion of memories (of pairs of *Opus clavicembalisticum*'s melody combinations) has an objective duration of at most 25 minutes and a subjective duration of roughly four hours.

Coughs are often unavoidable parts of hearing experiences but rarely parts of works considered as fusions of sounds. Memories of notes are often unavoidable parts of remembering experiences, but never parts of remembered works considered as fusions of remembered pairs of melody combinations.

Not just *any* fusion of remembered pairs of melody combinations will exhibit a symmetric local design or have a duration of at most 25 minutes; but more than one acceptable fusion exists.

(A picture created from *Opus clavicembalisticum*'s score can be cut into roughly a thousand melody shape combinations in more than one way. Hence there are different appropriate ways to remember *Opus clavicembalisticum*. The qualities of remembered melodies may or may not be invariant, relative to these ways.)

listicum on the *Fantasia contrappuntistica.* Busoni's piano piece takes around 25 minutes to hear.²¹

* * * * *

Others have composed large scores of unusual cogency and coherence, but only Sorabji managed to make compelling designs appear (instead of disappear) in memories of music of virtually unlimited duration.²²

No composer, of any period, has successfully attacked a musical problem of greater difficulty, or left behind a more valuable set of working methods. This makes Sorabji something other than a fabulous musical outsider. It makes him historically more germane than most of his contemporaries.

---

²¹The *Fantasia*'s musical design is compounded of notes, so it gains nothing in memories that lack remembered notes as parts.

Busoni's work and Sorabji's remembered work provide similarly ample opportunity for anticipation and surprise, and are in this important sense comparably organized.

²²Sorabji's symmetric designs can never be local in music of exceptional duration; but their counterparts can always be local in fusions of memories. Cf. footnote 18.

It has been suggested that single memories, having entire works as subjects, are also sometimes compelling:

> Gertrude Stein was fond of saying that paragraphs are emotional and sentences aren't. Each great structural and emotional paragraph of *Opus clavicembalisticum* is made up of an extraordinary number of minutely differing sentences: the representatives of some particular genus of melody. The paragraphs cannot be heard. All that can be heard are representatives of melodic genera, passing by in a welter of counterpoint. But the paragraphs can be remembered — as objects of poignant and rather terrifying unity. Everything passes by like *Finnegans Wake*, only to get recollected like *The Making of Americans.*
> (Kenneth Derus: Program notes for the performance of *Opus clavicembalisticum* by Geoffrey Madge on 24 April 1983 in Chicago, p. 3.)

Appendix 1

The Texts of Sorabji's Vocal Music

Paul Rapoport

The following are the texts set by Sorabji in his extant songs for voice and keyboard instrument, and voice and chamber ensemble, dating from 1915 to 1973. (A few songs are probably still missing.) The individual songs are listed alphabetically by the title Sorabji used, the alphabetization disregarding *The* and the French definite articles *Le, La, L',* and *Les*. The collection of five sonnets of Michelangelo is entered alphabetically under *Cinque sonetti di Michelagniolo Buonarroti*. After the song texts is the complete text for Sorabji's Third Symphony, *Jāmī*.

Most of the songs set poems by French parnassians or symbolists, such as Baudelaire and Verlaine, or followers of them, such as Gilkin and Tailhade. Mystery, the unattainable, decay, and darkness both literal and metaphorical are some of the themes found in these poems, but their varied styles and methods make any such list a bit misleading. Many of the poems attain their effect by indirectness, subtlety, and unusual interplay of images — well-known traits of French symbolism. Some of the poems are certainly better than others: the stark Satanic language of the Gilkin cannot mask its obviousness, nor can the directness of the Dowson mask its triteness. Why Sorabji set these particular poems is unknown, but the general attraction of French symbolist themes to a high-strung outsider like him is fitting.

The prose translations of the Sa'dī poems are an exception to the above: they deal with straightforward but intense emotions of basic human relationships in a manner which Sorabji could well relate to from his own makeup and experiences. He occasionally quoted the last few sentences of "La fidélité"; nothing could reflect better his belief in passion combined with forgiveness.

Most often the song title and the original title of the poem are the same; when they are not, this is indicated immediately after Sorabji's title. (See, for example, the song "I Was Not Sorrowful", which is not the poet's title.) For the French symbolists Baudelaire, Mallarmé, and Verlaine, the date of publication given is the earliest the poem appeared in a sizable collection, not necessarily the earliest publication date of the individual poem. This plan has also been followed for the other poets, with some less certain results in dating. The format of any poem given below (involving spelling, punctuation, and inclusion or omission of certain words or lines) is not necessarily that of the earliest published edition but, for the French symbolists, follows the editorial advice of various modern critical editions. For the lesser-known poets, reasonable editions have been used, keeping in mind Sorabji's text. This was especially significant for the *Trois poèmes du Gulistān de Sa'dī*, for which there are at least two different (prose) translations by the same person (Franz Toussaint), and for "Hymne à Aphrodite" by Laurent Tailhade, of which Sorabji set the uncommon early version.

A few comments in larger type on the texts as used by Sorabji follow the items to which they relate. If Sorabji made minor, easily correctable errors in his writing of a text, this is noted, although simple spelling mistakes are usually not described.

A short bibliography at the end of this appendix gives source information for the texts appearing in it.

À la promenade (Paul Verlaine; in *Fêtes galantes*, 1869)

    Le ciel si pâle et les arbres si grêles
    Semblent sourire à nos costumes clairs
    Qui vont flottant légers, avec des airs
4   De nonchalance et des mouvements d'ailes.

    Et le vent doux ride l'humble bassin,
    Et la lueur du soleil qu'atténue
    L'ombre des bas tilleuls de l'avenue
8   Nous parvient bleue et mourante à dessein.

    Trompeurs exquis et coquettes charmantes,
    Cœurs tendres, mais affranchis du serment,
    Nous devisons délicieusement,
12 Et les amants lutinent les amantes,

De qui la main imperceptible sait
Parfois donner un soufflet, qu'on échange
Contre un baiser sur l'extrême phalange
16   Du petit doigt, et comme la chose est

Immensément excessive et farouche,
On est puni par un regard très sec,
Lequel contraste, au demeurant, avec
20   La moue assez clémente de la bouche.

The word "légers" (line 3) is omitted in the published score, along with any music for it. This problem may well have come from Sorabji's manuscript, of which there is no trace.

L'allée (Paul Verlaine; in *Fêtes galantes*, 1869)

Fardée et peinte comme au temps des bergeries,
Frêle parmi les nœuds énormes de rubans,
3   Elle passe, sous les ramures assombries,
Dans l'allée où verdit la mousse des vieux bancs,
Avec mille façons et mille afféteries
6   Qu'on garde d'ordinaire aux perruches chéries.
Sa longue robe à queue est bleue, et l'éventail
Qu'elle froisse en ses doigts fluets aux larges bagues
S'égaie en des sujets érotiques, si vagues
10   Qu'elle sourit, tout en rêvant, à maint détail.
     — Blonde, en somme. Le nez mignon avec la bouche
Incarnadine, grasse et divine d'orgueil
Inconscient. — D'ailleurs, plus fine que la mouche
14   Qui ravive l'éclat un peu niais de l'œil.

Apparition (Stéphane Mallarmé; in "Premiers poëmes", from *Poésies*, 1887)

La lune s'attristait. Des séraphins en pleurs
Rêvant, l'archet aux doigts, dans le calme des fleurs
Vaporeuses, tiraient de mourantes violes
4   De blancs sanglots glissant sur l'azur des corolles
    — C'était le jour béni de ton premier baiser.
Ma songerie aimant à me martyriser
S'enivrait savamment du parfum de tristesse
8   Que même sans regret et sans déboire laisse
La cueillaison d'un Rêve au cœur qui l'a cueilli.
J'errais donc, l'œil rivé sur le pavé vieilli
Quand avec du soleil aux cheveux, dans la rue
12   Et dans le soir, tu m'es en riant apparue

       Et j'ai cru voir la fée au chapeau de clarté
       Qui jadis sur mes beaux sommeils d'enfant gâté
       Passait, laissant toujours de ses mains mal fermées
16 Neiger de blancs bouquets d'étoiles parfumées.

Sorabji set "de la tristesse" (line 7), which is his error. He also misspelled a few words.

Arabesque (Shamsu'd-Dīn Ibrāhīm Mīrzā; source not located)

    Une petite arabesque de flûte se déploye
    triste et nostalgique
    étalant dans ses courbes subtiles
    des désirs sans nom et des voluptés inouïes.

Sorabji indicated alternate words at two points in the score: "étalant" or "trahissant", "inouïes" or "dangereuses". He misspelled two words.

Benedizione di San Francesco d'Assisi

    Il Signore ti benedica e ti custodisca,
    Ti mostri la sua faccia e abbia misericordia di te,
    Volga a te il suo sguardo e ti dia pace.
    Il Signore ti benedica.

Sorabji set this modern version of St. Francis's Benediction, which comes from the Bible (Numbers 6: 24–26). He wrote the indicative "mostra" instead of the correct subjunctive "mostri" (line 2). The repetition (line 4) of the first part of the first line is Sorabji's.

Les chats (Charles Baudelaire; in "Spleen et idéal", from *Les fleurs du mal*, 1857)

      Les amoureux fervents et les savants austères
      Aiment également, dans leur mûre saison,
      Les chats puissants et doux, orgueil de la maison,
4   Qui comme eux sont frileux et comme eux sédentaires.

      Amis de la science et de la volupté,
      Ils cherchent le silence et l'horreur des ténèbres;
      L'Érèbe les eût pris pour ses coursiers funèbres,
8   S'ils pouvaient au servage incliner leur fierté.

464   Appendix 1

>   Ils prennent en songeant les nobles attitudes
>   Des grands sphinx allongés au fond des solitudes,
> 11 Qui semblent s'endormir dans un rêve sans fin;
>
>   Leurs reins féconds sont pleins d'étincelles magiques,
>   Et des parcelles d'or, ainsi qu'un sable fin,
> 14 Étoilent vaguement leurs prunelles mystiques.

Sorabji misspelled a few words.

Chrysilla (Henri de Régnier; in "Médailles votives", from *Les médailles d'argile*, 1900)

>   Lorsque l'heure viendra de la coupe remplie,
>   Déesse, épargne-moi de voir à mon chevet
>   Le Temps tardif couper, sans pleurs et sans regret,
> 4 Le long fil importun d'une trop longue vie.
>
>   Arme plûtot l'Amour; hélas! il m'a haïe
>   Toujours et je sais trop que le cruel voudrait
>   Déjà que de mon cœur, à son suprême trait,
> 8 Coulât mon sang mortel sur la terre rougie.
>
>   Mais non! que vers le soir en riant m'apparaisse,
>   Silencieuse, nue et belle, ma Jeunesse!
> 11 Qu'elle tienne une rose et l'effeuille dans l'eau;
>
>   J'écouterai l'adieu pleuré par la fontaine
>   Et, sans qu'il soit besoin de flèches ni de faulx,
> 14 Je fermerai les yeux pour la nuit souterraine.

Sorabji neglected to write in all the words in line 4 where there are notes in the vocal line which were presumably intended for them.

Cinque sonetti di Michelagniolo Buonarroti (Michelangelo Buonarroti: *Rime*, edited by Enzo Noè Girardi, 1960)

Although he indicated in 1979 that he had used the edition of Carl Frey, which reproduces Michelangelo's archaic spellings, Sorabji inconsistently modernized the spelling in some places only and made errors in others. The text given here, offering a modernization of some of the original spelling and punctuation (but not of other elements of the language), comes very close to what he probably intended throughout, with the exception of a few elisions, which may have their source in Frey's edition. Sorabji preferred the archaic spelling of the poet's name.

1.

    Tu sa' ch'i' so, signor mie, che tu sai
ch'i' vengo per goderti più da presso,
e sai ch'i' so che tu sa' ch'i' son desso:
4 a che più indugio a salutarci omai?
    Se vera è la speranza, che mi dai,
se vero è 'l gran desio che m'è concesso,
rompasi il mur fra l'uno e l'altra messo,
8 ché doppia forza hann' i celati guai.
    S'i' amo sol di te, signor mie caro,
quel che di te più ami, non ti sdegni,
11 ché l'un dell'altro spirto s'innamora.
    Quel che nel tuo bel volto bramo e 'mparo,
e mal compres' è dagli umani ingegni,
14 chi 'l vuol saper convien che prima mora.

2.

    Non so se s'è la desïata luce
del suo primo fattor, che l'alma sente,
o se dalla memoria della gente
4 alcun'altra beltà nel cor traluce;
    o se fama o se sogno alcun produce
agli occhi manifesto, al cor presente,
di sé lasciando un non so che cocente
8 ch'è forse or quel c'a pianger mi conduce.
    Quel ch'i' sento e ch'i' cerco e chi mi guidi
meco non è; né so ben veder dove
11 trovar mel possa, e par c'altri mel mostri.
    Questo, signor, m'avvien, po' ch'i' vi vidi,
c'un dolce amaro, un sì e no mi muove:
14 certo saranno stati gli occhi vostri.

Sorabji erroneously inserted "non" before "lasciando" (line 7).

3.

    A che più debb'i' omai l'intensa voglia
sfogar con pianti o con parole meste,
se di tal sorte 'l ciel, che l'alma veste,
4 tard' o per tempo alcun mai non ne spoglia?

A che 'l cor lass' a più languir m'invoglia,
   s'altri pur dee morir? Dunche per queste
   luci l'ore del fin fian men moleste;
8 c'ogni altro ben val men c'ogni mia doglia.
      Però se 'l colpo ch'io ne rub' e 'nvolo
   schifar non posso, almen, s'è destinato,
11 chi entrerà 'nfra la dolcezza e 'l duolo?
      Se vint' e preso i' debb'esser beato,
   maraviglia non è se nudo e solo
14 resto prigion d'un cavalier armato.

4.

   Veggio nel tuo bel viso, signor mio,
   quel che narrar mal puossi in questa vita:
   l'anima, della carne ancor vestita,
4 con esso è già più volte ascesa a Dio.
      E se 'l vulgo malvagio, isciocco e rio,
   di quel che sente, altrui segna e addita,
   non è l'intensa voglia men gradita,
8 l'amor, la fede e l'onesto desio.
      A quel pietoso fonte, onde sïan tutti,
   s'assembra ogni beltà che qua si vede
11 più c'altra cosa alle persone accorte;
      né altro saggio abbiàn né altri frutti
   del cielo in terra; e chi v'ama con fede
14 trascende a Dio e fa dolce la morte.

5.

   Se nel volto per gli occhi il cor si vede,
   altro segno non ho più manifesto
   della mie fiamma; addunche basti or questo,
4 signor mie caro, a domandar mercede.
      Forse lo spirto tuo, con maggior fede
   ch'i' non credo, che sguarda il foco onesto
   che m'arde, fie di me pietoso e presto,
8 come grazia c'abbonda a chi ben chiede.
      O felice quel dì, se questo è certo!
   Fermisi in un momento il tempo e l'ore,
11 il giorno e 'l sol nella su' antica traccia;
      acciò ch'i' abbi, e non già per mie merto,
   il desïato mie dolce signore
14 per sempre nell'indegne e pronte braccia.

Sorabji neglected to write in the words "signor mie" in line 4 where there are notes in the vocal line which were presumably intended for them.

Correspondances (Charles Baudelaire; in "Spleen et idéal", from *Les fleurs du mal*, 1857)

    La Nature est un temple où de vivants piliers
    Laissent parfois sortir de confuses paroles;
    L'homme y passe à travers des forêts de symboles
4   Qui l'observent avec des regards familiers.

    Comme de longs échos qui de loin se confondent
    Dans une ténébreuse et profonde unité,
    Vaste comme la nuit et comme la clarté,
8   Les parfums, les couleurs et les sons se répondent.

    Il est des parfums frais comme des chairs d'enfants,
    Doux comme les hautbois, verts comme les prairies,
11 — Et d'autres, corrompus, riches et triomphants,

    Ayant l'expansion des choses infinies,
    Comme l'ambre, le musc, le benjoin et l'encens,
14 Qui chantent les transports de l'esprit et des sens.

A few words are incorrect in the published score.

Crépuscule du soir mystique (Paul Verlaine; in "Paysages tristes", from *Poèmes saturniens*, 1866)

    Le Souvenir avec le Crépuscule
    Rougeoie et tremble à l'ardent horizon
    De l'Espérance en flamme qui recule
4   Et s'agrandit ainsi qu'une cloison
    Mystérieuse où mainte floraison
    — Dahlia, lys, tulipe et renoncule —
    S'élance autour d'un treillis, et circule
8   Parmi la maladive exhalaison
    De parfums lourds et chauds, dont le poison
    — Dahlia, lys, tulipe et renoncule —
    Noyant mes sens, mon âme et ma raison,
12 Mêle dans une immense pâmoison
    Le Souvenir avec le Crépuscule.

There are two incorrect spellings in the published score. At least one is probably a misprint.

Dans la grotte (Paul Verlaine; in *Fêtes galantes*, 1869)

    Là! je me tue à vos genoux!
    Car ma détresse est infinie,
Et la tigresse épouvantable d'Hyrcanie
4   Est une agnelle au prix de vous.

    Oui, céans, cruelle Clymène,
    Ce glaive qui, dans maints combats,
Mit tant de Scipions et de Cyrus à bas,
8   Va finir ma vie et ma peine!

    Ai-je même besoin de lui
    Pour descendre aux Champs-Élysées?
    Amour perça-t-il pas de flèches aiguisées
12   Mon cœur, dès que votre œil m'eut lui?

There is one incorrect accent in the published score which almost certainly comes from a later, incorrect edition of the poem.

La dernière fête galante (Paul Verlaine; in *Parallèlement*, 1889)

    Pour une bonne fois séparons-nous,
    Très chers messieurs et si belles mesdames.
    Assez comme cela d'épithalames,
4   Et puis là, nos plaisirs furent trop doux.

    Nul remords, nul regret vrai, nul désastre!
    C'est effrayant ce que nous nous sentons
    D'affinités avecque les moutons
8   Enrubannés du pire poétastre.

    Nous fûmes trop ridicules un peu
    Avec nos airs de n'y toucher qu'à peine.
    Le Dieu d'amour veut qu'on ait de l'haleine,
12   Il a raison! Et c'est un jeune Dieu.

    Séparons-nous, je vous le dis encore.
    Ô que nos cœurs qui furent trop bêlants,
    Dès ce jourd'hui réclament, trop hurlants,
16   L'embarquement pour Sodome et Gomorrhe!

Lines 9 to 12 were added by Verlaine in 1894. Sorabji set all 16 lines.

L'étang (Maurice Rollinat; in "Les spectres", from *Les névroses*, 1883)

    Plein de très vieux poissons frappés de cécité,
    L'étang, sous un ciel bas roulant de sourds tonnerres,
    Étale entre ses joncs plusieurs fois centenaires
4   La clapotante horreur de son opacité.

    Là-bas, des farfadets servent de luminaires
    À plus d'un marais noir, sinistre et redouté;
    Mais lui ne se révèle en ce lieu déserté
8   Que par ses bruits affreux de crapauds poitrinaires.

    Or, la lune qui point tout juste en ce moment,
    Semble s'y regarder si fantastiquement,
11   Que l'on dirait, à voir sa spectrale figure,

    Son nez plat et le vague étrange de ses dents,
    Une tête de mort éclairée en dedans
14   Qui viendrait se mirer dans une glace obscure.

Sorabji set "ne" (line 7) twice, which is his error. He also misspelled a few words.

Le faune (Paul Verlaine; in *Fêtes galantes*, 1869)

    Un vieux faune de terre cuite
    Rit au centre des boulingrins,
    Présageant sans doute une suite
4   Mauvaise à ces instants sereins

    Qui m'ont conduit et t'ont conduite,
    Mélancoliques pèlerins,
    Jusqu'à cette heure dont la fuite
8   Tournoie au son des tambourins.

La fidélité (Sa'dī; in *Gulistān*. Translation by Franz Toussaint: *Le jardin des roses*, 1923)

    Pendant des années, j'avais voyagé avec cet ami. Bien des fois, ensemble, nous avions partagé le pain et le sel. C'est vous dire que notre intimité était absolue. Un jour, désireux de réaliser un gain, il se permit de me blesser, et notre intimité cessa. Malgré ce pénible événement, nous nous aimions encore, lorsque j'appris qu'il récitait, dans les assemblées, cette kacida, que j'avais composée.
    «Lorsque mon ami pénètre dans ma demeure en souriant, il saupoudre de sel la plaie du blessé d'amour. Que se passerait-il, si une boucle de ses

cheveux venait à caresser mon front, comme l'aumône d'un homme riche tombe dans la main d'un pauvre?»

Plusieurs personnes avaient bien voulu applaudir ces vers, et mon ancien camarade les avait aussitôt louangés avec exagération. Il était allé jusqu'à gémir d'avoir perdu mon affection, n'hésitant point à se reconnaître coupable ...

Je me rendis compte qu'il voulait me revoir, et lui adressai les vers suivants, en témoignage de pardon:

«Nous sommes restés fidèles l'un à l'autre. Toi seul as été injuste. Je ne pouvais prévoir que tu t'éloignerais, et j'avais lié mon cœur au tien ... Il y avait tant d'autres cœurs, cependant! Reviens. Tu seras aimé comme jamais tu ne l'as été!»

Sorabji misspelled a few words.

Frammento cantato

    I bend to the rose.
    Its silence speaks what God above me knows.

No source for these lines has been discovered.

L'heure exquise (Paul Verlaine; untitled poem, no. 6 in *La bonne chanson*, 1870)

    La lune blanche
    Luit dans les bois;
    De chaque branche
    Part une voix
    Sous la ramée ...

6   Ô bien-aimée.

    L'étang reflète,
    Profond miroir,
    La silhouette
    Du saule noir
    Où le vent pleure ...

12   Rêvons, c'est l'heure,

Un vaste et tendre
Apaisement
Semble descendre
Du firmament
Que l'astre irise ...

18 C'est l'heure exquise.

Hymne à Aphrodite (Laurent Tailhade; in "Poèmes et bas-reliefs", from *Le jardin des rêves*, 1880)

Aphrodite, déesse immortelle aux beaux rires,
Qui te plais aux chansons lugubres des ramiers,
Les cœurs humains pour toi chantent comme des lyres
4 Et tes bras font pâlir la blancheur des pommiers.

Salut, dispensatrice auguste de la vie,
Qui courbes sous ton joug les fauves indomptés,
Qui fais voler la lèvre à la lèvre ravie,
8 Salut, blanche Cypris, reine des voluptés!

C'est par toi que, le soir, sous les myrtes propices,
S'enlacent doucement des groupes bienheureux,
Et qu'au bord des ruisseaux et près des précipices
12 Sanglotent dans la nuit les enfants amoureux.

C'est par toi que, brûlant d'ivresse, frémissante,
L'églantine se teint de son sang parfumé,
Et que la vierge apporte, heureuse et rougissante,
16 Sa couronne et son cœur aux bras du bien-aimé.

Et c'est toi qui, rythmant les divines étoiles,
Fais tressaillir d'amour le cœur de l'univers,
Afin que l'harmonie en qui tu te dévoiles,
20 Apprenne aux hommes purs à composer des vers.

Je t'implore, déesse immense et vénérable,
Soit que, glorifiant les rosiers rajeunis,
Sous les lilas en fleurs et les bosquets d'érable
24 Tu couvres de baisers les songes d'Adonis;

Soit que le dur Arès t'enchaîne à sa victoire,
Ou que, domptant les flots, ô mère des amours,
Les Cyclades en fleurs écoutent ton histoire:
28 Mon encens à tes pieds s'exhalera toujours.

Garde-moi de l'ennui, de la vieillesse immonde,
Garde-moi, si jamais l'espoir toucha ton cœur,
Ô reine qui maintiens et gouvernes le monde,
32 Avant tout, garde-moi de l'infâme laideur!

Fais que je tombe dans ma force et ma jeunesse,
Que mon dernier soupir ait un puissant écho,
Et, pour qu'un jour mon âme en plein soleil renaisse,
36 Que je meure d'amour comme Ovide et Sapho.

Sorabji misspelled a few words in both manuscripts. In the title and line 1, he wrote "Aphrodité" in place of "Aphrodite". Curiously, in a substantial revision of this poem which Sorabji did not set, Tailhade did use the less common "Aphrodité" in the poem, whose title he changed to "Hymne antique".

I Was Not Sorrowful (Ernest Dowson, poem titled "Spleen", 1905)

I was not sorrowful, I could not weep,
And all my memories were put to sleep.

I watched the river grow more white and strange,
4 All day till evening I watched it change.

All day till evening I watched the rain
Beat wearily upon the window pane.

I was not sorrowful, but only tired
8 Of everything that ever I desired.

Her lips, her eyes, all day became to me
The shadow of a shadow utterly.

All day mine hunger for her heart became
12 Oblivion, until the evening came,

And left me sorrowful, inclined to weep,
With all my memories that could not sleep.

Sorabji used "my" in place of "mine" (line 11).

L'irrémédiable (Charles Baudelaire; in "Spleen et idéal", from *Les fleurs du mal*, 1857)

    I

    Une Idée, une Forme, un Être
    Parti de l'azur et tombé
    Dans un Styx bourbeux et plombé
4   Où nul œil du Ciel ne pénètre;
    Un Ange, imprudent voyageur
    Qu'a tenté l'amour du difforme,
    Au fond d'un cauchemar énorme
8   Se débattant comme un nageur,

    Et luttant, angoisses funèbres!
    Contre un gigantesque remous
    Qui va chantant comme les fous
12 Et pirouettant dans les ténèbres;

    Un malheureux ensorcelé
    Dans ses tâtonnements futiles,
    Pour fuir d'un lieu plein de reptiles,
16 Cherchant la lumière et la clé;

    Un damné descendant sans lampe,
    Au bord d'un gouffre dont l'odeur
    Trahit l'humide profondeur,
20 D'éternels escaliers sans rampe,

    Où veillent des monstres visqueux
    Dont les larges yeux de phosphore
    Font une nuit plus noire encore
24 Et ne rendent visibles qu'eux;

    Un navire pris dans le pôle,
    Comme en un piège de cristal,
    Cherchant par quel détroit fatal
28 Il est tombé dans cette geôle;

    — Emblèmes nets, tableau parfait
    D'une fortune irrémédiable,
    Qui donne à penser que le Diable
32 Fait toujours bien tout ce qu'il fait!

II

    Tête-à-tête sombre et limpide
    Qu'un cœur devenu son miroir!
    Puits de Vérité, clair et noir,
36 Où tremble une étoile livide,

    Un phare ironique, infernal,
    Flambeau des grâces sataniques,
    Soulagement et gloire uniques,
40 — La conscience dans le Mal!

Sorabji misspelled a few words.

La jalousie (Saʿdī; in *Gulistān*. Translation by Franz Toussaint: *Le jardin des roses,* 1923)

Je me rappelle qu'un jeune homme et moi, jadis, étions aussi inséparables l'un de l'autre que deux amandes dans une même coque. Un jour, le destin voulut que je parte. Des années passèrent. À mon retour, cet ami m'adressa de violents reproches:
— Pourquoi ne m'as-tu pas jamais écrit, pourquoi n'as-tu jamais eu pitié de ma tristesse? gémit-il.
Je répondis:
— Je ne voulais pas que ta beauté embrasât le cœur du messager ...

Ô mon ancien ami, sois indulgent! Si tu savais combien j'ai été jaloux, combien j'ai souffert de penser que des étrangers pouvaient te contempler jusqu'à la satiété ... Mais, je me trompais. Cela n'était pas possible, car personne ne se lasse d'un spectacle ineffable!

La lampe (Saʿdī; in *Gulistān*. Translation by Franz Toussaint: *Le jardin des roses,* 1923)

Une certaine nuit, mon ami pénétra dans ma demeure. Je me levai avec une telle promptitude, que ma lampe tomba.
Mon ami m'accabla de reproches, disant:
— Pourquoi, dès que tu m'as aperçu, as-tu éteint la lampe?
Je répondis:
— J'ai cru que le soleil s'était levé ...
J'ai vu en songe celui dont la beauté illuminerait la nuit la plus obscure. À mon réveil, j'ai pensé: «D'où me vient ce bonheur?»

Si un fâcheux se place devant ta lampe, bondis et tue-le! Mais si, au contraire, le nouveau venu a des lèvres de miel et un sourire aussi doux que le sucre, saisis-le par le bras et éteins la lampe.

Sorabji misspelled a few words, probably in misconstruing their exact grammatical sense. For example, he wrote the imperfect "levais" instead of the past definite "levai" (second sentence). He also wrote the perfect "s'est levé" for the pluperfect "s'était levé" (just before the suspension points), although the music contains the notes for the additional syllable in the latter.

Le mauvais jardinier (Iwan Gilkin; in *La nuit*, 1897)

    Dans les jardins d'hiver, des fleuristes bizarres
    Sèment furtivement des végétaux haineux,
    Dont les tiges bientôt grouillent comme les nœuds
4   Des serpents assoupis aux bords boueux des mares.

    Leurs redoutables fleurs, magnifiques et rares,
    Où coulent de très lourds parfums vertigineux,
    Ouvrent avec orgueil leurs vases vénéneux.
8   La mort s'épanouit dans leurs splendeurs barbares.

    Leurs somptueux bouquets détruisent la santé
    Et c'est pour en avoir trop aimé la beauté
11   Qu'on voit dans les palais languir les blanches reines.

    Et moi, je vous ressemble, ô jardiniers pervers!
    Dans les cerveaux hâtifs où j'ai jeté mes graines,
14   Je regarde fleurir les poisons de mes vers.

Sorabji probably completed this song, but so far only one page has been found, setting the poem as far as line 5, word 5.

Pantomime (Paul Verlaine; in *Fêtes galantes*, 1869)

    Pierrot qui n'a rien d'un Clitandre
    Vide un flacon sans plus attendre,
3   Et, pratique, entame un pâté.

    Cassandre, au fond de l'avenue,
    Verse une larme méconnue
6   Sur son neveu déshérité.

    Ce faquin d'Arlequin combine
    L'enlèvement de Colombine
9   Et pirouette quatre fois.

Colombine rêve, surprise
De sentir un cœur dans la brise
12 Et d'entendre en son cœur des voix.

Three words are misspelled in the published score.

The Poplars (Jovan Dučić. Translation by Paul Selver, 1919)

Why are the poplars to-night so aquiver?
So eerily, wildly? What betokens their sound?
The sallow moon has faded long beyond the mound
4 Distant and dark as foreboding; on the river

Gloomily plunged in silence, leaden and grey
Visions have been scattered amid this dead night.
The poplars alone, upreared upon the height,
8 Rustle, rustle eerily and skyward sway.

Alone in the night by the silent water here
I stand, as the last mortal. It is my shadow that
Lies earthward before me. To-night I am in fear
12 Of myself, my own shadow, and I tremble thereat.

Sorabji misspelled one word.

Although this poem was published in 1919 and Sorabji set it in 1915, possibly it was also published earlier in an anthology other than the one given at the end of this appendix. It is equally likely that Sorabji could have seen an unpublished copy, as the translator was at the time a writer for *The New Age*, with which Sorabji was beginning to be associated.

Roses du soir (Pierre Louÿs, poem titled "Roses dans la nuit"; in "Bucoliques en Pamphylie", from *Les chansons de Bilitis*, 1895)

Dès que la nuit monte au ciel, le monde est à nous, et aux dieux. Nous allons des champs à la source, des bois obscurs aux clairières, où nous mènent nos pieds nus.

Les petites étoiles brillent assez pour les petites ombres que nous sommes. Quelquefois, sous les branches basses, nous trouvons des biches endormies.

Mais plus charmant la nuit que toute autre chose, il est un lieu connu de nous seuls et qui nous attire à travers la forêt: un buisson de roses mystérieuses.

Car rien n'est divin sur la terre à l'égal du parfum des roses dans la nuit. Comment se fait-il qu'au temps où j'étais seule je ne m'en sentais pas enivrée?

Sorabji misspelled a few words. He also changed the first "nuit" to "lune" and created his own title, perhaps forgetting Louÿs's title, even though it appears in the text itself.

Symphony [No. 3], *Jāmī*

Although not the text of a song (in the sense of a small-scale work for voice and keyboard instrument), the words sung by the baritone solo in the *Jāmī* Symphony are given here. They are from the poem *Yūsuf and Zuleykhā* by the Persian poet Jāmī, in the translation by Edward G. Browne.

      In solitude, where Being signless dwelt,
      And all the Universe still dormant lay
      Concealed in selflessness, One Being was
      Exempt from "I-" or "Thou-"ness, and apart
5   From all duality; Beauty Supreme,
      Unmanifest, except unto Itself
      By Its own light, yet fraught with power to charm
      The souls of all; concealed in the Unseen,
      An essence pure, unstained by aught of ill.
10 No mirror to reflect Its loveliness,
      Nor comb to touch Its locks; the morning breeze
      Ne'er stirred Its tresses; no collyrium
      Lent lustre to Its eyes; no rosy cheeks
      O'ershadowed by dark curls like hyacinth,
15 Nor peach-like down were there; no dusky mole
      Adorned Its face; no eye had yet beheld
      Its image. To Itself It sang of love
      In wordless measures. By Itself It cast
      The die of love.
                       But Beauty cannot brook
20 Concealment and the veil, nor patient rest
      Unseen and unadmired: 'twill burst all bonds,
      And from Its prison-casement to the world
      Reveal Itself. See where the tulip grows
      In upland meadows, how in balmy spring
25 It decks itself; and how amidst its thorns
      The wild rose rends its garment, and reveals
      Its loveliness. Thou, too, when some rare thought,
      Or beauteous image, or deep mystery
      Flashes across thy soul, canst not endure
30 To let it pass, but hold'st it, that perchance

          In speech or writing thou may'st send it forth
          To charm the world.
                              Wherever Beauty dwells
          Such is its nature, and its heritage
          From Everlasting Beauty, which emerged
     35   From realms of purity to shine upon
          The worlds, and all the souls which dwell therein.
          One gleam fell from It on the Universe,
          And on the angels, and this single ray
          Dazzled the angels, till their senses whirled
     40   Like the revolving sky. In divers forms
          Each mirror showed It forth, and everywhere
          Its praise was chanted in new harmonies.
          [The Cherubim, enraptured, sought for songs
          Of praise. The spirits who explore the depths
     45   Of boundless seas, wherein the heavens swim
          Like some small boat, cried with one mighty voice,
          "Praise to the Lord of all the universe!"]

          Each speck of matter did He constitute
          A mirror, causing each one to reflect
     50   The beauty of His visage. From the rose
          Flashed forth His beauty, and the nightingale
          Beholding it, loved madly. From that Light
          [The candle drew] the lustre which beguiles
          The moth to immolation. On the sun
     55   His Beauty shone, and straightway from the wave
          The lotus reared its head. Each shining lock
          Of Leylā's hair attracted Majnūn's heart
          Because some ray divine reflected shone
          In her fair face. 'Twas He to Shīrīn's lips
     60   Who lent that sweetness which had power to steal
          The heart from Parvīz, and from Ferhād life.

          His Beauty everywhere doth show itself,
          And through the forms of earthly beauties shines
          Obscured as through a veil. He did reveal
     65   His face through Joseph's coat, and so destroyed
          Zuleykhā's peace. Where'er thou seest a veil,
          Beneath that veil He hides. Whatever heart
          Doth yield to love, He charms it. In His love
          The heart hath life. Longing for Him, the soul
     70   Hath victory. That heart which seems to love
          The fair ones of this world, loves Him alone.

          Beware! say not, "He is All-Beautiful,
          And we His lovers." Thou art but the glass,
          And He the Face confronting it, which casts
     75   Its image on the mirror. He alone

Is manifest, and thou in truth art hid.
Pure Love, like Beauty, coming but from Him,
Reveals itself in thee. If steadfastly
Thou canst regard, thou wilt at length perceive
80 He is the mirror also — He alike
The Treasure and the Casket. "I" and "Thou"
Have here no place, and are but phantasies
Vain and unreal. Silence! for this tale
Is endless, and no eloquence hath power
85 To speak of Him. 'Tis best for us to love,
And suffer silently, being as naught.

Sorabji omitted lines 43–47, probably because he used an edition of Browne's translation (from his book *A Year amongst the Persians*) which did not contain them. The sentence immediately preceding them is repeated in Sorabji's setting. The bracketed words in line 53 Sorabji also omitted, probably in error.

Bibliography (for the poems printed in this appendix)

Baudelaire, Charles: *Œuvres complètes* (vol. 1), edited by Claude Pichois. Paris: Gallimard, 1975.

Browne, Edward G.: "Ṣúfíism". In *Religious Systems of the World*, 7th edition. London: Swan Sonnenschein, 1904. (For the *Jāmī* Symphony.)

Buonarroti, Michelangelo: *Rime,* edited by Enzo Noè Girardi. Bari: Giuseppe Laterza e figli, 1960. See also under Frey, below.

Dowson, Ernest: *The Poems of Ernest Dowson.* London: John Lane, 1905.

Frey, Carl (ed.): *Die Dichtungen des Michelagniolo Buonarroti herausgegeben und mit kritischem Apparate versehen.* Berlin: G. Grote'sche Verlagsbuchhandlung, 1897. See also under Buonarroti, above.

Gilkin, Iwan: *La nuit.* Paris: Librairie Fischbacher, [1897].

Ibrāhīm Mīrzā, Shamsu'd-Dīn: source not located.

Louÿs, Pierre: *Œuvres complètes* (vol. 2: *Les chansons de Bilitis*). Paris: Éditions Montaigne, 1929.

Mallarmé, Stéphane: *Œuvres complètes* (vol. 1: *Poésies*), edited by Carl Paul Barbier and Charles Gordon Millan. Paris: Flammarion, 1983.

Régnier, Henri de: *Les médailles d'argile.* Paris: Société du Mercure de France, 1900.

Rollinat, Maurice: *Les névroses.* Paris: Bibliothèque Charpentier, 1883.

Sa'dī: *Le jardin des roses,* translated by Franz Toussaint. Paris: Stock, 1923.

Selver, Paul: *Anthology of Modern Slavonic Literature in Prose and Verse.* London: Kegan Paul, Trench, and Trubner, 1919. (For the Dučić.)

Tailhade, Laurent: *Le jardin des rêves.* Paris: Alphonse Lemerre, 1880.

Verlaine, Paul: *Œuvres poétiques,* edited by Jacques Robichez. Paris: Garnier Frères, 1969.

Appendix 2

The Recordings of Sorabji's Music

Paul Rapoport

Sorabji's Performances on Private Tape Recordings

Tapes Made by Erik Chisholm

Erik Chisholm made these presumably monophonic tapes at 3¾ i.p.s. on a Grundig tape recorder at the home of Neil Solomon in London. There were two reels (in apparently poor sound) whose current existence is uncertain; they have apparently not been seen since Chisholm's death in 1965. According to letters from Chisholm to Norman Gentieu of 23 February 1962 and various dates in March 1962, the two sessions took place as follows:

1.   22 February 1962

Passeggiata veneziana
A short extemporization
Sorabji reading his artistic creed
Sorabji reading his chapter "Yoga and the Composer" from *Mi contra fa*
Third Symphony for Piano Solo (from beginning, ca. 45 mins.)

2.   27 February 1962

Third Symphony for Piano Solo (remainder)

Chisholm listed one of the readings as "the chapter Yoga and the Musician from his book <u>Around Music</u>", which is incorrect. Presumably Sorabji read excerpts from the chapter indicated above. The other reading (of the artistic creed) may have been of the statement from October 1959 beginning "I am not a 'modern' composer".[1]

Tapes Made by Frank Holliday

The following lists the sessions which Frank Holliday arranged on six trips to Sorabji's house in Dorset during which he recorded him playing his own music. All the recordings were made on a monophonic Ferrograph tape recorder, each time after elaborate experimentation with microphone placement, volume settings, and so on. The quality of performance varies considerably; more specifically, the results are usually unrehearsed, approximate readings rather than performances of the music as notated.

On one occasion the microphone was not working properly, and there were other problems from time to time which Holliday described in his detailed notes after each of the first five sessions. Nonetheless, the sound quality from most of the sessions is good.

The works and their parts are listed in the order in which they were recorded. The time of day is given in Holliday's notes but is not repeated here.

1. 5 May 1962

Concerto da suonare da me solo e senza orchestra, per divertirsi
Gulistān — Nocturne for Piano

6 May 1962

St. Bertrand de Comminges: "He was laughing in the tower"
"Quære reliqua hujus materiei inter secretiora"
Sorabji reading from his essay "Some Sacro-Sanct Modern Superstitions" (ca. 6 mins.)[2]
Sorabji reading about the Sicilian temperament from Francis Guercio's book *Sicily, the Garden of the Mediterranean: The Country and its People* (ca. 2 mins.)

---

[1]{See pp. xv and 345 for the essential part of the rest of the statement; p. 345 also gives the reference to all of it as printed seven years later.}
[2]{See pp. 327–30 for the entire text.}

2.   5 October 1962

Second Symphony for Piano, 1st movement (from beginning, ca. 64 mins.)
Second Symphony for Piano, 1st movement (remainder)
Second Symphony for Piano, 2nd movement
Second Symphony for Piano, 3rd movement

3.   9 September 1963

Second Symphony for Piano, 4th movement

10 September 1963

Second Symphony for Piano, 5th movement
Passeggiata veneziana

4.   25 September 1964

Fourth Symphony for Piano Alone, 1st movement (from beginning, ca. 40 mins.)
Fourth Symphony for Piano Alone, 1st movement (remainder)
Fourth Symphony for Piano Alone, 2nd movement (Chorale Prelude)
Fourth Symphony for Piano Alone, 2nd movement (Interlude, Ostinato, first eleven variations)

26 September 1964

Fourth Symphony for Piano Alone, 2nd movement (remainder)
Fourth Symphony for Piano Alone, 3rd movement

5.   26 March 1965

Gulistān — Nocturne for Piano
Fourth Symphony for Piano Alone, 2nd movement (Chorale Prelude)
Nocturne, *Jāmī*
Le jardin parfumé

6.   18 April 1968

Études transcendantes Nos. 13, 18, 20, 22, 26, 28, 40, 44, 66, 81, 69, 71

Others' Performances on Professional Recordings

This is a list of long-playing records, cassettes, and compact discs — in chronological order of issue (in the case of multiple formats, the issue of the first one). All formats are stereophonic and standard in size and speed, except for the six- and eight-inch records noted. Where there are multiple formats, only the month of issue of the first format is stated.

Michael Habermann

Opus clavicembalisticum: Introito, Preludio corale
Two Piano Pieces
Fantaisie espagnole
Fragment Written for Harold Rutland (third version)
Pastiche on the "Habanera" from Bizet's *Carmen*

Musical Heritage Society	MHS 4271	LP (issued in November 1980 in the USA)
	MHC 6271	cassette
Musicmasters	MM 20015	LP
	MM 60015	CD

Geoffrey Douglas Madge

Opus clavicembalisticum: Introito, Preludio corale

Side B of Radio Nederland Transcription Service LP 198051. Issued towards the end of 1980 in The Netherlands for broadcasting only (around the world). This is a recording of the performance given on 11 June 1980 in The Hague.

Michael Habermann

Nocturne, *Jāmī*
Pastiche on the "Hindu Merchant's Song" from Rimskiy-Korsakov's *Sadko*
Le jardin parfumé — Poem for Piano Solo
Pastiche on the Valse, Op. 64, No. 1 (the *Minute Waltz*) by Chopin

Musical Heritage Society	MHS 4811	LP (issued in November 1982 in the USA)
	MHC 6811	cassette
Musicmasters	MM 20019	LP
	MMD 60019	CD

Michael Habermann

Reissue of: *Opus clavicembalisticum: Introito; Le jardin parfumé* — Poem for Piano Solo (excerpt)

Side B of an eight-inch LP accompanying *The Piano Quarterly,* issue no. 122, vol. 31 (Summer 1983). Issued in July 1983 in the USA. The first item was taken from Michael Habermann's first recording and the second item from his second recording (see above).

Geoffrey Douglas Madge

Opus clavicembalisticum

Royal Conservatory Series RCS 4–800. Four LPs: record nos. 801–804. Issued in September 1983 in the Netherlands. Out of print.

Michael Habermann

Opus clavicembalisticum: Introito, Preludio corale (excerpt only of the latter)

Side A of a six-inch LP (*Soundpage* No. 19) accompanying *Keyboard,* issue no. 120, vol. 12, no. 4 (April 1986). Issued in March 1986 in the USA. Both items were taken from the performance given on 6 October 1978 in Midland, Michigan.

Michael Habermann

Prelude, Interlude, and Fugue for Piano
Valse-fantaisie
St. Bertrand de Comminges: "He was laughing in the tower"

Musical Heritage Society	MHS 7530	LP (issued in June 1987 in the USA)
	MHC 9530	cassette
Musicmasters	MM 20118	LP
	MM 40118	cassette
	MMD 60118	CD

Kevin Bowyer

Symphony No. 1 for Organ

Continuum CCD 1001/2. Two CDs: disc nos. 1001 and 1002. Issued in November 1988 in England.

Michael Habermann

Reissue of: *Le jardin parfumé* — Poem for Piano Solo; Prelude, Interlude, and Fugue; Nocturne, *Jāmī;* and the Pastiches on Rimskiy-Korsakov and Chopin

ASV	ZC AMM159	cassette
	CD AMM159	CD

Both were issued in December 1988 in England. The performances are taken from the second and third of Michael Habermann's Musicmasters recordings.

John Ogdon

Opus clavicembalisticum

Altarus AIR–CD–9075. Four CDs: disc nos. 9075(1) to 9075(4). Issued in May 1989 in England.

Marc-André Hamelin

Sonata No. 1 for Piano

Altarus AIR–CD–9050. CD "single". Issued in July 1990 in England.

There are plans for further recordings, by Yonty Solomon, Ronald Stevenson, Kevin Bowyer, and Marc-André Hamelin.

Appendix 3

The Sorabji Music Archive

Alistair Hinton

Worldwide interest in the works of Kaikhosru Shapurji Sorabji (1892–1988) has steadily developed since the mid-1970s. At that time, two myths which had long clung about him — his music's alleged unplayability and his socalled "ban" on public presentations of it — were finally laid to rest. His actual wish (which admittedly led to a "silence" of almost 40 years) was that none of his works be given publicly *without his express consent.* Performances, broadcasts, and commercial recordings have since shown that, given suitable circumstances, Sorabji was willing to permit, even encourage his music to be heard, and that musicians now exist who are capable of doing justice to his intentions.

Cognoscenti of his principal keyboard works would never imagine these compendia of fearsome difficulties becoming "standard" repertory for future piano and organ virtuosi. It is already clear, however, that despite the unique challenges which this music hurls at performers, it claims a powerful and immediate intellectual and emotional grip on listeners.

International artists of distinction who have performed, broadcast, or recorded Sorabji's music include pianists Yonty Solomon, John Ogdon, Marc-André Hamelin, Geoffrey Douglas Madge, Michael Habermann, Ronald Stevenson, Valerie Tryon, and Donna Amato; sopranos Jo Ann Pickens and Jane Manning; and organist Kevin Bowyer.

As well as almost seven decades of music composition, Sorabji, a prolific critic and essayist of great wit, contributed many brilliant and frequently controversial articles, reviews, and "letters to the editor" to several English journals. He published two volumes of collected essays, *Around Music* (1932) and *Mi contra fa* (1947), the latter reissued in 1986 by Da Capo Press.[1] The present volume, appearing at the time of the Sorabji centenary, is the first full-length published study about the composer and his music.

Sorabji's vast corpus of work remained mostly inaccessible to the public for many years. The foundation of the Sorabji Music Archive overcame this. Established in 1988, it houses many of Sorabji's original manuscripts and a substantial collection of literature by and about him, including correspondence; articles; essays; letters to the editor; reviews of books, music, concerts, and recordings; a performance/broadcast history and discography; and many other items of interest.

The Archive now issues copies of these remarkable scores and writings to the public worldwide and welcomes visits by appointment from performers and scholars. Several distinguished musicians have prepared definitive editions (some in manuscript, some printed) of Sorabji's works; more are in progress. It is hoped that the premiere publication of the *Fantasiettina* by Bardic Edition (1987) will encourage other publishers to print new editions of Sorabji's music.

All rights in all the musical and literary works of Sorabji are vested exclusively within the Archive.

An almost single-handed operation, the Archive is indebted to Terry Hinton, Grace Keaton, and Chris Rice for valuable voluntary assistance from time to time. Extensive and indispensable help from George Ross in preparing and indexing literature deserves special mention.

The Sorabji Music Archive continually updates all the information it provides and welcomes all enquiries concerning Kaikhosru Sorabji.

The Sorabji Music Archive
Easton Dene
Bailbrook Lane
Bath
Avon BA1 7AA
England

---

[1] {*Around Music* was reissued in 1979 by Hyperion Press in an edition which he did not authorize and did not like.}

Bibliography

al-Nafzāwī ('Umar ibn Muḥammad, al-Nafzāwī): *The Perfumed Garden*, translated by Richard F. Burton, introduced by Alan Hull Walton. London: Neville Spearman, 1963.
Allen, Warren Dwight: *Philosophies of Music History*. New York: American Book Company, 1939.
Anon.: *The Book of the Thousand Nights and a Night [Arabian Nights]*, translated by Richard Francis Burton (16 vols.). Benares: privately printed, 1885 (vols. 1–10), 1886–88 (vols. 11–16).
Anon.: *The Book of the Thousand Nights and One Night [Arabian Nights]*, translated by John Payne (13 vols.). London: privately printed, 1882–89.
Anon.: *Le livre des mille nuits et une nuit*, translated by J[oseph] C[harles] Mardrus (16 vols.). Paris: Éditions de la revue blanche (vols. 1–11), E. Fasquelle (vols. 12–16), 1900–04.
Anon.: *La reine de Saba*, translated by J[oseph] C[harles] Mardrus. Paris: Charpentier et Fasquelle, 1918.
Ashworth, Edward Clarke: "Music — *Opus clavicembalisticum*", in *The New English Weekly*, vol. 9 (30 April 1936), p. 55.
'Aṭṭār (Farīdu'd-Dīn 'Aṭṭār): *The Conference of the Birds*, translated by Afkham Darbandi and Dick Davis. Harmondsworth: Penguin Books, 1984.
Avalon, Arthur, ed.: *The Serpent Power*, 7th edition. Madras: Ganesh, 1964. Reprinted, New York: Dover, 1974, excluding the Sanskrit text and the colour in the plates.
———, ed.: *Tantra of the Great Liberation*. London: Luzac, 1913. Reprinted, New York: Dover Publications, 1972.
Belloc, Hilaire: *The Servile State*, 3rd edition. London: Constable, 1927.
Benda, Julien: *La trahison des clercs*. Paris: B. Grasset, 1927.
———: *The Treason of the Intellectuals*, translated by Richard Aldington. New York: W. Morrow, 1928.
Benson, Marjorie Maulsby: *The "Opus clavicembalisticum" by Kaikhosru Shapurgi [recte Shapurji] Sorabji: An Analysis, with References to its Model, the "Fantasia contrappuntistica" by Ferruccio Busoni* (DMA, American Conservatory of Music, 1987). Ann Arbor: University Microfilms International, 1987 (item no. 87–15706).
Bhimani, Nazlin: *Kaikhosru Sorabji's Writings on British Music in "The New Age" (1924–34)* (MA, University of British Columbia, 1985).
Blom, Eric: *Everyman's Dictionary of Music*. London: J. M. Dent, 1946.

Branson, David: "Kaikhosru Sorabji", in *The British Musician and Musical News*, vol. 5, no. 11 (November 1929), pp. 311–12.

Browne, Arthur G.: "The Music of Kaikhosru Sorabji", in *Music and Letters*, vol. 11 (January 1930), pp. 6–16.

Browne, Edward G.: *A Literary History of Persia* (4 vols.). Cambridge, England: Cambridge University Press, 1964.

———: "Ṣúfíism", in *Religious Systems of the World*, 7th edition, pp. 314–32. London: Swan Sonnenschein, 1904.

———: *A Year amongst the Persians*, 3rd edition. London: Adam and Charles Black, 1959.

Buonarroti, Michelangelo: *Rime*, edited by Enzo Noè Girardi. Bari: Giuseppe Laterza, 1960.

Busoni, Ferruccio: *Briefe an seine Frau*, edited by Friedrich Schnapp. Erlenbach-Zürich: Rotapfel, 1935.

———: *Letters to his Wife*, translated by Rosamond Ley. London: Edward Arnold, 1938.

———: *Selected Letters*, translated and edited by Antony Beaumont. New York: Columbia University Press, 1987.

Butler, Bill: *The Definitive Tarot*. London: Century, 1975.

Chisholm, Erik: "Kaikhosru Shapurji Sorabji". London: Oxford University Press, ca. 1938. Reprinted privately: n.pl., [ca. 1964].

——— and Holliday, Frank: "The Composer Sorabji" (transcript of a recorded talk). Printed privately: n.pl., [1970].

Cobbett, William: *A History of the Protestant Reformation in England and Ireland*. London: Burns Oates and Washbourne, 1925.

Coomaraswamy, Ananda K.: *The Dance of Śiva*. New York: The Sunwise Turn, 1924.

Copley, Ian Alfred: *The Music of Peter Warlock: A Critical Survey*. London: Dennis Dobson, 1979.

Dahlhaus, Carl: *Foundations of Music History*, translated by J. Bradford Robinson. Cambridge, England: Cambridge University Press, 1983.

Demuth, Norman: *Musical Trends in the 20th Century*. London: Rockliff, 1952.

Derus, Kenneth: "Another Alkan". A paper read to the members of the Alkan Society of Great Britain on 21 November 1977 in London. Unpublished.

———: Program notes for the performance of *Opus clavicembalisticum* by Geoffrey Douglas Madge on 24 April 1983 in Mandel Hall, Chicago. Chicago: Contemporary Concerts, 1983.

Douglas, Norman: *Alone*. London: Chapman and Hall, 1921.

———: *How about Europe?* London: Chatto and Windus, 1930.

———: *South Wind*. New York: Modern Library, 1925.

Dummett, Michael: *The Game of Tarot: From Ferrara to Salt Lake City* (London: Duckworth, 1980).

Duncan-Rubbra, Edmund: "Sorabji's Enigma", in *The Monthly Musical Record*, vol. 62 (September 1932), p. 148.

Eliot, T[homas] S[tearns]: "Tradition and the Individual Talent", in his *The Sacred Wood*, pp. 42–53. London: Methuen, 1920.

Ellis, Havelock: *Studies in the Psychology of Sex* (2 vols.). New York: Random House, ca. 1936.

Foreman, Lewis: *Bax: A Composer and his Times*, 2nd edition. London: Scolar Press, 1988.

Garvelmann, Donald M., ed.: *The Composer Sorabji (Postscript)*. Printed privately: [New York, 1971].

————: "Kaikhosru Shapurji Sorabji", in *Journal of the American Liszt Society*, vol. 4 (December 1978), pp. 18–22.

————: "Sorabji, Kaikhosru Shapurji", in *The New Grove Dictionary of Music and Musicians*, edited by Stanley Sadie, vol. 17, pp. 534–35. London: Macmillan, 1980.

————: *Thirteen Transcriptions for Piano Solo of Chopin's Waltz in D Flat, Op. 64, No. 1 (The Minute Waltz)*. Bronx, New York: Music Treasure Publications, 1969.

————: Transcript of the WNCN radio broadcast on Sorabji of 13 December 1970. Printed privately: [New York], 1970.

Gervais, Terence White: "Sorabji, Kaikhosru Shapurji", in *Grove's Dictionary of Music and Musicians*, 5th edition, edited by Eric Blom, vol. 7, pp. 970–71. London: Macmillan, 1954.

Gettings, Fred: *Encyclopedia of the Occult*. London: Rider, 1986.

Goddard, Scott: Review of *Around Music*, by Kaikhosru Sorabji, in *Music and Letters*, vol. 14, no. 3 (July 1933), p. 288.

Grant, Kenneth: *The Magical Revival*. London: Frederick Muller, 1972.

Gray, Cecil: *Musical Chairs: or, Between Two Stools*. London: Home and Van Thal, 1948.

————: *Peter Warlock: A Memoir of Philip Heseltine*. London: Jonathan Cape, 1934.

————: "Sorabji, Kaikhosru", in *Cobbett's Cyclopedic Survey of Chamber Music*, edited by Walter Cobbett, vol. 2, pp. 436–37. London: Oxford University Press, 1930.

————: *A Survey of Contemporary Music*. London: Oxford University Press, 1922.

Gray-Fisk, Clinton: "Kaikhosru Shapurji Sorabji", in *The Musical Times*, vol. 101 (April 1960), pp. 230–32. Reprinted privately: n.pl., 1960 and later.

Grew, Sydney: "Kaikhosru Sorabji — Le jardin parfumé: Poem for Piano", in *The British Musician*, vol. 4 (1928), pp. 85–86.

Guénon, René: *The Reign of Quantity and the Signs of the Times*, translated by Lord Northbourne. London: Luzac, 1953.

Guercio, Francis M.: *Sicily, the Garden of the Mediterranean: The Country and its People*, 2nd edition. London: Faber and Faber, 1954.

Gula, Robert J.: "Kaikhosru Shapurji Sorabji (1892–   ): The Published Piano Works", in *Journal of the American Liszt Society*, vol. 12 (December 1982), pp. 48–49.

Habermann, Michael: "Kaikhosru Shapurji Sorabji", in *The Piano Quarterly*, issue no. 122, vol. 31 (Summer 1983), pp. 36–37.

————: "Sorabji", in *Keyboard*, issue no. 120, vol. 12, no. 4 (April 1986), pp. 56–62.

―――――: *A Style Analysis of the Nocturnes for Solo Piano by Kaikhosru Shapurji Sorabji with Special Emphasis on "Le jardin parfumé"* (DMA, Peabody Institute of the Johns Hopkins University, 1985). Ann Arbor: University Microfilms International, 1985 (item no. 85–06576).

Hall, Radclyffe: *The Well of Loneliness.* London: Jonathan Cape, 1928.

Haynes, Edmund Sidney Pollock: *The Decline of Liberty in England.* London: G. Richards, 1916.

Heseltine, Philip: "Sorabji, Kaikhosru", in *A Dictionary of Modern Music and Musicians*, edited by A[rthur] Eaglefield-Hull, p. 469. London: J. M. Dent, 1924.

Hewart, Gordon (Lord Hewart of Bury): *The New Despotism.* London: E. Benn, 1929.

Hinton, Alistair: "Kaikhosru Sorabji — An Appreciation", in program notes for the concert by Yonty Solomon on 7 December 1976 in Wigmore Hall, London, pp. 11–13. London: Park Lane Group, 1976.

―――――: Letter to the Editor, in *Notes*, vol. 46, no. 4 (June 1990), pp. 1090–91.

Holliday, Frank: "A Contribution", in program notes for the concert by Yonty Solomon on 7 December 1976 in Wigmore Hall, London, p. 10. London: Park Lane Group, 1976.

Howes, Frank: *The English Musical Renaissance.* London: Secker and Warburg, 1966.

Huvé, Cyril and Geoffrey Douglas Madge: "L'éloge de la difficulté", in *Le monde de la musique*, no. 119 (February 1989), pp. 116–18.

James, M[ontague] R[hodes]: *Ghost-Stories of an Antiquary.* Harmondsworth: Penguin, 1937.

Lambert, Constant: *Music Ho! A Study of Music in Decline.* London: Faber and Faber, 1934.

Levy, Oscar: *The Idiocy of Idealism.* London: William Hidge, 1940.

Ludovici, Anthony: *Man: An Indictment.* London: Constable, 1927.

―――――: *Woman: A Vindication.* London: Constable, 1923.

MacDiarmid, Hugh: *The Company I've Kept.* London: Hutchinson, 1966.

Machen, Arthur: *The House of Souls.* London: E. G. Richards, 1906.

Mackerness, E[ric] D[avid]: *A Social History of English Music.* London: Routledge and Kegan Paul, 1964.

Mairet, Philip: *A. R. Orage: A Memoir.* New Hyde Park, New York: University Books, 1966.

Merriam, Alan P.: *The Anthropology of Music.* [Evanston]: Northwestern University Press, 1964.

Meyer, Leonard: *Music, the Arts, and Ideas.* Chicago: University of Chicago Press, 1967.

Nafzāwī: see al-Nafzāwī.

Naoroji, Dadabhai: "The Parsi Religion", in *Religious Systems of the World*, 7th edition, pp. 184–93. London: Swan Sonnenschein, 1904.

Payne, John: *The Poetical Works of John Payne* (2 vols.). London: privately printed, 1902. Reprinted, New York: AMS Press, 1970.

Peterkin, Norman: "A Note on Kaikhosru Sorabji", in program notes for the concert by Yonty Solomon on 7 December 1976 in Wigmore Hall, London, pp. 8–9. London: Park Lane Group, 1976.

Pirie, Peter: "The Search for Sorabji", in *Music and Musicians*, vol. 28, no. 3 (November 1979), pp. 16–20.

Portsmouth, Earl of: *Alternative to Death*. London: Faber and Faber, 1943.

Posner, Bruce: Response to the Letter to the Editor from Alistair Hinton printed in *Notes*, vol. 46, no. 4 (June 1990), in *Notes*, vol. 46, no. 4 (June 1990), pp. 1091–92.

───────: Review of *Fantasiettina [...]*, by Kaikhosru Sorabji, in *Notes*, vol. 46, no. 2 (December 1989), pp. 511–12.

───────: *Sorabji* (BSc, Fordham University, 1975). Unpublished.

Rapoport, Paul: *Opus est: Six Composers from Northern Europe*. London: Kahn and Averill, 1978. New York: Taplinger, 1979.

───────: "Sorabji returns?", in *The Musical Times*, vol. 117 (December 1976), p. 995.

Roberge, Marc-André: "The Busoni Network and the Art of Creative Transcription", in *Canadian University Music Review*, vol. 11, no. 1 (1991), pp. 68–88.

───────: "Kaikhosru Shapurji Sorabji (1892–1988)", in *Sonances*, vol. 8, no. 2 (Winter 1989), pp. 30–37.

───────: "Kaikhosru Shapurji Sorabji, compositeur *sui generis*", in *Sonances*, vol. 2, no. 3 (April 1983), pp. 17–21.

Rubbra, Edmund: see Duncan-Rubbra, Edmund.

Sanderson, William: *That which was Lost*. London: Constable, 1930.

Scholes, Percy, ed.: "Sorabji, Kaikhosru", in his *The Oxford Companion to Music*, 1st edition, pp. 885–86. London: Oxford University Press, 1938.

Scholes, Percy, ed.: "Sorabji, Kaikhosru", in his *The Oxford Companion to Music*, 8th edition, pp. 557–58. London: Oxford University Press, 1952.

Scholes, Percy, ed.: "Sorabji, Kaikhosru Shauprji", in his *The Oxford Companion to Music*, 9th edition, pp. 975–76. London: Oxford University Press, 1955.

Selver, Paul: *Orage and The New Age Circle: Reminiscences and Reflections*. London: George Allen and Unwin, 1959.

Sitwell, Sacheverell: "Kaikhosru Sorabji", in program notes for the concert by Yonty Solomon on 7 December 1976 in Wigmore Hall, London, p. 7. London: Park Lane Group, 1976.

Slonimsky, Nicolas, ed.: *Baker's Biographical Dictionary of Musicians*, 6th edition. New York: Schirmer, 1978.

───────, ed.: *Baker's Biographical Dictionary of Musicians*, 7th edition. New York: Schirmer, 1984.

───────, ed.: *Baker's Biographical Dictionary of Musicians*, 8th edition. New York: Schirmer, 1992.

───────: *Music Since 1900*, 4th edition. New York: Charles Scribner's Sons, 1971.

Sorabji, Kaikhosru Shapurji: *[Animadversions [...]]*. Essay written about his works, published and unpublished, on the occasion of the microfilming of some of his manuscripts. Lacking the first three pages. Unpublished, [1953].

───────: *Around Music*. London: Unicorn Press, 1932. Reprinted without the errata sheet, Westport, Connecticut: Hyperion Press, 1979.

———: *Collected Writings from Five Serial Publications*. Microfilm compiled by Paul Rapoport and Kenneth Derus. Unpublished, 1977.

———: "The Greatness of Medtner", in *Nicolas Medtner*, edited by Richard Holt, pp. 122–32. London: Dennis Dobson, 1954.

———: *Mi contra fa: The Immoralisings of a Machiavellian Musician*. London: Porcupine Press, 1947. Reprinted with an introduction by Donald Garvelmann, New York: Da Capo Press, 1986.

———: "Modern Piano Technique", in *The Sackbut*, vol. 1, no. 3 (July 1920), pp. 116–23.

———: "Oriental Influences in Contemporary Music", in *The Chesterian*, new series, no. 3 (December 1919), pp. 83–86.

———: "Sexual Inversion", in *The Medical Times* (London), vol. 49 (October 1921), pp. 148–49.

———: "The Songs of Francis George Scott", in *Scottish Art and Letters*, vol. 1 (1944), pp. 22–23.

———: "The Validity of the Aristocratic Principle", in *Art and Thought*, edited by K. Bharatha Iyer, pp. 214–18. London: Luzac, 1947.

Spengler, Oswald: *The Decline of the West*, translated by Charles Francis Atkinson. London: G. Allen, 1922.

Steane, John: "English Opera Criticism in the Interwar Years: Sorabji of *The New Age*", in *Opera*, vol. 36 (June 1985), pp. 623–31.

Stevenson, Ronald: "*Opus clavicembalisticum* — A Critical Analysis", in the booklet with the recording of *Opus clavicembalisticum* by John Ogdon, pp. 28–49. Sevenoaks: Altarus (AIR–CD–9075), 1989.

Storr, Anthony: *Solitude: A Return to the Self*. New York: The Free Press, 1988.

Tomlinson, Fred: *Warlock and Van Dieren*. London: Thames Publishing, 1978.

Treitler, Leo: *Music and the Historical Imagination*. Cambridge, Massachusetts: Harvard University Press, 1989.

Tripp, C. A.: *The Homosexual Matrix*, 2nd edition. New York: New American Library, 1987.

Van Dieren, Bernard: *Down among the Dead Men*. London: Oxford University Press, 1935.

Whistler, James McNeill: *The Gentle Art of Making Enemies, as Pleasingly Exemplified in Many Instances, wherein the Serious Ones of This Earth, Carefully Exasperated, Have Been Prettily Spurred onto Unseemliness and Indiscretion, while Overcome by an Undue Sense of Right*. London: Heinemann, 1936.

Whittall, Arnold: "Sorabjiana", in *The Musical Times*, vol. 107 (March 1966), pp. 216–17.

Williams, Christopher à Becket: "The Music of Kaikhosru Sorabji", in *The Sackbut*, vol. 4, no. 11 (June 1924), pp. 315–19.

Wilson, Colin: *The Occult*. St. Albans: Granada, 1979.

Zaehner, Robert Charles: *The Teachings of the Magi*. London: George Allen and Unwin, 1956.

Index of Sorabji's Compositions

Some of the titles given here are abbreviated or standardized; to represent Sorabji's titles completely *and* consistently is impossible. For fuller titles and variants, see the Detailed Catalog in Chapter 5.

Bold-face page numbers indicate the complete entry for each work in the Detailed Catalog. Italics indicate music examples, bold italics extended references.

2 Piano Pieces: 40 102 104 **120** 175 433 437–440 442 444 450 483
　In the Hothouse: 40–41 **120** 360 369 433–434 436–442 444 448–449
　Toccata No. 0: 40 102 **120** 433 439
2 Sutras sul nome dell'amico Alexis: **166–167** 176
3 Fêtes galantes de Verlaine: 104 **116–117** 178 432 440 445 449 461–462 468
3 Pastiches: 98 **123–124** 178 358 432–433
　No. 1, on the "Minute Waltz" (Chopin): 29 41 104 **123** 358 432 436 439–440 442 444 483 485
　No. 2, on the "Habanera" from "Carmen" (Bizet): 41 52 **123** 358 432 436–442 448 483
　No. 3, on the "Hindu Merchant's Song" from "Sadko" (Rimskiy-Korsakov): 52 **123–124** 358 432 444 483 485
3 Poèmes (1941): 26 **148–149** 178 463 468–469
3 Poèmes du "Gulistān" de Sa'dī: 99 **130–131** 178 190 303 461 469 474

3 Poèmes pour chant et piano (1918, 1919): 104 **118** 178 429 433 440 448–451 467 475
4 Frammenti aforistici: **170** 176 356 432 451
5 Sonetti di Michelagniolo Buonarroti: 44 **125–126** 178 428 432 441 443 448 450 460 464
20 Frammenti aforistici: **164–165** 167 176 356
100 Études transcendantes: see *Études transcendantes*
104 Frammenti aforistici: 165 **167** 176 356–357

Agonie, Le: **155–156** 176
Apparition, Op. 4, No. 3: **112** 178 462
Arabesque: **119–120** 178 463

Bell-Chorale for Saint Luke's Carillon: see *Suggested Bell-Chorale*
Benedizione di San Francesco d'Assisi: 37 **167–168** 178 463
Black Mass: **122–123** 177 247–248

Carmen (Bizet): see *3 Pastiches*
Cent études transcendantes: see *Études transcendantes*

Cento quattro frammenti aforistici: see *104 Frammenti aforistici*
Chaleur, Op. 5: **112–113** 177 180
Chromatic Fantasy (J. S. Bach): see *Transcription in the Light of Harpsichord Technique*
Chrysilla, Op. 1, No. 1: **109–110** 178 464
Cinque sonetti: see *5 Sonetti*
Concertino non grosso: 30 **166** 177
Concerto da suonare da me solo e senza orchestra, per divertirsi: 80 83 97 107 **152–153** 176 360 432 435 439–440 481
Concerto No. 1, Op. 3 (1915–16; piano, orchestra): **111** 177 220–221 223–225 233–234
Concerto No. 2, Op. 10 (1916–17; piano, orchestra): xi 94 **114–115** 175 177 181 220 226–227 229–230 233–234
Concerto No. 3 (1918; piano, chamber orchestra): 64 95 **114–115** 177 182 220
Concerto No. 4 (1918; piano, orchestra; formerly No. 1): 64 **115** 177 182 220 236–237 240
Concerto No. 5 (1920; piano, orchestra; published as No. 2): 20 64 94–95 104 **120–121** 177 182 221 240 334 362
Concerto No. 6 (1922; piano, chamber orchestra; formerly No. 3): 95 **124–125** 177
Concerto No. 7 (*Sīmurgh-'Anqā*, 1924; piano, chamber orchestra): 64 94 **126–127** 177 222
Concerto No. 8 (1927–28; piano, orchestra; formerly No. 5): 64 94–95 **131–132** 177

Désir éperdu: **114** 175 432 449
"Dies iræ" Variations: see *Variazioni e fuga triplice*

Étang, L', Op. 9: **114** 178 180 469
Études transcendantes: 52–53 64 90 100 **149–152** 176 355 358–360 433 440–441 449 482

Fantaisie espagnole: 29 40–41 77 104 **117** 175 358 428 432 435–440 442 444–445 448 450–451 483
Fantasia ispanica: 102 **139** 175
Fantasiettina atematica: **174** 177
Fantasiettina sul nome illustre dell'egregio poeta Christopher Grieve ossia Hugh M'Diarmid: xii 26 45 48 104 **162** 176 339 *343* 356 423 429 432 440 442–449 451 487 492
Faust (Goethe): see *Music for "Faust"*
Fragment Written for Harold Rutland: **142–143** 176 356 426 432
  1st version: **142–143** 433
  2nd version: **142**
  3rd version: **142–143** 356 439–440 442 449 483
Frammento cantato: **165–166** 178 470
Frammenti aforistici: see *4, 20,* or *104 Frammenti aforistici*
Fugue (J. S. Bach): see *Transcription in the Light of Harpsichord Technique*

Gallo d'oro, Il, da Rimskij-Korsakov: Variazioni frivole con una fuga anarchica, eretica e perversa: 65 97–98 **171–172** 176 192 350 352
Gulistān (Nocturne for piano): xii 52–53 89–90 **147–148** 176 189 319 *339* 360 365 *368–369* *380* 424 429 432 435 438 440 443 448 481–482

Habanera (Bizet): see *3 Pastiches*
"He was laughing in the tower": see *Saint Bertrand de Comminges*
Heure exquise, L', Op. 2, No. 2: **110** 178 470
Hindu Merchant's Song (Rimsky-Korsakov): see *3 Pastiches*
Hymne à Aphrodite, Op. 4, No. 2: **112** 178 180 461 471

I Was Not Sorrowful: **116** 178 180 461 473
In a Summer Garden (Delius): see *Transcription of "In a Summer Garden"*
In the Hothouse: see *2 Piano Pieces*
Irrémédiable, L': **131** 178 180 472

Jāmī (Nocturne for piano): **133** 175 186 360 369 *379* 381 384 *386* 432–435 442–445 482–483 485
Jāmī Symphony: see *Symphony No. 3, Jāmī*
Jardin parfumé, Le: ix 40 43 62 82 104 **125** 175 184 233 280 304 333 335 341 356 **360–388** 365 367 *370–378 380 382 385–387* 423 432–435 437–438 440–441 443–446 449–450 482–485 490–491

Konzertmäßige Übertragung der Schlußszene aus Salome von Richard Strauss: **153** 179 357

Mauvais jardinier, Le: 99 **116** 175 178 180 475
Medea: **111–112** 177 225 227
Messa alta sinfonica: 18 44 55 64 97 **162–163** 177 314 321
Minute Waltz (Chopin): see *3 Pastiches* or *Pasticcio capriccioso*
Movement (voice, piano): 111 **137** 178 180
Music for "Faust": **135** 179
Music to "The Rider by Night": **118–119** 175 178 235

Nido di scatole, Un: 64 98 **156–157** 176 192
Nocturne, Gulistān: see *Gulistān*
Nocturne, Jāmī: see *Jāmī*

One Hundred Transcendental Studies: see *Études transcendantes*
Opus archimagicum: see *Sonata No. 5*

Opus clavicembalisticum: ix xii 7 19 20–21 26 29–30 38–39 47–49 51–53 60–61 64–65 73 76 80 82 84 91 100 102 104 134 **135–136** 175 186–187 195 240 298 **300–310** 334 342 *351–352–353* 355 360 363 **390–419** 408–409 428–429 432 434 436 438–446 448–450 483–485 488–489 493
Opus clavisymphonicum: 64 **160–161** 177 192 424
Opus secretum: 101 **173–174** 176
Opus sequentiale: see *Opus clavicembalisticum*
Opusculum claviense: see *Opusculum clavisymphonicum*
Opusculum clavisymphonicum vel claviorchestrale: 37 65 **169** 177
Opusculum for Orchestra: 62 **125** 177 184
Organ Symphony: see *Symphony*

Passacaglia: 64 **134–135** 175 301
Passeggiata arclecchinesca: **174–175–176**
Passeggiata variata: 96 **174** 176
Passeggiata veneziana: **158** 176 358 424 432 435 441 480 482
Passion: 98
Pasticcio capriccioso sopra Op. 64, No. 1 dello Chopin: 29 123 **139** 178 358
Pastiche on the "Habanera" (Bizet): see *3 Pastiches*
Pastiche on the "Hindu Merchant's Song" (Rimskiy-Korsakov): see *3 Pastiches*
Pastiche on the "Minute Waltz" (Chopin): see *3 Pastiches* or *Pasticcio capriccioso*
Piano Pieces: see *2 Piano Pieces*
Piano Quintet: see *Quintet*
Piano Sonata: see *Sonata*
Piano Symphony: see *Symphony*
Poplars, The, Op. 2, No. 1: **109** 178 180 476 479
Prelude in E♭ (J. S. Bach): see *Transcription of Prelude in E♭*

Prelude, Interlude, and Fugue: 41 104 **124** 175 350 352 *354* 432–433 437–439 442–445 450 484–485

"Quære reliqua hujus materiei inter secretiora": **147** 176 355 481
Quasi habanera, Op. 8: **113** 175 358 432 449
Quattro frammenti aforistici: see *4 Frammenti aforistici*
Quintet No. 1: 104 **119** 177 192 428–429
Quintet No. 2: 18 64 103 **138–139** 177 192 301

Rapsodie espagnole (Maurice Ravel): see *Transcription de concert*
Rosario d'arabeschi: 75 **160** 176 192 358 432 440
Roses du soir, Op. 1, No. 2: **110** 178 476

Sadko (Rimskiy-Korsakov): see *3 Pastiches*
Saint Bertrand de Comminges: "He was laughing in the tower": 52 **148** 176 355 432 438 444 446 481 484
Salome (Richard Strauss): see *Konzertmäßige Übertragung*
Schlußszene aus Salome von Richard Strauss: see *Konzertmäßige Übertragung*
Sequentia cyclica super "Dies iræ" ex Missa pro defunctis: 64 96 100 **153–154** 176 190 307 *347–350* 356 359 361
Sonata No. 0, Op. 7: 95 **113** 175 229–230
Sonata No. 1: 51 104 **117–118** 175 230 236 238 242–244 253–255 333 355 433 444–446 448–451 485
Sonata No. 2: 64 104 **121** 175 183 236–238 240 242 243–245 255 355 433
Sonata No. 3: 42 104 **121–122** 175 183 243 245 355 438 446

Sonata No. 4: 45 64 79 **133–134** 175 187 298 302–304 360
Sonata No. 5, Opus archimagicum: 62 64 65 93 102 **141–142** 176 188
St. Bertrand de Comminges: see *Saint Bertrand de Comminges*
Suggested Bell-Chorale for Saint Luke's Carillon: **161–162** 178
Symphonia brevis: see *Symphony No. 5*
Symphonia magna: see *Symphony No. 6*
Symphonic High Mass: see *Messa alta sinfonica*
Symphonic Nocturne (piano): 64 **170–171** 176 360
Symphonic Variations (piano): 18 64 86 100 **143–145** 159 175–176
Symphonic Variations (piano, orchestra): 100 145 **158–160** 175 177
Symphony No. 1 (orchestra et al.): 62 64 **122** 177 183 238 240–241 243
Symphony No. 1 (organ): 48 51 64 104 **127** 176 280 333 428–429 432–433 446 448–450 485
Symphony No. 1, Tāntrik (piano): 62 102 **146** 176 187–188 247 346
Symphony No. 2 (orchestra et al.): 37 64 96 131 135–**136**–137 175 177 303 311
Symphony No. 2 (organ): 50 **138** 176 301 311
Symphony No. 2 (piano): 90 148 **157–158** 176 435 482
Symphony No. 3, Jāmī (orchestra et al.): 100 **155** 177 190 318–319 460 477 479
Symphony No. 3 (organ): 50 53 64 100 103 **156** 176 191
Symphony No. 3 (piano): 81 **161** 176 480
Symphony No. 4 (piano): 29 **163–164** 176 435 482
Symphony No. 5, Symphonia brevis (piano): 37 **168** 176 360

Symphony No. 6, Symphonia magna (piano): 38 44 65 **169–170** 176

Tāntrik Symphony: see *Symphony No. 1, Tāntrik*

Tessuto d'arabeschi, Il: 45 **173** 177 344 426 429 432 442–443 448–450

Three Pastiches: see *3 Pastiches*

Toccata No. 0: see *2 Piano Pieces*

Toccata No. 1: 37 90 **132–133** 175 185 187

Toccata No. 2: 21 64 78 **139 141** 145 175 434

Toccata No. 3: 101 103 **145–146** 175–176

Toccata No. 4: 29–30 64 90 101 **165** 176 312

Toccatinetta sopra C. G. F.: 64 **134** 175

Transcendental Studies: see *Études transcendantes*

Transcription de concert de "Rapsodie espagnole" (Maurice Ravel): **152** 179 357

Transcription in the Light of Harpsichord Technique for the Modern Piano of the Chromatic Fantasia of J.S. Bach, Followed by a Fugue: **146–147** 179 189 357–358 432 439

Transcription of "In a Summer Garden" (Delius): **109** 175 178 214

Transcription of Prelude in E♭ (J. S. Bach): **152** 179

Trois fêtes galante de Verlaine: see *3 Fêtes galantes*

Trois poèmes: see *3 Poèmes* (1918–19) or *3 Poèmes* (1941)

Trois poèmes du "Gulistān" de Sa'dī: see *3 Poèmes du "Gulistān"*

Two Piano Pieces: see *2 Piano Pieces*

Valse-fantaisie: 62 104 **128** 175 184 358 433 443–445 484

Variazione maliziosa e perversa sopra "La morte d'Åse" da Grieg: 98 **168–169** 176 358 433 451

Variazioni e fuga triplice sopra "Dies iræ": 64 **128–130** 175 184 303 305 307–308 310 352 356

Variazioni frivole con una fuga anarchica, eretica e perversa: see *Gallo d'oro*

Venti frammenti aforistici: see *20 Frammenti aforistici*

Villa Tasca: Mezzogiorno siciliano — Evocazione nostalgica: 45 **173** 176

Vocalise No. 1 (soprano fioriturata), Op. 2, No. 3: **110–111** 178 180 224

Vocalise No. 2: **111**–112 175 178 225 227

Waltz in D♭, Op. 64, No. 1 (Chopin): see *3 Pastiches* or *Pasticcio capriccioso*

Wienerische Weisen: see *Valse-fantaisie*

General Index

This is an index of persons (widely interpreted) and compositions by composers other than Sorabji. (For compositions by Sorabji, see the previous index, pp. 494–98.) Persons are indexed only if they are mentioned by name, with the exception of Sorabji's mother and father. For those with a reputation as a composer or whose music is mentioned in this book, dates are given in parentheses. Proper names contained in names of groups, religions, organizations, buildings, places, and foods are usually not indexed.

Keys of compositions are indicated as major mode by upper case (e.g. Concerto in D), minor mode by lower case (Concerto in d). Opus, Köchel, and similar catalog numbers are specified when their presence might help in locating a particular composition in other sources.

Bold-face page numbers indicate a complete chapter in the book by the person whose name is indexed. Italics indicate music examples, bold italics extended references to persons other than a chapter's author. The additional references sometimes found within the pages having numbers in bold or bold italics (i.e. references to the person so indexed) are printed in plain type.

The index uses English alphabetization.

The expression *a.* is an abbreviation of *alias.*

à Becket Williams, Christopher: *see* Williams
'Abdu'l Bahā: 63
Adonis: 471
Aikin, Jim: 334
Aitken, Robert: 126 431–432
al-Nafzāwi (*a.* 'Umar ibn Muḥammad, al-Nafzāwī): 125 360 488 491
al-Rashīd, Khalīfa Hārūn: 156
Albéniz, Isaac (1860–1909): 39 358
   Iberia: 39
Alberic of Mauléon, Canon: 148 355
Aldington, Richard: 488

Alice (of Carroll's *Alice in Wonderland*): 181
Alighieri, Dante: 328
Alkan, Charles Valentin (1813–88): 19–20 24 45 170 258 263 337 352 357 391 425 430 489
   Chemin de fer, Le: 352
Allāh: 62 182 184
Allan, Maud: 433
Allen, Warren Dwight: 11 488
Allinson, Adrian: 244
Amato, Donna: 53 429 431 451 486
Ampersand, Opus: xiii

Anscombe, Gertrude Elizabeth
    Margaret: 458
Antcliffe, Herbert: 72–73 84
Anthony, Saint: 222
Aphrodite: 112 178 180 461 471–472
Aprahamian, Felix: 41
Aquinas, Saint Thomas: 63 327 421
Arbuthnot, John: 25
Arès (*Eng.* Ares): 471
Arlequin (*Eng.* Harlequin): 475
Armstrong Gibbs, Cecil: *see* Gibbs
Arnold, Matthew: 420
Åse: *see* Grieg, Edvard: *Åse's Death*
Ashton, Lucia (Lucy): *see* Lucia
Ashworth, Edward Clarke: 79–80
    85–86 143 147 319 488
Asquith, Lady Cynthia: 220 233
Assisi, Saint Francis of: *see* Francis
Atkinson, Charles Francis: 493
'Aṭṭār (*a.* Farīdu'd-Dīn 'Aṭṭār): 488
Aubert, Louis (1877–1968): 216–217
Avalon, Arthur: 488
Aziz, Maqbool: xiii

Baba, Meher: *see* Meher Baba
Babbitt, Milton (b. 1916): 455
Bach, Johann Sebastian (1685–
    1750): 4 50 91 146–147 151–152
    179 189 225 266 334 340 344 346
    355 357–358 421 432 439
    Art of the Fugue, The: 91
    Chromatic Fantasia and Fugue,
        BWV 903: 146–147 151 179
        189 355 357–358 432 439
    French Suite, BWV 815a: 152
        Prelude in E♭: 152 179
    Fugue, BWV 948: 146–147 179
        189 357–358 432 439
    Mass in b: 266 272 421
Bahai, Abdul: *see* 'Abdu'l Bahā
Bailey, Derek: 40
Baker, Theodore: 102–103 379 492
Barbier, Carl Paul: 479
Barrymore, John: 313
Bartholomew-the-Great, Saint: 442
Bartók, Béla (1881–1945): 263–264
    278 338 362
Battle March of Delhi, The: 181

Baudelaire, Charles: 24 118 131 148
    460–461 463 467 473 479
Bax, Sir Arnold (1883–1953): viii 257
    270 **274–276** 274–276 281 341
    490
    Quartet No. 1 for Strings: 276
    Quintet for Oboe and Strings:
        274
    Quintet for Piano and Strings:
        274
    Sonata No. 2 for Piano: 274
    *Symphonic Variations for Piano
        and Orchestra:* 275 341
    Symphony No. 3: 276
    Symphony No. 6: 275–276
Beaumont, Antony: 254 489
Bechert, Paul: 242
Bechhofer Roberts, C. E.: 282
Beck, Franz (1734–1809): 5
Becker (of the printing firm
    Waldheim-Eberle): 242
Becket Williams, Christopher à: *see*
    Williams
Bedford, Duke of (*a.* John
    Plantagenet): 421
Beecham, Sir Thomas: 289
Beerbohm Tree, Sir Herbert: *see*
    Tree
Beethoven, Ludwig van (1770–1827):
    11 33 210 225 262 265–266 337
    399 412 443 455
    Große Fuge: 412
    Missa solemnis: 266
    *Sonata No. 29 for Piano,
        Hammerklavier:* 399
    Symphony No. 9: 11
Beiler, Jonathan: 173 432
Bellini, Giovanni: 421
Belloc, Hilaire: 259 488
Benda, Julien: 488
Bennett, Arnold: 259
Benson, Marjorie Maulsby: 488
Berg, Alban (1885–1935): 36 39–40
    240
    Sonata for Piano: 38
Berio, Luciano (b. 1925): 240
Berlioz, Hector (1803–69): 18 262
    265 273 338 340 344
    Damnation of Faust, The: 18

Grande messe des morts (Requiem): 265
Berry, Duc de (*a.* Jean de France): 421
Bertrand, Aloysius: 356
Bertrand de Comminges, Saint: 52 148 175 355 432 438 444 446 481 484
Best, Reginald Norman: 50 63 89 133 152 162–163 317 322 324–325
Bhimani, Nazlin: iii iv viii **256–284** 256 261 488
Bierce, Ambrose: 213
Bilitis: 476 479
Bizet, Georges (1838–75): see *Habanera* next
   Habanera (from *Carmen*): 41 123 358 432 436–442 448 483
Blake, William: 235
Bliss, Arthur (1891–1975): 241 279 324
Bloemendal, Coenraad: 432
Blom, Eric: 24 101 146 224 267 488 490
Booth, Davyd: 173 432
Boughton, Rutland (1878–1960) 279–280
   Immortal Hour, The: 280
Boulez, Pierre (b. 1925): 46 212–213 240 430
Bowen, York (1884–1961): 27 158 279–280
Bowyer, Kevin: 48–51 53 108 127 429 431 446 448–450 485–486
Brahms, Johannes (1833–97): 33 266–267 273 337 391
   Concerto No. 2 for Piano and Orchestra in B♭: 391
   Rhapsody for Piano in g (2 Rhapsodies, Op. 79, No. 2): 267
Branson, David: 431 434 489
Braque, Georges: 213
Bredell, Baldwin S.: 311
Brenan, Patricia: 198
Brian, Havergal (1876–1972): 3 5 11 13
   Symphony No. 1, The Gothic: 11 13
Bridge, Frank (1879–1941): 211
Brittain, Rex H.: 119–120 124
Britten, Benjamin (*a.* Lord Britten of Aldeburgh, 1913–76): 279
Bromage, Bernard: 62 88 125 132 142 317
Browne, Arthur G.: 80 334 489
Browne, Edward G.: 155 186 296 477 479 489
Bruce, Neely (b. 1944): 123 431 436
Bruckner, Anton (1824–96): 11
Brünnhilde (of Wagner's *Der Ring des Nibelungen*): 287
Brzeska, Henri Gaudier-: *see* Gaudier-Brzeska
Buonarroti, Michelagniolo (*or* Michelangelo): 44 125–126 178 326 428 432 441 443 448 450 460 464 479 489
Burton, Sir Richard Francis: 325 360 488
Burton-Page, Anthony: 174
Bury, Lord Hewart of: *see* Hewart
Bush, Alan (b. 1900): 257 278 280
Busoni, Ferruccio (1866–1924): viii 4 8 19 26 33 40 46 54 117 121 128 174 176 184 189 196 199 213 239 252–255 257–258 267 289 295 300–301 313–314 334 337 340 342 344 346 352 356–358 374 377 379 390–391 403 405 425 430 433 459 488–489 492
   Concertino for Piano and Orchestra, BV 292: 352
   Concerto for Piano and Orchestra with Male Chorus: 425
   Doktor Faust: 430
   Fantasia contrappuntistica: 300 301 344 374 459 488
   Indian Fantasy: 267 269
   Klavierübung: 356
   Konzertstück for Piano and Orchestra, BV 236: 352
   Perpetuum mobile, BV 293: 352
   Prélude et étude en arpèges: 374

Romanza e scherzoso, BV 290: 352
Rondò arlecchinesco: 174 176
Sonatina No. 6 for Piano: 358
Toccata: 344
Transcription for Piano of the Chromatic Fantasia (J. S. Bach): 189 358
Butler, Bill: 489
Buxtehude, Diderik (*or* Dietrich) (1637–1707): 50

Cabena, Barrie (b. 1933): xiii
Cage, John (b. 1912): 46 317
Cairns, Christine: 431 445
Caliban: 329
Caloveglia, Count: 190
Campbell, James: 432
Canterbury, 99th Archbishop of (*a.* Geoffrey Francis Fisher): 324
Cardus, Neville: 262 284
Carreño, María Teresa: 292
Carrington, Douglas: 48
Carroll, David: 432
Carter, Deborah: 173 432
Caruso, Enrico: 288
Casement, Roger David: 219
Cassandre (*Eng.* Cassandra): 475
Cecil, Hugh: xii 427
Chausson, Ernest (1855–99): 33 338
Chaykovskiy, Pëtr Il'ich (1840–93): 337
Chesterfield, Lord (10th Earl of Chesterfield, *a.* Edwin Francis Scudamore-Stanhope): 208
Chesterton, G[ilbert] K[eith]: 259
Chisholm, Alastair: xiii 23
Chisholm, Erik (1904–65): viii xi 20 23 27–28 38 39 52 63 65–66 78–82 87 89–90 100 105 130–131 134–135 137 146 240 257 **298–311** 298–300 303–304 307 311 317 321–322 346 360–361 389 426 428 435 480–481 489
Chisholm, Morag: xiii
Chopin, Fryderyk (*or* Frédéric) (1810–49): 29 33 41 56 104 123 139 144 171 178 225 296 352 358 369 432 439–440 442 444 483 485 490
Sonata No. 2 for Piano in b♭: 144 352
Waltz in D♭, Op. 64, No. 1, *The "Minute Waltz":* 29 41 104 123 139 178 358 432 439–440 442 444 483 485 490
Chopsticks: 151
Chorley, Henry F.: 262
Christ, Jesus: *see* Jesus Christ
Chrysilla: 109 178 464
Chrysostom, Saint John: *see* Gretchaninoff, Alexander: *Liturgy No. 2*
Clarke, Raymond: 429 431 444–445 448
Clitandre (*Eng.* Clitandra): 475
Clymène (*Eng.* Clymene): 468
Cobbett, Walter Willson: 335 490
Cobbett, William: 489
Coburn, Alvin Langdon: xi 12 198 231–232
Cohen, Harriet: 274
Coleridge-Taylor, Samuel (1875–1912): 231 233
Colles, H[enry] C[ope]: xi 228
Colombine (*Eng.* Columbine): 476
Conover, Roger L.: 213
Coomaraswamy, Ananda K.: 18 489
Cooper, Daniel G.: xiii 77
Cooper, James: 26 148
Cooper, Joy McArden: *see* McArden
Copley, Ian Alfred: 249 489
Corder, Frederick (1852–1932): 211
Cortot, Alfred: 120–121
Couperin, François: 148
Cravan, Arthur: 212–213
Crosby, Bing: 328
Crowley, Aleister: 62 233 243 245 247
Curtiss, Sidney: 173 432
Cypris: *see* Aphrodite
Cyrus (the Persian rulers of this name): 468
Czerny, Carl (1791–1857): 411

da Palestrina, Giovanni Pierluigi: *see* Palestrina

da Vinci, Leonardo: 326 328
Dahlhaus, Carl: 11 489
Dante: *see* Alighieri
Darbandi, Afkham: 488
d'Arcy, Father Martin: 327
Davies, E. Emlyn: 127 138 428 431 433
Davis, Dick: 488
Davison, James William: 262
de Falla, Manuel: *see* Falla
de Régnier, Henri: *see* Régnier
de Solis, Count Aldo Solito: 132
Dean, Winton: 262
Debussy, Claude (1862–1918): 4 154 230 238 263 265 270 334 338 358 360
  Ibéria: 265
  Mer, La: 265
  Nocturnes: 265
  Pelléas et Mélisande: 201 265
Delius, Frederick (1862–1934): viii 42 45 109 173 175 178 205 212 214 218 221 230–231 257 263 270 **271–273** 271–272 278 280–281 337–338 344 359–360 389 423 442
  Arabesque, An: 359
  Concerto for Cello and Orchestra: 272
  Concerto for Violin and Orchestra: 272
  Concerto for Violin, Cello, and Orchestra: 272
  In a Summer Garden: 109 178 214
  Mass of Life, A: 271 272
  Paris: 271
  Sea Drift: 271
  Sonata No. 2 for Violin and Piano: 272
  Song of the High Hills, A: 272
  Village Romeo and Juliet, A: 271
    A Walk to the Paradise Garden: 271
delle Sedie, Enrico: 218
Demuth, Norman: 275 489
Dennett, Daniel: 456
Derus, Kenneth: iii–iv viii–ix 19 38 47 112 122 135 173 **195–255**
195–196 199 201 203 215 218 221 225 229 233–235 240 243 245 248–249 255 **452–459** 452 457 459 489 493
Devil, The: 224 473
Dickie, Peter: xii 447
Diderot, Denis: 250
Dies iræ (chant): 8 64 96 128 142 153 175 176 184 190 303 305 307–308 310 352 356 359 361
Dietrich, Marlene: 218
Dietze, Georg: 454
Don Juan: *see* Juan
Douglas, Norman: 188 190 208 489
Dowson, Ernest: 116 460 472 479
Draeseke, Felix (1835–1913): 5
Drewett, Norah: 428
Dučić, Jovan: 109 476 479
Dummett, Michael: 489
Duncan-Rubbra, Edmund (1901–86): 334 489 492
Duparc, Henri (1848–1933): 338
Dürer, Albrecht: 260

Eaglefield-Hull, A.[rthur]: *see* Hull
Eblis: 304
Edroff-Smith, Emily: 33 127 146 292
Ehrlich, Paul: 245
Elgar, Sir Edward (1857–1934): viii 257 270 **273–274** 273 278
  Cockaigne: 273
  Concerto for Violin and Orchestra: 273
  Falstaff: 273–274
  Kingdom, The: 273
  Land of Hope and Glory: 273
  Symphony No. 2: 273
Eliot, Sir Charles: 247
Eliot, T[homas] S[tearns]: 11 239 489
Ellis, Havelock: 67 70–71 126 259 490
Epstein, Jacob: 216 231
Erasmi, Gabriele: xiii
Erdész, Rivka Golani: 432
Érèbe (*Eng.* Erebus): 463
Evans, Frederick H.: 231
Eve: 326
Ewing, Cecil: 431 434 440

Fabergé, Karl: 421
Fahey, Father Dennis: 329
"Fakreddin ul. Mulk": 307
Falla, Manuel de (1876–1946): 279
Falstaff, Sir John: 273–274
Farinelli (*a.* Carlo Broschi): 288
Fauré, Gabriel (1845–1924): 22 270
  Sonata for Violin and Piano in A, Op. 13: 270
Faust: 135 179 310
Feldman, Morton (1926–87): 453 457
  Triadic Memories: 457
Ferhād (of Jāmī's *Yūsuf and Zuleykhā*): 478
Fétis, François Joseph: 262
Fields, Gracie: 328
Finch, Douglas: 431 451
Finn, Robert: 335
Finnegan: 459
Flaubert, Gustave: 222
Flynn, George (b. 1937): 452
  Glimpses of Our Inner Selves: 452
Ford, Ford Madox: 216
Foreman, Lewis: 274–275 490
Francis of Assisi, Saint: 37 167 178 313 463
Franck, César (1822–90): 273
Frank, Alan: 38–39
Freud, Sigmund: 202 421
Frey, Carl: 464–465 479
Fricker, Peter Racine (1920–90): 324
Froese, Elvira: 431 451

Galilei, Galileo: 203
Galsworthy, John: 259
Gaṇès: *see* Gaṇeśa
Gaṇeśa: 62 184
Garvelmann, Donald M.: xiii 28–29 37–39 41 48 60–61 82 90–91 93 103 123 139 167 202 333 428 435–437 490 493
Gates, John: 29 77 428 431 435
Gaudier-Brzeska, Henri: 216
Gee, Ken: xiv
Gentieu, Norman P.: v viii xi xiii 27 43 45–46 60–61 63 81 94 115 126 156 161 173 187 222 278 298 *311–317* 311–312 315 321 344 480
Gervais, Terence White: 24 102 490
Gettings, Fred: 65 490
Gibbons, John: 431 448
Gibbs, Cecil Armstrong (1889–1960): 239–240
Gilbert (a naturopath physician to Kaikhosru Sorabji): 324
Gilda (of Verdi's *Rigoletto*): 287
Gilkin, Iwan: 99 116 460 475 479
Gilly, Dinh: 288 295
Girardi, Enzo Noè: 464 479 489
God: 23 62 69 72 134 162 187 190 201 222 244 292–293 304 306 310 316–317 321 323 325 411 463 466 468 470
Goddard, Scott: 212 490
Godowsky, Leopold (1870–1938): 20 41 46 51 295 340 342 356–357 406 425 430
  53 Studies on Chopin's Etudes: 356
Goethe, Johann Wolfgang von: 310
Golani, Rivka: *see* Erdész
Goldhan, Wolfgang: 198
Goossens, Eugène (1893–1962): 224
Gould, J. Cecil: xi 320
Gounod, Charles (1818–93): 286
Grace, Harvey: 244 333
Grainger, Percy (1882–1961): 217
  Arrangement of "Molly on the Shore": 217
Granados, Enrique (1867–1916): 358
Grant, Kenneth: 490
Gray, Cecil (1895–1951): 75 77 195 198 222–223 226 230–231 235 238–239 248–249 259 262 281 335 339 490
  The Temptation of Saint Anthony: 222
Gray, Pauline: 198
Gray-Fisk, Clinton: 27 78 82 101 134 141 145 175 258 281 308–309 342 360 420 490
Gretchaninoff, Alexander (1864–1956): 169
  Liturgy No. 2 of Saint John Chrysostom, Op. 29: 169

Nicene Creed: 169
Grew, Sydney: 341 361 490
Grieg, Edvard (1843–1907): *see Åse's Death* next
  Åse's Death (from *Peer Gynt*): 98 168 176 358 433 451
Grieve, Christopher Murray: 26–27 48 54 84 104 135 162 176 199 257–258 264 273 283 286 343 345 356 429 432 440 442–446 448–449 451 491
Grove, Sir George: 24 102–103 224 490
Grünbaum, Branko: 453
Guénon, René: 490
Guercio, Francis: 481 490
Gula, Robert J.: 342 355 490

Habermann, Michael: iii–iv ix xii 39 41 44 48–49 76 87 90 97 123–124 128 143 147 162 **333–389** 333 336 357 361 428–429 431 436–445 448 450 483–486 490–491
Ḥāfiẓ (*a.* Khwāja Shamsu'd-Dīn Muḥammad-i-Ḥāfiẓ-i-Shīrāzī): 424
Hall, David: 334
Hall, Radclyffe: 306–307 491
Hamelin, Marc-André (b. 1961): 51–53 253 429 431 449–451 485–486
Hanslick, Eduard: 262
Hardy, Thomas: 30
Harlequin: *see* Arlequin
Hartlieb, Marion v.: 198
Harty, Russell: 40
Hārūn al-Rashīd, Khalīfah: *see* al-Rashīd
Haydn, Franz Joseph (1732–1809): 41 266 337
Haynes, Edmund Sidney Pollock: 491
Heifetz, Jascha: 270
Heinsheimer, Hans: 198
Helmholtz, Hermann: 216–217
Henry, Leigh: 241
Henry VIII, King of England: 313
Hertzka, Emil: 238 240 242 254
Heseltine, Philip (1894–1930): viii xi 18 51 59 63 72–73 109 111–112 114 119 122 **195–252** 195–198 208 211–212 214 218–220 222–224 226 230–231 235 238–239 243 245 248–253 257 261 262 263 278 281 389 489–491 493
  Transcription of "In a Summer Garden" (Delius): 214
Hewart, Gordon (*a.* Lord Hewart of Bury): 491
Hindemith, Paul (1895–1963): 263
Hinton, Alistair (b. 1950): iii–iv vii ix xiii **17–57** 17 23 30 37 39 45–46 49 55 87 94–95 100–101 108 128 134 137 167–170 180 184 255 270 312 317 335 339 392 426 431 440 448 450 **486–487** 491–492
Hinton, Terry: 487
Hoffmann, E[rnst] T[heodor] A[madeus]: 404; *also see* Offenbach, Jacques: *Barcarolle*
Holbrooke, Joseph (1878–1958): 242 257
Holliday, Brenda: 318 324
Holliday, Frank: iii–v vii–ix xiii 26–29 34 37–39 42 56 60–61 63 68–70 76 80–82 87 **88–92** 88–90 101 105 132 147 156–158 161 163 165 184 200 282 297 **317–325** 317–318 320–325 327 330 362 **420–424** 420 423 428 435 481 489 491
Holmboe, Vagn (b. 1909): 3 5
Holst, Gustav (1874–1934): viii 239–240 270 **276–278** 276–279 281
  At the Boar's Head: 276
  Beni Mora: 278
  Choral Symphony: 277 281
  Hymn of Jesus, The: 277–278
  Hymns from the R̥g-Veda: 277
  Ode to Death: 277
  Planets, The: 239 277–278
Holt, Richard: 493
Honegger, Arthur (1892–1955): 264
  Roi David, Le: 264
Horace (*a.* Quintus Horatius Flaccus): 293
Horowitz, Vladimir: 217
Horus: 30

Howells, Herbert (1892–1983): 239–240 279
Howes, Frank: 261 491
Hughes, Herbert: 259
Hughes, Howard: 6 56
Hull, A[rthur] Eaglefield-: 235 491
Huvé, Cyril: 412 491
Huxley, Aldous: 23 220 291

Iblīs: see Eblis
Ibrāhīm Mīrzā, Shamsu'd-Dīn: 119 463 479
Imajishi, Fujiko: 432
Ingram, Henry: 126 431–432
Ireland, John (1879–1962): 27 125 160–161 257 278 280
Isaiah: 422
Isis: 311
Isolde (of Wagner's *Tristan und Isolde*): 287
Ives, Charles (1874–1954): 9 38–39 51 334–335 430
    Sonata No. 2 for Piano, Concord, Mass. 1840–1860: 38
Iyer, K. Bharatha: 493

Jackson, Laura Riding: see Riding
Jalālu'd-Dīn Rūmī: see Rūmī
James, M[ontague] [Rhodes]: 147–148 355 491
James, William: 454
James I, King of England: 310
Jāmī (*a.* Nūru'd-Dīn 'Abdu'r-Rahmān Jāmī): xv 100 133 155 175 177 186 190 319 328 360 369 379 381 384 386 421 432–435 442–445 460 477 479 482–483 485
Jeffry, Alix: xii 336
Jenkins, Theodore: 120
Jesus Christ: 90 187 190 200 310 322
John Chrysostom, Saint: *see* Gretchaninoff, Alexander: *Liturgy No. 2*
John of the Cross, Saint (*a.* Juan de Yepis y Álvarez): 63 328
Johns, Gloria: 173 432
Johnson, Edward: 22

Johnson, Joanna: xiv
Johnson, Roy Hamlin: 210
Jones, Robert: 334
Joseph: see Yūsuf
Juan (de Sevilla), Don: 249

Kalmus, Alfred: 240 242
Kann, Hans: 41
Katz, Maurice: 431 434
Keaton, Grace: 487
Keeler, Christine: 328
Keeley, Robert: 431 444
Kennamer, Stephen: 341
Khachaturyan, Aram (1903–78): 324
King, The (of Carroll's *Alice in Wonderland*): 181
Klein, Hans-Günter: 198
Knussen, Oliver (b. 1952): 22
Koczwara, František (ca. 1750–91)
    Battle of Prague, The: 181
Koechlin, Charles (1867–1950): 216
Korngold, Erich Wolfgang (1897–1957): 425

Lambert, Constant (1905–51): 269 278 491
Landis, Stephan: xiii
Landowska, Wanda: 189
Lane, Edward William: 241
Langford, Samuel: 284
Langgaard, Rued (1893–1952): 95
Langmaid, Pasco: 329
Lawrence, D[avid] H[erbert]: 219–220 223 233
Lawrence, Frieda: 219
Leski, Clemens: 390
Lesure, François: 198
Levy, Oscar: 491
Lewis, David: 454 456
Lewis, Janice: 431 451
Lewis, Wyndham: 216 231
Ley, Rosamund: 254 489
Leylā (of Jāmī's *Yūsuf and Zuleykhā*): 478
Liszt, Ferenc (*or* Franz) (1811–86): 4–5 20 41 152 265 334–335 337 340 342 357–358 363 369 430 439 443 451 490

Concerto No. 1 for Piano and
   Orchestra in E♭, R. 455: 369–
   370
  Études d'exécution
   transcendante: 152
  Préludes, Les: 5
Loermans, C. Marsel: xii 417
Lorenz, Robert: 244
Louÿs, Pierre: 110 476–477 479
Lowens, Irving: 335
Loy, Mina: 213
Lucia (of Donizetti's Lucia di
   Lammermoor): 287
Ludovici, Anthony: 491
Luke, Saint: 161 178 310

MacDiarmid, Hugh: see Grieve
MacDonald, Malcolm: xiii
MacDowell, Edward: 274
Machen, Arthur: 491
Machiavelli, Niccolò: viii 96 203 257
   290 325 337 453 493
Mackerness, Eric David: 261 491
Macleod, Garrard: 24
Madge, Geoffrey Douglas (b. 1941):
   iii–iv ix xii 46–49 51 52 54 82 87
   113 136 174 250 **390–419** 390
   394–395 412 419 429 431 441–
   446 448–449 459 483–484 486
   489 491
Madge, Truus: xiii
Maeterlinck, Maurice: 279
Magnard, Albéric (1865–1914): 5
Magnus de la Gardie, Count: 147
   355
Mahler, Gustav (1860–1911): 36 93
   211 241 258 263 265 267 271 295
   337 340
  Lied von der Erde, Das: 241
  Symphony No. 8: 265
Mairet, Philip: 259 491
Majnūn (of Jāmī's Yūsuf and
   Zuleykhā): 478
Malcolm, Norman: 456
Mallarmé, Stéphane: 112 461–462
   479
Manning, Jane: 42 46 392 431 440
   448–450 486
Marchesi, Blanche: 131 295

Mardrus, J[oseph] C[harles]: 191 488
Marguerite (of Berlioz's Damnation
   of Faust): 18
Marie, Jean-Bernard: 431 449
Maritain, Jacques: 327
Marrot, H. Vincent: 128
Marsh, William: 442
Martin, Victor: 432
Martine, Marthe: 118 429 431 433
Marx, Joseph (1882–1964): 33
Marx, Karl: 327
Mary (mother of Jesus): 68
Masefield, John: 88
Mathewson, Karen J.: xiii
Matthews, Denis: 267
Maurer, Charles: xiii
McArden, Joy: 26 148
McNaught, William Gray: 228
McWhirter, Norris: 7
Medea: 111–112 177 225
Medtner, Nicolas (1880–1951): 18 45
   204 258 263 295 337 344 430 493
  Sonata for Piano in e, Op. 25,
   No. 2, The Night Wind: 204
Meher Baba: 63
Melchior, Alain: xiii
Mellers, Wilfrid (b. 1914): 40
Mendelssohn-Bartholdy, Felix
   (1809–47): 262 337
Menter, Sophie: 292
Meppelink, Hieke: 431 451
Merriam, Alan P.: 491
Messiaen, Olivier (1908–92): 246 334
   366 430
Meyer, Leonard: 11 491
Michelangeli, Arturo Benedetti: 20
Michelangelo: see Buonarroti
Millan, Charles Gordon: 479
Miller, Elma (b. 1954): 46
Milton, John: xv 73 422
Mindszenty, Cardinal József (a.
   József Pehm): 327
"Mirza el. Akbari": 307
Mitropoulos, Dimitri (1896–1960):
   388
Moiseiwitsch, Benno: 210
Moore, Harry T.: 233
Morland, Harold: 147–148 157 164
   165–166

Morrell, Lady Ottoline: 219
Mozart, Wolfgang Amadeus (1756–91): 33 225 266–267 337
   Sonata for Piano in a, K. 310: 267
Musès, Charles: 198
Muspratt, Joan: xi
Myers, Rollo: 269

Nafzāwi, al-: *see* al-Nafzāwi
Nairn, Edward Gerard: xiii
Nancarrow, Conlon (b. 1912): 455
Naoroji, Dadabhai: 69 491
Nason, Edward: 148
Nasveld, Robert: 431 451
Nelson, Admiral Horatio: 314
Newman, Ernest: viii 196 213 252–253 258 262–263 266–267 282 284
Newmarch, Rosa: 200 204
Nichols, Robert: 119 235
Nietzsche, Friedrich: 214
Norma (of Bellini's *Norma*): 287
Northbourne, Lord (4th Baron of Northbourne, *a.* Walter Ernest Christopher James): 490
"Nureddior": 307

Offenbach, Jacques (1819–90): 158 358
   Barcarolle (from *Tales of Hoffmann*): 158 358 424
Offord, Martin: 431 444 450
Ogdon, John (1937–89): 20 49–53 76 82 87 91 187 298 389 428–429 431 434 446 448–450 485–486 493
Orage, A[lfred] [Richard]: 257–259 270 283 295 491–492
Ould, Barry Peter: xii 48 426 447
Ovid (*a.* Publius Ovidius Naso): 472

Palestrina, Giovanni Pierluigi da (ca. 1525–94): 422–423
Parvīz (of Jāmī's *Yūsuf and Zuleykhā*): 478
Payne, John: 185 488 491
Pepper, Joseph: 432
Perry, Douglas: 432

Peterkin, Marie: xi 140
Peterkin, Norman: xi 27 34–37 46 57 68 74 113 117 139–141 153 184 297 324–325 339 491
Petri, Egon: 26–27 75 154 260 295 301
Pfitzner, Hans (1869–1949): 270
   Concerto for Piano and Orchestra: 270
Picasso, Pablo: 213 421
Pichois, Claude: 479
Pickens, Jo Ann: 431 449 486
Pierrot: 475
Pirie, Peter: 492
Pius XII, Pope (*a.* Eugenio Pacelli): 327
Pohran, Alexandra: 432
Pope, Alexander: 25 89
Porpora, Nicola (1686–1768): 288
Portsmouth, 9th Earl of (*a.* Gerard Vernon Wallop): 492
Posner, Bruce: 492
Pound, Ezra: 216 259 262
Powell, John (1882–1963): 210–211
   Sonata teutonica for Piano: 210
Powell, Jonathan: 53 429 431 450–451
Procter, Robert William: 166–167 176
Prokof'ev, Sergey (1891–1953): 324
Prout, Ebenezer (1835–1909): 98 208
Purcell, Henry: 257

Queen of Sheba: *see* Sheba, Queen of
Quilter, Roger (1877–1953): 27

Rachmaninoff, Sergei (1873–1943): xiv 33 48 274 295 337 342
   Vocalise (*14 Songs*, Op. 34, No. 14): 48
Racine Fricker, Peter: *see* Fricker
Radclyffe-Hall, Marguerite (*a.* John): *see* Hall, Radclyffe
Rākṣasas (followers of a demon): 234
Rāmakṛṣṇa, Śrī: 63
Rapoport, Paul (b. 1948): iii–iv vii–ix xi **xiii–xiv 3–16** 3 28 31 35 39

43–44 46 **58–87** 59–61 68 70 83
85–86 **93–192** 95 101 165 168
198 256 261 **285–330** 312 363
390–419 390 426 436 440 442
460–479 480–485 492–493
Rashīd, Khalīfah Hārūn al-: *see* al-Rashīd
Ravel, Maurice (1875–1937): 152 179
229 263 265 270 334–335 338
356–358 360 377 388
  Daphnis et Chloë: 265
  Gaspard de la nuit: 360 377
  Rapsodie espagnole: 152 179 357
  Tombeau de Couperin, Le: 265–266
  Valse, La: 358
Rebikov, Vladimir (1866–1920): 277
Reed, Douglas: 329
Reger, Max (1873–1916): 4 46 337
  340 346 357 430
Régnier, Henri de: 109 464 479
Reid, Hugh: 360
"Rembrandt": xi 268
Réti, Rudolph: 388–389
Rexroth, Kenneth: 247
Reynolds, Reginald: 217–218
Rice, Chris: xiii 48–49 52 95 487
Richards, George: 161
Riding, Laura: 195 198
Rimskiy-Korsakov, Nikolay (1844–1908): 97–98 123 171–172 176
  192 279 358 483 485
  Golden Cockerel, The: 97–98
    171–172 176 192
  Hindu Merchant's Song (from *Sadko*): 123 358 432 483 485
Roberge, Marc-André: iii–iv ix xiii
  52–53 77 108 198 **425–451** 425
  492
Robichez, Jacques: 479
Robinson, J. Bradford: 11 489
Rollinat, Maurice: 114 469 479
Rosenthal, Moriz: 292
Ross, George: 53 487
Roussel, Albert (1869–1937): 216
Rowley, Alec (1892–1958): 27 139
Rubbra, Edmund Duncan-: *see* Duncan-Rubbra
Rudhyar, Dane (1895–1985): 246

Rūmī (*a*. Jalālu'd-Dīn Rūmī): 296
Rumson, Gordon: 170 431 451
Rushby-Smith, John (b. 1936): 40
Rutland, Harold: 27 56 142–143 157
  163–164 175 356 426 431–433
  439–440 442 449 483
Rycraft, Malcolm: 114 431 449

Sabaneev, Leonid (1881–1968): 215
Sabbaticus, H. N.: 183
Saʿdī (*a*. Muṣharrifu'd-Dīn b.
  Muṣliḥu'd-Dīn 'Abdu'llāh Saʿdī):
  99 130 148 178 189 303 360 460–461 469 474 479
Sadie, Stanley: 103 262 490
Sadko: *see* Rimskiy-Korsakov,
  Nikolay: *Hindu Merchant's Song*
Saint-Saëns, Camille (1835–1921):
  337
Sanderson, William: 492
Sangiorgio, Victor: 429 431 445
Saphir, Julian: 53 429 431 449–450
Sappho: 472
Satan: 62 184 304 316 474
Satie, Erik (1866–1925): 334
Saurat, Denis: 27 56 138 424
Savage, Stephen: 17 22
Scelsi, Giacinto (1905–88): 390 457
  Quattro pezzi per orchestra
    (ciascuno su una nota sola):
    457
Scheherazade: *see* Shahrazād
Schenkman, Peter: 432
Scherek, Mr.: 224
Schnabel, Artur (1882–1951): 274
Schnapp, Friedrich: 254 489
Schoenberg, Arnold (1874–1951): 4
  36 46 201 204–205 209 240–242
  263–264 267 269 275 281 334
  3 Piano Pieces, Op. 11: 201
  5 Orchestral Pieces, Op. 16: 204–205
  6 Little Piano Pieces, Op. 19: 205
  Buch der Hängenden Gärten,
    Das: 264
  Concerto for Cello and Orchestra
    (after Monn): 269
  Gurrelieder: 264
  Quartet No. 2 for Strings: 264

Verklärte Nacht: 264
Scholes, Percy: 59 492
Schreker, Franz (1878–1934): 425
Schubert, Franz (1797–1828): 33 225 280 337
  Symphony No. 4: 280
Schumann, Robert (1810–56): 33 225 273 337
Scipio (*a.* Publius Cornelius Scipio Africanus, Major *and* Minor, the Roman generals of these names): 468
Scott, Cyril (1879–1970): 210–211 229 233 279
Scott, Francis George (1880–1958): 27 45 133 295 493
Scott, Hugh Arthur: xi 225 228
Searle, Humphrey (1915–82): 17 20–21
Sedie, Enrico delle: *see* delle Sedie
Seed, Christopher: 431 449
Selver, Paul: 109 259 476 479 492
Shahrazād: 306
Shamsu'd-Dīn Ibrāhīm Mīrzā: *see* Ibrāhīm
Shaw, George Bernard: 258–259 262 282 284
Sheba, Queen of: 30 191
Shelley, Percy Bysshe: 205
Shephard, Geoffrey Colin: 453
Shīrīn (of Jāmī's *Yūsuf and Zuleykhā*): 478
Shiva: *see* Śiva
Shostakovich, Dmitriy (1906–75): 13 22 269–270 324
  Concerto No. 1 for Violin and Orchestra: 270
  Symphony No. 4: 13 270
  Symphony No. 10: 270
Sibelius, Jean (1865–1957): 265 269 272 278 344
  Symphony No. 5: 278
  Symphony No. 7: 265
Simons, Peter: 454
Simorg-Anka: *see* Sīmurgh-'Anqā
Simpkins, Brooks: 324–325
Sīmurgh-'Anqā: 126 177 222
Sitwell, Osbert: 27

Sitwell, Sir Sacheverell: 41 160 238–239 492
Śiva: 234 489
Skalkótas, Nîkos (1904–49): 46 390–391
  32 Piano Pieces: 391
Skinner, Jon R.: xiii
Skryabin, Aleksandr (1872–1915): xiv 4 90 149 199–200 218 229 246 334 338–339 345 384 430
  2 Danses, Op. 73: 218
  2 Poèmes, Op. 71: 218
  5 Préludes, Op. 74: 218
  Désir (*2 Pieces*, Op. 57, No. 1): 90
  Nocturne, Op. 9, No. 2: 384
  Poem of Ecstasy, The (*Symphony No. 4*): 200
  Prometheus, The Poem of Fire (*Symphony No. 5*): 199–200
  Vers la flamme, Op. 72: 218
Slonimsky, Nicolas (b. 1894): v 102–103 204 388–389 492
Smith, William: 173 431–432
Snook, Paul: xiii
Solis, Count Aldo Solito de: *see* de Solis
Solito de Solis, Count Aldo: *see* de Solis
Solomon, Neil: 480
Solomon, Yonty: 36 38–44 48–49 87 108 122 148 152–153 160 239 335 425 428–429 431 437–441 444–446 448–450 485–486 491–492
Sor, Fernando (1778–1839): 19
Sorabji, Kaikhosru Shapurji (1892–1988): *passim*
Sorabji, Madeleine Mathilde: xi 18 33 51 67–71 89–90 116 122 137 139 201 203 205 207 214–215 218 223–224 239 241 247 286 313–314 316 322 421
Sorabji, Shapurji: xi 17–18 24–25 67–68 71 103 203 206 214–215 247 260 313 421
Spencer, Herbert: 247
Spencer-Bentley, Clive: 96 174
Spengler, Oswald 493

General Index 511

Squarey, Reverend Gerald: 51
Stamford, 8th Earl of (*a.* Reverend Harry Grey): 233
Starr, Lady Mary: 233
Starr, Meredith: 198 233 243
Steane, John: 256 284 493
Stein, Gertrude: 459
Stevens, Bernard (1916–83): 27
Stevenson, Ronald (b. 1928): 5 26 45 49 51–52 87 104 162 173 389 425 428–431 434 442–446 448 485–486 493
Stewart-Murphy, Charlotte: xiii
Stieglitz, Alfred: 231
Stockhausen, Karlheinz (b. 1928): 46 240 366
Storr, Anthony: 7 493
Strauß, Johann II (1825–99): 62 98 128 171 358
Strauss, Richard (1864–1949): 22 153 179 201 263 265 273–274 357
  Elektra: 201 263–265
  Salome: 153 179 265 357
Stravinsky, Igor (1882–1971): xiv 221 263–264 269 277–278 281 362
  Sacre du printemps, Le: 263
Suhrawardy, Hasan: 219–220
Szymanowski, Karol (1882–1937): viii 19 33 46 258 263 **295–297** 296 337
  Symphony No. 3, The Song of the Night: 296

Tailhade, Laurent: 112 460–461 471–472 479
Taylor, Douglas: xiii 198
Taylor, John: 432
Tchaikovsky, Peter: *see* Chaykovskiy
Templeton, Edith: 420
Teresa of Ávila, Saint: 63
Terry, Sir Richard: 423
Thomas Aquinas, Saint: *see* Aquinas
Thorne, Russell: 198
Thoth: 311
Thüringer, Peter: 198
Thurston, William: xiii
Tippett, Sir Michael (b. 1905): 324
Tobin, John: 20 84 324 428 431 434

Toch, Ernst (1887–1964): *see Concerto* next
  Concerto No. 1 for Piano and Orchestra, Op. 38: 283
Tomlinson, Fred: 231 493
Toussaint, Franz: 130 461 469 474 479
Tree, Sir Herbert Beerbohm: 313
Treitler, Leo: 11 493
Trew, Charles A.: 18 115 201
Trine, Ralph Waldo: 245
Tripp, C. A.: 71 493
Trotter, Thomas: 127 429 431 446
Tryon, Valerie: 44 431 440–442 486
Tupper, Martin: 208
Tyutchev, Fëdor: 204
Tzara, Tristan: 213

V. Hartlieb, Marion: *see* Hartlieb
Van Beethoven, Ludwig: *see* Beethoven
Van Dieren, Bernard (1884–1936): 42 222 226 230–231 235–236 238 252 257–258 262 273 279 281 292–293 295 344 493
  "Chinese" *Symphony*: 279
  Diaphony: 230
  Overture, Op. 7: 230
  Tailor, The: 235
Van Dieren, Bernard II: 28 312
Varèse, Edgard (1883–1965): 428
Vaughan, Rebecca: 249–250
Vaughan, Thomas: 249–250
Vaughan Williams, Ralph (1872–1958): 278 281
  Symphony No. 4: 281
  Symphony No. 5: 281
Verdi, Giuseppe (1813–1901): *see Requiem* next
  Requiem Mass: 90
Verlaine, Paul: 24 104 110 116 118 148 178 433 440 445 449 460–462 467–470 475 479
Vicars, Adrian: 166
Vicars, Denise: 166 319
Vicars, Kevin: 166
Vicars, Mervyn: 138–139 155 166 319
Viinholt Nielsen, Bendt: 95

Vinci, Leonardo da: *see* da Vinci
Vinton, Patricia: xiv
Von Goethe, Johann Wolfgang: *see* Goethe
Von Weber, Carl Maria: *see* Weber
Von Webern, Anton: *see* Webern
Von Zemlinsky, Alexander: *see* Zemlinsky

Wagner, Richard (1813–83): 67 90 234 262 265 271 273 275 340
   Ring des Nibelungen, Der: 218 263 265 346
Walton, Alan Hull: 488
Walton, William (1902–83): 238–239 278 280
Warlock, Peter: *see* Heseltine, Philip
Watson, Ian (*a.* John S.): xiii
Weber, Carl Maria von (1786–1826): *see Sonata No. 1* next
   Sonata No. 1 for Piano in C, J. 138: 352
Webern, Anton (1883–1945): 11 356
Wellesz, Egon (1885–1974): 240 242
Wells, H[erbert] G[eorge]: 259
Welsh, Henry: 149
West, Rebecca: 216
Whistler, James McNeil: 493
Whitman, Walt: 279
Whittall, Arnold: 256 493

Widner, Marc: 432
Wilde, Oscar: 67 199 213 248
Wilkinson, Fiona: 432
Williams, Christopher à Becket (1890–1956): 123 125 230 233 342 360 454 493
Wilson, Colin: 243 493
Wolf, Hugo (1860–1903): 262
Wolpe, Stefan (1902–72): 51 390 430
Wolsey, Cardinal Thomas: 313
Wood, Sir Henry: 199 204 286
Wooters, David: 198
Wright, Erika: xiii
Wulkan-Stanley, Solomon: 328
Wundt, Wilhelm: 454

Xenakis, Iannis (b. 1922): 46 390 412 430

Yūsuf (of Jāmī's *Yūsuf and Zuleykhā*): xv 186 422 477–478

Zaehner, Robert Charles: 493
Zafer, David: 432
Zemlinsky, Alexander von (1871–1942): 425
Zimmermann, Walter: 453
Zoroaster: 51 214
Zuleykhā (of Jāmī's *Yūsuf and Zuleykhā*): xv 186 422 477

* * * * *

Deæ gratias maximas ac summas laudes, nam MCMXCII vere redactor huius Opusculi Sorabjilibrarioli dactylographiam confecit, domi suæ Ancastris, apud Canadenses bar-
barissimos et crapulosissimos.
{vide pp. 187, 191}

F i n e m
coronat
Opus